Legal Research
and Writing
for Paralegals

ASPEN COLLEGE SERIES

Legal Research and Writing for Paralegals

Sixth Edition

Deborah E. Bouchoux
Georgetown University
Washington, D.C.

Wolters Kluwer
Law & Business

Library of Congress Cataloging-in-Publication Data

Bouchoux, Deborah E., 1950–
  Legal research and writing for paralegals / Deborah E. Bouchoux. —
6th ed.
     p. cm.
  Includes bibliographical references and indexes.
  ISBN 978-0-7355-9865-2 (perfectbound : alk. paper)
1. Legal research — United States. 2. Legal composition. 3. Legal
assistants — United States — Handbooks, manuals, etc. I. Title.

  KF240.B68 2011
  340.072'073—dc22
                                                      2011009907

About Wolters Kluwer Law & Business

Wolters Kluwer Law & Business is a leading global provider of intelligent information and digital solutions for legal and business professionals in key specialty areas, and respected educational resources for professors and law students. Wolters Kluwer Law & Business connects legal and business professionals as well as those in the education market with timely, specialized authoritative content and information-enabled solutions to support success through productivity, accuracy and mobility.

Serving customers worldwide, Wolters Kluwer Law & Business products include those under the Aspen Publishers, CCH, Kluwer Law International, Loislaw, Best Case, ftwilliam.com and MediRegs family of products.

CCH products have been a trusted resource since 1913, and are highly regarded resources for legal, securities, antitrust and trade regulation, government contracting, banking, pension, payroll, employment and labor, and healthcare reimbursement and compliance professionals.

Aspen Publishers products provide essential information to attorneys, business professionals and law students. Written by preeminent authorities, the product line offers analytical and practical information in a range of specialty practice areas from securities law and intellectual property to mergers and acquisitions and pension/benefits. Aspen's trusted legal education resources provide professors and students with high-quality, up-to-date and effective resources for successful instruction and study in all areas of the law.

Kluwer Law International products provide the global business community with reliable international legal information in English. Legal practitioners, corporate counsel and business executives around the world rely on Kluwer Law journals, looseleafs, books, and electronic products for comprehensive information in many areas of international legal practice.

Loislaw is a comprehensive online legal research product providing legal content to law firm practitioners of various specializations. Loislaw provides attorneys with the ability to quickly and efficiently find the necessary legal information they need, when and where they need it, by facilitating access to primary law as well as state-specific law, records, forms and treatises.

Best Case Solutions is the leading bankruptcy software product to the bankruptcy industry. It provides software and workflow tools to flawlessly streamline petition preparation and the electronic filing process, while timely incorporating ever-changing court requirements.

ftwilliam.com offers employee benefits professionals the highest quality plan documents (retirement, welfare and non-qualified) and government forms (5500/PBGC, 1099 and IRS) software at highly competitive prices.

MediRegs products provide integrated health care compliance content and software solutions for professionals in healthcare, higher education and life sciences, including professionals in accounting, law and consulting.

Wolters Kluwer Law & Business, a division of Wolters Kluwer, is headquartered in New York. Wolters Kluwer is a market-leading global information services company focused on professionals.

For my husband, Don, and my children, Meaghan, Elizabeth, Patrick, and Robert, who have provided immeasurable support and inspiration in helping me achieve my goal of writing a legal research and writing textbook for paralegal students

Summary
of Contents

Section I Legal Research:
Primary Authorities   1

Section II Legal Research:
Secondary Authorities and
Other Research Aids   205

Section III
Legal Writing   579

Appendices

Contents

Chapter 2   The Federal and State Court Systems

31

Chapter 3   Statutory Law

65

Chapter 4   Case Law and Judicial Opinions   111

Chapter 5 The Use of Digests, Annotated Law Reports, and *Words and Phrases*

165

Section II
Legal Research: Secondary Authorities and Other Research Aids 205

Chapter 6   Encyclopedias, Periodicals, Treatises, and Restatements   207

Chapter 7   Miscellaneous Secondary Authorities   **259**

Chapter 8   Legal Citation Form   **299**

Chapter 10   Special Research Issues   415

Chapter 11   The Digital Library: Lexis, Westlaw, and Nonprint Research Sources

479

Chapter 12   E-Research: Legal Research Using the Internet   519

Chapter 13   Overview of the Research Process   549

Section III
Legal Writing 579

Chapter 14   Back to Basics 581

Chapter 15   Strategies for Effective Writing   609

Chapter 16   Legal Correspondence   647

Chapter 17   Legal Memoranda   671

Chapter 18   Legal Briefs   689

Chapter 19   Postwriting Steps   715

Appendices

Preface

You will soon discover that legal research is truly a "hands-on" subject. Although there are numerous books to be found that discuss methods and techniques, there is no substitute for actually performing the task of legal research. A simple analogy can be drawn to driving a car: You may find several manuals that discuss driving and provide tips on better driving, but simply reading about operating a car is not a substitute for actually driving a car yourself. Similarly, you will learn the most about legal research, about which shortcuts are invaluable, and about which techniques are non-productive, only by doing legal research. To that end, library assignments are placed at the conclusion of each chapter so you can see and use the books discussed in each chapter. You should never have to use a book or set of books that have not been discussed in the chapter you have finished reading or any preceding chapter. Take the time to explore the books by reviewing the foreword, table of contents, and index found in each volume. Familiarize yourself with all of the features of the books or electronic resources you use, and you will simplify your legal research.

Performing legal research can be both frustrating and gratifying. It can be frustrating because there is often no one perfect answer and because there are no established guidelines on how much research to do and when to stop. On the other hand, legal research is gratifying because you will be engaged in a task that requires you to do something and one in which you will be rewarded by finding the right case, statute, or other authority.

You should view legal research as an exciting treasure hunt—a search for the best authorities to answer a question or legal issue. In this sense, the task of using and exploring the law library or the Internet for answers to legal issues or questions should be a welcome relief from the assignments of other classes, which may be passive in nature and involve copious amounts of reading.

I would encourage you to research with other students if you are comfortable doing so. Often you will learn a great deal by comparing notes with others who may be able to share successful strategies for effectively

using various books or electronic resources or finding the answers to research problems. Naturally, sharing ideas and tips for research techniques should not be viewed as an excuse not to do the work yourself or a license to use answers discussed by others. In other words, you should research with other students (if you find it useful to do so), but you should never write together. Not only is this practice dishonest, but it will prevent you from effectively learning the skill of legal research. Ultimately, an employer is not interested in how many "points" you obtained on a class exercise or what grade you obtained, but in whether you can be depended upon to research an issue competently. As adult learners and professionals, you should concentrate on learning the skill of legal research rather than focusing on the number of right answers you can obtain.

Although this text shows case names and book titles in italics, underlining or underscoring is also acceptable according to *The Bluebook: A Uniform System of Citation* (Columbia Law Review Ass'n et al. eds., 19th ed. 2010) and ALWD & Darby Dickerson, *ALWD Citation Manual* (4th ed., Aspen Publishers 2010), which are the standard reference tools for citation form. There is variation among practitioners, so check with your firm or office to determine if there is a preference. Unless otherwise noted, all citations given in *Bluebook* form are displayed in the format used by practitioners, not in the LARGE AND SMALL CAP format used in academic writing. When only one citation is given in the text, it is given in *Bluebook* form.

When you begin reading this book, most of you will be unfamiliar with cases, statutes, constitutions, or the numerous other legal authorities. As you progress in class and through the chapters and assignments in this text, you will readily be able to measure your progress. When you complete this text and your legal research class, you will have gained thorough mastery of legal research and writing techniques as well as familiarity with the numerous sets of law books and electronic resources that you will be required to use in your profession.

This sixth edition of the text introduces several new features, including the following:

- Conformance of all citations in the text with the new 19th edition of *The Bluebook* and the new 4th edition of *ALWD*. Chapter 8 (relating to citation form) includes a list of the most significant changes made to the new 19th edition of *The Bluebook* and the new 4th edition of *ALWD*.
- Discussion of how to use Google's new feature "Google Scholar" to locate cases.
- Discussion of the migration of the government's website offering access to critical government documents from GPO Access to FDsys.
- Discussion of new websites FederalRegister.gov and Regulations .gov for free access to valuable government materials.
- Revamped section on conducting legislative history research in Chapter 10.

- New assignment in Chapter 11 requiring users to access and use Loislaw (the online legal research system to which readers of this text are provided free access for a period of time).
- New assignment in Chapter 11 requiring readers to Shepardize and KeyCite the same cases to illustrate the differences between Shepardizing and KeyCiting.
- Discussion in Chapter 11 of the following new features in Westlaw and Lexis:

  - West's new, easy-to-use, and intuitive platform WestlawNext, which allows searching similar to "Google"-type searching.
  - Lexis's new features: Easy Search and "Case in Brief."

- Discussion of the fee-based, computer-assisted research system Fastcase and its free app for iPhones (allowing free access to the largest free law library available on an iPhone or iPad), as well as discussion of other law-related "apps."
- All new Discussion Questions and Internet Legal Research Assignments.

Additionally, new charts and diagrams are included, such as a chart (see Figure 10-2) showing where and how to locate legislative history documents. Reflecting the continuing and dramatic effect of the Internet on legal research and the ever-increasing accessibility of resources in cyberspace, new material relating to amended Federal Rule of Appellate Procedure 32.1 (allowing the citation of unpublished decisions) is included in Chapter 4, and links for Web-based tutorials are given when applicable. Chapter 13 (which provides an overview of the legal research process) includes a full range of open-ended research questions, requiring readers to use and apply all skills learned in previous chapters to obtain answers to these research questions.

The vast number of legal authorities available both in a conventional law library and through digital law libraries means that effective legal researchers are flexible. Sometimes the materials you need are not on the shelves and you will need to switch directions. Sometimes new methods of locating materials emerge. In any event, you will find legal research an interesting hunt for the authorities you need, whether in conventional print sources, on Lexis or Westlaw (the computer-assisted legal research systems), or on the Internet.

At the time of the writing of this sixth edition, the Government Printing Office website (previously known as "GPO Access") was in the final stages of migrating its vast collections of federal documents and materials to a new system, called "Federal Digital System" (often referred to as "FDsys" and located at http://www.gpo.gov/fdsys). This site offers easy access to authenticated government documents, including our federal statutes, our Code of Federal Regulations, and numerous other primary sources. Some collections of government materials, however, remain accessible through the prior system, GPO Access, at http://www.gpoaccess.gov.

Textbook Resources

The companion website for *Legal Research and Writing for Paralegals* at www.aspenparalegaled.com/books/bouchoux_legalwriting research includes these additional resources for students and instructors:

- Study aids to help students master the key concepts for this course, including interactive StudyMate exercises such as flash cards, matching exercises, fill-in-the-blank exercises, and cross-word puzzles. (These activities are also available for download to an iPod, iPad, or other handheld device.)
- Instructor resources to accompany the text, including a comprehensive Instructor's Manual, Test Bank, and PowerPoint slides. (These resources are also available on a CD-ROM.)
- Blackboard and eCollege course materials to supplement the text, designed to streamline the teaching of the course and provide valuable resources from the book in an accessible, electronic format.
- Links to helpful websites and updates.

This text also comes packaged with four months of prepaid access to Loislaw's online legal research database at http://www.loislawschool.com.

Deborah E. Bouchoux

Spring 2011

Acknowledgments

I would like to express my deep appreciation to the many individuals who contributed greatly to the development of this text and its sixth edition. First, I would like to express my gratitude to Susan M. Sullivan, the Program Director of the University of San Diego Paralegal Program, who provided me with my first opportunity to teach and who suggested I write a legal research and writing text. She has been a good friend and colleague.

Thank you to Alex Butler for his assistance in obtaining photostats for the text and to Gayle P. Gregg of Kaufman & Canoles for providing numerous sample pages and forms.

Many thanks also to the various reviewers who evaluated the manuscript on behalf of the publisher. Throughout the more than 20 years I have taught I have also received continuing evaluation from my students, who have offered their comments and insight regarding methods of teaching, productive assignments, and effective writing strategies.

Finally, my deepest appreciation to my editor, Sarah Hains (Editorial Production Coordinator), and to the following individuals at Aspen Publishers: Carol McGeehan, Publisher; Betsy Kenny, Developmental Editor; and David Herzig, Associate Publisher—College Market, all of whom offered encouragement and support throughout the development of this text. Their thoughtful comments and suggestions were welcomed and greatly contributed to this sixth edition. Thanks also to Doug Gallaher (Project Manager) and Dane Torbeck (Sponsoring Editor) at Publication Services.

I would like to acknowledge the following publishers who permitted me to reproduce copyrighted material for this text.

Chapter 2: The Federal and State Court Systems

Figure 2-2: Reprinted with permission from *Federal Reporter Second Series*, copyright © 1998 by West, a Thomson Reuters business.

Most of the statistical information in this chapter was obtained from http://www.uscourts/gov and http://www.supremecourt.gov.

Chapter 3: Statutory Law
Figure 3-4: Reprinted with permission from Title 35 of U.S.C.A., copyright by West, a Thomson Reuters business.

Figure 3-5: 35 U.S.C.S. § 289. Copyright 2010 LexisNexis, a division of Reed Elsevier Inc. All rights reserved. Used with permission.

Figure 3-6: Cover of Cumulative Supplement, 42 U.S.C.A. § § 1983, 1984, copyright 2006 by West, a Thomson Reuters business.

Figure 3-7: Reprinted with permission of West, a Thomson Reuters business.

Figure 3-9a: U.S.C.A. General Index. Reprinted with permission of West, a Thomson Reuters business.

Figure 3-9b: U.S.C.S. General Index. Copyright 2010 LexisNexis, a division of Reed Elsevier Inc. All rights reserved. Used with permission.

Figure 3-10: Reprinted with permission from U.S.C.A. Popular Name Table, copyright © 2004 by West, a Thomson Reuters business.

Figure 3-11: Va. Code Ann. § 18.2-26. Reprinted with permission of West, a Thomson Reuters business, copyright © 1996.

Chapter 4: Case Law and Judicial Opinions
Figure 4-1: Reprinted with permission from 595 S.E.2d 697, copyright © 2004 by West, a Thomson Reuters business.

Figure 4-2: Reprinted with permission from 108 S. Ct. 2830, copyright © 1992 by West, a Thomson Reuters business.

Figure 4-3: Reprinted with permission from *West's Law Finder*, copyright © 1988 by West, a Thomson Reuters business.

Figure 4-6: Reprinted with permission from 33 L. Ed. 2d 363. Copyright 2010 LexisNexis, a division of Reed Elsevier Inc. All rights reserved. Used with permission.

Chapter 5: The Use of Digests, Annotated Law Reports, and *Words and Phrases*
Figure 5-2: Reprinted with permission of West, a Thomson Reuters business.

Figure 5-3: Reprinted with permission from Descriptive Word *Index to Ninth Decennial Digest*, Part 2, copyright © 1988 by West, a Thomson Reuters business.

Figure 5-4: Reprinted with permission from 29 *Ninth Decennial Digest*, Part 2, page 783, copyright © 1988 by West, a Thomson Reuters business.

Figure 5-5: Reprinted with permission from 44 *Ninth Decennial Digest*, Part 2, Table of Cases, page 1015, copyright © 1988 by West, a Thomson Reuters business.

Figure 5-6: Reprinted with permission from 29 *Ninth Decennial Digest*, Part 2, page 956, copyright © 1988 by West, a Thomson Reuters business.

Figures 5-7, 5-8, and 5-10: Reprinted with permission from American Law Reports, copyright by West, a Thomson Reuters business.

Figure 5-11: Reprinted with permission from *Words and Phrases*, copyright by West, a Thomson Reuters business.

Chapter 6: Encyclopedias, Periodicals, Treatises, and Restatements

Figure 6-1: Reprinted with permission from 87 C.J.S., copyright by West, a Thomson Reuters business.

Figure 6-2: Reprinted with permission from 25 Am. Jur. 2d, copyright by West, a Thomson Reuters business.

Figure 6-3: Reprinted with permission from *Deeds* § 87:77, *Am. Jur. Legal Forms 2d*, copyright by West, a Thomson Reuters business.

Figure 6-4: Reprinted with permission from General Index Update to Am. Jur. 2d, copyright by West, a Thomson Reuters business.

Figure 6-6: Reprinted with permission of the publisher, California Western Law Review, Vol. 44, Number 1, Fall 2007, copyright © 2007.

Figure 6-7: Reprinted with permission of *California Lawyer*, copyright © 2004.

Figure 6-8: Reprinted from "Subject and Author Index" and "Table of Cases" from *Index to Legal Periodicals & Books*, reprinted with permission of the H.W. Wilson Company.

Figure 6-9: Reprinted from *O'Neal's Close Corporations* (3d ed. 2003) copyright © 2003 by West, a Thomson Reuters business.

Figure 6-11: Restatement, Second, Torts, Copyright © 1965 by the American Law Institute. Reprinted with permission. All rights reserved.

Chapter 7: Miscellaneous Secondary Authorities

Figure 7-1: Reprinted with permission from *Black's Law Dictionary* 1002 (6th ed. 1990) copyright © 1990 by West, a Thomson Reuters business.

Figure 7-2: Reprinted with permission from *Martindale-Hubbell Law Directory* 1389B. Copyright © Martindale-Hubbell.

Figure 7-3A: Reprinted with permission from *Virginia Forms*, Vol. 3B, Form 9-1706, by Frank J. Gallo. Copyright 2010 LexisNexis, a division of Reed Elsevier Inc. All rights reserved. Used with permission.

Chapter 9: Updating and Validating Your Research

Figure 9-1: Reprinted with permission from *Shepard's United States Citations*, Eighth Edition, 2004, Bound Vol. 1-7, page 703. Copyright © 2004 LexisNexis, a division of Reed Elsevier Inc. All rights reserved. Used with permission.

Figure 9-4: Reprinted with permission from *Shepard's California Citations*, Vol. 88, July 2006, No. 7, page 461. Copyright © 2006 LexisNexis, a division of Reed Elsevier Inc. All rights reserved. Used with permission.

Figure 9-6: Copyright © 2010 LexisNexis, a division of Reed Elsevier Inc. All rights reserved. Used with permission.

Figure 9-7: Reprinted with permission from Westlaw, copyright by West, a Thomson Reuters business.

Figure 9-8: Reprinted with permission from Thomson/West, copyright by West, a Thomson Reuters business.

Chapter 11: The Digital Library: Lexis, Westlaw, and Nonprint Research Sources

Figures 11-1, 11-2, 11-3, and 11-4: Lexis screens. Copyright 2010 LexisNexis, a division of Reed Elsevier Inc. All rights reserved. Used with permission.

Figures 11-5, 11-6, 11-7, and 11-8: Westlaw screens. Reprinted with permission of West, a Thomson Reuters business.

Chapter 12: E-Research: Legal Research Using the Internet

Figure 12-1: FindLaw screen. Reprinted with permission of Thomson/West.

Figure 12-2: Reprinted with permission of Justia Inc.

Figure 12-3: Washlaw screen. Reprinted with permission of Washlaw.edu.

Public Domain Materials

No copyright is claimed in the material shown in the following figures: 3-2, 7-6, 10-1, 10-3, 10-4, 10-5, 10-6, 10-7, 10-8, 15-1, Appendix B, Appendix C, Appendix D.

Legal Research
and Writing
for Paralegals

Legal
Research

Primary Authorities

Finding the Law

We are under a Constitution, but the Constitution is what the judges say it is, and the judiciary is the safeguard of our liberty and of our property under the Constitution.

Charles Evans Hughes (1907)

Chapter Overview

In this chapter we will discuss the role of paralegals in legal research and writing, the ethical duty to perform research competently, types of law libraries and their uses, and the sources of law in the United States. We will also examine the classification of law books as either primary or secondary sources. Finally, there is a brief introduction to the major law book publishers, who will be compared in greater detail in later chapters.

A. The Paralegal's Role in Legal Research and Writing

1. Legal Research and Writing as Core Competencies

Paralegals are expected to perform the task of legal research competently and cost effectively. In fact, the American Association for Paralegal

Education ("AAfPE"), a national organization that serves the needs of paralegal educators and institutions offering paralegal education programs, identifies legal research as one of the "core competencies" that a successful paralegal must possess.

Performing legal research today is both easier and more difficult than it was just a generation ago. It is easier because many materials are available through electronic sources and on the Internet, making it quick and easy to find statutes, cases, and other legal authorities. It is more difficult because these new materials make so many sources accessible that tracking down the right authority can seem like finding a needle in a haystack.

Today's paralegals are expected to know how to use conventional print sources, the computer-assisted research services Lexis and Westlaw, and the Internet to find the best answer to a research problem as quickly and effectively as possible.

Once you have conducted legal research, you will need to communicate the results of that research. In fact, the cornerstone of the legal profession is communication—communication with a colleague, client, adverse party, or judge. In most cases the communication will be in written form. Even in those instances in which you communicate orally, you will often follow up with a written letter or memo to a file. Effective legal writing is not only a task expected of paralegals but also one of the core competencies identified by AAfPE for success in the paralegal profession.

2. *Ethical Duty to Research Accurately*

Perhaps the most fundamental aspect of the attorney-client relationship is the client's absolute trust and confidence in the competence of the attorney. This duty of competence is imposed on paralegals as well who are required to exercise the ordinary skill and knowledge that would be expected of similar paralegals in similar circumstances. In fact, Guideline 1 of the American Bar Association's Model Guidelines for the Utilization of Paralegal Services specifically requires that attorneys take reasonable measures to ensure that a paralegal's conduct is consistent with the attorney's obligations, meaning that obligations imposed on attorneys are likewise imposed on paralegals. Thus, attorneys are responsible for ensuring that their paralegals are competent to perform assigned work, including legal research and writing.

Although it is important to "know" the law, particularly in a field in which you may intend to specialize, it is even more important to be able to "find" the law. In this sense, proficiency in legal research is the foundation for a successful career as a paralegal. Your employer will not be as interested in your final grade in any specific class as much as your ability to find accurate answers to questions relating to topics even though you may not have been exposed to those topics in school. If you cannot perform legal research tasks accurately and efficiently, you will not be a successful paralegal despite excellent grades in your coursework.

In fact, the duty to perform accurate legal research has been addressed in a number of cases, including *People v. Ledesma*, 729 P.2d 839, 871 (Cal. 1987), in which the court noted that an attorney's first duty is to investigate the facts of a client's case and to research the law applicable to those facts. In sum, the ethical duty to conduct adequate research required of attorneys is shared by paralegals as well.

Moreover, the failure to research adequately may lead to liability for legal malpractice. In one of the earliest cases on this subject matter, *Smith v. Lewis*, 530 P.2d 589 (Cal. 1975), *overruled on other grounds*, 544 P.2d 561 (Cal. 1976), the California Supreme Court affirmed a lower court decision awarding $100,000 to be paid to a former client by an attorney who had failed to conduct adequate legal research. The court held that the attorney was obligated to undertake reasonable research and stated, "[e]ven as to doubtful matters, an attorney is expected to perform sufficient research to enable him to make an informed and intelligent judgment on behalf of his client." 530 P.2d at 596. In sum, you will be expected to perform competent legal research not only because your employer will insist on it but also because ethical standards demand it. Finally, as further evidence of the importance of legal research, in spring 2006, the National Conference of Bar Examiners announced plans to consider adding a component to the bar exam that will focus on legal research methods and skills. Now that we have established the role of paralegals in legal research and writing and the ethical duty shared by paralegals with attorneys to conduct competent legal research, we can address two critical questions: where legal research is performed and what sources are used.

B. Law Libraries

1. *Types of Law Libraries*

As noted in the introduction to this text, legal research is a "hands-on" skill, requiring you to know how to use a law library. Your first task, therefore, is to locate a law library that you may use. There are approximately 3,600 law libraries in the United States. Following is a list of the most common types of law libraries with a brief description of each:

> *Law School Libraries* All accredited law schools have their own law libraries, most of which will have tens of thousands of volumes in print and nonprint forms such as Lexis, Westlaw, CD-ROM, microforms, and the Internet. If you are attending a paralegal program at a four-year university that is affiliated with a law school, you will undoubtedly have access to the law library at the law school. Even if you do not attend a paralegal program affiliated with a law school, you may have access to a law school library if it has been designated as a Federal Depository Library,

or a partial or selective depository, meaning that certain publications of the United States government, generally statutes and court decisions, will be sent to the library for review and access by the general public. In many cases, local public libraries or university libraries are designated as federal depositories. You can easily determine whether a library is a Federal Depository Library by calling the reference librarian at the library and inquiring. The locations of the approximately 1,350 depository libraries can be found at the Government Printing Office's website: http://www.gpo.gov/libraries.

Paralegal School Libraries Some paralegal programs maintain their own law libraries, although these are typically much smaller and contain far fewer volumes than law school libraries. Generally, only students who attend these programs have access to these law libraries.

Local Law Libraries Often a county or city will maintain a law library, and these are usually open to members of the general public. These law libraries vary in size, with the largest law libraries being found in the largest counties. Often they are located near a courthouse. The American Association of Law Libraries provides a list of state, county, and court law libraries at the following website: http://www.aallnet.org/sis/sccll.

Government or Agency Law Libraries Various governmental agencies, such as the Department of Justice, maintain their own law libraries. These law libraries typically serve only agency employees, and members of the general public will have no access. The Library of Congress, located in Washington, D.C., was established by the United States Congress in 1800 primarily to provide reference and research assistance to members of Congress. It has an excellent law library, which is open to any member of the general public.

Courthouse Law Libraries Many courts, both federal and state, maintain their own law libraries. Court law libraries are often found in the courthouse for the county seat. Some law libraries are open to the public while others restrict access to courthouse personnel, attorneys, and their paralegals.

Bar Association and Private Group Law Libraries Often bar associations or private groups, such as insurance companies or real estate boards, will maintain law libraries. These are usually open only to members of the association or group.

Law Firm Libraries Almost every law firm will maintain a law library, some of which are nearly as extensive as a law school or courthouse law library. These law libraries are available for use only by members or employees of the firm.

You should consult a telephone book or use a general Internet search engine, such as Google, and contact law schools, courthouses, and county offices in your area to determine whether members of the general public have access to those law libraries and to obtain the hours for each. Be particularly careful of law school libraries that tend to schedule their hours of operation around the law school calendar and will often close unannounced after final exams or during semester breaks.

Additionally, many public and college or university libraries are increasing their collections of law books. While these libraries typically offer only the major sets of books, such as the cases of the United States Supreme Court, federal statutes, and statutes from the state in which they are located, these public or college libraries may afford a quick answer to some legal research questions.

Finally, law libraries now exist in computer databases such as those offered by Lexis or Westlaw and in cyberspace with vast collections of legal materials available for free "24/7." These virtual law libraries afford quick and easy access to a significant number of legal resources. Conducting legal research using Lexis and Westlaw is discussed in Chapter 11, and conducting legal research in cyberspace through the Internet is discussed in Chapter 12.

2. Arrangement of Law Libraries

There is no one standard arrangement for law libraries. Each law library is arranged according to the needs of its patrons or by decision of the law librarian. The best introduction to a law library is a tour given by a staff member, and you should inquire whether orientation tours of the law library are given. If you cannot arrange for a tour, obtain a copy of the library handbook or guide that will describe the services offered, set forth the library's rules and regulations, and provide a floorplan of the law library. Spend an hour wandering around the law library and familiarizing yourself with its arrangement, organization, and collections. You will notice that there may be duplicate volumes of some books or even duplicate sets of books. In general, books that are widely used will have duplicates to ensure ease of use and accessibility. In many cases you can judge legal books by their titles, which usually describe their contents. The law library's website may offer a "virtual" tour.

Although a few law libraries still use a card catalog (identical in its alphabetical organization and arrangement to the card catalogs you may have used through your schooling) to help you locate the books, treatises, and periodicals in the library, the more modern approach is the online catalog or OPAC (online public access catalog).

Most of the online catalogs are very easy to use, and you should not be intimidated. The law library staff is usually quite willing to provide instruction, and training sessions can be completed in only a few minutes. Typically, you will type in or "enter" the title, author, or subject matter you desire in the search box displayed on the screen, and you will then be provided with the "call number." The shelves or "stacks" in the law library

are clearly marked, and locating a book is merely a matter of matching up the call number provided by the card catalog or online catalog with the appropriate stack label.

Most law school and large law firm law libraries use the Library of Congress classification system to arrange their books. The Library of Congress classification system arranges books on the shelves in subject order. Materials are organized according to twenty-one branches of knowledge. Each book is marked with a three-line classification number, consisting of an alphanumeric combination, which includes letters, a whole number, and a decimal. For example, a book may be classified as "KF503.181." The designation "KF" is the Library of Congress identifier for American legal publications, and "503.181" refers to the book's location in the stacks.

An unusual feature of law libraries is that, in general, they are not circulating libraries. That is, unlike other libraries that circulate their volumes by allowing one to check out books, law libraries seldom allow patrons to check out books. You can imagine your frustration if you were unable to read a case because someone had already checked out the volume containing the case. Books that are not widely used, however, may often be checked out by individuals who possess library identification cards.

Practice Tip

The Law Library

Familiarize yourself with your law library by investing half an hour to wander through the stacks and gain a sense of how the library is arranged. Experiencing the way the stacks are organized will imprint itself on your memory. This initial investment will save time for you later when you need to recall, for example, where the books relating to corporate law or litigation are located.

---

3. Law Library Staff

Most of the larger law libraries are serviced by full-time law librarians who not only are lawyers who have been awarded a Juris Doctor degree but also possess a Master's Degree in Library Science. Most library staff are extremely helpful and responsive to questions; however, you should diligently try to locate a book or answer before you approach library staff for help. In law school libraries, the individuals who sit at the front desk are often law students who may not be thoroughly knowledgeable about the arrangement of the library or its collections. Therefore, if you have a question, be sure to address it to one of the professional law librarians (in this regard, the reference librarians are particularly helpful) rather than a student who may be more interested in studying at the front desk than

helping you locate a book. Many reference librarians are available for research consultations by appointment. Although law librarians will provide useful research tips and suggestions, they will not provide legal advice.

4. Law Library Courtesy

You should assume that everyone who uses the law library is as busy as you, and therefore you should observe standard library etiquette by reshelving properly every book you use (unless the law library you use prohibits reshelving or has a separate preshelving stack for books that are to be reshelved). Nothing is more frustrating than taking time out of a busy schedule to drive to a law library and search for the appropriate sources only to realize that a needed volume is missing. If you take books to a study carrel to read or to the photocopier to reproduce a page, you must reshelve them when you are finished. This is particularly true in school situations in which your fellow classmates will in all likelihood have the same assignments as you and will thus need to use the same books.

Do not deface the books by turning pages down or marking an answer. Finally, do not resort to unfair conduct by hiding or intentionally misplacing books. There is no excuse for such overzealous tactics that not only impede learning but also reflect poorly on one who is purporting to be a member of a profession devoted to the law.

Ethics Alert

Researching Economically

Because legal researchers have so many sources from which to choose when conducting a research project, it is critical to consider which sources best serve the client's interests. Rather than rushing to begin a project the minute it is assigned, spend some time thinking things through. Should you begin with the conventional print sources? Lexis or Westlaw? The Internet? Your ethical duty to research accurately includes the duty to research economically as well.

---

5. Other Library Services

Most law libraries offer a variety of other services to ensure students can conduct productive research. For example, if you are working on an extensive project, your law library may reserve a carrel for you and allow you to store books and materials there. Similarly, you may be able to reserve a group study room so you can meet with other students to brainstorm a research project. Law librarians can provide you with

permits and letters of introduction to other law libraries in the area so you can retrieve materials not available at your law library. If certain materials are not maintained at your law library, the reference librarian may assist you in borrowing materials from other institutions through interlibrary loans. The ease of facsimile and online transmission results in ready access to a wealth of materials from all over the nation and the world. Most law libraries also offer tutorials though their websites.

Practice Tip

Legal Abbreviations

In the beginning of your legal career, you may become confused by the numerous abbreviations used for legal books, case reports, and journals. To determine the meaning of abbreviations such as "Ala." (for *Alabama Reports*) or "C.J.S." (for *Corpus Juris Secundum*), check Appendix A in *Black's Law Dictionary* (9th ed. 2009), which provides an extensive list of abbreviations commonly used in law. Additionally, be patient. Within just a few weeks you will likely learn about 90 percent of all of the abbreviations you are likely to encounter. See Chapter 4 for a list of some other common legal abbreviations.

C. Sources of Law in the United States

1. Cases and Our Common Law Tradition

If your task is to be able to find the law, one may well ask, "What is the 'law' we are talking about?" There are numerous definitions of the word "law." On an academic or philosophical level, law is a system of rules that governs society so as to prevent chaos. On a practical level, on the other hand, as indicated by the quotation at the beginning of this chapter, Governor of New York, and later United States Supreme Court Chief Justice, Charles Evans Hughes suggested that the law "is what the judges say it is." This second view may give you cause for concern. If the law is what a judge says, what if the judge rules against you because of your race, or sex, or religion? What if the judge is not familiar with an area of the law? The American legal system has certain safeguards built into it to protect litigants from such scenarios.

The American legal system is part of what is referred to as the "common law" tradition. "Common law" is defined in part by *Black's Law Dictionary* 313 (9th ed. 2009) as that body of law that derived from judicial decisions rather than from statutes or constitutions. Common law is thus often referred to as "judge-made law."

This common law system began in England several hundred years ago. Since at least 1300 A.D., people who may have been training to be lawyers began "taking notes" on what occurred during trials. When judges were called upon to decide cases, they then began referring to these written reports of earlier cases and following the prior cases in similar situations. The English referred to this system as the "common law" because it was applied equally all throughout England and replaced a less uniform system of law. This system of following similar previous cases was considered the most equitable way of resolving disputes: People who are involved in like situations should be treated in the same manner.

This concept of following previous cases, or precedents, is called *stare decisis*, which is a Latin phrase meaning "to stand by things decided." In its broadest sense, the doctrine of stare decisis means that once courts have announced a principle of law, they will follow it in future cases that are substantially similar. It is this doctrine of stare decisis that serves to protect litigants from judges who may not be familiar with an area of the law. If the judge is required to follow precedent, he or she cannot rule against you based on your race, sex, or religion. Similarly, these precedents will guide a judge who is unacquainted with a certain area of the law. In this way, stare decisis advances fairness and consistency in our legal system.

Moreover, stare decisis promotes stability in our judicial system. It would not only be chaotic but manifestly unfair if judges treated each case that came before them as being severed from our great body of legal tradition and then rendered different and inconsistent rulings on a daily basis. You can imagine the frustration of a client who seeks advice of counsel on the division of property in a dissolution of a marriage only to be informed that the division depends on which judge hears the case: that Judge Jones divides property in a marital dissolution on a 50/50 basis; Judge Smith divides the property on a 40/60 basis; and Judge Anderson divides the property differently each day depending upon his mood. The client's rights would be totally dependent upon an arbitrary assignment to a judge. Such a result is not only unjust but also unpredictable. Thus, stare decisis not only encourages stability in our legal system but also aids those in the legal profession in advising clients as to the likely disposition of their cases.

Under this system or doctrine of precedent following, "the law" was thus found in the written decisions of the judges, and these decisions served as precedents that were followed in later cases involving substantially similar issues. Thus, the first source of law in the United States is judge-made case law.

2. *Constitutions*

The second source of law in the United States is constitutions. A constitution sets forth the fundamental law for a nation or a state. It is the document that sets forth the principles relating to organization and

regulation of a federal or state government. We have a United States Constitution, our supreme law of the land, and each state has its own constitution.

3. *Statutes*

The third source of law in the United States is statutes. A statute, or law, is defined by *Black's Law Dictionary* 1542 (9th ed. 2009) as "a law passed by a legislative body." In the United States, legislatures did not become particularly active in enacting statutes until the early to mid-nineteenth century, when the United States economy began changing from a very rural base to a more urban base. This major change in American society was coupled with a tremendous population growth, due largely to immigration, and it became clear that rather than having a system that decided disputes on a case-by-case basis, which was slow and cumbersome at best, enacting broader laws that would set forth rules to govern behavior of the public at large would best serve the needs of a growing society. For example, when people live miles apart from one another and interact on a sporadic basis, few disputes will arise. On the other hand, when people are crowded into apartment buildings and work in densely populated urban areas, the number of problems greatly increases, and there is a concomitant need for general regulation by law or statute.

4. *Administrative Regulations*

A fourth source of law in the United States is found in the vast number of administrative rules and regulations promulgated by federal agencies such as the Federal Communications Commission ("FCC"), the Food and Drug Administration ("FDA"), the Occupational Safety and Health Administration ("OSHA"), and numerous other agencies. Agencies exist in the individual states as well, and these also enact rules and regulations.

The agencies play a unique role in our legal system because they function quasi-legislatively and quasi-judicially. You may recall from basic history and civics classes that our government is divided into three branches: the legislative branch, which makes laws; the judicial branch, which interprets laws; and the executive branch, which enforces laws. Each division is to exercise its own powers, and, by a system known as "checks and balances," each functions separately from the others.

The agencies, on the other hand, perform two functions: They act as a legislature by promulgating rules and regulations that bind us; and they act as a judiciary by hearing disputes and rendering decisions.

Although you may not have given a great deal of thought to the impact of the agencies in your daily life, their influence is significant and far-reaching. For example, the radio you listen to and the television you watch are regulated by the FCC; the cosmetics you use and the food or aspirin you ingest are regulated by the FDA; and the safety of your workplace is regulated by OSHA.

5. *The Executive Branch*

Although the primary function of the federal executive branch is to enforce the law, it does serve as a source of law in three ways. First, treaties are entered into by the executive branch with the advice and consent of the United States Senate. These agreements between two or more nations do affect your daily life and serve as a source of law because they may relate to trade and import matters, economic cooperation, or even international boundaries and fishing rights. Second, the president, our chief executive, can issue executive orders to regulate and direct federal agencies and officials. State governors may also issue executive orders. Third, the executive branch exerts influence on the law through policies on enforcing laws.

For example, if various federal laws relating to possession of small amounts of drugs are rarely enforced, the *effect* is as if the law does not exist despite the fact that a statute clearly prohibits such acts. Nevertheless, although such an approach by the executive branch influences the law as well as societal behavior, such influence on the law is indirect and remote. In the event the government then prosecutes an individual for violation of such a previously unenforced law, the individual usually cannot raise the previous laxity as a defense. In a related example, in 1980, when the Selective Service System was reinstated to require United States males born in 1960 or later to register with the Service, several conscientious objectors refused to register. The federal government immediately prosecuted some of these individuals, who then asserted as a defense that they had been singled out for prosecution because they had been vigorous opponents of this draft registration. This defense, commonly known as "selective enforcement," is rarely successful and was not successful in the draft registration cases. To use a simple analogy, if you are cited for speeding, you cannot successfully assert that either all people who speed should be likewise cited or that none should. You would accept that you had simply been unluckier than other speeders. On the other hand, if only women are cited or only Hispanics are cited, such would appear to be the result of discrimination based on sex or ethnic origin, and a defense of selective enforcement alleging such invidious discrimination might well be successful.

D. Legal Systems of Other Countries

Although every country has its own system of law, most systems are classified as being either part of the common law tradition, described above, or part of the civil law tradition. Civil law systems developed from Roman law. The Roman emperor Justinian I commissioned a comprehensive code of laws known as *Corpus Juris Civilis*, meaning "Body of Civil Law," to set forth all of the law of the Roman Empire. As a result,

countries whose systems of law follow the Roman scheme of law with thoroughly comprehensive codes are said to be part of the civil law tradition. Even today many countries' codes of civil law are derived from the original Roman codes.

In general, civil law countries place much heavier reliance on their collections of statutes than on their much smaller collections of cases. These statutes are designed to address every conceivable legal issue that might arise, and it is these statutes that provide the ultimate answers to legal questions. Cases considered by judges rarely form the sole basis for any decision in civil law countries. Austria, China, France, Germany, Greece, Italy, Japan, Mexico, the Russian Federation, South Korea, Spain, and many of the countries of Latin America are considered civil law countries.

In general, English-speaking countries or those that are prior British Commonwealth colonies are part of the common law system, which is greatly dependent on cases used as precedents, which in turn are followed in future cases that are substantially similar. Non-English-speaking countries are usually part of the civil law system, which is greatly dependent on codes or statutes intended to apply to every legal question or dispute. Because of the thoroughness of the Roman codes, statutes came to be known as the "written" law while the common law, relying as it does on judge-made case law, is often referred to as the "unwritten" law.

It is interesting to note that every state in the United States, except Louisiana, and every Canadian province, except Quebec, is part of the common law tradition. Because Quebec and Louisiana were settled by the French, their legal systems are largely patterned after the law of France, a civil law country. In fact, the Civil Code of Louisiana is closely based on the Code Napoleon, the French legal code enacted in 1804. In practice, however, even in many countries with systems based on civil law, case law still plays a significant role. Table T.2 of *The Bluebook* identifies more than 40 foreign countries as either common law or civil law countries.

E. Legal System of the United States

The nature of our federalist system of government seeks to apportion power between our central or federal government and the 50 separate states and the District of Columbia. The founders of the Constitution feared that an overly strong federal government with concentrated power would ultimately engulf the separate states. Therefore, the Tenth Amendment to the Constitution was adopted. This amendment reserves to the individual states any powers not expressly granted or delegated to the federal government.

As a result, although the United States adheres to a uniform common law tradition, there is no one single legal system in this country.

We have federal laws enacted by the United States Congress and federal cases decided by our federal courts, including the United States Supreme Court. Moreover, unless an area of the law has been preempted by the United States Constitution or the federal government, each state and the District of Columbia is free to enact laws as well as decide cases dealing with state or local concerns. Even within each state are smaller political subdivisions such as cities and counties, which enact local ordinances and regulations.

Thus, there is a tremendous body of legal literature on the shelves of law libraries: federal cases and federal statutes; Connecticut cases and Connecticut statutes; Florida cases and Florida statutes; Utah cases and Utah statutes; and so forth. Additionally, both the federal government and state governments promulgate administrative regulations, attorneys general issue opinions regarding legal problems, and experts publish commentary regarding the law. As early as 1821, Supreme Court Justice Joseph Story complained, "The mass of law is . . . accumulating with an almost incredible rapidity . . . . It is impossible not to look without some discouragement upon the ponderous volumes, which the next half century will add to the groaning shelves of our jurists." This statement was made about the time volume 19 of the *United States Reports* was published. As of 2010, the *United States Reports* covered more than 550 volumes.

All of the great mass of legal authorities can be classified as either primary authority or secondary authority. That is, every book in any law library is a primary authority or a secondary authority. See Figure 1-1.

Primary authorities are official pronouncements of the law by the executive branch (treaties and executive orders), legislative branch (constitutions, statutes, and administrative regulations and decisions), and judicial branch (cases). The key primary authorities are cases, constitutions, statutes, and administrative regulations. Thus, primary sources are those created by a governmental entity.

If a legal authority does not fall within one of the previously mentioned categories, it is a *secondary* authority. Secondary authorities may consist of legal encyclopedias, which provide summaries of many areas of the law; law review articles written about various legal topics; books or other treatises dealing with legal issues; law dictionaries; annotations, or essays about the law; and expert opinions on legal issues. In general, the secondary authorities are not the law but rather provide comment, discussion, and explanation of the primary authorities and, more important, help you locate the primary authorities.

It is critical to understand thoroughly the differences between primary and secondary authorities because only the primary authorities are *binding* upon the court, agency, or tribunal that may be deciding the legal issue you are researching. That is, if your argument relies upon or cites a case, constitution, statute, or administrative regulation that is relevant to a legal issue, it *must* be followed. All other authorities, for example, the secondary authorities, are *persuasive* only. If your argument cites *Black's Law Dictionary* for the definition of *negligence*, a court might

be *persuaded* to adopt such a definition, but it is not *bound* to do so. On the other hand, if you cite a relevant case that defines *negligence*, a court must follow that definition.

Even though the secondary authorities are not binding on a court, they are often extremely effective research tools and provide excellent introductions to various legal topics. Nevertheless, you should keep in mind the purpose of the secondary authorities—to explain the primary authorities and locate the primary authorities that, if relevant, must be followed by a court.

In addition to the various authorities previously discussed, there are other books in the law library that are in the nature of practical guides or finding tools. These include books such as digests, which help you locate cases (see Chapter 5), form books, which provide forms for various legal documents such as wills, deeds, and contracts (see Chapter 7), and sets of books (and their electronic counterparts) called *Shepard's Citations*, which help you update the authorities you rely upon in any legal writing (see Chapter 9). Although these books are not true secondary authorities, their principal function is either to assist in locating primary sources or to serve as practical or finding guides for those in the legal profession.

The Final Wrap-Up

Using and Citing Primary and Secondary Authorities

Use: Use primary authorities to support the legal assertions you make. Use secondary authorities to summarize and explain the primary authorities and to help you locate the primary authorities.

Citation: You may cite to any primary authority. If a primary authority is on point, it must be followed in your jurisdiction. You may cite to most secondary authorities. Many are highly authoritative (such as the Restatements and many treatises). Others, however, are elementary and weak (for example, most legal encyclopedias) and should be used to familiarize yourself with an area of law and to direct you to the primary authorities.

F. Law Book Publishing

As shown in Figure 1-1, the collection and variety of books in a law library are incredibly extensive.

Compared to the litigation explosion of the last 30 years, the early period of American history produced a fairly small number of cases. But just as the change in American society from agrarian and rural to an industrial and urban population resulted in a need for statutes to establish standards for behavior, this change also resulted in increased litigation and attendant case decisions.

For example, in the United States Courts of Appeal alone, the number of cases filed between 2003 and 2006 increased by more than 9 percent. According to the National Center for State Courts, the nation's state courts process more than 85 million cases each year. In fact, this same organization reports that approximately 95 percent of all legal cases initiated in the United States are filed in the state courts, and has concluded that the "trend for most types of state court cases is characterized by rapid growth." Most cases filed in the trial courts, approximately 90 percent, never come to trial. Of those state court cases that go to trial, only slightly more than 10 percent are appealed and result in a published opinion due to the fact that trial court opinions are rarely published. Nevertheless, even that number, added to the cases decided and published by the federal courts, results in approximately 50,000 cases being published each year. Additionally, Congress and the state legislatures publish thousands of pages of statutes, and thousands of pages of administrative rules and regulations are also published annually.

Figure 1-1
Primary Authorities (binding)

Authorities	*Source*
Cases (federal and state)	Judiciary
Constitutions (federal and state)	Legislature
Statutes (federal and state)	Legislature
Administrative regulations (federal and state)	Administrative agencies
Executive orders (federal and state)	Executive branch
Treaties (federal only)	Executive branch

Secondary Authorities (persuasive)

Authorities	*Finding Tools*
Encyclopedias	Digests
Law review articles	
Periodical publications	*Updating Tools*
Treatises and texts	*Shepard's Citations* and KeyCite
Dictionaries	
Attorneys general opinions	
Restatements	
Annotations	
Foreign sources	
Form books	
Practice guides (such as jury instructions or non-judicial opinions on ethics)	

Thus, a tremendous amount of publication of legal authorities, both primary and secondary, occurs each year. You cannot expect to know all of the law contained in these authorities; however, you can be reasonably expected to be able to locate and use these legal authorities. That is the goal of legal research.

The actual publication of these authorities is conducted by only a handful of publishing companies. The giant in the legal publishing industry is West, a Thomson Reuters business, headquartered in Eagan, Minnesota ("West") and founded in 1872.

In 1996, West was purchased for $3.4 billion by The Thomson Corporation, a Canadian publishing and information conglomerate. In the United States, the company retained its identification as "West." In the mid-1990s, West then merged with or purchased a number of other large law book publishers, namely Bancroft-Whitney, Clark Boardman Callaghan, and Lawyers Cooperative Publishing. West's more than 8,500 employees make it the preeminent provider of information to the legal market in the United States. In 2001, West acquired FindLaw (http://www.findlaw.com), which is a leader in free online legal information and services and the highest-trafficked legal website. In addition to being the provider of Westlaw, West annually publishes over 60 million books.

The merger of Lawyers Cooperative Publishing ("Lawyers Co-op") into West has been of particular interest inasmuch as these two companies were for years the major publishers in the law book industry, offering competing products and services. For example, West has published federal statutes in a set known as U.S.C.A. while Lawyers Co-op published the same statutes in its set, U.S.C.S. Similarly, West has published cases from the United States Supreme Court in a set called *Supreme Court Reporter* while Lawyers Co-op published those same cases in a set called *United States Supreme Court Reports, Lawyers' Edition*. Lawyers and other legal professionals would purchase one set rather than the other based on price, convenience, habit, and ease of use, or perceived advantages of one set over the other.

Because the possibility of West acquiring a virtual monopoly on legal publication existed, West was ordered to divest itself of some of the publications it acquired through its merger. Thus, U.S.C.S. is now owned by LexisNexis Group ("Lexis"), a division of Reed Elsevier PLC, and will continue to compete head-on with West for readers of federal statutes. You will likely notice some differences in the presentation of Lexis's name in its various publications. For example, some of its publications are marked "LexisNexis," others are marked "LEXIS Publishing," and still others are marked "LEXIS Law Publishing." For simplicity, this text will generally use "Lexis" to refer both to the company's print publications and to its online or computer-assisted legal research system.

The numerous combinations and acquisitions of publishing companies have resulted in changes in some features of some law books. For example, for years a set of books called *American Law Reports* was published by Lawyers Co-op. It therefore referred its users to other Lawyers Co-op books. In 1998, the set was acquired by West, and thus it now directs readers to West-owned law books. Moreover, some of the

features of the set changed slightly after West acquired it. Thus, as books are described in this text, it is possible that some of their features and layout have changed over the years with recent books in a set appearing slightly different from earlier published books in the set.

Another major law book publisher is Wolters Kluwer, which is headquartered in the Netherlands and includes a number of other "brands," including Aspen Publishers and Commerce Clearing House. Wolters Kluwer's computer-assisted research system is called Loislaw and is of particular benefit to sole practitioners and smaller law offices.

Law book publishers also face increasing competition from emerging technologies. As discussed in Chapter 11, many cases now appear in CD-ROM format at a price significantly less than print versions, or on the Internet at no cost. These inroads on print publication have caused decreases in circulation of print materials. For example, subscriptions to West's *South Western Reporter*, publishing decisions from Texas, Missouri, Arkansas, Kentucky, and Tennessee, have fallen 21 percent since 1993.

Finally, the acquisition of West by Thomson comes amid increasing competition and consolidation in the legal publishing arena. In 1994, Dutch publisher Wolters Kluwer purchased legal and tax publisher Commerce Clearing House Inc. In 1994, Anglo-Dutch publishing power-house Reed Elsevier PLC purchased Lexis, the online legal research system, from Mead Corporation for $1.5 billion. In sum, the world of legal publishing, long dominated by the giants West and Lawyers Co-op, is changing, partly due to increased competition and conglomeration and partly due to pressures brought to bear by the Internet, which allows 24-hours-a-day free access to many legal materials.

West publishes primary and secondary sources, for example, cases, statutes, and constitutions, as well as encyclopedias and other nonbinding authorities. Throughout the chapters ahead, there are frequent discussions and comparisons of West and other publishers, including analyses of similarities and distinctions between methods and organization of their publications.

In general, there are three major "families" of legal publishers, each of which incorporates other law book publishers: The Thomson Corporation (including West and Westlaw, Bancroft Whitney, and Clark Boardman Callaghan); Reed Elsevier PLC (including Lexis, Matthew Bender, Michie Company, Shepard's, and Martindale-Hubbell); and Wolters Kluwer (including Aspen Publishers, Inc. and Commerce Clearing House). More information on legal publishers can be found at the following Internet site: *A Legal Publishers List: Corporate Affiliations of Legal Publishers* (2d ed. 2006), *available at* http://www.aallnet.org/committee/criv/resources/tools/list.

Additionally, some companies such as Commerce Clearing House, Clark Boardman Callaghan, and Bureau of National Affairs specialize in the publication of looseleaf services—that is, sets of books dealing with various legal topics and contained in ringed binders. The hallmark of these looseleaf volumes is that they publish information on legal topics that are subject to frequent change and that if placed in hardback volumes would quickly become out-of-date. Publication of materials in

looseleaf binders allows frequent updating by replacement of individual outdated pages with current pages. The looseleaf sets are thus "evergreen."

One of the common features shared by the primary sources (cases, constitutions, statutes, and regulations) as they are initially published is that they are arranged in chronological order. That is, cases are published in the order in which the court issued the decisions. A court will not designate a month as landlord-tenant month and only hear cases dealing with landlord-tenant law before moving on to some other topic, but rather may hear a case involving burglary followed by a contract dispute followed by a probate matter. The cases appear in volumes of books, called "court reports," in chronological order.

Similarly, during any given session, a legislature will enact laws relating to motor vehicles, regulation of utilities, and licensing of real estate salespeople. The initial publication of these statutes is in the order in which they were enacted rather than according to subject matter.

This type of organization makes research difficult. If you were asked to locate cases dealing with landlord-tenant law, you would find that they have not been brought together in one specific location but rather may be scattered over several hundred volumes of cases. It is clear then that a method of obtaining access to these primary authorities is needed and, in general, the secondary authorities and digests will assist you in locating the primary authorities. For example, a secondary source such as a legal encyclopedia will describe and explain landlord-tenant law and will then direct you to cases that are primary or binding authorities relating to this area of the law. These cases, when cited in a legal argument, under the doctrine of stare decisis, must be followed by a court, whereas the encyclopedia discussion is persuasive only and need not be followed by a court.

G. Nonprint Research Media

Until fairly recently, almost all legal research was performed using conventional print volumes in law libraries. With the advent of computer-assisted legal research (see Chapter 11) and Internet legal research (see Chapter 12), legal professionals use a variety of media to get the right answers to their research questions and are no longer tied to the law library. Good researchers must be adept at both methods of performing legal research: using conventional print sources and using newer technology sources such as CD-ROM, commercial databases such as Lexis and Westlaw, and the Internet. Using newer technologies allows legal professionals to perform research at their desks and on the road.

Some methods are more efficient and cost-effective than others. For example, if you need general background information about an area of law, you should consider browsing an encyclopedia or treatise in print form. If you need information about a new or evolving area of law, computer-assisted legal research will likely provide the most current

information. If you need to refresh your memory about a statutory provision, it may be more cost-effective for the client if you quickly review the statute in print form rather than going to the expense of logging on to Lexis or Westlaw. Moreover, you need to be flexible in using all methods of legal research if case materials are unavailable: Books can disappear from library shelves and networks can crash.

Thus, effective legal researchers are creative and adaptable. A 2004-2005 survey by the American Bar Association reported that the responding attorneys used fee-based services, such as Lexis and Westlaw, and free Internet sites more than any other sources (although print sources were used nearly 60 percent of the time as secondary sources). Legal Technology Resource Center, American Bar Association.

Successful legal researchers thus combine research media to obtain information for clients. Knowing which media to use requires an analysis of many factors, including the complexity of your task, the costs involved, and time constraints. Many teachers urge students first to become familiar with the conventional print tools before becoming too wedded to computer-assisted or Internet legal research. Strong skills in manual legal research provide a good foundation for using Lexis, Westlaw, and the Internet more effectively. Thus, this text will fully examine the conventional print research tools before discussing newer technologies such as computer-assisted legal research and Internet legal research.

— Practice Tip —

Access to Government Publications

The Government Printing Office website (previously known as "GPO Access") is in the final stages of migrating its vast collections of federal documents and materials to a new system, called "Federal Digital System" (often referred to as "FDsys" and located at http://www.gpo.gov/fdsys). This site offers easy access to authenticated government documents, including our federal statutes, our Code of Federal Regulations, and numerous other primary sources. Some materials, however, remain accessible through the prior system, GPO Access at http://www.gpoaccess.gov.

H. Change in Our Legal System

Although stare decisis promotes stability, fairness, and uniformity in our legal system, blind adherence to established precedents in the face of changing societal views and mores may result in injustice. For example, in 1896, the United States Supreme Court held that "separate but equal" public facilities for blacks and whites were lawful. *Plessy v. Ferguson*, 163 U.S. 537 (1896). This precedent served to justify segregation for more than 50 years. In 1954, however, in *Brown v. Board of Education*,

347 U.S. 483, 495 (1954), the Supreme Court overruled its earlier decision and held that segregation solely according to race in public schools violated the United States Constitution. A strict adherence to stare decisis would have precluded a second look at this issue and would have resulted in continued racial segregation.

Similarly, the view of women has changed in our case law. In *Bradwell v. State*, 83 U.S. (16 Wall.) 130, 141 (1872) (Bradley, J., concurring), the Justice noted: "The paramount destiny and mission of woman are to fulfil the noble and benign offices of wife and mother. This is the law of the Creator." One hundred years later, Justice Brennan acknowledged, "There can be no doubt that our Nation has had a long and unfortunate history of sex discrimination. Traditionally, such discrimination was rationalized by an attitude of 'romantic paternalism' which, in practical effect, put women, not on a pedestal, but in a cage." *Frontiero v. Richardson*, 411 U.S. 677, 684 (1973).

Thus, it is clear that as society changes, the law must also change. A balance must be struck between society's need for stability in its legal system and the need for flexibility, growth, and change when precedents have outlived their usefulness or result in injustice. In discussing the fact that the United States Supreme Court can overrule its precedents to correct an injustice, Woodrow Wilson remarked that the Court sits as "a kind of constitutional convention in continuous session." It is the function of our courts to achieve both of these seemingly contradictory goals: the need for stability and the need for change.

In recent years the United States Supreme Court has shown an increased willingness to depart from its previous rulings. From 1789 to 1954 the United States Supreme Court overruled only 88 of its precedents. From 1954 to 2007, however, the Court overruled more than 140 of its precedents.

Nevertheless, you should not view these changes as abrupt and unsettling frequent events. Change often occurs slowly and always occurs in an ordered framework. This order is a result of the structure of our court systems into a hierarchy of lower courts, which conduct trials, and higher courts, which review the conduct of those trials by appeal.

Change in established legal precedent comes about by rulings of higher courts, which then bind lower courts in that judicial system or hierarchy. For example, a small claims court in Portland, Oregon, cannot overrule *Brown v. Board of Education*. Because *Brown v. Board of Education* was decided by the United States Supreme Court, it can only be overruled by the United States Supreme Court. Similarly, a decision by the highest court in Minnesota binds all of the lower courts in Minnesota, and a decision by the Ninth Circuit Court of Appeals is binding on all courts within that circuit, but not in other circuits. Nevertheless, lower courts often attempt to evade precedents by striving to show those precedents are inapplicable to the cases then before them. For example, a lower court might hold that a precedent established by a court above it dealing with the interpretation of a written contract is not binding because the lower court is interpreting an oral contract. Lower courts thus often reject precedent or refuse to follow precedent on the basis that

those precedents are inapplicable to their case or can be distinguished from their case. This flexibility in reasoning results in a rich, complex, and often contradictory body of American case law. According to *Hart v. Massanari*, 266 F.3d 1155, 1173 (9th Cir. 2001), "This ability to develop different interpretations of law among the circuits [and courts] is considered a strength of our system. It allows experimentation with different approaches to the same legal problem so that when the Supreme Court eventually reviews the issue it has the benefit of 'percolation' within the lower courts."

Thus, stare decisis means more than simply following settled cases. It means following settled cases that are factually similar and legally relevant to the case or problem you are researching. Such a factually similar and legally relevant case from a court equivalent to or higher than the court that will hear your particular case is said to be "on point" or "on all fours" with your case. The goal of legal research is to be able to locate cases on point with your particular case. Such cases are binding upon and must be followed by the court hearing your case.

In the event you cannot locate cases on point in your judicial hierarchy (possibly because your case presents a novel issue not yet considered in your jurisdiction), you should expand your search for cases on point to other jurisdictions. That is, if your case presents an issue not yet decided by the Minnesota courts, often called a case "of first impression," search for on-point cases in other states. If you locate a Wisconsin case on point, it is *not* binding in Minnesota. It may, however, be *persuasive* to the Minnesota court. If the Minnesota court adopts the view espoused in the Wisconsin case, it is then a precedent in Minnesota and according to the doctrine of stare decisis is binding upon that Minnesota court and all others lower than it in Minnesota.

Among the factors that may be considered by the Minnesota court in adopting the Wisconsin view are whether the Wisconsin case is well reasoned and well written, whether Minnesota and Wisconsin have some tradition in relying upon and respecting each other's cases, whether the Wisconsin case was issued by one of the higher Wisconsin courts, and whether the Wisconsin view is shared by other jurisdictions or approved by legal scholars. See Figure 1-2.

Change in our legal system can occur not only as a result of judges expanding or overruling precedents found in cases but also through repeal or amendment of a statute by a legislature or even through judicial interpretation of a statute. You may notice as you read statutes that many are broadly written, ambiguous, or vague. In such a case, judges may interpret the meaning of the statute, clarify ambiguous terms, explain the language of the statute, or declare the law invalid. For example, a statute may require a landlord to provide 30 days' notice to a tenant before evicting the tenant for nonpayment of rent. A question may arise as to the meaning of this provision if the thirtieth day occurs on a national holiday. If the statute does not address this issue, a court is free to determine that if the thirtieth day occurs on a Sunday or holiday, the tenant will be given an extra day's notice. Although a court cannot *change* the plain meaning of a statute, it is free to *interpret* the statute. Thus,

Figure 1-2
Stare Decisis and Our Judicial Hierarchy

- Primary law consists of cases, constitutions, statutes, treaties, executive orders, and administrative regulations. All other legal authorities are secondary.
- Primary law from your state or jurisdiction is binding within your state or jurisdiction.
- Primary law from another state or jurisdiction is persuasive only in your state or jurisdiction.
- If your state or jurisdiction adopts the law or position of another state or jurisdiction, then that position is now binding within your judicial hierarchy.
- Secondary law (no matter where it originates) is persuasive only.
- Higher courts in any given judicial hierarchy bind lower courts in that hierarchy.
- Higher courts can depart from a previously announced rule if there are compelling and important reasons for doing so.

even when you locate a statute that appears directly to address your research problem, you cannot stop researching. You must read the cases that have interpreted the statute because it is judicial interpretation of a statute rather than the naked language of a statute that is binding under the doctrine of stare decisis. This research requirement brings us full circle to the practical definition of "the law" given before—that the law is what the judges say it is. In statutory construction, the law is not always what the statute says but rather what a judge says it means.

You have seen that a case from a higher court in one state or jurisdiction is binding upon lower courts in that state or jurisdiction and may be persuasive authority in other states. In contrast, a statute has no effect whatsoever anywhere other than in the jurisdiction that enacted it. When the Kansas legislature is enacting statutes relating to the licensing of real estate salespersons, it is unaffected by statutes in Nevada relating to the same topic. Any Nevada statutes on this topic lack even persuasive effect outside Nevada's jurisdictional boundaries.

I.   Identifying the Holding in a Case

You can readily see that the foundation of the American legal system lies in its rich and varied body of case law. While analysis of cases will be discussed in great detail in Chapter 4, you should be aware that under the concept of stare decisis, only the actual rule of law announced in a case is binding. That is, only the holding of the case is authoritative. The holding is referred to as the *ratio decidendi* or "reason of the decision."

The remainder of the language in the case is referred to as *dictum,* which is usually used as an abbreviated form of *obiter dictum,* meaning a remark "in passing." *Black's Law Dictionary* 519 (9th ed. 2009) provides that dictum is "a statement of opinion or belief considered authoritative because of the dignity of the person making it." Dictum in a case is persuasive only.

On some occasions, a court may speculate that its decision would be different if certain facts in the case were different. This type of discussion is dictum and although it may be persuasive in other cases, it is not binding authority.

In many cases, distinguishing the holding from the dictum is easily done. Often a court will set the stage for announcing its holding by using extremely specific language similar to the following: "We hold that a landlord may not commence an action to evict a tenant for nonpayment of rent without providing the tenant with a written notice to either pay rent or forfeit possession of the leased premises." On other occasions, finding the holding requires a great deal more persistence and probing.

You may notice that some cases are difficult to read and are written using archaic and outmoded language. Do not get discouraged. Reading cases takes a great deal of patience and experience. You will find, however, that the more cases you read, the more skillful you will become at locating the holding, distinguishing dicta from the holding, and understanding the relevance of the case for the future.

J. How the Legal Research Process Works: A Research Scenario

Just as it is nearly impossible to put together a puzzle without first seeing a picture of the finished product, it is difficult to understand the process of legal research before actually performing a legal research project. To understand what you will be able to do when you have completed your research class, consider the following scenario, which is typical of the type of task a researcher often encounters.

> Peggie, a paralegal, was recently hired by a law firm and asked by her supervising attorney to do some legal research. The attorney met with a client, Grace, whose husband Phil died two years ago. Grace is the mother of a ten-year old boy. The son spends occasional time with Phil's parents. Grace is remarrying, and although the grandparents are kind and loving, Grace has decided that it would be better to limit any visits by her son with Phil's parents so that she can begin her new marriage and start her new family. Phil's parents have told Grace that they will go to court to seek visitation. The attorney wants Peggie to find out how the courts in the state handle grandparent visitation. After getting the assignment, Peggie went back to her office to begin the research process. First, she thought about the places she might need to look to find an answer to this question. Because Peggie is unfamiliar with family law, she realized that she would need to learn a bit more about grandparent visitation in general so that she would

have the background to understand the materials she would be reading as she worked on this research assignment. Peggie thus reviewed some introductory information in a legal encyclopedia (Chapter 6) to "get her feet wet." Next, she looked to see whether her state had any statutes (Chapter 3) that address this issue. After reading the statutes, Peggie realized that she needed a better understanding of the meaning of some of the language in the statute, so she looked up some court cases (Chapter 4) that interpreted the statute. One case in particular was relevant to this question, so she used a digest (Chapter 5) to find other cases that dealt with the same issue. She then reviewed a set of books on family law in general and read the chapters relating to grandparent visitation (Chapter 6). Peggie also decided to use Lexis or Westlaw to locate the most current information and other specialized articles or texts on grandparent visitation (Chapter 11). Next, she made sure that the statutes and cases were still in effect and had not been modified or overturned (Chapter 9). Finally, Peggie wrote her attorney a memorandum (Chapter 17) describing what she had found out from her research, being careful to use correct citation form (Chapter 8).

Peggie's approach to her research problem is only one way that the problem could be solved; another researcher might well approach the problem differently, but both would reach the same conclusion.

It is thus important for researchers to understand thoroughly all of the legal research resources that are available, so that when a project is received, it can be completed efficiently and correctly. Moreover, researchers need to understand the American legal system and court structures (Chapters 2 and 4) so that cases can be put into context and researchers therefore understand which authorities are binding.

Legal research is not so much about following a predictable formula as it is about understanding how the numerous resources fit together so that researchers can make intelligent decisions about performing legal research. Thus, the next chapters will afford you an in-depth understanding of the available resources so that you will know how and where to look for answers, allowing you to fulfill your ethical duties to perform research accurately and efficiently and help clients with their legal problems.

K. Case Citation Form

Although case citation will be discussed in depth in Chapter 8, the sooner you begin examining the books in which our cases are published or reported and the sooner you begin reading those cases, the more confident you will become about your ability to research effectively.

All cases follow the same basic citation form: You will be given the case name, the volume number of the set in which the case is published, the name of the set in which the case appears, the page on which it begins, and the year it was decided (and the deciding court, if not apparent from the name of the set). For example, in "reading" the citation to the United States Supreme Court case *Brown v. Board of Education*, 347 U.S. 483 (1954), you can readily see the following:

1. The case name is *Brown v. Board of Education*;
2. It is located in volume 347;
3. It is found in a set of books entitled *United States Reports*;
4. It begins on page 483 of volume 347; and
5. It was decided in 1954.

State court cases are cited much the same way. The citation *State v. Paul*, 548 N.W.2d 260 (Minn. 1996) informs you that:

1. The case name is *State v. Paul*;
2. It is located in volume 548;
3. It is found in a set of books entitled *North Western Reporter, Second Series*;
4. It begins on page 260; and
5. It is a Minnesota Supreme Court case decided in 1996.

Although this text shows case names and book titles in italics, underlining or underscoring is also acceptable according to *The Bluebook: A Uniform System of Citation* (Columbia Law Review Ass'n et al. eds., 19th ed. 2010) ("*The Bluebook*") and ALWD & Darby Dickerson, *ALWD Citation Manual* (4th ed., Aspen Publishers 2010) ("*ALWD*"). As discussed in Chapter 8, although *The Bluebook* is the standard reference tool for citation form, *ALWD* has gained in popularity due to its commonsense rules and user-friendly format. The citation examples given previously comply with both *Bluebook* and *ALWD* rules. There are additional citation systems as well and variation among practitioners, so check with your firm or office to determine if there is a preference.

CyberSites

http://west.thomson.com	Information about West products and services
http://www.lexisnexis.com	Information about Lexis products and services
http://www.lectlaw.com	The 'Lectric Library, a variety of legal information together with links to other law-related sites
http://www.ilrg.com	Internet Legal Research Group, a comprehensive guide to legal resources available online
http://www.hg.org/publishers.html	HG.org website, offering a list of legal publishers together with their addresses and telephone numbers
http://www.lawguru.com/ilawlib	Internet Law Library (formerly the U.S. House of Representatives Internet Law Library) with useful links to a large number of legal resources

(continued)

CyberSites *(Continued)* ██████████████████

http://www.loc.gov/law/guide	Guide to Law Online, prepared by the U.S. Law Library of Congress, Public Services Division, providing an annotated guide to sources of information and law available online and links to useful and reliable sites for legal information
http://www.bc.edu/schools/ law/library/research/ researchguides.html	Boston College Law Library's legal research guides
http://www.ll.georgetown.edu/ research/index.cfm	Georgetown University Law Library's legal research tutorials and guides
http://www.gpo.gov/fdsys	The Government Printing Office website, offering secure and authentic government documents and publications. Known as Federal Digital System ("FDsys"), it replaces GPO Access (found at http://www.gpoaccess.gov).

Writing Strategies

Always support arguments with cases on point. Precedents that differ significantly from your case will not only *not* be helpful, they may actually hurt your case by causing the reader to believe that there is no authority to support the position you advocate.

Carefully scrutinize the cases you find for their weight (what level is the court that rendered the decision?), their date (when was the case decided?), their issues (are the legal issues involved in the cases you find similar or identical to ones in your case?), and the facts (are the facts involved in the cases you find similar or analogous to the ones in your case?).

Use only the "best" decisions to support your argument. Be merciless. Discard cases that provide the adversary with any ammunition. When you have selected the cases that will best advance your position, use analogy to show the reader how similar they are to your case so the reader can easily see why these cases are controlling.

Use active voice and vivid and forceful language when constructing your argument. Personalize your clients by identifying them by name ("Jean White") and depersonalize adverse parties by referring to them by a "label" (the "defendant," the "company").

Assignment for Chapter 1

1. a. Give the name of the case located at 543 U.S. 111 (2006).
   b. Who argued the cause and filed briefs for the petitioner?
2. a. Give the name of the case located at 551 U.S. 264 (2007).
   b. Who delivered the opinion of the Court?
   c. Who dissented in this case?
3. a. Give the name of the case located at 549 U.S. 225 (2007).
   b. Who delivered the opinion of the Court?
   c. Was the lower court's ruling affirmed or reversed?
4. a. Give the name of the case located at 546 U.S. 212 (2006).
   b. Give the date the case was argued.
   c. Give the date the case was decided.
   d. In brief, what general subject matter or topic does this case discuss?
   e. Locate a case in this volume in which the defendant's name is *Schmidt* and give its citation.
   f. What part did Justice Thomas take in this case?

Internet Assignment for Chapter 1

1. Use Table T.1 of *The Bluebook* or access http://www.ncsc.org (the website for the National Center for State Courts), and access the website for your state's highest court.
   a. Give the name of the Court.
   b. Identify how many judges or justices sit on the bench.
   c. Identify your state's chief justice or chief judge.
   d. Identify the city in which your court is located.
2. Access the site for GPO Access or FDsys (at http://www.gpo.gov/fdsys).
   a. How many federal depository libraries are located in your state?
   b. Why did Congress establish the federal depository library system?
3. Access Cornell Law School's Legal Information Institute at http://www.law.cornell.edu. Select "Wex Legal Dictionary/Encyclopedia." Provide the definition for "common law."
4. Access the website for the American Bar Association and review the Model Rules of Professional Conduct. Specifically, review Rule 5.3. Assume that Sam is the supervising attorney for Penny, a new paralegal. Sam knows that Penny is planning to breach confidential client information by disclosing it to another law firm and yet fails to do anything to avoid this situation. Is Sam liable for Penny's actions? What section of Rule 5.3 governs your answer?

The Federal
and State
Court Systems

*To have standing, a complainant must have a dog in the hunt; if
complainant has no such dog, then complainant cannot object to
things occurring in the hunt.*

Tex. Disposal Sys. Landfill, Inc. v. Tex. Comm'n on Envtl. Quality,
259 S.W.3d 361, 363 (Tex. App. 2008)

A. Federalism
B. Establishment of Federal Court Structure
C. Jurisdiction
D. Ground Rules for Cases
E. The Federal Court Structure
F. State Court Organization
G. Citation Form

Chapter Overview

As discussed in Chapter 1, there is no one legal system in the United
States. There are 52 legal systems: one system composed of cases and
statutes decided and enacted by federal courts and the federal legislature,
namely the United States Congress, and another system composed of
cases and statutes decided and enacted by the state courts and state
legislatures for each of the 50 states and the District of Columbia.

This chapter will provide an overview of the federal and state court
systems. To perform research tasks, you should understand these court
structures so that when you are confronted with a research assignment or
a case citation you will readily understand the hierarchy of cases within
a given court structure, giving greater emphasis to cases from higher
courts such as the United States Supreme Court and the United States
Courts of Appeal than to cases from the federal trial courts, the United
States District Courts, or the lower state courts.

A. Federalism

As you no doubt remember from basic American history or civics classes, there are three branches in the federal government: the legislative branch, which is charged with making federal law; the executive branch, which is tasked with enforcing the law; and the judicial branch, whose function is interpreting the law. A chart showing the organization of the government of the United States can be found at http://bensguide .gpo.gov/files/gov_chart.pdf.

That we have federal courts that exist separate and apart from state courts is a result of a feature of our system of government called federalism. The principle of federalism developed from the time of the drafting of the Constitution.

At the time of the Constitutional Convention in 1787, there were two conflicting ideas held by the framers of the Constitution. On the one hand, the framers recognized the need for a strong central or "federal" government to act in matters of national concern and to reduce George Washington's fear that the fledgling nation had "thirteen heads, or one head without competent powers." On the other hand, the delegates to the Convention were wary of delegating too much power to a centralized government; after all, almost all of the delegates had served as soldiers in the Revolutionary War, which had been fought against a monolithic government insensitive to the rights of the newly emerging colonies. This principle of states' rights was seen as the best protection against an encroaching central government.

The solution was a compromise: For those delegates opposed to a strong national government, the principle developed that the national government could exercise only those powers expressly delegated to it. These powers were specifically enumerated in Article I, Section 8 of the Constitution, which states that, among other things, the federal government has the power to borrow money, collect taxes, coin money, establish post offices, declare war, raise and support armies, and make any other laws "necessary and proper" for carrying out these delegated powers. This "necessary and proper" clause is often called the "elastic" clause as it makes clear that the federal government not only has the powers expressly delegated to it in Article I, Section 8 but can also take action that is not specifically mentioned so long as it is "necessary and proper" to enable it to carry out the delegated powers.

As is readily seen, these specifically enumerated powers are extremely important, and those delegates in favor of states' rights were concerned that, as a result of the compromise, the federal government was too strong and would eventually "swallow up" the states. In fact, Patrick Henry refused to attend the Convention because of his opposition to granting any additional power to the national government and expressly warned that the Constitution "squints toward monarchy. . . . Your President may easily become King." However, the Constitution was immediately modified by the addition of ten amendments collectively known as the Bill of Rights, which were designed to protect individual

liberties. The Tenth Amendment, in particular, was enacted to reassure those in favor of states' rights that the federal government would not be able to encroach on the rights of the 13 new states or their citizens. The Tenth Amendment, often referred to as the "reserve" clause, provides that any powers not expressly given to the national government are reserved to, or retained by, the individual states.

The result of the historic Constitutional Convention is our "living law"—a unique federalist system in which the states have formed a union by granting the federal government power over national affairs while the states retain their independent existence and power over local matters. In a system based on federalism, power is shared between the national and state governments.

B. Establishment of Federal Court Structure

Article III, Section 1 of the Constitution created the federal court system. This section provides in part that "the judicial power of the United States shall be vested in one Supreme Court and in such inferior courts as Congress may from time to time ordain and establish." Thus, only the existence of the Supreme Court was ensured. It was left up to Congress to determine its composition and to create any other federal courts. In fact, the very first Congress began to work on establishing a functioning federal court system and enacted the Judiciary Act of 1789. This Act created 13 district courts in prominent cities with one judge apiece, three circuit courts to be presided over by no more than two Supreme Court Justices and a district court judge, and above these, the United States Supreme Court consisting of a Chief Justice and five Associate Justices. Although the Judiciary Act of 1789 has been amended several times (among other reasons, to increase the number of Supreme Court Justices), the basic structure of our federal court system remains as it was in 1789: district courts, intermediate circuit courts of appeal, and one United States Supreme Court. Judges appointed to these courts are often referred to as "Article III judges."

C. Jurisdiction

The jurisdiction (or power to act) of the federal courts does not extend to every kind of case or controversy but only to certain types of matters. You will learn a great deal more about this topic in your litigation or civil procedure classes, but a brief explanation is in order here for you to understand fully why some research assignments will be researched through the exclusive use of federal law, and others will be researched through the exclusive use of the law of a particular state.

There are two types of cases that are resolved by federal courts: those based on federal question jurisdiction and those based on diversity jurisdiction.

1. Federal Question Jurisdiction

The federal courts are empowered to hear cases that involve a federal question, namely, any case arising under the United States Constitution, a United States (or federal) law, or any treaty to which the United States is a party. Additionally, federal courts may decide controversies between states or between the United States and foreign governments and any cases involving the U.S. government. Cases arising under the Constitution include cases alleging racial, sexual, or age discrimination; cases involving freedom of speech, freedom of the press, freedom of religion; cases involving a defendant's right to a fair trial; cases involving federal crimes such as bank robbery or kidnapping; and any other such actions pertaining to a federal law or the Constitution.

It may be easier for you to remember the scope of federal question cases (sometimes called "subject matter jurisdiction" cases) if you keep in mind a simple analogy. If a 7-11 convenience store in your neighborhood were burglarized, you would expect your local law enforcement officials to investigate the crime. On the other hand, if a bank in your area were burglarized, you would expect the investigation to be handled by the FBI, our federal law enforcement officials. Similarly, *federal* questions, namely those arising under federal law or the Constitution, are resolved by *federal* courts while more local matters are typically resolved by state courts.

2. Diversity Jurisdiction

The other category of cases that is handled by federal courts is determined not by the issue itself (as are federal question cases) but by the status of the parties to the action.

Imagine you are a New York resident on vacation in Montana where you become involved in an automobile accident with a Montana resident. You may have some concern whether a court in Montana would treat you, an outsider, the same as it would treat its own residents, particularly in a locality in which the residents elect the judge.

To ensure that litigants are treated fairly and to eliminate any bias against an out-of-state litigant, the federal courts may resolve cases based on the diversity of the parties; that is, in general, federal courts may hear cases in civil actions between: (i) citizens of different states; and (ii) citizens of a state and citizens of a foreign nation. Diversity cases accounted for more than 30 percent of the total filings in federal district courts in 2008.

Note that diversity jurisdiction is conditioned upon satisfying another key element: The amount in controversy must exceed $75,000 exclusive of interest and court costs. For example, if a resident of Oregon sues a resident of Nevada for breach of contract and alleges (in good faith) damages in the amount of $80,000, the matter may be instituted in federal court.

Diversity must be complete; all plaintiffs must be citizens of different states from all defendants. A federal court in a diversity case will apply the state law of the state in which it is located. For example, if an Ohio resident sues a Texas resident for $100,000 for breach of contract in a Texas federal court, the federal court will rely on Texas's law in reaching its decision. In early 2005, Congress passed the Class Action Fairness Act of 2005, which amended the federal diversity statute (28 U.S.C. § 1332) by granting district courts original jurisdiction in civil actions in which the matter in controversy exceeds $5 million. The legislation was intended to reduce forum shopping by sending most large multistate class actions to federal court (although the matter will be heard in state court if the primary defendant and more than one-third of the plaintiffs are from the same state).

Over the years, the federal courts have increased the monetary amount in diversity cases in order to prevent the federal courts from becoming inundated with cases. Until 1988, the monetary amount was $10,000. When it became apparent that almost any routine "fender bender" resulted in damages in excess of $10,000, Congress increased the monetary limit to the amount of $50,000. In October 1996, the limit was increased again to its present requirement of $75,000. There is no monetary jurisdictional limit for cases instituted in federal court based on federal questions; that is, if a plaintiff alleges she has been wrongfully discharged from her employment due to sexual discrimination, she need not allege damages in excess of $75,000. Congress has periodically considered automatically increasing the monetary limit in diversity cases based on changes in the Consumer Price Index.

Diversity jurisdiction has its detractors, notably former Chief Justice William H. Rehnquist, who had urged elimination of diversity jurisdiction as a basis for initiating an action in federal court. Because total elimination of diversity jurisdiction appeared unlikely, Rehnquist alternatively suggested that diversity jurisdiction be curtailed so as to prevent citizens of one state from suing citizens from another state in federal court. It is believed such a modification to diversity jurisdiction would eliminate "forum shopping," that is, the selection of a particular federal court for certain perceived advantages, among them the strategy of making it difficult for individuals to defend themselves in a court not located near their residences.

Another criticism of diversity jurisdiction, especially in cases brought by a citizen of one state against a citizen of another state, is that the federal courts are becoming "clogged up" deciding non-federal questions such as routine automobile accident cases, which are better resolved by the state courts.

If a plaintiff brings a case in state court that could have been brought in federal court (based on either subject matter or diversity jurisdiction), the defendant may remove it to federal court. If removal was improper (because the court lacked jurisdiction), the case must be remanded or returned back to the state court.

See Figure 2-1 for chart of federal jurisdiction.

Figure 2-1
Federal Jurisdiction

Federal jurisdiction may be based upon the following:

- **Federal question:** Any case arising under the U.S. Constitution or any federal law or treaty (28 U.S.C. § 1331 (2006)); or
- **Diversity:** Generally, cases in which all plaintiffs are from different states from all defendants and in which the matter in controversy exceeds $75,000. (28 U.S.C. § 1332 (2006)).

Additionally, cases originally filed in state court may be removed to a federal court, as follows:

- **Removal:** If a case is originally filed by a plaintiff in state court and federal jurisdiction exists, the case may be removed to federal district court by the defendant. (28 U.S.C. § 1441 (2006)).
- **Remand:** If it appears that a district court lacks subject matter jurisdiction, the case must be remanded or returned to the state court. (28 U.S.C. § 1447 (2006)).

3. *Concurrent Jurisdiction*

Often one hears about cases that are being litigated in a state court when it seems clear the action involves a federal question, for instance, racial discrimination. In such cases, concurrent jurisdiction may exist, meaning the plaintiff alleged a cause of action that violated both state law and federal law. In the example mentioned above, the basis for the action, racial discrimination, violates both California law and federal law. The plaintiff in such a case then has a choice whether to proceed in state court or federal court. In fact, unless Congress vests exclusive jurisdiction of a matter in the federal courts, any claim arising under federal law may be heard in either federal or state court.

The decision in which court to bring an action when concurrent jurisdiction exists is often made on the basis of tactics and strategy. For example, a plaintiff may wish to proceed in a federal court because it is not as crowded with cases as the local state court, thus resulting in a more speedy trial and resolution. Moreover, any diversity jurisdiction case regardless of the amount of money involved may be brought in a state court rather than a federal court.

4. *Exclusive Jurisdiction*

Some matters are handled exclusively by federal courts and are never the subject of concurrent jurisdiction. For example, by federal law all bank-ruptcy cases are resolved by the United States Bankruptcy Courts

(discussed below). Other examples of cases that are handled exclusively by federal courts are maritime, copyright infringement, and patent infringement cases. Generally, statutes govern which cases are subject to such *exclusive jurisdiction*.

Because issues relating to jurisdiction are often complex, always ask your supervising attorney if you have a question relating to the jurisdiction of a case.

D. Ground Rules for Cases

Even if a federal question is involved or even if the requirements for diversity jurisdiction are satisfied, there still remain some ground rules that must be satisfied before a federal court will hear a case.

In large part, these ground rules are rooted in Article III of the Constitution, which establishes the jurisdiction of federal courts and restricts federal courts to resolving "cases" and "controversies." This limitation has been construed to mean that federal courts will only resolve an actual controversy. Moreover, the actual controversy must exist throughout the matter, and not merely at the date the action is initiated. With very few exceptions, federal courts will not consider issues that are "moot" or already resolved. In fact, it is a fraud on a court to continue with a case that is moot. An exception to this requirement is demonstrated by the well-known case *Roe v. Wade*, 410 U.S. 113 (1973), in which a pregnant plaintiff challenged a Texas law prohibiting abortion. By the time the case reached the United States Supreme Court, the plaintiff had given birth and placed the baby for adoption. The United States Supreme Court could have dismissed the case claiming it was moot—namely, that the issue had already been effectively decided upon the birth of the child and that even if the court awarded the relief the plaintiff had requested, declaring abortion lawful, the plaintiff's situation would not be affected by the ruling. However, in *Roe* the United States Supreme Court, realizing that such a case would inevitably be rendered moot by the time it would reach the Court, made an exception and heard the case.

A close corollary to this ground rule that federal courts will not consider questions that are moot is that federal courts will not render advisory opinions, even if asked by the president. The federal courts view themselves as constitutionally bound to resolve actual ongoing disputes, not to give advice. For example, President George Washington once sent the Supreme Court 29 questions on treaties and international law, asking for advice. The Justices refused on the dual bases that under the Constitution, they could not share powers and duties with the executive branch and that they were forbidden to issue advisory opinions.

Finally, a plaintiff must have personally suffered some actual or threatened injury; that is, the plaintiff must be adversely affected by some conduct of the defendant and cannot base a claim on the rights or interests of some other persons. No matter how convinced you may be that a law is unconstitutional, you cannot challenge it unless *your* rights

are directly affected. This requirement is referred to as "standing." For example, in *Sierra Club v. Morton*, 405 U.S. 727 (1972), the Sierra Club brought an action to prevent development of Mineral King Valley into a commercial resort. The Court concluded that the Sierra Club lacked standing as it had not alleged that it or any of its members would be affected by the defendant's activities in developing Mineral King Valley. The Court noted that standing does not exist merely because one has an interest in a controversy or a matter is personally displeasing; one must have a personal stake in the outcome of the controversy.

In a more recent example, in late 2009, the United States District Court for the District of Columbia entered judgment in favor of defendant's Ringling Bros. circus in an action brought by a former circus employee who alleged that the circus's conduct toward its elephants violated the Endangered Species Act. The court ruled that the plaintiff lacked standing to sue because he did not prove he had a strong attachment to the elephants and that their treatment caused him to suffer injury. The court also found that he lacked credibility because he was essentially a "paid" plaintiff. *ASPCA v. Feld Entm't, Inc.*, 677 F. Supp. 2d 55, 67 (D.D.C. 2009).

E.   The Federal Court Structure

1.   *District Courts*

The district courts are the trial courts in our federal system. At present, there are 94 district courts scattered throughout the 50 states, the District of Columbia, and the territories and possessions of the United States. There is at least one district court in each state, and the more populous states, namely California, New York, and Texas, have four within their territorial borders. Other less populous states, such as Alaska, Idaho, and Utah, each have only one district (although they may have branches or divisions in other parts of the state to allow easy access for litigants). There are also district courts located in Puerto Rico, Guam, the Northern Mariana Islands, and the Virgin Islands. Although there may not be a federal district court located in your hometown, there is at least one in your state, thus providing you with ready access to the federal courts. See Figure 8–1 in Chapter 8 for a list of all district courts.

These district courts have jurisdiction over a wide variety of cases. One day a district court judge may hear a case involving a bank robbery and the next day may resolve a civil rights question followed by a case involving a crime committed on an Indian reservation. Bankruptcy courts are considered units of our district courts with judges appointed by the courts of appeal for terms of 14 years. Each of our 94 districts includes a United States bankruptcy court.

The more than 670 judges who sit in federal district courts are, as are all of the judges in the federal court system, nominated by the president and confirmed with the advice and consent of the United States

Senate. The number of judges assigned to a particular district court will vary depending upon the number of cases the court is called upon to adjudicate. There may be as few as one district court judge assigned to a district court, or there may be nearly 50, as is the case for the increasingly busy Southern District of New York. In the event of a shift in the population that increases the caseload of a district, the United States Congress will add or approve new judgeships to enable the district court to keep pace with its increasing demands.

The district court judges, who are paid $174,000 per year, usually sit individually; that is, they hear cases and render decisions by themselves rather than as a panel or group as the judges for our intermediate courts of appeal and our United States Supreme Court Justices sit.

The vast majority of all federal cases end at the district court level; only approximately 10 percent of these federal cases are appealed. Civil filings in the district courts were relatively stable between 2005 and 2008. Recent studies estimate that less than 2 percent of all federal civil cases go to trial, fewer than did in 1962, partly because of out-of-court settlements and partly because of alternatives to litigation, such as mediation and arbitration. Many experts are dismayed by the lack of trials, believing that the trial system is central to democracy and to developing our common law. Additionally, prisoner petitions declined after the enactment of the Prisoner Litigation Reform Act, aimed at reducing prisoner petitions. Finally, product liability cases such as those involving breast implants and asbestos cause moderate fluctuations from year to year.

2. *United States Courts of Appeal*

The 13 United States Courts of Appeal, sometimes called the circuit courts, are the intermediate courts in our federal system. The theory of our judicial system is that a litigant should have a trial in one court before one judge and a right to an appeal in another court before a different judge or judges. This structure serves to satisfy the cause of justice and to ensure that a litigant who may have been denied any rights at the trial in the district court will have a second opportunity before a different panel of judges in these intermediate courts of appeal. In fact, a statute directs that no judge may hear an appeal of a case originally tried by him or her.

In a civil case, either side may appeal the verdict. In a criminal case, the defendant may appeal a guilty verdict, but the government may not appeal if a defendant is found not guilty. Either side in a criminal case may appeal with respect to the sentence that is imposed after a guilty verdict.

It is critical to distinguish between the district courts, where the trial occurs, evidence is presented, witnesses testify, and a decision is rendered, and the courts of appeal, whose primary function is to review cases from these district courts. The courts of appeal do not retry a case. They do not receive additional evidence or hear witnesses. They merely review the record and the briefs of counsel to determine if a prejudicial error of law was made in the district court below. A second important function of the United States Courts of Appeal is to review and enforce

decisions from federal administrative agencies such as the National Labor Relations Board or the Securities and Exchange Commission. Judicial review in cases involving certain federal agencies or programs, for example, disputes over Social Security benefits, may occur first in a federal district court rather than in one of the courts of appeals.

The United States is divided into 12 geographical areas, often called "circuits," and there is a court of appeal in each of these circuits. Additionally, there is a Court of Appeals for the Federal Circuit, as discussed below. Figure 2-2 shows the grouping of states that make up each circuit. It is not critical to know which states or district courts fall within the boundaries of which circuits. Maps of the circuit courts are readily available in the front of each volume of West's *Federal Reporter*. You should certainly know which circuit covers the state in which you will be working and that each circuit is assigned a number and will have several states (and their district courts) within it. For example, the Ninth Circuit covers California and most of the western states.

Thus, if a trial occurs in the Northern District of California, the appeal is filed in the Ninth Circuit. Similarly, if a trial occurs in the Southern District of New York, the appeal is filed in the Second Circuit. All lower federal district courts that fall within the jurisdiction of a federal circuit court are bound by its decisions. Each of the intermediate circuit courts of appeal is free to make its own decisions independent of what other circuits have held; however, in practice, the circuit courts are often guided by decisions from other circuits. Decisions by the U.S. Supreme Court often resolve conflicts among the circuits—not only those in the lower circuit courts but in all other courts in the nation.

The Eleventh Circuit was created in 1981 to relieve some of the pressure the Fifth Circuit was facing due to an ever-increasing caseload caused by population growth. The Fifth Circuit, which had covered Texas, Louisiana, Mississippi, Alabama, Georgia, and Florida, was split, and a new Eleventh Circuit was created by the United States Congress to handle cases from Alabama, Georgia, and Florida (leaving only Texas, Louisiana, and Mississippi in the Fifth Circuit).

Since the 1940s, several proposals have been made to split the huge Ninth Circuit in two. At the time of writing of this text, legislation is pending in the 111th Congress (H.R. 191 and S. 1727) that would reorganize the Ninth Circuit by leaving California, Guam, Hawaii, and the Northern Mariana Islands in the Ninth Circuit and create a new Twelfth Circuit (to be composed of Alaska, Arizona, Nevada, Idaho, Montana, Oregon, and Washington). The primary reason advanced for dividing the Ninth Circuit is that it is simply too large, making for inconsistent law. Many of the judges in the Ninth Circuit are opposed to the split, including former Chief Judge Mary Schroeder, who testified before the 109th Congress that advances in technology, including computer-assisted legal research, e-mail, and an automated docketing system, have improved the circuit's efficiency. Many experts believe that because most of the judges in the Ninth Circuit oppose the split, Congress should not effect it. As former Chief Judge Schroeder remarked in July 2004, "Divorce is expensive. This family is going to stay together."

Figure 2-2

The Thirteen Federal Judicial Circuits (See 28 U.S.C.A § 41)

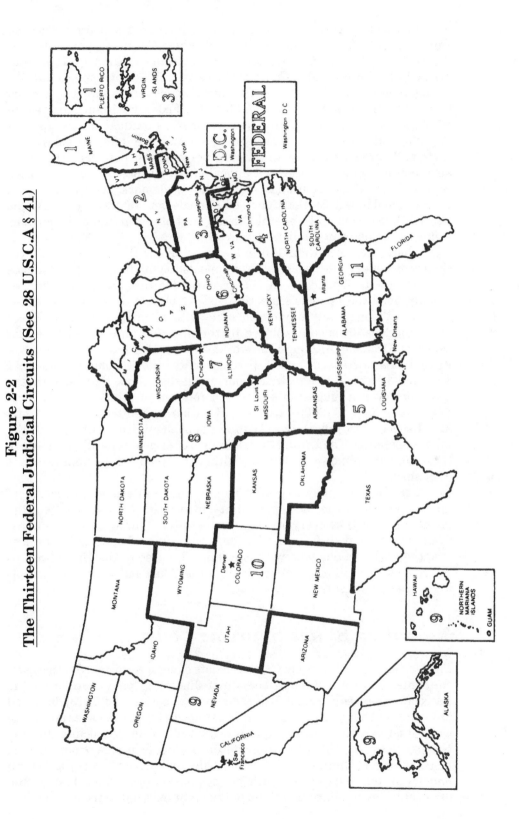

In addition to the 11 "numbered" circuits (First Circuit, Second Circuit, and so forth), there is a United States Court of Appeals for the District of Columbia Circuit and a circuit court created in 1982 that merged the United States Court of Customs and Patent Appeals and the appellate division of the United States Court of Claims into a new court known as the Court of Appeals for the Federal Circuit, located in Washington, D.C. This court has exclusive jurisdiction over patent appeals, and many practitioners believe it has strengthened our patent system. Patent cases make up about 30 percent of its caseload. This court also handles certain specialized appeals such as those from the United States Court of International Trade, the Trademark Trial and Appeal Board, the United States Court of Appeals for Veterans Claims, the United States Court of Federal Claims, and other specialized courts as well as appeals from all district courts.

There are more than 170 judges who sit for the 13 United States Courts of Appeal, with each court of appeals having from six to 29 judges assigned to it, depending on the caseload for the circuit. The judges usually hear the appeals from the District Courts as a panel of three judges, although they may sit *en banc* with all judges present. These federal judges are also appointed by the president and earn an annual salary of $184,500. Although the workload of the United States Courts of Appeal has increased by 42 percent since 1990, Congress has not authorized any additional circuit court judgeships since that time. In late 2009, however, a judgeship bill was introduced in the Senate (S. 1653, 111th Cong. §§ 2, 3 (2009)) that would authorize additional circuit court and district court judgeships. At the time of the writing of this text, the bill was pending. The United States Courts of Appeal typically issue more than 25,000 opinions each year, although about 80 percent are not published.

For the vast majority of litigants, these intermediate courts of appeal represent the last opportunity to prevail. As you will see, the popular notion that everyone has access to the United States Supreme Court is unfounded; for most litigants the court of appeals is the last chance to win, as one who wishes to appeal a case to the United States Supreme Court is largely dependent on the Court's discretion in accepting a case for review.

3. *United States Supreme Court*

The United States Supreme Court consists of eight Associate Justices and one Chief Justice. Although the Chief Justice is paid more than the Associate Justices ($223,500 to their annual salaries of $213,900), and although he has prestige and certain authority by virtue of seniority, the Chief Justice's vote counts equally with that of any Associate Justice. Nevertheless, as the presiding officer of the Supreme Court, he is responsible for administration of the Court and leadership of the federal judicial system. Upon the death or resignation of a Chief Justice, the president may either appoint one of the eight existing Associate Justices

to the position of Chief Justice or may appoint an "outsider" as Chief Justice. That is, there is no seniority system whereby an Associate Justice works his or her way up to the Chief Justice position.

As are all Article III judges in the federal system, the Supreme Court Justices are appointed by the president and hold office "during good behavior." This means they are not subject to mandatory retirement and may sit as federal judges until they voluntarily resign or die. As an example of the lack of a mandatory retirement, Judge Giles Rich, of the United States Court of Appeals for the Federal Circuit, sat on the bench until his death in 1999 at age 95. Although federal judges can be impeached by the Congress, this drastic remedy is seldom used, and only a handful of judges have been removed through impeachment and conviction by Congress of treason, bribery, or other high crimes and misdemeanors. To further ensure the independence of the federal judiciary, the Constitution prohibits any decrease in federal judges' salaries during their term in office. These two protections ensure that an independent judiciary decides cases free from popular passion and political influence.

The individuals who sit on the United States Supreme Court (or state supreme courts) are usually referred to as "Justices" while the individuals who sit on lower courts are referred to as "judges." Occasionally, individuals who sit on intermediate appellate courts are also referred to as "justices," although in general the term "justice" is reserved for individuals on the United States Supreme Court or a state supreme court.

The Supreme Court has not always had nine Justices. When the Court was established in 1790, there were only six Justices. The number of Justices has changed several times; at one point there were ten Justices. The present composition of nine Justices has existed since 1869. The most recent attempt to alter the size of the Supreme Court occurred in 1937 when President Franklin D. Roosevelt presented a plan to the Senate for reorganization of the Court. President Roosevelt's proposal called for adding an additional Justice each time any Justice reached the age of 70 and did not voluntarily retire, to a maximum of 15 Justices. Fierce public outcry immediately met this attempt to "pack" the Supreme Court and there has been no serious discussion of altering the number of Justices since that time.

Federal Court Caseloads

- The last year that new judgeships were authorized for the federal appellate courts was 1990; since that year, appeals filings have increased nearly 45 percent.
- Sixty percent of federal judges come from the public sector; fewer than 40 percent come to the bench from private practice.
- Of the appeals commenced in the federal courts of appeal in 2008, most came from the Ninth Circuit (22 percent), while the fewest came from the District of Columbia Circuit (only 2 percent).
- In 2009, bankruptcy filings increased more than 35 percent over filings in 2008.

(continued)

> ## Federal Court Caseloads *(Continued)*
>
> - The number of criminal cases filed in the United States district courts rose to 76,655 in 2008, its highest level since 1932 (primarily due to increases in cases related to immigration, fraud, marijuana trafficking, and sex offenses).
> - Most of the work of the United States district courts relates to its civil caseload. In 2008, civil cases constituted approximately 79 percent of total filings, and criminal cases accounted for 21 percent. Of the civil cases, actions brought under statutes (such as social security cases) make up the majority, followed by contract actions and civil rights cases. Of the criminal cases, most involve drugs, property law offenses, and immigration law violations.
> - The Department of Justice (which is responsible for prosecuting federal crimes and representing the government in civil actions) is the most frequent litigator in the federal court system.
> - Between 1990 and 2008, the number of cases filed in the United States District Courts climbed nearly 35 percent.

Because there is no mandatory retirement for federal judges, many have served for extremely long periods—notably Chief Justice John Marshall, widely regarded as the finest jurist produced by the United States, who served 34 years, Associate Justice William O. Douglas, who served for 36 years, and Associate Justice John Paul Stevens who announced his retirement in 2010 at age 90 after 35 years on the bench. Since 1970, Supreme Court Justices have served for approximately 26 years.

In addition to their primary activities of hearing Supreme Court cases and writing opinions, each Justice is assigned to one of the federal judicial circuits for the purpose of handling special and emergency matters such as stays of execution and injunctions. For example, in mid-2000, Associate Justice Anthony Kennedy, then assigned to the Eleventh Circuit, which includes Florida, rejected an emergency request to allow Elian Gonzales, a Cuban child, to remain in the United States. Similarly, in spring 2005 Justice Kennedy (after his referral to the Court) denied an application by Floridian Terri Schiavo's parents to reinsert her feeding tube. Because there are 13 federal circuits and only 9 Supreme Court Justices, some Justices are assigned to more than one circuit. Assignment to the circuits is made by the Chief Justice at the beginning of each term. A listing of the assignments is found in the front of each volume of *United States Reports*.

The United States Supreme Court is currently located in Washington, D.C. Initially, the Court met in New York City, the original capital of the United States. When the national capital was relocated to Philadelphia, the Court established its offices there. When Washington, D.C., became the permanent national capital in 1800, the Court again moved and was located in the United States Capitol. In 1929, former President William Howard Taft, who had been appointed as Chief Justice of the Court after his presidential term, persuaded Congress to construct a

permanent building for the Court. The Supreme Court building was completed in 1935, almost 150 years after the Court was created.

By federal law the term of the United States Supreme Court commences on the first Monday in October. Typically the term ends at the end of June nine months later. During the summer recess the Justices continue working and reviewing the many petitions for relief the Court receives during the year. The last month of the term is often referred to as the "June crunch" as the Court struggles to finalize and release opinions before the summer recess. In the last two months of the Court's 2008-2009 term, it produced decisions in nearly 50 percent of its cases, some of which were the most complex on its docket.

Many interesting traditions endure in the Court. The Justices are seated at the bench by seniority: The Chief Justice occupies the center seat and the most senior Associate Justice sits to his right; the next most senior Associate Justice sits to his left, and this procedure continues, with the newest member of the Court occupying the chair at the extreme right (as seen by one facing the bench). Formal pictures of the Justices also reflect this seniority arrangement.

Though seldom used, white quill pens are still placed on the tables in the Court, just as was done 200 years ago. They are given to the attorneys as souvenir gifts. One of the more impressive traditions is the "conference handshake," which was instituted by Chief Justice Melville W. Fuller in the late 1800s. As the Justices take their seats on the bench and at the beginning of the case conferences at which they meet to review cases, each Justice formally shakes hands with each of the other Justices. This handshake serves as a visible reminder that while the Justices may offer differing views of the law, they are united in their purpose of interpreting the United States Constitution. Because the Court has retained so many traditions, one legal historian has called it "the first Court still sitting."

Until William H. Rehnquist became Chief Justice, the caseload of the United States Supreme Court increased dramatically each year. In just the nine-year period between 1994 and 2003, the number of cases appealed in the federal system grew more than 20 percent. In recent years, however, the Court has been reducing its docket and producing far fewer opinions. During the 1980s, the Court routinely decided roughly 150 cases per term. In its 2008-2009 term, the Court decided only 79 cases.

By the authority of the Constitution, the United States Supreme Court has the jurisdiction to act not only as an appellate or reviewing court but also, in very limited instances, as a court of original jurisdiction or a trial court for cases involving controversies between two states and many cases affecting ambassadors, public ministers, and consuls. Although the Supreme Court can conduct a trial in these cases, it prefers that trials be conducted in the district courts below. As might be expected, few litigants elect to have their trial conducted in this highest court as there is no avenue for an appeal if a party loses a trial before the United States Supreme Court. In cases involving controversies between two or more states, the United States Supreme Court has original and exclusive

jurisdiction. For example, in 2005, New Jersey initiated an action in the Supreme Court against Delaware regarding each state's rights to the Delaware River. The Supreme Court typically hears only one or two original jurisdiction cases per term. See Figure 2-3 for an outline of jurisdiction of the United States Supreme Court.

The most important function of the United States Supreme Court is its appellate jurisdiction; that is, its authority to review decisions from lower courts. Cases may come to the Supreme Court from the lower federal courts or from the highest court in any state.

Although a few cases, such as some cases under the Interstate Commerce Act, are directly appealable from the district courts to the United States Supreme Court, the vast majority of federal cases that the Supreme Court reviews proceed to the Court in the expected "stair-step" fashion: trial in the district court, an intermediate appeal to the appropriate circuit court, and a final appeal to the United States Supreme Court. In the 2008-2009 term, 62 of the Court's 79 written cases came from the federal appellate courts, 1 from the federal district courts, and 15 from state appellate courts (and 1 case was an original jurisdiction case).

Additionally, special statutes might allow for direct appeal to the Supreme Court. For example, you might recall that in mid-2000, the Department of Justice asked that the United States Supreme Court review the Microsoft antitrust case under a special federal statute that would have resulted in the case moving from the United States District Court directly to the Supreme Court, skipping over the intermediate court of appeals. The Supreme Court declined the case, and it was sent to the Court of Appeals for the District of Columbia Circuit. In nearly 30 years, only two such cases have gone directly to the Supreme Court under

Figure 2-3
Jurisdiction of United States Supreme Court

I. ORIGINAL JURISDICTION (28 U.S.C. § 1251 (2006))
  A. Controversies between two or more states (exclusive jurisdiction)
  B. Actions in which ambassadors or other public ministers of foreign states are parties (non-exclusive jurisdiction)
  C. Controversies between the United States and a state (non-exclusive jurisdiction)
  D. Actions by a state against the citizens of another state (non-exclusive jurisdiction)
II. APPELLATE JURISDICTION (28 U.S.C. §§ 1253, 1254, 1257 (2006))
  A. Cases from federal courts
    1. United States District Courts (special statutes allow some direct appeals as well as appeals from three-judge district courts granting or denying injunctive relief to be directly appealed to United States Supreme Court)
    2. United States Courts of Appeal
      (a) Certiorari
      (b) Certification (granted only in exceptional cases)
  B. Cases from highest state courts that present a federal question

special legislation (15 U.S.C. § 29(b)(2006)) that provides that government-initiated antitrust cases of general public importance should receive direct consideration by the Court.

The most widely used means to gain access to the United States Supreme Court from the lower circuit courts of appeal is the writ of *certiorari*. *Certiorari* is a Latin word meaning "to be more fully informed." *Black's Law Dictionary* 258 (9th ed. 2009). A litigant who has lost an appeal in the intermediate circuit court will file a document or petition with the Supreme Court called a Petition for Writ of Certiorari. The fee for filing the Petition for Writ of Certiorari is $300. This petition will set forth the litigant's (or petitioner's) basis for appeal and will enumerate the errors that were allegedly committed by the lower court(s). The Supreme Court will either grant the petition and direct the lower court to send its records and files to the Supreme Court for review (in which instance the case is often referred to as being "cert worthy") or will deny the petition, meaning that the lower court decision will stand. In the vast majority of cases, issuance of the writ, or "granting cert," is discretionary with the Supreme Court, and seldom does a litigant have an absolute right to have the Supreme Court review a case.

Approximately 8,000 petitions for certiorari are filed with the United States Supreme Court each year, and the Justices typically grant cert in fewer than 100 of these cases. Full written opinions are issued in about 75 cases, and the remaining cases are disposed of without oral argument or formal written opinions.

Deciding which of the approximately 8,000 petitions for certiorari to grant (which will result in the United States Supreme Court's hearing the appeal) may be as important as the actual decision ultimately reached. The Justices contend that their screening function in determining which appeals to hear is critical in importance. A Supreme Court historian once stated that deciding which petitions for certiorari should be granted is "arguably the most important stage in the entire Supreme Court process."

Each Associate Justice is entitled to four law clerks (and the Chief Justice is entitled to five) who are usually top graduates of the nation's best law schools. Many of the Justices themselves, including Chief Justice Roberts and Associate Justices Breyer and Kagan, have served as law clerks. These law clerks routinely work 70 to 90 hours per week (as do many of the Justices) and prepare memoranda for the Justices summarizing the petitions for certiorari that have been filed. Eight of the nine present Justices make use of a "cert pool," pooling their law clerks, who take turns evaluating the cert petitions and writing memos. Justice Alito prefers to rely on his own clerks. All of the Justices review all of the petitions or the clerks' memoranda discussing the petitions, and they meet on Wednesdays and Fridays in "conference" to discuss the petitions for certiorari. Once again, the Justices sit in prescribed order by seniority at the conference table with the Chief Justice sitting at the east end. No notes are taken, and no one other than the nine Justices is ever present at these confidential case conferences. For certiorari to be granted, only four of the nine Justices need vote to accept the case for review. This process is often referred to as "the rule of four."

There are no clearly articulated or published criteria followed by the Justices in determining which petitions will be deemed "cert worthy." The guideline most frequently given is that certiorari will be granted when there are "compelling" reasons for doing so. These "compelling" reasons are, of course, determined by the Justices. In general, however, a review of the cases accepted by the Supreme Court reveals some common threads: If the lower federal courts of appeal are in conflict on a certain issue and are issuing contradictory opinions, the Supreme Court often grants certiorari so that it can resolve such conflicts; if a case is of general importance, the Court will grant certiorari; or if a state court of last resort has decided an important federal question in a way that conflicts with a decision of another court, certiorari is often granted. These three factors considered by the Court are also set forth in Rule 10 of the Rules of the Supreme Court.

Denial of the writ of certiorari is not to be viewed as a message to the petitioner from the Court that it has fully reviewed and researched all aspects of the case and it is satisfied the lower court's ruling is correct but rather that for reasons of judicial economy not every case can be heard. The Supreme Court cannot possibly review every case that litigants desire to appeal, and the appeal process must end somewhere. In most cases originating in the federal court system, the litigant had a trial conducted by a judge who was appointed by the president and confirmed by the Senate; an appeal then followed in one of the circuit courts of appeal before a panel of judges appointed by the president and confirmed by the Senate. This should be sufficient to satisfy the cause of justice. In fact, in 1925, Chief Justice William Howard Taft (formerly President Taft) stated, "[N]o litigant is entitled to more than two chances, namely, to the original trial and to a review." Denial of a writ of certiorari is the chief means the Justices have of controlling their caseload and ensuring they continue to issue opinions on a timely basis.

Practice Tip

Denials of Certiorari

Be a savvy reader. Understand that the denial of certiorari is not an endorsement or affirmance of lower court action but merely a determination by a court that it will not take a case.

Once the petition for certiorari has been granted, the attorneys or parties are notified and instructed to submit their written arguments, called briefs, which are then filed with the Court and made available to the public.

Oral arguments are heard two weeks of every month on Mondays, Tuesdays, and Wednesdays through April. Thursdays and Fridays are generally reserved for discussion of cases and voting on petitions for certiorari. A typical day begins with a case at 10:00 A.M, and another at 11:00 A.M. followed by a lunch break from 12:00 noon to 1:00 P.M. The afternoon session will also be devoted to two cases, one at 1:00 P.M. and

another at 2:00 P.M. In recent years, however, the Court has not heard cases in the afternoon, probably due to its decreased caseload. At least six Justices must be present to hear a case. The two-week sessions when the Court hears arguments and delivers opinions are called "sittings," and the two-week sessions when the Justices consider business before the Court and write opinions are called "recesses."

Usually only one-half hour is allotted to each side for oral argument. Timing is regulated by a lighting system. After 25 minutes, a white light is turned on, notifying the speaker that only five minutes remain for oral argument. A red light signals the end of the 30-minute oral argument period. During the oral argument, the Justices usually ask questions and often interrupt the speaker. It is rare for a case to exceed the one hour allotted for oral argument. Cameras, computers, PDAs, and cell phones are not authorized in the courtroom, and spectators are not permitted to take notes.

After oral argument, the Justices again meet in conference and discuss the case. A preliminary vote is taken to determine the Court's disposition of the case. This is the time when the power and prestige of the Chief Justice are shown. If the preliminary vote is 5–4 with the majority in favor of affirming and the Chief Justice is in the majority, he may assign the opinion to be drafted by any of the Associate Justices in the majority group or may decide to author the opinion himself. When the Chief Justice is not in the majority, the senior Associate Justice in the majority group will make the assignment.

While one Justice is drafting the majority opinion, others may be writing separate dissents or concurring opinions (see Chapter 4). Drafting the majority opinion may take weeks or months, and the law clerks often write the first drafts. Justice Brennan once disclosed that he circulated ten drafts of an opinion before one was approved. When the opinion is complete, it is circulated to the other Justices for comments. Justices who were originally in the majority may, after reviewing the opinion, change their votes, and it is possible that what initially appeared to be a majority may vanish and the original dissenters may become the majority. While the average length of time between oral argument and issuance of the opinion is only a few months, in some instances there may be a period of nearly a year before the final opinion is released. Generally, all cases argued during a term are decided before the summer recess begins.

Finally, the last revisions are made to the opinion and it is released to the public and authorized for printing in the *United States Reports*, the official publication of the Court's work. Only the final version of the opinion is printed and only it is the law, serving as a legal precedent under the doctrine of stare decisis.

In its 2008-2009 term, the Court continued its practice of overturning lower court judgments in the vast majority of the cases that it fully reviewed. Specifically, the Court reversed or vacated lower court rulings approximately 75 percent of the time. The U.S. Court of Appeals for the Ninth Circuit is often the most frequently reversed court (it was reversed 81 percent in the 2008-2009 term), and it continued to face heavy scrutiny

by the Supreme Court. Cases from the Ninth Circuit accounted for about 20 percent of the decisions issued by the Supreme Court in its 2008-2009 term.

Although the popular view of the Supreme Court is that the Justices are often divided, with few exceptions, their unanimity rate has generally remained above 30 percent since the early 1990s (although it was only about 20 percent in the 2008-2009 term). When the Court is evenly divided (as may be the case if a Justice has recused himself or herself due to a conflict of interest), the ruling of the lower court stands, and no nationwide precedent is set.

Although the vast majority of cases arrive at the United States Supreme Court from the various United States courts of appeal by means of the writ of certiorari, there is one other means by which cases from the United States Courts of Appeal may be reviewed by the United States Supreme Court: certification. Certification is the process by which a court of appeals refers a question to the United States Supreme Court and asks for instructions. Certification is not done for the benefit of the parties to the case. It is done at the desire of the court and typically involves questions of grave doubt. The Court itself refers to its certification jurisdiction as "exceptional."

One example of certification occurred in mid-2004, after the Supreme Court issued a decision relating to federal criminal sentencing guidelines. The Court of Appeals for the Second Circuit certified the case to the Supreme Court and issued a set of three questions for the Court. The Second Circuit noted the rarity of the certification process by remarking that it had not certified a case for more than twenty years and stating that a prompt answer to the questions was needed to avoid a major disruption in the administration of criminal justice.

The certification procedure does not play a significant role in the Court's caseload. Certification is discretionary with the Court and is granted only for exceptional cases. In addition, a party may appeal directly to the United States Supreme Court from an order granting or denying injunctive relief in any case determined by a three-judge district court.

Cases from state courts may be appealed to the United States Supreme Court from the highest court in a state if and only if a federal question is involved. Even then, the Court may, in its discretion, refuse to grant certiorari, thus rendering the state court decision final. State court cases seeking access to the United States Supreme Court have no absolute right to an appeal and are entirely dependent on the Court granting certiorari. In the 2008-2009 term, the Court took only 15 cases from the state courts. See Figure 2-4 for a diagram of federal court structure.

Figure 2–4
Structure of Federal Court System

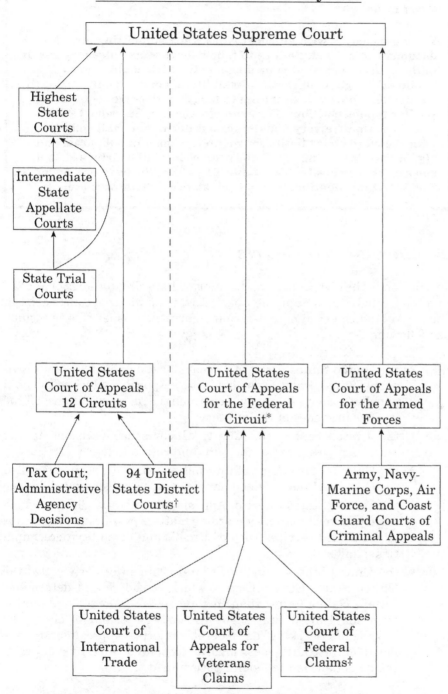

*The Court of Appeals for the Federal Circuit also receives cases from the Patent and Trademark Office, the Board of Contract Appeals, the Merit Systems Protection Board, and the International Trade Commission as well as other agencies.

†A few cases are directly appealed from the United States District Courts to the United States Supreme Court.

‡Formerly, the United States Claims Court.

———— Ethics Alert ————

Court Rules

You must comply with all court rules when submitting any
document to a court. Failure to follow local court rules may result
in the court's refusal of your document, which could lead to
liability for legal malpractice. In addition, you may not
circumvent court rules relating to length of documents by using
smaller typeface or font. For example, the U.S. Supreme Court
rules that that "[e]very booklet-format document shall comply
with the word count limits shown on the chart in subparagraph
1(g) of this Rule." Sup. Ct. R. 33(1)(d). Nearly all courts post their
rules on their websites. See Table T.1 of *The Bluebook* or Appendix
2 of *ALWD* for identification of each state's judicial website.

---

4. *Specialized Courts*

In addition to the district courts, the intermediate circuit courts of appeal,
and the United States Supreme Court, certain specialized courts exist in
the federal judicial system to determine particular issues. These include
the following:

- the United States Court of Appeals for the Armed Forces (previously United States Court of Military Appeals), which is the final
  appellate court to review court-martial determinations of the
  various branches of the military;
- the United States Tax Court, which issues decisions in tax
  matters relating to income, gift, and estate taxes;
- the United States Court of International Trade (previously called
  the Customs Court), which handles trade and customs disputes;
- the United States Court of Appeals for Veterans Claims, which
  reviews determinations regarding matters pertaining to veterans
  of the armed services such as benefit and disability determinations; and
- the United States Court of Federal Claims (formerly called the
  United States Claims Court), which considers and determines
  certain claims (other than in tort) seeking monetary damages
  from the United States government, for example, claims by
  contractors working on federal projects. Approximately one
  fourth of the court's cases involve tax refund suits. In every case,
  the defendant is the federal government.

A review of some recent Court of Federal Claims cases reveals cases
involving the collapse of the savings and loan industry, cases involving
Native American tribes claiming that the government had breached its
fiduciary responsibilities to them, and those cases seeking damages

under the National Vaccine Injury Compensation Program. In fiscal year 2008, the court rendered judgments in more than 1,000 cases and awarded $1.3 billion in damages. The average claim made against the government is more than $1 million.

As a matter of historical perspective, it is useful to know that the district courts, the intermediate courts of appeal, and the United States Supreme Court are referred to as "constitutional courts" as they exist under Article III of the Constitution, and their judges (the "Article III judges") are protected as to tenure and salary reductions. Most of the specialized courts described above are created under Article I of the Constitution and are referred to as "legislative courts" or Article I courts; their judges are appointed for specific terms.

F. State Court Organization

In addition to the federal court structure discussed earlier in this chapter, each of the 50 states and the District of Columbia has its own arrangement for its court system. Although the names of these courts vary, the general organization is the same in each state and in the District of Columbia: A trial is held in one court and the losing party will have the right to at least one appeal in an appellate (or reviewing) court. Some state courts are courts of "limited" or "special" jurisdiction, meaning they can hear only certain types of cases, such as probate cases, tax cases, or cases involving certain amounts of money, while other state courts are courts of "general" jurisdiction, meaning they hear a wide variety of cases.

Some state courts are extremely busy. For example, the National Center for State Courts has noted that the State of California has the largest court system in the world. The Superior Court of Los Angeles County alone is larger than the court systems of several countries. Remember that state courts handle approximately 98 percent of all cases processed each year. More than 18 million civil cases were processed in the state trial courts in 2007.

California's court system is typical of many states and is shown in Figure 2-5. Different states assign differing names to their trial courts, such as superior court, circuit court, or district court. Intermediate appeals are heard by the court of appeals, with the California Supreme Court serving as the state court of last resort. You can see that this structure is extremely similar to the federal court structure in which a trial is held in the district court, an intermediate appeal follows in the United States Courts of Appeal, and a final appeal may occur in the United States Supreme Court.

Figure 2–5
California Court Structure

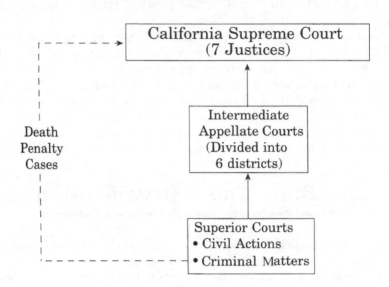

Although the majority of courts have a two-tier appellate system, in eleven jurisdictions (Delaware, District of Columbia, Maine, Montana, Nevada, New Hampshire, Rhode Island, South Dakota, Vermont, West Virginia, and Wyoming) there is no intermediate court of appeal, and dissatisfied litigants proceed directly from the state trial court to the court of last resort in the state, usually called the supreme court. For example, in South Dakota a breach of contract case alleging damages of $50,000 would be tried in the South Dakota Circuit Court. The party who loses would appeal directly to the South Dakota Supreme Court. (See Figure 2-6.)

In almost all states, the highest state court is called the supreme court. Maryland, however, calls its highest court the court of appeals. New York also calls its highest court the court of appeals and calls one of the courts below it, which handles felonies and miscellaneous civil actions, the supreme court, which can cause a great deal of confusion. When reading cases from New York, therefore, exercise a great deal of caution and remember that the decisions of its highest court, the court of appeals, bind all other courts in New York, while its supreme court is not New York's highest court despite its name. Similarly, the decisions of Maryland's highest court, the court of appeals, bind all other courts in Maryland. Likewise, the court of last resort in the District of Columbia is called the court of appeals.

Figure 2–6
<u>South Dakota Court Structure</u>

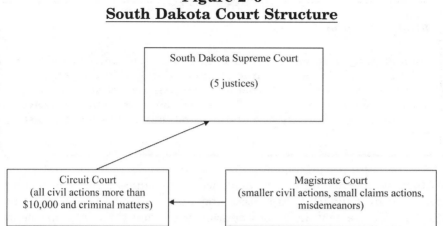

Decisions by the highest courts in all states are rendered by odd-numbered panels of judges (or justices) who function in a collective manner similar to the Justices of the United States Supreme Court. Seventeen of the 50 states have a five-member supreme court; 28 of the states have a seven-member supreme court; and five of the states (and the District of Columbia) have a nine-member supreme court.

As of 2010, the median salary for justices on the highest state courts is $146,917. The median salary for judges sitting on the state intermediate appellate courts is $140,732; and the median salary for state trial court judges is $132,500. Note that most of these salaries are lower than the starting salaries paid to new attorneys in the nation's largest law firms, which range from $125,000 to $140,000 or more.

Although all judges in the federal system are appointed by the president and are confirmed by the United States Senate, there is great variation among the states with regard to the selection of state court judges. Many states use a merit selection method (somewhat similar to the federal presidential appointment method) in which the governor appoints a judge from a list of nominees provided to him or her by a judicial nominating commission. Other states elect their judges by vote of either the state legislature or the general population for specific terms.

For information about all federal and state courts, see *Federal-State Court Directory* (previously *Want's* directory, now available through CQ Press at http://www.cqpress.com). This annual directory provides thorough information about federal and state courts and judges and also provides charts showing the organization of each state court system. Generally, each state's judicial website also includes basic information about the judicial system in that state. Table T.1 of *The Bluebook* and Appendix 2 of *ALWD* provide a reference to each state's judicial website.

——— Practice Tip ———

Reading Citations

Gain as much information from citations as you can. When you see the word "App." in a case citation, immediately think to yourself that the case is likely not from the state's highest court. Similarly, the absence of the word "App." in a citation is probably a signal that the case is a strong one and is from your state's court of last resort.

The state trial courts are often referred to as courts of first resort: Witnesses appear and testify, evidence is introduced, and a decision is rendered by a judge or jury. State appellate courts do not retry a case. Rather, they review the record or transcript from the trial court below, read the written briefs submitted by the attorneys for each party, listen to oral arguments in some cases, and then render a decision. No evidence is presented and no witnesses testify. It is often said that appellate courts cannot make factual determinations and are restricted to deciding issues of law. For example, if a jury convicts Defendant Smith of manslaughter, the appellate court cannot overturn or reverse this judgment on the basis that Smith seems like a fine, upstanding individual and the appellate court cannot believe Smith would have committed such an atrocious act. The trial court has already determined a fact: Smith killed the victim. With few exceptions, it is not within the province of an appellate court to substitute its judgment for that of the jury. The appellate court may, however, reverse the judgment and order a new trial on the basis that prejudicial hearsay was incorrectly admitted at trial, that the jury instructions were improper, or that evidence used at the trial to convict Smith was obtained without a search warrant. Such issues are ones of law rather than fact. Appellate courts typically review only questions of law, not factual determinations that have already been made by a judge or jury at the trial below. Thus, it is often said that trial courts try cases whereas appellate courts try trial courts.

G. Citation Form

1. Federal Cases (The Bluebook *and* ALWD)

    a. United States Supreme Court cases:
        Vestron, Inc. v. Lowell, 347 U.S. 483 (1965). (Note that *ALWD* allows parallel citations.)
    b. United States Courts of Appeal cases:
        Bailey v. Talbert, 585 F.2d 968 (8th Cir. 1989).
    c. United States District Court cases:
        Peters v. May, 697 F. Supp. 101 (S.D. Cal. 1988).

2. *State Cases* (The Bluebook *and* ALWD)

Cite to the regional reporter for the region in which the court is located, if the opinion appears in that reporter. Otherwise, cite to the state's official report. Do not use parallel citations unless required by local rules:

Janson v. Keyser, 415 N.E.2d 891 (Mass. 1976).

Supreme Court Dicta

- In its 2008 term, the Supreme Court reversed 81 percent of the cases it received from the Ninth Circuit, 11 percent of the cases it received from the Second Circuit, and 73 percent of the cases it received from the state courts.
- In 2000, when the Supreme Court heard *Bush v. Gore*, 531 U.S. 98 (2000), just four days elapsed between the time the Court agreed to hear the case and when it issued its decision, which represented the quickest turnaround in the Court's history.
- For the past 30 years, about one-third of the Court's sitting Justices have been former clerks. For the past 14 terms, between 19 and 40 percent of the clerks have been women.
- From 1999-2004, the Justices recused themselves more than 500 times. Justice Stephen Breyer led the list with 181 recusals (primarily in cases involving rulings by his brother, a federal judge).
- The annual salary of the first Chief Justice was $4,000. The salary of the current Chief Justice is $223,500.
- By law, the Chief Justice sits on the boards of three significant Washington cultural institutions, including the Smithsonian Institution.
- William Howard Taft is the only Chief Justice in history to have previously served as president.
- The United States Supreme Court reverses cases from the United States Courts of Appeal approximately 75 percent of the time.
- In the Court's 2008-2009 term, the Justices were split 5-4 in about 30 percent of the cases they decided.
- Supreme Court Justice Sonia Sotomayor took her judicial oath in 2009 using the Bible signed by every Justice who has served in the past 100 years.
- The private law firm Latham & Watkins landed six Supreme Court clerks in 2006, offering them about $165,000 in salary and a signing bonus of about $200,000.
- In 1999, Justice Breyer used the pronoun "I" in a Supreme Court opinion, violating a 200-year-old tradition, begun by Chief Justice John Marshall, of speaking collectively by using the pronoun "we" in Majority opinions.
- Each October before the Court begins its session, several Justices attend a "Red Mass" (named for the red vestments of its celebrants) at the Roman Catholic Cathedral of St. Matthew (where President Kennedy's funeral Mass was held), where the church blesses the forthcoming term as well as the work of other civic leaders.
- Chief Justice John G. Roberts, Jr.'s replacement of Chief Justice Rehnquist was the first time that a Chief Justice's former law clerk succeeded him.

(continued)

Supreme Court Dicta *(Continued)*

- A 2010 poll by FindLaw revealed that two-thirds of Americans cannot name any of the Justices of the United States Supreme Court.
- In 2005, due to financial reasons, the Supreme Court closed its barbershop, which had been in use since the 1940s.
- Although 47 states have allowed television coverage of at least some court proceedings, television coverage of oral arguments has been forbidden by continuous order of the Supreme Court. Cameras, computers, cell phones, and PDAs are also forbidden.
- After leaving office, President John Adams stated, "My gift of John Marshall [appointed by Adams as Chief Justice in 1801] to the people of the United States was the proudest act of my life." One Court observer remarked that to try to describe Marshall's eloquence "would be to attempt to paint the sunbeams."
- According to Justice Joseph Story, on rainy days the early Justices would enliven case conferences with wine. On other days, even if the sun was shining, Chief Justice John Marshall would order wine anyway, saying, "Our jurisdiction is so vast that it must be raining somewhere."
- Injuries suffered by Chief Justice Marshall, often referred to as "the man dissenting the Court Supreme," in a stagecoach crash while riding circuit court were said to have hastened his death.
- Harlan Fiske Stone (appointed Chief Justice in 1941), a former farm boy, once said, "Had I realized what I'd be doing later in my career I'd have hung on to that pitchfork."

CyberSites ▬▬▬▬▬▬▬▬▬▬▬▬▬▬▬

http://www.supremecourt.gov	The website of the United States Supreme Court provides information about the Court, its docket, a schedule of oral arguments, opinions, Court rules, visitor information, and bar admission forms.
http://www.uscourts.gov	The Federal Judicial home page provides information about the U.S. federal courts and links to the U.S. Supreme Court, the U.S. Courts of Appeal (with a map of the Federal circuits), U.S. District Courts, and U.S. Bankruptcy Courts.
http://www.fjc.gov	The Federal Judicial Center provides educational and research services relating to the federal courts, including online access to numerous publications and statistical reports.
http://www.usa.gov	USA.gov (formerly FirstGov) is the federal government's official web portal with links to all units of the federal judicial branch and a vast array of excellent information about the federal government.
http://www.scotusblog.com	This website features information, posts, statistics, and comments about the Supreme Court, its caseload, and the Justices.
http://www .supremecourthistory.org	The site of the Supreme Court Historical Society offers excellent information about the history and background of the Supreme Court, with several useful guides explaining how the Court works and its traditions.
http://www.loc.gov/law/ guide/us.html	The Library of Congress site provides excellent information about the United States judiciary as well as various online guides to law and legal issues.
http://www.ncsc.org	The National Center for State Courts offers information about state courts, including statistical tables for state court caseloads and an organizational chart for each state's judicial system.
(202) 479–3360	Today's Supreme Court decisions.
http://www.findlaw.com	FindLaw, a well-known legal site, provides easy access to federal and state cases as well as a wide variety of other law-related information and links.

(continued)

CyberSites *(Continued)* ▬▬▬▬▬▬▬▬▬▬▬▬▬▬▬▬▬▬

http://www.law.cornell.edu   This website provides decisions of the
                              Supreme Court, cases from other federal
                              courts, and some state court cases.

Writing Strategies

When selecting cases to discuss and analyze in your writing, examine citations carefully for the signals they will give you about the level of the court that rendered the decision. When viewing a "U.S." citation, immediately think "highest court in the country"; when viewing an "F.2d" or "F.3d" citation, immediately think "intermediate federal appellate courts"; when viewing an "F. Supp." or "F. Supp. 2d" citation, immediately think "trial court—lowest court in the federal system."

Although there is nothing wrong with district court cases, you should prefer cases from higher courts over lower courts, everything else being equal.

Examine opinions for clues regarding the strength and viability of a case. If the precedent you rely on was a 9–0 decision, refer to it as a "unanimous decision" or a decision by an "undivided court." Refer to cases relied upon by an adversary, if applicable, as decisions rendered by a "bare majority" or a "divided court."

If you cannot find cases as recent as you would like, try to enhance the stature of older cases by describing them as "well-established," "well-settled," or "landmark" cases. Select cases from your circuit and remind the reader of this in your writing by stating, "This circuit has held . . . " or "Since 1967, the law in this circuit has been . . . ."

Discuss *your* argument. Do not shift the focus away from your position to your adversary's by spending all of your time refuting your adversary's contentions.

Assignment for Chapter 2

1. a. Give the name of the case in volume 544 of the *United States Reports* in which the defendant's name is *Abrams* and give the citation for the case.
   b. Who was the U.S. Attorney General at the time this case was decided?
   c. During the period of time covered by this volume, which United States Supreme Court Justice was assigned or allotted to the Second Circuit?
   d. Locate a case in this volume in which the plaintiff's name is *Moussaoui*. What was the result reached in this case?
2. Locate and review the case *Poster Exchange Inc. v. National Screen Service Corp.*, 362 F.2d 571 (5th Cir. 1966). What did the court say about the meaning of the denial of certiorari?
3. Locate and review the case *Rutherford v. American Medical Ass'n*, 379 F.2d 641.
   a. In which circuit was this case decided?
   b. Review the portion of the case relating to certification of cases. Is a court of appeals required to certify a case to the U.S. Supreme Court? Why or why not?
4. Locate and review the case *Mudd v. White*, 309 F.3d 819 (D.C. Cir. 2002). Why was the appeal denied?
5. a. Give the name of the case at 599 F. Supp. 2d 712.
   b. In which district court was this case decided.
   c. Briefly, summarize the holding of the court.

Internet Assignment for Chapter 2

1. Access the website of the U.S. Supreme Court.
   a. Select "Opinions" and then "2008 Term Opinions of the Court." Select the case *Yeager v. United States*. When was this case decided and who delivered the opinion of the Court?
   b. Review the Rules of the Supreme Court. How does Rule 10 begin?
   c. Select "About the Supreme Court" and then "The Court and Its Procedures." How many petitions seeking review do the Justices review each week?
   d. Select "About the Supreme Court" and then review the biographies of the current Justices. Where did Justice Elena Kagan attend college? When did she assume her role on the Court?

2. Access the website for the National Center for State Courts. Review the state court structure charts and give the name of the court in your state in which a small claims action would be initiated.
3. Access the website U.S. Courts (www.uscourts.gov). Select U.S. District Courts and then the "County/District Court Locator." Search by details by county code and indicate the district court and circuit for the following localities: Monterey, California; Escambia County, Florida; Douglas, Minnesota; and El Paso, Texas.
4. Access the website for the Federal Judicial Center (www.fjc.gov). Select "Federal Judicial History" and then "Landmark Judicial Legislation." When was the 5th judicial circuit divided and the 11th circuit established?

Statutory Law

Nearly all legislation involves a weighing of public needs as against private desires; and likewise a weighing of relative social values.

Louis D. Brandeis (year unknown)

A. **Federal Legislation**
B. **State Legislation**
C. **Statutory Research Overview**
D. **Citation Form**

Chapter Overview

Recall from Chapter 1 that courts are free to interpret statutes. Thus, this chapter focuses on statutory law because the logical progression many researchers follow when given a task is to first determine whether a statute relates to the issue. If so, they begin by reading the statute itself and then reviewing the cases and other sources that interpret it.

In this chapter we will thus discuss the enactment of federal and state legislation and will then focus on the publication and codification of statutes. In order to conduct research efficiently and effectively, you will need a clear understanding of the procedure by which laws are passed and the sets of books in which they are found. Following this, we will focus on research techniques that will enable you to locate statutes.

A. Federal Legislation

1. *Enactment of Federal Statutes*

The chief function of the Congress of the United States is its lawmaking task. Congress is a bicameral (two-chamber) legislature. It consists of

100 members of the Senate and 435 members of the House of Representatives ("House").

The framers of the Constitution anticipated that most legislation would originate in the House. This expectation arose from the fact that the House is considered more representative of the country's population and its desires. Every state, without regard to its size, sends two senators to Congress. On the other hand, states that are less populous, such as Montana or Alaska, send far fewer representatives to the House than heavily populated states such as New York or California. Although the Senate can introduce most types of legislation, the drafters of the Constitution correctly anticipated that most legislation would commence in the House. For example, during the first session of 111th Congress, from January 6, 2009, until December 31, 2009, 4,404 bills were introduced in the House whereas 2,920 were introduced in the Senate. The Constitution provides that only the House of Representatives can originate revenue-raising bills. By tradition, the House also initiates appropriation bills. Legislation can be proposed by anyone, including members of Congress, executive departments of the federal government, private individuals, or lobbyists. These individuals or groups transmit their proposals to their representative.

There are several steps in the enactment of legislation (we will assume legislation is originating in the House):

- A bill, which is a proposed law, is introduced by its sponsor in Congress by being handed to the Clerk of the House or by being placed in a wooden box called the "hopper."
- The bill is numbered. If the bill originated in the House, it will be labeled "H.R." Those bills introduced in the Senate are labeled "S."

Examples

(i) H.R. 412 (from the first session of the 108th Congress): "To enhance the operation of the AMBER Alert communications network in order to facilitate the recovery of abducted children, to provide for enhanced notification on highways of alerts and information on such children, and for other purposes."

(ii) S. 1160 (from the first session of the 110th Congress): "A bill to ensure an abundant and affordable supply of highly nutritious fruits, vegetables, and other specialty crops for American consumers and international markets by enhancing the competitiveness of United States-grown specialty crops."

The numbering of the bills is always sequential; that is, "H.R. 41" indicates the forty-first bill introduced in a particular congressional session.

- The bill is now printed in slip form (as an individual pamphlet) by the Government Printing Office and given to each representative and sent to the appropriate committee. For example, if the bill deals with the military, it will be referred to the House (or Senate) Armed Services Committee. If it involves the judiciary, it will be referred to the House (or Senate) Judiciary Committee. The House has 20 permanent or "standing" committees, and the Senate has 16. Additionally, several select committees exist, such as the Senate Select Committee on Ethics. Much of the work involved in enacting federal legislation is done by these committees or by their subcommittees. Until 1975, the Speaker of the House could refer a bill to only one committee. In modern practice, the Speaker may refer an introduced bill to multiple committees for consideration of those provisions of the bill within the jurisdiction of each committee concerned. Generally, the Speaker must designate a primary committee of jurisdiction on bills referred to multiple committees.

- The committee will now place the bill on its calendar. The committee's initial action is usually to request interested agencies of the government to comment upon the proposed legislation. The committee may hold hearings regarding the proposed legislation, and interested parties, lobbyists, experts, and consumer advocates may testify either voluntarily or by subpoena. Cabinet officers and high-ranking civil and military officials of the government may also testify.

- After studying the legislation and holding hearings, the committee will take one of three actions: It will report (recommend) the bill without any revisions; it will report the bill with revisions and modifications; or it may "table" the bill, or fail to take any action on it, which effectively kills the bill. The committee will hold a "markup" session and then issue a written statement, called a report, which explains the purpose of the bill, the intent of the bill, and why the bill has been approved or modified. Generally, a section-by-section analysis is given. Committee reports are perhaps the most valuable single element of the legislative history of a law. They are used by the courts, executive departments, and the public as a source of information regarding the purpose and meaning of the law.

- After the bill has been returned to the chamber in which it originated, it is placed on the calendar and scheduled for debate on the floor of the House (or Senate, if the bill was introduced in the Senate). Although there are certain limits for the duration of debate in the House, debate in the Senate is usually not subject to any limits. The House Rules Committee may call for the bill to be voted on quickly if it is important or urgent.

- Voting occurs after debate, typically by electronic voting device.

- After a bill is passed in the chamber in which it originated, it is sent to the other chamber, which may pass the bill in its then present form. When a final bill is passed by one chamber, it is called an "engrossed" bill. More likely, however, the bill will be sent to the appropriate committee for analysis. This committee may also approve the measure, modify it, or table it. A report will be issued by the committee explaining the action taken by it.
- After the bill is reported out of the committee, it will be scheduled for debate and voting in the second chamber.
- If the bill is passed and the version agreed to by the second chamber is identical to the one passed by the first chamber, it will be sent to the president for signature.
- If the versions passed by the House and Senate differ, the measure is sent to "conference," the function of which is to reconcile these differing versions and produce compromise legislation acceptable to both chambers. The conference is typically made up of senior members or "conferees" of the House and Senate committees that studied the bill, although in recent years junior members of the committee have been appointed as well as other members interested in the measure who were not on the committees. This has led to increased conference sizes, such as the 1981 conference on a budget reconciliation bill in which 250 members of Congress, divided into 58 subgroups, participated.
- The conference may continue for weeks or months as the conferees struggle to harmonize the conflicting versions of the bill. After agreement is finally reached, the conferees will prepare a report setting forth their conclusions and recommendations. This compromise measure must again be voted on by both the House and Senate.
- When the reconciled bill has been passed by both the House and Senate, it is printed by the Government Printing Office in a process called "enrollment" and is then certified as correct and signed by the Speaker of the House and then the vice president.
- The bill is now sent to the president for signature. If the president approves the bill, he will sign it, date it, and usually write the word "approved" on the bill, which has now been printed on parchment. Once the president has signed the bill, it is referred to as a "law" or a "statute" rather than a "bill." (An "act" is a series of statutes related to the same topic, such as the Lanham Act, which consists of numerous statutes all dealing with federal trademark law.) If the president fails to take action within ten days, excluding Sundays, while Congress is in session (January 3 until mid-summer), the bill will become law without his signature. If Congress adjourns before this ten-day period and the president fails to sign the bill, it will die. This is often referred to as the "pocket veto."

- If the president vetoes the bill or rejects the bill by refusing to sign it, Congress may override this veto and enact the measure if both the House and Senate vote to approve it by a two-thirds majority. Failure to secure this two-thirds vote will result in the president's veto being upheld.
- When the bill is signed, it is assigned a number in sequential order. For example, Pub. L. 110-120 would indicate the 120th public law enacted during the One Hundred Tenth Congress.
- A bill that is not enacted in a particular Congress does not carry over to the next Congress; it must be re-proposed in a following Congress if legislation is desired. For example, the Brady Bill, dealing with the sale of firearms, was introduced in several Congresses before finally being enacted into law. Far more bills are introduced in any session than are passed. For example, between January 6, 2009, and December 31, 2009, 7,324 bills were introduced in the House and Senate, but only 119 (about two percent) had become law.

See Figure 3-1 for a diagram showing how a bill becomes a law.

2. *Classification of Federal Statutes*

After the bill is enacted into law by the president signing it or by act of the United States Congress in overriding a presidential veto by a two-thirds vote of each chamber of Congress, it is sent to the Archivist of the United States, who will classify each law as public or private and will direct its publication.

Public laws are those that affect the public generally, such as tax laws, laws relating to federal lands, laws relating to bankruptcy, and the like.

Private laws are those that affect only one person or entity or a small group of persons, granting them some special benefit not afforded to the public at large. The most common private laws are those dealing with immigration or naturalization; for instance, those allowing an individual or a family to enter the United States even though the immigration quota of that country has been met. Other private laws might deal with forgiveness of a debt owed to the United States or allowance of a claim against the United States government that would ordinarily be barred due to sovereign immunity (the principle that government entities are not subject to or are "immune" from certain types of claims). Only a handful of private laws are passed in any congressional session. See Figure 3-2 for an example of private legislation.

Figure 3-1
How a Bill Becomes Law

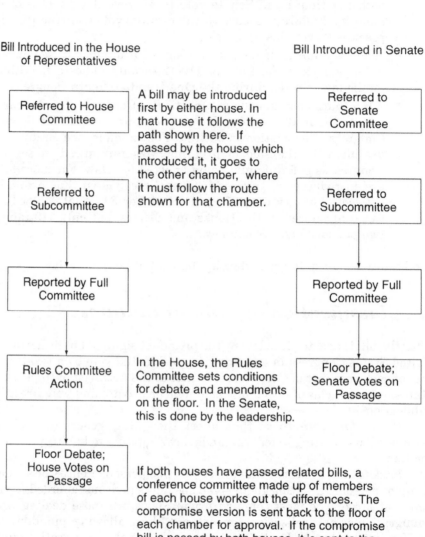

Bill Introduced in the House of Representatives

Bill Introduced in Senate

Referred to House Committee

A bill may be introduced first by either house. In that house it follows the path shown here. If passed by the house which introduced it, it goes to the other chamber, where it must follow the route shown for that chamber.

Referred to Senate Committee

Referred to Subcommittee

Referred to Subcommittee

Reported by Full Committee

Reported by Full Committee

Rules Committee Action

In the House, the Rules Committee sets conditions for debate and amendments on the floor. In the Senate, this is done by the leadership.

Floor Debate; Senate Votes on Passage

Floor Debate; House Votes on Passage

If both houses have passed related bills, a conference committee made up of members of each house works out the differences. The compromise version is sent back to the floor of each chamber for approval. If the compromise bill is passed by both houses, it is sent to the president, who can sign it into law or veto it. If vetoed, the Congress may override the veto by a two-thirds majority in both houses. The bill then becomes law.

Figure 3-2
Private Law

PRIVATE LAW 108–6—DEC. 23, 2004

Private Law 108–6
108th Congress

An Act

For the relief of Tanya Andrea Goudeau.

Dec. 23, 2004
[H.R. 530]

Be it enacted by the Senate and House of Representatives of the United States of America in Congress assembled,

SECTION 1. IMMEDIATE RELATIVE STATUS FOR TANYA ANDREA GOUDEAU.

(a) IN GENERAL.—Tanya Andrea Goudeau shall be classified as a child under section 101(b)(1)(E) of the Immigration and Nationality Act for purposes of approval of a relative visa petition filed under section 204 of such Act by her adoptive parent and the filing of an application for an immigrant visa or adjustment of status.

(b) ADJUSTMENT OF STATUS.—If Tanya Andrea Goudeau enters the United States before the filing deadline specified in subsection (c), she shall be considered to have entered and remained lawfully and shall, if otherwise eligible, be eligible for adjustment of status under section 245 of the Immigration and Nationality Act as of the date of the enactment of this Act.

(c) DEADLINE FOR APPLICATION AND PAYMENT OF FEES.—Subsections (a) and (b) shall apply only if the petition and the application for issuance of an immigrant visa or the application for adjustment of status are filed with appropriate fees within 2 years after the date of the enactment of this Act.

(d) REDUCTION OF IMMIGRANT VISA NUMBER.—Upon the granting of an immigrant visa or permanent residence to Tanya Andrea Goudeau, the Secretary of State shall instruct the proper officer to reduce by 1, for the current or next following fiscal year, the worldwide level of family-sponsored immigrants under section 201(c)(1)(A) of the Immigration and Nationality Act.

(e) DENIAL OF PREFERENTIAL IMMIGRATION TREATMENT FOR CERTAIN RELATIVES.—The natural parents, brothers, and sisters of Tanya Andrea Goudeau shall not, by virtue of such relationship, be accorded any right, privilege, or status under the Immigration and Nationality Act.

SEC. 2. ELIGIBILITY FOR CITIZENSHIP.

For purposes of section 320 of the Immigration and Nationality Act, Tanya Andrea Goudeau shall be considered to have satisfied the requirements applicable to adopted children under section 101(b)(1) of such Act.

Approved December 23, 2004.

Laws can also be classified as permanent or temporary. *Permanent laws* remain in effect until they are expressly repealed, while *temporary laws* have limiting language in the statute itself (often called "sunset clauses"), such as the following: "This law shall have no force or effect after December 31, 2010."

As you might expect, the vast majority of laws are permanent, as it would be extraordinarily inefficient for lawmakers to pass legislation that continually expires. Nevertheless, there are situations in which temporary legislation is enacted. For example, in 1998, the U.S. Congress enacted the Internet Tax Freedom Act (Public Law 105-277). To encourage Internet commerce, the Act established a three-year moratorium (until October 2001) on the imposition of new state and local taxes on Internet access, as well as on multiple or discriminatory taxes on electronic commerce. The Act has been extended three times since its original enactment and currently extends to 2014. Various spending measures, appropriations bills, and tax laws are often temporary.

3. *Publication of Federal Statutes*

a. *United States Statutes at Large*

As each law is passed, it is published by the United States Government Printing Office as a looseleaf unbound pamphlet or sheet of paper (or several sheets, depending upon the length of the law), referred to as a "slip." At the end of each congressional session, these slips are taken together and are placed in chronological order in a hardback set of volumes called *United States Statutes at Large*. Keep in mind that a session is one year and that there are two sessions for each Congress because a new Congress comes into existence every two years upon the election of the members of the House of Representatives. All of our federal laws since 1789 are contained in more than 120 volumes of *United States Statutes at Large*. This set is often referred to as our "session laws," because it includes all the slips from one legislative session in chronological order.

Because it can take as long as a year after the end of a congressional session for the applicable volume of *United States Statutes at Large* to arrive at a law library, you should know there are several alternate sources available that will provide you with the exact wording of a federal statute. In this regard, you should never rely on a summary or synopsis of any legislation. You must obtain and analyze the exact wording of the statute in order to ensure that your research is correct because a mere summary, in a news publication or otherwise, cannot convey the explicit nature of statutory language.

To obtain the exact wording of a federal statute without waiting as long as one year for the hardback bound volumes of *United States Statutes at Large* to become available, consult the following:

(1) Slip Laws

The slips themselves are available in certain libraries throughout the United States. Nearly 1,300 libraries scattered throughout the nation (including law libraries) have been designated as United States Government Depository Libraries, which will receive certain selected government materials, notably slip laws. In a large city there may be several depository libraries. For example, there are nine in Los Angeles, California. Often these depositories are large law school libraries, public libraries, or the libraries in courthouses in a county seat. To find out if a library is a depository library, simply call the reference librarian at a few of the libraries in your area (both law school libraries and at the largest courthouse in your region). The reference librarian will inform you if the library has been designated as a government depository. If so, any member of the public will have access to the depository materials, including the slip laws. These slips may be available as early as five to seven days after the law is enacted. Alternatively, to locate federal depository libraries, access http://www.gpo.gov/libraries.

(2) **United States Code Congressional and Administrative News (***"USCCAN"***)**

This publication is issued monthly by West, which prints in a softcover or pamphlet form the complete text of all of the public laws passed during the previous month as well as newly enacted federal regulations, executive orders, and presidential proclamations. A law firm or law library subscribes to this publication in much the same way an individual might subscribe to *Time Magazine, Sports Illustrated,* or *Wired,* although the cost is substantially higher-for example, nearly $900 per year for 12 issues of USCCAN, as opposed to approximately $15 per year for 12 issues of *Wired.* At the end of each congressional session, the pamphlets making up USCCAN are published in hardback volumes.

(3) **United States Law Week**

This weekly publication is a product of the Bureau of National Affairs, which prints the complete text of the more significant public laws enacted during the previous week (as well as summaries of recent cases decided). Although *United States Law Week* will thus give you more rapid access than USCCAN (because *United States Law Week* is weekly and USCCAN is published only monthly), *United States Law Week* does not provide you with *all* of the public laws passed during the week preceding its publication but only those the publisher deems most important. Similar to USCCAN subscriptions, law firms and law libraries will subscribe to *United States Law Week* much the same way individuals arrange to receive publications they may be interested in (once again, however, the cost may be significantly higher—the current subscription rate for *United States Law Week* is approximately $700 per year). E-mail summaries are now routinely provided to subscribers.

(4) Government Printing Office

Slip laws can be purchased from the United States Government Printing Office. Call toll free at (888) 293-6498 or (202) 512-1800 to place an order.

(5) U.S.C.S. Advance *Pamphlets*

A monthly pamphlet issued by the publisher of U.S.C.S. and called *U.S.C.S. Advance* publishes the text of newly enacted public laws passed during the previous month. There are no hardbound volumes. Summaries of proposed legislation are also given, together with tables that pinpoint the sections of the United States Code that have been affected by recent legislation or regulatory action.

(6) Congressional Representatives

You should also consider contacting the sponsor of the legislation or your congressional representative(s) to ask for the complete text of a recently enacted law. Most representatives have local telephone numbers, which can be found in your telephone book or local newspaper, and most of them have assistants or "staffers" who are very helpful and skillful in locating the information you need and sending it to you at no cost. Alternatively, access the THOMAS site (http://thomas.loc.gov) and select either "House of Representatives" or "Senate" to locate phone numbers and addresses of all members of Congress. All congressional representatives and their staffers have immediate access to Congressional Research Service, a division of the Library of Congress, the primary function of which is to provide research and reference assistance to the United States Congress. If your first request for information is not successful, call again. Often the information you request will be provided to you within a matter of days.

(7) The Internet

Rapid access to federal statutes can also be found on the Internet. One of the best sites for legislative information is "THOMAS," a site provided by the Library of Congress that offers the text of proposed and enacted legislation, committee information, calendars for hearings scheduled, and House and Senate Directories. Access http://thomas.loc.gov. Searching may be done by keyword or bill number. Alternatively, access GPO's Federal Digital System "FDsys," previously known as "GPO Access," at http://www.gpo.gov/fdsys). A sample page from THOMAS is shown as Figure 10-1 in Chapter 10. Research using the Internet will be fully discussed in Chapter 12.

(8) Lexis and Westlaw

You can also gain rapid access to federal statutes (together with their legislative history, including committee reports and debates)

through either of the two online legal research services, Lexis and Westlaw. These services are fully described in Chapter 11.

As discussed above, at the end of each congressional session, the slip laws are compiled chronologically into the bound set of volumes called *United States Statutes at Large*. *United States Statutes at Large* contains both public and private laws, although private laws are typically found in a much smaller section near the end of each volume.

Although *United States Statutes at Large* offers a wonderful historical overview of the order in which the United States Congress has enacted laws for the previous 220 years, it suffers from glaring deficiencies from a legal researcher's point of view:

- The arrangement of *United States Statutes at Large* is chronological rather than by subject or topic. Thus, if you were asked to find all of the federal laws relating to trademarks, you might find them scattered over more than 120 volumes rather than being contained in volumes devoted solely to the topic of trademarks.
- Subsequent amendments to or even a repeal of a previously passed law will not appear together with that law but will appear in the volumes relating to the session in which those amendments or repeals were enacted. That is, if a law enacted in 1990 was amended in 2000 and repealed in 2009, you would need to look at three separate volumes of *United States Statutes at Large*—those for 1990, 2000, and 2009—to obtain the complete history and current status of this legislation.
- There is no one comprehensive index to *United States Statutes at Large*. Even though each volume of *United States Statutes at Large* contains an index and a table of contents, there is no one cumulative index to tell you which specific volumes to examine if you were charged with the responsibility of locating all of the federal laws relating to copyrights, for example. Rather, you would be forced to pick up each volume of the set and examine its index to determine if any laws relating to copyrights were contained in that volume.

b. *United States Code*

Because the organization of *United States Statutes at Large* makes research using the set so difficult, it became readily apparent that a set of books should be developed to eliminate these barriers to efficient research. The process of developing a set of books that compiles the currently valid laws on the same subject together with any amendments to those laws is referred to as "codification."

The first codification of *United States Statutes at Large* occurred in the mid-1870s. A second codification or edition followed a few years thereafter but the set or "code" in current use originates from 1925, when Congress authorized preparation of the *United States Code* (U.S.C.).

All of the statutes enacted into law and contained in *United States Statutes at Large* were analyzed and categorized by subject matter so that at the completion of this project there were 50 categories or "titles" of federal statutes. For instance, Title 7 contains statutes dealing with agriculture; Title 25 contains statutes dealing with Indians; Title 38 contains statutes dealing with veterans' benefits; and Title 50 contains statutes dealing with war and national defense. The 50 titles are further divided into chapters and sections. A citation to any statute in the *United States Code* indicates the number of the title, the name of the set, the section number, and the year of the code, as follows:

42	U.S.C.	§	1396	(2006)
Title	*Set*	*Abbr. for section*	*Section no.*	*Year of code*

It is not important to know what subject each of the 50 titles refers to. It is sufficient to understand that there are, in fact, 50 groups of statutes or titles, that they are arranged alphabetically, and that these 50 titles are permanently established, meaning that any federal statute relating to agriculture will always be found in Title 7, that any federal statute dealing with Indians will always be found in Title 25, and so on. See Figure 3-3 for a listing of the 50 titles of the *United States Code*.

Figure 3-3
Titles of *United States Code*

1. General Provisions
2. The Congress
3. The President
4. Flag and Seal, Seat of Government, and the States
5. Government Organization and Employees
6. Surety Bonds
7. Agriculture
8. Aliens and Nationality
9. Arbitration
10. Armed Forces
11. Bankruptcy
12. Banks and Banking
13. Census
14. Coast Guard
15. Commerce and Trade
16. Conservation
17. Copyrights
18. Crimes and Criminal Procedure
19. Customs Duties
20. Education
21. Food and Drugs
22. Foreign Relations and Intercourse
23. Highways
24. Hospitals and Asylums
25. Indians
26. Internal Revenue Code
27. Intoxicating Liquors
28. Judiciary and Judicial Procedure
29. Labor
30. Mineral Lands and Mining
31. Money and Finance
32. National Guard
33. Navigation and Navigable Waters

34. Navy (see Title 10,
Armed Forces)
35. Patents
36. Patriotic Societies and
Observances
37. Pay and Allowances of
the Uniformed Services
38. Veterans' Benefits
39. Postal Service
40. Public Buildings,
Property, and Works
41. Public Contracts
42. The Public Health and
Welfare

43. Public Lands
44. Public Printing and
Documents
45. Railroads
46. Shipping
47. Telegraphs, Telephones,
and Radiotelegraphs
48. Territories and Insular
Possessions
49. Transportation
50. War and National
Defense

The *United States Code* is "official," a term whose sole meaning is that publication of the set is directed by a statute or that the set is designated as "official" by a statute or court order. The actual printing of the set is done either by the United States Government Printing Office or at its express instruction. In fact, West has helped organize and maintain the *United States Code* since 1926. The *United States Code* is revised and a new edition published by the Government Printing Office every six years. During this six-year period, statutes may be amended or even repealed. Changes to federal statutes during the course of the six years are reflected in annual hardbound supplements placed on the shelf after Title 50. However, these annual cumulative supplements often take eight months to two years to be printed. Thus, researchers often rely on one of the annotated versions of the *United States Code* for more rapid updating and other useful research features, as described below.

c. Annotated Versions of the *United States Code*

Although the *United States Code* is an efficiently organized set in that all federal statutes relating to bankruptcy have been brought together, all federal statutes relating to crimes have been brought together, and so forth, researchers typically want something more than a mere recitation of a statute. If you will remember the point made in Chapter 1, that under the concept of stare decisis, it is not the naked statutory language that controls but a court's interpretation of that statute (particularly in instances in which the statute is vague or ambiguous), you can readily see why the *United States Code*, although organized in an easy-to-understand scheme, is still unsatisfactory to researchers. That is because researchers prefer to read a statute and immediately be directed to cases that have construed or interpreted that statute.

Because the *United States Code* simply recites the exact text of a federal statute and immediately thereafter recites the exact text of the next federal statute without providing any comment regarding the law or any reference to any cases that may have interpreted that law, two private publishers, West and Lexis, have separately assumed the task of

providing this necessary information to those in the legal profession. Because the publication of these two sets is not directed by statute, these publications are referred to as "unofficial." Note that the terms "official" and "unofficial" relate to whether the publication of a set is government-approved or not. The terms do not relate to the accuracy or credibility of a set. Both U.S.C.A. and U.S.C.S. are referred to as "annotated" codes, meaning they contain "notes" referring readers to cases interpreting statutes.

Note that the classification and organization of all of the federal statutes, both official and unofficial, is identical so that once a statute is assigned to a title and given a section number, it retains those designations for all purposes.

> Example: 17 U.S.C. § 105 (2006)
>   17 U.S.C.A. § 105 (West 1996)
>   17 U.S.C.S. § 105 (LexisNexis 2001) (for *The Bluebook*)
>   17 U.S.C.S. § 105 (Lexis 1994) (for *ALWD*)

(1) United States Code Annotated

West publishes an annotated version of the *United States Code* titled *United States Code Annotated*, universally referred to as "U.S.C.A." The word "annotated" means "with notes," and one of the most useful features of U.S.C.A. is the notes provided to researchers who use U.S.C.A. These include references to additional primary and secondary materials.

U.S.C.A. is a set of more than 350 volumes, all of which are relatively small in size for law books (approximately 5½"×9½") and all of which are a deep maroon color. U.S.C.A. is divided into the very same groupings or 50 "titles" as the *United States Code* and reproduces the exact wording of the federal statutes contained in the *United States Code*. There is a multivolume general index to U.S.C.A.

The front of each volume of U.S.C.A. contains a list of the 50 titles of the *United States Code*. Therefore, you need not memorize which statutes are contained within each title because you can readily determine this information.

You may have observed that there are only 50 titles to the *United States Code* (and U.S.C.A.), and yet U.S.C.A. comprises more than 350 volumes. This arrangement arises out of the fact that some titles, such as Bankruptcy, contain numerous statutes and "spill over" into more than one volume, while other titles, such as Coast Guard, have far fewer statutes and can be contained in less than one volume. Thus, 14 volumes of U.S.C.A. are devoted to bankruptcy statutes while the statutes relating to Highways and then Hospitals and Asylums are combined in one volume.

U.S.C.A. is not valuable because it provides the exact text of federal statutes—the *United States Code* provides that as well. U.S.C.A. is valuable because of the "extra" features provided to researchers. Those are displayed in Figure 3-4 and are as follows:

Figure 3-4
<u>Sample Pages from U.S.C.A. (Title 35)</u>

35 § 288   PATENTS; PROTECTION OF RIGHTS   PT. III
Note 21

21. Scope of review

Where there has been disclaimer of infringement and trial court has not adjudicated issue of validity, court of appeals is not required to rule on question. Broadview Chemical Corp. v. Loctite Corp., C.A.Conn. 1973, 474 F.2d 1391.

22. Dismissal

Dismissal of patent infringement action is not appropriate absent failure of proof of bad faith or deceptive intent on part of patentees in procuring patents from Patent and Trademark Office. National Business Systems, Inc. v. AM Intern., Inc., D.C.Ill.1982, 546 F.Supp. 340.

Text of Statute

§ 289.   **Additional remedy for infringement of design patent**

Whoever during the term of a patent for a design, without license of the owner, (1) applies the patented design, or any colorable imitation thereof, to any article of manufacture for the purpose of sale, or (2) sells or exposes for sale any article of manufacture to which such design or colorable imitation has been applied shall be liable to the owner to the extent of his total profit, but not less than $250, recoverable in any United States district court having jurisdiction of the parties.

Nothing in this section shall prevent, lessen, or impeach any other remedy which an owner of an infringed patent has under the provisions of this title, but he shall not twice recover the profit made from the infringement.

(July 19, 1952, c. 950, 66 Stat. 813.)

Historical and Statutory Notes

Historical and Revision Notes

Reviser's Note. Based on Title 35, U.S.C., 1946 ed., §§ 74, 75 (Feb. 4, 1887, c. 105, §§ 1, 2, 24 Stat. 387, 388). Language is changed.

Cross References

Cross References

Attorney fees, see section 285 of this title.
Burden of proof of invalidity of patent, see section 282 of this title.
Damages recoverable in action for—
    Copyright infringement, see section 504 of Title 17, Copyrights.
    Patent infringement, see section 284 of this title.
Defenses to action for infringement of patent, see section 282 of this title.
Infringement of patent, see section 271 of this title.
Patented articles marked as such and notice of infringement, see section 287 of this title.
Patents for design, generally, see section 171 et seq. of this title.

Federal Rules

One form of action, see rule 2, Federal Rules of Civil Procedure, Title 28, Judiciary and Judicial Procedure.

West's Federal Practice Manual

Infringement—remedies for, see § 3969.

Library References

Library References

Patents ⚎252, 316 to 320.   C.J.S. Patents §§ 304, 330, 353, 357, 358, 360.

Figure 3-4 *(Continued)*

CH. 29   INFRINGEMENT—DESIGN PATENT   35 § 289

Notes of Decisions

he shall not twice recover the profit made from the infringement" was to insure that a design patentee may not recover both the profit of an infringer and some additional damages remedy from the same infringer, such as a reasonable royalty, and the "shall not twice recover the profit" language should not be taken out of context to preclude recovery of financial gains made by a separate infringer whose only nexus with the manufacturer is by virtue of a sales contract. Bergstrom v. Sears, Roebuck and Co., D.C.Minn. 1980, 496 F.Supp. 476.

4. Infringement

Design patent is infringed if, in eye of ordinary observer, giving such attention as purchaser usually gives, two designs are substantially the same, and resemblance is such as to deceive such an observer, inducing him to purchase one supposing it to be the other. Sunbeam Lighting Co. v. Pacific Associated Lighting Inc., C.A.Cal.1964, 328 F.2d 300.

Identity of a single line in designs comprising many lines, where such line is in no way peculiar or novel, and does not determine character of the whole, does not constitute "infringement". Sears, Roebuck & Co. v. Talge, C.C.A.Mo.1944, 140 F.2d 395.

It is similarity in the peculiar or distinctive appearance which constitutes "infringement" of a design patent rather than identity in the details producing such appearance. S. Dresner & Son v. Doppelt, D.C.Ill.1941, 120 F.2d 50.

Where in the eye of an ordinary observer, giving such attention as a purchaser usually gives, two designs are substantially the same and the resemblance is such as to deceive such an observer and sufficient to induce him to purchase one, supposing it to be the other, the one first patented is infringed by the other. National Nut Co. of California v. Sontag Chain Stores Co., C.C.A.Cal.1939, 107 F.2d 318, reversed on other grounds 60 S.Ct. 961, 310 U.S. 281, 84 L.Ed. 1204. See, also, Sanson Hosiery Mills, Inc. v. Warren Knitting Mills, Inc., C.A.N.J.1953, 202 F.2d 395.

Changes producing substantially different effect on eye will avoid infringement. American Fabrics Co. v. Richmond Lace Works, C.C.A.N.Y.1928, 24 F.2d 365.

Confusion resulting from similarity of use of bottles would not convert into infringement design which otherwise would not be infringement. Coca-Cola Co. v. Whistle Co., D.C.Del.1927, 20 F.2d 955.

Annotations

1. Constitutionality

This section is not unconstitutional in that it imposes a penalty for infringement, and authorizes the enforcement thereof by a court of equity in an injunction suit. Untermeyer v. Freund, N.Y.1893, 58 F. 205, 7 C.C.A. 183.

2. Prior law

Since in 1946 revision of the damages provision of patent law Congress restricted a utility patentee's recovery to damages alone but left undisturbed preexisting law with respect to right of a design patentee to also recover profits, the pre-1946 case law on the subject of recovery of profits by utility patentees is entitled to substantial weight in the design patent context. Bergstrom v. Sears, Roebuck and Co., D.C.Minn.1980, 496 F.Supp. 476.

3. Purpose

Purpose of language, "[n]othing in this section shall * * * lessen * * * any other remedy" available to a design patentee "but

(a) Historical and Statutory Notes

Following the statute you will find an overview of the history of a particular statute, including the Public Law Number, the effective date of the statute, its citation to *United States Statutes at Large*, an indication of the date certain parts or subsections of the statute were added or deleted, and a basic summary of the evolution of this particular federal law.

(b) Cross References

Following the historical notes you will be sent to other federal statutes that may be of assistance in helping you understand this federal statute.

(c) Library or Research References

In its section called "Library References," U.S.C.A. directs you to other sources in the law library, including form books, practice manuals, texts and treatises, jury instructions, encyclopedias, A.L.R. annotations, and law review articles that also deal with the topic covered by the statute. Additionally, you will be given West's topic name and key number assigned to the subject covered by the statute so you may access West's digests (discussed in Chapter 5). Some volumes of U.S.C.A. title this feature "Research References." If there are an unusually large number of law review articles that discuss a statute, they may be listed in a separate section called "Law Review and Journal Commentaries."

(d) Westlaw Electronic Research

U.S.C.A. may provide you with some guidance in developing search queries so you can conduct further research relating to the statute on Westlaw, West's computerized legal research system (see Chapter 11).

(e) Code of Federal Regulations

Following the library references you may be directed to sections of the *Code of Federal Regulations* (see Chapter 10) that relate to this statute.

(f) Notes of Decisions

These notes or "annotations" are the most valuable part of U.S.C.A., for it is these notes that will direct you to cases that have interpreted the statute you have just read.

Because a case citation standing alone might not be particularly helpful to a researcher, you will not only be given the case citation but also a brief one-sentence description of the case so you do not waste time pulling endless cases off the library shelves but instead can make an informed decision as to which cases to review based upon the quick summary or "annotation." Although West's goal is to serve as a comprehensive tool for researchers, U.S.C.A. will not send you to every case that

may interpret or mention a statute. Nevertheless, you will be sent to a sufficient cross-section of cases so you can embark upon your research tasks.

Because some statutes have been interpreted in hundreds of ways
on hundreds of occasions, U.S.C.A. does not merely give you a long list of
annotations but organizes or indexes these annotations for you under
numbered catchlines. For instance, if you have read a statute and want to
read cases that interpret the statute generally, you may be directed to
read the annotations listed under the catchline called "Note 1." Note 1
will then give you quick summaries of several cases that discuss this
statute in a general fashion. The annotations are arranged alphabetically
under numbered notes so you can readily locate court decisions on any
section or portion of the statute you are researching. For example,
suppose you are researching 42 U.S.C.A. § 1395(y) (West 2006), relating
to exclusions from health insurance coverage. The annotations are
arranged, in part, as follows:

> *Notes of Decisions*
>
> Purpose   5
> Group health plans   12
> Construction   2
> Custodial or supportive care   16-18
> Estoppel   34
> Evidence   33
> Persons liable   31
> Jurisdiction   26

Thus, if you are interested in custodial care, you would review the
annotations listed under Notes 16-18. You must then read the cases to
which you are directed. Although the brief digests or summaries are
extremely well done and are written by attorney-editors, they cannot
convey the subtle nuances of a case and are never a substitute for full
analysis of a case. It is possible there may be no annotations following a
statute, which would indicate that the statute has not been the subject of
litigation and thus has not been interpreted or construed by any cases.

Finally, U.S.C.A. not only contains a multivolume general index at
the end of the set, but each title is separately indexed, and each volume
in the set is kept current by an annual cumulative pocket part or by
separate softcover supplements, the importance of which will be
discussed below.

(2) United States Code Service

Lexis also publishes an annotated version of the *United States Code*
entitled *United States Code Service Lawyers Edition* and referred to as
"U.S.C.S." Similar in arrangement to U.S.C.A., U.S.C.S. is a set of more
than 230 volumes, which conform in size to most law books in that they
are approximately 7"×10". The U.S.C.S. volumes are black and have aqua
trim that is displayed on the spines of the books. Like U.S.C.A., this set

also contains a multivolume general index. U.S.C.S. is divided into the same 50 titles as U.S.C. and U.S.C.A. and contains the identical wording of the federal statutes published in *United States Statutes at Large.*

Although U.S.C.A. contains more than 350 volumes and U.S.C.S. contains more than 230 volumes, you should not make the assumption that U.S.C.A. is more valuable than U.S.C.S. or that U.S.C.A. gives you far more information than U.S.C.S. provides. Rather, the individual volumes in U.S.C.S. are quite large compared to the smaller size volumes used for U.S.C.A., and therefore, although the number of books in each set differs, the material contained within the books is substantially similar.

Like U.S.C.A., U.S.C.S. is "unofficial," meaning that it is published by a private publishing company without any government direction or mandate. Just as provided by U.S.C.A., U.S.C.S. contains the text of the federal statutes. If you are curious why these various sets (U.S.C., U.S.C.A., and U.S.C.S.) are all available, all of which provide the wording of the federal statutes, you should note a simple analogy to automobiles. All automobiles provide the same service: transportation. Yet consumers develop distinct preferences for Chevrolets, Fords, or Hondas and may select one make of automobile over another based on habit, perceived differences, or various options available.

Similarly, all of the codifications mentioned herein (U.S.C., U.S.C.A., and U.S.C.S.) provide the same coverage: federal statutes. Yet consumers, namely law firms and law libraries, may choose to purchase one set over another based on various perceived advantages or options available.

Among the features provided by U.S.C.S. are the following:

(a) History; Ancillary Laws and Directives

Immediately following the text of the federal statute you will be provided with information relating to the effective date of the statute and amendments and revisions made to the statute. A citation to *United States Statutes at Large* is provided. This feature of U.S.C.S. is virtually identical to that feature of U.S.C.A. titled "Historical Notes," as both features show the evolution and development of the statute.

(b) *Code of Federal Regulations*

U.S.C.S. will direct you to sections of the *Code of Federal Regulations* that relate to this statute.

(c) Cross References

U.S.C.S. will direct you to other federal statutes that refer to your statute.

(d) Research Guide

U.S.C.S. will direct you to other sources in the library (books, forms, encyclopedias, annotations, law review articles, for example) that may be

helpful in construing and interpreting this statute. This feature of U.S.C.S. is equivalent to the feature of U.S.C.A. titled "Library References," although it is somewhat broader in scope than the Library References given by U.S.C.A. in that you are often directed to a wider variety of law review articles.

(e) Interpretive Notes and Decisions

These notes or annotations are the most important of the features offered by U.S.C.S. Functioning identically to the annotations found in U.S.C.A., these notes will direct you to cases that have interpreted or discussed the statute being researched. Just as given by U.S.C.A., U.S.C.S. will provide you not only the citations to cases that have construed this statute but also a short digest or summary of the cases to enable you to research more efficiently by selecting only those cases that appear promising. Just as seen in U.S.C.A., U.S.C.S. will organize the annotations for you by numbering them so that all of the cases discussing one part of the statute are brought together, all of the cases discussing another part of the statute are brought together, and so on. See Figure 3-5 for sample pages from U.S.C.S.

As you can see, the unofficial sets, U.S.C.A. and U.S.C.S., are substantially similar: Both provide the exact wording of the public federal statutes; both provide information relating to the history of the statute; both direct you to other sources in the library to enhance your understanding of the statute; and both provide you with citations and summaries or "annotations" of cases interpreting the statute.

Beyond this, both sets share additional features in common:

- The front of each volume of U.S.C.A. and U.S.C.S. contains a listing of the 50 titles of the *United States Code*;
- The citations to U.S.C.A. and U.S.C.S. are nearly identical in form. For instance, if a statute is found at Title 42, Section 1352, it will be cited: 42 U.S.C. § 1352 (2006), 42 U.S.C.A. § 1352 (West 2003), and 42 U.S.C.S. § 1352 (LexisNexis 2000). Thus, once a law is categorized within one of the 50 titles of the United States Code and assigned a section number, it will retain this title and section number for U.S.C.A. and U.S.C.S.;
- Both U.S.C.A. and U.S.C.S. have conversion tables that allow you to locate a federal statute if the only information you have is the public law number or the *U.S. Statutes at Large* citation. You can convert these citations into a citation to U.S.C.A. or U.S.C.S. For example, if you know a statute is 108 Stat. 381, tables in the last volumes of U.S.C.A. and U.S.C.S. located after the volumes for Title 50 will convert this citation to 20 U.S.C. § 1085 so you can readily locate the statute; and

Figure 3-5
Sample Pages from U.S.C.S. (Title 35)

35 USCS § 289   PATENTS

§ 289.   Additional remedy for infringement of design patent

Text
of
Statute

Whoever during the term of a patent for a design, without license of the owner, (1) applies the patented design, or any colorable imitation thereof, to any article of manufacture for the purpose of sale, or (2) sells or exposes for sale any article of manufacture to which such design or colorable imitation has been applied shall be liable to the owner to the extent of his total profit, but not less than $250, recoverable in any United States district court having jurisdiction of the parties.

Nothing in this section shall prevent, lessen, or impeach any other remedy which an owner of an infringed patent has under the provisions of this title [35 USCS §§ 1 et seq.], but he shall not twice recover the profit made from the infringement.

(July 19, 1952, ch 950, § 1, 66 Stat. 813.)

History
Notes

HISTORY; ANCILLARY LAWS AND DIRECTIVES

Prior law and revision:
This section is based on 35 USC, 1946 ed., §§ 74, 75 (Feb. 4, 1887, ch 105, §§ 1, 2, 24 Stat. 387, 388).
Language is changed.

Cross
References

CROSS REFERENCES

Court of Appeals jurisdiction of appeals from judgments in civil actions for patent infringement which are final except for accounting, 28 USCS § 1292(a)(4).
Venue of civil action for patent infringement, 28 USCS § 1400(b).
Action by owner against United States in Court of Claims where invention described in and covered by patent is used or manufactured by or for United States without license of owner, 28 USCS § 1498(a).
Infringement of patents, generally, 35 USCS § 271.
Injunction to prevent violation of right secured by patent, 35 USCS § 283.
Damages for infringement, generally, 35 USCS § 284.

Research
Guide

RESEARCH GUIDE

Am Jur:
1 Am Jur 2d, Abatement, Survival, and Revival § 101.
20 Am Jur 2d, Costs § 63.
60 Am Jur 2d, Patents § 481.

Forms:
14 Am Jur Legal Forms 2d, Patents §§ 196:264–196:267.
19 Am Jur Pl & Pr Forms (Rev), Patents, Forms 21.

Annotations:
Propriety of reference under Federal Civil Procedure Rule 53(b). 1 L Ed 2d 1796.
Right to jury trial in patent infringement action in federal court. 18 ALR Fed 690.

Figure 3-5 *(Continued)*

INFRINGEMENT AND OTHER REMEDIES   **35 USCS § 289, n 2**

Modern status of federal rules of res judicata in patent litigation. 4 ALR Fed 181.

Res judicata effect of federal consent decree in patent cases. 4 ALR Fed 214.

Texts:

2 Deller's Walker on Patents (2d ed) § 184.

4 Deller's Walker on Patents (2d ed) § 223.

Law Review Articles:

Zarley, Jury Trials in Patent Litigation. 20 Drake L Rev 243.

Newitt & Nelson, The Patent Lawyer and Trial by Jury. 1 John Marshall J of Practice & Procedure 59.

INTERPRETIVE NOTES AND DECISIONS

Index to Numbered Annotations

1. Generally
2. Recovery of profits

1. Generally

Annotations

Generally, in law action for damages for patent infringement, examination of defendant's cost records was irrelevant since recovery was limited to damages as distinguished from profits; wilful infringer of design patent was liable for $250 plus profits over $250, recovery to be either at law or in equity; it was not necessary to allege plaintiff based claim on statute; examination of cost records was proper but not on examination before trial. Swarthmore, Inc. v Miss Greeley Junior Frocks, Inc. (1943, DC NY) 52 F Supp 992, 59 USPQ 300.

35 USCS § 289 makes total profits of infringer one of the measures of damages in design patent cases; if plaintiff had shown further general damages under § 284, such as forced price reduction, lost profits in excess of those made by defendant, or loss of good will, it would be entitled to compensation for these other general damages as well, but, in view of failure of proof on these items, infringer's profits are taken as measure of general damages; since these exceed reasonable royalty, plaintiff has been fully compensated under § 284, and may not recover reasonable royalty; conversely, if plaintiff should recover reasonable royalty, it could not obtain infringer's profits; plaintiff is entitled to compensatory award, not a vindictive one. Sel-O-Rak Corp. v Henry Hanger & Display Fixture Corp. (1958, DC Fla) 159 F Supp 769, 117 USPQ 245, affd (CA5 Fla) 270 F2d 635, 123 USPQ 3.

2. Recovery of profits

In case of patent for design for ornamental figures in carpet, entire profit from manufacture and sale of the carpet should not have been allowed as damages unless it was shown by

reliable evidence that the entire profit was due to figure or pattern. Dobson v Hartford Carpet Co. (1885) 114 US 439, 29 L Ed 177, 5 S Ct 945.

This penalty attached only where infringer knew the article exposed for sale had upon it a design protected by patent. Fuller v Field (1897, CA7 Ill) 82 F 813.

Where patent was on piano case, plaintiff was not entitled to entire profits made from sale of pianos. Bush & Lane Piano Co. v Becker Bros. (1915, CA2 NY) 222 F 902; Bush & Lane Piano Co. v Becker Bros. (1916, CA2 NY) 234 F 79.

Recovery of total profit of infringer under 35 USCS § 289 is intended to place patentee in shoes of infringer to receive full benefit of infringement; income taxes paid by infringer are not deductible in calculating total profit recovery of patentee, but portion of fixed costs of infringer factually found under circumstances to be attributable to infringement are deductible, and trial court's deduction of ⅔ of fixed expenses is affirmed as not clearly erroneous. Schnadig Corp. v Gaines Mfg. Co., Inc. (1980, CA6) 206 USPQ 202.

Dealer who was fully aware when he sold article covered by design patent that manufacturer had no license from patentee, was liable for entire penalty. Anderson v Saint (1891, CC Pa) 46 F 760.

Wilful infringement was necessary to recovery under penalty clause. General Gaslight Co. v Matchless Mfg. Co. (1904, CC NY) 129 F 137.

Considering willful or grossly negligent infringement of design patent on furniture, court awards full profits of infringer with deductions for income tax and portion of overhead attributable to infringing manufacturer, and includes portion of profits derived from unpatented corner table that accompanies infringing piece. Schnadig Corp. v Gaines Mfg. Co. (1977, DC Tenn) 200 USPQ 453.

- Both U.S.C.A. and U.S.C.S. are kept current by the most typical method of updating legal research volumes: annual cumulative pocket parts. Statutes are subject to frequent repeal or amendment, and this method allows the codes to be kept current without requiring the entire set of volumes in U.S.C.A. or U.S.C.S. to be replaced. A slit or "pocket" has been created in the back cover of each volume of U.S.C.A. and U.S.C.S. Sometime during the first quarter of each year the publishers of U.S.C.A. and U.S.C.S. mail small, softcover pamphlets called "pocket parts" to law firms, agencies, and law libraries that have subscribed to U.S.C.A. and U.S.C.S. These pocket parts slip into the slits in the back of each volume of U.S.C.A. and U.S.C.S. and provide current information about the statutes in that volume, including changes or amendments to the statute and references or annotations to cases decided since the hardback volume of U.S.C.A. or U.S.C.S. was placed on the library shelf.

  Pocket parts are prepared annually. When the pocket part is received for 2010, for example, the law librarian removes and discards the old 2009 pocket part and replaces it with the new 2010 pamphlet. The pocket parts are *cumulative*, meaning that if a hardback volume was received in 2006, the 2010 pocket part found in the back of that volume will have all of the changes and updates relating to the statutes in that volume from 2007, 2008, and 2009. See Figure 3-6 for a sample cover from a pocket part.

On occasion, and over a period of time, the pocket parts may become too thick to fit into the slit cut into the back of each hardbound volume of U.S.C.A. or U.S.C.S. On such occasions, the publishers will issue a softcover supplement that functions in the same way as a pocket part but sits on the library shelf next to the volume it updates.

There are few invariable or inflexible rules in legal research, but one of them is that you must always consult a pocket part (or softcover supplement) if the volume you are using is updated by a pocket part pamphlet. If you wish, you may elect to check the pocket part before reviewing the hardbound volume itself. *When* you review the pocket part is not critical; *that* you review it is critical. Oftentimes, research in a university law library can be frustrating as a volume will contain a slit or opening for a pocket part and yet no pocket part is found. If this is so, you should assume that a pocket part does exist but that it has been misplaced, because the publishers of both U.S.C.A. and U.S.C.S., as a courtesy to researchers, will provide either a pocket part for each volume or a notice, which slips into the pocket and will inform you "this volume contains no pocket part." See Figure 3-7.

Figure 3-6
Front Page of Pocket Part to U.S.C.A.

UNITED STATES CODE ANNOTATED

Title 42
The Public Health and Welfare
§§ 1983 to 1984

2006
Cumulative Annual Pocket Part

Replacing 2005 pocket part in back of 2003 bound volume

Includes the Laws of the
109th CONGRESS, First Session (2005)

For close of Notes of Decisions
See page III

For Later Laws and Cases
Consult
USCA
Interim Pamphlet Service

THOMSON
✱ ™
WEST

Mat #40454238

Figure 3-7
Notice That No Pocket Part Exists

This Volume
Contains
No Pocket Part

Refer to
Separate
Soft Bound Supplement
to this Volume
for
Latest Updating Material

S1291b

You can easily see the advantage of the pocket parts and supplements: rapid supplementation of the statutes and annotations at a cost much lower than replacing the more than 350 volumes of U.S.C.A. or the approximately 230 volumes of U.S.C.S. each year. Nevertheless, the expenses associated in maintaining any law library are substantial.

To enhance the updating of U.S.C.A., West provides an additional pamphlet service. These Statutory Supplements are designed to accelerate the updating of statutes in U.S.C.A. before the publication of next year's pocket part. They include the public laws passed since the publication of the most recent pocket part and that relate to sections of the *United States Code*. Therefore, after you check the pocket part (published yearly) or supplement to determine if a statute has been amended or repealed, check the Statutory Supplements (published periodically) to determine if even more recent changes have occurred. Because the Statutory Supplements are not cumulative, you will have to check each one. These Statutory Supplements update all 50 titles of U.S.C.A., and thus are shelved after the end of Title 50. When new pocket parts are published at the beginning of each year, they will include all of the information previously included in the Statutory Supplements, which are then discarded.

The publishers of U.S.C.S. also issue a monthly pamphlet to each subscriber of U.S.C.S. This is the *U.S.C.S. Advance*, and it includes materials such as newly enacted (but not yet codified) public laws, presidential proclamations and executive orders, and other presidential documents. Each monthly issue of *Advance* includes a cumulative index. A section titled "Current Awareness Commentary" includes highlights of new legislation, summaries of pending legislation, and "Supreme Court Update" discusses recent United States Supreme Court cases and cases accepted for review by the Court. See Figure 3-8 for a chart showing how to update research of federal statutes.

When a statute is located under a particular title and section, for example, 42 U.S.C.A. § 1223 or 42 U.S.C.S. § 1223, any amendment or further information relating to it in the pocket parts (or supplementary pamphlets) will also be located under the same title and section number. Similarly, the pocket parts use the same annotation titles or catchlines as the hardbound volumes so researchers can readily locate the latest decisions interpreting a statute.

When necessary, the publishers of U.S.C.A. and U.S.C.S. will issue replacement volumes for the hardback volumes in the set by simply mailing the law firm, agency, or law library a new volume together with a bill for the new volume.

Finally, you may be able to do some updating using various online sources. For example, the site for the Office of the Law Revision Counsel at http://uscode.house.gov/lawrevisioncounsel.shtml lists the sections of the United States Code affected by recently enacted laws. Similarly, the site FDsys, maintained by the Government Printing Office at http://www.gpo.gov/fdsys, ensures that its online references to the U.S. Code are always current. Of course, the online research services Lexis and Westlaw provide current statutory language and alert you to any pending statutory changes.

Figure 3-8
Updating Federal Statutory Research

U.S.C.	U.S.C.A.	U.S.C.S.
Read statute in main hardbound volume.	Read statute in main hardbound volume.	Read statute in main hardbound volume.
Check annual hard bound supplements.	Check annual pocket part or softcover supplements.	Check annual pocket part or softcover supplements.
Check slip laws, *U.S. Law Week*, or USCCAN.	Check U.S.C.A.'s Statutory Supplements.	Check U.S.C.S.'s *Advance* pamphlets.
	Check slip laws, *U.S. Law Week*, or USCCAN.	Check slip laws, *U.S. Law Week*, or USCCAN.
Check the FDsys website at http://www.gpo.gov/fdsys or the website http://uscode.house.gov/lawrevisioncounsel.shtml.	Check the FDsys website at http://www.gpo.gov/fdsys or the website http://uscode.house.gov/lawrevisioncounsel.shtml.	Check the FDsys website at http://www.gpo.gov/fdsys or the website http://uscode.house.gov/lawrevisioncounsel.shtml.

d. Use of U.S.C., U.S.C.A., and U.S.C.S.

As you now know, there are three sets of codes you may use to locate and interpret federal statutes: U.S.C., U.S.C.A., and U.S.C.S. It is unlikely you will use U.S.C. very often because U.S.C.A. and U.S.C.S. provide you with the exact wording of the federal statutes found in U.S.C. together with extremely useful annotations, which refer you to cases interpreting and construing the statutes. Moreover, the updating of U.S.C. is much slower than that for U.S.C.A. or U.S.C.S. Nevertheless, you may choose to use U.S.C. when you are primarily interested in reviewing only the statutory language itself rather than any judicial decisions interpreting the statutes.

When you are interested in researching the history of a statute, finding other sources in the law library that discuss or refer to that statute, and, most important, reviewing judicial decisions that have interpreted the statute, use U.S.C.A. or U.S.C.S. There are some differences between them. For example, U.S.C.S.'s section titled "Research Guide" refers you to far more sources in the library than does U.S.C.A.'s comparable section titled "Library References." In general, U.S.C.A. will direct you to other West publications, and U.S.C.S. will direct you to other Lexis or Reed Elsevier publications. Additionally, the organization of the annotations within each set differs in that U.S.C.A. uses an alphabetical arrangement whereas U.S.C.S. uses a topic approach. Finally, U.S.C.A.

and U.S.C.S. may each refer you to cases that the other set does not. In general, West's publication, U.S.C.A., attempts to be as comprehensive as possible, sending you to nearly all cases interpreting or discussing a federal statute, while the publisher of U.S.C.S. aims to provide researchers with the most significant cases, eliminating what it believes to be outmoded or repetitive cases, stating that U.S.C.S. contains "no vague or marginal cases to wade through and weigh before getting to the heart of [a] problem."

Another difference is that the language contained in U.S.C.A. is identical to the official text of the *United States Code* while the language in U.S.C.S. is identical to the text of *United States Statutes at Large*. Thus, the language found in U.S.C.S. replicates the language of statutes as enacted by Congress. Only on rare occasions, however, will an error in reprinting a statute occur in the *United States Code*, and this difference may be more imagined than real.

Most experts agree that these differences are not significant for most research projects. Therefore, for the typical research project you will ordinarily use U.S.C.A. or U.S.C.S. but not both. Using both sets would be analogous to driving to work in a Ford and then walking home and driving to work again in a Chevrolet. In most respects, U.S.C.A. and U.S.C.S. are *competitive* sets, meaning they are equivalent. The choice of which set you ultimately use may depend on habit or convenience. If your first employer has purchased U.S.C.A. and you become familiar with the organization and arrangement of this set, you may find that you prefer to use U.S.C.A. Many people prefer U.S.C.S. due to the larger size of the books and larger and bolder typeface, which is easy to read. Some researchers prefer an integrated approach to all legal research and will consistently use all West publications when possible, thereby gaining access to all of West's books and its proprietary key number/digest system (see Chapter 5), whereas others prefer to use books published by Lexis to obtain access to its other publications.

In summary, if you are engaged in an extremely detailed research project, you should consult both U.S.C.A. and U.S.C.S. Ordinarily, however, one set will be sufficient for most of your research needs, and most law firms, corporations, and agencies purchase only one set or the other.

The exercise placed at the end of this chapter will require you to use both U.S.C.A. and U.S.C.S., and you may find you have an immediate preference for one set over the other.

Practice Tip

Annotations

Never fully rely on the one-sentence annotations or descriptions of cases provided by U.S.C.A., U.S.C.S., or any other annotated set. It is not possible to convey complex case analysis in one sentence. Similarly, never quote from an annotation. They are not the law but rather very brief summaries of the law found in the cases.

e. Research Techniques

There are three primary techniques you may use to locate federal statutes: the descriptive word approach, the title/topic approach, and the popular name approach.

(1) Descriptive Word Approach

This method of locating statutes is one that you have undoubtedly used before in other research projects. For example, if you were asked to find out how far Earth is from Mars, you might elect to use an encyclopedia; however, you would not simply start reading at page 1 of volume 1, hoping you would eventually stumble upon the information. You would consult the general index at the end of the encyclopedia set and look for various words that describe the problem such as "Earth," "Mars," "planets," or "solar system." The index would then direct you to the appropriate volume and page number. This is the descriptive word approach.

Both U.S.C.A. and U.S.C.S. have a multivolume general index, which is arranged alphabetically and is usually located after Title 50, the last volume in both U.S.C.A. and U.S.C.S. These index volumes are softcover books that are replaced each year. When you have been assigned a legal research problem, you should try to think of key words or phrases that describe this problem. To assist in developing descriptive words or phrases, consider the following questions: *Who* is involved? *What* is the issue under consideration? *Where* did the action take place? *When* did the action occur? *Why* did the issue develop? *How* did the problem arise? You should then look up these words or phrases in the general index of U.S.C.A. or U.S.C.S., which will then direct you to the appropriate title and section of the code. See Figure 3-9.

The indices for U.S.C.A. and U.S.C.S. are both very "forgiving." For example, if you selected "landlord" and the statute is indexed under "tenant," both U.S.C.A. and U.S.C.S. will guide you to the appropriate word, as follows:

Landlord. Tenant, this index.

U.S.C.A. and U.S.C.S. will direct you to the appropriate statute by listing the title first and then identifying the specific statute section, as follows:

Citizenship, 8 § 1409

You are thus directed to Title 8, Section 1409.

If you have difficulty thinking of an appropriate word to look up in the index, you might consider using a thesaurus to provide you with synonyms or antonyms. Generally, however, such a practice will not be necessary as the indices for both U.S.C.A. and U.S.C.S. are excellent finding tools and have indexed statutes under numerous words or topics. Thus, you need not distill your research problem into one perfect word; even phrases such as "sudden infant death syndrome" are found in the general index to U.S.C.A. and U.S.C.S., and there are typically numerous cross-references and entry words in these indices that will lead you to the correct statute.

Figure 3-9
Sample Page from U.S.C.A. General Index

STEEL—Cont'd
Exports and imports,
  Chromium, certificate of origin, release
      from customs custody for entry into
      U.S., exemptions, 22 § 287c
  Delegation of Presidential functions, 19
      § 2901 nt, EON 12661
  Emergencies, loans, 15 § 1841 nt
  Enforcement, international trade, 19 § 2253
      nt
  Voluntary limitations, 19 § 2485
Income tax,
  Accelerated cost recovery system, property
      used in the production of, transitional
      safe harbor lease property, 26 § 168 nt
  Carrybacks and carryforwards, depreciable
      property, tax credits, 26 § 38 nt
Interest, emergencies, loans, 15 § 1841 nt
International Trade, this index
Labor and employment, emergencies, loans,
    15 § 1841 nt
Loan Guarantee Board, emergencies, 15
    § 1841 nt
Loans, emergencies, 15 § 1841 nt
Proclamations, Steelmark Month, 36 § 139
Reports, emergencies, loans, 15 § 1841 nt
Rivers of Steel National Heritage Area, 43
    § 1451 nt
Sheet and plate steel, standard gauge, 15
    § 206 et seq.
  Preparation of standard, 15 § 207
Steelmark Month, 36 § 139
Water pollution, list, categories, sources of
    pollution, inclusion, manufacturing of, 33
    § 1316

STEEL IMPORT STABILIZATION ACT
Generally, 19 § 2253 nt

STEEL INDUSTRY
Definitions, international trade, 19 § 2253 nt

**STEEL INDUSTRY COMPLIANCE EXTEN-
  SION ACT OF 1981**
Generally, 42 §§ 7401 nt, 7410, 7413

**STEEL TRADE LIBERALIZATION PRO-
  GRAM IMPLEMENTATION ACT**
Generally, 19 § 2101 nt

STEELE BAYOU MS
Non-navigable waters, 33 § 59g

STEELHEAD (RAINBOW TROUT)
Conservation, 16 §§ 1823 nt, 3301 et seq.

**STEENS MOUNTAIN COOPERATIVE MAN-
  AGEMENT AND PROTECTION ACT
  OF 2000**
Generally, 16 § 460nnn et seq.

STEERAGE PASSENGERS
Explosives, fines, penalties and forfeitures, 18
    § 3671

STEERING
Inland navigational rules, 33 § 2004 et seq.

**STEESE NATIONAL CONSERVATION
  AREA**
Generally, 16 § 460mm et seq.

STEINERT'S DISEASE
Muscular Dystrophy, generally, this index

> Reference to other part of U.S.C.A. Index

STELLER SEA LIONS
Conservation, 16 §§ 1383b, 1851 nt

**STELLWAGON BANK NATIONAL MARINE
  SANCTUARY**
Generally, 16 § 1433 nt

STENNIS, JOHN C.
John C. Stennis Center For Public Service
    Training and Development, generally, this
    index

STENOGRAPHERS
Agriculture Department, contracts, 7 § 2232
Board of Veterans Appeals, 38 § 7101
Compensation and salaries,
  Courts, increase, 28 § 603 nt
  Fixed by Director of Administrative Office
      of U.S. Courts, 28 § 604
Congressional Committees, this index
Contested elections, House of Representatives
    members, testimony taken, deposition
    upon oral examination, 2 § 386
Farm Credit Administration, contract for, ex-
    penditures, 12 § 2249
Federal agencies, temporary or intermittent
    employment, 5 § 3109
  Salary limitations, requirement of public in-
      spection, 5 § 3109 nt
Transcripts, generally, this index

STEPHEN FOSTER MEMORIAL DAY
Generally, 36 § 140

STEPHEN MATHER WILDERNESS
Generally, 16 § 1132 nt

STEPLADDER MOUNTAINS WILDERNESS
Generally, 16 § 1132 nt

STEPPARENTS AND STEPCHILDREN
Social security, 42 § 416

> Reference to 42 U.S.C.A. § 416

STEREO PLATES
Postage stamps, sales, 39 § 405

STERILIZATION
Coercion and duress, 42 §§ 300a–7, 300a–8
Foreign assistance,
  Human rights, 22 § 2151n
  Involuntary sterilization, 22 § 2151b
Human rights,
  Foreign assistance, 22 § 2151n
  Military assistance and sales, 22 § 2304
Military assistance and sales, human rights, 22
    § 2304
Physicians and Surgeons, this index

**STERLING ACT (CIVIL SERVICE RETIRE-
  MENT)**
See Popular Name Table

Figure 3-9 *(Continued)*
Sample Page from U.S.C.A. General Index

GENERAL INDEX

CHIRICAHUA NATIONAL MONUMENT

Chiricahua National Monument Wilderness, designation, 16 § 1132 note
Establishment, 16 § 431 note

CHIROPRACTORS

Social security, services included under medical assistance programs, 42 § 1396d

CHISTOCHINA

Public lands, Copper River, native village subject to withdrawal of public lands from appropriation under Alaska Native claims settlement, 43 § 1610

CHITINA

Public lands, Copper River, native village subject to withdrawal of public lands from appropriation under Alaska Native claims settlement, 43 § 1610

CHLORACNE

Veterans' benefits, disability and death compensation, 38 § 1116

CHLORAMPHENICOL

Food, Drug, and Cosmetic Act (this index)

CHLORIDES OF POTASSIUM

Mineral leasing and prospecting permits, 30 § 281

CHLORINE

Water Supply Systems (this index)

CHLOROFLUORCARBONS

Air pollution control, nonessential products containing, 42 § 7671i

CHLORTETRACYCLINE

Food, Drug, and Cosmetic Act (this index)

CHOCTAW-CHICKASAW SUPPLEMENTAL AGREEMENT

Generally, 16 § 151

CHOCTAW TRIBE

Choctaw-Chickasaw Supplemental Agreement, 16 § 151
Disposition of estates, 25 § 375d
Minerals, reservation of, 25 § 414
Per capita payments, 25 § 120

CHOICE

Election or Choice (this index)

CHOLERA

Anti-Hog-Cholera Serum and Hog-Cholera Virus (this index)
Veterans' benefits, cholera included in term chronic disease, 38 § 1101

CHONDROSARCOMA

Veterans' benefits, disability and death compensation, 38 § 1116

CHORAL PERFORMANCES

National Foundation on the Arts and the Humanities Act of 1965, 20 § 952

CHRISTA MCAULIFFE FELLOWSHIP PROGRAM

Generally, 20 § 1113 et seq.
Evaluation of applications, 20 § 1113d
Repayment provisions, 20 § 1113e
Selection of fellowships, 20 § 1113c
Use of funds, 20 § 1113a

CHRISTIAN SCIENCE

Income tax, 26 § 1402
Medicare, post-hospital extended care in Christian Science skilled nursing facilities, defined, 42 § 1395x
Sanatoriums. **Social Security** (this index)

CHRISTMAS DAY

Patriotic customs, display of flag, 36 § 174

CHRISTMAS ISLAND

Trade Agreement Acts, designation under trade act as beneficiary developing country, 19 § 2462 note

CHROME

Southern Rhodesia, prohibition, importation into U.S., suspension of operation of amendments concerning by President, 22 § 287c note

CHRONIC DISEASES

Disease (this index)

CHRONIC ECONOMIC DEPRESSION

Public works, research into causes, 42 § 3151

CHRONIC HAZARD ADVISORY PANEL

Consumer product safety, 15 § 2077

CHRYSLER CORPORATION LOAN GUARANTEE

Generally, 15 § 1861 et seq.
Aggregate amount of nonfederally guaranteed assistance, computation and components, 15 § 1863
Agreement between board and Chrysler Corporation for employee stock ownership plan, 15 § 1866
Annual comprehensive assessments by Transportation Secretary, 15 § 1871
Appropriations, authorization, 15 § 1874
Assignment or sale of guarantee to foreign entity prohibited, 15 § 1864
Assistance from other than federal government to fund employee stock ownership plan, 15 § 1866
Audits by General Accounting Office, 15 § 1869

CHRYSLER CORPORATION LOAN GUARANTEE—Cont'd

Authority of board
generally, 15 § 1863
– limitations, 15 § 1867
– protection of government's interest, 15 § 1870
– termination, 15 § 1875
Automobile industry
– federal regulations, assessment of economic impact by Transportation Secretary, 15 § 1873
– long-term study and annual comprehensive assessment by Transportation Secretary, 15 § 1871
Bankruptcy, 15 § 1870
Benefits. Wages and benefits, infra
Board
generally, 15 § 1862
– agreement with Chrysler Corporation for employee stock ownership plan, 15 § 1866
– authority
generally, 15 § 1863
– – limitations, 15 § 1867
– – protection of government's interest, 15 § 1870
– – termination, 15 § 1875
– defined, 15 § 1861
– investigatory powers, 15 § 1869
Capital, defined, 15 § 1863
Cash to be obtained from disposition of corporate assets, defined, 15 § 1863
Chrysler Corporation Loan Guarantee Act of 1979, 15 § 1861 et seq.
Collective bargaining agreements, modification
generally, 15 § 1865
– maximum reductions in wages and benefits, 15 § 1865
Commitments
generally, 15 § 1863
– terms, 15 § 1864
Common stock, employee stock ownership plan, 15 § 1866
Compensation. Wages and benefits, infra
Computation of aggregate amount of nonfederally guaranteed assistance, 15 § 1863
Concessions
– defined, 15 § 1863
– employees to make, 15 § 1865
Contracts, 15 § 1864
Contracts entered into by corporation, effect, 15 § 1870

Reference to 15 U.S.C.S. §§ 1864 and 1870

Definitions
generally, 15 § 1861
– board, 15 § 1861
– borrower, 15 § 1861
– capital, 15 § 1863
– cash to be obtained from disposition of corporate assets, 15 § 1863
– concession, 15 § 1863
– corporation, 15 § 1861
– financial commitment, 15 § 1863
– financing plan, 15 § 1861
– fiscal year, 15 § 1861
– labor organization, 15 § 1861
– operating plan, 15 § 1861
– persons with existing economic stake in health of corporation, 15 § 1861
– wages and benefits, 15 § 1861

References to the Code are to Title and Section 575

After you have been directed to the appropriate title and section, you can readily locate the statute by scanning the library shelves. U.S.C.A. and U.S.C.S. are arranged by titles 1 through 50, and the spine of each volume that faces you is clearly marked to facilitate your research efforts.

This descriptive word approach (sometimes called the "index method" because you use the general index to find statutes) is usually the easiest and most efficient way to locate a statute, particularly for beginning researchers. This is the technique you should use until you are extremely familiar with the organization of U.S.C.A. and U.S.C.S. and feel comfortable using the next method of statutory research: the title/topic approach.

(2) Title/Topic Approach

As you know, all of the statutes in U.S.C.A. and U.S.C.S. are divided or categorized into 50 titles. It is possible that you may be so familiar with the contents and organization of U.S.C.A. and U.S.C.S. that when presented with a legal research problem, you bypass the general index, and immediately proceed to remove the appropriate title from the library shelf.

Thus, if you consistently performed research in the area of bankruptcy and were asked a question relating to the filing of a petition under the United States Bankruptcy Act, you may be able to immediately recognize that this subject is covered by Title 11. You would proceed to the appropriate volume(s) relating to Title 11, and begin examining the statutes and annotations therein.

At the very beginning of Title 11 is a table of contents, which gives you an outline of the bankruptcy statutes to follow so you can select the appropriate one. Additionally, after the very last bankruptcy statute you will be given an index to all of the preceding bankruptcy statutes in Title 11, and you may use this to focus in on the specific statute you are seeking.

This title/topic method is best employed by researchers who are sufficiently familiar with U.S.C.A. and U.S.C.S. that they can confidently select the one particular title of the 50 titles available and review the statutes therein. Because it is possible that some statutes may be covered under more than one title and because this title/topic approach presumes a great deal of knowledge about U.S.C.A. and U.S.C.S., you should avoid using this method when you are just beginning to perform legal research.

(3) Popular Name Approach

Many of our federal statutes are known by a popular name—either that of the sponsors of the legislation (McCain-Feingold Act, Taft-Hartley Act, Sarbanes-Oxley Act of 2002) or that given to the legislation by Congress or the public (USA PATRIOT Act, TARP Program, AMBER Alert Act). If you are asked to locate one of these statutes, you can easily do so in either U.S.C.A. or U.S.C.S.

To find such a statute in U.S.C.A., locate the volume(s) entitled *Popular Name Table*, which lists in alphabetical order federal laws known by their popular names. Simply look up the law you are interested in, and you will be directed to the appropriate title and section. See Figure 3-10 for a sample page from the *Popular Name Table*.

To locate such a statute in U.S.C.S., you should consult the *Popular Name Table* found in a separate volume of U.S.C.S., which lists the federal statutes known by a popular name in alphabetical order. Just as with U.S.C.A., you will be directed to the appropriate title and section.

The *United States Code* also includes a table, "Acts Cited by Popular Name," in the volume for Title 50.

Shepard's Acts and Cases by Popular Name: Federal and State organizes federal and state statutes in alphabetical order, providing you with citations to federal as well as state laws and cases known by popular names. For federal laws, this compact set also provides a citation to *United States Statutes at Large* and gives the public law number as well as the year the statute was enacted. *Shepard's Acts and Cases* is kept current by softcover supplements.

Finally, if you have only a public law number (such as P. L. 110-114) or a reference to the statute from *Statutes at Large* (such as 86 Stat. 471), both U.S.C.A. and U.S.C.S. have separate volumes marked "Tables" after Title 50 of the respective sets, allowing you to translate and convert a public law number or a *Statutes at Large* citation into a citation to U.S.C.A. or U.S.C.S.

Practice Tip

Infra and Supra

When using indexes for almost any set of law books, you may encounter the words *infra* (meaning "below") and *supra* (meaning "above"). These are signal terms that direct you to other pages within the index. For example, if you look up the word "tenant" in an index, you may see the instruction "See landlord, *supra*," meaning that you should look at the entries listed under the word "landlord" given previously in the index.

---

f. Final Research Steps

After you locate the statute you are interested in, read it carefully. Examine the historical notes, and review the library references to determine whether other sources in the library provide further information on this statute or the subject matter it discusses. Then read the annotations carefully, and decide which cases you will read in full based on your initial reading of the brief descriptions of these cases. Finally, check the pocket part and any of the interim pamphlets or supplements (which are usually arranged exactly like the numbering used in the hardback volumes) to determine if the statute has been amended or

Figure 3-10
Sample Page from U.S.C.A. Popular Name Table

117   POPULAR NAME TABLE

Black Lung Benefits Act (BLBA)—Continued
   Pub.L. 97–119, Title I, §§ 101 to 104, Title II, Dec. 29, 1981, 95 Stat. 1635 to 1639, 1643 (26
      §§ 1 note, 501, 4121, 9500, 9501, 9601, 9602; 30 §§ 801 note, 901, 902, 921 to 923, 925,
      932, 934, 934a, 940)
   Pub.L. 98–426, § 28(h)(2), Sept. 28, 1984, 98 Stat. 1655 (30 § 932)
   Pub.L. 101–509, Title V, § 529, [Title I, § 104(d)(3)] Nov. 5, 1990, 104 Stat. 1447 (30 § 938)
   Pub.L. 103–296, Title I, § 108(i), Aug. 15, 1994, 108 Stat. 1488 (30 §§ 902, 921 to 925, 936,
      945, 957)
   Pub.L. 104–66, Title I, Subtitle J, § 1102(b)(2), Dec. 21, 1995, 109 Stat. 723 (30 § 936)
   Pub.L. 107–275, § 2(a), (b)(1) to (4), (c)(1), Nov. 2, 2002, 116 Stat. 1925, 1926 (30 §§ 902, 923
      to 925, 936, 945)

Black Lung Benefits Act of 1972
   Short title, see 30 USCA § 801 note
   Pub.L. 92–303, May 19, 1972, 86 Stat. 150 (30 §§ 901, 902, 921 to 924, 931 to 934, 936 to 940,
      951)
   Pub.L. 97–119, Title I, § 104, Dec. 29, 1981, 95 Stat. 1639 (30 §§ 902, 925, 932, 934)
   Pub.L. 98–426, § 28(h)(2), Sept. 28, 1984, 98 Stat. 1655 (30 § 932) ——————— *Reference to*
                                                                                  30 U.S.C.A § 932

Black Lung Benefits Amendments of 1981
   Short title, see 30 USCA § 801 note
   Pub.L. 97–119, Title II, Dec. 29, 1981, 95 Stat. 1643 to 1645 (30 §§ 801 note, 901, 902, 921,
      922, 923, 932, 940)

Black Lung Benefits Reform Act of 1977
   Short title, see 30 USCA § 801 note
   Pub.L. 95–239, Mar. 1, 1978, 92 Stat. 95 (26 § 4121 note; 29 § 675 note; 30 §§ 801 note, 901,
      902, 903, 904, 921, 922, 923, 924, 924a, 931, 932, 932a note, 933, 937, 940, 941, 942, 943,
      944, 945)
   Pub.L. 107–275, § 2(c)(2), Nov. 2, 2002, 116 Stat. 1926 (30 § 924a)

Black Lung Benefits Revenue Act of 1977
   Short title, see 26 USCA § 1 note
   Pub.L. 95–227, Feb. 10, 1978, 92 Stat. 11 (26 §§ 192, 501, 4121, 4218, 4221, 4293, 4946, 4951,
      4952, 4953, 6104, 6213, 6405, 6416, 6501, 6503, 7454; 30 §§ 934, 934a)
   Pub.L. 95–488, § 1(a) to (d), Oct. 20, 9178, 92 Stat. 1637, 1638 (26 §§ 192, 6104)
   Pub.L. 96–222, Title I, § 108(b)(2)(A), (3)(A), Apr. 1, 1980, 94 Stat. 226 (30 §§ 934, 934a)
   Pub.L. 97–119, Title I, § 103(b), Dec. 29, 1981, 95 Stat. 1638 (30 § 934a)

Black Lung Benefits Revenue Act of 1981
   Short title, see 26 USCA § 1 note
   Pub.L. 97–119, Title I, Subtitle A, Dec. 29, 1981, 95 Stat. 1635 (26 §§ 1 note, 501, 4121, 9500,
      9501, 9601, 9602; 30 §§ 902, 925, 932, 934, 934a)

Black Lung Consolidation of Administrative Responsibility Act
   Pub.L. 107–275, Nov. 2, 2002, 116 Stat. 1925 (30 §§ 801 note, 902, 904, 921 to 924, 924a, 925,
      932a, 936, 945)

Black-McKellar Act
   See, also, Air Mail Acts
   June 12, 1934, ch. 466, 48 Stat. 933

**Black Rock Desert-High Rock Canyon Emigrant Trails National Conservation Area Act of
   2000**
   See, also, Consolidated Appropriations Act, 2001
   See, also, Miscellaneous Appropriations Act, 2001
   Pub.L. 106–554, § 1(a)(4) [Div. B, Title I, § 125], Dec. 21, 2000, 114 Stat. 2763, 2763A–228,
      2763A–353 (16 §§ 460ppp, 460ppp–1 to 460ppp–7, 1132 note)
   Pub.L. 107–63, Title I, § 135, Nov. 5, 2001, 115 Stat. 443 (16 §§ 460ppp–2, 460ppp–3,
      460ppp–6)

Blackstone River Valley National Heritage Corridor Act of 1986
   Pub.L. 99–647, Nov. 10, 1986, 100 Stat. 3625 (16 § 461 note)
   Pub.L. 101–441, Oct. 18, 1990, 104 Stat. 1017 (16 § 461 note)
   Pub.L. 102–154, Title I, § 118, Nov. 13, 1991, 105 Stat. 1013 (16 § 461 note)
   Pub.L. 104–208, Div. A, Title I, § 101(d), [Title I, § 115], Sept. 30, 1996, 110 Stat. 3009–201
      (16 § 461 note)
   Pub.L. 105–355, Title V, § 501, Nov. 6, 1998, 112 Stat. 3261 (16 § 461 note)

repealed and to look for annotations or references to cases that have interpreted the statute subsequent to the publication of the hardbound volume. If you have any difficulty performing statutory research, you may call either Lexis ((800) 897–7922) or West ((800) 733–2889) to receive personal assistance from reference attorneys.

```
──────────────────── Ethics Alert ────────────────────

Updating the Annotated Codes

Always examine the pocket parts or softcover supplements to the
annotated codes. They provide the only way you can ensure that
your statutory research is complete. Failure to review the pocket
parts and supplements is a breach of your ethical duty to research
accurately and thoroughly.
```

g. United States Constitution

Although the United States Constitution is not one of the 50 titles of the *United States Code*, nevertheless both U.S.C.A. and U.S.C.S. contain volumes for the Constitution. You will be provided with the text of the Constitution and its amendments and then, by the use of annotations, you will be referred to cases that interpret the Constitution. For example, after you read the First Amendment, you will be directed to thousands of cases that have construed the First Amendment. You will also be provided with reference guides and cross-references to other materials to help you better understand the constitutional provision you are researching. Unannotated versions of the United States Constitution can be found in U.S.C. and in the *Am. Jur. 2d Desk Book* (see Chapter 6) and at various Internet sites, such as http://thomas.loc.gov.

Depending upon the arrangement of the law library you use, the volumes for the Constitution may precede Title 1 on your library shelves, may be located as the last volumes after Title 50, or may appear alphabetically within the set between the volumes for Conservation and those for Copyrights.

The three primary research approaches discussed above, namely, the descriptive word approach, the title/topic approach, and the popular name approach, should also be used when you are presented with a constitutional research issue. Be sure to refer to the pocket parts or softcover supplements for the applicable volumes to locate the newest cases interpreting constitutional provisions.

B. State Legislation

1. Enactment of State Statutes

The process of enacting and publishing legislation at the state level is substantially similar to the process described above for the federal level. Most state legislatures closely conform to the United States Congress with regard to their organization and manner of enacting law. Just as the United States Congress is divided into two chambers—the Senate and the House of Representatives—each state (except Nebraska) has a legislature divided into two chambers. Such a legislature is referred to as a bicameral legislature. Nebraska has a one-house or unicameral legislature. The names given to the two chambers may vary from state to state. For example, the two bodies in California are the Senate and the Assembly; the two chambers in Louisiana are the Senate and the House of Representatives; and the two bodies in Maryland are the Senate and the House of Delegates. More than four-fifths of the state legislatures meet on a yearly basis, while the remaining legislatures meet every two years.

Similar to the process of enacting federal law, much of the work in enacting state law is done by committees. When a final version of a bill is agreed upon, it will be sent to the governor of the state for signature, at which time it is referred to as a "law" or "statute" rather than a bill.

Additional information regarding the names of the lawmaking bodies for each of the states and the process of enacting legislation can be obtained from almost any general information encyclopedia or at the website of the National Conference of State Legislatures at http://www.ncsl.org.

2. Publication and Codification of State Statutes

Many states, particularly the most populous ones, initially publish their laws in slip form, similar in appearance to federal slip laws. At the end of the state's legislative session, these slips are taken together and compiled into books, which are generally referred to as "session laws." Although some states may not use the words "session laws" and may name their compiled statutes "acts and resolves," "laws," or "statutes," or some other name, the generic title given to volumes that set forth a state's laws in chronological order is "session laws."

These session laws are analogous to *United States Statutes at Large*. That is, the volumes of session laws will contain the laws of a particular state in the order in which they were enacted. Just as researchers required *United States Statutes at Large* to be better arranged, or "codified," in order to bring together all the current laws on the same subject and eliminate laws that had been repealed, codification of the session laws of each state has also taken place. These state codifications

may be called "codes," "statutes," "general laws," "compilations," "revisions," or "consolidations," depending on the state.

Most states arrange their statutes by titles and chapters, such as Virginia: Va. Code Ann. § 8.01-108 (2000). A few states, usually the more populous ones, arrange their statutes in named titles, such as California: Cal. Evid. Code § 312 (West 1995). Thus, numbering and format vary from state to state.

Most states have annotated codes, meaning that after you are provided with the wording of the state statute, you will be directed to cases that interpret the statute. West publishes annotated codes for approximately 30 states and Lexis publishes for most of the remaining states. A few states use other (or both) publishers. An identification of the publisher for each state's statutes can be found in Table T.1 of *The Bluebook* and Appendix 1 of *ALWD*.

Although the publication of each state's statutes will vary somewhat and although the publication may be official or unofficial, most state codes share the following features:

(i) The constitution of the state will be contained in the code;

(ii) The statutes will be organized by subject matter so that all of the corporation statutes are together, all of the penal statutes are together, all of the workers' compensation statutes are together, and so forth;

(iii) There will be a general index to the entire set and often each title will be separately indexed, so that after you read the last evidence statute you are given an index to all of the evidence statutes, and so forth;

(iv) The statutes are kept current by annual cumulative pocket parts, which will be placed in the back of each hardback bound volume, or by supplements placed on the shelves next to the volumes being updated;

(v) Annotations will be provided to direct you to cases interpreting the statutes, typically through the use of a one-sentence summary of the case and its citation, similar to the arrangement and organization of annotations provided by U.S.C.A. and U.S.C.S.;

(vi) Historical notes, which explain the history and amendments to the statute, and library references, which will direct you to other sources in the law library to assist you in interpreting the statute, will typically be provided (see Figure 3-11 for a sample page of a state statute); and

(vii) Conversion tables are provided in each volume so that if a state statute has been repealed or renumbered, you will be informed of the repealing or provided with the new section number of the statute.

Figure 3-11
<u>**Sample Page from Code of Virginia**</u>

§ 18.2-26. Attempts to commit noncapital felonies; how punished. —
Every person who attempts to commit an offense which is a noncapital felony
shall be punished as follows:

(1) If the felony attempted is punishable by a maximum punishment of life
imprisonment or a term of years in excess of twenty years, an attempt thereat
shall be punishable as a Class 4 felony.

(2) If the felony attempted is punishable by a maximum punishment of
twenty years' imprisonment, an attempt thereat shall be punishable as a Class
5 felony.

(3) If the felony attempted is punishable by a maximum punishment of less
than twenty years' imprisonment, an attempt thereat shall be punishable as a
Class 6 felony. (Code 1950, §§ 18.1-17, 18.1-18; 1960, c. 358; 1975, cc. 14, 15;
1994, c. 639.)

Law Review. — For survey of Virginia criminal law for the year 1973-1974, see 60 Va. L. Rev. 1499 (1974). For survey of Virginia criminal law for the year 1974-1975, see 61 Va. L. Rev. 1697 (1975). For article discussing the legislative history of sexual assault law reform in Virginia, see 68 Va. L. Rev. 459 (1982).

Double jeopardy considerations. — Multiple punishments for the crimes of attempted murder and malicious wounding do not violate the double jeopardy clause when the convictions are obtained in a single trial. Creamer v. Commonwealth, No. 1298-91-3 (Ct. of Appeals Dec. 15, 1992).

The word "punishable," as here used, means the maximum punishment which may be imposed. Slusher v. Commonwealth, 196 Va. 440, 83 S.E.2d 719 (1954).

No retroactive assignment of punishment. — Although the amendments to this section subsequent to defendant's misconduct included attempts at § 18.2-32 offenses, the revised statute may not retroactively assign punishment to prior acts. Cook v. Commonwealth, 20 Va. App. 510, 458 S.E.2d 317 (1995).

Section inapplicable to attempt to commit act of sodomy for money. — The General Assembly, by its amendment of § 18.2-346 to

3. *Research Techniques*

The same techniques used to locate federal statutes are used to locate
state statutes. They are as follows:

a. Descriptive Word Approach

This method requires you to determine which words or phrases relate to
the issue you are researching and then locate those words or phrases in
the general index, which will then direct you to the appropriate statute.

b. Title/Topic Approach

This technique may be used when you have become so familiar with your
state code that you bypass the general index, and immediately locate the
particular title or chapter that deals with the research problem.

c. Popular Name Approach

This method of locating statutes is used in those instances in which a state statute is known by a popular name, such as the "Megan's Law" in your state. You can locate this statute by simply looking up the name of the act or statute in the alphabetically arranged general index.

For example, suppose you wish to determine whether the directors of a corporation may conduct a board meeting by conference call. If you elect to use the descriptive word approach, you should consider looking up some of the following words in the general index in order to be directed to the appropriate statute: "directors," "board of directors," "corporations," "meetings," or "conference calls." Researchers who are familiar with their state's code may use the topic approach and immediately locate the volumes in the state code that contain statutes dealing with corporations, and review the separate index at the end of all of the corporations statutes or the table of contents, which appears at the beginning of the statutes dealing with corporations.

After locating the statute, read it carefully, examine the historical notes and library references, if any, analyze the annotations you believe appear promising, and examine the pocket part (or supplements) to ensure the statute is still in force and to locate newer cases that may have interpreted the statute. You must then read the relevant cases in full.

You may observe that the numbering system for some state codes is unusual, with large gaps between some sections; for example, § 1815 might be followed by § 1832. Such a gap may indicate that sections 1816 through 1831 have been repealed or renumbered. Consult any conversion tables that appear in the volume to determine whether sections 1816 through 1831 have been repealed or whether they have been renumbered and subsumed within some other title or chapter in the code.

On other occasions you may notice that the numbering of state statutes is not by whole numbers but rather by decimals or subsections. For instance, § 410 may not be followed by § 411, but by § 410.10, § 410.20, § 410.30, and then by § 411. This numbering scheme typically indicates that after the state legislature enacted statutes that were numbered as § 410 and § 411, other statutes were enacted that dealt with the same general topic or subject matter and thus needed to be inserted between § 410 and § 411.

Finally, there is no one set of books that will provide you with all of the laws for all 50 states. Such a set would be unwieldy, expensive, and generally not very useful, as researchers in one state are usually not interested in the statutes of another state.

The Final Wrap-Up

Use and Citation of Annotated Codes

Use: Use annotated codes to find relevant statutes. Then use the annotations or one-sentence case summaries to locate cases on point. You may also use the various research references to expand and supplement your research efforts because these will direct you to useful forms, helpful law review articles, and so forth.

Citation: You may (and should) cite to and quote from the statutes you find in an annotated code, but you may never cite to or quote from the annotations (case summaries) or any research references. You must retrieve the cases and references cited, read and analyze them, and then you may cite to these sources.

4. *Uniform and Model Laws and Court Rules*

Uniform or model laws are those drafted for topics of the law in which uniformity is desirable and practical. For example, a set of laws relating to the formation, operation, and dissolution of partnerships, called the Uniform Partnership Act (1914 & 1997), has been adopted in every state but Louisiana. Once adopted in a state, a Uniform Law is then a state statute like any other and can be located using any of the research techniques discussed above. Many states, however, often make changes and modifications to the Uniform Laws, resulting in laws that are highly similar from state to state but that are not perfectly uniform. Uniform and model acts are discussed in detail in Chapter 7.

Rules of procedure and court rules bind those practicing in a given jurisdiction. These rules of procedure and court rules are fully discussed in Chapter 10.

C. Statutory Research Overview

When you are undecided whether to begin a project by examining federal or state statutes, keep in mind that some matters are exclusively presumed to be federal in nature. For example, establishing a uniform currency system is the province of the federal government, which eliminates the confusion that would result if each state developed its own types of coins. On the other hand, states have the power to enact laws relating to local concerns, such as establishing the death penalty in the state, residency laws for obtaining a divorce, and statutes of limitation for

breach of contract matters. If you are uncertain whether an area is governed by federal or state law, examine the federal statutes first. If the topic is not covered by federal statute, proceed to examine your state statutes.

When you locate a statute, quickly review the entire scope of the statutes governing the topic. Generally, terms used in the act or statutory scheme are first defined. Definitions are usually followed by the rules announced in the statute and then by penalties for violations of the statute. Assume that each word in the statute is there for a purpose, and the words are to be given their plain meaning. If the statute is vague or ambiguous, examine the cases that discuss the statute to determine how courts have interpreted the statute. You can also examine the legislative history of the statute by reviewing the documents considered by the legislature when it enacted the law, such as the transcripts of committee hearings and committee reports. Legislative history research is fully discussed in Chapter 10. Remember that it is the court's interpretation of a statute rather than the naked statutory language that is controlling under our system of law. It is the province of our courts to apply and interpret statutes and even strike down statutes as unconstitutional.

D. Citation Form

1. *Federal Statutes* (The Bluebook *and* ALWD)

11 U.S.C. § 1327 (2006).
11 U.S.C.A. § 1327 (West 2004).
The Bluebook: 11 U.S.C.S. § 1327 (LexisNexis 2001)
ALWD: 11 U.S.C. § 1327 (Lexis 2000)

2. *State Statutes* (The Bluebook *and* ALWD)

Ind. Code Ann. § 14-201 (West 1998).
Wash. Rev. Code § 8.907 (1997).

CyberSites ■■■■■■■■■■■

http://thomas.loc.gov	THOMAS contains full text of pending bills, key legislation, committee and congressional information, references to the Congressional Record, the text of historical documents, and information about the legislative process and legislators.
http://www.gpo.gov/fdsys	The United States Government Printing Office site offers access to authenticated bills, public and private laws, United States Code, United States Constitution, *U.S. Statutes at Large*, and various congressional documents, reports, and bills.
http://www.findlaw.com	FindLaw, one of the best-known legal sites, provides easy access to federal and state statutes as well as a wide variety of other law-related information and links to other sites.
http://uscode.house.gov/ lawrevisioncounsel.shtml	The site for the Office of the Law Revision Counsel provides information about the United States Code, allows searching of the United States Code, and provides classification tables listing sections of the United States Code affected by new laws.
http://www4.law.Cornell.edu/ uscode	The site of Cornell Law School provides easy access to the United States Constitution and to federal statutes, including a list of titles of the United States Code, a list of federal statutes by popular names, and a form allowing rapid access to specific sections of the Code.
http://www.loc.gov/law/guide	The Guide to Law Online, offered by the Library of Congress, provides links to the United States Code, to *U.S. Statutes at Large*, and to state statutes.
http://www.senate.gov/ legislative/common/generic/ Doc_Room.htm; (202) 224–7791	The Senate Document Room provides information on the status and availability of Senate legislative documents. Documents can be ordered by fax or online at orders@sec.senate.gov.
http://clerk.house.gov/about/ offices_lrc.html; (202) 226–5200	The Legislative Resource Center for the House of Representatives provides public access to all published House documents.
http://www.ncsl.org/ ?tabid=17173	The National Conference of State Legislatures offers direct links to all state legislatures, their constitutions, bills, statutes, and other legislative information.

Writing Strategies

Examine statutes as carefully as possible. Every word and phrase is meaningful. If the statute is contrary to the client's position, look to see if your issue fits within any exceptions to the statute. Review the law review articles you are directed to by the cross-references to determine if any guidance is given as to what situations the statute was designed to address or remedy.

Statutes can be long and complex. To avoid having to reproduce all of a lengthy statute in your writings, say "in pertinent part New York General Business Law section 26 (McKinney 2004) provides . . . ."

If the statute supports the client's position, say so forcefully: "California Government Code section 426 (West 1995) [requires] or [mandates] or [imposes] . . . ."

If the statute contradicts the client's position, try to shift the focus away from the statute and toward the cases interpreting the statute that may provide you with more latitude due to vague or imprecise language: "In the seminal case interpreting Indiana Code Annotated section 14-11-1-6 (West 1998), the court . . . ."

Assignment for Chapter 3

1. What volume of the United States Code relates to Education?
2. Use U.S.C.A. and cite the title and section that govern the following:
   a. Payment to jurors serving on a grand jury of their parking fees.
   b. Removal of shark fins.
3. Use either U.S.C.A. or U.S.C.S. and cite the title and section that govern the following:
   a. Harbor lines in the Potomac River
   b. Hate crimes (either conduct constituting hate crimes or guidelines)
4. Use the popular name tables as directed and cite the title and section for the following:
   a. Use U.S.C.A. and give the citation for the Cooper-Hawes Act.
   b. Use U.S.C.A. and give the citation for the short title of the Immigration Marriage Fraud Amendments of 1986.
   c. Use U.S.C.S. and give the citation for the Hart Scott Rodino Antitrust Improvements Act of 1976.
   d. Use either U.S.C.A. or U.S.C.S. and give the citation for the Telemarketing Fraud Prevention Act of 1998.
5. Use U.S.C.A. How is "arson" defined?
6. Use either U.S.C.A. or U.S.C.S. Give the citation for the statute that relates to creation of a registry for Alzheimer's disease.
7. Use the U.S.C.A. volumes for the Constitution. Answer the following questions and cite the best case to support your answer. Give case names only.
   a. Under the First Amendment (Freedom of Religion—Public Schools), did a school district's allowing an elementary student to distribute literature concerning the impact of religion in her life foster an excessive entanglement with religion so as to violate the Establishment Clause? Cite the newest case that supports your answer.
   b. Under the Eighth Amendment (Cruel and Unusual Punishment), does depriving a convicted felon of voting rights in North Carolina constitute cruel and unusual punishment?
8. Use U.S.C.A.
   a. Under 7 U.S.C.A. § 2015, if a recipient of food stamps refuses to accept employment without good cause, may he lose his food stamps? Answer the question and cite the best case to support your answer. Give the case name only.
   b. What Utah law review article are you directed to in order to better understand this statute? Give the citation only.
   c. Give the first public law designation for this statute.

9. Use U.S.C.S.
    a. Under 18 U.S.C.S. § 3559, does the three strikes law violate the double jeopardy clause?
    b. Under 29 U.S.C.S. § 164, does the NLRB have jurisdiction over newspapers and other publications?
10. Use *U.S. Statutes at Large*.
    a. What is the short title of Public Law 110-140?
    b. Give the citation for this law in *U.S. Statutes at Large*.
    c. What was its designation in the House of Representatives?
11. Use *U.S. Statutes at Large*.
    a. For whose relief was Private Law 108-3 enacted?
    b. What was the purpose of this private law?

Internet Assignment for Chapter 3

1. Access one of the Internet sites for the United States House of Representatives and select "Committees."
    a. When was the Committee on Homeland Security made permanent?
    b. How many Democratic and Republican members are there in the Committee?
2. Access the National Conference on State Legislatures (http://www.ncsl.org). Select the links for your state's legislators and identify your state's President pro tempore of the Senate. If your state does not have a President pro tempore, identify your state's first listed Senate leader.
3. Access THOMAS and locate information relating to bill number H.R. 4331 introduced in the 111th Congress.
    a. What is the full title of this bill?
    b. What is the short title of this bill?
    c. To what committee was this bill assigned?
4. Access THOMAS and locate the Patent Reform Act introduced in the 109th Congress.
    a. What was the Senate Number assigned to this bill?
    b. Locate information relating to its status. What was the latest major action taken on this legislation?
5. Access the website for GPO Access (or FDsys). Browse Title 18 of the United States Code. Select Part I.
    a. What is the general subject matter of Section 1504?
    b. What was this statute's original public law number?
6. Access the website for GPO Access (or FDsys). Browse the public and private laws for the 107th Congress.
    a. For whose relief was private law 107-005 enacted?
    b. What is the general subject matter or topic of this private law?

Case Law and Judicial Opinions

It is evident that I consider stare decisis essential to the rule of law.

Supreme Court Associate Justice Lewis F. Powell, Jr. (1990)

Chapter Overview

This chapter will discuss judicial opinions and provide you with an understanding of the publication of cases, the elements of a typical court case, and the types of opinions written by judges. We will present the elements of analyzing and briefing cases and introduce the *National Reporter System*, a thorough and comprehensive series of case reporters, which publishes decisions from state and federal courts.

A. Selective Publication

1. Standards for Publishing Cases

At the conclusion of Chapter 1, you were required to locate certain
published cases. This emphasis on locating cases is a cornerstone of the
legal profession, primarily because of our common law tradition of
reliance on case law as precedent. You will recall from Chapter 1 that the
concept of stare decisis requires that a court follow a previous case from
that jurisdiction if the case is materially similar to the case then before
the court, although higher courts may depart from previously decided
cases if a change in the law is deemed important. Each year approximately 60,000 new cases are published, and each one of these adds to the
great number of cases or precedents that you may need to locate to
persuade a court to rule in a client's favor. Although previous assignments have required you to locate cases, it was easy to accomplish
because the citations to the cases were given to you.

Seldom, if ever, does such a lucky event occur in the workplace.
Generally, you will be provided only with an overview of the legal problem
or question involved, and you will then be required to locate cases on
point without the aid of a specific citation or often any direction whatsoever. In Chapters 5, 6, and 7 you will read about several publications that
will help you locate relevant cases. Before you begin to locate cases,
however, you will need a clear understanding of the elements of a typical
court case and the process of publication of cases.

You may be surprised to learn that not all cases are published or
"reported." In general, and with the exception of some trial cases from our
federal courts, trial court decisions are not published. If you consider the
overwhelming number of routine assault and battery cases, divorce or
dissolution actions, prosecutions for driving while intoxicated, or cases
relating to the possession of narcotics, you can readily see why trial court
decisions are not usually published. Many of these cases add little to our
body of precedents and relate only to the litigants themselves. If we were
to publish the more than 90 million cases that are processed annually in
our state courts, our bookshelves would soon collapse of their own weight.
As a result, usually only decisions of appellate courts are published.
Because approximately 10 percent of cases are appealed, even the
reporting of appellate court decisions results in a mass of publication.
Therefore, in general, only appellate court cases that advance legal
theory are published. More than 80 percent of cases disposed of by federal
courts are unpublished. Generally, only the decisions of the courts of last
resort in a jurisdiction are published in full. For example, all of the
decisions of the United States Supreme Court and the California Supreme Court are published in full officially, but the decisions of the lower
federal courts and lower California courts are not. Similarly, the State of
Washington publishes only about 25 percent of its Court of Appeals
opinions.

In many instances, the courts themselves decide whether a case merits publication. For example, in California, California Rule of Court 8.1105 provides that cases that meet the following criteria, among others, should be considered by appellate courts in determining which cases should be officially published:

- those that establish a new rule of law or alter or criticize an existing rule;
- those that address an apparent conflict of authority in the law;
- those that involve a legal issue of continuing public interest; or
- those that make a significant contribution to legal literature.

In many jurisdictions, including California, unpublished cases cannot be cited or used as precedents except in extraordinary circumstances. You should not interpret the fact that many cases are not published as a conspiracy to prevent people from obtaining access to cases. Unless a case is sealed (usually for national security reasons, to maintain trade secrets, or for the protection of a minor), the case file is readily accessible at the courthouse that handled the case. If you know the name of the case, you can determine its docket number in a Plaintiff-Defendant Index at the courthouse. You may then ask a court clerk to allow you to review the file, and you will have access to all of the pleadings filed in the case as well as the judge's decision and the final judgment. If you need a case from another jurisdiction, consult your yellow pages directory and locate an "attorneys service" company. These companies will locate and copy case files and pleadings for you for payment of a fee.

You can see, therefore, that publishing every case decided in the United States this year would not be of any great value to researchers and would simply result in needless publication. Thus, a certain amount of "weeding out" or selectivity occurs in the publication of cases.

2. The Controversy Surrounding Unpublished Opinions

As discussed above, generally a court decides which cases to publish by certifying them for publication after determining that the cases meet the court's standards for publication. In recent years, however, the issue of selective publication of cases has sparked a great deal of controversy. In *Anastasoff v. United States*, 223 F.3d 898, 905 (8th Cir. 2000), the court ruled that allowing judges to ignore unpublished cases was unconstitutional and gave them arbitrary power. Although *Anastasoff* was later vacated as moot on other grounds, *see Anastasoff v. United States*, 235 F.3d 1054 (8th Cir. 2000), the issue regarding the precedential value of published decisions continued to engender heated debate.

Remember that "unpublished" does not mean "unavailable"; it simply means that the case will not be printed in a conventional hardbound book. As courts have published their opinions on their own

websites and released them to Lexis and Westlaw, the online legal research systems, the public has been able to access these otherwise unpublished decisions, and attorneys and litigants have wanted to refer to, cite to, and rely upon these unpublished decisions to support their arguments and their clients' positions. Moreover, in 2001 West created the *Federal Appendix,* a set that prints the unpublished federal courts of appeals decisions, together with headnotes, key numbers, and topic names, making these unpublished cases even more readily available to researchers. Finally, pursuant to the E-Government Act of 2002, 44 U.S.C. § 3601 (2006), all federal appellate courts must provide access over the Internet to all of their written opinions, regardless of whether such opinions are to be published. Thus, researchers were able to locate and access these "unpublished" cases through numerous means and demanded the right to cite to them in their briefs.

After several years of discussion and debate, with some circuits (such as the Ninth Circuit Court of Appeals) vehemently opposed to allowing parties to cite unpublished cases, the issue was resolved on January 1, 2006, when the Federal Rules of Appellate Procedure were amended to add Rule 32.1, which prohibits courts from restricting parties and attorneys from citing unpublished federal judicial opinions issued after January 1, 2007. (You may cite pre-2007 unpublished cases if local federal rules permit such.) Because the new rule applies only to unpublished cases issued after January 1, 2007, it may take some years to determine its full effect. In any event, although you may cite to an unpublished case issued after January 1, 2007, its precedential effect is questionable. Such cases generally have persuasive effect only, and thus some experts believe that researchers will likely cite to these unpublished cases only when they can locate no precedential decisions.

You may wonder whether you have an obligation to locate and cite to one of these numerous unpublished authorities if it supports a client's position. At present there is no legal obligation to locate authorities that may be persuasive only; thus, failure to cite to such unpublished opinions would likely not constitute malpractice.

State courts also differ in their treatment of unpublished decisions, with about one-half of the states allowing citation of unpublished decisions, although most of these concur that these unpublished decisions are not binding precedent under the theory of stare decisis. Others, such as California (which publishes only about 10 percent of its appellate cases each year), strictly prohibit courts and parties from citing or relying upon opinions not certified for publication except in extraordinary circumstances. Cal. R. Ct. 8.1115.

As a researcher, you will have access to unpublished decisions (from the courts' own websites, through Lexis and Westlaw, and through various Internet sources). You will need to know and comply with your state and applicable federal rules regarding citing to these unpublished cases when you prepare documents for filing with courts.

B.   Elements of a Case

When an appellate court has reviewed the transcript of the trial below, read the written arguments (called "briefs"), which were submitted by the parties, and perhaps heard oral argument, the court will render its decision in a written opinion. It is this opinion that will be published (assuming it advances legal knowledge) and that will now serve as a precedent under the doctrine of stare decisis.

Cases that are published or reported typically contain the following elements (See Figure 4-1):

1.   *Case Name*

The name or title of a case identifies the parties involved in the action and also provides additional information about the nature of the proceeding. There are several types of case names.

> *Smith v. Jones.* This case name is the most common and indicates by the use of the signal "v." (for "versus") that the matter is adversarial in nature. The first listed party, Smith, is the plaintiff, who has instituted this action against Jones. Usually the case name will remain the same if the case is appealed, although some courts may reverse the order by placing the name of a defendant who lost the trial below and instituted the appeal first. For example, if Jones lost the trial and appealed the decision, the case might then be identified as *Jones v. Smith*, even though the original plaintiff was Smith. *The Bluebook* and *ALWD* require that only the first listed plaintiff and first listed defendant be identified in a case citation. Nevertheless, a case may involve several plaintiffs and defendants or may be a consolidation of several cases so a court can resolve cases dealing with the same legal issue at one time.
>
> *In re Smith.* The phrase "in re" means "regarding" or "in the matter of." This case name designates a case that is not adversarial in nature. That is, rather than one party instituting an action against another, this case involves only one matter or party, such as a bankruptcy proceeding, a conservatorship, disbarment, or a probate matter that relates to the rights of one individual. Additionally, "in re" is used to designate civil cases involving multiple claims that are transferred to one federal court for coordinated and consistent handling, such as the case *In re Vitamin Antitrust Litigation.*
>
> *State v. Smith* (or *United States v. Smith*). This case name generally indicates a criminal proceeding. In our legal system, when a crime is committed, the state will prosecute the action on behalf of its citizens, all of whom have been injured by the crime. Some jurisdictions identify these cases as *People v. Smith*, and four

Figure 4-1
Sample of a Published Case

STATE v. BOYD   N.C. **697**
Cite as 595 S.E.2d 697 (N.C.App. 2004)

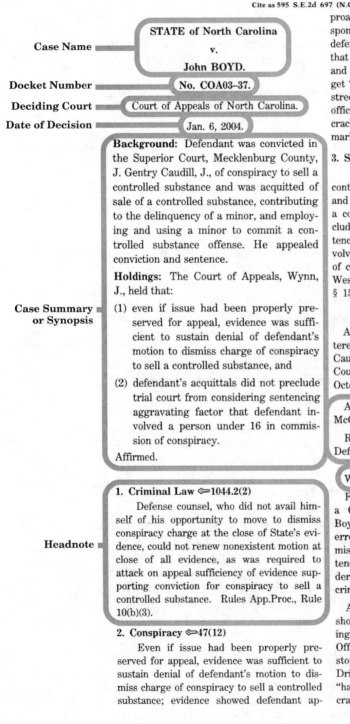

Case Name

STATE of North Carolina
v.
John BOYD.

Docket Number — No. COA03–37.

Deciding Court — Court of Appeals of North Carolina.

Date of Decision — Jan. 6, 2004.

Background: Defendant was convicted in the Superior Court, Mecklenburg County, J. Gentry Caudill, J., of conspiracy to sell a controlled substance and was acquitted of sale of a controlled substance, contributing to the delinquency of a minor, and employing and using a minor to commit a controlled substance offense. He appealed conviction and sentence.

Holdings: The Court of Appeals, Wynn, J., held that:

Case Summary or Synopsis

(1) even if issue had been properly preserved for appeal, evidence was sufficient to sustain denial of defendant's motion to dismiss charge of conspiracy to sell a controlled substance, and

(2) defendant's acquittals did not preclude trial court from considering sentencing aggravating factor that defendant involved a person under 16 in commission of conspiracy.

Affirmed.

Headnote

1. Criminal Law ⬚1044.2(2)

Defense counsel, who did not avail himself of his opportunity to move to dismiss conspiracy charge at the close of State's evidence, could not renew nonexistent motion at close of all evidence, as was required to attack on appeal sufficiency of evidence supporting conviction for conspiracy to sell a controlled substance. Rules App.Proc., Rule 10(b)(3).

2. Conspiracy ⬚47(12)

Even if issue had been properly preserved for appeal, evidence was sufficient to sustain denial of defendant's motion to dismiss charge of conspiracy to sell a controlled substance; evidence showed defendant ap-

proached undercover police officers in response to juvenile's call, that officer told defendant he wanted to find some cocaine, that defendant told officer to pull his car over and wait while he went down the street to get "it," that defendant and juvenile crossed street, and that juvenile returned and handed officer clear plastic bag containing a rock of crack cocaine, which officer paid for with a marked twenty dollar bill.

3. Sentencing and Punishment ⬚98

Fact that defendant was acquitted of contributing to the delinquency of a minor and employing and using a minor to commit a controlled substance offense did not preclude trial court from considering the sentencing aggravating factor that defendant involved a person under 16 in the commission of conspiracy to sell a controlled substance. West's N.C.G.S.A. § 15A–1340.16(d)(13); § 15A–1340.4(a) (Repealed).

Appeal by Defendant from judgment entered 13 August 2002 by Judge J. Gentry Caudill in Superior Court, Mecklenburg County. Heard in the Court of Appeals 28 October 2003.

Assistant Attorney General Martin T. McCracken, for the State.

Robert W. Ewing, Winston-Salem, for the Defendant.

Na
Cou

WYNN, Judge.

Aut
Opi

From his conviction for Conspiracy to Sell a Controlled Substance, Defendant, John Boyd, argues on appeal that the trial court erred by failing to grant his motion to dismiss, and considering as an aggravating sentencing factor that he involved a person under 16 years of age in the commission of a crime. We find no error in Defendant's trial.

At trial, the State's evidence tended to show that on 25 October 2001, while conducting undercover drug buys, Charlotte Police Officers Eric Duft and Susan O'Donohue stopped two juveniles in the Colony Acres Drive neighborhood and asked for some "hard" or "rock"—slang terms for the drug crack cocaine. In response, Quintine Hamp-

Figure 4-1 *(Continued)*

ton, one of the youths, pointed across the street and yelled for "J.B." to come over to the car. Responding to Hampton, Defendant approached the officers' car. Officer Duft reiterated his desire to find some "hard," but before discussing the drug request, Defendant asked the officers whether they were police. Officer Duft denied being a police officer and assured Defendant he "just wanted to get hooked up." Apparently satisfied, Defendant told Officer Duft to pull his car over and wait while he went down the street to get "it."

The officers then observed Hampton and Defendant cross Colony Acres Drive before losing sight of them. After two or three minutes, Hampton returned alone and handed Officer Duft a clear plastic bag containing a rock of crack cocaine. Officer Duft paid Hampton with a marked twenty dollar bill. Thereafter, Defendant and Hampton were arrested separately.

After estimating that he had conducted approximately 200–300 similar undercover drug buy stings, Officer Duft testified that "it is common for more than one person to be involved in the [drug] transaction" and sometimes, "they will use a younger person to sell them [because] [t]here is less consequences for a juvenile than there is for an adult." The arresting officer testified that, when Defendant was apprehended, "He stated to me; and I, quote, 'I did not sell shit. All I did was get a piece of the rock.'" At the close of the State's evidence, defense counsel did not "care to be heard" on the conspiracy charge, but did move to dismiss all remaining charges; the motions were denied.

In his defense, Defendant denied the statement attributed to him by the arresting officer. Rather, Defendant testified that he was walking towards Hampton to warn him that Officers Duft and O'Donohue were police officers. When Defendant "couldn't catch [Hampton's] bicycle" he turned around to go home. Defendant maintained "I don't have nothing to do with it."

1. N.C.G.S. § 14.316.1: "to knowingly or willfully cause, encourage or aid any juvenile within the jurisdiction of the court to be in a place or condition, or to commit an act whereby the juvenile could be adjudicated delinquent, undisciplined, abused or neglected."

Ultimately, the jury convicted Defendant of Conspiracy to Sell a Controlled Substance but acquitted him of the remaining charges of Sale of a Controlled Substance, Contributing to the Delinquency of a Minor [1], and Employing and Using a Minor to Commit a Controlled Substance Offense.[2] The trial judge found one aggravating factor (that Defendant involved a person under the age of 16 in the commission of the offense) outweighed mitigating factors (that Defendant had a support system in the community and was gainfully employed) and sentenced Defendant in the aggravated range of 18 to 22 months imprisonment. Defendant appealed.

[1] Defendant first argues the trial court erred by denying his motion to dismiss the charge of Conspiracy to Sell a Controlled Substance. For procedural reasons, we disagree.

N.C.R.App. P. 10(b)(3) provides that "a defendant in a criminal case may not assign as error the insufficiency of the evidence to prove the crime charged unless he moves to dismiss the action...." The rules further provide that by presenting evidence after the close of the State's case, a defendant waives any previous motion to dismiss, and in order to preserve an insufficiency of the evidence argument for appeal, defendant must renew his motion to dismiss at the close of all evidence.

[2] At the close of the State's case, the trial judge in the instant case asked defense counsel whether he cared to make "any motions for the defendant?" Defense counsel responded:

Yes, Your Honor. I think, taking the evidence in the light most favorable to the state, their strongest case seems to be for conspiracy. And so, I don't care to be heard on that ... I'll ask you to dismiss the sale, at the close of evidence.

2. N.C.G.S. § 90–95.4: "to hire or intentionally use a minor to violate G.S. § 90–95(a)(1)."

Figure 4-1   *(Continued)*

STATE v. BOYD   N.C. **699**
Cite as 595 S.E.2d 697 (N.C.App. 2004)

At the close of all evidence, Defense counsel renewed prior motions to dismiss: "We would rest and renew our motions to dismiss; and, re-adopt our arguments, special as they relate to the sale, conspiracy, contributing to the delinquency of a minor; and, the engaging a minor in drug trafficking." By that statement, defense counsel renewed his argument that he "didn't care to be heard" on the conspiracy charge because "their strongest evidence seems to be for conspiracy." Defense counsel did not avail himself of his opportunity to move to dismiss the conspiracy charge at the close of the State's evidence, and thus, he could not renew a nonexistent motion at the close of all evidence. Accordingly, we are precluded from reviewing the merits of Defendant's argument. *See State v. Stocks,* 319 N.C. 437, 439, 355 S.E.2d 492, 492 (1987) (holding that "a defendant who fails to make a motion to dismiss at the close of all the evidence may not attack on appeal the sufficiency of the evidence at trial."). We note, however, that even if this issue had been properly preserved for appeal, the evidence in the record sustains the trial court's denial of Defendant's motion to dismiss this charge.

[3] Defendant next argues that because Hampton's age was an element of the crimes for which he was acquitted, Contributing to the Delinquency of a Minor and Employing and Using a Minor to Commit a Controlled Substance Offense, the trial court erred by considering the sentencing aggravating factor that he "involved a person under 16 in the commission of a crime." We disagree.

In North Carolina, a trial court may consider any aggravating factors it finds proved by the preponderance of the evidence that are reasonably related to the purposes of sentencing.   N.C.G.S.   § 15A–1340l.4(a). N.C.G.S § 15A–1340.16(d)(13) allows a court to aggravate a defendant's sentence from the presumptive range when "defendant involve[s] a person under the age of 16 in the commission of the crime."

In *State v. Marley,* 321 N.C. 415, 424, 364 S.E.2d 133, 138 (1988), our Supreme Court stated that "once a defendant has been acquitted of a crime he has been set free or judicially discharged from an accusation; re-

leased from ... a charge or suspicion of guilt." Therefore, our Supreme Court held "to allow the trial court to use at sentencing an essential element of a greater offense as an aggravating factor, when the presumption of innocence was not, at trial, overcome as to this element, is fundamentally inconsistent with the presumption of innocence itself." In *Marley,* the defendant had been tried for first degree murder upon the theory of premeditation and deliberation. The jury found the defendant guilty of second degree murder. Thus, one can infer from the jury's verdict in *Marley* that the jury determined there was insufficient evidence of premeditation and deliberation.

In this case, it cannot be inferred from the jury's acquittal of Defendant on the contributing to the delinquency of a juvenile and employing and intentionally using a minor to commit a controlled substance offense charges that it found there was insufficient evidence to conclude beyond a reasonable doubt that Hampton was a minor. Indeed, the parties in this case stipulated Hampton was thirteen years old. Unlike Marley, where the difference between first degree murder and second degree murder was the jury "decided that there [was] not sufficient evidence to conclude beyond a reasonable doubt that defendant premeditated and deliberated the killing," *Marley,* 321 N.C. at 424, 364 S.E.2d at 138, in this case, we are unable to explain rationale behind the jury's verdict. Thus, by convicting Defendant of conspiracy to sell a controlled substance, the jury concluded that Johnny Boyd and Quintinie Hampton were conspirators. Therefore, we uphold the trial court's consideration as an aggravating sentencing factor that Defendant involved a person under the age of 16 in the commission of a crime.

No error.   **Decision**

Judges TIMMONS–GOODSON and ELMORE concur.

jurisdictions (Kentucky, Massachusetts, Pennsylvania, and Virginia) are known as "Commonwealths" and will identify their criminal cases as *Commonwealth v. Smith.*

In re Johnny S. Case names that indicate only a party's first name or initials (such as *In re J.B.*) are typically used to designate matters that involve minors. Often these cases relate to delinquency actions involving minors, adoption proceedings, or child custody proceedings. For purposes of privacy, the minor's surname is omitted from the published opinion.

Ex rel. Smith. The phrase "ex rel." is short for "ex relatione" meaning "upon relation or information." Such a case name indicates a legal proceeding instituted by an attorney general or some other state or governmental official on behalf of a state but at the instigation of a private party who has an interest in the matter. For example, a case involving a serviceman's refusal to obey a lawful order was titled *United States ex rel. New v. Rumsfeld.*

Ex parte Smith. "Ex parte" means "on one side only" and usually refers to an action by or for one party without notice to or any contest by the other party.

Complaint of M/V Vulcan. A case with this type of title will·involve maritime or admiralty matters or will deal with a ship or sailing vessel. "M/V" means "motor vessel."

United States v. 22,152 Articles of Aircraft Parts. Such an oddly named case typically involves the forfeiture or seizure of illegal goods or contraband. For example, this case was a forfeiture action brought by the United States government, which sought title to aircraft parts that a purchaser had attempted to illegally export to Libya. *United States v. $200,000 in United States Currency* was an action brought by the government seeking forfeiture to the government of $200,000 seized by the United States Customs Department at Miami International Airport.

Practice Tip

Citations in Cases

The citations that appear in published cases are generally not in correct *Bluebook* or *ALWD* form. For space reasons, these published cases often take shortcuts in citing cases and other authorities. Similarly, the cases available or cited on Lexis or Westlaw often violate *Bluebook* or *ALWD* citation rules. Rely on *The Bluebook* or *ALWD* when citing legal authorities.

2. *Docket Number and Deciding Court*

Immediately beneath the case name you will be provided the docket number of the case. When the first paper or pleading in a case is filed, the clerk of the court will stamp a number on the papers. This number, referred to as a docket number, serves to identify and track this case as it progresses through the court. Courts do not identify cases by name, primarily due to the possibility of duplication and confusion. To request information about a case or obtain copies of the pleadings or motions submitted in a case, you must provide the docket number to the clerk, who will then retrieve the file for you. Often docket numbers provide information about a case. For instance, a docket number of "CV-09-862-CAJ" indicates the case was a civil case filed or instituted in 2009, it was the 862nd case filed that year, and it has been assigned to Judge Carolyn A. Jackson. Following the docket number, the deciding court is often identified.

3. *Date of Decision*

The date the case was decided by the court will be given. If two dates are given, one will be identified as the date the case was argued, and the other will be the date the decision was issued by the court. For citation purposes, the critical date is the year of decision.

4. *Case Synopsis or Summary*

Before you are given the actual opinion of the court, you will be provided with a paragraph summarizing the nature and background of the case, an identification of the parties, the name of the lower court judge, a description of what occurred at the court(s) below, the name of the judge authoring this opinion, and what this court's decision is. This introductory paragraph, often referred to as a case synopsis (or occasionally as a "syllabus"), provides a quick overview of the general nature of the case and by what procedure it arrived at this court. This summary is typically prepared not by the court that issued the opinion but rather by the editors at West, Lexis, or some other publishing company and is intended to serve merely as a convenience to legal professionals. Thus, although it serves as a quick introduction to the case, it may never be quoted from or relied upon as authority. A case synopsis merely helps you weed out irrelevant cases.

5. *Headnotes*

Before the actual opinion of the court, you will be provided with short paragraphs, each of which is assigned a number and a name. These are called headnotes or digest paragraphs. (For the present time, ignore the

pictorial design of the "Key" followed by another number. This Key Number System will be thoroughly described in Chapter 5.) For instance, you may be presented with the following headnote:

3. Criminal Law
To convict defendant of aiding and abetting offense against the United States, Government must prove defendant was associated with criminal venture, participated in it as something defendant wished to bring about, and sought by his or her actions to make it succeed.

Each point of law discussed in the case is assigned a headnote. If a case discusses 20 issues of law, there will be 20 headnotes. These headnotes usually are prepared by the editors of the companies that publish the court reports and serve as a table of contents or index to the case. They allow you to determine, usually in less than one minute, whether the case is worthy of additional analysis. For example, someone in your law office may realize you are researching an assault and battery issue and may recommend that you read the case *Gingles v. Edmisten*, 590 F. Supp. 345 (E.D.N.C. 1984). When you retrieve this case, you discover the case is 40 pages long. It is possible that you could spend two hours reading this case only to realize, on the last page, that *Gingles v. Edmisten* is not at all on point and that you were steered in the wrong direction.

Headnotes help reduce the time you might spend reading a case that ultimately proves to be of no value to you and serve to give you a brief glimpse at the legal topics discussed in a case. By examining the headnotes, each of which is only a sentence in length, you can make an informed decision whether to read the case in full or whether to put the case aside.

If the issues you are researching are assault and battery, quickly scan the headnotes looking for the words "assault" or "battery." If none of the headnotes deal with these issues but rather deal solely with "licenses," "deeds," and "trusts," you can make a quick determination to set the case aside rather than spend hours reading a case that does not discuss the issues in which you are interested.

If your examination of the headnotes reveals that headnote 6 discusses battery, you should then examine the case and locate a boldface, bracketed "6." This **[6]** corresponds with and directs you to the portion of the case devoted to the discussion of battery. Because the headnote is usually only a single sentence, you should now read this section **[6]** of the case in full. If this reading looks promising, you should return to the beginning of the case and read the entire case.

Because the headnotes are typically prepared by publishers rather than judges, you cannot rely on the headnotes as authoritative, and you should never quote from the headnotes. You should rather use the headnotes to assist you in making an initial determination whether the case will be helpful to you and then to locate the most relevant portion of the case. Like the case synopsis, use the headnotes to help you weed out irrelevant decisions.

6. *Names of Counsel*

You will be provided with the names and locations of the law firms and the individual attorneys in those firms who represented the parties in the case. You may wish to contact the attorneys, especially if the case presents a novel issue or represents a change in the law. Although you can readily obtain copies of the briefs and papers filed in a court case from the clerk of the court, discussing the case with the attorney involved may be of particular help to you, and often the attorneys may be flattered that they are being contacted as experts in this field.

7. *Opinion*

The commencement of the opinion of the court is almost always marked by an identification of the judge or justice who authored the opinion. For example, "Petersen, C.J." would indicate Chief Judge or Chief Justice Petersen. Everything that follows the identification of the author is the court's opinion. Some sets of case reports include introductory summaries before the case begins. For example, the set *United States Reports*, which publishes decisions of the U.S. Supreme Court, includes a *Syllabus* before most opinions, which is a summary of the decision to follow. The Syllabus is prepared by the Court, and most cases include the following disclaimer: "The Syllabus constitutes no part of the opinion of the Court but has been prepared . . . for the convenience of the reader." Similarly, some older sets of case reports and some of the unofficial sets include summaries of the arguments advanced by each party or summaries of the opinion to follow. Make sure you understand the difference between these useful editorial enhancements and the actual opinion. Only the court's opinion is binding; summaries or syllabi are helpful overviews of the case to follow, but they are usually prepared by a court official or a private publisher, and you may not quote from them or rely on them.

Most opinions start with a recital of the facts in the case because without factual background, the rest of the opinion exists in a vacuum. The court will then apply the law of the jurisdiction involved to the facts in this particular case. Precedents may be cited and statutes or other authorities may be relied upon.

As you read the opinion in the case, keep in mind the key distinction between the holding in the case and *dicta*, extraneous comments made by the court that cannot serve as binding authority. You will notice that there are different types of opinions:

> *Majority opinions* are those written by a member of the majority after the court has reached its decision. A majority opinion is one in which more than half of the judges or justices agree. The holding, or ratio decidendi, announced in the majority opinion is the law and serves as binding authority on lower courts in that jurisdiction.

Per curiam *opinions* are opinions issued by the whole court and no specific author will be identified. Per curiam decisions are usually short, often deal with uncontroversial matters, and are often said to establish no precedent for future cases. Per curiam decisions are not necessarily unanimous. One highly controversial decision, *Bush v. Gore*, 531 U.S. 98 (2000), was a nonunanimous per curiam decision. After the opinion, Chief Justice Rehnquist (with whom Justices Scalia and Thomas joined in a concurring opinion) wrote, "We join the *per curiam* opinion. We write separately because we believe there are additional grounds that require us to reverse the Florida Supreme Court's decision." *Id.* at 111.

Concurring opinions are opinions written by justices who agree with the actual result reached in a case, for example, that the case should be reversed, but would rely on authorities other than those depended upon by the author of the opinion. A concurring opinion often uses language such as the following: "I agree the lower court erred and its decision should be reversed; however, while my learned brethren rely on Civil Code § 52, I would rely on Probate Code § 901." For example, in *Lynch v. Donnelly*, 465 U.S. 668, 687 (1984), Justice O'Connor's concurring opinion began as follows: "I concur in the opinion of the Court. I write separately to suggest a clarification of our Establishment Clause doctrine." A concurring justice is essentially telling others in the majority, "You got the right answer but for the wrong reason." Although most concurring justices set forth an actual opinion giving the reasons they concur, others may simply state, "I concur," and give no opinion.

Plurality opinions are those in which a result is reached but due to the existence of numerous concurring opinions, there is no common legal ground upon which the majority has agreed. If no opinion receives more than half of the justices' votes, the opinion receiving the most number of votes is called a plurality opinion. Although a plurality opinion resolves the dispute between the litigating parties, it is a weak opinion because it does not reflect the will of a majority. In fact, the reasoning of the plurality is not binding in future cases although it may be highly persuasive.

Dissenting opinions are those written by members of the minority who disagree with the result reached. Just as is seen with concurring opinions, a dissenting judge may write a full opinion giving the reasons for the dissent or may simply indicate, "I dissent." If a certain case hurts your legal position, read the dissent carefully, as it may suggest arguments against the majority opinion.

Memorandum opinions report routine decisions. They provide a holding or result but little, if any, reasoning therefor. The decisions of the United States Supreme Court that merely reflect that a writ of certiorari has been denied are examples of memorandum opinions. Other memoranda opinions may state only, "For the reasons given by the court below, we also affirm." See Figure 4-2 for examples of memorandum opinions.

Figure 4-2
Sample Page from West's *Supreme Court Reporter* Showing Memorandum Decisions

---

2830   108 SUPREME COURT REPORTER   486 U.S.

1

486 U.S. 1058, 100 L.Ed.2d 930

**Hugh J. SHANNON, petitioner,
v. UNITED STATES. No.
87–6952.**

Case below, 836 F.2d 1125.

Petition for writ of certiorari to the United States Court of Appeals for the Eighth Circuit.

June 13, 1988. Denied.

2

486 U.S. 1059, 100 L.Ed.2d 930

**Frans Jacobus Smit THERON,
petitioner, v. UNITED STATES
MARSHAL. No. 87–6954.**

Case below, 832 F.2d 492.

Petition for writ of certiorari to the United States Court of Appeals for the Ninth Circuit.

June 13, 1988. Denied.

3

486 U.S. 1059, 100 L.Ed.2d 930

**ALBERTA GAS CHEMICALS LIMITED,
et al., petitioners, v. E.I. du PONT de
NEMOURS AND COMPANY, et al.
No. 87–652.**

Former decision, 484 U.S. 984, 108 S.Ct. 499.

Case below, 826 F.2d 1235.

Memorandum
Opinion

June 13, 1988. The motion of petitioners to file reply brief under seal is granted. Petition for writ of certiorari to the United States Court of Appeals for the Third Circuit denied.

4

486 U.S. 1059, 100 L.Ed.2d 930

**NATIONWIDE CORPORATION and Nationwide Mutual Insurance Company,
petitioners, v. HOWING COMPANY, et al. No. 87–1047.**

Former decision, 484 U.S. 1056, 108 S.Ct. 1008.

Case below, 625 F.Supp. 146; 826 F.2d 1470.

Petition for writ of certiorari to the United States Court of Appeals for the Sixth Circuit.

June 13, 1988. Denied.

Justice WHITE took no part in the consideration or decision of this petition.

5

486 U.S. 1059, 100 L.Ed.2d 930

**N.W. ENTERPRISES, INC., petitioner,
v. TEXAS. No. 87–1370.**

Petition for writ of certiorari to the Court of Appeals of Texas, Fourteenth District.

June 13, 1988. Denied.

Justice BRENNAN and Justice MARSHALL would grant the petition for a writ of certiorari and reverse the judgment of conviction.

6

486 U.S. 1059, 100 L.Ed.2d 931

SECURITIES INDUSTRY ASSOCIATION, petitioner, v. BOARD OF GOVERNORS OF the FEDERAL RESERVE SYSTEM, et al. No. 87–1513.

Case below, 839 F.2d 47.

Chamber or *in-chambers opinions* are written by a United States
Supreme Court Justice in his or her capacity as the Justice
assigned to a circuit rather than in the capacity of writing for the
majority. An in-chambers opinion is usually used to dispose of an
application by a party requesting some form of interim relief,
such as a temporary injunction or a stay of a judgment or order of
a lower court. For example, in a matter arising out of the Kobe
Bryant sexual assault case, the trial court issued an order
prohibiting the press from publishing certain transcripts that the
press received by an inadvertent e-mail transmission. The press
requested a stay of the order, and Justice Breyer, writing an
in-chambers opinion as Circuit Justice, denied the application for
a stay. *Associated Press v. Dist. Ct. for the Fifth Dist. of Colo.*, 542
U.S. 1301 (2004). For another example, a decision by a Supreme
Court Justice to stay an execution of a convicted murderer in his
or her assigned circuit is a chamber opinion. A chamber opinion
begins with words such as the following: "Justice Scalia, Circuit
Justice."

En banc *opinions* are those in which all judges in a court of appeals
participate. For example, if all of the judges in the Ninth Circuit
sit together to decide a case (rather than the case being heard by
a panel of three judges, as is the usual procedure), the decision is
said to be rendered *en banc*, literally "in the bench."

Some Supreme Court cases, such as *Bush v. Gore*, produce several
separate opinions and sorting them out can be difficult. Remember that
only the majority opinion is the law that is binding on lower courts.
Dissenting opinions and concurring opinions are not the law and although they may be persuasive, they are not mandatory authorities that
must be followed.

Practice Tip

Headnotes

**Never quote from either the synopsis or the headnotes in a
published case. Although these editorial enhancements are very
helpful to researchers, they are not the law but rather the
publisher's interpretation and summary of the law. Recognize
these features for what they are — tools to help you pick the right
cases to read and focus on the most pertinent parts of the case.**

---

8. Decision

The final element in a case is the actual decision reached by the court.
The final decision may be to *affirm* or uphold the determination of the
lower court, to *reverse* or overturn the determination reached below, or to

remand or return the case to the lower court for further action consistent with the court's findings. A court may also *vacate* a case or dismiss it entirely. Although, strictly speaking, the word "decision" refers only to the final disposition of a case, in many instances and in common usage, the words "opinion," "judgment," "decision," "case," and "holding" are often used interchangeably to refer to an entire case from the name of the case to the final decision.

———— Ethics Alert ————

Reliance on Non-Majority Opinions

Whenever you cite a case in a document, the reader will assume that you are relying on the majority opinion. If you are relying on anything other than the majority opinion, such as a dissent or a concurring opinion, you must inform the reader by indicating such, as follows: *Circuit City Stores v. Adams*, 532 U.S. 105, 125 (Stevens, J., dissenting).

C. Publication of Cases

1. *Official and Unofficial Publication*

Now that you are familiar with the elements of a case, you should become familiar with the publication of cases and the features provided in the casebooks, which will assist you in your research efforts. The books in which cases are published are referred to as "reporters," and each one has a specific abbreviation. If cases are published pursuant to some statutory directive or court rule, the sets of books in which they are collected are referred to as "official" reports. Cases published without this type of governmental mandate are collected in sets of books referred to as "unofficial" reporters. Although the terms "report" and "reporter" are often used interchangeably, the term "report" usually refers to an official set of cases, such as the *U.S. Reports* or *California Reports*, whereas the term "reporter" usually refers to an unofficial set, such as the *Supreme Court Reporter* or *Pacific Reporter*.

Keep in mind that the terms "official" and "unofficial" have nothing to do with the quality or accuracy of the cases. Cases found in "official" sets are neither better nor more precise than those found in "unofficial" sets. The terms "official" and "unofficial" relate solely to the method of publication, not to the legal status of the cases. In the rare event of some discrepancy between two versions of a case, however, the official or government-approved version will govern.

When decisions are rendered by a court, they are initially available in slip form; that is, as looseleaf sheets of paper, or in small pamphlets. For example, a decision released by the highest court in North Carolina,

the North Carolina Supreme Court, will initially be published in slip form. It may also be published on the court's website and on various Internet sites and will be available on Lexis and Westlaw. At this stage, the opinion will consist solely of the case name, date of decision, names of attorneys, opinion (and concurring or dissenting opinions, if any), and decision. Many of the extra features discussed above, such as the headnotes and the introductory paragraph or synopsis, will not yet be present. North Carolina publishes all of its decisions officially and therefore the case will appear next in softcover temporary volumes called *advance sheets* and thereafter in hardbound volumes known as *North Carolina Reports*.

Because the case itself is not copyrighted and is in the public domain, you would be free to take the case, photocopy it, perhaps add a few extra features, such as your own form of headnotes, place it in a set of volumes that you publish, and give the set your name. Such a publication would be "unofficial," as there is no statute that directs you to publish this case. The case in your privately published volume would be word for word the same as that which appeared in the official *North Carolina Reports* — after all, what the judge has said in issuing the opinion is "etched in stone." What may distinguish your unofficial set of case reporters from the official set would be the "extra" features such as headnotes, the case summary or syllabus, and the like. These extra features are often called "editorial enhancements."

This type of duplication of case publishing by private individuals (or companies) is exactly what has occurred, and there now exist official and unofficial sets, each of which might publish the same case and each of which might add special or extra features to the sets. This is why you cannot quote from or rely exclusively on the headnotes or case synopsis — they are not usually prepared or written by the court but by a publishing company, and therefore are not the law. Similarly, the availability of cases on the Internet (see Chapter 12) arises out of the fact that cases are not copyrightable. Thus, they can be copied, posted on the Internet, and disseminated to others.

2. *Series of Cases*

You may have observed that some of the case reports on the shelves are marked *Atlantic Reporter* or *Federal Reporter*, while others indicate *Atlantic Reporter 2d Series* or *Federal Reporter 3d Series* on the spine. In some states, such as California, where there is an abundance of reported cases, some of the spines indicate *California Reports 3d Series* and even *California Reports 4th Series*.

The switch to a new series does not occur at regularly scheduled intervals, and you cannot predict when the next series will commence. It is believed that the change to a new series is done to prevent the volume numbers from getting too high. For example, volume 300 of the *South Western Reporter* is followed by volume 1 of the *South Western Reporter, Second Series*, and volume 999 of the *Federal Reporter, Second Series* is

followed by volume 1 of the *Federal Reporter, Third Series*. If the volume numbers were to reach 1806, for example, the likelihood of transposing the numbers and making an error in citation form are much greater.

You do not need to know which years are covered by which series. It is sufficient that you know, for example, that any case published in *Southern Reporter 2d Series* is newer than any case published in *Southern Reporter*, and so forth.

3. Advance Sheets

After a case is released by a court in slip form, publishers correct minor errors, add the editorial enhancements such as the headnotes, and then gather and publish the cases in temporary softcover books or pamphlets referred to as "advance sheets." These advance sheets are published to provide rapid access to cases and are often available within a few weeks after a decision is issued by a court. West publishes advance sheets for its reporters (usually each week) and sends them to law libraries, agencies, and law firms that subscribe to its services, much the same way you might subscribe to *Time Magazine* or *Sports Illustrated*.

The advance sheets are placed on the shelves next to the hardbound volumes they relate to and are meant to last only until a permanent hardbound volume is published, typically a few months. Upon receipt of the permanent volume, the advance sheets are discarded. The permanent volumes will share the identical volume number and pagination as the earlier advance sheets. Therefore, you may readily rely upon and quote from cases appearing in the advance sheets because the citation to the page a quote appears on in the advance sheet will be identical to the page a quote appears on in the later published hardbound volume. West is so exacting that if a word is hyphenated between pages 242 and 243 of an advance sheet, it will likewise be hyphenated between pages 242 and 243 of the later permanent volume. After a case is printed in a West advance sheet but before publication in hardbound form, West returns the case to the authoring judge for additional comments or corrections, which are then included in the final print version.

D. Publication of State Cases

1. West's National Reporter System

In 1879, brothers John and Horatio West created and published the *North Western Reporter*. The *North Western Reporter* is unofficial; it is published by West, now a publicly traded company, which is acting independently and without any direction or order from any governmental authority. In most instances, the cases "picked up" by West and published in its *North Western Reporter* were already being published officially. West, however, believed that by grouping neighboring states together from the northwest

region of the United States and by adding extra features to its sets of books, it could provide better service to those in the legal profession and could create a market for its publications. The set was so successful that West followed it by creating reporters for other geographical regions of the United States. The sets of books published by West that collect state and federal cases are collectively referred to as the *National Reporter System*. In these sets of books West publishes all the cases released by courts for publication as well as adding thousands of cases not released for official publication and those that were reported as memorandum decisions.

The states that make up each unit of the *National Reporter System* can be readily seen in the map shown as Figure 4-3 and are as follows:

North Western Reporter N.W., N.W.2d	Iowa, Michigan, Minnesota, Nebraska, North Dakota, South Dakota, and Wisconsin
Pacific Reporter P., P.2d, P.3d	Alaska, Arizona, California, Colorado, Hawaii, Idaho, Kansas, Montana, Nevada, New Mexico, Oklahoma, Oregon, Utah, Washington, and Wyoming
North Eastern Reporter N.E., N.E.2d	Illinois, Indiana, Massachusetts, New York, and Ohio
Atlantic Reporter A., A.2d	Connecticut, Delaware, Maine, Maryland, New Hampshire, New Jersey, Pennsylvania, Rhode Island, Vermont, and Washington, D.C.
South Western Reporter S.W., S.W.2d, S.W.3d	Arkansas, Kentucky, Missouri, Tennessee, and Texas
Southern Reporter So., So. 2d, So. 3d	Alabama, Florida, Louisiana, and Mississippi
South Eastern Reporter S.E., S.E.2d	Georgia, North Carolina, South Carolina, Virginia, and West Virginia

These geographical units were the first units created by West. It is not important to memorize or know which state is published or covered in which unit. It is sufficient if you understand the general structure of West's *National Reporter System*: It is a set of books, published unofficially, which reports many cases already published officially by many states themselves. You should know, however, which unit covers the state in which you will be working. As you can see from the map in Figure 4-3, West's grouping of the states is not a perfect geographical division. Certainly no one would view Kansas or Oklahoma as Pacific states, and yet their cases have been placed in the *Pacific Reporter*. Thus, although a knowledge of geography may be helpful in considering which unit publishes decisions from a certain state, you cannot be absolutely certain unless you review the list that is found in the front of each and every volume of the books in the *National Reporter System* units.

Figure 4-3
National Reporter System Map Showing the
States Included in Each Reporter Group

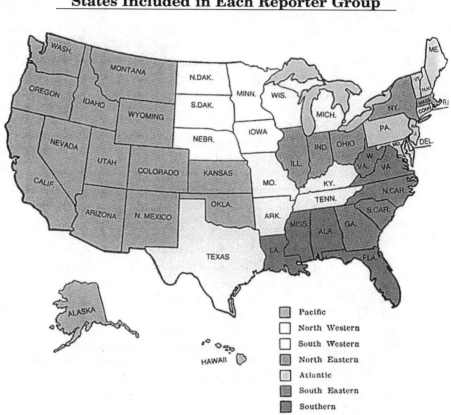

The National Reporter System also includes the Supreme Court Reporter, the Federal Reporter, the Federal Supplement, Federal Rules Decisions, West's Bankruptcy Reporter, the New York Supplement, West's California Reporter, West's Illinois Decisions, West's Military Justice Reporter and the Federal Claims Reporter.

No one state has ruled on every issue, and researchers in a state are often required to search for cases outside their home or forum jurisdiction. West's grouping of cases from neighboring states affords legal practitioners the ability to engage in such research. Although a case from one state is not binding outside its jurisdictional borders (see Chapter 1), in the absence of its own binding authority a state might adopt the position announced by another state. If it does, under our concept of stare decisis, the principle then binds the lower courts within that state.

Because West believed that New York, California, and Illinois published so many cases, it created units just for those states: the *California Reporter* (created in 1959 to publish cases from the California Supreme Court, the California Court of Appeal, and the Appellate Departments of California's Superior Courts); the *New York Supplement* (created in 1956, which publishes decisions of various New York courts);

and *Illinois Decisions* (created in 1976 to publish cases from the Illinois Supreme Court and Appellate Court). Thus, a case citation to a California case may appear as follows:

> *Taylor v. Conrad*, 34 Cal. 3d 102, 698 P.2d 109, 206 Cal. Rptr. 911 (1983).

This citation indicates there are three sets of books in which you could locate this California case: the official *California Reports*, the unofficial *Pacific Reporter*, and the unofficial *California Reporter*. These three citations are called "parallel" citations. The publication of cases in more than one location can be a great service to a researcher: If the volume of *California Reports* that you need is missing from the shelf, you can elect to read the case in the *Pacific Reporter* or the *California Reporter*. Remember that the opinion issued by the court in *Taylor v. Conrad* will be the same no matter which of the three sets you select to locate the case. What the judge has stated in the opinion will not be revised by West's books in any manner. What will differ, however, may be the color of the set, the quality of the paper used, the typeface, and the editorial enhancements such as headnotes and the case summary or synopsis.

As is common with well-established and popular sets, all of the regional units have reached the second series (S.E.2d, A.2d, N.E.2d, N.W.2d, and So. 2d), and three reporters have reached their third series (P.3d, S.W.3d, and So. 3d).

If you are puzzled why multiple sets of case reporters are needed, you should simply bear in mind that many different types of automobiles are also available in the United States. It is possible to buy a Ford, a Chevrolet, a Nissan, or a Honda. Each car will provide the same function: transportation. Yet an individual may develop a preference for one manufacturer or may select one model over another based on considerations of price or available options. The same is true for law firms, corporations, and agencies. Some may elect to purchase official reports rather than unofficial reporters based upon price or some other consideration, and some may prefer the many extra and integrated features found in West's *National Reporter System*.

One of the advantages of the *National Reporter System* units lies in its grouping of states. A law firm in South Carolina that purchases the official *South Carolina Reports* will acquire a set of books that contains cases from South Carolina. If that firm purchases the *South Eastern Reporter*, however, it will acquire a set of books that contains decisions not only from South Carolina but also from Georgia, North Carolina, Virginia, and West Virginia. This allows legal professionals in states without a rich or complex body of case law to review decisions from other states, which decisions might be relied upon if a case of first impression arises in South Carolina. West also markets about 30 state-specific versions of its regional reporters. For example, in Massachusetts a law firm can purchase a set called *Massachusetts Decisions* comprising only the Massachusetts cases from the *North Eastern Reporter*. Lists of the sets of books published by West are available on its website at http://west.thomson.com.

West's *National Reporter* units often publish cases that would not otherwise be published in the official state reports. This is because West will publish cases that have been designated "not for publication" due to the fact that these cases do not advance legal theory or are duplicative of other already published cases.

Interestingly enough, and perhaps because of its publishing expertise, West has been recognized as the official or primary source of decisions in a majority of the states. Thus, although *Arizona Reports* and *Ohio State Reports* are the official sets of the respective states, the actual publication of the books is accomplished by West. Similarly, some states have adopted West's regional reporters as their official state reporters.

Additionally, the availability of unpublished opinions on the computerized legal research systems, Lexis and Westlaw, on the Internet, and in the newly published *Federal Appendix* has contributed to the increasing proliferation of cases. As noted earlier, some courts attempt to reduce the mass of legal publication by enacting court rules prohibiting citation of cases in court documents unless those cases have been marked "for publication." Others require authors citing unreported cases to include a copy of the case together with any document citing the case. In any event, at present, an unreported case is not binding precedent under the doctrine of stare decisis but is rather persuasive authority only. As noted, the issue whether researchers should be allowed to cite to unpublished opinions in documents submitted to courts has generated considerable controversy, leaving state courts highly divided as to whether to allow such citation.

2. Citation Form

Although citation form will be covered in depth in Chapter 8, at this point you should know one importance of distinguishing an official citation from an unofficial citation. Many state citation rules require that citations to state court cases include a citation to the official state report followed by a citation to West's regional reporter. Thus, you will need to know the units in West's *National Reporter System* so that when you are confronted with a case citation such as *Neibarger v. Universal Cooperatives*, 439 Mich. 512, 486 N.W.2d 612 (1992), you will know that because the *North Western Reporter* is one of West's *National Reporter System* unofficial regional units, the citation to it should follow the official *Michigan Reports* citation. Under *The Bluebook* and *ALWD* (unless local rules require otherwise), the citation would include only the West regional reporter and not the official citation, as follows: *Neibarger v. Universal Cooperatives*, 486 N.W.2d 612 (Mich. 1992).

3. Discontinuation of Some Official Reports

Because of the success and accuracy of West's *National Reporter System*, and because many researchers preferred using and buying the regional

reporters with their convenient grouping of cases from neighboring states and user-friendly editorial enhancements, many states have ceased publishing their cases officially. In fact, between 1948 and 1981, 20 states discontinued officially publishing their cases. Another reason for the discontinuation of official reports in many states is the expense of publishing cases that West will also be publishing. In the states shown below there are no longer parallel citations, and the only citation to cases from these states is to the appropriate geographical unit of West's *National Reporter System* (although, as noted above, for about 30 of these states, West publishes specialized state-specific reporters, for example, the *Alabama Reporter, Florida Cases*, and the *Maine Reporter*):

State That Never Published Cases Officially	*States That Have Discontinued Official Publication and Year of Discontinuance*	*States That Continue to Publish Officially*
Alaska	Alabama (1976)	Arizona
District of Columbia	Arkansas (2009)	California
	Colorado (1980)	Connecticut
	Delaware (1966)	Georgia
	Florida (1948)	Hawaii
	Indiana (1981)	Idaho
	Iowa (1968)	Illinois
	Kentucky (1951)	Kansas
	Louisiana (1972)	Maryland
	Maine (1965)	Massachusetts
	Minnesota (1977)	Michigan
	Mississippi (1966)	Montana
	Missouri (1956)	Nebraska
	North Dakota (1953)	Nevada
	Oklahoma (1953)	New Hampshire
	Rhode Island (1980)	New Jersey
	South Dakota (1976)	New Mexico
	Tennessee (1972)	New York
	Texas (1962)	North Carolina
	Utah (1974)	Ohio
	Wyoming (1959)	Oregon
		Pennsylvania
		South Carolina
		Vermont
		Virginia
		Washington
		West Virginia
		Wisconsin

E. Publication of Federal Cases

1. *United States Supreme Court Cases*

a. *Publication*

United States Supreme Court cases are published in the following three sets of books. Most law firms or offices will purchase only one set.

(1) United States Reports (U.S.)

The *United States Reports* is official. It is published by private firms under contract with the United States Government Printing Office and comprises more than 550 volumes. Approximately 5,000 pages are published each year. Initially, cases from the United States Supreme Court were published in sets of books named after the individuals responsible for publishing the set. Thus, the initial 90 volumes of this set have names on the spines such as Dallas, Cranch, Wheaton, and Peters. In 1875, it became apparent that it was unsatisfactory to name a set after an individual who would inevitably retire or die. Therefore, in 1875, the set that reported United States Supreme Court cases was named the *United States Reports*. The older volumes were later numbered consecutively. Citations to these older cases appear as follows: *Turner v. Fendall*, 5 U.S. (1 Cranch) 117 (1801). When you observe such a citation, you should simply realize the case is very old. Cases in *United States Reports* appear initially as bench opinions, which are small pamphlets issued to the press and the public on the day opinions are announced by the Court. Several days later the case will be printed in slip form and then in brown softcover advance sheets. Some months later, the hardbound volumes are published and sent to law firms, law libraries, and other subscribers.

(2) Supreme Court Reporter (S. Ct.)

The *Supreme Court Reporter* is published by West and is unofficial. It is another unit of West's *National Reporter System*. This set began its coverage in 1882 and reports in full every decision rendered by the United States Supreme Court since that time. Cases initially appear in advance sheets, which are issued twice a month. The advance sheets are later discarded and replaced by semi-permanent volumes, which remain on the bookshelves for two or three years until the final permanent corrected and hardbound volumes are available.

(3) United States Supreme Court Reports, Lawyers' Edition (L. Ed.)

United States Supreme Court Reports, Lawyers' Edition (and *Lawyers' Edition 2d*), is published by Lexis and is unofficial. It was created in response to a need among lawyers for less expensive books reporting Supreme Court cases than the official ones then being published. It

contains all decisions issued by the Supreme Court since 1789. This set contains many useful editorial features such as quick summaries of the holdings of the cases, summaries of the briefs of counsel for the parties in the cases (given for older cases), research references, and, for some cases, annotations or essays written by Lexis's staff attorneys on significant legal issues raised in the case. Be careful when reading older cases reported in *Lawyers' Edition*, as it may be easy to confuse the arguments being advanced by counsel with the actual opinion of the Court. Make sure you rely only on information appearing after the authoring Justice's name. Any information that precedes the majority opinion has usually been prepared by the publisher, and although it is extremely valuable and useful, it is not the law. Cases initially appear in advance sheets about twice per month, and these advance sheets are discarded when the permanent volumes are received.

There are thus three parallel cites for all United States Supreme Court cases, and you can locate the 1986 case, *Batson v. Kentucky*, in three locations: 476 U.S. 79, 106 S. Ct. 1712, and 90 L. Ed. 2d 69. In the event of any conflict in versions of the cases reported in these volumes, the version of a case found in the official *U.S. Reports* governs.

All three sets reporting cases from the United States Supreme Court (U.S., S. Ct., and L. Ed.) include a section called "Syllabus," given before each opinion published in the set. The Syllabus is a comprehensive summary of the case to follow. Although it is prepared by the Court's Reporter of Decisions, it is not the opinion of the Court itself. Therefore, it is a useful feature but cannot be quoted from. Be careful to rely only on the case itself, not on any of the editorial enhancements that accompany a case. Locate the name of the author of the majority opinion. This name signals the start of the opinion. Everything given after it is "fair game."

b. Rapid Access to United States Supreme Court Cases

As described above, all of the sets that publish United States Supreme Court cases issue advance sheets. Nevertheless, even the advance sheets may take four to six weeks to be received. Very rapid access to United States Supreme Court cases can be achieved through the following sources:

(1) Slip Opinions

After the bench opinion is made available to the public, the United States Supreme Court issues its opinion in slip form. These slip opinions are available at the United States Supreme Court the day a decision is announced. The slips are then immediately sent to law libraries, law book publishers, and other subscribers. The slip opinions can typically be located in law libraries within five to ten days after the date of decision. The slips will contain only the decision of the Court and the Court's Syllabus; they will not include any editorial features such as headnotes.

(2) Computer-Assisted Research

As we will discuss more fully in Chapter 11, the computer-assisted research services Lexis and Westlaw usually have the full text of a United States Supreme Court case within one hour after the decision is released. Other computer-assisted legal research services such as Loislaw also offer immediate access to these cases.

(3) United States Law Week

You may recall from Chapter 3 that *United States Law Week*, a weekly publication of The Bureau of National Affairs, Inc. ("BNA"), publishes some of the federal laws passed during the previous week. *United States Law Week* is perhaps better known, however, for publishing in looseleaf form (for example, looseleaf pamphlets, which are then maintained in ringed binders), the full text of United States Supreme Court opinions from the preceding week. Just as you may subscribe to *Architectural Digest* or *In Style*, law firms and law libraries subscribe to *United States Law Week* to obtain rapid access to recent United States Supreme Court decisions. In addition to publishing the United States Supreme Court cases, *United States Law Week* also indicates which cases have been docketed or scheduled for hearing by the Court and includes summaries of cases recently filed with the Court, a calendar of hearings scheduled, and summaries of oral arguments made before the Court. *United States Law Week*'s print service is complemented by its e-mail notification service, called *Supreme Court Today, Case Alert and Legal News*, which provides subscribers with e-mail alerts every day the Court decides a case or grants or denies review. Highlights and summaries of arguments are also included.

(4) Newspapers

Many law firms and law libraries subscribe to legal newspapers, which report news of interest to legal professionals. Often these newspapers will print United States Supreme Court cases in full as well as cases from lower federal courts or cases from the courts in the state in which the newspaper is published. These newspapers are generally available within a few days after the decision is rendered.

(5) West Document Research & Retrieval

West provides a variety of services allowing ready access to cases. Specifically, West Document Research & Retrieval provides public records, court documents, and so forth by overnight delivery, e-mail, or fax. Call 1-877-DOC-RETR.

(6) Internet

As discussed in Chapter 12, Supreme Court cases are now available at no cost on many Internet sites. Cases appear on the Internet within a day of their release. The most authoritative site is that of the Supreme Court itself at http://www.supremecourt.gov. The text of each opinion is posted to the Court's site within an hour after the opinion is announced.

2. *United States Courts of Appeal Cases*

The set of books that publishes cases from the intermediate courts of appeal (for example, First Circuit, Second Circuit, and so forth) is the *Federal Reporter* (abbreviated "F.") and the *Federal Reporter, Second Series* and *Third Series* (abbreviated as "F.2d" and "F.3d"). The *Federal Reporter* was created by West in 1880 to publish decisions from the United States Courts of Appeal. Although the primary function of the *Federal Reporter* is to publish decisions from these intermediate federal courts, it has published cases from various other courts as well. See Figure 4-4.

This set of reporters is unofficial and is yet another of the units in West's *National Reporter System*. In fact, the *Federal Reporter* is the *only* set that reports decisions from these intermediate courts of appeal. Although only approximately 20 percent of the cases for the Courts of Appeal are published, the *Federal Reporter* grows by about 20 to 25 hardbound volumes each year. There is no official reporter for these cases. Thus, there are no parallel cites for cases from our federal courts of appeal. The only citation that you will encounter is to the *Federal Reporter* or *Federal Reporter, Second Series* or *Third Series*. As is typical of publication of court decisions, the cases are initially published in softcover advance sheets that are later replaced by hardbound permanent volumes.

Although the overview of the *Federal Reporter*, as shown in Figure 4-4, is a useful historical guide, it is sufficient to know that the chief role of the *Federal Reporter* is to report decisions from the United States Courts of Appeal.

As discussed earlier, in 2001 West began publishing a new set of books, the *Federal Appendix*, which reports unpublished courts of appeals cases. Each case begins with the announcement, "This case was not selected for publication in the Federal Reporter." The set is part of the *National Reporter System*. Each case includes West's editorial enhancements, such as case synopses, key numbers, headnotes, and so forth. As a researcher, you will be able to access unpublished federal decisions (through Lexis and Westlaw, the online legal research systems, on the Internet, and now through the *Federal Appendix*), but you must understand and comply with all federal and court rules regarding citation to such opinions when you submit documents to a court.

3. *United States District Court Cases*

You will recall from Chapter 2 that the United States District Courts are the trial courts in our federal system. You may also recall that Section A of this chapter noted that trial court decisions are not usually published. An exception to this general rule lies in the *Federal Supplement* and *Federal Supplement, Second Series* (abbreviated as "F. Supp." and "F. Supp. 2d"), created in 1932 by West and which publish decisions from the United States District Courts, our federal trial courts. Although the

Federal Supplement and *Federal Supplement, Second Series* publish decisions from other courts as well (see Figure 4-5), their key function is to report decisions from these United States District Courts, although they publish only about 15 percent of the cases heard by our federal district courts. The *Federal Supplement* and *Federal Supplement, Second Series* are other unofficial West publications and are a part of West's *National Reporter System*. The *Federal Supplement* and *Federal Supplement, Second Series* are the only sets of books that publish United States District Court cases. Thus, there are no parallel citations for United States District Court cases. Just as with other case reports, cases appear first in advance sheets and later in hardbound volumes.

Figure 4-4
Coverage of the *Federal Reporter*

1880-1912	U.S. Circuit Court Cases
1911-1913	Commerce Court of the United States (Court abolished in 1932)
1880-1932	U.S. District Courts (after 1932, cases reported in *Federal Supplement*)
1929-1932, 1960-1982	U.S. Court of Federal Claims
1891-Date	U.S. Courts of Appeal
1929-1982	U.S. Court of Customs and Patent Appeals (covers years court was in operation)
1943-1961	U.S. Emergency Court of Appeals
1972-1993	Temporary Emergency Court of Appeals

Figure 4-5
Coverage of the *Federal Supplement*

1932-1960	U.S. Court of Claims
1932-Date	U.S. District Courts
1956-Date	U.S. Court of International Trade (formerly the United States Customs Court)
1968-Date	Judicial Panel on Multidistrict Litigation
1973-1996	Special Court, Regional Rail Reorganization Act (abolished in 1996)

4. *Cases Interpreting Federal Rules*

Yet another unit in West's *National Reporter System*, the *Federal Rules Decisions* set, publishes United States District Court cases since 1939 that interpret the Federal Rules of Civil Procedure and, since 1946, cases

that interpret Federal Rules of Criminal Procedure, cases interpreting Federal Rules of Evidence, Federal Rules of Appellate Procedure, Federal Sentencing Guidelines, and other rules. *Federal Rules Decisions* (abbreviated as "F.R.D.") publishes these cases in advance sheets and then in replacement hardbound volumes. These cases do not otherwise appear in the *Federal Supplement*. Thus, the name of this set, *Federal Rules Decisions*, is perfectly descriptive of its function: It publishes cases that construe federal rules, whether those rules are rules of procedure for civil cases, rules of procedure for criminal cases, rules of evidence, or others. Articles that provide comment on the federal rules are also included.

Practice Tip

Common Legal Abbreviations in Law Books

Newcomers to the legal profession are often bewildered by the numerous odd abbreviations found in law books. With just a little time and effort, you will be able to understand and translate the quirky abbreviations you see. *Black's Law Dictionary* (9th ed. 2009) includes a table of abbreviations, and both *The Bluebook* and *ALWD* are helpful in interpreting legal abbreviations. Following are some of the more common abbreviations you will encounter:

A.	Atlantic	Crim.	Criminal
P.	Pacific (or Procedure)	Ct.	Court
S.E.	South Eastern	Super.	Superior
S.W.	South Western	D.	District
N.E.	North Eastern	C.D.	Central District
N.W.	North Western	E.D.	Eastern District
So.	Southern	M.D.	Middle District
F.	Federal	N.D.	Northern District
R.	Rule, Rules	S.D.	Southern District
Supp.	Supplement	W.D.	Western District
App.	Appellate	J.	Judge, Justice (or Journal)
Dist.	District	JJ.	Judges, Justices
Div.	Division	A.J.	Associate Judge, Associate Justice
Ch.	Chapter or Chancery	C.J.	Chief Judge, Chief Justice
Cl.	Claims	P.J.	Presiding Judge
Cir.	Circuit	L.	Law
Civ.	Civil		

F. Star Paging

Citation form will be thoroughly discussed in Chapter 8, but for now it is sufficient if you are aware that many court rules require that citation to cases include all parallel cites. Thus, if you are referring to the case *Guysinger v. K.C. Raceway, Inc.*, in a brief for a court in Ohio, which requires parallel citations, the correct citation form is as follows: *Guysinger v. K.C. Raceway, Inc.*, 54 Ohio App. 3d 17, 560 N.E.2d 584 (1990).

The Bluebook requires that for United States Supreme Court cases, you are to cite only to the official *United States Reports*. That is, for citation form purposes, it is as if the unofficial sets, West's *Supreme Court Reporter* (S. Ct.) and Lexis's *Supreme Court Reports, Lawyers' Edition* (L. Ed.), do not exist (unless the citation to the *United States Reports* is unavailable). The *ALWD* rule is substantially similar, although *ALWD* permits parallel citations for United States Supreme Court cases.

Obviously, therefore, the publishers at West and Lexis were in a dilemma. It would be extremely difficult for these publishers to attempt to market their sets of books because no matter how wonderful and useful the extra features contained in these unofficial sets might be, law firms and other users would be highly unlikely to purchase a set of books that could not be cited or quoted.

The publishers at West and Lexis thus developed a technique of continually indicating throughout their sets which volume and page a reader would be on if that reader were using the official *United States Reports*. This technique of indicating page breaks in the official set is called "star paging" because the early method of indicating when a new page commenced was through the use of a star or asterisk (*).

Lexis indicates its page breaks with a boldface reference in brackets, as in **[516 US 14]**. West uses an inverted "T." For example, if you are reading a case in West's *Supreme Court Reporter*, each page therein will provide you with the parallel citation to the official *United States Reports*. This citation is usually found in the upper corner of each page. As you are reading through the opinion, you might see language such as the following:

"We therefore hold|that the law of implied indemnity . . . ."
             218

Such an indication informs you that if you were reading this case in the *United States Reports*, after the word "hold" you would have turned the page to page 218. The first word on page 218 in that volume of the *United States Reports* would be "that."

Star paging is entirely self-correcting. If you have any doubt that you are converting the page numbers accurately, you can always retrieve the appropriate volume of the *United States Reports* and verify that the first word on page 218 is "that." As a result, no matter which set of unofficial books you use for United States Supreme Court cases, you can

Figure 4-6
Sample Page from Lexis's *Lawyers' Edition,* *Second Series* Showing "Star Paging"

Parallel Citations for Case

FURMAN v GEORGIA   363
408 US 238, 33 L Ed 2d 346, 92 S Ct 2726

Livermore thus agreed with Holmes and Henry that the Cruel and Unusual Punishments Clause imposed a limitation upon the legislative power to prescribe punishments.

[408 US 263]
However, in contrast to Holmes and Henry, who were supporting the Clause, Livermore, opposing it, did not refer to punishments that were considered barbarous and torturous. Instead, he objected that the Clause might someday prevent the legislature from inflicting what were then quite common and, in his view, "necessary" punishments—death, whipping, and earcropping.[6] The only inference to be drawn from Livermore's statement is that the "considerable majority" were prepared to run that risk. No member of the House rose to reply that the "considerable majority" was prohibit torture.

Several conclusions thus emerge from the history of the adoption of the Clause. We know that the Framers' concern was directed specifically at the exercise of legislative power. They included in the Bill of Rights a prohibition upon "cruel and unusual punishments" precisely because the legislature would otherwise have had the unfettered power to prescribe punishments for crimes. Yet we cannot now know exactly what the Framers thought "cruel and unusual punishments" were. Certainly they intended to ban torturous punishments, but the available evidence does not support the further con-

clusion that *only* torturous punishments were to be outlawed. As Livermore's comments demonstrate, the Framers were well aware that the reach of the Clause was not limited to the proscription of unspeakable atrocities. Nor did they intend simply to forbid punishments considered "cruel and unusual" at the time. The "import" of the Clause is, indeed, "indefinite," and for good reason. A constitutional provision "is enacted, it is true, from an experience of evils, but its general language

[408 US 264]
should not, therefore, be necessarily confined to the form that evil had theretofore taken. Time works changes, brings into existence new conditions and purposes. Therefore a principle to be vital must be capable of wider application than the mischief which gave it birth." Weems v United States, 217 US, at 373, 54 L Ed at 801.

It was almost 80 years before this Court had occasion to refer to the Clause. See Pervear v The Commonwealth, 5 Wall 475, 479–480, 18 L Ed 608, 609, 610 (1867). These early cases, as the Court pointed out in Weems v United States, supra, at 369, 54 L Ed at 799, did not undertake to provide "an exhaustive definition" of "cruel and unusual punishments." Most of them proceeded primarily by "looking backwards for examples by which to fix the meaning of the clause," id., at 377, 54 L Ed at 802, concluding simply that a punishment would be "cruel and unusual"

Star Paging (the word "language" appears on page 263 of volume 408 of the *United States Reports,* and the word "should" appears on page 264 of the volume)

---

judges? What is understood by excessive fines? It lies with the court to determine." Since Livermore did not ask similar rhetorical questions about the Cruel and Unusual Punishments Clause, it is unclear whether he included the Clause in his objection that the Eighth Amendment "seems to have no meaning in it."

6. Indeed, the first federal criminal statute, enacted by the First Congress, prescribed 39 lashes for larceny and for receiving stolen goods, and one hour in the pillory for perjury. Act of April 30, 1790, §§ 16–18, 1 Stat 116.

readily tell the page you would be on if you were holding the official *United States Reports*. Figure 4-6 shows a sample page illustrating star paging. Star paging is also found in some other West sets, such as in *California Reporter* and in the *New York Supplement*, directing you to pagination for the official California and New York reports. When you read cases on the Lexis or Westlaw screens, star paging is also provided so that you can determine where the page breaks occur in the print versions of the cases you are viewing on the screen.

G. Specialized *National Reporter System* Sets

There are additional sets of books that are also a part of West's *National Reporter System* series. These reporters, however, publish very specialized cases and are as follows:

1. *West's* Military Justice Reporter

This set publishes decisions from the United States Court of Appeals for the Armed Forces and the Military Service Courts of Criminal Appeals.

2. *West's* Veterans Appeals Reporter

This set publishes cases decided by the United States Court of Appeals for Veterans Claims, created in 1988, and previously named the United States Court of Veterans Appeals.

3. *West's* Bankruptcy Reporter

The *Bankruptcy Reporter* publishes selected decisions that are not found in the *Federal Supplement* and that are decided by the United States Bankruptcy Courts, the Bankruptcy Appellate Panels, and the United States District Courts. Additionally, this set reprints bankruptcy appeals handled by the United States Courts of Appeal and the United States Supreme Court.

4. *West's* Federal Claims Reporter

This set (previously called *United States Claims Court Reporter*) publishes decisions from the United States Court of Federal Claims (formerly called the United States Claims Court) from 1982 as well as Court of Federal Claims appeals handled by the United States Courts of Appeal

and the United States Supreme Court. Cases include tax refund suits, government contracts cases, environment and natural resource disputes, and civilian and military pay questions.

5. *West's* Federal Cases

Until 1880, when West began publishing cases from the lower federal courts, there was no one comprehensive set of books that reported decisions from these courts. Although several sets existed, none were adequate. Therefore, in 1880, West collected all of these lower federal court cases together and republished them in a set of books titled *Federal Cases*. *Federal Cases* is a very unusual arrangement of cases as it publishes these lower federal court cases that preceded the establishment of the *National Reporter System* in *alphabetical* order rather than *chronological* order, as is the usual format. If you examine *Federal Cases*, you will note that each case is assigned a consecutive number, with the first case referred to as No. 1, *The Aalesund*, and the last case referred to as No. 18,222, *In re Zug*.

Due to the fact it covers much older cases, *Federal Cases* is typically available at only larger law libraries. You should compare the relatively small number of volumes, 30, which cover lower federal court cases from 1789 to 1879 in *Federal Cases*, with the current total of approximately 3,000 volumes covering cases from 1880 to the present in the *Federal Reporter* and *Federal Supplement*, thus demonstrating again the dramatic increase in litigation and case publication in this country.

━━━━━━ Practice Tip ━━━━━━

Google Scholar

A new feature introduced by Google, "Google Scholar," allows free and easy searching of court opinions from federal and state courts. Access http://scholar.google.com and select the "Legal opinions and journals" button. Type in your case name or your search terms in plain English and you will be directed to cases relating to your topic. You may also explore related cases and cases that have cited your case.

H. Features of West's *National Reporter System*

The case reporters in West's *National Reporter System* possess a number of useful editorial features that aid in and simplify legal research. These

features are found in both the advance sheets and the permanent hardbound volumes (except as noted) and are as follows:

1. Tables of Cases Reported

There will be at least one alphabetical table of cases in each volume of West's *National Reporter System* sets. For example, in any volume of the *Supreme Court Reporter*, there will be a complete alphabetical list of all of the cases in that volume. This feature is useful if you know the approximate date of a Supreme Court case and need to examine a few volumes of the set to locate the specific case itself. Additionally, you may have inadvertently transposed the numbers in a citation and be unable to locate the case you need. The table of cases will allow you to look up the case you desire, and then locate the specific page on which it appears. Cases can be found by using either the plaintiff's or the defendant's name.

Some sets of books have two tables of cases. For instance, any volume in the *Pacific Reporter* will contain one complete alphabetical list of the cases in that volume as well as an alphabetized list of the cases arranged by state so that the Alaska cases are separately alphabetized, the Arizona cases are separately alphabetized, and so on. Similarly, any volume in the *Federal Reporter* will possess one complete alphabetical list of the cases in that volume and will also separately arrange and alphabetize the First Circuit cases, then the Second Circuit cases, for example.

2. Tables of Statutes and Rules

The Table of Statutes will direct you to cases in a volume that have interpreted or construed any statutes or constitutional provisions. Thus, if you are interested in whether any recent cases have interpreted N.Y. Banking Law § 317 (McKinney 2001), you can consult the table of statutes in any recent volume of the *North Eastern Reporter*, and you will be directed to the specific page in the volume that interprets that statute.

Similarly, there are tables listing all federal rules of civil and criminal procedure, federal rules of appellate procedure, and federal rules of evidence that are construed by any cases in a particular volume. This feature is not found in all volumes or sets.

3. Table of Words and Phrases

This table alphabetically lists words or phrases that have been interpreted or defined by any cases in a volume of the *National Reporter System*. For example, you can consult the Table of Words and Phrases and determine if the words "abandonment," "negligence," or "trustee" have been defined by any cases in a volume, and you will be directed to the

specific page in a volume on which such a word is judicially defined. This feature is not found in all volumes or sets.

4. List of Judges

This feature is found only in the hardbound volumes of the *National Reporter System* and lists all of the judges sitting on the courts covered by that particular volume. Thus, any hardbound volume of the *Federal Reporter* will provide a list of First Circuit judges, Second Circuit judges, and so on.

5. Key Number System

Although West's Key Number System will be described in full in the next chapter, for the present it is sufficient to know that in the back of each hardbound volume in West's *National Reporter System* (except the *Bankruptcy Reporter* and the *Federal Claims Court Reporter*), West will provide a brief summary of each case in the volume arranged by topic and key number. All of the books in the *National Reporter System* are participants in the Key Number System, West's integrated research system that helps you find cases discussing similar points of law.

I.   Finding Parallel Cites

You have seen that many cases can be found in more than one place. This is because many cases are published officially and unofficially. The different citations to a case are known as *parallel cites*.

On some occasions, you may have one cite and may need the other parallel cite. This could be due to the fact that court rules require all parallel cites or it could be for the very practical reason that the volume you need is missing from the library bookshelf, and you must obtain the parallel cite to locate the case you need. There are several techniques you can use to find a parallel cite.

1. Cross-References

Many cases provide all parallel cites. For example, if you open a volume of *California Reports* to the case you need, at the top of each page you are given all parallel cites for this case. Similarly, most of West's reporters will provide the official citation for cases they report unofficially. Note that all parallel citations are shown at the top of Figure 4-6. Additionally, Lexis and Westlaw screens display parallel citations.

2. National Reporter Blue Book *and State Blue and White Books*

If you have an official cite for a state court case and you need the unofficial parallel cite, you can use a set published by West and titled the *National Reporter Blue Book*. This set contains complete conversion tables showing parallel cites. For example, if you look up the official cite, 321 N.C. 111, you are immediately provided with the unofficial citation, 361 S.E.2d 562.

Similarly, most states that continue to publish their cases officially (about one-half of the states) have available what are known as "State Blue and White Books," which provide conversion tables with parallel citations. For example, the *Nebraska Blue and White Book* is a single volume with blue pages giving citations from the official reports to the unofficial regional reporter (when you have an official citation) and the white pages giving the parallel citation from the regional reporter back to the official reports. The various Blue and White Books are published by West. Most law libraries include only the Blue and White Book for the state in which they are located.

3. Shepard's Citations *and* KeyCite

As you will learn in Chapter 9, when you Shepardize or KeyCite either an official or an unofficial citation, you are given the parallel cite.

The Final Wrap-Up

Using and Citing Cases

Use:	Use cases to support the legal assertions you make. Focus on the relevant facts and the reasoning relied upon by the deciding court. Did the court establish a new rule of law? Is the holding limited to the particular facts of the case, or is it broad enough to serve as a precedent in later cases? Also use cases to direct you to other authorities, both primary and secondary. Most court opinions cite numerous other legal authorities, many of which may be helpful to you.
Citation:	Because cases are primary authority and because they are binding in your jurisdiction (assuming they are on point), your documents will probably cite cases more than any other authorities. Use proper citation form (according to *The Bluebook*, *ALWD*, or local rules).

4. State Digests

West has published sets of books called "digests" for each state except Delaware, Nevada, and Utah. These digests (discussed in detail in the next chapter) contain tables of cases, which provide parallel citations. Thus, if you look up a case by name in the Table of Cases for the *Wisconsin Digest*, you will be provided with the citation for the case in the *Wisconsin Reports* as well as in the *North Western Reporter*.

J. Summary of West's *National Reporter System*

West's *National Reporter System* is a series of sets of case reporters that publishes cases from state appellate courts and from federal trial and appellate courts. All of the sets of books in the *National Reporter System* are unofficial because the books are published privately by West rather than pursuant to some statutory directive or mandate. Although West's *National Reporter System* is the largest collection of case reporters, West is not the only publisher of cases. For example, Lexis publishes United States Supreme Court cases in its set *United States Supreme Court Reports, Lawyers' Edition*.

West publishes state court cases in various regional units, each of which contains cases from a particular geographical area. The regional units are as follows:

> *North Western Reporter*
> *Pacific Reporter*
> *North Eastern Reporter*
> *Atlantic Reporter*
> *South Western Reporter*
> *Southern Reporter*
> *South Eastern Reporter*

Because the states of New York, California, and Illinois decide so many cases, West also created the following separate sets just for these states:

> *New York Supplement*
> *California Reporter*
> *Illinois Decisions*

Federal cases are published in these sets of books:

Supreme Court Reporter	(cases from the United States Supreme Court)
Federal Reporter	(cases from the United States Courts of Appeal)

Federal Supplement   (cases from the United States
                                      District Courts)
Federal Rules Decisions   (cases interpreting federal rules of
                                      civil and criminal procedure and
                                      other rules)

West also publishes four other sets, each of which is descriptively titled: the *Military Justice Reporter*, the *Veterans Appeals Reporter*, the *Bankruptcy Reporter*, and the *Federal Claims Reporter*. The *Federal Appendix* reports unpublished decisions from the United States Courts of Appeal. Specialized sets exist for several states, such as *Kentucky Decisions* and *Texas Cases*.

All of the books in West's *National Reporter System* possess a variety of useful features and all are participants in West's Key Number System, which is described in full in Chapter 5.

You can readily see that there are numerous sets of reporters, each identified by its own particular abbreviation. There is an excellent reference tool of abbreviations and acronyms used in legal literature, from "Ct. Cl. R." (for Court of Claims Rules) to "S.L.R.B." (for State Labor Relations Board). *See* Mary Miles Prince, *Prince's Bieber Dictionary of Legal Abbreviations* (6th ed. 2009), published by William S. Hein & Co., Inc., of Buffalo, New York. A copy may be kept in the reference section of your law library. Additionally, the front of each volume of West's general encyclopedia, *Corpus Juris Secundum* (C.J.S.), includes a thorough table of legal abbreviations. Finally, the new *Black's Law Dictionary* (9th ed. 2009) includes an extensive list of legal abbreviations in its Appendix A. See Figure 4-7 for a summary of case law publication.

K. Briefing Cases

The importance of cases in our common law system has already been discussed. You will also recall that in our legal system it is not sufficient to merely read a statute assuming that it will provide the answer to a question or problem because it is the task of our courts to interpret and construe statutory language. Thus, reading, interpreting, and analyzing cases are of critical importance to all involved in the legal profession.

Few people find it natural to read cases. The language used by courts is often archaic, and the style of writing can make it difficult to comprehend the court's reasoning. Moreover, the topics discussed in cases are often complex. The most common technique used to impose some order or structure on the confusing world of case law is case briefing. Do not confuse the word "brief" in this context, in which it means a summary of the key elements of a case, with the written argument an attorney presents to a court, which is also called a "brief." A case brief is a short, written summary and analysis of a case.

Figure 4-7
Summary of Case Law Publication

	Highest Court	Intermediate Appellate Courts	Trial Courts
Federal Cases	United States Supreme Court a. *United States Reports** b. *Supreme Court Reporter* c. *United States Supreme Court Reports, Lawyers' Edition* d. *United States Law Week*	United States Courts of Appeal cases are published in *Federal Reporter* (F., F.2d, and F.3d)	United States District Court cases are published in *Federal Supplement* (F. Supp. and F. Supp. 2d)
State Cases	State Supreme Courts Examples of official sets are *California Reports** and *Georgia Reports**. Unofficial sets are *Pacific Reporter, California Reporter*, and *South Eastern Reporter*.	State Appellate Courts Examples of official sets are *California Appellate Reports** and *Georgia Appeals Reports**. Unofficial sets are *Pacific Reporter, California Reporter*, and *South Eastern Reporter*.	Generally, trial court cases are not published

(*designates official set)

Practice Tip

Finding Authorities

Be a smart researcher. When you read cases, be alert to references to other cases and legal authorities cited in the opinion. These may help you in your research tasks.

It is extremely common for law students to brief cases so in the event they are called upon in class to discuss a case, they will have a convenient summary to use. Moreover, practicing attorneys often desire to have cases briefed so they may save time by reading the briefs first and then, based

upon the initial reading, analyze only selected cases in full. In some instances, months can go by between hearings in court, or new attorneys and paralegals may join the legal team. The case briefs for a matter handled by the team should be sufficiently readable and useful that new team members can be immediately brought "up to speed" by reviewing the briefs.

Perhaps the primary reason for briefing cases, however, is to learn how to focus on the important parts of the case in order to obtain a thorough understanding of the case and its reasoning. Although you may be tempted to view case briefing as busywork and may believe you can understand a case by simply reading it through, research has shown that people tend to read quickly and see words in groupings. Briefing a case will force you to slow down and concentrate on the critical aspects of the case.

Preparing a case brief requires you to tear the case apart and rebuild it in a structure that helps you and others understand it. Case briefing helps develop your analytical skills and forces you to focus on the critical parts of a court's opinion. In a sense, you are taking notes on the cases you read, and just as explaining a difficult concept to another helps you understand it better, preparing a case brief will help clarify your comprehension of the case. As discussed below, after you have mastered case briefing and thus trained yourself to analyze cases properly, you may be able to dispense with separately prepared written briefs and be able to brief cases by merely underlining or highlighting the key portions of cases.

The first briefs you prepare may be nearly as long as the case itself. This is because it takes practice to learn to recognize the essential elements of a case. Initially, every part of the case will seem critical to you. With time, however, you will develop skill at briefing and will be able to produce a concise summary of cases. Ideally, a case brief should be no more than one typed page, although longer and more complex cases may require a longer brief.

There is no one perfect form for a case brief. Some large law firms provide suggested formats. If no form is given to you, you should use a style that best suits you and helps you understand the case and its significance as a precedent for the research problem on which you are working. Read through a case at least once before you begin to brief it so you will have a general idea as to the nature of the issues involved and how the court resolved these issues. Resist the temptation to read only the headnotes or to skim the case. A close scrutiny of the case may reveal critical analysis likely to be overlooked in a cursory reading. See Figure 4-8 for some reading strategies.

It may take you several readings of a case to understand it thoroughly. You may need to take notes, and prepare a diagram or flowchart showing the path the case followed in reaching this court and the relationship of the parties to each other.

Figure 4-8
Case Reading Strategies

Consider the following strategies to help you better understand the cases you read and to help prepare case briefs.

- During your first reading, focus on who the parties are and what relief they wanted from the court. Ask, "What is the plaintiff's gripe?" and "What is the defendant's defense?"
- Figure out what happened at the court(s) below and then determine what this reviewing court's decision is. Knowing the court's decision in advance will help you make sense of the case when you read it more thoroughly.
- Look for clues. Watch for language in the court's opinion such as "It is critical to note that," "although we have previously held that," and other signals that what follows such expressions is key to the court's decision.
- Look up all Latin words and any words you don't understand.

Good case briefs share the following elements:

- They use complete sentences.
- They do not overquote from the opinion.
- They do not include unnecessary, distracting citations.
- They do not include the writer's personal opinions.
- They are brief, ideally one page in length.

The most common elements to be included in a case brief are the following:

1. *Name of case.* Give the case name following *Bluebook* or *ALWD* rules or as it appears in the running head on the top of each page of the case.
2. *Citations.* All parallel citations should be included as well as the year of decision. These citations will enable you and others to retrieve the case later if you need to relocate it. Use correct citation form.
3. *Procedural history.* This is a brief summary of the holdings of any previous court(s) and usually includes the disposition of the case by this court. A procedural history describes how the case got to this court and how this court resolved the case. It will be significant whether the prior decision is a trial court decision or an appellate court decision. Consider briefly identifying the parties and stating the nature of the action, the relief they were

seeking, or the defenses they raised. Then proceed to discuss what the court(s) below held and the final disposition by this reviewing court. In many instances, the procedural history or background can be summed up in one or two brief sentences.

Example: The case was appealed by the defendant to the Georgia Court of Appeals after a jury verdict in the Superior Court awarded monetary damages to the plaintiff employee for sexual harassment. The Georgia Court of Appeals affirmed the decision of the Superior Court.

Practice Tip

Determining Procedural History

Westlaw has added a new feature called "Graphical History" to enable you to view the procedural background of cases. When you access a case on Westlaw, click on "Direct History (Graphical View)," which will be displayed on the screen. You will be given a flowchart, showing the path a case has followed through the courts. These easy-to-understand timelines display in graphical manner, with boxes and arrows, a case's route through the court system, allowing you to grasp a case's procedural history visually. Although Lexis does not show the procedural history of a case in a flowchart format, it includes a brief description of a case's subsequent and prior history when a case is displayed on the screen.

---

4. *Statement of facts.* A case brief should include a concise summary of the facts of the case. You need not include all facts but rather only the significant facts relied on by the court in reaching its decision. Facts that affect the outcome of a case are called "relevant facts" or "material facts." Identify the parties by name and indicate whether a party is a plaintiff, defendant, and so forth. The facts are more readable if they are presented in a narrative rather than outline or "bullet" format. Discuss facts in the past tense. A chronological presentation of the facts is usually the most helpful to a reader. Thus, tell a story in plain English, giving enough facts that the issue the court is being called upon to decide is apparent from reading these facts. Although a chronological presentation is the most typical way facts are presented, if the facts have no temporal relationship to each other, consider grouping the facts by topic or by the claims or causes of action presented by the plaintiff. If certain facts are

disputed, note such. Some case briefs present the statement of facts before the procedural history; this can be helpful if the procedural history is complex, and putting the statement of facts first can help the reader better understand the procedural history.

5. *Issue(s).* You must formulate the question(s) or issue(s) being decided by this court. Focus on what the parties asked the court to determine. In some instances, courts will specifically state the issues being addressed. In other instances, the issues are not expressly provided, and you will have to formulate the issue being decided. Phrase the issue so that it has some relevance to the case at hand. Thus, rather than stating the issue in a broad fashion ("What is an assault?" or "Did the lower court err?"), state the issue so it incorporates some of the relevant facts of the case ("Does a conditional threat constitute an assault?"). Keep each issue or question to one sentence in length.

   If you have trouble determining the issue, locate the rule the court announces and then convert this into question form.

   Example of rule: The goodwill of a celebrity is a marital asset that can be evaluated and distributed in a marriage dissolution.

   Example of issue: Is a celebrity's goodwill acquired during a marriage a property asset that can be evaluated and distributed in a proceeding dissolving the marriage?

   In any event, the issue should be phrased so that it can be answered "yes" or "no." If there are several issues, number each one and place each at the left margin. Do not number a single issue.

   There are three ways issues can be phrased: a direct question, the "whether" format, or the "under" format. A direct question might ask, "Is pointing an unloaded gun at a person an assault?" The "whether" format would phrase the same question as follows: "Whether pointing an unloaded gun at a person is an assault." The "under" format would result in the following phrasing: "Under California law, is pointing an unloaded gun at a person an assault?" Generally, any of these formats is acceptable, although some attorneys dislike the "whether" form of issue because it results in a fragment rather than a complete sentence.

6. *Answer(s) or Holding(s).* Provide an answer(s) to the question(s) being resolved by this court. Rather than merely stating "yes" or

"no," phrase the answer in a complete sentence and incorporate some of the reasons for the answer. For example, if the issue is "Does a conditional threat constitute an assault?," rather than merely stating "no," state, "A conditional threat does not constitute an assault because a condition negates a threat so the hearer is in no danger of present or immediate harm." If you have set forth three issues, you will need three separate answers. Each answer should be no more than two sentences in length. Strive for one-sentence answers. Do not include citations. A brief answer or holding such as "the court below did not err in distributing the value of a celebrity's goodwill" is not helpful to the reader. Each answer should directly respond to the issues you have phrased.

Example: Yes. All assets acquired during a marriage are subject to division. The goodwill earned by a celebrity is no different from any other asset acquired during a marriage.

7. *Reasoning.* The reasoning is the most important part of a brief. This is the section in which you discuss *why* the court reached the conclusions it did. Were prior cases relied upon? Did the court adopt a new rule of law? Is the decision limited to the facts of this particular case, or is the decision broad enough to serve as binding precedent in similar but not identical cases? Did the court discuss any social policy that would be served by its decision? Fully discuss the reasons why the court reached its decision and the thought process by which it arrived at this decision. Make sure you apply the court's reasoning to the facts of your case. Re-read your issue(s) and answer(s) and then ensure that the reasoning is directly responsive to these and answers the *why* question. Citations may be included in this section but are often not necessary. Use your own words in summarizing and explaining the court's reasoning rather than overquoting from the case. This will help ensure that you understand the rationale for the court's decision. Many briefs include the authoring judge's name. Don't be concerned that there will be repetition in your case brief. As you have seen, the brief answer or holding nearly parrots the language of the issue. The same or similar language will reappear as part of your reasoning section. A case brief is not meant to be a thrilling work of literature. It is meant to help you develop your analytical skills and provide a convenient summary of a case.

8. *Decision.* Include the actual disposition of this case, such as "affirmed" or "reversed."

Practice Tip

Formulating Issues

To gain experience in formulating issues for case briefs and other court documents, review the briefs filed with the U.S. Supreme Court, and examine the "Questions Presented." The Supreme Court requires all petitions for writs of certiorari and all principal briefs to set forth the questions the Court is asked to review. Review these questions to sharpen your skills at writing your own question and issue statements. The briefs may be accessed through the Supreme Court's website at http://www.supremecourt.gov. Select "Merits Briefs." Alternatively, the briefs may be accessed through FindLaw at http://supreme.lp.findlaw.com/supreme_court/briefs/index.html.

You may include an additional section in your brief summarizing concurring or dissenting opinions.

Following is a suggested format for a typical case brief, briefing *State v. Boyd*, the case shown as Figure 4-1.

State v. Boyd,
162 N.C. App. 159, 595 S.E.2d 697 (2004)

Procedural History

Defendant Boyd was convicted of conspiracy to sell a controlled substance but acquitted of the crimes of sale of a controlled substance, contributing to the delinquency of a minor, and employing and using a minor to commit a controlled substance offense. He appealed his conviction and sentence. The Court of Appeals affirmed.

Statement of Facts

Defendant was convicted of conspiracy to sell crack cocaine arising out of a police undercover operation. The evidence at trial showed that Defendant supplied the cocaine to a minor, Hampton, who actually conducted the sale to the undercover officers. At the close of the State's evidence, Defendant's attorney did not move to dismiss the conspiracy charge but did move to dismiss all other charges. Counsel renewed all motions at the conclusion of all evidence. The motions were denied. The jury convicted Defendant of the conspiracy charge and acquitted him of the remaining charges. In sentencing the Defendant, the trial judge found one aggravating factor, that Defendant involved a person under the age of 16 in the commission of a crime.

Issues

1. May Defendant appeal his conspiracy conviction if he did not make a motion to dismiss the conspiracy charge at trial?

2. If Defendant is acquitted of certain charges relating to a minor, may the minor's age be considered as an aggravating sentencing factor when Defendant is sentenced for conspiracy to sell a controlled substance?

Answers

1. No. A Defendant may not attack on appeal the sufficiency of evidence at trial unless he makes a motion to dismiss at trial.
2. Yes. A trial court may consider any aggravating factors that it finds proved by a preponderance of evidence that are reasonably related to the purposes of sentencing.

Reasoning

North Carolina's rules of appellate procedure provide that to preserve an issue for appeal, a defendant must make a motion to dismiss the action at trial. Defendant's counsel moved to dismiss all charges against Defendant *except* the conspiracy charge at the close of the State's case. At the close of all evidence, he could not renew a nonexistent motion. Thus, the appellate court was precluded from reviewing the merits of Defendant's argument.

If a defendant is acquitted of a crime, it cannot be used as an aggravating sentencing factor. However, in this case, Defendant was convicted of conspiracy to sell a controlled substance; thus, Defendant and Hampton were conspirators. Moreover, the parties expressly stipulated that Hampton was a minor. Thus, the trial court could consider Hampton's age as an aggravating sentencing factor when sentencing Defendant on the conspiracy count.

Decision

The Court of Appeals affirmed the conviction and sentence.

After you have gained experience in case briefing, you may be able to use a technique some experts have referred to as "Technicolor briefing," in which you use colored pens and highlighters to mark sections of cases as you read them. You will photocopy or print the cases you need to brief, and annotate the critical sections in the margins. For example, use "PH" to mark the procedural history section of the case, "I" to designate the issue to court is deciding, and so forth. In law school, this technique is usually called "book briefing" because you brief the cases in your textbooks by these notes rather than preparing a separate brief. See Figure 4-9 for a form for a case brief.

Develop a system of abbreviations to help you mark and annotate the cases you read. See Figure 4-10 for a list of commonly used legal abbreviations.

Case Brief Assignment

Prepare a brief of the case *Kirk v. Harter*, 188 F.3d 1005 (8th Cir. 1999).

Figure 4-9
<u>Case Brief Form</u>

Case Name: _____

Case Citation: _____

Procedural History: _____

_____

_____

_____

Statement of Facts: _____

_____

_____

_____

Issues:

1. _____

2. _____

3. _____

Answers:

1. _____

2. _____

3. _____

Reasoning: _____

_____

_____

_____

Holding: _____

L. Citation Form

1. *Federal Cases* (The Bluebook *and* ALWD)

    a. Cases from the United States Supreme Court:
        Roe v. Wade, 410 U.S. 113 (1973) (*ALWD* allows parallel citations).
    b. Cases from the United States Courts of Appeal:
        Traylor v. Cohen, 597 F.2d 109 (4th Cir. 1988).
    c. Cases from the United States District Courts:
        Allen v. Carr, 686 F. Supp. 207 (W.D. Tex. 1980).

2. *State Cases* (The Bluebook *and* ALWD)

Local state rules often require citation to the official report followed by a parallel citation to a regional reporter, as follows:
    Baker v. Dolan, 281 Mich. 114, 204 N.W.2d 909 (1995).

    Both *The Bluebook* and *ALWD* require legal professionals to follow all applicable local rules. Unless local rules require parallel citations, under both *The Bluebook* and *ALWD*, the citation would include only West's regional reporter and not all parallel citations, as follows:
    Baker v. Dolan, 204 N.W.2d 909 (Mich. 1995).

Figure 4-10
Common Legal Abbreviations

Π	plaintiff
Δ	defendant
§	section
C	complaint
K	contract
x, x/c	cross, cross-complaint
app	appeal
atty	attorney
c/a	cause of action
cert	certiorari
dep	deposition, deponent
J, J'ment	judgment
JNOV	judgment notwithstanding the verdict
Re:	regarding
SJ	summary judgment
S/F	statute of frauds
S/L	statute of limitations
v., vs.	versus, as opposed to
w/	with
w/o	without

CyberSites

http://www.uscourts.gov	Federal Judiciary home page with links to federal courts and information about the federal court system.
http://www.supremecourt.gov	The website of the United States Supreme Court provides information about the Court, its docket, Court rules, and access to its opinions.
http://www.loc.gov/law/guide	This site, called Guide to Law Online, provides access to cases from the United States Supreme Court, the Courts of Appeal, and the District Courts, as well as links for state cases.
http://scholar.google.com	Google Scholar offers free and easy access to federal and state court cases. Search by case name or topic.
http://www.law.cornell.edu	This site provides United States Supreme Court rulings since 1990 and 600 important Court cases prior to 1990. Cases from lower federal courts are also provided as are links to state court cases.
http://www.washlaw.edu	Washburn Law School's site offers links to federal and state cases as well as links to numerous excellent law-related sites.
http://lp.findlaw.com	FindLaw, one of the best-known legal sites, provides easy access to federal and state cases as well as providing a wide variety of other law-related information and links to other sites.
http://www.lawschool.westlaw.com/highcourt/HowToBrief.doc	Westlaw's site for law students offers a guide to briefing cases.
http://www.lib.jjay.cuny.edu/research/brief.html	John Jay College of Criminal Justice offers a guide to briefing cases.

Writing Strategies

In discussing cases, it is not enough to merely summarize or repeat the court's holding. You must *analyze* the case and show the reader why and how it applies to your situation.

By briefing cases, you will force yourself to concentrate on the critical elements of a case: its procedural background, the facts, the issues, the reasoning, and the holding. When you later discuss the case in a memo or court brief, you will be "pre-programmed" to analyze the case properly by virtue of the training you acquired by preparing case briefs.

In written projects, discuss cited cases in the past tense. Any discussion in a project in the present tense ("the Defendant argues," "a duty is owed," "the Plaintiff appeals") will be interpreted as referring to *your* case, not a cited case on which you are relying.

In discussing cases, you need not give all of the facts. Give sufficient facts, however, so a reader can see why the case is controlling. If the facts are strikingly similar to those in your case, recite them in greater detail to allow the reader immediately to grasp why the result reached in the cited case governs your case.

Confront cases that are contrary to your position head-on. Assume the adversary will locate these cases. You will minimize their impact if you discuss them yourself. Emphasize why such cases are not controlling by distinguishing them from your case. Show the reader that the facts and issues in such unfavorable cases are so different from those in your case that they cannot be relied upon.

Use "location" to minimize the impact of unfavorable cases. Discuss them briefly and only after you have set forth your strongest arguments. Discuss them in the middle of a project rather than at the beginning or end, where they will draw more attention.

Assignment for Chapter 4

1. a. Give the name of the case located at 53 P.3d 119.
   b. Give the parallel citations for this case.
2. Review volume 595 N.W.2d.
   a. What case in this volume construes Neb. Rev. Stat. § 48-824?
   b. Review the case. Generally, to what topic does the statute relate?
3. a. Give the name of the case located at 804 A.2d 34.
   b. Review the case synopsis. Describe the procedural background of the case.
   c. What topic name and key number have been assigned to headnote 2?
   d. Look up the topic name and key number in the Key Number Digest in the back of the volume. To what case are you directed?
4. a. Give the name of the case located at 789 A.2d 607.
   b. Give the parallel citation for the case.
   c. What does headnote 10 of the case discuss?
5. a. Give the name of the case located at 504 F.3d 206.
   b. Give the full name of the author of the opinion.
6. a. Give the name of the case located at 517 F. Supp. 2d 792.
   b. What is the general topic of this case?
   c. What case in this volume construes the phrase "genuine issue"?
7. a. What is the name of the case located at 645 F. Supp. 141 (D. Del. 1986)?
   b. Give a brief description of the type of action the case involved.
   c. Describe the defendant.
8. Locate the case located at 548 U.S. 1301 (2006). In what capacity did the author of the opinion act?
9. Locate the case located at 101 F. Supp. 2d 866 (S.D. Ohio 1999). How many headnotes does the case include?
10. a. Give the name of the case published at 228 F.R.D. 617 (2005).
    b. What type of opinion does this case report?
11. Give the parallel citations for the case located at 545 U.S. 193.
12. Give the name of the case located at:
    a. 668 N.W.2d 16
    b. 24 S.W.3d 101
    c. 200 So. 294
13. Locate the case at 123 S. Ct. 371. How does page 37 of the parallel *United States Reports* begin?

14. Locate the case at 161 L. Ed. 2d 876. How does page 534 of the parallel *United States Reports* begin?

15. Use the *National Reporter Blue Book* (2010 Permanent Supplement), and give the parallel citations for the following cases:
   a. 272 Conn. 653
   b. 352 N.C. 287
   c. 227 Mich. App. 614
   d. 144 Wash. App. 371

16. Locate the case at 228 P.3d in which the defendant's name is *Rowland*.
   a. Give the case name and citation.
   b. Who argued the case for the appellant?
   c. Who was the Chief Justice of the Nevada Supreme Court during the period of time covered by this volume?
   d. What case in this volume construes the phrase "final judgment"? On which page is this phrase discussed?

Internet Assignment for Chapter 4

1. Access the U.S. Supreme Court website and locate "Opinions," specifically "2008 Term Opinions of the Court."
   a. Review the case with the docket number 08-479. Give the name of the case.
   b. In which volume of the *United States Reports* will the case be published?
   c. Did the search in question violate the Fourth Amendment?

2. Access the U.S. Supreme Court website and review the Chief Justice's Year-End Report on the Federal Judiciary for 2009.
   a. Give the percentage of the decrease in total number of case filings in the U.S. Supreme Court in the 2008 Term.
   b. Did civil filings in the U.S. District Courts increase or decrease in the 2008 Term? Why?

3. Access the site WashLaw (Washburn University School of Law).
   a. Select "Florida" and review decisions of the District Courts of Appeal (Fourth District). Access the opinions for 2010. Review the decision released February 3, 2010, as 4D09-4708. Give the name of the case and state why the petition in question was denied.
   b. Select "Washington" and review Washington Supreme Court cases. Locate the case 11 Wash. 2d 88 (1941). Give the name of the case, its parallel citation, and indicate what headnote 7 discusses.

4. Access the website www.law.cornell.edu and locate opinions from the Second Circuit Court of Appeals. Review the case assigned docket number 08-3331-cv.
   a. Give the name of the case.
   b. In which U.S. District Court was the trial heard?
   c. Under what names did the defendant offer its coffee?
5. Access Google Scholar and search for cases relating to the display of a cross on public land.
   a. What is the first case to which you are directed?
   b. How many times has this case been cited?
   c. Give the parallel citations for this case.
   d. Was the cross permitted to be displayed on the public land?

The Use of Digests, Annotated Law Reports, and *Words and Phrases*

Binding authority . . . cannot be considered and cast aside; it is not merely evidence of what the law is. Rather, case law on point is the law.

Hart v. Massanari, 266 F.3d 1155, 1170 (9th Cir. 2001)

A. **Using Digests to Locate Cases**
B. ***American Law Reports***
C. ***Words and Phrases***
D. **Citation Form**

Chapter Overview

This chapter will complete the discussion of the major primary authorities (statutes, constitutions, and cases) by explaining the use of digests, which serve as comprehensive casefinders. Additionally, you will be introduced to annotated law reports, which can "speed up" the research process and provide you with an exhaustive overview of an area of the law. These annotated law reports combine elements of both primary and secondary sources and thus form a bridge between the primary sources of statutes, constitutions, and cases, which have been discussed, and the secondary authorities of encyclopedias, law reviews, treatises, and other sources, which follow. Finally, you will be provided with a discussion of *Words and Phrases*, a set of books created by West, which can be used to determine the legal meaning of certain words and phrases, and then direct you to primary authorities supporting those interpretations.

A. Using Digests to Locate Cases

1. Introduction

It is improbable that an individual with whom you work will simply hand you a list of citations and ask you to retrieve and photocopy the cases cited. It is far more likely that you will be presented with a description of a research problem and be tasked with determining the answer. For example, an attorney might describe a client's current problems with her landlord by posing the following scenario: The firm's client rented a house from her landlord. Two months later the client noticed the roof was leaking and notified the landlord repeatedly of this problem to no avail. A recent storm caused water to leak through the roof, causing $20,000 damage to the client's expensive furniture and rug. You may be asked to research whether the landlord is liable for the damage and whether the tenant may withhold rent from the landlord until the $20,000 damage amount is satisfied.

This common type of research assignment requires you to search for cases that are "on point," which will serve as precedents and provide an answer to the client's questions. Of course, if an area of the law is likely to be dealt with by statutes, you should remember to consult initially your annotated code to review the applicable statutes, and then examine the annotations following the statutes, which will direct you to cases that interpret the statute.

You will recall that cases are usually published in chronological order. That is, there is no one set of books called *Landlord and Tenant Law* that will contain all cases dealing with landlords and tenants. Such cases are scattered throughout the numerous sets of books. For instance, each volume in the *Nevada Reports* may contain a few cases covering this particular subject matter. You cannot simply start with Volume 1 of the *Nevada Reports* or some other set of reports hoping to eventually stumble upon the right case. Such a research technique is not only inefficient and time-consuming, it may well be ineffective, as it is possible you could examine the more than 100 volumes of the *Nevada Reports* only to discover that Nevada has not yet considered this particular issue.

Legal research requires a much more systematic approach to locating pertinent cases, and this systematic approach is aided through the use of sets of books called "digests." Although there are different types of digests, all of them function in a similar fashion: Digests assist you by arranging cases by subject matter so that all of the assault cases are brought together, all of the bribery cases are brought together, all of the contract cases are brought together, and so on. These digests, however, do not reprint in full all of the assault cases, but rather print a brief one-sentence summary or "digest" of each assault case and then provide you with a citation so you can determine which cases you should retrieve and examine in full. In this way, digests serve as guideposts, which help direct you to the specific cases you need so you can research as efficiently and effectively as possible. Because the digests are written by publishers

(primarily West) and are mere summaries of cases, the digest entries cannot be quoted from or relied upon. The cases the digests direct you to, however, will serve as binding authority.

2. *The American Digest System*

Although there are different types of digests, the majority are published by West, which realized shortly after it introduced its *National Reporter System* that legal professionals needed a method of finding the cases published therein. The most comprehensive digest set published by West is the *American Digest System*, which will be described here in detail. Once you understand how to use the *American Digest System*, you will also understand how to use the other West digests because all digests are organized in substantially the same manner.

The *American Digest System* is an amazingly thorough set of books that aims at citing and digesting every reported case so you can readily locate all cases in a given area of law, such as corporations, trusts, negligence, or landlord-tenant law. In the *American Digest System*, West brings together all cases relating to a legal issue from all of the units of the *National Reporter System*. Thus, if you were researching the defenses to battery, you would be able to locate cases from the *Supreme Court Reporter*, *Federal Reporter*, *Federal Supplement*, *North Western Reporter*, *Pacific Reporter*, and others, all of which deal with defenses to battery. The *American Digest System* is therefore most useful when you have an extensive research project and you desire to know how several jurisdictions (both federal and state) have treated a specific legal topic.

West describes its combination of headnotes and topics and Key Numbers as part of the "greatest time-saving system ever invented to help [researchers] find cases worthy of further analysis."

3. *Organization of the* American Digest System

To understand how to locate cases using West's *American Digest System*, it is necessary to understand how the System is organized. You will recall from Chapter 4 that when a decision is issued by a court, it consists of a case name, a docket number, a date of decision, names of counsel, and the opinion itself. West receives a copy of the case, scans or keyboards it on Westlaw, and assigns it to its editors. These editors are attorneys who thoroughly read the case and, through a 26-step process, draft the brief synopsis (which appears after the case name and which concisely summarizes the case) and the headnotes for the case. If the case discusses seven areas of law, it will have seven headnotes. If the case discusses 12 areas of the law, it will have 12 headnotes. These headnotes are the brief paragraphs that precede the opinion of the court. Each headnote is given a consecutive number, a topic name (Insurance, Covenants, Deeds, Venue, for example) based on the area of law the headnote deals with, and

a "Key Number" (a pictorial design of a key and a number). Thus, a typical headnote in a case published in any West set of court reports looks like the following:

7. Gifts ⚷ **22**
Constructive delivery is sufficient where donor's intention to make the gift plainly appears and the articles intended to be given are not present or, if present, are incapable of manual delivery.

Such a headnote is the seventh one in the case, its topic is "Gifts," and its Key Number is 22.

The case is now complete, consisting of the original elements as provided by the court and the additional features (synopsis and headnotes) provided by West's editors. The case will be printed in an advance sheet, which is mailed to agencies, judges, law firms, law libraries, and other subscribers. The headnotes alone, however, are taken by West and published in a monthly pamphlet called the *General Digest*. Last month's *General Digest*, therefore, contains all of the headnotes of all cases published by West in its *National Reporter System* (*North Western Reporter*, *Pacific Reporter*, *California Reporter*, *Federal Reporter*, and so on). The headnotes are arranged alphabetically by topic name such as Abandoned and Lost Property, Abatement and Revival, Abortion and Birth Control, and Absentees. Within each topic name, the headnotes are arranged by Key Number, such as Absentees 1, Absentees 2, and Absentees 3.

The monthly softcover issues of the *General Digest* are later brought together ("cumulated") and published in hardcover volumes. West then began bringing together and publishing the hardcover volumes of the *General Digest* in ten-year groups called "Decennials." The word "decennial" is literally defined as a ten-year period. Thus, the *First Decennial* contains all headnotes from all of the units of the *National Reporter System* for the period 1897-1906. *The Second Decennial* contains all headnotes from all of the units of the *National Reporter System* for the ten-year period 1906-1916. For obvious reasons, the *American Digest System* is sometimes called the *Decennial Digest System*.

You should be aware that West has also created a set of books called the *Century Digest* to cover the time period 1658 to 1897 (the date coverage of the *First Decennial* commences). The *Century Digest* uses a classification scheme different from the Key Number System used in the *Decennials*. It is unlikely you will use the *Century Digest* very often, if ever, as it digests cases that are very old. West does, however, provide cross-reference tables in the *First* and *Second Decennial Digests* so you can readily locate cases in the *Century Digest* if you have a topic name and a Key Number. Figure 5-1 shows the time period covered by each of the *Decennials*.

As you can see, starting in 1976, West began issuing the *Decennials* in two five-year parts (and recently began issuing *Decennials* in three parts). This change was brought about by the explosion in case law.

Figure 5-1
Coverage of Decennial Units

Century Digest	1658-1897
First Decennial	1897-1906
Second Decennial	1907-1916
Third Decennial	1916-1926
Fourth Decennial	1926-1936
Fifth Decennial	1936-1946
Sixth Decennial	1946-1956
Seventh Decennial	1956-1966
Eighth Decennial	1966-1976
Ninth Decennial, Part 1	1976-1981
Ninth Decennial, Part 2	1981-1986
Tenth Decennial, Part 1	1986-1991
Tenth Decennial, Part 2	1991-1996
Eleventh Decennial, Part 1	1996-2001
Eleventh Decennial, Parts 2 and 3	2001-2004
General Digest, 12th Series	2004-Date

General Digest is the name of the set of books currently in use. As soon as the next five-year time period is completed, the name of the *General Digest, 12th Series*, will likely change to *Twelfth Decennial, Part 1*, and the current set will then be called the *General Digest, 13th Series*.

It is not necessary to memorize the time periods covered by each *Decennial* unit. It is sufficient to understand the general structure of the *Decennial* units: Each *Decennial* covers approximately a ten-year period and each *Decennial* will contain all of the headnotes from all of the units of the *National Reporter System* for its particular time period.

If you possess the headnote presented earlier relating to constructive delivery of gifts (**Gifts 22**), you can locate all American cases from 1658 until last month that relate to this specific subject matter. You can accomplish this task by taking the following actions:

- Locate the *Decennial* volumes for a recent time period such as the *Eleventh Decennial, Parts 1, 2,* or *3*.
- Find the volume covering the letter "G" (for "Gifts").
- Look up "Gifts" (using guide words at the top of each page).
- Locate Gifts 22 (presented in numerical order).

You will now be presented with all United States Supreme Court cases decided between 1996-2004 relating to constructive delivery of gifts, then all United States Court of Appeals cases relating to this subject, all United States District Court cases, all Alabama cases, all Alaska cases, all Arizona cases, and so on. Each case will be described with a one-sentence summary (the "digest") and you will be provided a case citation, enabling you to locate the case and read it in full if you

determine the case may be helpful. The one-sentence entries in the digest are the headnote paragraphs from the cases in West's reporters, now rearranged by subject matter.

After you have located cases in the *Eleventh Decennial, Parts 1, 2 and 3*, follow the same strategy for the *Tenth Decennial, Part 2*, the *Tenth Decennial, Part 1*, the *Ninth Decennial*, and so forth. In this way you will be able to find all cases decided in federal and state courts from 1658 (using the *Century Digest*) until last month (using the *General Digest, 12th Series*), which relate to constructive delivery of gifts.

4. West's Digest Topics

The fact that you can locate all cases on a similar point of law from 1658 until last month arises from West's remarkable consistency in assigning topic names and Key Numbers to legal issues. In order to efficiently and systematically organize cases under topic names and Key Numbers, West developed its own outline of the law. It should be noted that this outline of the law was developed exclusively by West for its own purposes. You may or may not agree with the organization scheme developed by West. You may believe additional topic names should exist. West's outline is not an official pronouncement of the subjects discussed in cases. It has no judicial or academic authority. It is simply West's organizational blueprint for its Key Number System, representing its decision that there are more than 400 topics of law that a case may discuss.

A complete list of West's Digest Topics is shown in Figure 5-2. The list is also found at the beginning of any West Digest volume.

A case may discuss one of these more than 400 topics in a variety of ways. For example, cases may discuss infants in many different respects. The Key Numbers are assigned as follows: Each Key Number relates to the manner in which a point of law is discussed. This subtopic is represented by a number, the "key number." Thus, if a case relates to the prevention of cruelty to an infant, West will title the pertinent headnote **Infants 15;** if a case relates to the effect of marriage of an infant (in a legal sense, an "infant" is simply someone who has not yet attained the age of majority), West will title the pertinent headnote **Infants 10;** and if a case relates to emancipation of an infant by a parent, West will give the pertinent headnote the topic and Key Number **Infants 9**. Each topic name and Key Number combination thus represents a specific point of law, and each provides links to other similar cases.

It is unnecessary to commit to memory the list of topic names; it is sufficient if you have a general understanding of West's system. It may be easiest to understand West's system if you imagine that West possesses an immense chart with all of the topics and Key Numbers listed on it. Every time a portion of *any* case in *any* unit of the *National Reporter System* discusses prevention of cruelty to infants, the headnote will be given the topic name "Infants" and the Key Number 15. The headnote will then be printed initially in the monthly pamphlet *General Digest* and will later be printed in the hardbound copies called *Decennials*. You will be

Figure 5-2
West's List of Digest Topics

The West Key Number System

ALPHABETICAL LIST OF DIGEST TOPICS

1	Abandoned and Lost Property	69	Cancellation of Instruments	131	District and Prosecuting Attorneys
2	Abatement and Revival	70	Carriers	132	District of Columbia
4	Abortion and Birth Control	71	Cemeteries	133	Disturbance of Public Assemblage
5	Absentees	72	Census		
6	Abstracts of Title	73	Certiorari	134	Divorce
7	Accession	74	Champerty and Maintenance	135	Domicile
8	Accord and Satisfaction			135h	Double Jeopardy
9	Account	75	Charities	136	Dower and Curtesy
10	Account, Action on	76	Chattel Mortgages	137	Drains
11	Account Stated	76a	Chemical Dependents	138	Drugs and Narcotics
11a	Accountants	76h	Children Out-of-Wedlock	141	Easements
12	Acknowledgment	77	Citizens	142	Ejectment
13	Action	78	Civil Rights	143	Election of Remedies
14	Action on the Case	79	Clerks of Courts	144	Elections
15	Adjoining Landowners	80	Clubs	145	Electricity
15a	Administrative Law and Procedure	81	Colleges and Universities	146	Embezzlement
		82	Collision	148	Eminent Domain
16	Admiralty	83	Commerce	148a	Employers' Liability
17	Adoption	83h	Commodity Futures Trading Regulation	149	Entry, Writ of
18	Adulteration			150	Equity
19	Adultery	84	Common Lands	151	Escape
20	Adverse Possession	85	Common Law	152	Escheat
21	Affidavits	88	Compounding Offenses	154	Estates in Property
23	Agriculture	89	Compromise and Settlement	156	Estoppel
24	Aliens			157	Evidence
25	Alterations of Instruments	89a	Condominium	158	Exceptions, Bill of
26	Ambassadors and Consuls	90	Confusion of Goods	159	Exchange of Property
27	Amicus Curiae	91	Conspiracy	160	Exchanges
28	Animals	92	Constitutional Law	161	Execution
29	Annuities	92b	Consumer Credit	162	Executors and Administrators
30	Appeal and Error	92h	Consumer Protection		
31	Appearance	93	Contempt	163	Exemptions
33	Arbitration	95	Contracts	164	Explosives
34	Armed Services	96	Contribution	165	Extortion and Threats
35	Arrest	97	Conversion	166	Extradition and Detainers
36	Arson	98	Convicts	167	Factors
37	Assault and Battery	99	Copyrights and Intellectual Property	168	False Imprisonment
38	Assignments			169	False Personation
40	Assistance, Writ of	100	Coroners	170	False Pretenses
41	Associations	101	Corporations	170a	Federal Civil Procedure
42	Assumpsit, Action of	102	Costs	170b	Federal Courts
43	Asylums	103	Counterfeiting	171	Fences
44	Attachment	104	Counties	172	Ferries
45	Attorney and Client	105	Court Commissioners	174	Fines
46	Attorney General	106	Courts (see also Topic 170b Federal Courts)	175	Fires
47	Auctions and Auctioneers			176	Fish
48	Audita Querela	107	Covenant, Action of	177	Fixtures
48a	Automobiles	108	Covenants	178	Food
48b	Aviation	108a	Credit Reporting Agencies	179	Forcible Entry and Detainer
49	Bail	110	Criminal Law	180	Forfeitures
50	Bailment	111	Crops	181	Forgery
51	Bankruptcy	113	Customs and Usages	183	Franchises
52	Banks and Banking	114	Customs Duties	184	Fraud
54	Beneficial Associations	115	Damages	185	Frauds, Statute of
55	Bigamy	116	Dead Bodies	186	Fraudulent Conveyances
56	Bills and Notes	117	Death	187	Game
58	Bonds	117g	Debt, Action of	188	Gaming
59	Boundaries	117t	Debtor and Creditor	189	Garnishment
60	Bounties	118a	Declaratory Judgment	190	Gas
61	Breach of Marriage Promise	119	Dedication	191	Gifts
62	Breach of the Peace	120	Deeds	192	Good Will
63	Bribery	122a	Deposits and Escrows	193	Grand Jury
64	Bridges	123	Deposits in Court	195	Guaranty
65	Brokers	124	Descent and Distribution	196	Guardian and Ward
66	Building and Loan Associations	125	Detectives	197	Habeas Corpus
		126	Detinue	198	Hawkers and Peddlers
67	Burglary	129	Disorderly Conduct	199	Health and Environment
68	Canals	130	Disorderly House	200	Highways

Figure 5-2 (Continued)

201	Holidays	256	Mayhem	313a	Products Liability	360	States
202	Homestead	257	Mechanics' Liens	314	Prohibition	361	Statutes
203	Homicide	257a	Mental Health	315	Property	362	Steam
204	Hospitals	258a	Military Justice	316	Prostitution	363	Stipulations
205	Husband and Wife	259	Militia	316a	Public Contracts	365	Submission of Controversy
205h	Implied and Constructive	260	Mines and Minerals	317	Public Lands	366	Subrogation
	Contracts	265	Monopolies	317a	Public Utilities	367	Subscriptions
206	Improvements	266	Mortgages	318	Quieting Title	368	Suicide
207	Incest	267	Motions	319	Quo Warranto	369	Sunday
208	Indemnity	268	Municipal Corporations	319h	Racketeer Influenced and	370	Supersedeas
209	Indians	269	Names		Corrupt Organizations	371	Taxation
210	Indictment and Information	270	Navigable Waters	320	Railroads	372	Telecommunications
211	Infants	271	Ne Exeat	321	Rape	373	Tenancy in Common
212	Injunction	272	Negligence	322	Real Actions	374	Tender
213	Innkeepers	273	Neutrality Laws	323	Receivers	375	Territories
216	Inspection	274	Newspapers	324	Receiving Stolen Goods	376	Theaters and Shows
217	Insurance	275	New Trial	325	Recognizances	378	Time
218	Insurrection and Sedition	276	Notaries	326	Records	379	Torts
219	Interest	277	Notice	327	Reference	380	Towage
220	Internal Revenue	278	Novation	328	Reformation of Instruments	381	Towns
221	International Law	279	Nuisance	330	Registers of Deeds	382	Trade Regulation
222	Interpleader	280	Oath	331	Release	384	Treason
223	Intoxicating Liquors	281	Obscenity	332	Religious Societies	385	Treaties
224	Joint Adventures	282	Obstructing Justice	333	Remainders	386	Trespass
225	Joint-Stock Companies and	283	Officers and Public	334	Removal of Cases	387	Trespass to Try Title
	Business Trusts		Employees	335	Replevin	388	Trial
226	Joint Tenancy	284	Pardon and Parole	336	Reports	389	Trover and Conversion
227	Judges	285	Parent and Child	337	Rescue	390	Trusts
228	Judgment	286	Parliamentary Law	338	Reversions	391	Turnpikes and Toll Roads
229	Judicial Sales	287	Parties	339	Review	392	Undertakings
230	Jury	288	Partition	340	Rewards	393	United States
231	Justices of the Peace	289	Partnership	341	Riot	394	United States Magistrates
232	Kidnapping	290	Party Walls	342	Robbery	395	United States Marshals
232a	Labor Relations	291	Patents	343	Sales	396	Unlawful Assembly
233	Landlord and Tenant	292	Paupers	344	Salvage	396a	Urban Railroads
234	Larceny	294	Payment	345	Schools	398	Usury
235	Levees and Flood Control	295	Penalties	346	Scire Facias	399	Vagrancy
236	Lewdness	296	Pensions	347	Seals	400	Vendor and Purchaser
237	Libel and Slander	297	Perjury	348	Seamen	401	Venue
238	Licenses	298	Perpetuities	349	Searches and Seizures	402	War and National Emergency
239	Liens	299	Physicians and Surgeons	349a	Secured Transactions	403	Warehousemen
240	Life Estates	300	Pilots	349b	Securities Regulation	404	Waste
241	Limitation of Actions	302	Pleading	350	Seduction	405	Waters and Water Courses
242	Lis Pendens	303	Pledges	351	Sequestration	406	Weapons
245	Logs and Logging	304	Poisons	352	Set-Off and Counterclaim	407	Weights and Measures
246	Lost Instruments	305	Possessory Warrant	353	Sheriffs and Constables	408	Wharves
247	Lotteries	306	Postal Service	354	Shipping	409	Wills
248	Malicious Mischief	307	Powers	355	Signatures	410	Witnesses
249	Malicious Prosecution	307a	Pretrial Procedure	356	Slaves	411	Woods and Forests
250	Mandamus	308	Principal and Agent	356a	Social Security and Public	413	Workers' Compensation
251	Manufactures	309	Principal and Surety		Welfare	414	Zoning and Planning
252	Maritime Liens	310	Prisons	357	Sodomy	450	Merit Systems Protection
253	Marriage	311	Private Roads	358	Specific Performance		(Merit Systems Protection
255	Master and Servant	313	Process	359	Spendthrifts		Board Reporter)

able to locate other cases on this area of the law by taking this topic name and Key Number (**Infants 15**) and looking it up in the various *Decennial* units. You will then be directed to other cases, both federal and state, that discuss this issue and that were decided within the relevant ten-year periods. According to West, "the beauty of the . . . [s]ystem is that the key number assigned to a point of law is uniform throughout all of West's digests."

You may have noticed that some of the Key Numbers have been subdivided, such as **Criminal Law 1169.1(5).** This occurs as an area of the law expands and novel theories are developed. West will categorize its Key Numbers, such as **Criminal Law 1169,** into subdivisions to reflect the varying and developing ways in which this topic is discussed by courts, as shown by the following list:

Criminal Law 1169	Admission of evidence
Criminal Law 1169.1	Admission of evidence in general
Criminal Law 1169.1(5)	Admission of evidence relating to arrest and identification

Similarly, as new causes of action or new defenses arise, West will add new topics, such as "Racketeer-Influenced and Corrupt Organizations," "Abortion and Birth Control," and "Franchises." In this way, West keeps current with case law as it expands and develops. Finally, some head-notes have more than one key number because they relate to more than one legal topic. At present, there are more than 100,000 individual key numbers.

5. *Locating a Topic and Key Number*

Until now, we have assumed that you knew a topic name and Key Number and looked it up in the various *Decennial* units to locate cases. We will now assume that you are starting your research project from "square one" and that the only information you have is the description of the research problem, for example, the landlord-tenant issue described in the beginning of this chapter. There are four strategies you can use to obtain a topic and Key Number that you can use to locate on-point cases.

a. Descriptive Word Approach

Each of the *Decennial* units includes a volume (or volumes) titled "Descriptive Word Index." West has selected certain words and phrases and listed these alphabetically in its Descriptive Word Indexes. You use these indexes exactly as you do the indexes for U.S.C.A. and U.S.C.S. as described in Chapter 3. That is, you simply brainstorm by thinking of words and phrases that describe the problem you are researching, such as landlord, tenant, or lease. Remember to consider the Who, What, Where, When, Why, and How questions discussed in Chapter 3 to assist you in developing a list of descriptive words or phrases. Look up these words in

any Descriptive Word Index, and you will be provided with a topic and Key Number just as you were given a title and section when you located statutes in U.S.C.A. or U.S.C.S.

If you have difficulty thinking of words to use, think of synonyms (renter), antonyms (owner), defenses a party might assert (consent, waiver), the type of relief a party might seek (injunctive relief, damages, rescission of the lease), or the cause of action a plaintiff might plead (breach of contract, negligence). These should assist you in thinking of words to look up in the index. Just as you have seen with the indexes for U.S.C.A. and U.S.C.S., the Descriptive Word Indexes in the *American Digest System* are very "forgiving." Many topics are indexed under more than one entry, making it easy for you to locate the all-important topic name and Key Number.

When attempting to locate a topic name and a Key Number by using this Descriptive Word Index method, you should use the Descriptive Word Index to one of the newer Decennial units such as the *Eleventh Decennial Digest, Parts 1, 2,* or *3.* If you cannot locate a topic name and a Key Number in the *Eleventh Decennial Digest, Parts 1, 2,* or *3,* try the *Tenth Decennial (Parts 1* and *2)* as it is possible that no cases discussed this particular legal issue during 1996-2004, the time period covered by the *Eleventh Decennial Digest, Parts 1, 2,* and *3.* You could also use one of the Descriptive Word Indexes for the *General Digest.* There is a cumulative Descriptive Word Index in every tenth volume of the *General Digest.*

The Descriptive Word method is the easiest and most reliable way of locating a topic name and a Key Number, and this should be the approach you use until you have become thoroughly familiar with West's Key Number System. In fact, West advises that this method of search will generally prove most useful and should always be used first unless the researcher knows the specific topic. See Figure 5-3 for a sample page from the Descriptive Word Index to the *Ninth Decennial Digest, Part 2,* which demonstrates how to locate a topic name and a Key Number through the Descriptive Word approach.

b. Topic Approach

You may recall that in locating statutes, the topic approach calls for you to bypass the general index at the end of a set of statutes, and go directly to the appropriate title and begin examining the statutes. The topic approach to locating a topic name and a Key Number is exactly the same. Thus, if you were using the topic approach for the landlord-tenant problem described herein, you would bypass the Descriptive Word Index and go immediately to the "L" volume of a *Decennial* unit such as the *Eleventh Decennial Digest, Part 1,* and look up the phrase "Landlord and Tenant." Prior to the digest listing of the headnotes (**Landlord & Tenant 1, Landlord & Tenant 2,** and so on) you will be given an overview of the coverage of this topic, Landlord and Tenant, much like a book's table of contents. All of the Key Numbers digested under **Landlord & Tenant** will be identified in an index or outline fashion, and you may then scan the entries to determine the appropriate Key Number and proceed to look

Figure 5-3
Sample Page from Descriptive Word Index

43–9th D Pt 2—77

LANDLORD — Guide Word

LANDLORD AND TENANT—Cont'd
GUIDE dogs, waiver of pet restriction inapplicable to dog neither trained nor used as guide dog. **Land & Ten 134(1)**
HABITABILITY. **Land & Ten 125**
Implied warranty—
Coextensive with Residential Rental Agreements Act. **Land & Ten 125(1)**
HEALTH regulations, see this index **Health and Environment**
HEAT, see this index **Heat**
HEAT violation, notice as condition precedent to prosecution. **Health & E 39**
HOLDING over—
Damages—
Landlord's proper measure of damages for tenant's willful holdover. **Land & Ten 144**
Estoppel, effect on. **Land & Ten 62(4)**
Extension by. **Land & Ten 90**
Month to month tenancy. **Land & Ten 115(3)**
Renewal by. **Land & Ten 90**
Rent, amount while holding over. **Land & Ten 200.9**
Sufficiency to create new tenancy. **Land & Ten 90(4)**
Tenancy at sufferance, creation by. **Land & Ten 119(2)**
Tenancy at will, creation by. **Land & Ten 118(4)**
Year-to-year tenancy. **Land & Ten 114(3)**
HOMESTEAD, see this index **Homestead**
HOMICIDE conviction arising from death of tenant's guest—
Due process guarantees. **Const Law 258(3)**
HOTELS—
Duties owed to renter's patrons—
Providing guard for coat rack. **Inn 11(3)**
HUNTING rights. **Land & Ten 134(3)**
HUSBAND and wife—
Lease of community property. **Hus & W 267(3)**
Administration of community. **Hus & W 276(6)**
Separate property of wife, see this index **Separate Estate of Wife**
ICE and snow—
Generally, see this index **Ice and Snow**
ILLUSORY tenancy—
Effect—
Protecting against speculative profiteering by tenants of rent controlled apartment. **Land & Ten 278.4(6)**
Summary proceedings to dispossess, right to maintain. **Land & Ten 298(1)**
ILLUSORY tenants—
Entering into sublease in order to evade rent stabilization requirements. **Land & Ten 200.16**
IMPLIED contracts, see this index **Implied Contracts**
IMPLIED covenants. **Land & Ten 45**
IMPLIED tenancy, see this index **Implied Tenancy**
IMPROVEMENTS. **Land & Ten 150–161**
Actions. **Land & Ten 159**
Claims for. **Land & Ten 223(7)**

LANDLORD AND TENANT—Cont'd
IMPROVEMENTS—Cont'd
Compensation. **Land & Ten 157(6–8)**
Damages for failure to make. **Land & Ten 223(6)**
Lien. **Land & Ten 157(10)**
Ownership in general. **Land & Ten 157(2)**
Reimbursing tenant for repair of boiler made at request of tenant. **Impl & C C 40**
Remedy for failure to make. **Land & Ten 159**
Removal. **Land & Ten 157(4)**
INCOME tax, see this index **Income Tax**
INCUMBRANCES. **Land & Ten 145–149**
Reasonable rent, incumbrances as factor in determining. **Land & Ten 200.25**
INDEMNITY against liability for negligence. **Indem 8.1(2)**
INDORSEMENT, extension or renewal on lease. **Land & Ten 89**
INFANT'S property, lease of. **Infants 44**
INJUNCTION—
Assessing tenants nonrefundable rental fees. **Inj 136(2)**
Communication by tenant by signs or notices—
Free speech. **Const Law 90.1(1)**
Covenants as to use of leased premises. **Inj 62(2)**
Disturbance of possession of tenant. **Land & Ten 132(2)**
Preliminary injunction, tenant's consent to sale of building's air rights. **Inj 136(2)**
Summary proceedings. **Land & Ten 299**
Unlawful detainer, action for. **Land & Ten 290½**
Violation of laws relating to suspension of right of reentry and recovery of possession by landlord. **Land & Ten 278.16**
⎯⎯⎯⎯⎯**nd & Ten 55(4)**
INJURIES—
⎯⎯⎯⎯⎯**nd & Ten 139(4)**
Dangerous or defective condition. **Land & Ten 162–170**
Mobile home parks, see this index **Trailer Parks or Camps**
Employees of tenant. **Land & Ten 165, 169(5)**
Patrons of lessee—
Liability of lessee. **Land & Ten 167(8)**
Premises. **Land & Ten 140–142**
Eviction. **Land & Ten 176**
Property of tenant. **Land & Ten 166**
⎯⎯⎯⎯⎯trance of trespassers and vandals. **Land & Ten 166(6)**
Property of third persons. **Land & Ten 167(9)**
Reversion. **Land & Ten 55**
Scalding of cleaning woman when steam pipe burst—
Liability of tenant. **Land & Ten 167(2)**
Tenants or occupants. **Land & Ten 164**
INNKEEPERS—
See this index **Innkeepers**

LANDLORD AND TENANT—Cont'd
INNKEEPERS—Cont'd
Membership in metropolitan hotel industry stabilization association. **Inn 2**
INSANE persons, see this index **Mental Health**
INSOLVENCY, termination of lease. **Land & Ten 101½**
INSURANCE—
Covenants to insure. **Land & Ten 156**
Insurable interest. **Insurance 115(4)**
Landlord's liability insurance—
Risks and causes of loss. **Insurance 435.34**
Nature and cause of injury or damage. **Insurance 435.35**
Lessee's good-faith efforts to obtain—
Preventing cancellation of lease. **Land & Ten 103(1)**
Right to proceeds. **Insurance 580(4)**
INTERFERENCE with—
Possession of tenant. **Land & Ten 131–133**
Relationship. **Land & Ten 19**
Use of premises. **Land & Ten 134(4), 172(2)**
INTERVENTION, see this index **Intervention**
INTOXICATING liquors, see this index **Intoxicating Liquors**
INTRUDER—
Lessor's liability for lessee's injuries inflicted by. **Land & Ten 164(1)**
INVALIDITY as affecting action for unlawful detainer. **Land & Ten 290(4)**
JOINT tenants, implied tenancy between. **Land & Ten 8**
JUDGMENT—
Conclusiveness. **Judgm 684**
Recovery of possession, action for. **Land & Ten 285(6)**
Summary proceedings for possession, post
Unlawful detainer, action for. **Land & Ten 291(17)**
JURISDICTION, see this index **Jurisdiction**
⎯⎯⎯⎯⎯
Justices of the Peace
KEY to leased premises, see this index **Keys**
KNOWLEDGE of defects affecting liability for injuries. **Land & Ten 164(6, 7), 165, 166(10)**
LACHES, affecting rescission of lease. **Land & Ten 34(4)**
LANDLORD'S title, estoppel dependent on. **Land & Ten 62(2)**
LARCENY of property from landlord or tenant, see this index **Larceny**
LEASES. **Land & Ten 20–49**
Bankruptcy proceedings. **Bankr 3086–3088**
Farm lease. **Land & Ten 322**
Female tenant's right to possession of apartment though not married to signing tenant—
Civil R 11.5
Land & Ten 43
Nonassignment clauses—
Restraints on alienation, policy against. **Perp 6(17)**
Protection leases—
Nature of. **Mines 56**

Subtopic Heading

Topic Name and Key Number

up and examine the headnotes listed or digested under **Landlord & Tenant.** To select topics, you can review an alphabetical list of the more than 400 digest topics that appears in the front of any West Digest volume.

Just as the topic method should be used with caution to find statutes, it should be used with caution to locate topic names and Key Numbers because you may miss other topics and Key Numbers under which this area of the law may be digested. Because West's *American Digest System* has more than 400 topics, this method should be used only after you have become thoroughly familiar with West's Key Number classification system. Each topic discussion begins with an overview of its coverage as well as an identification of subjects included and subjects excluded, which will help ensure you are searching within the correct topic. See Figure 5-4 for a sample page from the *Ninth Decennial Digest, Part 2*, showing a partial list of Key Numbers within the topic Landlord & Tenant. Once again, you can see that if you need to review cases relating to damage to a tenant's property, West has organized these under the topic name "Landlord & Tenant" and the Key Number 166.

c. Table of Cases Approach

If you know the name of a case, you can look it up in an alphabetically arranged master Table of Cases, which will provide you with the citations to the case (although not in *Bluebook* or *ALWD* form) and a list of the topics and Key Numbers under which it has been classified. For example, if you have the name of the case *DeGracia v. Huntingdon Associates, Ltd.*, and you know it was decided between 1981 and 1986, you can use the Table of Cases in the *Ninth Decennial Digest, Part 2* (which covers the time period 1981-1986). When you look up this case, you will be given all citations to the case, the history of the case (for example, whether it has been affirmed or reversed), and all of the topics and Key Numbers under which it is digested or classified. See Figure 5-5.

Each *Decennial* unit and each volume of the *General Digest* contains its own Table of Cases listed alphabetically by plaintiff. The Table of Cases is usually located after the last volume in a *Decennial* set. Some of West's earlier Digests contain an additional Table of Cases, the Defendant-Plaintiff Table, so if you know only the name of a defendant, you can determine the exact case name and parallel citations (although you will not be given topic names and key numbers). This may be useful if you wish to locate other cases involving a certain defendant. More recent digest sets integrate the two tables, allowing you ready access to cases whether you know the name of the plaintiff or defendant.

d. "Case on Point" Approach

If you have already located a case on point, its headnotes will display applicable topic names and Key Numbers. If one of these headnotes is relevant to your research, you can then use that headnote to locate other similar cases by looking up your topic name and Key Number in the various units of the *Decennial Digest System*. For example, review

Figure 5-4
Sample Page from *Ninth Decennial Digest, Part 2*

29 9th D Pt 2—783

LANDLORD & TENANT ► Topic name

VII. PREMISES, AND ENJOYMENT AND USE THEREOF.—Cont'd

(D) REPAIRS, INSURANCE, AND IMPROVEMENTS.

⬅150. Right and duty to make repairs in general.
  (1). In general.
  (2). Duty to rebuild on destruction of property.
  (3). Landlord's right of entry to make repairs.
  (4). Rights of subtenants.
  (5). Right of tenant to repair at landlord's cost.
151. Statutory provisions.
152. Covenants and agreements as to repairs and alterations.
  (1). In general.
  (2). Consideration for agreement.
  (3). Construction and operation of covenants in
    general.
  (4). Nature of repairs included in covenant or
    agreement.
  (5). Duty to rebuild on destruction of property.
  (6). Right of landlord to notice that repairs are
    necessary.
  (7). Agreement by landlord to pay for repairs.
  (8). Rights and liabilities of assignees and subten-
    ants.
  (9). Waiver of claims under or stipulations in cove-
    nant or agreement.
  (10). Right of tenant to repair and recover cost.
  (11). Alterations by tenant.
153. Mode of making repairs.
154. Remedies for failure to make repairs and alterations.
  (1). Nature and form of remedy.
  (2). Right of action and defenses.
  (3). Pleading and evidence.
  (4). Damages.
  (5). Trial.
155. Maintenance of boundaries and fences.
156. Covenants and agreements as to insurance.
157. Improvements by tenant and covenants therefor.
  (1). Covenant by lessee to make improvements.
  (2). Ownership of improvements in general.
  (4). Right to remove and agreements for removal
    of improvements.
  (5). Forfeiture or waiver of right to remove im-
    provements.
  (6). Right to compensation in general.
  (7). Covenants and agreements to pay for improve-
    ments.
  (8). Liabilities of successors of lessor.
  (9). Mode of termination of tenancy as affecting
    right to compensation.
  (10). Lien for value of improvements.
  (11). Determination of compensation.
  (12). Actions for compensation.
158. Improvements by landlord and covenants therefor.
159. Remedies for failure to make improvements.
  (1). Actions for breach of tenant's covenant to
    make improvements.
  (2). Actions for breach of landlord's covenant to
    make improvements.
160. Condition of premises at termination of tenancy.
  (1). In general.
  (2). Covenants and agreements as to condition of
    premises on termination of tenancy.

  (3). Duty of tenant to rebuild or replace personal
    property.
  (4). Actions for breach of covenant.
161. Personal property on premises at termination of
  tenancy.
  (1). Rights and liabilities as to property on premis-
    es in general.
  (2). Care of property left on premises by outgoing
    tenant.
  (3). Actions to recover property or value.

(E) INJURIES FROM DANGEROUS OR
    DEFECTIVE CONDITION.

⬅162. Nature and extent of landlord's duty to tenant.
163. Mutual duties of tenants of different portions of
  same premises.
164. Injuries to tenants or occupants.
  (1). Injuries due to defective or dangerous condi-
    tion of premises in general.
  (2). Injuries due to failure to repair.
  (3). Injuries due to negligence in making repairs.
  (4). Injuries due to unlighted passageways.
  (5). Liability for injuries to subtenant.
  (6). Liability of landlord as dependent on knowl-
    edge of defects.
  (7). Notice to or knowledge of tenant as to de-
    fects.
165. Injuries to employé of tenant.
  (1). Injuries due to defective or dangerous condi-
    tion of premises in general.
  (2). Injuries due to failure to repair.
  (3). Injuries due to unlighted passageway.
  (4). Liability of landlord as dependent on knowl-
    edge of defects.
  (5). Failure to guard dangerous places.
  (6). Operation or condition of elevators.
  (7). Notice to or knowledge of tenant as to de-

166. Injuries to property of tenant on premises.
  (1). Nature and extent of the duties of landlord
    and tenant respectively.
  (2). Injuries due to defective condition of premises
    in general.
  (3). Injuries due to failure to repair.
  (4). Injuries due to negligence in making repairs.
  (5). Injuries due to defective water pipes or drains.
  (6). Injuries due to negligent acts of landlord.
  (7). Injuries due to negligence of third persons in
    general.
  (9). Injuries due to negligence of cotenant.
  (10). Liability of landlord as dependent on knowl-
    edge or notice of defects.

► Outline of topics and key numbers listed under "Landlord & Tenant"

  (1). Duties of landlord and tenant to third persons.
  (2). Injuries due to defective or dangerous condi-
    tion of premises in general.
  (3). Injuries due to failure to repair.
  (4). Failure to light or guard dangerous places.
  (5). Injuries due to openings, defects, or obstruc-
    tions in walks or streets.
  (6). Injuries caused by fall of snow or ice from
    roof.
  (7). Injuries due to the negligence of tenant.

Figure 5-5
Sample Page from Table of Cases to
Ninth Decennial Digest, Part 2

References are to Digest Topics and Key Numbers

DeFulmer, People ex rel., v. Scully, NYAD 2 Dept, 487 NYS2d 401, 110 AD2d 671. See People ex rel. DeFulmer v. Scully.

de Furgalski v. Siegel, DCIll, 618 FSupp 295.—Civil R 13.3(1), 13.4(1), 18.5(1), 13.10, 13.12(3); Courts 100(1); Equity 67, 72(1), 84; Fed Cts 425.

DeFusco v. Giorgio, RI, 440 A2d 727.— Judgm 90, 91, 344; Usury 104; Witn 198(2), 205.

DeGarcia v. I.N.S., CA9, 783 F2d 931. See Magallanes-Damian v. I.N.S.

DeGarmo v. State, TexCrApp, 691 SW2d 657, cert den 106 SCt 337, 474 US 973, 88 LEd2d 322.—Crim Law 409(5), 662.65, 983, 986.2(2), 1134(1), 1144.13(6), 1213.8(1), 1213.8(8); Homic 253(1), 342.

DeGase v. DeGase, MoApp, 690 SW2d 485.—App & E 80(4), 1008.1(5), 1010.1(6), 1012.1(1); Partners 328(3), 336(3).

De Gasperis v. De Gasperis, NYAD 2 Dept, 469 NYS2d 469, 98 AD2d 758.—Compromise 21.

DeGay v. State, TexApp-Beaumont, 711 SW2d 419, review gr.—Const Law 75; Crim Law 982.9(1).

DeGay v. State, TexApp 9 Dist, 663 SW2d 459.—Ind & Inf 166; Weap 17(4).

Degelos, Succession of, LaApp 4 Cir, 450 So2d 682.—Ex & Ad 92; Spec Perf 106(3).

Degelos, Succession of, LaApp 4 Cir, 446 So2d 412.—Des & Dist 109; Wills 11.

Degen v. General Coatings, Inc., Tex-App 14 Dist, 705 SW2d 784.—Courts 81, 85(1); Pretrial Proc 587.

Degenaars v. Degenaars, NJSuperCh, 452 A2d 222, 186 NJSuper 233.—Divorce 87; Infants 18.

Degenaars Co. v. U.S., ClCt, 2 ClCt 482 —U S 70(21), 73(15), 74(11).

Degenaars Co. v. U.S., ClCt 1 ClCt 129, 555 FSupp 403.—Fed Cts 1101.

Degener, In re Marriage of, IllApp 2 Dist, 75 IllDec 878, 458 NE2d 46, 119 IllApp3d 1079.—Divorce 72, 252.3(4).

Degeneres v. Burgess, LaApp 1 Cir, 486 So2d 769.—Contracts 108(1), 186(3), 205.15(3), 280(3), 322(4), 324(1); Damag 123, 188(1); Evid 445(1); Lim of Act 32(1); Neglig 1; Sales 391(3), 394; Subrog 30; Ven & Pur 3(1).

DeGenova v. Board of Review, Ohio App, 493 NE2d 287, 24 Ohio App3d 125, 24 OBR 196.—Social S 473.

DeGeorge v. Bernier, CAFed, 768 F2d 1318.—Pat 90(1), 99, 106(2), 106(3), 314(5), 328(2).

Degerlia v. First Bank and Trust Co., IllApp 5 Dist, 77 IllDec 238, 460 NE2d 97, 121 IllApp3d 658.—Venue 2, 8(2), 22(1).

DeGette v. Mine Co. Restaurant, Inc., CAColo, 751 F2d 1143.—Lim of Act 95(1).

De Gheldre Hoorn, Matter of, BkrtcyAla, 44 BR 23. See Childers, Matter of.

De Giacomo v. Regan, NYAD, 444 NYS2d 273, 84 AD2d 629.—Offic 101.5(2).

Degideo v. Com., Unemployment Compensation Bd. of Review, PaCmwlth, 433 A2d 607, 61 PaCmwlth 268.—Social S 728.

DeGidio v. Perpich, DCMinn, 612 FSupp 1383.—Civil R 13.3(1), 13.7, 13.12(6); Fed Civ Proc 172, 181, 186.10; Fed Cts 265, 266, 267, 268, 269; Judgm 567.

DeGier v. Commissioner of Public Safety, MinnApp, 387 NW2d 908.—Autos 144.1(1); Const Law 262.

DeGirolamo v. U.S., DCNY, 518 FSupp 778.—Lim of Act 55(3), 95(1); U S 113, 125(6).

Degiman v. Degiman, SC, 281 SE2d 123, 276 SC 600.—Divorce 235, 240(2), 240(4), 286(3), 287.

Deglopper, In re, BkrtcyIdaho, 53 BR 95.—Bankr 396(5), 399(1); Home 80.

Degnan v. Executive Homes, Inc., Mont, 696 P2d 431.—Contracts 188.5(1), 205.35(2), 205.40, 322(1); Torts 1.

Degnan v. Monetti, NJSuperAD, 509 A2d 277, 210 NJSuper 174.—Zoning 487, 489, 512, 610, 623, 709.

Degolyer Co., Inc. v. Standard & Poor's Corp., CATex, 672 F2d 433. See Municipal Bond Reporting Antitrust Litigation, In re.

DeGraaf v. General Motors Corp., MichApp, 352 NW2d 719, 135 MichApp 141, appeal den.—Prod Liab 96.5.

DeGrace v. Shelby Tp. Police and Fire Civil Service Com'n, MichApp, 389 NW2d 137, 150 MichApp 587.—Mand

DeGracia v. Huntingdon Associates, Ltd., GaApp, 336 SE2d 602, 176 Ga-App 495.—Judgm 185(3), 185.3(14); Land & Ten 164(1).

phone Co., KanApp, 687 P2d 1380.— App & E 930(1), 931(1), 989, 994(1), 1001(1), 1010.1(6); Damag 50, 50.10; Neglig 136(14); Pub Ut 103; Tel 278, 284.

DeGraff, Matter of Compensation of, OrApp, 630 P2d 895, 52 OrApp 1023.— Work Comp 1545.

DeGraff v. Kaplan, IllApp, 65 IllDec 75, 440 NE2d 930, 109 IllApp3d 711.—App & E 984(5); Costs 173(1); Evid 455; Partners 81, 86, 121.

DeGraff's Estate, Matter of, MoApp, 637 SW2d 277.—Ex & Ad 218, 459, 495(3), 496(1), 501; Jury 19(7).

DeGraffenreid v. Curtwright, MoApp, 652 SW2d 310.—Judgm 334.

DeGraffenreid, State ex rel. v. Keet, MoApp, 619 SW2d 873. See State ex rel. DeGraffenreid v. Keet.

de Graffenried v. U.S., ClCt, 2 ClCt 640. —Fed Cts 1112; Pat 203, 292.1(2), 292.2, 328(2).

DeGrand v. Alton Tel. Printing Co., Inc., BkrtcyIll, 15 BR 367. See Alton Tel. Printing Co., Inc., In re.

Degree v. Degree, NCApp, 325 SE2d 36, 72 NCApp 668, review den 330 SE2d 607, 313 NC 598.—Hus & W 279(2), 281; Stip 8.

De Gregorio v. CBS, Inc., NYSup, 473 NYS2d 922, 123 Misc2d 491.—Const Law 90.1(8); Damag 50.10; Libel 6(1); Torts 1, 8.5(6), 8.5(8).

De Gregorio v. Pennsylvania Public Utility Com'n, PaCmwlth, 481 A2d 1241, 85 PaCmwlth 354.—Autos 87, 106; Pub Ut 194.

DeGrio v. American Federation of Government Employees, Fla, 484 So2d 1.—Courts 489(1); Labor 221.

DeGroat v. Ingles, CalApp 1 Dist, 191 CalRptr 761, 143 CA3d 399.—Judgm 181(2), 181(6), 188.

DeGroat v. New York State Higher Educ. Services Corp., NYAD, 456 NYS2d 159, 90 AD2d 616.—Lim of Act 66(11).

Degroat v. State, FlaApp 5 Dist, 489 So2d 1163, review den 496 So2d 142.— Crim Law 986.2(4), 1208.1(3).

DeGroff v. Bethlehem Cent. School Dist., NYAD, 460 NYS2d 680, 92 AD2d 702.—Mun Corp 741.1(8); Schools 112.

DeGroot v. American Legion Post No. 1247, IllApp 1 Dist, 86 IllDec 199, 475 NE2d 5, 130 IllApp3d 735. See Monsen v. DeGroot.

DeGroot v. Arizona Racing Com'n, ArizApp, 686 P2d 1301, 141 Ariz 331. —Admin Law 349, 360, 669, 754, 760, 763, 786, 791; Const Law 287.2(1), 318(1); Theaters 3.10.

DeGroot v. Employment Sec. Com'n, SCApp, 328 SE2d 668, 285 SC 209.— Admin Law 791; Const Law 278.7(3); Social S 584.5, 660.

DeGrow v. DeGrow, MichApp, 315 NW2d 915, 112 MichApp 260.—Divorce 303(6), 303(7); Infants 19.3(6); Parent & C 2(3.4).

De Gryse v. De Gryse, Ariz, 661 P2d 185, 135 Ariz 335.—App & E 982(2); Divorce 163, 165(2), 194, 252.3(4); Hus & W 279(2); Judgm 346.

Deguffroy & Associates, Inc. v. W.C.A.B. (Blanchetti), PaCmwlth, 503 A2d 994, 94 PaCmwlth 566.—Work Comp 504, 1981.

DeHart v. A.C. and S. Co., Inc., DelSuper, 484 A2d 521. See Sheppard v.

DeHart v. Aetna Life Ins. Co., Ohio, 431 NE2d 644, 69 Ohio St2d 189, 23 003d 210.—App & E 962, 1092; Courts 78, 85(1); Pretrial Proc 551.

DeHart v. Diversified Services, NYAD, 442 NYS2d 255, 83 AD2d 685.—Work Comp 1536, 1676, 1939.8.

DeHart v. Moore, DCFla, 424 FSupp 55.—Exchanges 11(11).

DeHart v. Ritenour Consolidated School Dist., MoApp, 663 SW2d 332.— Deeds 144(1); Quiet T 46; Schools 65.

DeHart v. R/S Financial Corp., NCApp, 337 SE2d 94, 78 NCApp 93, review den 342 SE2d 893.—App & E 263(1); Evid 267, 402; Judgm 199(1), 199(3.9); Pretrial Proc 44; Trial 139.1(5), 143, 178; Usury 117.

DeHart v. R/S Financial Corp., NCApp, 311 SE2d 694, 66 NCApp 648, appeal after remand 337 SE2d 94, 78 NCApp 93, review den 342 SE2d 893, 316 NC 376.—Plead 427; Trial 139.1(16), 168, 178; Usury 11, 119.

DeHart v. State, IndApp 3 Dist, 471 NE2d 312, reh den; transfer den.— Const Law 199; Crim Law 150; Health & E 25.5(5), 25.5(5.5), 37, 39, 41; Statut 190.

DeHart v. State, OrApp, 637 P2d 1311, 55 OrApp 254.—Const Law 268.1(6).

DeHart v. U.S., BkrtcyPa, 50 BR 685. See Metropolitan Metals, Inc., In re.

DeHaven v. Dan-Co FS Co-op., WisApp, 383 NW2d 509, 128 Wis2d 472.—Social S 241.

DeHaven v. DeHaven, La, 412 So2d 537. —App & E 185(1); Divorce 387; Hus & W 279(2); Parent & C 3.3(8); Ven & Pur 1.

DeHaven v. DeHaven, LaApp, 401 So2d 418, writ gr 406 So2d 624, rev 412 So2d 537.—App & E 185(1); Courts 37(2), 39, 472.1; Divorce 297, 311.5; Hus & W 279(2); Parent & C 3.1(8), 3.3(8).

DeHaven v. Gant, WashApp, 713 P2d 149, 42 WashApp 666, review den.— App & E 232(2), 241, 754(1); Evid 555.10; Phys 18.80(8); Trial 388(3).

DeHaven v. Thomas D. Gant, M.D., P.S., WashApp, 713 P2d 149, 42 WashApp 666. See DeHaven v. Gant.

De Hay v. Town of West New York, NJSuperAD, 460 A2d 157, 189 NJSuper 340, certification den 468 A2d 227, 94 NJ 591.—Equity 72(1); Mun Corp 191, 220(8).

Note topics and key number under which case is digested

4-1, where the case *State v. Boyd*, 162 N.C. App. 159, 595 S.E.2d 697 (2004), appears. Note headnote number 3, which is given the topic name **Sentencing and Punishment** and the Key Number **98**. If you read the *Boyd* case and determine that this section of the case relating to sentencing and punishment is relevant to your research, you can take the topic name and Key Number **Sentencing and Punishment 98** and look it up in the various *Decennial* units to locate other similar cases. Alternatively, you can sign on to Westlaw and search for other cases classified to this same topic name and Key Number.

6. *Using Digests*

Once you have obtained a topic and a Key Number, such as **Landlord & Tenant 166(1)**, you merely look this up in the various units of the *American Digest System* and you will unlock the door to cases from 1658 until last month, all of which relate to injuries to a tenant's property.

Because the *Decennials* are arranged alphabetically, you simply retrieve the "L" volume in any of the *Decennial* units and look up **"Landlord & Tenant 166(1)."** Topics are listed in alphabetical order, and Key Numbers within those topics are listed in numerical order, making it easy for you to find the information you need. At this point, West will do more than merely list the digest headnotes in a haphazard fashion. West has carefully arranged the entries, giving you federal cases, first from the highest federal court, the United States Supreme Court, through cases from the United States Courts of Appeal to the lowest federal courts, the United States District Courts. After all of the federal cases have been digested, you will be given the entries for state court cases. Again, West will order and list the states alphabetically, making it easy for you to quickly locate cases from Arkansas, Louisiana, Minnesota, or South Carolina. West's listing of cases from South Carolina will be in order of the South Carolina court hierarchy and then in reverse chronological order so you will proceed from the newer South Carolina Supreme Court cases to the older South Carolina Supreme Court cases and then from the newer South Carolina Court of Appeals cases to the older South Carolina Court of Appeals cases. Consider browsing adjacent Key Numbers to determine if another Key Number may be helpful. See Figure 5-6 for a sample page from the *Ninth Decennial Digest, Part 2*, showing the organization of cases.

In looking up your topic and Key Number in the *Decennial* units, you should start with the most recent *Decennial* unit. If you cannot find the cases you need, proceed to the older *Decennial* units. You should never exclusively rely on the brief summaries or digests of the cases. Although they are usually very clearly and concisely presented, you must read a case in full to really understand it. Similarly, you should *never* cite a digest as legal authority. Its sole function is to locate cases for you, not to serve as support for an assertion you make.

In your review of the various West publications and case reporters, you may have observed that there are diagrams or drawings of "keys" on

Figure 5-6
Sample Page from *Ninth Decennial Digest, Part 2,*
Showing Digests of Cases

⊷166 LANDLORD & TENANT   29 9th D Pt 2—956

⊷166. Injuries to property of tenant on premises.

Library references

C.J.S. Landlord and Tenant § 423 et seq.

⊷166(1). Nature and extent of the duties of landlord and tenant respectively.

Cal.App. 1 Dist. 1983. Where lessee of storage space was afforded option, by operator of space, of greater monthly payments under lease with insurance or of purchasing insurance elsewhere, and she was not subjected to an adhesive contract under which she had to accept exculpatory clause or forego lease, storage lease did not involve the public interest so as to render exculpatory clause in lease invalid under Civil Code section providing, inter alia, that all contracts which have as their object to exempt anyone from responsibility for his own fraud or willful injury to person or property of another are against policy of the law. West's Ann.Cal.Civ. Code § 1668.—Cregg v. Ministor Ventures, 196 Cal.Rptr. 724, 148 C.A.3d 1107.

Cal.Super. 1982. Apartment building owners and managers had no affirmative duty to secure parking facilities, which they never represented as being protected, merely because they had notice of previous instances of vandalism to parked cars and thus tenant could not recover from owners and managers for destruction by fire of tenant's automobile in building parking area.—Jubert v. Shalom Realty, 185 Cal.Rptr. 641, 135 C.A.3d Supp. 1.

D.C.App. 1983. Exculpatory clause in lease which purported to relieve landlord of liability for personal property damage caused by any source, including defective roofing and plumbing, was ineffective to bar recovery of damages from landlord inasmuch as clause amounted to waiver or modification of tenant's rights under implied warranty of habitability.—George Washington University v. Weintraub, 458 A.2d 43.

Kan. 1982. Landlord, having leased premises in their entirety to tenants, did not have control over portion of premises wherein fire started and had no duty to inspect same, and thus failure of landlord to inspect wiring and failure to discover and correct latent defect on premises could not, as a matter of law, constitute negligence.—Moore v. Muntzel, 642 P.2d 957, 231 Kan. 46.

There were no warranties flowing from landlord to tenants on which liability for fire damage could be predicated.—Id.

La.App. 4 Cir. 1982. Alleged failure of lessee to present evidence of negligence by ultimate building owner or lessor had no effect on her right to recover for loss of personal property destroyed in fire at apartment under statutes which base liability on status, either as owner or lessor, rather than on personal fault. LSA-C.C. arts. 2322, 2695.—Barnes v. Housing Authority of New Orleans, 423 So.2d 750.

Minn.App. 1984. Lease provision exculpating landlords from liability for water damage was not ambiguous, even though contract's reference to "premises" varyingly referred to entire building or to first floor and basement.—Fena v. Wickstrom, 348 N.W.2d 389.

N.Y.A.D. 1982. Where the tenant had notice that water would be turned off in building on a Friday and knew that water would be turned on before he reopened his shop on the following Monday, and where building owner did not have access to tenant's premises, it was tenant's responsibility to be particularly careful in closing all the faucets, and his failure to do so was proximate and sole cause of flooding.—Arthur Richards, Inc. v. 79 Fifth Ave. Co., 450 N.Y.S.2d 13, 88 A.D.2d 517, reversed 455 N.Y.S.2d 596, 57 N.Y.2d 824, 441 N.E.2d 1114.

Pa. 1986. Exculpatory clause in commercial lease agreement relieving lessor of liability for injury or damage to personal property in premises caused by fire in any part of building of which demised premises was a part, was valid and enforceable; the clause did not contravene any policy of the law, commercial lease related entirely to parties' own private affairs, there was no disparity in bargaining power between parties, and clause, as modified, spelled out intention of parties with particularity.—Princeton Sportswear Corp. v. H & M Associates, 507 A.2d 339, 510 Pa. 189, appeal after remand 517 A.2d 963, 358 Pa.Super. 325.

Pa.Super. 1984. Exculpatory clauses in lease were valid and enforceable where lease was commercial lease, there was no disparity in bargaining power between the parties, exculpatory clauses had been reviewed, negotiated and modified by both parties and their counsel, and clauses, as modified, evidenced clear and unambiguous intent to release landlords from liability for damages caused by fire when such fire was not the result of any negligence on landlords' part.—Princeton Sportswear Corp. v. H & M Associates, 484 A.2d 185, 335 Pa.Super. 381, reversed 507 A.2d 339, 510 Pa. 189, appeal after remand 517 A.2d 963, 358 Pa.Super. 325.

Landlords were not liable for damages tenant suffered as result of fire which damaged building's power center and thereby deprived tenant of heat, electricity and water, where under exculpatory clauses in lease, it was clear that landlords were not liable for any property damage caused by fire in any portion of the building of which demised premises was a part unless such fire was caused by landlords' negligence, power center constituted portion of building in which demised premises was a part, and lower court specifically found that landlords' conduct was not tortious.—Id.

⊷166(2). Injuries due to defective condition of premises in general.

C.A.La. 1983. Not every defect in leased premises will serve as a basis for a claim of damages against lessor under Louisiana law; instead, vices and defects must be substantial and of such nature as are likely to cause injury to a reasonably prudent individual. LSA-C.C. art. 2695.—Volkswagen of America, Inc. v. Robertson, 713 F.2d 1151.

D.C.App. 1983. While landlords clearly bear burden of maintaining rented premises in compliance with housing code provisions, liability is not imposed upon landlords for losses arising from all conditions that violate the code.—George Washington University v. Weintraub, 458 A.2d 43.

Fla.App. 1 Dist. 1984. Lessee's complaint, which alleged making of the lease and lessor's covenant to keep the roof in good repair, the undertaking by lessor through services of a roofing contractor to keep the roof in good repair, a breach of that covenant by reason of the roof collapsing during course of repairs due either to defects in the structure or to overloading of the roof by the contractor, and resulting damages to lessee's property, was sufficient to state cause of action against lessor for breach of contract.—Cisu of Florida, Inc. for Use and Benefit of Aetna Cas. and Sur. Co. v. Porter, 457 So.2d 1118.

Ill.App. 1 Dist. 1985. Under common law, landlord is not liable for injury to property of tenant caused by defects in demised premises absent express warranty as to condition of premises or covenant to repair.—Wanland v. Beavers, 86 Ill.Dec. 130, 474 N.E.2d 1327, 130 Ill. App.3d 731.

Ill.App. 1982. Warranty of habitability implied in lease of building does not give rise to a cause of action for permanent injuries or proper-

ty damage.—Auburn v. Amoco Oil Co., 61 Ill. Dec. 939, 435 N.E.2d 780, 106 Ill.App.3d 60.

La.App. 1 Cir. 1986. Lessee and its property insurer were not required to show negligence on the part of the lessor in order to recover damages resulting from a fire caused by a defect in the premises. LSA-C.C. arts. 2322, 2695.— Great American Surplus Lines Ins. Co. v. Bass, 486 So.2d 789, writ denied 489 So.2d 245.

Even if lessee assumed responsibility for electricity, lessor was liable for damages resulting from the destruction of the lessee's property due to a fire caused by a defect in the building's electrical system where there was no proof of negligence on the part of the lessee and where the lessor knew or should have known of the defect. LSA-R.S. 9:3221.—Id.

La.App. 3 Cir. 1985. Under LSA-C.C. art. 2695, lessor is liable to lessee for any losses sustained as result of "vice and defects" in premises, provided they did not arise as result of lessee's fault.—Freeman v. Thomas, 472 So.2d 326.

La.App. 3 Cir. 1984. Mere fact that common wall between premises leased for jewelry store purposes and adjacent premises was constructed of sheetrock and thus susceptible to breach by burglars did not render the condition a "vice" under statute so as to render owner lessor liable to lessees for damages arising out of the burglary. LSA-C.C. arts. 2322, 2703.—Hall v. Park Dell Terrace Partnership, 452 So.2d 342.

La.App. 4 Cir. 1985. Tenant's allegation that security services provided by landlord were inadequate did not provide basis for landlord's liability for arson damage, where all security services promised in lease were provided.—U.S. Fidelity and Guar. Ins. Co. v. Burns Intern. Sec. Services, Inc., 468 So.2d 662, writ denied 470 So.2d 882.

Implied warranty of fitness for intended use and freedom from defects, applicable to leased office building, did not extend to fire damage caused by arson, in light of provisions in lease waiving landlord's liability for damage caused by fire or unauthorized persons.—Id.

La.App. 4 Cir. 1984. Clause in lease clearly and unambiguously transferred liability of lessor to lessee for damage caused by leaks in roof, and thus lessor and its managing partner could not be held liable to lessee for damage which occurred when roof of premises failed under the burden of a heavy rainstorm.—St. Paul Fire & Marine Ins. Co. v. French Eighth, 457 So.2d 35, writ denied 462 So.2d 195 and Oreck v. French Eighth, 462 So.2d 195, reconsideration not considered 462 So.2d 1240, two cases.

La.App. 4 Cir. 1983. Tenants of building destroyed by fire were entitled to recover damages from landlord, despite fact that defect in leased premises was alleged not to have been in building in which tenants leased premises, but within the building, owned by same landlord, next door to tenants' building, unless landlord could exculpate himself. LSA-C.C. arts. 660, 2322.—Broome v. Gauthier, 443 So.2d 1127, writ denied 445 So.2d 449.

N.J.Super.A.D. 1982. Exculpatory clause in commercial lease which exempted landlord from liability for damage or injury resulting from carelessness or negligence or improper conduct of landlord or others, but did not exclude liability for damage flowing from defective design and construction of major structural aspects of building, did not immunize landlord from liability for water damage to tenant's computer equipment caused by defective design of roof.—Ultimate Computer Services, Inc. v. Biltmore Realty Co., Inc., 443 A.2d 723, 183 N.J.Super. 144, 30 A.L.R.4th 963.

Where exculpatory clause did not clearly express intention to exclude liability for injuries resulting from improper construction, landlord, in

For references to other topics, see Descriptive-Word Index

Note alphabetical arrangement of cases from states and arrangement from higher to lower courts within a state

the spines of many books in the law library. This diagram indicates the volume is a participant in West's Key Number System.

Ethics Alert

Using Digests

Digests are wonderful sources to find cases; however, you may not cite to them, and you must read the cases to which you are directed. Never quote from or rely on the digest or summary of a case; you must read the case itself and analyze it. Only then may you cite it as authority.

---

7. *Other West Digests*

As you have seen, the *American Digest System* is the most comprehensive digest system, with its coverage of all federal and state cases. It is entirely likely, however, that you may not need such extensive coverage. In this regard, there are several specialized digests published by West that will assist you in locating cases from a specific region, jurisdiction, or state, or covering a certain topic. The following digests are kept up to date by annual cumulative pocket parts.

a. *United States Supreme Court Digest*

This digest is published by West and classifies its headnotes according to the Key Number System. As its name indicates, this set provides brief summaries, or digests, only to United States Supreme Court cases. A Table of Cases is included.

b. **Federal Practice Digests**

There are several West Digests that serve as casefinders for cases from all federal courts, for example, the United States Supreme Court, the United States Courts of Appeal, and the United States District Courts. Each digest covers a specific time period, similar to the manner in which the *Decennials* each cover a ten-year period.

> *Federal Digest:* Federal Courts (1754-1938)
> *Modern Federal Practice Digest:* Federal Courts (1939-1961)
> *West's Federal Practice Digest 2d:* Federal Courts (1961-1975)
> *West's Federal Practice Digest 3d:* Federal Courts (1975-1984)
> *West's Federal Practice Digest 4th:* Federal Courts (1984-Date)

Thus, if you are interested only in recent cases from the Third Circuit, you could consult West's *Federal Practice Digest 4th* and West's *Federal Practice Digest 3d*. Cases are arranged in groups by court, circuits, and districts, making it easy for you to locate cases from the

United States Supreme Court, cases from the Third Circuit, or cases from the United States District Court for the Eastern District of Pennsylvania. All of the *Federal Practice Digests* include a Table of Cases.

c. Regional Digests

West has created regional digests for some of its regional geographic units.

> *Atlantic Digest*—digests cases reported in the *Atlantic Reporter*
> *North Western Digest*—digests cases reported in the *North Western Reporter*
> *Pacific Digest*—digests cases reported in the *Pacific Reporter*
> *South Eastern Digest*—digests cases reported in the *South Eastern Reporter*

Thus, if you were interested in locating cases from several neighboring states, you could consult the *North Western Digest*, which would assist you in finding cases from Iowa, Michigan, Minnesota, Nebraska, North Dakota, South Dakota, and Wisconsin. Again, the *Digest* will arrange the cases for you so that under **Criminal Law 1169.1(5)** all of the digest headnotes for Iowa cases are grouped together, all of the digest headnotes for North Dakota cases are grouped together, and all of the digest headnotes for Wisconsin cases are grouped together.

You will note there are no current digests for the *Southern Reporter, South Western Reporter*, and *North Eastern Reporter*. This should not be considered a drawback, however, as cases from states within these reporters are included within the all-inclusive *American Digest System* and also in their own respective state digests.

d. State Digests

West publishes digests for 47 of the states and the District of Columbia. Only Delaware, Nevada, and Utah do not have a digest. Additionally, Virginia and West Virginia are combined in one digest, as are North Dakota and South Dakota. Even though there is no separate digest for Delaware, Nevada, or Utah, you may locate cases from these states in the appropriate regional digest (*Atlantic Digest* or *Pacific Digest*) as well as in the comprehensive *Decennial* units, which arrange the digests or summaries of the cases alphabetically by state.

The state digests are all similarly named (*Alabama Digest, Missouri Digest, Tennessee Digest*), and each digests cases from a particular state according to West's Key Number System. Moreover, each state digest includes cases decided by the lower federal courts and the United States Supreme Court that arose in that state jurisdiction, that were appealed from that state, or that pertain to that state's law. The state digests also include a Table of Cases.

There is overlap and duplication in the digest entries. For example, a digest entry for a 2000 California case will be located in the *California Digest*, the *Pacific Digest*, and the *Eleventh Decennial Digest, Part 1*.

Which digest should you use? Generally, if your issue involves California law, start with the *California Digest*. If you do not find helpful cases, perhaps because the issue is one of first impression in California, expand your search by using the *Pacific Digest* and then the *Decennial* units.

e. Specialized Digests

In addition to the digests for federal court cases, the regional digests, and the state digests, West publishes various specialized digests, each of which digests cases relating to a specific topic or from a particular court. The function of each specialized digest is fully described by its name. Some of these specialized digests are as follows:

> *West's Bankruptcy Digest*
> *West's Military Justice Digest*
> *Federal Claims Digest*
> *West's Education Law Digest*
> *United States Merit System Protection Board Digest*
> *West's Veterans Appeals Cumulative Digest*

Practice Tip

Digests

When researching, think small. Start with the smallest digest unit that will be helpful to you. For example, when researching Oregon law, start with the *Oregon Digest*. If it is not helpful, then review the *Pacific Digest*, and then the various *Decennial* units.

---

8. *Common Features of West's Digests*

a. Uniform Classification

All of West's Digests are classified to West's uniform topic and Key Number System. Thus, once a legal issue is assigned the topic and Key Number **Landlord & Tenant 166(1)**, later cases that deal with this issue will also be digested under **Landlord & Tenant 166(1)**, whether they appear in a *Decennial* unit, *West's Federal Practice Digest 4th, the South Eastern Digest*, or the *Wyoming Digest*.

b. Descriptive Word Indexes

All of West's Digests include Descriptive Word Indexes arranged in similar fashion that provide you with topic names and Key Numbers, which you then look up in the pertinent digest. The indexes use words describing facts, places, things, and legal principles from actual cases.

c. Table of Cases

All of the West Digests contain a Table of Cases by plaintiff, so you may look up a case by the plaintiff's name and obtain parallel citations, the topic names, the Key Numbers under which it has been digested, and the subsequent history of the case. Additionally, some digests also contain a Defendant-Plaintiff Table of Cases listing the defendant's name first, so if you know a case only by the defendant's name, you will still be able to locate the case. These tables are usually located after the last volumes in a set. Newer digest sets integrate the two tables, allowing you to find cases by either the plaintiff's name or the defendant's name.

d. Table of Words and Phrases

The digest sets (the *United States Supreme Court Digest*, the *Federal Practice Digests*, the regional digests, the state digests, and the specialized digests) contain a Table of Words and Phrases, which alphabetically lists words and phrases that have been construed or defined by cases. Thus, if you look up the word "conspiracy" in the *Colorado Digest*, you will be provided with citations to all of the cases decided in Colorado that define or interpret this word.

e. Supplementation

The *United States Supreme Court Digest*, the *Federal Practice Digests 3d* and *4th*, the regional digests, and the state digests are kept current by annual cumulative pocket parts and supplemental pamphlets. The *American Digest System*, of course, is supplemented by the *General Digest*. If a pocket part or supplement exists, you must consult it to locate more recent cases and to determine if any new topics have been added. Additionally, the most current information is found in digest pages located in West's reporters (in both the recent hardbound volumes and their advance sheets). Each volume includes back-of-the-book Key Number Digest sections that catalog headnotes and Key Numbers for all of the cases in that volume.

f. Cross-Referencing

Because West's Key Number System is a truly integrated research approach, other West publications will give you topic names and Key Numbers, allowing easy access into the system. Thus, West's encyclopedias (discussed in Chapter 6) *Corpus Juris Secundum* (C.J.S.) and *American Jurisprudence, Second Series* (Am. Jur. 2d) routinely provide you with topic names and Key Numbers. Similarly, West's set *American Law Reports* (discussed below) directs you to relevant topic names and Key Numbers. Finally, the Key Number System is also used in West's online legal research system called Westlaw. Thus, this cross-referencing by West continually helps you gain access to its digests to allow you to find all cases on a similar point of law.

9. *Other Digests*

Although West is the largest publisher of digests and although its Key Number System provides easy access to all reported cases relating to a particular legal issue, it is not the only publisher of digests. The best known of the non-West Digests is the *United States Supreme Court Digest, Lawyers' Edition 2d*, published by Lexis. This digest uses its own classification scheme to direct readers to cases in *United States Supreme Court Reports, Lawyers' Edition* because only West may use its copyrighted Key Number System. Use the descriptive-word approach or table of cases approach to access this digest. Because this digest is published by Lexis, it provides references to other Lexis publications.

There are also a few state digests published by companies other than West. These non-West Digests also use their own classification schemes. Nevertheless, the basic system is the same: The researcher locates topics and subtopics and uses those to find citations to relevant cases.

Practice Tip

Using the Key Number System Online

To locate cases on Westlaw using the Key Number System, you can search Westlaw's Key Number Digest Outline, browsing the list of more than 400 topics, until you find the right key number. On Westlaw, key numbers are displayed as follows: "233k166."

The topic name "Landlord & Tenant" is replaced with the topic number "233" on Westlaw. (See Figure 5-2, which shows you that the entry "Landlord & Tenant" is assigned the number "233" in West's list of topic names.) The key number "166" remains the same whether in the print world or the online world and represents cases relating to injuries to property of tenants.

Topic Name and Key Number in Print: Landlord & Tenant 166

Topic Number and Key Number on Westlaw: 233k166

The Final Wrap-Up

Using and Citing Digests

Use:	Use digests to help you find all cases from your state, region, jurisdiction, or the entire nation on a similar point of law.
Citation:	Never cite to or quote from digests. Retrieve the cases you are directed to by the digests, and cite to these.

B. *American Law Reports*

1. *Introduction*

The *American Law Reports* ("A.L.R.") is a West product that publishes selected appellate court decisions from all over the nation as well as comprehensive and objective essays relating to the legal issues raised in a case. For this reason, A.L.R. forms a logical bridge between the primary sources (cases, constitutions, and statutes), which have been discussed, and the secondary sources (encyclopedias, law review articles, treatises, and so on), which will be discussed in the next chapters. A.L.R. combines features of primary sources (in that it publishes cases) with features of secondary sources (in that it publishes articles, called "annotations," which explain and expand upon the issues raised by the cases published in A.L.R.).

West's lawyer-editors review both state and federal appellate court decisions from all over the country and publish certain selected decisions that they believe are of widespread significance to legal professionals. You may recall that West's *American Digest System* digests *all* reported cases. A.L.R., on the other hand, does not have such a goal. Its aim is to publish only leading cases rather than cases of purely local interest or those that do not represent a new trend in the law.

The significance of A.L.R. does not lie in the fact that it publishes cases. After all, if A.L.R. selects a recent California Supreme Court case to be published, that case will already be published officially in the *California Reports* and unofficially in both the *Pacific Reporter* and *California Reporter*. The true value of A.L.R. lies in its scholarly and comprehensive articles (the "annotations"), which comment on each case A.L.R. selects to publish. Often the case that is published is of average length—perhaps seven or eight pages. The annotation that explains and analyzes the issues raised in the case may exceed 150 pages. Not all annotations are this long, although all are thorough and well researched.

For example, assume A.L.R. elects to publish an appellate court case relating to the liability of a blood bank for providing tainted blood. A.L.R. will also provide an exhaustive and objective analysis of the development of this area of law and how courts in other jurisdictions are treating this subject. The editors may spend months researching this legal issue and writing the annotation, which in many respects is a scholarly research brief thoroughly examining this area of the law and looking at both sides of the issue. A.L.R.'s thorough coverage includes cases from all jurisdictions that have examined the issue, and then A.L.R. arranges these cases according to jurisdiction so you can easily find the cases of interest to you. Each volume of A.L.R. includes about ten cases and their respective ten annotations.

If you are researching a certain area of the law and an A.L.R. annotation has been written regarding your topic, you should immediately retrieve the annotation and view it as "free research," as seldom, if ever, will you have the luxury of being able to devote as much time to an

analysis of a legal topic as the A.L.R. editors have in their annotations. In fact, the publisher of A.L.R. reports that A.L.R. is quoted from and cited more often than any other secondary authority.

2. A.L.R. Organization

A.L.R. is published in eight series and consists of more than 800 volumes.

A.L.R. This set consists of 175 volumes and covers federal cases and state appellate court cases decided between 1919 and 1948.

A.L.R.2d. This set consists of 100 volumes and covers federal cases and state appellate court cases decided between 1948 and 1965.

A.L.R.3d. This set consists of 100 volumes and covers state appellate court cases decided between 1965 and 1980 and federal court cases decided between 1965 and 1969.

A.L.R.4th. This set consists of 90 volumes and covers state appellate court cases from 1980 to 1991.

A.L.R.5th. This set consists of about 120 volumes and covers state appellate court cases from 1992 to 2005.

A.L.R.6th. This set was introduced in 2005 and covers state appellate court cases from 2005 to date.

A.L.R. Federal. As its name indicates, this set exclusively covers federal court cases from 1969 to 2005. It includes approximately 200 volumes.

A.L.R. Federal 2d. This set was introduced in 2005 and covers federal court cases from 2005 to date.

As you can see, until A.L.R. Federal ("A.L.R. Fed.") was introduced in 1969, federal court cases were published and analyzed in A.L.R., A.L.R.2d, and A.L.R.3d. A.L.R. Fed. and A.L.R. Fed. 2d follow the format of the other A.L.R. series: Significant federal court cases are selected for publication, and annotations thoroughly analyze the legal topics raised in the case and discuss the treatment of this topic by other federal courts.

A.L.R. is not published in advance sheets and the first volumes that appear on the library shelves are hardbound.

3. Features of A.L.R.

The following are all current features of the *American Law Reports*. Note, however, that not all features are found in all of the eight units that make up A.L.R. The set was recently purchased by West from Lawyers Co-op, and thus newer volumes in the A.L.R. sets direct you to relevant West Digest topic names and Key Numbers and give you tips on using Westlaw, whereas earlier volumes do not because Lawyers Co-op would never direct its users to a West publication.

Cases. All of the volumes in each A.L.R. series publish contemporary cases illustrating new developments or significant changes in the law. A brief synopsis of the case (called "Summary of Decision") is provided together with headnotes summarizing the issues in the case.

Annotations. A complete essay or annotation analyzing the case and the issues therein is presented. Before 1992, the lead case precedes the article; after this date, all cases are printed at the end of each volume.

Research References. Before the annotation begins, you will be directed to additional sources relating to the topic to be discussed, including other books, law review articles, form books, encyclopedias, and texts. Additionally, you will be given suggestions for drafting electronic search queries so you can find additional information on Westlaw and Lexis, the computerized research systems. Finally, you are directed to relevant West topic names and Key Numbers so you can gain access to West's Digests to find other similar cases.

Outline. An article outline is presented that shows how the annotation is organized so you can easily locate and read the sections that may be of the most interest to you.

Index. An alphabetical word index is presented for each annotation, which references the various issues and topics discussed in the annotation, enabling you to readily locate the sections of the annotation that are relevant to the issues of most interest to you.

Table of Cases, Laws, and Rules. Because you may be more interested in the manner in which the topic under discussion has been treated in some jurisdictions than in others, you will be provided with a table showing you which sections in the annotation discuss cases and statutes from individual states. Analogous information in A.L.R. Fed. and A.L.R. Fed. 2d is found in its Table of Courts and Circuits.

Scope Note. The annotation begins with a section titled "Scope," which briefly describes the matters discussed in the annotation and then refers to earlier annotations discussing the topic that are superseded. You will also be informed what topics are not included in the annotation.

Related Annotations Section. This section directs you to other annotations that might be of interest.

Summary. A concise and useful summary of the entire annotation is presented, setting the stage for the extensive annotation that follows. Additionally, annotations often contain "practice pointers," which provide practical tips on how to handle a case dealing with the subject matter under discussion.

See Figure 5-7 for features of A.L.R.

Figure 5-7
Sample Pages from A.L.R. Annotation
Showing Features of Annotations

Annotation

WHAT CONSTITUTES DEMISE OR BAREBOAT CHARTER OF VESSEL IMPOSING ON CHARTERER LIABILITIES OF OWNER PRO HAC VICE

by

Jean F. Rydstrom, LL.B.

Annotation analyzes issues raised by leading case

I. INTRODUCTION

Annotation outline shows overall organization of annotation

Total Client-Service Library® References

Am Jur, Shipping 1st ed §§ 297–300, 326, 327, 335–337, 340

3 Am Jur Legal Forms 2d, Boats and Boating § 42:43

11 Am Jur Legal Forms, Shipping, Forms 11:1916 et seq.

ALR Digests, Shipping §§ 5, 7–8.5

US L Ed Digest, Shipping §§ 21, 24, 25

ALR Quick Index, Ships and Shipping

Federal Quick Index, Ships and Shipping

TCSL provides references to other helpful sources (not found in all volumes)

Consult POCKET PART in this volume for later cases and statutory changes

Figure 5-7 *(Continued)*

I. Introduction

§ 1. Generally

[a] Scope

Scope section describes topics to be addressed

In some circumstances, one who contracts for the use of a vessel may be held subject to the various liabilities of ownership of that vessel. This results when the contract is a "demise" or "bareboat" charter party, under which the charterer takes possession from the owner and exercises control of the vessel for a certain time. The courts call such a charterer the "owner pro hac vice" (for this occasion), and whether the charterer becomes the owner pro hac vice depends upon the terms of the agreement between the parties, and the conduct of the parties under the agreement in respect to operation of the vessel.

While the characteristics of a formal demise or bareboat charter party are by now well-established, there are situations in which liability has been asserted against the owner of a vessel, or against her charterer, or both, and resolution of the question of liability has depended upon whether the particular agreement constituted such a demise charter. It is the purpose of this annotation to collect those cases in which the courts have had to construe the terms of a contract between the parties for the use of a vessel in order to determine whether the charterer was the owner pro hac vice so that he, rather than the owner, should be charged with a particular liability usually attendant upon ownership of a vessel.

[b] Related matters

References to other pertinent annotations

Presumption and burden of proof in action for injury to or loss of ship or vessel during bailment or charter. 65 ALR2d 1228.

Express agreement by charterer to return vessel, or to return it in a specified condition, as enlarging his common-law liability. 150 ALR 269 at page 294.

Construction of "and/or" as used in charter party. 118 ALR 1367 at page 1370, 154 ALR 866.

Charterer of ship as independent contractor with relation to owner. 19 ALR 1168 at page 1208.

✦

Norris, The Law of Maritime Personal Injuries 2d ed.

§ 2. Summary and comment

[a] Generally

Brief summary of annota

Charter parties include contracts of affreightment (for the carriage of goods) and demises of the vessel herself (§ 3, infra), under which the charterer takes over possession and control of the vessel (§ 5[a], infra), mans her (§ 6, infra), and is treated as the owner for the period of the charter (§ 7, infra). These charter parties are generally in standard forms and are readily distinguishable from each other as well as from "general agency" agreements between the owners of vessels and those retained by them and having the duties of a ship's "husband" (§ 7, infra). Contracts of affreightment may be time charters[1] under which the owner of the vessel mans and navigates her but the charterer takes her carrying capacity for a certain time to go anywhere he wishes, so having the vessel under his orders as to ports to be visited and cargoes to be loaded during that time; or they may be voyage charters[2] un-

---

1. For the terms of a standard time charter, see Gilmore and Black, The Law of Admiralty p 802.

2. For the terms of a voyage charter, see the Uniform General Charter, set out in Gilmore and Black, The Law of

Figure 5-8
Sample Page from *A.L.R. Index*

NUISANCES—Cont'd

Lewdness, indecency, and obscenity —Cont'd
- porno shops or similar places disseminating obscene materials as nuisance, 58 ALR3d 1134
Life tenant's right of action for injury or damage to property, 49 ALR2d 1117
Lights and lighting, casting of light on another's premises as constituting nuisance, 5 ALR2d 705
Limitation of actions, when statute of limitations begins to run as to cause of action for nuisance based on air pollution, 19 ALR4th 456
Liquors, see group Intoxicating liquors in this topic
Litter and debris, what constitutes special injury that entitles private party to maintain action based on public nuisance—modern cases, 71 ALR4th 13
Livestock, see group Animals in this topic
Location, funeral home as private nuisance, 8 ALR4th 324
Loudspeakers
- bells, carillons, and the like as nuisance, 95 ALR3d 1268
- use of phonograph, loud-speaker, or other mechanical or electrical device for broadcasting music, advertising, or sales talk from business premises, as nuisance, 23 ALR2d 1289
Massage parlor as nuisance, 80 ALR3d 1020
Merry-go-round as nuisance, 75 ALR2d 803
Mines and Minerals (this index)
Minors, see group Children in this topic
Motel or hotel as nuisance, 24 ALR2d 571

Index references to A.L.R. annotations

Motion pictures
- drive-in theater as nuisance, 93 ALR2d 1171
- obscene motion pictures as nuisance, 50 ALR3d 969
Motor vehicles, see group Automobiles in this topic
Moving of buildings on highways as nuisance, 83 ALR2d 478

NUISANCES—Cont'd

Mufflers or similar noise-preventing devices on motor vehicles, aircraft, or boats, validity of public regulation requiring, 49 ALR2d 1202
Municipal corporations
- attractive nuisance doctrine, liability of municipality for injury to children by fire under, 27 ALR2d 1194
- dump, municipal liability for maintenance of public dump as nuisance, 52 ALR2d 1134
- rule of municipal immunity from liability for acts in performance of governmental functions as applicable to personal injury or death as result of, 56 ALR2d 1415
- swimming pools, public swimming pool as a nuisance, 49 ALR3d 652
Music and musicians
- bells, carillons, and the like as nuisance, 95 ALR3d 1268
- drive-in theater or other outdoor dramatic or musical entertainment as nuisance, 93 ALR2d 1171
- use of phonograph, loud-speaker, or other mechanical or electrical device for broadcasting music, advertising, or sales talk from business premises, as nuisance, 23 ALR2d 1289
Neighborhood, see group Residential area or neighborhood in this topic
Noise or sound
- air conditioning, existence of, and relief from, nuisance created by operation of air conditioning or ventilating equipment, 79 ALR3d 320
- bells, carillons, and the like as nuisance, 95 ALR3d 1268
- carwash as nuisance, 4 ALR4th 1308
- coalyard, noise caused by operation of, as nuisance, 8 ALR2d 419
- dogs, keeping of dogs as enjoinable nuisance, 11 ALR3d 1399
- electric generating plant or transformer station as nuisance, 4 ALR3d 902
- special injury, what constitutes special injury that entitles private party to maintain action based on public nuisance—modern cases, 71 ALR4th 13
- windmill as nuisance, 36 ALR4th 1159
- zoo as nuisance, 58 ALR3d 1126

4. *Finding A.L.R. Annotations*

a. Index or Descriptive Word Approach

A multi-volume alphabetical index called *A.L.R. Index* exists that directs you to annotations in all A.L.R. sets. Using this index is similar to using any other index. Use the descriptive word approach and look up words or phrases that describe the problem or issue you are researching, and you will be directed to the appropriate annotation. The *A.L.R. Index* is another "forgiving" index allowing you to locate an annotation by using various words or phrases rather than requiring you to reduce your legal issue to one perfect word. For example, if your research task is to determine whether an obscene movie constitutes a nuisance, you simply look up the word "nuisance" in the *A.L.R. Index*, and you will be directed to the appropriate annotation. See Figure 5-8 for a sample page from the *A.L.R. Index*. After using the *Index*, check the pocket supplement (updated quarterly) located in the back of each volume of the *A.L.R. Index*, which will provide you with references to more recent annotations.

The *A.L.R. Index* also contains a Table of Laws, Rules, and Regulations directing you to annotations that cite particular federal and state statutes, rules, and regulations. Thus, if you are researching 42 U.S.C.A. § 248 (West 2003), you can look this up in the Table of Laws, Rules, and Regulations, and you will be directed to any annotation that mentions or discusses this statute.

West also provides a one-volume softcover index called *Quick Index*, which is easy to use and directs you to annotations in A.L.R.3d, A.L.R.4th, A.L.R.5th, and A.L.R.6th. *The Quick Index* does not provide as much detail as the *A.L.R. Index*, but it is a useful starting place for many research problems. A similar index called *A.L.R. Federal Quick Index* will direct you to annotations dealing with the federal law collected in A.L.R. Fed. and A.L.R. Fed. 2d and is usually shelved after the last volume in A.L.R. Fed. 2d.

b. Digest Approach

A 22-volume set called *A.L.R. Digest* classifies A.L.R. articles according to West's Key Number System, organizing areas of the law into more than 700 topics and presenting them alphabetically. For example, if you look up the topic "nuisance" in the *A.L.R. Digest*, you will be presented with detailed summaries of the various annotations relating to this topic. Because this digest is "synched" into West's Key Number System, if you have a Key Number, you can easily locate any companion annotation (and vice versa).

c. Miscellaneous Approaches

You will see in Chapter 6 that another of West's publications, its encyclopedia Am. Jur. 2d, often refers readers to A.L.R. annotations. Similarly, when you Shepardize a case either by using conventional print volumes of *Shepard's Citations* or by using Lexis or check its validity

through West's electronic updating service called "KeyCite," as discussed in Chapter 9, you will be informed whether the case has been published in any of the A.L.R. series. If A.L.R. has published a case you are interested in, this is a signal that an exhaustive and analytical annotation will be provided on the general topic discussed in that case.

A separate volume called *Table of Cases* directs you to annotations published in A.L.R.5th and A.L.R.6th that mention any cases. Thus, if you know a case name, you can look it up in this alphabetically arranged table of cases to be directed to any page in A.L.R.5th or A.L.R.6th that mentions it.

Each volume of A.L.R.4th to 6th and A.L.R. Fed. and A.L.R. Fed. 2d includes instructions explaining how to find an A.L.R. annotation, how to use an A.L.R. annotation, and a graphic showing how to update annotations.

A.L.R. annotations are also available on Lexis and Westlaw. Updates are added weekly, making researching A.L.R. annotations timely and easy. Computerized legal research is discussed in Chapter 11.

5. *Updating A.L.R. Annotations*

If a case was decided in 1990 and an A.L.R. annotation was prepared that year analyzing that case, it is possible that a case may have been decided after 1990 that has modified or limited the original case or that a newer annotation has been prepared that discusses the changes in the law since 1990. West has developed systems to help you locate newer cases or newer annotations relating to the topic you have researched. In fact, after you have located an annotation, you *must* update it to determine if the annotation remains an accurate interpretation of the law.

> *A.L.R.* If you have read an annotation in A.L.R. (that is, an annotation written between 1919 and 1948), you update it by checking a source named *A.L.R. Blue Book of Supplemental Decisions*. These volumes are usually located close to the A.L.R. volumes. Thus, if you have read an annotation at 168 A.L.R. 204, you simply look up this reference in the *A.L.R. Blue Book of Supplemental Decisions*, and you will be informed if the annotation has been supplemented or superseded by any later annotation in any A.L.R. series. You will also be directed to cases decided after the date your annotation was published and that relate to the issues discussed in your annotation.
>
> *A.L.R.2d.* Annotations written between 1948 and 1965 and that appear in A.L.R.2d are updated by a set of books called *A.L.R.2d Later Case Service*, which are typically located near A.L.R.2d. If your annotation was located at 80 A.L.R.2d 368, you simply look up that citation in the *A.L.R.2d Later Case Service*, and you will be directed to cases decided after 80 A.L.R.2d 368 that relate to the issues discussed in that annotation. These cases will be briefly summarized so you may easily determine which cases will

be most helpful to you. The *A.L.R.2d Later Case Service* will also direct you to more recent annotations relating to the subject matter discussed by the annotation at 80 A.L.R.2d 368. *A.L.R.2d Later Case Service* is itself updated by annual cumulative pocket parts placed in the back of each volume that must be consulted.

A.L.R.3d, A.L.R.4th, A.L.R.5th, A.L.R.6th, A.L.R. Fed. and A.L.R. Fed. 2d. Updating annotations in A.L.R.3d, A.L.R.4th, A.L.R.5th, A.L.R.6th, A.L.R. Fed., and A.L.R. Fed. 2d is easier than updating annotations in A.L.R. or A.L.R.2d (which require you to use separate books) because these more recent sets are kept current by the more conventional method of updating: annual cumulative pocket-part supplements inserted in the back of each volume. After you read an annotation in A.L.R.3d, A.L.R.4th, A.L.R.5th, A.L.R.6th, A.L.R. Fed., or A.L.R. Fed. 2d, you simply turn to the pocket part in that volume, which will direct you to more recent annotations and more recent cases relating to the topic discussed by your annotation. See Figure 5-9.

Annotation History Table. Each volume in the *A.L.R. Index* contains an Annotation History Table. This table will inform you whether the annotation you have been researching has been "supplemented," meaning that additional information has been collected in a later annotation, or whether it has been "superseded," meaning that the topics discussed in your annotation have been so significantly changed by later cases that only the new annotation should be relied upon. See Figure 5-10 for a sample page from the Annotation History Table.

Latest Case Service Hotline. The front of each softcover pocket-part supplement in A.L.R.3d, A.L.R.4th, A.L.R.5th, A.L.R.6th, A.L.R. Fed. and A.L.R. Fed. 2d will provide you with a toll-free telephone number (1-800-225-7488), which you can call to obtain the most recent information regarding annotations.

Lexis and Westlaw. Annotations in A.L.R. are available on Lexis and on Westlaw. One helpful feature of locating A.L.R. annotations online is that the supplementation is completely integrated with the annotation. Using A.L.R. in conventional print form requires that you supplement and update A.L.R. annotations using either separate books or pocket parts. When you access A.L.R. online, the supplements or updates are included together with the annotation, saving you time and effort.

Figure 5-9
Updating A.L.R Annotations

Location of Annotation	Method of Updating
A.L.R.	A.L.R. Blue Book of Supplemental Decisions
A.L.R.2d	A.L.R.2d Later Case Service
A.L.R.3d	Pocket Part in each volume
A.L.R.4th	Pocket Part in each volume
A.L.R.5th	Pocket Part in each volume
A.L.R.6th	Pocket Part in each volume
A.L.R. Fed.	Pocket Part in each volume
A.L.R. Fed. 2d	Pocket Part in each volume

The Final Wrap-Up

Using and Citing A.L.R. Annotations

Use: Use A.L.R. annotations to read comprehensive analyses of various topics and to locate other primary and secondary sources.

Citation: You may cite to A.L.R. annotations in memos and court documents. Although the annotations are a secondary source, they are credible and well written. A better approach, however, is to allow the A.L.R. annotations to direct you to binding primary authorities that you then cite in your documents.

Practice Tip

Pocket Parts

When using sets of books that are updated by pocket parts (such as A.L.R. 2d, 3d, 4th, 5th, 6th, Fed., and Fed. 2d, and *Words and Phrases*), always check the pocket part. It is malpractice not to do so. Don't forget that some books are also updated by softcover supplements placed on the shelves next to them. Check these too.

C. Words and Phrases

In the mid-1980s in Southern California, two young men attended a party at which one of them consumed a great deal of alcohol. This individual, recognizing he should not drive, asked his friend to drive him home and

Figure 5-10
Sample Page from Annotation History Table

29 ALR3d 1021
Superseded 13 ALR4th 52

29 ALR3d 1407
Superseded 96 ALR3d 195
24 ALR Fed 808

29 ALR3d 1425
§ 3[a], 3[b], 3[g], 3[i] Superseded 100
ALR3d 1205

30 ALR3d 9
§ 6 Superseded 76 ALR3d 11
§ 14.1 Superseded 90 ALR4th 859
§ 16, 19[d] Superseded 67 ALR3d 308
100 ALR3d 10
100 ALR3d 940
§ 19[c] Superseded 99 ALR3d 807
99 ALR3d 1080
§ 25 Superseded 7 ALR4th 308
§ 26[c] Superseded 11 ALR4th 241
§ 29 Superseded 69 ALR3d 1162

30 ALR3d 203
§ 18 Superseded 46 ALR3d 900

30 ALR3d 1352
Superseded 110 ALR Fed 211

32 ALR3d 508
Superseded 22 ALR4th 294

32 ALR3d 1446
Superseded 20 ALR4th 63

33 ALR3d 1417
Superseded 38 ALR4th 538

34 ALR3d 1256
§ 5 Superseded 81 ALR4th 259
§ 6 Superseded 85 ALR4th 19
§ 8, 11, 13, 15 Superseded 74 ALR4th
388
§ 14 Superseded 71 ALR4th 638

35 ALR3d 412-486
§ 19 Superseded 27 ALR4th 568

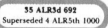
35 ALR3d 692
Superseded 4 ALR5th 1000

Indication that annotation at 35 A.L.R. 3d 692 has been superseded or replaced by a later annotation

35 ALR3d 1129
§ 3, 4 Superseded 2 ALR5th 475
§ 6 Superseded 12 ALR4th 611

35 ALR3d 1404
§ 10.5 Superseded 8 ALR5th 463

36 ALR3d 405
§ 7, 8 Superseded 85 ALR4th 979

36 ALR3d 735
Superseded 43 ALR4th 1062

36 ALR3d 820
Superseded 74 ALR4th 277

37 ALR3d 1338
Superseded 22 ALR4th 237

38 ALR3d 363
Superseded 61 ALR4th 27

39 ALR3d 222
Superseded 68 ALR4th 294

39 ALR3d 1434
Superseded 1 ALR5th 132

40 ALR3d 856
Superseded 85 ALR4th 365

41 ALR3d 455
§ 3[e, f] Superseded 91 ALR Fed 547

41 ALR3d 904
Superseded 6 ALR4th 1066

42 ALR3d 560
§ 8 Superseded 96 ALR3d 265

44 ALR3d 1108
Superseded 58 ALR4th 402

45 ALR3d 875
§ 13 Superseded 58 ALR4th 559

45 ALR3d 1181
§ 1-4 Superseded 61 ALR4th 615
§ 5-7 Superseded 61 ALR4th 464

45 ALR3d 1364
Superseded 20 ALR4th 136
24 ALR4th 508

46 ALR3d 680
Superseded 50 ALR4th 787

46 ALR3d 733
Superseded 46 ALR4th 220

46 ALR3d 900
§ 11 Superseded 58 ALR4th 902

46 ALR3d 979
§ 7[b] Superseded 35 ALR4th 225

46 ALR3d 1024
§ 5 Superseded 52 ALR4th 18

46 ALR3d 1383
Superseded 53 ALR4th 231

47 ALR3d 909
Superseded 47 ALR4th 134

47 ALR3d 971
Superseded 47 ALR4th 100

47 ALR3d 1286
Superseded 81 ALR3d 1119

49 ALR3d 915
Superseded 97 ALR3d 294

49 ALR3d 954
Superseded 49 ALR4th 1076

50 ALR3d 549
§ 4 Superseded 70 ALR4th 132

51 ALR3d 8
§ 2 [b] Superseded 65 ALR4th 346

51 ALR3d 520
Superseded 65 ALR4th 1155

52 ALR3d 636
§ 9 Superseded 87 ALR Fed 177

52 ALR3d 1289
Superseded 48 ALR4th 229

52 ALR3d 1344
Superseded 76 ALR4th 1025
79 ALR4th 171

53 ALR3d 731
Superseded 4 ALR5th 273

53 ALR3d 1285
Superseded 97 ALR3d 528

53 ALR3d 1310
Superseded 2 ALR5th 396

55 ALR3d 581
§ 9[c,d] Superseded 86 ALR3d 1116

57 ALR3d 584
§ 5 Superseded 86 ALR Fed 866

58 ALR3d 533
Superseded 45 ALR4th 949

59 ALR3d 138
Superseded 76 ALR4th 22

59 ALR3d 321
§ 5, 6, 13 Superseded 83 ALR4th 1056

slid into the passenger side of the vehicle. Before the driver could get into the car, however, the car began rolling down the hill on which it was parked. The passenger grabbed wildly for the steering wheel and managed to move his leg enough to apply the brake. Nevertheless, the car struck another vehicle, and the passenger was issued a citation by the police officer who arrived at the scene for "driving while under the influence of an alcoholic beverage," a violation of the California Vehicle Code.

The entire case depended on the interpretation of the word "driving," for if the passenger was not "driving," he could not be in violation of the statute. The definition of the word "driving" can obviously be found in any dictionary. How this word has been defined and construed in a legal sense by case law can be found in a set of books consisting of more than 100 volumes published by West called *Words and Phrases*. It arranges words and phrases in alphabetical order from Volume 1 ("A" to "Abuses") to Volume 46 (also called Book 132, "Without Heirs" to "Zygoma"), making the set as easy to use as any dictionary. *Words and Phrases* aims at providing the definition of words and phrases as interpreted by state and federal cases from 1658 to the present time. *Words and Phrases*, like digests, is thus an excellent casefinder. It contains no narrative treatment as secondary sources do, but rather focuses exclusively on locating cases. It is the last "bridge" to the secondary sources to be discussed in Chapters 6 and 7.

In the case described above, a review of the definition of the term "driving" revealed that "driving" required one to have control of a vehicle. The court hearing the case in California determined that the passenger was not "driving" under the meaning of the California statutes because he had no true ability to control the vehicle. The case was dismissed.

Once again, West will do more than merely list citations for the cases defining words such as "assessment," "clemency," "distress," "guardian," or "petition." *Words and Phrases* will provide you with a brief summary of the cases that have defined these words so you may easily determine which cases you should read in full.

Words and Phrases is kept current by annual cumulative pocket parts. Thus, once you have reviewed the cases in the main volume that define a word—for example, "guardian"—examine the pocket part to determine if newer cases have interpreted or construed the word "guardian." See Figure 5-11 for a sample page from *Words and Phrases*.

The Final Wrap-Up

Using and Citing Words and Phrases

Use:	Use *Words and Phrases* to help you find cases that have construed and defined terms, words, and phrases, whether those are legal terms or everyday terms.
Citation:	Never cite to or quote from *Words and Phrases*. Read the cases to which you are directed, and rely on and cite to these.

Figure 5-11
Sample Page from West's *Words and Phrases*

GUARDED

    Cross References

Appropriately Guarded
Sufficiently Guarded

GUARDIAN   Word to be
                                      defined

In general—p. 700
Appointed by court—p. 702
Appointed by will—p. 702
Conservator distinguished—p. 703
Natural guardians—p. 703
Next friend—p. 704
Trustee—p. 704

    Cross References   Cross
                                       references

Action to Remove a Guardian
Agent
Committee
De Facto Guardian
Discharge
Express Trust
General Guardian
Legal Guardian
Legal Representative
Natural Guardian
Next Friend
Occupant; Occupier
Owner
Quasi Guardian
Special Guardian
Trustee of Express Trust
Unsuitable Guardian
Voidable

In general

    A guardian is one who is entitled to the
custody of the person of an infant. Wilson
v. Me-ne-chas, 20 P. 468, 469, 40 Kan. 648.

    A guardian is a person upon whom the   Judicial
law imposes the duty of looking after the   definitions
pecuniary interests of his ward. Sparhawk   of
v. Allen, 21 N.H. 27, 1 Fost. 27.   "guardian"

    The term "guardian", as defined in stat-
ute governing adoptions, embraces within its
meaning the custodial guardianship resulting
from a final committal of dependent or neg-

D. Citation Form

Digests and *Words and Phrases* are used solely to locate cases. You may never cite to them. You may, however, cite to an A.L.R. annotation:

The Bluebook:	Francine L. Harris, Annotation, *The Battered Spouse Syndrome as a Defense in Manslaughter Cases*, 96 A.L.R.4th 797 (1988).
ALWD:	Francine L. Harris, *The Battered Spouse Syndrome as a Defense in Manslaughter Cases*, 96 A.L.R.4th 797 (1988).

CyberSites

http://www.ll.georgetown.edu/ guides/digests.cfm	Georgetown University Law Library offers an excellent description of using digests to find case law.
http://www.ll.georgetown.edu/ tutorials/index.cfm	Georgetown University Law Library offers a number of tutorials to teach and explain legal research. Select "Secondary Sources" for a tutorial on A.L.R.
http://www.bu.edu/lawlibrary/ research/guides/guidesatoz .html	Boston University Law Library offers several guides to legal research, including ones for digests and A.L.R.
http://lexisnexis.com/infopro/ zimmerman	"Zimmerman's Research Guide" is provided by Lexis and offers descriptions of hundreds of legal topics, including digests and A.L.R.
http://law.scu.edu/library/ legal-research-guides.cfm	Santa Clara Law School offers research guides on numerous topics, including the use of digests and A.L.R.

Writing Strategies

In any research project, remember the key distinction between primary and secondary authorities: If on point, primary authorities must be followed and are binding, while secondary authorities are persuasive at best. Therefore, you should always cite at least one primary authority to support each of your arguments. Secondary authorities such as A.L.R. annotations should be used only in conjunction with primary authorities, namely, as "extra" support for a contention.

Use some variety in the manner in which you discuss your authorities. If each paragraph begins with the phrase "In [case name] or [authority] . . ." or if each paragraph discusses one topic and always concludes with a citation, your writing will have one rigid and structured appearance. Introduce citations, paragraphs, and sentences in varying ways. This variety will enhance readability. Your project must not only be right—it must be read.

Assignment for Chapter 5

1. Use the Table of Cases for the *Eleventh Decennial Digest, Part 1*.
   a. Under which topic and key numbers is the case *Fry v. Mount* digested?
   b. Give the citation to the case in which the defendant's name is *Tueros*.

2. Use the Descriptive Word Index to the *Eleventh Decennial Digest, Part 1*.
   a. Which topic and key number discuss trespass ab initio?
   b. Look up this topic and key number in the *Eleventh Decennial Digest, Part 1*. Which 1998 Minnesota Court of Appeals case discusses this?

3. Use the Descriptive Word Index to the *Tenth Decennial Digest, Part 2*.
   a. Which topic and key number discuss actions for wrongful search or seizure?
   b. Look up this topic and key number in the *Tenth Decennial, Part 2*. Which 1995 Louisiana Court of Appeal case discusses this general topic?
   c. Which 1999 Louisiana Court of Appeal case updates this general topic?

4. Use the Descriptive Word Index to West's set *Federal Practice Digest, 4th Series*.
   a. Which topic and key number discuss whether identity of a client is subject to the attorney-client privilege?
   b. Review this topic and key number. Which 2007 case from the Ninth Circuit Court of Appeals held that a client's identity is not ordinarily privileged?
   c. Review the case. What headnote discusses this issue?

5. Use the Words and Phrases volumes for West's set *Federal Practice Digest, 4th Series*. What is the most recent federal case from the District Court of Connecticut to construe the term "indefinite"?

6. Use West's set *United States Supreme Court Digest*.
   a. What is the most recent case that interprets the phrase "disparate impact"? Give the case name only.
   b. Give the official citation to the case *State of Missouri v. Dockery* and its topic and key numbers.

7. Use the *South Eastern Digest, 2d Series*.
   a. What topic and key number discuss insanity as a ground for divorce?
   b. Review the topic and key number. What 1969 North Carolina Court of Appeals case discusses this area of law?

8. Use the *Atlantic Digest, 2d Series*.
   a. Generally, what topic and key number discuss stock dividends?
   b. Review this topic and key number. What 1998 Maryland Court of Special Appeals case discusses this topic?
   c. Use the Words and Phrases volumes for this set. What 1971 Rhode Island case construes the term "reckless driving"?
9. Use the Table of Words and Phrases for the *California Digest, 2d Series*.
   a. What case interprets the meaning of the word "clerical errors"?
   b. Under what topic and key number is the case digested?
10. Use the Descriptive Word Index for the *New York Digest, 4th Series*.
    a. Which topic and key number discuss treble damages for legal malpractice?
    b. Review this topic and key number. Which 1993 case from the Northern District of New York allowed punitive damages against an attorney when the attorney engaged in willful and intentional misrepresentation, among other conduct?
11. Use the A.L.R. Quick Index and answer the following questions.
    a. Which annotation deals with the expungement of adult criminal records for shoplifting?
    b. Review the annotation. Who is the author? What Am. Jur. Proof of Facts reference are you directed to that relates to this topic? Review Section 3[a] of this annotation. What is the most recent Pennsylvania Superior Court case that discusses that in the absence of an applicable statute, the court is without authority to grant expungement or expunction?
12. Use the A.L.R. Quick Index and answer the following questions.
    a. What annotation deals with whether First Amendment protections of privacy are afforded to blogs and bloggers?
    b. Review the annotation. Generally, if a school district employee is punished for posting a blog criticizing school personnel has a First Amendment claim been established? What section discusses this? Review the 2008 Western District of Washington case discussed. Did the employee establish that her blog was protected speech under the First Amendment?
13. Use the A.L.R. Federal Quick Index for A.L.R. Fed and A.L.R. Fed 2d.
    a. What annotation deals with the Foreign Intelligence Surveillance Act?
    b. Review Section 2.5 of this annotation. What does it provide?

14. Use A.L.R. Table of Cases for A.L.R.5th and A.L.R.6th.
    a. In which annotation is the case *Machulsky v. Hall* discussed?
    b. Review the annotation. What is the general subject matter of the annotation?
15. Use West's set *Words and Phrases*. What is the most recent case that construes the meaning of the phrase "used exclusively"? Give the case name only.

Internet Assignment for Chapter 5

1. Access West's website at http://www.west.thomson.com. Search for the most current digest for your state. Use the format "West's Ohio Digest" if you have difficulty. Review the "Summary of Contents" for your state's digest. How many volumes are dedicated to the Descriptive Word Index for your state?
2. Access Georgetown Law Library's website at http://www.ll.georgetown.edu. Select "Research Guides" (by Title) and then locate "Digests, Using—Research Guide." What are the three steps in using a digest?
3. Access Boston University's law library website and review the Research Guide for Digests. How can a researcher find cases that provide judicial definitions of words?
4. Access Santa Clara University law library's Legal Research Guides. Locate "Using a Case Digest." Which secondary sources might provide you with a West Key Number?
5. Access Zimmerman's Research Guide. What is A.L.R.?

Legal
Research

*Secondary Authorities and
Other Research Aids*

Encyclopedias, Periodicals, Treatises, and Restatements

For centuries, the most important sources of law were not judicial opinions themselves, but treatises that restated the law, such as the commentaries of Coke and Blackstone.

Hart v. Massanari, 266 F.3d 1155, 1165 (9th Cir. 2001)

A. Encyclopedias
B. Legal Periodicals
C. Texts and Treatises
D. Restatements
E. Citation Form

Chapter Overview

Section I of this text discussed the major primary legal authorities: statutes, constitutions, and cases. Administrative rules and regulations, executive orders, and treaties are discussed in Chapter 10. All other sources are secondary authorities. In general, the secondary sources serve to explain, summarize, analyze, and locate primary sources.

If you know a legal question can be answered by a statute, you can and should begin your research in one of the annotated codes by locating and reading the statute and then examining the annotations following it to find cases that interpret and construe the statute. Often, however, when presented with a legal issue, you may not know where to begin. In these instances, many experts recommend that you start your research projects by using a secondary source. Secondary sources provide you with analysis of an issue and then direct you to the relevant primary authorities.

Always keep in mind that primary sources are binding on a court or tribunal. If on point, these primary authorities must be followed. Secondary sources lack this mandatory authority. Although they are often highly respected, the secondary sources are persuasive only. A court may elect to

adopt a position set forth in a secondary authority or may reject it. Thus, your goal is always to locate relevant primary sources. The secondary authorities will assist you in this task.

The secondary authorities discussed in this chapter are those most frequently used: encyclopedias, periodicals, treatises, and Restatements. The following chapter will discuss miscellaneous secondary authorities, including opinions of attorneys general, dictionaries, directories, form books, uniform laws, looseleaf services, and jury instructions.

A. Encyclopedias

1. *Introduction*

Just as *Encyclopaedia Britannica* or *The World Book* encyclopedia are reference works that alphabetically arrange topics ostensibly covering all human knowledge, legal encyclopedias exist that alphabetically arrange topics related to legal issues, from abandonment to mortgages to zoning. Legal encyclopedias are easy to use and serve as an excellent introduction to an area of the law. In addition to providing summaries of hundreds of legal topics, encyclopedias will direct you to cases through the use of footnotes. That is, as you read about an area of the law such as corporations, deeds, or trusts, you will be referred continually to cases dealing with these areas of the law. Generally, the narrative statements or summaries of the legal topics will cover the top half of each page in the set, and the bottom half of each page will be devoted to case and other citations that support the narrative statements of the law.

One of the hallmarks of encyclopedias is their noncritical approach, meaning that encyclopedias explain the law as it is, without any critical comment or recommendations for changes in the law. Many other secondary sources offer critical opinion and suggestions for change in the law.

The treatment of legal topics in encyclopedias is general and somewhat elementary. For this reason, encyclopedias are seldom cited in court documents such as briefs. They are rather most useful for providing an overview of an area of law and sending you to cases that will provide more thorough analysis. They give you the background you need on a legal topic before reading cases. Encyclopedias are excellent casefinders (although the cases you are sent to are often criticized for being older cases) and tools for introducing you to an area of law. Moreover, they are readily available; even small law libraries usually have one, if not both, of the general sets.

It is unlikely that you will need to use both sets. Your choice of which set to use will likely depend upon convenience or habit.

There are three types of encyclopedias: general sets, local sets, and special subject sets.

2. *General or National Encyclopedias*

A general or national encyclopedia is a set that aims at discussing all of American law, civil and criminal, state and federal, substantive and procedural. That is, a discussion of false imprisonment will include a complete overview of this area of the law, including summaries of the majority and minority views, and then send you to federal cases as well as various state cases dealing with this topic.

There are two general or national encyclopedias: *Corpus Juris Secundum* (C.J.S.) published by West, and *American Jurisprudence 2d* (Am. Jur. 2d) previously published by Lawyers Co-op and now also published by West.

a. C.J.S.

C.J.S. is an encyclopedia consisting of more than 150 dark blue volumes, which discusses more than 400 different topics of the law. These topics are arranged alphabetically, making it easy for you to locate the discussions on covenants, franchises, or trial.

C.J.S. is an extremely thorough and comprehensive set, which aims at providing you with references to all cases that support any narrative statement of the law. The narrative material is articulately presented and is easy to understand. The cases that support the narrative statements are arranged in the footnotes alphabetically by state so you can readily locate cases from your jurisdiction or from neighboring states. Often, the "leading case" in an area of the law is summarized briefly for you.

Each topic begins with a thorough outline to provide you with quick access to the most pertinent parts of the discussion. Each section within a topic begins with a boldface "Black Letter" summary of the rule discussed in the section. By reading this preview of the section, you can quickly determine whether you should proceed to read the section in full.

As its very name indicates (*Corpus Juris Secundum*, meaning "Body of Law Second"), C.J.S. was preceded by an earlier set, *Corpus Juris*. Although some law libraries still maintain *Corpus Juris* (C.J.), it is unlikely you will use this older set, and you should always begin your research in C.J.S. rather than C.J.

C.J.S. contains a multi-volume index, usually found after the last volume in the set, and is kept current by annual cumulative pocket parts, which will inform you if the narrative statement of the law found in the main volume has changed and will refer you to newer cases supporting the text statement. C.J.S. also now includes a Table of Cases so you can readily find a discussion of a case if you know the case name.

Because C.J.S. is a West publication, it is a participant in West's Key Number System. As each discussion begins, in a section called "Library References," West provides you with the pertinent topic and Key Number to enable you to locate all cases on this area of the law, particularly the most recent cases, through the use of West's *General Digest*. See Figure 6-1 for a sample page from C.J.S.

Figure 6-1
Sample Page from C.J.S.

§ 182   **TRADE-MARKS, ETC.**   87   C.J.S.

§ 182.   Abandonment and Nonuser

     a. Abandonment in general
     b. Nonuser
     c. Miscellaneous acts or omissions
     d. Operation and effect
     e. Evidence

a. Abandonment in General

Summary of rule discussed in section to follow

> Trade-marks and trade-names may be lost by abandonment; abandonment requires the concurrence of both an intention to abandon and an act or omission by which such intention is carried into effect.

The title to a trade-mark or trade-name acquired by adoption and user may be lost by an abandonment of such use,[5] although abandonment is not favored.[6] An actual intention permanently to give up the use of a name or mark is necessary to constitute abandonment of it.[7] Abandonment requires the concurrence of both an intention to abandon and an act or omission by which such intention is carried into effect.[8] Abandonment must have been voluntary,[9] and an involuntary deprivation of the use of the name or mark does not in itself constitute abandonment.[10] Failure to affix a trade-mark to goods through inadvertence is not abandonment where no intention to abandon is shown;[11] nor can an undisclosed intention constitute abandonment.[12] Despite the fact that abandonment depends in a large part on the intention of the parties, an ineffective attempt to assign a trade-mark ordinarily results in its abandonment.[13]

b. Nonuser

Nonuser of a trade-name or trade-mark is not of itself an abandonment thereof; however, where intention to abandon is shown by other circumstances and conditions, nonuser is a sufficient act of relinquishment and effectuates the abandonment.

While trade-marks and trade-names may be lost through nonuser,[14] mere disuse, although for a con-

5. U.S.—Greyhound Corp. v. Rothman, D.C.Md., 84 F.Supp. 233, affirmed, C.A., 175 F.2d 893—G. F. Heublin & Bro. v. Bushmill Wine & Products Co., D.C.Pa., 55 F.Supp. 964—Bisceglia Bros. Corp. v. Fruit Industries, D.C.Pa., 20 F.Supp. 564, affirmed, C.C.A., Fruit Industries v. Bisceglia Bros. Corp., 101 F.2d 752, certiorari denied 59 S.Ct. 1043, 307 U.S. 646, 83 L.Ed. 1526.
Ky.—Corpus Juris cited in Stratton & Terstegge Co. v. Stiglitz Furnace Co., 81 S.W.2d 1, 4, 258 Ky. 678.
N.Y.—Winthrop Chemical Co. v. Blackman, 268 N.Y.S. 647, 150 Misc. 229.
Wash.—Foss v. Culbertson, 136 P.2d 711, 17 Wash.2d 610—Seattle Street Railway & Municipal Employees Relief Ass'n v. Amalgamated Ass'n of Street Electric Railway & Motor Coach Employees of America, 101 P.2d 338, 3 Wash.2d 520.
63 C.J. p 523 note 17.

6. U.S.—Du Pont Cellophane Co. v. Waxed Products Co., D.C.N.Y., 6 F. Supp. 859, modified on other grounds, C.C.A., 85 F.2d 75, certiorari denied E. I. Dupont De Nemours & Co. v. Waxed Products Co., 57 S.Ct. 194, 299 U.S. 601, 81 L.Ed. 443.

7. Ky.—Corpus Juris cited in Stratton & Terstegge Co. v. Stiglitz Furnace Co., 81 S.W.2d 1, 4, 258 Ky. 678.
N.Y.—Neva-Wet Corp. of America v. Never Wet Processing Corp., 13 N. E.2d 775, 277 N.Y. 163.
63 C.J. p 523 note 18.
Letter assuring noncontest
Where plaintiff ordering trademarked razors from manufacturer sent to lender a letter which consented to manufacturer's pledge of razors as security for loan to manufacturer and which stated that plaintiff would not assert any claims contrary to lender's right to realize on security in event of nonpayment of loan, letter was abandonment of all plaintiff's trade-mark and fair trade rights.—Stahly, Inc. v. M. H. Jacobs Co., C.A.Ill., 183 F.2d 914, certiorari denied 71 S.Ct. 239, 340 U.S. 896, 95 L.Ed. 650.

8. U.S.—E. I. DuPont De Nemours & Co. v. Celanese Corp. of America, 167 F.2d 484, 35 C.C.P.A., Patents, 1061, 3 A.L.R.2d 1213—Greyhound Corp. v. Rothman, D.C.Md., 84 F. Supp. 233, affirmed, C.A., 175 F.2d 893—Hygienic Products Co. v. Judson Dunaway Corp., D.C.N.H., 81 F. Supp. 935, vacated on other grounds, C.A., 178 F.2d 461, certiorari denied 70 S.Ct. 802, 803, 339 U. S. 948, 94 L.Ed. 1362—Colonial Radio Corp. v. Colonial Television Corp., D.C.N.Y., 78 F.Supp. 546—Coca-Cola Co. v. Dixi-Cola Laboratories, D.C.Md., 31 F.Supp. 835, modified on other grounds, C.C.A., Dixi-Cola Laboratories v. Coca-Cola Co., 117 F.2d 352, certiorari denied Coca-Cola Co. v. Dixi-Cola Laboratories, 62 S.Ct. 60, 314 U.S. 629, 86 L.Ed. 505—Bisceglia Bros. Corp. v. Fruit Industries, D.C.Pa., 20 F. Supp. 564, affirmed, C.C.A., Fruit Industries v. Bisceglia Bros. Corp., 101 F.2d 752, certiorari denied 59 S.Ct. 1043, 307 U.S. 646, 83 L.Ed. 1526—Du Pont Cellophane Co. v. Waxed Products Co., D.C.N.Y., 6 F. Supp. 859, modified on other grounds, C.C.A., 85 F.2d 75, certiorari denied E. I. Dupont De Nemours & Co. v. Waxed Products Co., 57 S.Ct. 194, 299 U.S. 601, 81 L.Ed. 443.

Ky.—Stratton & Terstegge Co. v. Stiglitz Furnace Co., 81 S.W.2d 1, 258 Ky. 678.
Wash.—Foss v. Culbertson, 136 P.2d 711, 17 Wash.2d 610.
63 C.J. p 524 note 19.
9. U.S.—E. I. Du Pont De Nemours & Co. v. Celanese Corp. of America, 167 F.2d 484, 35 C.C.P.A., Patents, 1016, 3 A.L.R. 2d 1213—DuPont Cellophane Co. v. Waxed Products Co., C.C.A.N.Y., 85 F.2d 75, certiorari denied E. I. DuPont De Nemours & Co. v. Waxed Products Co., 57 S.Ct. 194, 299 U.S. 601, 81 L.Ed. 443.
10. U.S.—Fraser v. Williams, D.C. Wis., 61 F.Supp. 763—Reconstruction Finance Corp. v. J. G. Menihan Corp., D.C.N.Y., 28 F.Supp. 920.
Md.—American-Stewart Distillery v. Stewart Distilling Co., 177 A. 473, 168 Md. 212.
Wash.—Washington Barber & Beauty Supply Co. v. Spokane Barbers' & Beauty Supply Co., 18 P.2d 499, 171 Wash. 428.
11. U.S.—Chrysler Corp. v. Trott, Cust. & Pat.App., 83 F.2d 302.
12. Wash.—Olympia Brewing Co. v. Northwest Brewing Co., 35 P.2d 104, 178 Wash. 533.
13. D.C.—Old Charter Distillery Co. v. Ooms, D.C., 73 F.Supp. 539, affirmed Continental Distilling Corp. v. Old Charter Distillery Co., 188 F.2d 614, 88 U.S.App.D.C. 73.
14. U.S.—G. F. Heublin & Bro. v. Bushmill Wine & Products Co., D. C.Pa., 55 F.Supp. 964—Bisceglia Bros. Corp. v. Fruit Industries, D. C.Pa., 20 F.Supp. 564, affirmed, C.C. A., Fruit Industries v. Bisceglia Bros. Corp., 101 F.2d 752, certiorari denied 59 S.Ct. 1043, 307 U.S. 646, 83 L.Ed. 1526.

b. Am. Jur. 2d

American Jurisprudence 2d (Am. Jur. 2d) consists of more than 100 green volumes, which discuss more than 400 areas of the law. Similar to the arrangement of C.J.S., Am. Jur. 2d arranges its topics (or "titles") alphabetically, enabling you to quickly locate the discussion you need. While C.J.S. historically has aimed at directing you to *all* cases that support any legal principle, Am. Jur. 2d will direct you to a representative cross-section of cases that support a legal principle. In fact, its editors have prided themselves on "weeding out" irrelevant, redundant, or obsolete cases and selecting the best cases that support the narrative summaries of the law. As previously stated in the Foreword in volume one of Am. Jur. 2d, "[W]e do not devote pages to listing multiple citations to mere platitudes which no court would deny or doubt."

Many of the features of Am. Jur. 2d are similar to those seen in C.J.S. That is, the narrative statements of the law are clearly and concisely presented in an easy-to-read manner. The cases you are sent to in the footnotes are often briefly summarized for you. Each topic begins with an outline to allow you to locate readily the parts of the discussion of greatest interest to you.

Am. Jur. 2d is the successor to *American Jurisprudence* (Am. Jur.), which is still in existence but seldom used due to the expanded coverage of Am. Jur. 2d. Am. Jur. 2d contains a multi-volume general index and, similar to C.J.S., is kept current by annual cumulative pocket parts, which describe changes in the law and send you to newer cases than those found in the main hardbound volumes. Like C.J.S., Am. Jur. 2d also includes research references, which lead you to other West publications, including the valuable A.L.R. annotations discussed in Chapter 5.

Am. Jur. 2d also features two unique books in its encyclopedia system:

Am. Jur. 2d Desk Book. This book serves as a legal almanac and is a unique collection of miscellaneous legal and historical information. The Desk Book contains the text of the United States Constitution, the Declaration of Independence, the United Nations Charter, and the Monroe Doctrine. Additionally, there are diagrams showing the organization of various federal agencies, such as the Departments of Labor and Transportation, and directories with addresses, telephone numbers, and website addresses of the agencies and of the United States Courts of Appeal, United States District Courts, and United States Bankruptcy Courts. Various statistical charts are given, such as suicide rates, life expectancy tables, and marriage and divorce statistics. The Desk Book also contains other miscellaneous tables, data, charts, diagrams, statistics, and glossaries of terms of interest in the legal profession. The Desk Book is updated by pocket parts.

Am. Jur. 2d New Topic Service. The New Topic Service is a looseleaf binder volume of pamphlets designed to provide you with information relating to new and emerging areas of the law, such as

Computers and the Internet, the Americans with Disabilities Act, and Terrorism. The articles discussed in the pamphlets are merged into the appropriate hardbound volumes when volumes are replaced or revised.

See Figure 6-2 for a sample page from Am. Jur. 2d.

c. Features Common to C.J.S. and Am. Jur. 2d

The following features are common to both C.J.S. and Am. Jur. 2d:

(i) Both C.J.S. and Am. Jur. 2d discuss more than 400 topics of the law, which are arranged alphabetically (Abandonment, Assault, Banks, Contracts, Deeds, and so forth).

(ii) Only C.J.S. includes an alphabetized Table of Cases (with references to more than one million cases). There is no Table of Cases for Am. Jur. 2d.

(iii) Although there is some discussion of statutes in the narrative discussions of the law, neither C.J.S. nor Am. Jur. 2d provides in-depth analyses of statutes. Detailed discussion of all state and federal statutes on each of the more than 400 areas of the law discussed would make the sets too cumbersome and unwieldy to use. In general, Am. Jur. 2d emphasizes statutory law more than C.J.S. Each set, however, includes a separate volume usually called "Table of Laws and Rules," which directs you to specific sections within each set that discuss or cite federal statutes, various rules, the *Code of Federal Regulations*, and Uniform Laws.

(iv) The narrative statements of the law are presented concisely in both sets. The style of writing is similar, and the discussion of the law is straightforward. For this reason, it cannot be said that one set is clearly superior to the other. Each set has its advantages, and your choice of which set to use will be based largely on habit and personal preference. Although the sets do have some distinguishing features, they are more alike than not, and for most purposes you should research in either C.J.S. or Am. Jur. 2d, but not both. Moreover, now that both sets are published by West, both provide you with West topics and Key Numbers and give references to other West resources.

(v) Each set contains a multivolume general index usually located after the last volume in the set, and each of the more than 400 topics or titles begins with its own table of contents or index allowing you to locate quickly the sections of the discussion of greatest interest to you.

Figure 6-2
Sample Page from Am. Jur. 2d

§ 40 EJECTMENT 25 Am Jur 2d

IX. EVIDENCE [§§ 40–43]

Research References

ALR Digest: Ejectment § 23

ALR Index: Ejectment, Eviction, and Ouster

9 Am Jur Pl & Pr Forms (Rev), Ejectment, Forms 10, 65-68

46 Am Jur POF2d 695, Intent of Parties to Ambiguous Deeds

§ 40. Burden of proof

Since, in an action in ejectment, the plaintiff must, as a general rule, recover on the strength of his own title and not on the weakness of his adversary's title,[22] when his title is disputed, the burden of proof is on the plaintiff to establish title in himself,[23] and the plaintiff in ejectment must show title to the precise land in controversy.[24] Thus, when the property was not specifically listed in the deed in question, but the deed purported to convey all property owned by the grantor not previously sold, plaintiffs had the burden to show that the specific parcel in controversy had not been previously sold.[25] But the failure of a plaintiff in an ejectment action to sustain his burden of proof does not, without more, form the basis for a determination that the defendant has good title to the property.[26]

When the plaintiff and the defendant do not trace their title to a common source,[27] the burden is on the plaintiff to trace his title to the commonwealth or to some grantor in possession,[28] or to show in some other way his legal title to the property as against the defendant.[29]

IIII *Reminder:* In addition to a legal estate in himself, the plaintiff in ejectment must, as a general rule, establish his right to the immediate possession of the premises in dispute.[30]

After the plaintiff has established a prima facie case entitling him to a

Reference to A.L.R. annotation

Annotations: Defense of adverse possession or statute of limitations as available under general denial or plea of general issue in ejectment action, 39 ALR2d 1426 § 3[a].

References to forms

Forms: Answer—Defense—Defendant in adverse possession under claim of title founded on written instrument. 9 Am Jur Pl & Pr Forms (Rev), Ejectment, Form 43.

Counterclaim or cross-complaint—Allegations—Prayer—Adverse possession—For value of improvements and taxes. 9 Am Jur Pl & Pr Forms (Rev), Ejectment, Form 47.

22. § 7.

Note alphabetical arrangement of cases by state

23. MacMillan Bloedell, Inc. v Ezell (Ala) 475 So 2d 493; Snipes v Douglass (Dist Col App) 319 A2d 326; Janoske v Friend, 261 Md 358, 275 A2d 474; Sheriff's Meadow Foundation, Inc. v Bay-Courte Edgartown, Inc., 401 Mass 267, 516 NE2d 144; King v Lee, 279 NC 100, 181 SE2d 400; Bertha v Smith, 26 Tenn App 619, 175 SW2d 41.

Since the record established that the plaintiff in ejectment had title, it was entitled to recover the property in question. Adams v Mark Oil, Inc. (Miss) 431 So 2d 489.

Plaintiff in an action for ejectment must show title, and there is no burden on the defendant to show title. K & K Farming, Inc. v Federal Intermediate Credit Bank, 237 Neb 846, 468 NW2d 99.

24. Banks v Underwood, 156 W Va 118, 190 SE2d 438.

25. Ritchey v Underwood (Ala) 479 So 2d 1223.

Practice References: Ambiguous deeds, burden of proof as to ejectment. Intent of Parties to Ambiguous Deeds, 46 Am Jur POF2d 695 § 1.

Reference to *Proof of Facts*

26. Frost v Markham, 86 NM 261, 522 P2d 808.

27. § 17.

28. § 8.

29. §§ 12 et seq.

As to title by estoppel, see §§ 15-17.

30. § 18.

746

(vi) Each topic discussion in both sets begins with a "scope" paragraph, which briefly outlines what will be discussed in the topic and what specific subjects may be treated or discussed elsewhere in the set. These "scope notes" enable you to determine rapidly whether you are researching the correct topic or whether you should direct your attention to some other topic in the set.

(vii) Both sets support the narrative discussion of the law with footnotes that provide citations to cases, although, as discussed previously, C.J.S. generally purports to send you to all cases that support any statement of the law, whereas Am. Jur. 2d will send you to selected leading cases. You will first be sent to federal cases and then to state cases, listed alphabetically by state to allow easy access to the law of selected states and jurisdictions. When presented with a statement of the law and numerous case citations that support it, there are some techniques you can use effectively to select cases when time or budget constraints prevent you from examining all cases. Select and read cases from your jurisdiction before reading cases from other jurisdictions; review newer cases before older cases; and review cases from higher courts before those from lower courts. Do not misinterpret these guidelines as saying that "old cases are bad." Old cases are *not* bad; however, when presented with numerous cases and when pressed for time, you should develop effective research strategies, and these guidelines will help you research more efficiently. After all, it may not be productive to review cases from the 1930s only to discover that the law substantially changed in the 1990s, rendering the earlier cases outmoded or invalid statements of the law.

(viii) Both sets will refer you to other sources to enhance your understanding of the law. C.J.S. has always included references to topic names and Key Numbers and the new replacement volumes of Am. Jur. 2d do as well. Both sets will refer you to pertinent and useful A.L.R. annotations, form books, and law reviews.

(ix) Each set is kept current by annual cumulative pocket parts and by replacement volumes when needed. For example, because the law relating to internal revenue and federal taxation changes so often, both C.J.S. and Am. Jur. 2d replace their tax volumes on an annual basis. Moreover, new topics, such as "Pipelines," "Products Liability," and "Energy," are often added to the sets, and these additions necessitate replacement volumes.

(x) Both C.J.S. and Am. Jur. 2d are available in CD-ROM form and on Westlaw. Only Am. Jur. 2d is available on Lexis.

(xi) Both sets are cited in the same manner: 1A C.J.S. *Actions* § 9 (2005). 1 Am. Jur. 2d *Actions* § 9 (2004).

d. Total Client-Service Library

Lawyers Co-op, the former publisher of Am. Jur. 2d, created a number of other sets of books, which it referred to as the Total Client-Service Library (TCSL), which are now published by West. The books in TCSL are designed to be used with Am. Jur. 2d, although they are not encyclopedias. See Figure 5-7 for a reference to TCSL sources. One of the sets in TCSL has already been discussed (the A.L.R. system). Most of the remaining units of the TCSL deal primarily with litigation and trial practice. Many are available in CD-ROM as well as print form (see Chapter 11). These very practical sets routinely refer you to Am. Jur. 2d and are as follows.

(1) Am. Jur. Proof of Facts

This set of more than 130 volumes (*Proof of Facts, Proof of Facts 2d,* and *Proof of Facts 3d*) is designed to assist in the preparation for and proving of facts at trials, both civil and criminal trials. The set is also available on Westlaw and in CD-ROM form. The articles in *Proof of Facts* are kept current by annual pocket parts and the addition of new volumes each year. *Proof of Facts* provides practical information regarding conducting client interviews, preparing witnesses for trial, conducting discovery, negotiating settlements, examining witnesses, and introducing evidence at trial. Each article provides background information regarding certain types of cases, for instance, personal injury, employment discrimination, or real estate litigation, and will then succinctly set forth the elements of such a case, which must be proved to prevail at trial. Sample interrogatories (written questions directed at parties in litigation) and other sample discovery forms will be provided together with model questions for examining witnesses. Each article includes a checklist providing an outline of the essential facts that must be established to prevail in a case or in asserting a defense. Diagrams and drawings that may be suitable for enlargement into poster-size courtroom exhibits are often included.

Access to this useful and practical guide to trial techniques is gained through a multivolume General Index. You only need to look up words that describe the issue or case you are researching and you will be directed to the appropriate article. That is, use the descriptive word approach to gain access to a pertinent article in this set.

(2) Am. Jur. Trials

This set of books consists of more than 100 volumes that focus on trial tactics and strategies. The articles in *Am. Jur. Trials* are authored by experienced litigators and provide a step-by-step approach to trial practice.

The first six volumes of the set, titled "Practice, Strategy, Controls," are devoted to matters common to all trials, such as fee agreements,

investigating cases, managing publicity, discovery, settlement, jury selection, and closing arguments. Information is often presented by easy-to-follow checklists, which outline steps to be taken in litigation matters.

The remaining volumes in *Am. Jur. Trials* are titled "Model Trials" and are devoted to specific kinds of cases, such as elevator accident cases, dental malpractice cases, or contact sports injury cases and will analyze in depth the strategy of conducting trials of these specific types of cases, from the first meeting with a client through appeal. The articles in *Am. Jur. Trials* are kept current by annual pocket-part supplements. West states that the articles are authored by "a virtual 'Who's Who' of the American trial bar."

Access to the articles is achieved through the General Index, which is best utilized through the descriptive word approach. To locate a pertinent article, simply look up words or phrases that describe your research problem or trial, and the General Index will direct you to the appropriate volume and page of an article. Remember to use the supplement to the General Index.

Following are examples of actual topics covered by *Am. Jur. Trials*:

- Disputed Paternity Cases
- Stockbroker Liability Litigation
- Pharmacist Malpractice
- Automobile Airbag Malfunction Litigation: Practice and Strategy

West also offers this set on Westlaw.

(3) Am. Jur. Pleading and Practice Forms Annotated

This set of books consists of more than 70 volumes that provide forms for every stage of state and federal litigation, including forms for complaints, answers, interrogatories, jury instructions, motions, and orders. These forms are extremely useful and serve as excellent "how to" guides for drafting forms. Practical checklists are included to remind you of items to be included in various forms. If your state does not have its own sets of form books, this set will provide several examples of litigation documents, which you can tailor to your state's requirements and a client's needs. If you are asked to prepare a complaint or a set of interrogatories, consult *Am. Jur. Pleading and Practice Forms Annotated*, which contains numerous forms you can use as models. Case notes indicate the proper usage for each form, and references to topic names and Key Numbers and other West resources, such as A.L.R. annotations, help you expand your research. More than 40,000 forms are included in this set, which is kept up to date by pocket part supplements. To locate a form, retrieve the multivolume General Index to the set and then use the descriptive word technique. You will then be directed to the appropriate form. The set is available in CD-ROM form and on Westlaw, enabling you to export forms directly to your word processor and print forms instantly.

(4) Am. Jur. Legal Forms 2d

There are many documents prepared in the legal profession that are not litigation-oriented. These documents are often used in connection with a client's personal or business needs, such as a will, a trust, a lease, or minutes of corporate meetings. *Am. Jur. Legal Forms 2d* provides more than 22,000 such forms together with checklists, tips, and advice for preparing various forms and documents. For example, if you are drafting a lease, *Am. Jur. Legal Forms 2d* will provide you with a list setting forth the elements required for a valid lease. As is the case with *Am. Jur. Pleading and Practice Forms Annotated*, described above, you should customize the forms you find to comply with the client's needs and your state statutes. Often, optional or alternative clauses are provided, allowing you to pick and choose clauses to construct the best document for the client. A "caution" section is included to help you avoid common errors in document drafting. Tax checkpoints and information are also included. References to West's Key Number System, A.L.R., and other West resources are provided.

As in the other sets in TCSL discussed herein, this set is kept current by the use of pocket parts, which will provide new forms, checklists, or other pertinent material. Locating an appropriate form is accomplished by using the General Index to the set and then looking up words or phrases that describe the problem or matter with which you are dealing. You will then be directed to the appropriate form. Alternatively, because the set is arranged alphabetically, you may use the topic approach and easily locate the section of interest to you. See Figure 6-3 for a sample page from *Am. Jur. Legal Forms 2d*. This set is also available in CD-ROM form and on Westlaw, allowing you to export forms to your word processor for printing and drafting.

e. Research Strategies for Using General Encyclopedias

There are several techniques used in locating the discussion of an area of law in C.J.S. or Am. Jur. 2d. The most commonly used research techniques, the descriptive word approach and the topic approach, are ones you are already familiar with and that you have used before in locating statutes in the annotated codes and cases in the digests.

(1) Descriptive Word Approach

The editors at West have selected certain words and phrases that describe the topics discussed in the encyclopedias and have listed these alphabetically in the multivolume general indexes to C.J.S. and Am. Jur. 2d. To use this approach, simply think of words or phrases that describe the issue you are researching. Look up these words in the volumes of the general index for C.J.S. or Am. Jur. 2d, and you will be directed to the appropriate topic and section. You should read the section to which you

Figure 6-3
Sample Page from *Am. Jur. Legal Forms 2d*

---

§ 87:76   **DEEDS**

Cross reference: For form of acknowledgment, see § 7:46. For forms of acknowledgments under the Uniform Recognition of Acknowledgments Act, see §§ 7:281 et seq.

§ 87:77 Connecticut—Quitclaim deed

Quitclaim deed made on __1_____, 19_2_. To all people to whom these presents come, greeting:

Know ye, that I, __3_____, of __4_____ *[address]*, City of __5_____, County of __6_____, State of __7_____, for the consideration of __8_____ Dollars ($____) received to my full satisfaction, do remise, release, and forever quitclaim unto __9_____, of __10_____ *[address]*, City of __11_____, County of __12_____, State of __13_____, his heirs, and assigns forever, all the right, title, interest, claim, and demand whatsoever that I have or ought to have in or to the following premises which are situated in the City of __14_____, County of __15_____, State of Connecticut: __16_____ *[set forth legal description of property]*.

To have and to hold the premises, with all the appurtenances, unto the releasee, his heirs, and assigns forever, so that neither I, the releasor, nor my heirs nor any other person under myself or them shall hereafter have any claim, right, or title in or to the premises or any part thereof, but therefrom I and they are by these presents forever barred and excluded.

In witness whereof, I have hereunto set my hand and seal on the day and year first above written.

[Signature]

[Seal]

[Attestation]

[Acknowledgment]

☑ **Tax Notes:**

(See Tax Notes following § 87:61)

☑ **Notes on Use:**

(See also Notes on Use following § 87:61)

Statutory reference: This form reflects generally the provisions of **Conn** Gen S § 47-5. Statutory deed forms have not been enacted in Connecticut.

Text reference: For general discussion of drafting requirements of deeds, see 23 Am Jur 2d, Deeds §§ 18–40.

Cross reference: For form of acknowledgment, see § 7:46. For forms of acknowledgments under the Uniform Recognition of Acknowledgments Act, see §§ 7:281 et seq.

(For Tax Notes and Notes on Use of form, see end of form)

are referred for the background information relating to your legal issue and then begin reading in full the cases cited in support in the footnotes. Be sure to supplement your research by checking the pocket part to ensure that the narrative statement of the law is correct and to locate cases more recent than those cited in the footnotes in the main volume. See Figure 6-4 for a sample page from an index to Am. Jur. 2d.

Because volumes in Am. Jur. 2d are replaced as needed, and because the replacement volumes may add new sections and discussions, it is possible that the General Index may send you to a section in an older volume that does not exist in a newer replacement volume. In such a case, check the Table of Parallel References found in the front of each volume. This feature is called the Correlation Table in newer volumes and is now found in the back of the hardback volumes. These tables will convert the old section number to the new section you should read in the replacement volume.

(2) *Topic Approach*

Because the more than 400 legal topics discussed in C.J.S. and Am. Jur. 2d are arranged alphabetically, it is often possible to use the topic approach successfully in locating a discussion of the area of law in which you are interested. To use the topic approach, simply think of the area of law related to your issue, for instance, Corporations, Landlord and Tenant, or Partnerships, and immediately retrieve that volume from the shelf. You should then examine the "scope note" to ensure that the specific issue you are interested in is included in the discussion to follow. The next step is to review the outline of the topic under discussion, which will refer you quickly to the appropriate section.

(3) *Table of Statutes Approach*

Because both Am. Jur. 2d and C.J.S. include a separate volume titled "Table of Laws and Rules," you can use this volume to look up specific statutes, administrative regulations, or Uniform Laws in which you are interested, and you will be directed to the appropriate volume, topic, and section within the encyclopedia set. The Table is usually shelved at the end of the set.

(4) *Table of Cases Approach*

Because C.J.S. now includes an alphabetical table of cases (found in softcover volumes shelved after the main volumes in the set), you can readily locate a discussion of a case if you know its name. Am. Jur. 2d does not include a table of cases, so this approach will not work if you are using Am. Jur. 2d.

Figure 6-4
Sample Page from General Index Update to Am. Jur. 2d

GENERAL INDEX UPDATE

JOB DISCRIMINATION —Cont'd
Pregnancy discrimination
    generally, **JobDiscrim § 135-146**   References to Sections 135–146
    benefits during pregnancy. Pregnancy benefits, above   of topic *Job Discrimination*
    fetal protection plans, selection and screening practices, **JobDiscrim § 397**
    health insurance
        benefits provided, **JobDiscrim § 709, 710**
        pregnancy benefits, above
    maternity leave, above
    no-pregnancy requirement, selection and screening practices, **JobDiscrim § 396**
    sex bias, pregnancy discrimination as, **JobDiscrim § 138**
    sick leave, **JobDiscrim § 756**
    state statutes, pregnancy leave and associated benefits, **JobDiscrim § 146**
    transfers and job assignments, **JobDiscrim § 801-804**
    weight restriction, selection and screening practices, **JobDiscrim § 435**
Preliminary injunctions. Injunctions, above
Preliminary motions
    generally, **JobDiscrim § 2265-2283**
    dismissal, motions for, above
    judgments on the pleadings, **JobDiscrim § 2279**
    more definite statement, **JobDiscrim § 2280**
    sanctions under FRCP 11, motions for, **JobDiscrim § 2282, 2283**
    stay of proceedings, **JobDiscrim § 2281**
    strike, motions to, below
    summary judgment motions, below
President of United States
    Government Employee Rights Act, presidential appointees, judicial proceedings on employment
        determinations, **JobDiscrim § 1809**
    religious discrimination, presidential appointees, prohibition, **JobDiscrim § 126**
Pretext
    generally, **JobDiscrim § 2505-2510**
    attacking employer's credibility, **JobDiscrim § 2509**
    comparison with similarly situated individuals, **JobDiscrim § 2507**
    direct evidence of discriminatory intent, **JobDiscrim § 2508**
    discharge and discipline, **JobDiscrim § 946, 947**
    disparate treatment, standard in individual case, **JobDiscrim § 2505, 2506**
    liquidated damages, **JobDiscrim § 2669**
    pattern and practice cases, **JobDiscrim § 2510**
    retaliation, **JobDiscrim § 251**
Pretrial conferences and orders
    generally, **JobDiscrim § 2312-2314**
    individual cases, **JobDiscrim § 2313**
    pretrial orders, **JobDiscrim § 2314**
    strategic considerations, **JobDiscrim § 2313**
Pretrial pleadings and motions
    generally, **JobDiscrim § 2220-2295**
    admissibility of testimony, summary judgment motions, **JobDiscrim § 2289**
    affirmative defenses in answers, **JobDiscrim § 2257**
    business necessity defense, summary judgment motions, **JobDiscrim § 2292**
    continuance of summary judgment motions, **JobDiscrim § 2290**
    counterclaims, **JobDiscrim § 2258**

Ethics Alert

Using Encyclopedias

The discussion of a topic of the law in an encyclopedia can seem complete, leading some researchers to conclude that reading the encyclopedia and consulting a few cases to which they are directed by the encyclopedia completes their research task. Remember that encyclopedias are meant to be introductions to an area of the law. Moreover, the cases to which you are directed are often somewhat older cases. Thus, you are obliged to go beyond encyclopedias when you research, and use other materials, including periodicals, Restatements, and, of course, the primary sources.

---

3. Local or State Encyclopedias

a. Introduction

You have seen that C.J.S. and Am. Jur. 2d are general encyclopedias that provide a national overview of more than 400 areas of the law. It is possible, however, that you may not need such broad coverage of a topic and are interested only in the law for your particular state. In this instance, you should consult an encyclopedia for your state, *if* one is published for your state. Not every state has its own encyclopedia. Generally, you will find encyclopedias published for the more populous states.

To determine if an encyclopedia exists for your state, check the card catalog in the law library, ask a reference librarian, or simply look at the shelves in the law library devoted to the law of your state. Carefully examine the books you find, as some state encyclopedias may label themselves "digests."

Most of the local sets are published by West (either because West was the original publisher of the set or acquired the set when it purchased Lawyers Co-op). The West sets are arranged much like C.J.S. and include references to other West resources, including A.L.R. annotations and various sets in the TCSL, such as *Am. Jur. Legal Forms 2d*. Many include references to topic names and key numbers, allowing easy access into West's digests. A few sets are published by Lexis. If your state does not have a local encyclopedia, use C.J.S. or Am. Jur. 2d and research your state's law by locating cases in the footnotes from your state. See Figure 6-5 for a list of the local encyclopedias and their publishers.

b. Features Common to State Encyclopedias

The following features are common to most state encyclopedias:

(i) *Coverage.* The discussion of the law presented will relate only to the law of a particular state, and the cases you will be directed to will be from that state and from federal courts that have construed that state's law.

(ii) *Arrangement.* The various topics covered in a state encyclopedia are arranged alphabetically. The narrative statements of the law are clearly presented, and you will be directed to cases and other authorities through the use of supporting footnotes.

(iii) *Table of Cases.* Unlike Am. Jur. 2d, which does not contain a table of cases, many local sets will contain tables that alphabetically list the cases discussed or cited in the set. Thus, if you know the name of a case in your state, you can readily locate the text discussion of it or the area of law with which it deals by using the Table of Cases.

(iv) *Table of Statutes.* Although C.J.S. and Am. Jur. 2d refer you only to selected federal statutes or uniform laws, many state encyclopedias contain a detailed table of statutes, which will direct you to a discussion or reference of a statute in which you are interested. Thus, if you are interested in Section 50 of the California Probate Code, you simply look this up in the table of statutes and you will be referred to any titles and sections in Cal. Jur. 3d where this statute is discussed.

(v) *Indexing.* Most state encyclopedias have a multi-volume general index usually located after the last volume in the set. Additionally, many encyclopedias precede the discussion of a topic with an index or outline of the various subjects discussed within the topic.

(vi) *Supplementation.* State encyclopedias are supplemented or kept up to date in the same manner as the general encyclopedias, C.J.S. and Am. Jur. 2d, that is, by cumulative pocket parts and replacement volumes.

Figure 6-5
List of Local Encyclopedias

Encyclopedias Published by West	*Encyclopedias Published by Lexis*
California Jurisprudence, Third	Illinois Jurisprudence
Florida Jurisprudence, Second	Michigan Law and Practice
Georgia Jurisprudence	Encyclopedia, Second
Illinois Law and Practice	Pennsylvania Law Encyclopedia
Indiana Law Encyclopedia	Tennessee Jurisprudence
Kentucky Jurisprudence (ceased	Michie's Jurisprudence of Virginia
in 2001)	and West Virginia
Maryland Law Encyclopedia	
Massachusetts Jurisprudence	
(ceased in 1998)	
Michigan Civil Jurisprudence	
Encyclopedia of Mississippi Law	
(successor to *Grant's Summary*	
of Mississippi Law)	
New York Jurisprudence, Second	
Ohio Jurisprudence, Third	
Summary of Pennsylvania	
Jurisprudence, Second	
South Carolina Jurisprudence	
Texas Jurisprudence, Third	

c. Research Strategies for Using State Encyclopedias

The research techniques used to access the state or local encyclopedias are as follows:

(i) *Descriptive Word Approach.* By selecting words and phrases that describe the issue you are researching and then looking these up in the general index, you will be directed to the appropriate topic and section.

(ii) *Topic Approach.* Think of the topic or area of law your issue deals with and then retrieve this specific volume from the shelf. Examine the outline of the topic preceding the narrative discussion of the law to determine the specific section you should read.

(iii) *Table of Cases Approach.* If you are interested in a discussion of a particular case from your state, look up the case name in the table of cases for your set, and you will be referred to the topic and section that discuss it.

(iv) *Table of Statutes Approach.* If you are researching a particular statute in your state, you can look it up in the table of statutes, and you will be directed to the relevant topic and section in the encyclopedia.

Practice Tip

Encyclopedias

When using legal encyclopedias, start small. Use a set for your state (if one is available) before using either of the national sets (C.J.S. or Am. Jur. 2d). Similarly, when presented with a list of cases in footnotes, read the ones from your jurisdiction before reading those from other jurisdictions.

---

4. Special Subject Encyclopedias

The encyclopedias previously discussed, C.J.S., Am. Jur. 2d, and the local encyclopedias, discuss hundreds of areas of the law. There are, however, a few encyclopedias that are devoted to just one area of the law. For example, *Fletcher Cyclopedia of the Law of Corporations* contains more than 30 volumes and discusses in depth the law relating to corporations. Check the card catalog at your law library to determine if an encyclopedia exists for a particular subject. Many of these "encyclopedias," however, are more accurately classified as treatises, as discussed in Section C of this chapter. The best research strategy to employ when using a special subject encyclopedia is the descriptive word approach. Either the encyclopedia will contain a separate index volume or the index will be found in the last volume of the set. The alphabetically arranged index will contain numerous words and phrases describing topics discussed in the set and will refer you to the appropriate volume and section of the set describing the area of law in which you are interested.

5. Summary of Encyclopedias

Encyclopedias provide excellent introductions to numerous areas of the law as well as easy-to-understand summaries of the law. You must remember, however, to read the primary sources you are directed to by the encyclopedias, as these mandatory authorities *must* be followed by courts, and the encyclopedias are merely persuasive authorities, which *may* be followed. If you are assigned a research project and you are uncertain where or how to begin, begin with an encyclopedia. Be sure this is the beginning, however, and not the end of your research, as the information presented to you in encyclopedias is generally introductory rather than analytical. Encyclopedias generally tell you what the law is,

not what it should be. Although you may readily rely on encyclopedias to provide an accurate overview of the law, you should not cite an encyclopedia as authority in any brief or project you prepare unless there are no primary authorities or no other more creditable secondary authorities, such as Restatements, treatises, or law review articles, on which to rely. Although encyclopedias are helpful resources, they are not sufficiently scholarly to serve as the sole support for an argument you advance. If you remember these guidelines, encyclopedias will serve as excellent starting points for your legal research.

The Final Wrap-Up

Using and Citing Legal Encyclopedias

Use:　　Use legal encyclopedias to "get your feet wet" and gain background information about a topic. Encyclopedias provide a general overview rather than an exhaustive treatment of a topic. Rely on the cases encyclopedias refer you to rather than on the encyclopedia itself.

Citation:　　Do not cite to encyclopedias in any court documents or other legal writings unless there are no primary authorities on which you can rely. A citation to a legal encyclopedia is a signal to a reader that your argument is so weak that there are no mandatory authorities that support your viewpoint.

B.　Legal Periodicals

1.　Introduction

Just as you might subscribe to a periodical publication such as *Time Magazine, People,* or *Sports Illustrated,* law firms, paralegals, law libraries, legal departments of businesses, and agencies subscribe to a variety of publications that are produced on a regular or periodic basis and which discuss a wide range of legal topics.

There are four broad categories of legal periodicals: publications of law schools; publications of bar associations and paralegal associations; specialized publications for those in the legal profession sharing similar interests; and legal newspapers and newsletters. All of these publications are secondary sources. Although many of them, particularly the publications of law schools, are very well respected and scholarly, they remain persuasive authorities whose views *may* be followed rather than primary or mandatory authorities that *must* be followed, if relevant.

The legal periodicals typically direct you to primary authorities (cases, statutes, regulations, and constitutions) through the use of extensive footnotes. In fact, sometimes half of each page of a law school periodical consists of footnotes. The footnotes will also direct you to other relevant secondary authorities and practice guides.

The periodical publications serve many functions. Some provide extensive analyses of legal topics; some serve to keep practitioners current on recent developments in the law; and some provide practical information relating to problems and issues facing those in the legal profession.

2. *Law School Publications*

Most law schools produce a periodical publication generally referred to as a "law review," such as the *Montana Law Review, University of Cincinnati Law Review*, or *William and Mary Law Review*, although some title their publications "journals," such as the *Emory Law Journal, Rutgers Law Journal*, and *Yale Law Journal*. These are typically published three or more times each year, initially in softcover pamphlet form and later in hardbound volumes. More than 100 law schools publish these reviews, which contain articles on a variety of legal topics. Because the law reviews are published so frequently, they often provide topical analysis of recent cases or recently enacted legislation.

The law reviews are published by law students who have been selected to write for the law review based on academic distinction or writing samples submitted to the board of editors of the law review. These editors are typically second- and third-year law students who bear the primary responsibility for editing and publishing the law review, although faculty members often advise the students. Despite the fact that the law reviews are principally the product of students, they have a high degree of respectability due to the exacting and rigorous standards of the editors. Do not equate these law reviews with the newspapers or newsletters produced at a college. The law reviews provide scholarly analysis of legal topics and are routinely cited with approval by courts. The law reviews differ greatly from encyclopedias, which are noncritical in their approach and usually focus on merely explaining the law. The law reviews offer a critical approach and often advocate reform and change in the law.

A law review usually has several sections:

(i) *Articles.* "Articles" are usually scholarly monographs or essays written by professors, judges, or practicing attorneys. Often exceeding 30 pages in length, an article examines a topic in depth. The topics explored are diverse and may range from an analysis of the California Agricultural Relations Act to a study of discrimination against handicapped persons to an examination of the legal rights of the mentally ill. Despite the fact that these articles are authored by professors, judges, and attorneys, the students on the review's board of editors edit the articles, check the accuracy of the citations in the article, and make suggestions for revisions. Shorter articles may be called "Essays."

(ii) *Comments* and *Notes*. "Comments" and "Notes" are generally shorter pieces authored by students. These shorter analyses typically examine diverse legal topics, such as warranties in the sale of goods, conflicts of interest for former government attorneys, or tort liability for defective products.

(iii) *Case Comments/Recent Cases/Recent Developments*. This section is also authored by students and examines the impact of a recent case or newly enacted legislation.

(iv) *Book Reviews*. Just as *Newsweek Magazine* reviews recent works of fiction in each issue, some law reviews contain a section that reviews books or texts relating to legal issues, such as *Hazardous Product Litigation, Handbook of the Law of Antitrust,* or *Justice by Consent: Plea Bargains in the American Courthouse.* A critical analysis of the book is provided together with an identification of the publisher and the price of the book.

Almost all law schools publish one of these general types of law reviews; that is, a review containing articles on a variety of topics, such as corporate law, civil law, criminal law, trademark law, and so forth. In addition to these general law reviews, many law schools also provide other law reviews devoted to a specific area, such as international law or civil rights. For example, Boston College Law School publishes the following reviews in addition to its general law review, called the *Boston College Law Review*:

Boston College Environmental Affairs Law Review
Boston College International and Comparative Law Review
Boston College Third World Law Journal

Often law reviews are arranged alphabetically in a law library, so that the *Akron Law Review* is followed by the *Alabama Law Review*, which is then followed by the *Alaska Law Review*, and so forth, making the task of locating a law review easy and efficient. Law reviews are cited as follows:

Article (*The Bluebook* for practitioners and *ALWD*): Anne L. Alstott, *Equal Opportunity and Inheritance Taxation*, 121 Harv. L. Rev. 469 (2007).
Signed Student Note (*The Bluebook*): Sylvia T. Parker, Note, *Debtors' Rights to Debt Counseling*, 98 Tul. L. Rev. 1604 (1988).
Signed Student Note (*ALWD*): Sylvia T. Parker, Student Author, *Debtors' Rights to Debt Counseling*, 98 Tul. L. Rev. 1604 (1988).

See Figure 6-6 for a sample cover of a law review.

Figure 6-6
Sample Cover from Law Review

Fall 2007   Volume 44 Number 1

CALIFORNIA
WESTERN
LAW REVIEW

CALIFORNIA WESTERN
SCHOOL OF LAW | San Diego

ARTICLES

AMERICAN REPARATIONS THEORY AND PRACTICE AT THE
    CROSSROADS   *Eric K. Yamamoto,*
                                                    Sandra Hye Yun Kim
                                                    & Abigail M. Holden

XBRL AND THE SEC: HOW THE COMMISSION USES
    INTERACTIVE DATA TO INVESTIGATE ILLEGAL STOCK
    OPTIONS BACKDATING AND WHAT INTERACTIVE DATA
    MEANS FOR THE FUTURE OF FEDERAL SECURITIES LAW
    ENFORCEMENT   *Susan M. Brunka*

UNITED STATES V. FORT AND THE FUTURE OF WORK
    PRODUCT IN CRIMINAL DISCOVERY   *Anne Shaver*

"WHO ARE THOSE GUYS?": THE RESULTS OF A SURVEY
    STUDYING THE INFORMATION LITERACY OF INCOMING
    LAW STUDENTS   *Ian Gallacher*

OPPORTUNITY LOST: HOW LAW SCHOOL DISAPPOINTS LAW
    STUDENTS, THE PUBLIC, AND THE LEGAL PROFESSION   *Jason M. Dolin*

COMMENTS

POWERED BY GREASE: THE CASE FOR STRAIGHT VEGETABLE
    OIL IN THE NEW FUEL ECONOMY   *Robert Scott Norman*

A TANGLED SITUATION OF GENDER DISCRIMINATION:
    IN THE FACE OF AN INEFFECTIVE ANTIDISCRIMINATION
    RULE AND CHALLENGES FOR WOMEN IN LAW FIRMS—
    WHAT IS THE NEXT STEP TO PROMOTE GENDER
    DIVERSITY IN THE LEGAL PROFESSION?   *Lea E. Delossantos*

3. Bar Association and Paralegal Association Publications

Each state and the District of Columbia has a bar association. Usually an attorney cannot practice law in a jurisdiction without becoming a member of that state's bar association. The dues paid to the association often fund various legal programs such as services for indigents, disciplinary proceedings, and the periodical publication of a journal for the members of the bar. Some bar associations publish monthly journals while others publish every other month. The *ABA Journal* is a very professional-looking publication that is sent to members of the American Bar Association each month.

These publications usually offer a very practical approach to practicing law in a jurisdiction and feature articles on ethics; changes in local court rules, local cases, or local legislation; provide human interest biographies of judges or practitioners in the state; publish lists of attorneys who have been suspended or disbarred from the practice of law; and review books, software, and other materials of interest to practitioners. These journals usually resemble nonlegal publications such as *Time Magazine* or *Newsweek Magazine*. Their size (8½" × 11") is the same as the popular press publications, and they often feature a photograph of a judge or lawyer on a glossy front page. A table of contents is included as well as a variety of advertisements for products and services aimed at the legal profession, such as office furniture, software programs, seminars, and books.

The articles published in these bar association publications are far more practical in their approach than the academic articles published in law reviews. For example, an article in a law review relating to child support might well examine the development and evolution of cases and legislation in that area of the law, analyze the social policies served by child support, and advocate for reform, if needed. In contrast, an article in a bar association publication might be titled "How to Calculate Child Support" and would provide no such scholarly analysis, but rather would focus on the practical aspects of the process of calculating the amount of child support a noncustodial parent should pay.

Just as there are state bar associations, many local jurisdictions will often have city or county bar associations, such as the Bar Association of Montgomery County, Maryland. Many specialized groups may form local associations, such as the Women's Bar Association of the District of Columbia. These associations also produce periodical publications: Some are pamphlets, and others are informal newsletters or flyers. Generally, these publications are very practical and informal in approach. Articles relate solely to local matters, such as changes to the local rules of court, and they often serve to inform the membership of educational or social functions. Job postings are often included.

Figure 6-7
Sample Cover from Bar Association Periodical

In summary, the publications of bar associations tend to focus on practical guidelines for law practice. It is unlikely that you would conduct substantive research using these publications. It is far more likely that your use of these publications will be aimed at keeping you current on legal issues facing your jurisdiction. See Figure 6-7 for a sample cover from a bar association periodical.

Just as bar associations are composed of attorneys and produce a periodical publication, there are associations composed of paralegals that produce periodical publications. For example, the National Association of Legal Assistants publishes a bi-monthly journal called *Facts & Findings.* Similarly, the National Federation of Paralegal Associations issues a bimonthly publication called the *National Paralegal Reporter.* Other periodicals and journals exist for paralegals and are published independently of any association. One of the better-known publications is *Legal Assistant Today* (see http://www.legalassistanttoday.com). These publications publish articles of interest to paralegals, such as information on licensing and certification issues; articles offering practical approaches to paralegal tasks such as interviewing, document control, and discovery; and data on average salaries and benefits. Advertisements feature books, software, and seminars. If you belong to a local paralegal association, you will see that its newsletter will undoubtedly contain announcements of job vacancies.

Similar in approach to the journals and periodicals published by bar associations, the journals and periodicals published for paralegals share a practical focus and are oriented to providing useful information to practicing paralegals.

4. *Specialized Publications*

Just as individuals who are interested in fashion might subscribe to *Vogue,* individuals interested in home decorating might subscribe to *Better Homes and Gardens,* and individuals interested in aviation and defense might subscribe to *Aviation Week & Space Technology,* legal practitioners who have an interest in a specialized area of the law might subscribe to a specialized periodical. Thus, numerous journals and periodicals exist to provide practitioners who focus on a certain area of the law with the information of most interest to them. The numerous specialized periodicals vary in their approach, with some being more analytical and academic, such as the *SMU Science and Technology Law Review,* which explores legal issues in intellectual property, science, and technology, and others being more practical in approach such as the *Medical Trial Technique Quarterly,* which contains useful articles on topics such as how to cross-examine an expert cardiologist or how effectively to review medical records. Other examples of specialized periodicals are the *American Bankruptcy Law Journal,* the *Entertainment and Sports Lawyer,* the *Transportation Law Journal,* the *Practical Real Estate Lawyer,* and the *Journal of Taxation.* Practitioners interested in keeping current with developments in these fields subscribe to these publications.

Additionally, many periodicals are published for individuals who may share common interests, such as the *Chicano-Latino Law Review*, the *Journal of Catholic Legal Studies*, the *Women's Rights Law Reporter*, the *National Black Law Journal*, and the *American Indian Law Review*. Some periodicals focus on the interplay between law and other fields of endeavor, such as the *Journal of Health Law and Policy*, the *Journal of Law & Politics*, and the *Ecology Law Quarterly*. These journals or periodicals focus on issues that have implications for the legal field as well as some other field.

5. *Legal Newspapers and Newsletters*

In large cities such as New York and Los Angeles, you will find daily legal newspapers such as the *New York Law Journal* and the *Los Angeles Daily Journal*. These newspapers, published every weekday, contain the text of recent appellate cases from the state, publish the court calendar or docket for the courts in that locality, and contain articles of general interest to lawyers and paralegals practicing in that jurisdiction. They usually contain extensive classified advertisements and serve as a useful source of job announcements and vacancies.

Other smaller metropolitan areas, such as San Diego, often publish a newspaper every weekday that combines information about law with general business information. Thus, the *San Diego Daily Transcript* contains the court docket, information, and articles of interest to those in the legal profession as well as information relating to bankruptcy filings, the recording of mechanics' liens, and bidding dates for various construction projects in the area.

Some legal newspapers do not restrict their coverage to any locality; they are national in scope, such as the *National Law Journal*, which is published weekly. This weekly newspaper for legal professionals includes articles on a variety of legal topics including ethics, law school admissions, and criminal law matters. Additionally, recent state court and federal court decisions are highlighted. Professional announcements such as those relating to law firm mergers or formations and advertisements for career opportunities are included. Many legal publications offer both print and online subscriptions. For example, *The American Lawyer*, a monthly magazine, offers content in both conventional print form and online. Legal materials available on the Internet are discussed in Chapter 12.

In addition to legal newspapers, more than 2,000 legal and law-related newsletters are published in the United States. Some of these newsletters are one-page bulletins; others are multiple-page newsletters; and others are looseleaf reporting services, which are stored in ringed binders. Some newsletters offer only short articles, while others provide in-depth analysis of legal issues. Examples of these newsletters include *Jury Trials and Tribulations* (published twice per month and containing

summaries of civil jury trials in Florida) and *Bank Bailout Litigation News* (a monthly publication reporting on bank litigation and related banking matters).

6. *How to Locate Periodical Articles*

Although each issue of a law review, bar association publication, specialized periodical, or legal newspaper will contain its own table of contents, it would be extremely ineffective to conduct research by retrieving each of these hundreds of publications and scanning its table of contents in the hope that you will eventually stumble upon an article of interest to you. To locate an article in a periodical publication, you must consult one of several published indexes that will direct you to articles published in periodicals. There are several well-known indexes you can use.

a. *Index to Legal Periodicals & Books*

If you think back to the research you did for high school or college term papers, you may recall using *The Readers' Guide to Periodical Literature*, which directed you to articles in the popular press such as *Time Magazine*, *U.S. News & World Report*, or *Forbes Magazine*. Your technique was to think of words and phrases that described the topic you were researching and look those up in *The Readers' Guide*. You would then be directed to a relevant article in a particular issue of a periodical.

The *Index to Legal Periodicals & Books* is substantially similar in format to *The Readers' Guide*. In fact, both are published by the same company, so if you have used *The Readers' Guide*, you will be comfortable using the *Index to Legal Periodicals & Books* ("I.L.P."). I.L.P. indexes articles and books published in the United States, Australia, Canada, Great Britain, Ireland, and New Zealand. The articles, case notes, and biographies must be at least two pages in length to be included. I.L.P. is initially published in softcover monthly pamphlets that are later bound in hardcover volumes.

To locate an article you may use any of the following techniques:

(i) *Subject-Author Approach.* The subject approach calls for you to think of words describing the topic you are interested in, such as bankruptcy, divorce, or emotional distress. Look for these words in I.L.P.'s alphabetically arranged Subject and Author Index. You will then be directed to periodicals that have published articles regarding this topic. Alternatively, if you happen to know that author Deborah L. Rhode is an expert on gender bias, you can look up "Rhode" in this Index and you will be directed to articles written by her.

(ii) *Table of Cases Approach.* If you want to read articles that have discussed certain cases, such as *Bush v. Gore*, you can look up this case name in I.L.P.'s Table of Cases. Case names can be

located by either the plaintiff's or the defendant's name. You will then be directed to pertinent periodical articles written about this case.

(iii) *Table of Statutes Approach.* If you are interested in whether any articles have analyzed a particular statute, you can look the statute up in I.L.P.'s Table of Statutes, which will direct you to articles discussing this statute.

(iv) *Book Review Approach.* If you are looking for a review of a certain book, locate the title of the book in the Book Review Index in I.L.P., and you will be directed to periodicals that have reviewed this book.

See Figure 6-8 for sample pages from I.L.P.

Because I.L.P. is cumulated on a monthly, quarterly, and annual basis, you may need to check several pamphlets and several bound volumes for the years you are interested in. Thus, if you are interested in nuisances, you may have to check the softcover pamphlets for this year, looking up "nuisance" in each one, and then continue by looking up "nuisance" in last year's bound volume of I.L.P., then the previous year's bound volume of I.L.P., and so forth. Although this process is a bit time-consuming, it will yield great rewards, as I.L.P. indexes more than 1,000 periodicals and dates back to 1908. When using I.L.P., start with the current issues and work backward in time.

I.L.P. is also available in CD-ROM. If your library has purchased I.L.P. in CD-ROM, this will make your search easier by eliminating the need to look at several pamphlets or volumes of the set. An online or web-accessible version of I.L.P. is called "Index to Legal Periodicals Full Text." It is updated on a monthly basis and encompasses everything included in I.L.P. since 1982. Researching using the online index is much easier than using the conventional I.L.P. print volumes because the online version is completely cumulative. Once you type in the appropriate search terms (topic, author, case, and so forth) you will be directed to all pertinent articles from 1983 until last month. I.L.P. is also available on Lexis and Westlaw.

b. *Current Law Index, Legal Resources Index, and LegalTrac*

Current Law Index. ("C.L.I.") is a comprehensive index of more than 900 legal periodicals from the United States, Australia, Canada, Ireland, New Zealand, and the United Kingdom. C.L.I. is published in monthly softcover pamphlets that are cumulated each quarter and then again at year end. C.L.I. indexes all articles from the periodicals it covers, unlike I.L.P., which does not index shorter articles. There are four approaches to locating articles in C.L.I.

Figure 6-8
Sample Pages from *Index to Legal Periodicals & Books*

Coal
The Phasing Constraint: Who May Request Relief and When? J. O. Moreno. *Journal of Transportation Law, Logistics and Policy* v71 no4 p419-33 2004

Coalbed methane
Northern Plains Resource Council v. Fidelity Exploration and Development Co., 325 F.3d 1155 (9th Cir. 2003), cert. denied, 124 S. Ct. 434 (2003). *Environmental Law* v34 no3 p845-8 Summ 2004

Coastal zone
New Zealand
Coastal Management and the Environmental Compensation Challenge. S. Turner. *New Zealand Journal of Environmental Law* v4 p181-200 2000

Coburn, David H.
Rail Construction Cases: Environmental and Other Issues. *Journal of Transportation Law, Logistics and Policy* v71 no4 p379-92 2004

Cochrane, Drew J.
Disability Law in Wisconsin Workplaces. *Wisconsin Lawyer* v77 no10 p8-10, 53-5 O 2004

Codes and codification
History
Special Issue on Comparative Legal History. *The Journal of Legal History* v25 no2 p99-194 Ag 2004
Two Early Codes, the Ten Commandments and the Twelve Tables: Causes and Consequences. A. Watson. *The Journal of Legal History* v25 no2 p129-49 Ag 2004
Canada
Of Codifications, the Uniform Trust Code and Quebec Trusts: Lessons for Common Law Canada? A. Grenon. *Estates Trusts & Pensions Journal* v23 no3 p237-65 Ag 2004
China
Structures of Three Major Civil Code Projets in Today's China. G. Xu. *Tulane European and Civil Law Forum* v19 p37-56 2004
European Union countries
European Code of Contract [Special Issue] *Edinburgh Law Review* v8 Special Issue p I-IX, 1-89 2004
Explanatory Note [European Code of Contract: Special Issue] H. McGregor. *Edinburgh Law Review* v8 Special Issue p IX-X 2004
Introduction [European Code of Contract: Special Issue] J. A. D. H. Hope of Craighead. *Edinburgh Law Review* v8 Special Issue p I-VIII 2004
The Optional European Code on the Basis of the Acquis Communautaire—Starting Point and Trends. S. Grundmann. *European Law Journal* v10 no6 p698-711 N 2004
The Politics of a European Civil Code. M. W. Hesselink. *European Law Journal* v10 no6 p675-97 N 2004
France
Thoughts from a Scottish Perspective on the Bicentenary of the French Civil Code. E. Clive. *Edinburgh Law Review* v8 no3 p415-20 S 2004
Great Britain
Codification in England: The Need to Move from an Ideological to a Functional Approach—A Bridge too Far? E. Steiner. *Statute Law Review* v25 no3 p209-22 2004
Louisiana
Interpretations of the Louisiana Civil Codes, 1808-1840: The Failure of the Preliminary Title. T. W. Tucker. *Tulane European and Civil Law Forum* v19 p57-182 2004
Mapping Society Through Law: Louisiana Civil Law Recodified. D. Gruning. *Tulane European and Civil Law Forum* v19 p1-36 2004
Middle East
History
Wrongs and Responsibility in Pre-Roman Law. D. Ibbetson. *The Journal of Legal History* v25 no2 p99-127 Ag 2004
Québec (Province)
German influences
Imported Books, Imported Ideas: Reading European Jurisprudence in Mid-Nineteenth-Century Quebec. E. H. Reiter. *Law and History Review* v22 no3 p445-92 Fall 2004
History
Imported Books, Imported Ideas: Reading European Jurisprudence in Mid-Nineteenth-Century Quebec. E. H. Reiter. *Law and History Review* v22 no3 p445-92 Fall 2004
Scotland
Thoughts from a Scottish Perspective on the Bicentenary of the French Civil Code. E. Clive. *Edinburgh Law Review* v8 no3 p415-20 S 2004

Codicils *See* Wills
Coerced treatment *See* Involuntary treatment
Cogeneration of electric power *See* Electricity
Cohabitation *See* Unmarried couples

Cohen, Adam I.
Rules 33 and 34: Defining E-documents and the Form of Production. Panel Discussion. *Fordham Law Review* v73 no1 p33-51 O 2004

Cohen, Elizabeth J.
The Meaning of 'Forever'. *American Bar Association Journal* v90 p28 N 2004

Cohen, Fred
Silence of the experts. *Trial* v40 no10 p20-2, 24-5, 27-9 O 2004

Cohen, Jerry
The new Massachusetts Business Corporation Act, chapter 127, Acts of 2003. *Massachusetts Law Review* v88 no4 p213-17 Sp 2004

Colb, Sherry F.   → Entry by author
A World without Privacy: Why Property Does Not Define the Limits of the Right against Unreasonable Searches and Seizures. *Michigan Law Review* v102 no5 p889-903 Mr 2004

Collateral estoppel
See also
Res judicata
The U.N. Convention on the Recognition and Enforcement of Foreign Arbitral Awards and Issue Preclusion: A Traditional Collateral Estoppel Determination. S. M. Sudol, student author. *University of Pittsburgh Law Review* v65 no4 p931-50 Summ 2004

Collecting societies (Copyright)
European Union countries
Collective hysteria? A. Hobson. *Copyright World* no143 p15-17 S 2004

Collective bargaining
See also
Employee benefits
Promoting Labour Rights in International Financial Institutions and Trade Regimes. P. Barnacle. *Saskatchewan Law Review* v67 no2 p609-36 2004
Canada
ILO Freedom of Association Principles as Basic Canadian Human Rights: Promises to Keep. K. Norman. *Saskatchewan Law Review* v67 no2 p591-608 2004
"Labour is Not a Commodity": The Supreme Court of Canada and the Freedom of Association. J. Fudge. *Saskatchewan Law Review* v67 no2 p425-52 2004

Collective security *See* International security
Collectivism
Yugoslavia
The Fate of the Yugoslav Model: A Case Against Legal Conformity. K. Medjad. *The American Journal of Comparative Law* v52 no1 p287-319 Wint 2004

College admissions *See* Colleges and universities—Admission
College and university libraries
Exclusion or Efficient Pricing? The "Big Deal" Bundling of Academic Journals. A. S. Edlin, D. L. Rubinfeld. *Antitrust Law Journal* v72 no1 p119-57 2004

College athletics *See* College sports
College sports   → Entry by topic
With the First Pick in the 2004 NFL Draft, the San Diego Chargers Select . . . ?: A Rule of Reason Analysis of What the National Football League Should Have Argued in Regards to a Challenge of Its Special Draft Eligibility Rules under Section 1 of the Sherman Act. J. M. Ganderson, student author. *University of Miami Business Law Review* v12 no1/2 p1-33 Spr/Summer 2004

Colleges and universities
See also
Academic freedom
College sports
Colleges and universities—Finance
Fraternities and sororities
Law schools
Does the Tax Law Discriminate against the Majority of American Children?: The Downside of Our Progressive Rate Structure and Unbalanced Incentives for Higher Education. L. B. Snyder. *San Diego Law Review* v41 no3 p1311-35 Summ 2004
Dreaming of an Equal Future for Immigrant Children: Federal and State Initiatives to Improve Undocumented Students' Access to Postsecondary Education. A. Stevenson, student author. *Arizona Law Review* v46 no3 p551-80 Fall 2004
Admission
Litigators and Communities Working Together: Grutter v. Bollinger and the New Civil Rights Movement. M. Massie. *Berkeley Women's Law Journal* v19 no2 p318-23 2004
Finance
Florida
Monetary and Regulatory Hobbling: The Acquisition of Real Property by Public Institutions of Higher Education in Florida. C. L. Zeiner. *University of Miami Business Law Review* v12 no1/2 p103-68 Spr/Summer 2004

Figure 6-8 *(Continued)*

TABLE OF CASES

A

Acuff-Rose Music, Inc.; Campbell v., 114 S. Ct. 1164 (1994)
The Trademark Reporter v94 no5 p979-1016 S/October 2004

Adam; New Angel Court Ltd. v., [2004] S.T.C. 779
British Tax Review no4 p297-303 2004

Adams; Troyer v., 77 P.3d 83 (Haw. 2003)
University of Hawaii Law Review v26 no1 p275-307 Wint 2003

ADI Ltd.; Advanced Data Initegratiton Pty. Ltd. v., [2004] F.C.A. 731
Intellectual Property Forum no58 p48-50 S 2004

Admin. Rev. Bd.; Williams v., 376 F.3d 471 (5th Cir. 2004)
Louisiana Bar Journal v52 no3 p221-3 O/November 2004

Advanced Data Initegratiton Pty. Ltd. v. ADI Ltd., [2004] F.C.A. 731
Intellectual Property Forum no58 p48-50 S 2004

Agnew v. Comm'r of Inland Revenue, [2001] 3 W.L.R. 454
The Law Quarterly Review v120 p533-41 O 2004

Agrobin, Inc. v. Botanica Dev. Assocs., 861 So. 2d 445 (Fla. 2003)
The Florida Bar Journal v78 no9 p7 O 2004

Air Foyle Ltd. v. Center Capital Ltd., [2002] E.W.H.C. 2535
Lloyd's Maritime and Commercial Law Quarterly v2004 pt3 p303-12 Ag 2004

Ake v. Oklahoma, 105 S. Ct. 1087 (1985)
Cornell Law Review v89 no6 p1305-419 S 2004

Aley v. North Shore City Council, [1998] N.Z.R.M.A. 361
New Zealand Journal of Environmental Law v2 p274-9 1998

Alpine Land & Reservoir Co.; United States v., 340 F.3d 903 (9th Cir. 2003)
Environmental Law v34 no3 p900-2 Summ 2004

Alpine land & Reservoir Co.; United States v., 341 F.3d 1172 (9th Cir. 2003)
Environmental Law v34 no3 p902-5 Summ 2004

Alsey Valley Alliance v. Dep't of Commerce, 358 F.3d 1181 (9th Cir. 2004)
Environmental Law v34 no3 p926-8 Summ 2004

Am. Family Ins. Co.; De Ruyter v., 2004 WI App. 162 (2004)
Wisconsin Lawyer v77 no10 p46-7 O 2004

Ameritech Corp., Inc.; Lugo v., 629 N.W.2d 384 (Mich. 2001)
The Michigan Bar Journal v83 no10 p32-3 O 2004

Anchor Inn Seafood Rest.; Montgomery County v., 374 Md. 327 (2003)
University of Baltimore Journal of Environmental Law v11 no2 p231-4 Spr 2004

Andre M., In re, 88 P.3d 552 (Ariz. 2003)
Arizona Law Review v46 no3 p601-6 Fall 2004

Andrx Corp.; Kos Pharms., Inc. v., 369 F.3d 700 (3rd Cir. 2004)
Intellectual Property Forum no58 p84 S 2004

Anson; State v., 2004 WI App. 155 (2004)
Wisconsin Lawyer v77 no10 p45-6 O 2004

Antoine; United States v., 318 F.3d 919 (9th Cir. 2003)
Environmental Law v34 no3 p929-59 Summ 2004

AOL Time Warner Inc.; Noah v., 261 F. Supp. 2d 532 (E.D. Va. 2003)
Albany Law Journal of Science & Technology v14 no3 p775-97 2004

Apotex Inc.; Ciba-Geigy Can. Ltd. v., [1992] 44 C.P.R.3d 289
The Trademark Reporter v94 no5 p1086-104 S/October 2004

Arai Helmet; Howerton v., 597 S.E.2d 674 (N.C. 2004)
Trial v40 no10 p80, 82 O 2004

Arriba Soft Corp.; Kelly v., 336 F.3d 811 (9th Cir. 2003)
Jurimetrics v44 no4 p487-98 Summ 2004

Ashcroft; Eldred v., 123 S. Ct. 769 (2003)
Albany Law Journal of Science & Technology v14 no2 p309-57 2004
Jurimetrics v44 no4 p465-86 Summ 2004

Entry by case name

Atkins v. Virginia, 122 S. Ct. 2242 (2002)
American University Journal of Gender, Social Policy & the Law v12 no2 p361-89 2004
George Mason Law Review v11 no4 p805-81 Summ 2003

Authorson v. Canada, [2001] 58 O.R.3d 417
The Canadian Bar Review (Online) v82 no2 59165 bytes Ag 2003

Auton v. British Columbia, [2002] 6 B.C.L.R.4th 201
The Canadian Bar Review (Online) v82 no2 133790 bytes Ag 2003

B

B. v. Minister for Immigration & Multicultural & Indigenous Affairs, [2004] 206 A.L.R. 130
Australian Journal of Family Law v18 no2 p193-207 Jl 2004

Badgley; Ctr. for Biological Diversity v., 335 F.3d 1097 (9th Cir. 2003)
Environmental Law v34 no3 p876-7 Summ 2004

Bagri; R. v., [2004] 240 D.L.R.4th 147
The Criminal Law Quarterly v49 no2 p137-9 S 2004

Bagri; R. v., [2004] 240 D.L.R.4th 81
The Criminal Law Quarterly v49 no2 p136-7 S 2004

Bakewell Mgmt. Ltd. v. Brandwood, [2004] 2 All E.R. 305
Australian Law Journal v78 no10 p650-1 O 2004

Bank One, NA v. Borse, 812 N.E.2d 1021 (Ill. 2004)
Illinois Bar Journal v92 no10 p514 O 2004

Barker v. Saint Gobain Pipelines plc, [2004] E.W.C.A. Civ. 545
The Law Quarterly Review v120 p566-71 O 2004

Bartel v. Rural Mut. Ins. Co., 2004 WI App. 166 (2004)
Wisconsin Lawyer v77 no10 p43-4 O 2004

Bazzle; Green Tree Fin. Corp. v., 123 S. Ct. 2402 (2003)
North Carolina Law Review v82 no6 p2128-41 S 2004

Bd. of Educ.; Brown v., 74 S. Ct. 686 (1954)
Berkeley Women's Law Journal v19 no2 p210-332 2004
Berkeley Women's Law Journal v19 no2 p210-14 2004
Berkeley Women's Law Journal v19 no2 p276-82 2004
Berkeley Women's Law Journal v19 no2 p302-7 2004
Berkeley Women's Law Journal v19 no2 p324-32 2004
St. John's Law Review v78 no3 p515-67 Summ 2004
Virginia Law Review v90 no6 p1537-751 O 2004
Virginia Law Review v90 no6 p1537-77 O 2004
Virginia Law Review v90 no6 p1579-99 O 2004
Virginia Law Review v90 no6 p1601-12 O 2004
Virginia Law Review v90 no6 p1613-33 O 2004
Virginia Law Review v90 no6 p1635-47 O 2004
Virginia Law Review v90 no6 p1649-65 O 2004
Virginia Law Review v90 no6 p1667-91 O 2004
Virginia Law Review v90 no6 p1693-720 O 2004
Virginia Law Review v90 no6 p1721-51 O 2004

Bd. of Regents of the Univ. of Ga.; Lapides v., 122 S. Ct. 456 (2002)
San Diego Law Review v41 no3 p1057-98 Summ 2004

Beals v. Saldanha, [2003] 3 S.C.R. 416
Lloyd's Maritime and Commercial Law Quarterly v2004 pt3 p288-92 Ag 2004

Beder v. Cleveland Browns, Inc., 717 N.E.2d 716 (Ohio 1998)
Villanova Sports & Entertainment Law Journal v11 no2 p411-43 2004

Behrns v. Behrns, 835 A.2d 68 (Conn. 2003)
American Journal of Family Law v18 no3 p179 Fall 2004

Behrns; Behrns v., 835 A.2d 68 (Conn. 2003)
American Journal of Family Law v18 no3 p179 Fall 2004

Benchmark Bldg. Supplies Ltd. v. Mitre 10 (N. Z.) Ltd., [2004] 1 N.Z.L.R. 26
European Intellectual Property Review v26 no10 p N173-N174 O 2004

Bennett v. Human Rights & Equal Opportunity Comm'n, [2003] 204 A.L.R. 119
Australian Journal of Labour Law v17 no2 p197-203 O 2004

Big Meadows Grazing Ass'n v. United States ex. rel. Veneman, 344 F.3d 940 (9th Cir. 2003)
Environmental Law v34 no3 p917-19 Summ 2004

Blakely v. Washington, 124 S. Ct. 2531 (2004)
Louisiana Bar Journal v52 no3 p213-15 O/November 2004

(i) *Subject Approach.* The Subject Index lists entries alphabetically by subject name, such as contracts, franchises, or health insurance. By looking up the subject you are interested in you will be referred to a relevant periodical article.

(ii) *Author-Book Title Approach.* The Author-Book Title Index alphabetically indexes articles written by certain authors, such as Laurence H. Tribe. When you look up the author's name, you will be directed to periodicals containing articles by that author. This section also indexes book reviews by title of the book and the author's name.

(iii) *Table of Cases Approach.* If you are interested in cases that have been the focus of an article, you can look up the case in the Table of Cases by either the plaintiff's name or the defendant's name, and you will be directed to pertinent periodical articles.

(iv) *Table of Statutes Approach.* If a statute has been analyzed in depth in an article, you can locate it in the alphabetically arranged Table of Statutes, which will refer you to any article that has concentrated on treating that statute.

C.L.I. is also available on Lexis and Westlaw as "Legal Resources Index." Finally, C.L.I. is available through the Internet as a product called LegalTrac. LegalTrac is an online index to the articles found in C.L.I. together with articles found in business and general interest periodicals. Many law libraries subscribe to LegalTrac, allowing you desktop computer access so you can easily search for and locate relevant articles by subject matter, author name, or key words. Because LegalTrac is a web-based product, it is continuously updated.

One of the advantages of Legal Resources Index (or LegalTrac) over C.L.I. has to do with cumulation. C.L.I. (the conventional printed set) is arranged very similarly to I.L.P., thus requiring you to look at several pamphlets and hardbound volumes to find articles of interest to you. Because the electronic version of C.L.I., Legal Resources Index (and its Internet version, LegalTrac) is completely cumulative, once you locate the topic, author, case, or subject you are interested in, you will be presented with all relevant articles written since 1980, the year this index was created.

C.L.I. has one drawback: It was created in 1980, and therefore its coverage does not extend to any article written before 1980. To locate articles before 1980, use I.L.P. or one of the other indexes discussed herein.

c. Other Indexes

Although I.L.P. and C.L.I. (and their online versions) are the most comprehensive indexes because they send you to hundreds of periodicals, there are several other indexes you should know about that may help you locate periodical articles.

(i) *Index to Periodical Articles Related to Law*. The indexes previously discussed will direct you only to legal publications. It is possible, however, that articles related to law may appear in the popular press such as *Time Magazine*, *U.S. News & World Report*, or *Fortune*. The *Index to Periodical Articles Related to Law*, published quarterly, will direct you to such articles through its indexes arranged alphabetically by subject and author.

(ii) *Index to Foreign Legal Periodicals*. You may have noticed that I.L.P. and C.L.I. index articles from common law countries. The *Index to Foreign Legal Periodicals* will direct you to periodical articles from countries other than the United States and the British Commonwealth. This index is issued quarterly and indexes articles longer than four pages that relate to international law, comparative law, and the municipal law of non-common law countries. Access is gained through an alphabetically arranged subject index (which is in English), a geographical index, and an index by author. If you are interested in reviewing articles written in foreign countries, the *Index to Foreign Legal Periodicals* is an excellent starting place.

(iii) *Current Index to Legal Periodicals*. This weekly publication provides very rapid access to recent periodical articles.

(iv) *Jones-Chipman Index to Legal Periodicals*. As you know, I.L.P. will index and direct you to periodical articles written since 1908. To locate articles written before 1908, consult this index.

d. Special Subject Indexes

There are numerous other indexes, some of which index articles related to specific legal topics such as the following: *Criminal Justice Periodicals Index*; *Index to Federal Tax Articles*; and *Index to Canadian Legal Periodical Literature*. These indexes typically are arranged alphabetically by subject.

e. Other Finding Techniques

Often you may be directed to a particular law review or periodical article in the course of your research. For example, following a statute in U.S.C.S. is a "Research Guide," which typically recommends various A.L.R. annotations and law review articles relating to the statute you are researching. (See Figure 3-5.) These references to law reviews are found in U.S.C.A. and other annotated codes as well. Similarly, when you Shepardize or KeyCite cases or statutes, you will be directed to periodical articles written about them. Additionally, after you locate an article, you

can Shepardize or KeyCite it and be directed to later cases and other articles that have mentioned the article you have read, leading to an ever-increasing collection of legal resources. Shepardizing and KeyCiting are discussed in Chapter 9. Periodical articles can also be located through Lexis and Westlaw, the computer-assisted research systems discussed in Chapter 11. Searching may be done by citation, author name, or key words.

Finally, an astounding number of articles are available on the Internet. For example, the University Law Review Project (http://www .lawreview.org) offers links to hundreds of law reviews and periodicals. The site allows searching for journal articles by key words inserted into a search box at the Internet site. Moreover, many law reviews have their own websites. For example, the Duke Law Journal offers the full text of each published issue online (at www.law.duke.edu/journals/dlj). Moreover, a number of specialty journals exist only on the Internet, as discussed in Chapter 12.

7. *Summary of Legal Periodicals*

All of the legal periodicals (law reviews, bar association and paralegal journals, specialized periodicals, and newspapers and newsletters) are secondary authorities. A court is not required to adhere to the view expressed in a periodical, though it may be persuaded to do so. Periodicals range in approach from the scholarly law reviews to the more practical bar association and paralegal association journals to brief bulletins and newsletters. Locating periodical articles is best accomplished by using one of the separately published comprehensive indexes such as the *Index to Legal Periodicals* or the *Current Law Index*. You may use the descriptive word approach, the author approach, the table of cases approach, or table of statutes approach to locate relevant articles. Consider using LegalTrac, the online index of legal periodicals since 1980, or Lexis or Westlaw to avoid having to examine several volumes.

Generally, if a periodical article has been written about a topic of interest to you, you should view it as "free research," because the article may well examine the area of law in depth, comparing and contrasting cases in various jurisdictions and analyzing all facets of the topic, thus reducing your research tasks. You can then Shepardize or KeyCite the article to locate newer articles or cases that mention the article you have read. Although periodical publications are not primary authorities, they are frequently cited (especially the authoritative academic journal articles) in briefs and court documents to clarify and lend support to primary authorities such as cases.

The Final Wrap-Up

Using and Citing Periodicals

Use:	Use legal periodicals to obtain a thorough analysis of a legal topic. Many periodicals (especially the law reviews) are highly regarded and will provide extensive information about a subject you are researching. Legal periodicals can provide a fresh and creative approach and are published more quickly than other books so they can offer information on current developments in the law.
Citation:	Although all periodicals are secondary sources, some are highly persuasive. As you gain familiarity in reading cases, you will obtain greater insight into which periodicals are the most credible. Use *Shepard's Law Review Citations* to direct you to cases that cite your periodical with approval. You should primarily cite to the academic law reviews and special subject journals. Avoid citing to bar association publications, newspapers, and newsletters, which you should use to keep current in your field.

C. Texts and Treatises

1. Introduction

Texts written by legal scholars that focus on one topic of the law are referred to as treatises. Treatises comment upon and analyze an area of law. They are secondary sources. The authors may be academics or practicing attorneys. Treatises vary a great deal in scope and depth. A treatise may be a one-volume work on a fairly narrow legal topic, such as *The Law of Water Rights and Resources*, or an analysis of a newly emerging area of the law, such as *Animals and the Law: A Sourcebook*, or an extremely well-known multivolume set on a broader topic, such as the 25-volume set *Collier on Bankruptcy, 15th Edition Revised*.

As you have seen, an encyclopedia typically examines hundreds of topics of law from abandonment to zoning and provides introductory information on these topics. Treatises, on the other hand, are devoted to one area of the law and usually examine it in depth. For example, if you were to read all of the sections of C.J.S. on Contracts, you would be presented with approximately 2,000 pages of material. If you were to review a well-known treatise on contracts, titled *Williston on Contracts*, you would be presented with more than 30 volumes and approximately 18,000 pages of material.

You may recall that encyclopedias are noncritical summaries of the law, meaning that the information you are given merely summarizes the law relating to that topic. Treatises, however, may be "critical" in the

sense that they may boldly criticize case law or question the logic of a judicial opinion. For example, the following language is found in 6 J. Thomas McCarthy, *McCarthy on Trademarks and Unfair Competition* § 32:156 (4th ed. 2004): "In the author's opinion, the Third Circuit's view is a peculiar, illogical, and unsupported misreading of the § 33(b) [trademark] incontestability provisions." Such a statement is far different in tone from that of the encyclopedias, which merely present the law without any such disapproving commentary.

The narrative statements found in a treatise are typically more analytical than those found in encyclopedias. One feature treatises share in common with encyclopedias, however, is that they serve as casefinders. The format of many treatises is also similar to that of encyclopedias: Narrative discussions of the law are found on the top portion of each page with citations to cases and other authorities located through the use of supporting footnotes in the lower portion of each page. One particular type of treatise is called a "hornbook," a one-volume text devoted to one area of the law, such as contracts, torts, or real property. Hornbooks are primarily designed for use by law students and offer broad and fairly academic coverage of a topic. Cases discussed tend to be the landmark cases in the field.

Remember that texts and treatises come in many forms: from one volume to a multivolume set; from analysis of very narrow topics, such as *Standby and Commercial Letters of Credit*, to analysis of a broader topic, such as criminal law, corporations, or bankruptcy; from recently published analysis of newer legal topics, such as *Americans with Disabilities Act Handbook*, to the extremely well-known and respected treatise, *Prosser and Keeton on Torts*, which was first published in 1941 and is still the premier authority on torts; and from volumes that are in hardbound form to looseleaf binders to softcover pamphlets. Many treatises are now available in CD-ROM form and on Lexis and Westlaw. See Figure 6-9 for a sample page from a treatise.

In fact, if you are unsure what "category" a law book falls in, it is probably a treatise. No matter what kind of treatise it may be, however, it remains a secondary authority, meaning that although a court may choose to follow a position advanced by a well-known and highly regarded treatise such as John H. Wigmore's *Wigmore on Evidence*, the court is not required to do so. Courts have, however, cited numerous treatises with approval, and some treatises such as *Prosser and Keeton on Torts* have been cited thousands of times, partly because of the caliber of the authors. You should feel free to rely upon and quote from treatises in memoranda and briefs that you prepare so long as you also have at least one "on point" primary authority to support your position. If you are unsure as to the credibility of the treatise, you can consult a source titled *Who's Who in American Law* and review the author's credentials. Alternatively, you can look up the author's name in the *Index to Legal Periodicals & Books* or in the *Current Law Index* to determine if the author has produced other writings on this topic, or you can ask the reference librarians in your law library for their opinions on the expertise of the author and the treatise's overall reputation in the courts. Finally, if the treatise has been published in multiple editions, this is a signal it is widely accepted and used.

Figure 6-9
Sample Page from a Treatise

value of the estate without weakening his or her control over the business.

§ 2.06 Corporation Taxed as Partnership: S Corporation.

A closely held enterprise with a simple capital structure can obtain the limited liability for shareholders that comes with corporate status and the conduit or "pass through" tax effect of a partnership by incorporating and electing to be taxed under Subchapter S of the Internal Revenue Code.[1] Speaking broadly, a corporation that elects this tax status (an "S Corporation"—formerly referred to as a "Subchapter S" corporation) is not subject to federal tax on its income; instead, its income or losses are considered for tax purposes to be the income or losses of its shareholders. Most small enterprises will find it advantageous to incorporate and elect Subchapter S status or the use the LLC form described in the next section because of the possibility of double taxation previously discussed.

To be eligible to elect the tax status provided in Subchapter S a company must: be a domestic corporation with only one class of stock

---

In earlier years, the risk was great that the entire income of a family partnership would be taxed to the partner who actively participated in earning the income. See Lusthaus v. Commissioner, 327 US 293, 90 L Ed 679, 66 S Ct 539 (1946); Commissioner v. Tower, 327 US 280, 90 L Ed 670, 66 S Ct 532 (1946). The chance that a family partnership can be used successfully to split up family income is better since Commissioner v. Culbertson, 337 US 733, 93 L Ed 1659, 69 S Ct 1210 (1949). But a family partnership still involves risks. See Packel, The Next Inning of Family Partnerships, 100 U Pa L Rev 153 (1951).

See also Estate of Gilman v. Commissioner, 547 F2d 32 (CA2 1976) (court upheld a settlor's setting up for his sons an inter vivos trust of a controlling block of a corporation's voting stock). For a discussion of the implications of the Gilman decision on estate planning for officers and shareholders of closely held corporations, see Pressmen, Effect of Tax Court's Gilman Decision on Estate Planning for the Close Corporation, 44 J Tax'n 160 (1976).

But see Foglesong v. Commissioner, 621 F2d 865 (CA7 1980), revg 35 TCM 1309 (1976) (discussing the IRS' power to reallocate income and other items under IRC Sec 482) (discussing the IRS' power to reallocate income and other items under IRC Sec 482).

See Hood, Kurtz & Shors, Closely Held Corporations in Business and Estate Planning (1982); Comment, Advising the Family Business Owner in Succession Planning: The "Daughter Option," 36 Clev St L Rev 597 (1988).

[Section 2.06]

[1] IRC §§ 1361–1379. See generally Eustice & Kuntz, Federal Income Taxation of S Corporations.

Practice Tip

Books and Treatises

Treatises are primarily found in conventional book or print format, although many are available on Lexis and Westlaw. They are not available on the Internet (as are cases, statutes, constitutions, and other legal authorities).

---

2. *Common Features of Treatises*

Treatises usually share the following features:

    (i) *Format.* Treatises are essentially "expert opinions" on one topic of the law. The analysis of the law is presented in narrative form, and readers are usually directed to cases and other authorities through the use of footnotes. Generally, treatises are arranged by chapters and then by sections or paragraphs within those chapters.

    (ii) *Index.* An index to the treatise consisting of an alphabetical arrangement of the topics, subjects, words, and phrases discussed in the treatise will be located in the last volume of the set or as a separate index volume after the last volume in the set.

    (iii) *Table of Contents.* A table of contents will usually be presented in the front of each volume showing how the discussion of this area of the law is arranged by chapter.

    (iv) *Table of Cases.* Most treatises contain an alphabetically arranged table of cases so you may readily locate a discussion of a certain case.

    (v) *Table of Statutes.* Some treatises contain a table of statutes so you can locate the discussion of a certain statute.

    (vi) *Appendices.* Many treatises include the text of statutes and regulations that are relevant to the area of law covered by the treatise. For example, the appendix to the treatise *McCarthy on the Law of Trademarks and Unfair Competition* includes the full text of the United States Trademark Act.

    (vii) *Updating.* Most treatises are maintained by the traditional method of updating of legal books: an annual cumulative pocket part. If the treatise consists of looseleaf binders, it will be updated by periodically issued supplements placed in the binder or by replacement pages sent to the law library on a periodic basis. The law library will be provided with a set of instructions to, for example, "replace old page 41 with new

page 41 and discard old page 41." Some treatises are kept current by a separate softcover supplement, which will be placed next to the main volume(s) of the treatises. Check the copyright year of any hardback volumes to make sure they are current.

You must *always* check the pocket part or supplement to determine if the narrative statement of the law presented in the main hardbound volume is still an accurate statement of the law and to locate cases and other authorities more current than those found in the footnotes in the hardbound volume.

3. *Use of Treatises*

Although encyclopedias serve as excellent introductions to a wide variety of legal topics, a treatise usually serves as a thorough examination of one area of the law. Although you are discouraged from citing encyclopedias, you are encouraged to cite treatises, particularly those with established reputations. For a comprehensive analysis of a topic with thoughtful evaluation of case law, consult a treatise.

If you are unsure whether a treatise has been written regarding the topic of law you are interested in, you can try various strategies:

(i) Check the catalog in your law library for your topic (bankruptcy, contracts, trusts, and so forth). The catalog, which may be in print or online, will list every treatise the library contains relating to this topic and will direct you to the particular "stack" where the treatise is located.

(ii) You can also go directly to the shelves where the books relating to this area of law are maintained. For example, all of the books relating to criminal law are generally shelved together, and all of the books relating to real property are generally shelved together. By skimming the titles of the books in the stacks and randomly inspecting these books, you may well "stumble upon" an excellent treatise.

(iii) Ask the reference librarian for assistance. Even if your law library does not contain the treatise you need, you may be able to obtain one via an interlibrary transfer, that is, a "loan" from another library.

(iv) Because many treatises are in high demand, check the reserve room at your law library, which may keep the most frequently consulted treatises on reserve.

4. *Research Strategies for Using Treatises*

There are several alternative methods you can use to locate a discussion in a treatise on an issue in which you are interested. Most of these are familiar to you.

(i) *Descriptive Word Approach.* This method simply calls for you to select a word or phrase describing the issue you are researching and locate this word or phrase in the index. The index will then direct you to the appropriate volume, paragraph, or section in the treatise.

     For example, if the index directs you to **4:12,** this is a signal for you to review section 12 of chapter 4 of the set. As always, the descriptive word approach is the most reliable research technique for beginning researchers.

(ii) *Topic Approach.* If you are relatively familiar with the treatise or subject matter you are researching, you may elect to bypass the index to the treatise and proceed directly to the table of contents. You would then scan the list of chapter titles and subdivisions and proceed immediately to the appropriate chapter.

(iii) *Table of Cases / Table of Statutes Approach.* If you are interested in locating a discussion of a particular case, you can look up the case name in the alphabetically arranged table of cases, which will direct you to that section of the treatise that analyzes, evaluates, and discusses that case. Similarly, if your treatise includes a table of statutes, it will direct you to text discussion of specific statutes.

(iv) *Other Approaches.* It is possible that you may be referred to a treatise through another source entirely. Thus, if you are reading a pertinent case on an issue you are researching and the case comments favorably and relies upon a treatise, you should then retrieve and examine the cited treatise. Similarly, other sources (encyclopedias, periodical articles, and library references found in U.S.C.A. and U.S.C.S.) may refer you to a treatise. See Figure 3-5 for references in U.S.C.S. to treatises on patents.

The Final Wrap-Up

Using and Citing Treatises

Use: Use treatises to find detailed and usually scholarly information on one topic of the law. A treatise will explain the law, provide commentary and practice tips, and will refer you to other authorities, generally through the use of footnotes. Use a treatise to obtain more in-depth analysis of a topic than that given by an encyclopedia and to help you locate cases on point.

Citation: Many treatises are highly regarded. In fact, some are so influential that they are known only by an author's name, such as "Prosser" or "Williston," and are given great credence in their respective fields. You may freely cite to treatises so long as you also cite to primary authority for your argument. Thus, cite a treatise to lend additional support to your argument, not as the sole support for your argument.

D. Restatements

1. Introduction

In 1923, a group of law scholars established the American Law Institute, which is composed of judges, law professors, eminent lawyers, and other jurists. The Institute was created in response to the ever-increasing volume of court decisions, which the members of the Institute believed produced both uncertainty and complexity in the law. The Institute's solution to this mass of irreconcilable and ambiguous case law was to "present an orderly statement of the general common law of the United States."

To accomplish this task, legal scholars called "Reporters" were appointed by the Institute for various subject matters such as torts, property, contracts, conflict of laws, and agency. Individuals are selected for membership in the Institute on the basis of their professional accomplishments and their commitment to improving the law. Membership is currently limited to 3,000, with the United States Supreme Court Justices and chief judges of all United States Courts of Appeal and highest state courts as ex officio members. Each Reporter, together with his or her assistants and advisors, was assigned to one of these topics of the law to analyze carefully the assigned subject matter and thoroughly examine pertinent cases.

Figure 6-10
Chart of Restatements

Topic	Series
Agency	First,* Second,* and Third
Conflict of Laws	First* and Second
Contracts	First* and Second
Foreign Relations Law of the United States	Second* and Third
Judgments	First* and Second
Law Governing Lawyers	Third
Property (includes volumes for Landlord & Tenant, Wills and Other Donative Transfers, Mortgages, and Servitudes)	First, Second, and Third
Restitution	First
Suretyship and Guaranty**	Third
Torts (includes volumes for Apportionment of Liability, Products Liability, and Liability for Physical and Emotional Harm)	First,* Second, and Third
Trusts	First,* Second, and Third
Unfair Competition	Third
(**Replaces superseded Restatement of Security)	(*The original work on this subject is now out of print and has been replaced by the current series.)

The Reporters then prepared and presented preliminary drafts, restating American common law in a terse and nearly rule-like fashion, to the Institute. Various revisions to the drafts were made, and ultimately the Institute directed the publications of various final "Restatements," such as Restatement of Torts, Restatement of Contracts, and Restatement of Agency. Restatements do not exist for all areas of the law but only for selected topics. See Figure 6-10 for a chart of Restatements. Some of the Restatements have been updated or newly created in a second or third series, such as Restatement (Second) of Torts, Restatement (Second) of Contracts, and Restatement (Third) of Foreign Relations Law of the United States. For example, the Restatement (Third) of the Law Governing Lawyers (dealing with regulation of the legal profession and the attorney-client relationship) was created in 2000 in its third series with no preceding first or second edition or series. All of the series of Restatements are subject to rigorous drafting and review, making them highly credible and reputable. The Institute has several projects in draft status, including the proposed Restatement (Third) of Employment Law.

The goal of the Institute, to restate American case law in a clear and certain manner, has largely been accomplished due to the authority and repute of the members of the Institute. Although the initial focus of the Institute was merely to restate American case law in an unambiguous manner, the current emphasis is on predicting what courts might do in the future as well as restating what courts have held in the past.

2. *Arrangement of Restatements*

Each Restatement typically consists of two to six volumes. Each volume is arranged in chapters, and the chapters are arranged in titles and numbered sections. Each section relates a principle of the law in clear straightforward language printed in bold typeface. These Restatement sections are followed by "comments" and "illustrations." The comments section provides general analysis of the legal principle previously given. The illustrations section exemplifies the legal principle by providing articulately written examples demonstrating the application of the principle. The Reporter's Notes then complete each section by providing general discussion and explanations, together with references to cases that support the Restatement position. Each Restatement includes updating volumes called "Appendix" volumes that direct you to cases that have cited Restatement sections. Recent volumes include cross-references to West's Key Number System and A.L.R. annotations.

The Restatements are updated by pocket parts, cumulative annual supplements, and the Interim Case Citation service, which are semiannual pamphlets providing Restatement citations more recent than those covered in the current pocket part. See Figure 6-11 for a sample page from Restatement (Second) of Torts.

3. *Research Strategies*

To locate a pertinent Restatement provision, you can use either the descriptive word approach or the topic approach. To use the descriptive word approach, consult the alphabetically arranged index to the pertinent Restatement, generally found in the last volume of the Restatement set. Look up words or phrases that describe your research problem and you will be directed to the appropriate section of the Restatement.

To use the topic approach, simply scan the table of contents located in the first volume of any Restatement volume. By quickly viewing the table of contents you will be sent to the pertinent section.

Because there is an alphabetical Table of Cases for the newer Restatements, you can use this to locate pertinent Restatement sections. The Table of Cases is usually located in the Index volume for the relevant Restatement. Look up case names in the Table of Cases and you will be directed to particular Restatement sections that mention or cite those cases.

Figure 6-11
Sample Page from Restatement (Second) of
Torts Copyright 1965 by the American Law Institute.
Reprinted with permission. All rights reserved.

§ 312   TORTS, SECOND   Ch. 12

as a secondary consequence illness or other bodily harm, such as a miscarriage, by its internal operation upon the well-being of the other. As to acts which are negligent because they are intended or likely to cause an emotional disturbance which the actor should recognize as likely so to affect the action of the other or a third person as to cause bodily harm to the other, see § 303. As to acts which threaten bodily harm, but result in emotional disturbance alone, see § 435 A. As to acts which otherwise threaten bodily harm, but result in such harm only through emotional disturbance, see § 436. As to emotional disturbance as an element of damages where there is other harm, see § 905.

§ 312. Emotional Distress Intended

If the actor intentionally and unreasonably subjects another to emotional distress which he should recognize as likely to result in illness or other bodily harm, he is subject to liability to the other for an illness or other bodily harm of which the distress is a legal cause,

(a) although the actor has no intention of inflicting such harm, and

(b) irrespective of whether the act is directed against the other or a third person.

See Reporter's Notes.

Comment:

a. The rule stated in this Section does not give protection to mental and emotional tranquillity in itself. In general, as stated in § 436 A, there is no liability where the actor's conduct inflicts only emotional distress, without resulting bodily harm or any other invasion of the owner's interests. The emotional disturbance is important only in so far as its existence involves a risk of bodily harm, and as affecting the damages which may be recovered if the bodily harm is sustained. See § 905.

b. There is a considerable degree of duplication between the rule stated in this Section and that stated in § 46, which deals with the intentional or reckless infliction of emotional distress by extreme and outrageous conduct. In most of the cases in which the intentional infliction of emotional distress results in foreseeable bodily harm, the known risk of such bodily harm is sufficient in itself to make the act one of extreme out-

See Appendix for Reporter's Notes, Court Citations, and Cross References

Alternatively, you may be directed to a Restatement section in the course of your research. For example, a case you may be reading may refer to a Restatement section. In this instance you should review the section mentioned.

Be sure to check the Appendix volume for the section you are researching and the pocket part therein to determine if the Restatement section has been modified or limited and to locate cases supporting the Restatement section.

Finally, the Restatements are available on CD-ROM from West and on Lexis and Westlaw.

Practice Tip

Restatements

- **At present, there is no one index to all of the Restatements. To conduct research in the Restatements, you must know which is the pertinent Restatement for your research task.**
- **The American Law Institute has now published** *Concise Restatement of Torts, Concise Restatement of the Law Governing Lawyers,* **and** *Concise Restatement of Property,* **one-volume softcover books that include the most critical information from their respective Restatements and which are meant to be especially helpful for students. Check to see if your library has any of these concise Restatements.**

---

4. *Effect of Restatements*

The Restatements are a secondary source. Courts are not required to adopt or follow the Restatement positions. Nevertheless, the Restatements have been cited in cases more than 165,000 times. In fact, to determine if a Restatement section you are interested in has been cited by a court, you can consult the pocket parts and Appendix volumes of the individual Restatements. For more recent cases, you can also review Shepard's *Restatement of the Law Citations*, which will direct you to federal and state cases, as well as other authorities, that have cited Restatement provisions. Finally, if you are viewing a Restatement provision on Lexis or Westlaw, you may Shepardize or KeyCite the provision to be directed to cases that have mentioned it or interpreted it.

Many legal experts believe the Restatements are the most highly regarded of all of the secondary authorities, and you are encouraged to rely upon them and cite to them in research projects you prepare. In fact, in ordering citations to secondary authorities, only the uniform and model codes are cited before the Restatements, according to *The Bluebook* (Rule

1.4(i)), which provides rules for citation form. This preeminence of the Restatements in the *Bluebook* order of listing secondary materials confirms their authority.

The Final Wrap-Up

Using and Citing Restatements

Use: Use Restatements to obtain clear and concise statements of the law as well as comments upon and illustrations of those rules of law. Make sure you read the cases the Restatements direct you to, especially those in your jurisdiction.

Citation: Although the Restatements are a secondary authority, they are probably the most highly regarded of the secondary authorities. Thus, you should feel free to cite to them in your research memos and projects.

E. Citation Form

Encyclopedias (The Bluebook and ALWD):
   46 C.J.S. *Mechanics Liens* § 121 (1986).
   79 Am. Jur. 2d *Trusts* § 42 (1980).

Periodicals (The Bluebook and ALWD):
   John M. Golden, *Principles for Patent Remedies,*
      88 Tex. L. Rev. 505 (2010).

Treatises:
   The Bluebook: Susan L. Baker, *Federal Sentencing Guidelines*
      § 12:06 (2d ed. 1988).
   ALWD: Susan L. Baker, *Federal Sentencing Guidelines* § 12:06 (2d
      ed., West 1988).

Restatements:
   The Bluebook: Restatement (Second) of Torts § 13 (1976).
   ALWD: Restatement (Second) of Torts § 13 (1976).

CyberSites ▬▬▬▬▬▬▬▬▬▬▬▬▬▬▬▬▬▬▬▬▬▬▬▬▬

Some law school websites offer useful guides and tutorials for performing legal research using secondary sources. Use the following sites:

http://www.ll.georgetown.edu/ tutorials	Georgetown's Research Tutorials provide an overview of secondary sources and helpful research tips and strategies on using encyclopedias, treatises, periodicals, and Restatements.
http://library.kentlaw.edu/ Research/guides.htm	The website for Chicago-Kent College of Law provides tutorials on the use of secondary sources.
http://www.law.harvard.edu/ library/research/ guides/index.html	Harvard Law School offers several useful Research Guides that provide research tips for using secondary sources.

Encyclopedias

Encyclopedias are not available on the Internet. The legal encyclopedia Am. Jur. 2d is available both in CD-ROM form and on Westlaw and Lexis. C.J.S. is also available on Westlaw. Some state encyclopedias are also available on both Lexis and Westlaw and in CD-ROM form.

Treatises

Due to their voluminous content, treatises are not available on the Internet. Although numerous articles and law-related discussions are available on the Internet, there has been no effort to put comprehensive treatise collections on the Internet, likely due to authors' reluctance to have their materials distributed globally with a concurrent loss of royalty revenue. Numerous treatises are available on Lexis and Westlaw.

Periodicals

Following are Internet addresses that will allow you to retrieve various articles relating to law.

http://www.lawreview.org	The University Law Review Project, a coalition of legal educators, provides links to hundreds of law reviews, legal periodicals, newsletters, and so forth. Searching may be done by key words, topics, and specific journal names.
http://stu.findlaw.com/ index.html	The FindLaw website offers access to a wide variety of legal materials, including periodicals.
http://www.hg.org/ journals.html	The website HG.org is a comprehensive law and government portal with links to hundreds of law reviews and journals.

(continued)

CyberSites *(Continued)* ▄▄▄▄▄▄▄▄▄▄▄▄▄▄▄▄▄▄▄▄▄▄▄

Restatements

The Restatements are not available on the Internet. All of the Restatements currently in print are, however, available in CD-ROM form from West and on Lexis and Westlaw. Additionally, the website of the American Law Institute (http://www.ali.org) lists the Restatements currently in print and discusses the status of Restatements under consideration and in the drafting or revising process.

Writing Strategies

Writing is neither as mechanical nor as precise as mathematics. You cannot write by formula, assuming that "one primary authority plus one secondary authority equals one winning argument." In fact, constructing a writing using such an approach will result in a rigid and choppy project.

There is no easy answer to the question, "How many authorities are enough?" For some straightforward issues, a reference to one statute may be sufficient. Complex issues will require more in-depth analysis and expanded discussion of authorities.

Vary the authorities you rely upon. If your entire writing consists of references only to the Restatements, the reader will assume you are a lazy researcher who is uninterested in thoroughly researching the issues and content to rely upon one source. Thorough analysis calls for a combination of primary and secondary sources.

If you are relying upon primary sources as well as secondary sources to discuss an issue, analyze the primary authorities first. After you have shown the reader why the statutes, regulations, cases, or constitutional provisions control, enhance your discussion by providing additional support from a periodical, Restatement, annotation, or treatise.

Assignment for Chapter 6

1. Use Am. Jur. 2d.
   a. Which title and section deal with the inscription of the phrase "In God We Trust" on coins?
   b. Review the section to which you are directed. What topics and key numbers relate to this area of law?
   c. Which 1996 case held that the inscription did not violate the U.S. Constitution?
2. Use Am. Jur. 2d.
   a. Which title and section deal with breach of condition of parole?
   b. Review this section. May conduct that is not criminal be a ground for revocation of parole? Answer the question and cite a 1999 Eastern District of Virginia case that supports your answer.
3. Use C.J.S.
   a. Use the Table of Cases. Under which topic and section is the case *Tieberg v. Superior Court for Los Angeles County* discussed?
   b. Which topic and section generally discuss personal injuries sustained as a result of skiing?
   c. Read the section in part b. What is the general duty owed by ski resorts to skiers?
   d. To which A.L.R. annotation are you directed by the above section?
   e. Give a short summary of the definition of "demurrer."
4. Use *Am. Jur. Proof of Facts (3d)*.
   a. Give the citation to an article relating to the liability of a hospital for staph and other hospital acquired infections.
   b. Review the article. What does section 51 provide?
5. Use *Index to Legal Periodicals & Books* (volume 102, number 1, for October 2008).
   a. Cite an article written by Eric Goldman in 2008 relating to teaching cyberlaw.
   b. Cite an article written in 2007 relating to the insanity defense.
   c. Cite an article published in 2008 about a case in which a party's name is *Mannie*.
6. Use the Subject Index for *Current Law Index* for September 2008 and give the title and author of an article relating to American Indian mascots.
7. Locate the Fall 2009 article located at 49 Ga. L. Rev. 1.
   a. Give the title and the author of the article.
   b. Whose publicity rights are discussed on pages 26 and 27 of the article?

8. Locate the treatise *Chisum on Patents*.
   a. Use the Table of Cases and give the citation for *Gillette Co. v. Energizer Holdings*.
   b. Use the Index to the set. What section relates to express abandonment of a patent application?
   c. Review the section in part b. Which C.F.R. provision allows a patent applicant to expressly abandon a patent application?
9. Locate the treatise *Fletcher Cyclopedia of the Law of Private Corporations*.
   a. Which section discusses calling an annual shareholders' meeting?
   b. Review the section. Why doesn't the notice of an annual shareholders' meeting need to state the business to be transacted?
   c. Which 1994 case supports your answer?
10. Locate Restatement (Second) of Torts § 561.
   a. What is the topic of this Restatement section?
   b. Review the illustrations and comments to this Restatement section. May a nonprofit corporation be defamed? Why or why not?
   c. Use the appropriate Appendix volume to locate a 2007 case from the District of Columbia Court of Appeals relating to this topic. Give the name of this case.

Internet Assignment for Chapter 6

1. Access the website for Georgetown University Law Center at http://www.ll.georgetown.edu. Select "Research Guides" (by "Title") and then "Secondary Sources Research Guides."
   a. Review the information on periodicals. Briefly, why should one use a periodical index?
   b. What is a treatise?
2. Access the University Law Review Project at http://www.lawreview.org. Locate the New York University Law Review. Access the December 2009 issue (Volume 84, No. 6).
   a. Who authored the article *The Rights of Migrants: An Optimal Framework*?
   b. Review the Introduction to the article. In what 1976 case did the United States Supreme Court recognize that constitutional rights of noncitizens are limited?
3. Access the Washington and Lee Law School study on the most cited legal periodicals at http://lawlib.wlu.edu/LJ/index.aspx.

Sort the table by "Combined Rank." As of 2009, which were the top four most-cited periodicals? What was the one-hundredth most-cited periodical?

4. Access the website of the American Law Institute at http://www.ali.org.

   a. Review "Projects." What is the main difference between Restatements and model codes?

   b. Locate ALI's annual report for 2004. Review the table or annex that indicates how many times published cases cite to the Restatements.

      (i) How many times has your state cited to the Restatement of Property?

      (ii) Review the total number of times states have cited the Restatements. Which state has cited the Restatements the most?

Miscellaneous Secondary Authorities

Even trained lawyers may find it necessary to consult legal dictionaries, treatises, and judicial opinions before they may say with any certainty what some statutes may compel or forbid.

Rose v. Locke, 423 U.S. 48, 50 (1975)

Chapter Overview

The previous chapters discussed the most frequently used secondary authorities: A.L.R. annotations, encyclopedias, periodicals, treatises, and Restatements. There are, however, several other authorities that are used by legal researchers. These include opinions of attorneys general, dictionaries, directories, form books, uniform laws, looseleaf services, and jury instructions.

These sources summarize and explain the law as well as assist you in locating primary sources. The sources discussed in this chapter are often more practical in their approach and content than encyclopedias, periodicals, treatises, and Restatements. For example, dictionaries help you find the meaning of a word in its legal sense; form books provide information so you can effectively draft complaints, contracts, and other legal documents; and looseleaf services provide an "a" to "z" approach to understanding certain specialized areas of the law.

At the conclusion of this chapter you will be familiar with all of the tools you will need in order to locate answers for most research questions.

A. Attorneys General Opinions

1. *Introduction*

An attorney general is the chief law enforcement officer in a government. The United States attorney general is appointed by the president and is confirmed by the United States Senate. The United States attorney general is the head of the Department of Justice and serves as a member of the president's Cabinet and is the only cabinet member without the title "Secretary." Each of the 50 states and the District of Columbia also has an attorney general. In most states, the attorney general is elected by the voters. As the chief law enforcement officer, an attorney general issues written opinions on a variety of legal topics, including the interpretation of statutes and the duties and operations of government entities. These opinions typically are written in response to questions by legislators, the executive branch, or other government officials. The Attorney General has delegated responsibility for preparing formal opinions to the Department of Justice's Office of Legal Counsel; thus, recent opinions are almost always issued by the "O.L.C."

For example, the United States attorney general represents the United States in legal matters generally and gives advice and opinions to the president and to the heads of the executive departments of the government when requested. The attorney general may appear in person to represent the government before the United States Supreme Court in cases of exceptional importance.

Any large law library in your area will collect the opinions of the United States attorney general. However, your law library will likely collect only the opinions of the attorney general from your state and will not have any of the attorneys general opinions from other jurisdictions.

The opinions of attorneys general are secondary authority because they are not cases, constitutions, or statutes. Thus, a court is not required to follow an opinion of an attorney general. Because, however, these opinions are written by the chief legal advisor to the executive branch, whether federal or state, and are usually followed, they are highly persuasive, and you should feel free to rely upon them and cite them in briefs and memoranda that you write because courts view them as respectable and creditable commentaries on case law and legislation. In fact, the opinions carry the weight of law unless a court rules otherwise or legislation changes a statute being interpreted.

2. *Research Strategies*

Most sets of opinions of attorneys general will have an index, which you can use by the descriptive word approach; that is, by selecting words that

describe the issue you are researching, looking up these words in the alphabetically arranged index, and then being directed to the appropriate opinion. Unfortunately, these indexes are often not well-maintained and may be out of date.

It is more likely that you will be directed to a pertinent attorney general opinion by another source you are using. For example, if you are researching a particular statute in U.S.C.A. or U.S.C.S., you will be provided with a reference to any attorney general opinion that has interpreted or construed this statute. Similarly, when you are researching a state statute in your state's annotated code, you may be directed to a state attorney general opinion analyzing this state statute. Additionally, as you will see in Chapter 9, when you Shepardize or KeyCite a case, you will be directed to any attorneys general opinions that have mentioned this case.

Finally, many opinions are now available on the Internet. The assistant attorney general in charge of the U.S. Office of Legal Counsel assists the attorney general in his function as legal advisor to the president and all the executive branch agencies. The Office of Legal Counsel drafts legal opinions of the United States attorney general. Many of these can be found at its website at http://www.justice.gov/olc/opinions.htm. Searching is by date.

Similarly, the vast majority of states now offer their attorneys general opinions through their respective websites. Access the site of the National Association of Attorneys General at http://www.naag.org/attorneys_general.php to link to your state's attorneys general opinions.

B. Legal Dictionaries and Thesauri

Just as you would use a standard dictionary to determine the spelling, pronunciation, and meaning of a word with which you are unfamiliar, you can use a legal dictionary to determine the spelling, pronunciation, and meaning of a legal word or phrase with which you are unfamiliar. Thus, if you need to know the meaning of a word in its legal sense, such as "negligence," or the translation of a Latin phrase such as *damnum absque injuria* ("harm without injury in the legal sense"), or the meaning of a phrase such as "watered stock," you should consult a legal dictionary, which is an alphabetical arrangement of legal words and phrases. Many legal dictionaries will not only provide the definition of a word but will then give you a citation to a case or secondary authority in which the word was defined. So if you look up the word "mistrial" in a legal dictionary, you will not only be given its meaning but often will be directed to a case that defines the word "mistrial." This is another example of a secondary source not only explaining the law but also directing you to primary sources. Remember that when you define a word in a research project, cite to the case defining the word rather than the dictionary if the case is relevant and on point.

Perhaps the best known of the legal dictionaries is *Black's Law Dictionary*, a one-volume book published by West, which has been in

existence since 1891. *Black's* not only includes more than 45,000 definitions but also provides a guide to pronunciation of Latin terms, a chart showing the composition of the United States Supreme Court from 1789 to date, definitions of legal maxims, a Table of British Regnal Years listing the sovereigns of England for the last 900 years, the text of the United States Constitution, an extensive table of legal abbreviations, and references to West's Key Numbers to make researching easier. *Black's Law Dictionary* is available in hardcover, paperback, and on Westlaw. A new edition is released every several years. See Figure 7-1 for a sample page from *Black's Law Dictionary* (6th ed. 1990).

Another of the well-known legal dictionaries is *Ballentine's Law Dictionary*, a one-volume book published by the former Lawyers Co-op, which defines more than 45,000 words and phrases. Like *Black's, Ballentine's* also contains guides to pronunciation of Latin terms. Moreover, because it was formerly a Lawyers Co-op publication, it contains thousands of references to the Lawyers Co-op publications, *United States Supreme Court Reports, Lawyers' Edition*, A.L.R., and Am. Jur. 2d. *Ballentine's*, however, has not released a new edition since 1969, and thus *Black's* is far more current and should likely be consulted in preference to *Ballentine's*.

There are numerous other legal dictionaries that you can use, including specialized dictionaries such as Bryan A. Garner's *A Handbook of Criminal Law Terms*, which provides definitions of criminal law terms. Most legal dictionaries are located in the reference section of the law library, and you should make a point of browsing the shelves in the reference section to discover which dictionaries are available.

You may recall that the set *Words and Phrases* will provide you with definitions of words and phrases. Its coverage, however, is limited to words and phrases that have been defined in cases, and therefore you will not be able to find a word in *Words and Phrases* unless it has been the subject of court action. Moreover, because *Words and Phrases* is a multivolume set, it is more unwieldy than the more standard one-volume legal dictionaries such as *Black's* and *Ballentine's*. One of the advantages of *Words and Phrases*, however, is that it is supplemented by pocket parts, easily allowing for the addition of new words that enter the legal field. *Black's* and *Ballentine's* are similar to other traditional dictionaries and are not supplemented on an annual basis.

Many legal dictionaries such as *Black's* publish an abridged softcover version at a moderate price. These dictionaries are excellent resources for beginning researchers.

A legal thesaurus provides synonyms and antonyms for legal words and terms. When writing a letter, memorandum, or legal document, you may become tired of using the same word or may need to think of another way of expressing a legal term. A thesaurus will help you select the right word you need. One of the best known of the legal thesauri is *Burton's Legal Thesaurus* by William C. Burton, which provides more than 8,000 legal terms, synonyms, and definitions. For example, if you wish to find another word for "abandon," the thesaurus will suggest "forsake," "abdicate," "retract," and other terms.

Figure 7-1
Sample Page from *Black's Law Dictionary*
(6th ed. 1990)

MISTAKE   1002

Unilateral mistake. A mistake by only one party to an agreement and generally not a basis for relief by rescission or reformation.

Mister. A title of courtesy. A trade, craft, occupation, employment, office.

Mistery. A trade or calling.

Mistrial. An erroneous, invalid, or nugatory trial. A trial of an action which cannot stand in law because of want of jurisdiction, or a wrong drawing of jurors, or disregard of some other fundamental requisite before or during trial. Trial which has been terminated prior to its normal conclusion. A device used to halt trial proceedings when error is so prejudicial and fundamental that expenditure of further time and expense would be wasteful if not futile. Ferguson v. State, Fla., 417 So.2d 639, 641. The judge may declare a mistrial because of some extraordinary event (*e.g.* death of juror, or attorney), for prejudicial error that cannot be corrected at trial, or because of a deadlocked jury.

"Mistrial" is equivalent to no trial and is a nugatory trial while "new trial" recognizes a completed trial which for sufficient reasons has been set aside so that the issues may be tried de novo. People v. Jamerson, 196 Colo. 63, 580 P.2d 805, 806.

Misuse. As defense in products liability action, requires use in a manner neither intended nor reasonably foreseeable by manufacturer. Smith v. Sturm, Ruger & Co., Inc., 39 Wash.App. 740, 695 P.2d 600, 604.

Misuser /misyúwzər/. An unlawful use of a right. Abuse of an office or franchise. 2 Bl.Comm. 153.

Mitigating circumstances. Such as do not constitute a justification or excuse for the offense in question, but which, in fairness and mercy, may be considered as extenuating or reducing the degree of moral culpability. For example, mitigating circumstances which will reduce degree of homicide to manslaughter are the commission of the killing in a sudden heat of passion caused by adequate legal provocation. People v. Morrin, 31 Mich.App. 301, 187 N.W.2d 434, 438.

Those that affect basis for award of exemplary damages, or reduce actual damages by showing, not that they were never suffered, but that they have been partially extinguished.

In actions for libel and slander, refer to circumstances bearing on defendant's liability for exemplary damages by reducing moral culpability, or on liability for actual damages by showing partial extinguishment thereof. The "mitigating circumstances" which the statute allows defendant in libel action to prove are those which tend to show that defendant in speaking the slanderous words acted in good faith, with honesty of purpose, and not maliciously. Roemer v. Retail Credit Co., 44 C.A.3d 926, 119 Cal.Rptr. 82, 91.

See also Comparative negligence; Extenuating circumstances; Extraordinary circumstances.

Mitigation. To make less severe. Alleviation, reduction, abatement or diminution of a penalty or punishment imposed by law.

Mitigation of damages. Doctrine of "mitigation of damages," sometimes called doctrine of avoidable consequences, imposes on party injured by breach of contract or tort duty to exercise reasonable diligence and ordinary care in attempting to minimize his damages, or avoid aggravating the injury, after breach or injury has been inflicted and care and diligence required of him is the same as that which would be used by man of ordinary prudence under like circumstances. Darnell v. Taylor, La.App., 236 So.2d 57, 61. Mitigation of damages is an affirmative defense and applies when plaintiff fails to take reasonable actions that would tend to mitigate his injuries. Mott v. Persichetti, Colo.App., 534 P.2d 823, 825. See Restatement, Contracts § 336(1); U.C.C. § 2–603. *See also* Avoidable consequences doctrine.

Mitigation of punishment. A judge may reduce or order a lesser sentence in consideration of such factors as the defendant's past good behavior, his family situation, his cooperation with the police and kindred factors.

Mitior sensus /míshiyər sénsəs/. Lat. The more favorable acceptation.

Mitius imperanti melius paretur /míshiyəs impərántay míyl(i)yəs pəríytər/. The more mildly one commands, the better is he obeyed.

Mitter. L. Fr. To put, to send, or to pass; as, *mitter l'estate,* to pass the estate; *mitter le droit,* to pass a right. These words are used to distinguish different kinds of releases.

Mitter avant /mítər əvǽnt/. L. Fr. In old practice, to put before; to present before a court; to produce in court.

Mittimus /mítəməs/. The name of a precept in writing, issuing from a court or magistrate, directed to the sheriff or other officer, commanding him to convey to the prison the person named therein, and to the jailer, commanding him to receive and safely keep such person until he shall be delivered by due course of law. State v. Lenihan, 151 Conn. 552, 200 A.2d 476, 478. Transcript of minutes of conviction and sentence duly certified by court clerk. United States ex rel. Chasteen v. Denmark, C.C.A.Ill., 138 F.2d 289, 291.

Old English law. A writ enclosing a record sent to be tried in a county palatine; it derives its name from the Latin word *mittimus,* "we send." It is the jury process of these counties, and commands the proper officer of the county palatine to command the sheriff to summon the jury for the trial of the cause, and to return the record, etc.

Mixed. Formed by admixture or commingling; partaking of the nature, character, or legal attributes of two or more distinct kinds or classes.

As to mixed Action; Blood relations *(Mixed blood)*; Contract; Government; Jury; Larceny; Marriage; Nuisance; Policy; Presumption; Property; Tithes; and War, see those titles.

Note reference to case interpreting "mistrial"

A recent trend is publication of glossaries of legal terms on the Internet. For example, the website Law.Com offers a legal dictionary at http://dictionary.law.com. As of the date of this text, most online glossaries are not particularly comprehensive. They may, however, be helpful in providing you with a quick understanding of a legal term or Latin phrase. The full text of Bouvier's well-known legal dictionary is available at http://www.constitution.org/bouv/bouvier.htm.

The Final Wrap-Up

Use and Citation of Attorneys General Opinions, Dictionaries, and Thesauri

Use: Use attorneys general opinions as strong persuasive authorities that often clarify and interpret statutes and regulations. Although they are secondary authorities, they are highly credible. Use dictionaries and thesauri to obtain a quick definition of an unknown legal term.

Citation: Cite freely to attorneys general opinions because of their renown and highly persuasive nature. You may cite to dictionaries and thesauri, but consider citing instead to the primary authorities to which these sources usually direct you.

C. Directories

1. Introduction

A directory is simply a list of lawyers. Some law directories, such as the extremely well-known and highly regarded *Martindale-Hubbell Law Directory*, aim at listing all lawyers admitted to all jurisdictions. Other directories are more limited in coverage and may list only lawyers in a particular geographic region or locality. Still other directories focus on law schools, law libraries, or courts. Law directories are usually kept in the reference section of a law library.

2. Martindale-Hubbell Law Directory

a. Overview of *Martindale-Hubbell*

The best-known law directory in the United States is *Martindale-Hubbell Law Directory*, which has been in existence for more than a century. The initial goal of the directory was to publish an address for a lawyer, a banker, and a real estate office in every city in the United States. At

present, most major U.S. law firms pay to be listed in *Martindale-Hubbell*. The set is currently published annually in hardbound volumes and is also available on CD-ROM. Additionally, the set is available online through Lexis and on the Internet. (See Chapter 12.) The CD-ROM discs enable one to find attorneys solely by name without requiring the user to know the city in which the attorney practices. In fact, search criteria can be constructed so that you can readily locate an attorney who graduated from a specific school, such as Yale Law School, is fluent in French, and concentrates in the field of health law. The CD-ROM set costs approximately $1,000 and is updated quarterly. Finally, much of the information in *Martindale-Hubbell* is free on the Internet (http://www.martindale.com).

There are more than 10 volumes in *Martindale-Hubbell*, arranged alphabetically by state. For instance, Volume 1 covers the states Alabama, Alaska, Arizona, and Arkansas. Within the listing for each state, cities are arranged alphabetically from Abbeville, Alabama, to Wetumpka, Alabama. Within each city, law firms and attorneys are arranged alphabetically as well. Thus, if you were interested in locating a firm in Minneapolis, Minnesota, to handle a transaction for you or to refer a case to, you could scan through the law firms located in Minneapolis and select a firm that you believe could best represent the client's interests. See Figure 7-2 for a sample page from the *Martindale-Hubbell Law Directory*.

Each firm that has an entry will list its attorneys and provide biographical information about them. The date of birth, colleges and universities attended, honors awarded, and articles authored by the attorneys in the firm are given. Moreover, the firm's address, phone number, website, a sample of its representative clients, and the areas in which it practices will be noted. The firm may also include a firm profile, discussing its achievements and expertise. By reviewing *Martindale-Hubbell* you may be able to select a firm that focuses on a particular practice area such as franchise law, securities litigation, or white-collar criminal defense. Law firms pay a fee for these biographical entries, and therefore not every firm or attorney may elect to participate.

On the other hand, the front of each volume of *Martindale-Hubbell* contains a list of all attorneys licensed to practice in the states covered by that volume. Attorneys are listed in this blue pages section free of charge, and the biographical information given is limited to name, year of birth, address, education, date of bar admission, and the area of practice specialized in by the attorney. *Martindale-Hubbell* also lists corporate law departments by company name and indicates the city and state in which the corporate law department is located. In 1995, *Martindale-Hubbell* began assigning identification numbers to the more than 850,000 attorneys in its database, including former President Clinton and former Chief Justice William Rehnquist. These universal numerical identifiers are designed to make it easier to track attorneys disciplined for misconduct. *Martindale-Hubbell* also rates attorneys based on their legal ability and ethical standards. These ratings are developed by confidential polling of members of the bar.

Figure 7-2
Sample Page from *Martindale-Hubbell Law Directory*

DRATH, CLIFFORD, MURPHY, WENNERHOLM
& HAGEN

A PROFESSIONAL CORPORATION
1999 HARRISON STREET, SUITE 1900
OAKLAND, CALIFORNIA 94612-3578
Telephone: 510-287-4000
Telefax: 510-287-4050
Email: dcmwh@msn.com

San Diego, California Office: 600 B Street, Suite 1550. Telephone: 619-595-3060. Fax: 619-595-3066.

Areas of practice   *Civil Litigation with an emphasis in the fields of insurance and self-insured defense, insurance coverage analysis, construction, employment, environmental, products liability, personal injury and professional liability defense.*

FIRM PROFILE: *Drath, Clifford, Murphy, Wennerholm & Hagen is a Martindale-Hubbell Bar Register of Preeminent Lawyers firm.*

JOHN M. DRATH, born Portland, Oregon, November 14, 1944; admitted to bar, 1970, California; 1971, Colorado; 1993, Montana. *Education:* University of Washington (B.A., 1965); University of San Francisco (J.D., 1969). *Member:* State Bar of California; Association of Defense Counsel, Northern California (President, 1992-1993); Defense Research Institute; American Board of Trial Advocates; Federation of Insurance and Corporate Counsel. **PRACTICE AREAS:** Professional Liability Defense; Personal Injury Defense; Insurance Coverage; Bad Faith Defense; Complex Litigation. *Email:* dcmwh@msn.com

RICK J. MURPHY, born San Francisco, California, March 26, 1951; admitted to bar, 1976, California. *Education:* University of California at Davis (B.A., cum laude, 1973); University of Santa Clara School of Law (J.D., cum laude, 1976). *Member:* State Bar of California; Association of Defense Counsel; American Board of Trial Advocates. **PRACTICE AREAS:** Insurance Defense; Accident and Personal Injury; Business Litigation. *Email:* dcmwh@msn.com

TRACI E. WENNERHOLM, born Los Angeles, California, July 13, 1960; admitted to bar, 1985, California. *Education:* University of California at Riverside (B.A., 1982); Hastings College of the Law, University of California (J.D., 1985). *Member:* State Bar of California; Association of Defense Counsel; Defense Research Institute. **PRACTICE AREAS:** Construction Law; Personal Injury Defense; Asbestos Defense. *Email:* dcmwh@msn.com

DAVID F. BEACH, born Jackson, Michigan, March 31, 1955; admitted to bar, 1980, California. *Education:* College of San Mateo (A.A., 1975); University of California at Berkeley (B.S., 1977); University of San Diego (J.D., magna cum laude, 1980). *Member:* State Bar of California; American Arbitration Association; Association of Defense Counsel; Defense Research Institute. **PRACTICE AREAS:** Personal Injury Defense; Insurance Coverage; Construction Litigation; Asbestos Litigation. *Email:* dcmwh@msn.com

GRETCHEN W. LATIMER, born Berkeley, California, August 8, 1965; admitted to bar, 1992, California. *Education:* University of Puget Sound (B.A., 1987), Seattle University (J.D., 1992). *Member:* San Francisco Bar Association; Contra Costa County Bar Association. **PRACTICE AREAS:** Construction Defect; Insurance Defense. *Email:* dcmwh@msn.com

Representative clients   REPRESENTATIVE CLIENTS: Allstate Insurance Co.; American Equities Insurance Co.; American States Insurance Co.; Cooper Industries; First Financial Insurance Company; First Mercury Syndicate; Motors Insurance Co.; Nationwide Insurance Co.; Nautilus Insurance Co.; National General Insurance Co.; Northbrook Insurance Co.; Preferred Risk Mutual Insurance Co.; Scottsdale Insurance Co.; Super Computer, Inc,; TOPA Insurance Co.; USS-POSCO Industries, USX Corporation; Unicare Insurance Co.; Willis Corroon.

(For complete Biographical Data on Additional Personnel, see Professional Biographies at San Diego, California)

A separate volume in the *Martindale-Hubbell* set called "Corporate Law Directory" provides information on more than 35,000 in-house attorneys and corporate law departments. Thus, if you needed a list of the attorneys working in-house for Exxon-Mobil, you would consult this volume for their names, biographical information, and current responsibilities. Lists of government lawyers and academic programs are also included. Finally, *Martindale-Hubbell* also includes an international law directory, which lists thousands of lawyers and law firms around the world.

These features of *Martindale-Hubbell* make it an excellent source of information for career opportunities. You should consider directing a resume to a law firm that focuses on an area of law in which you are interested. There is no point in applying for a position with a law firm that is exclusively engaged in bankruptcy work if you have no interest in this area of law. Similarly, before interviewing with a firm, always review *Martindale-Hubbell* to familiarize yourself with the firm's practice areas, its office locations in other cities, and the general profile of the firm.

Most law firms maintain sophisticated websites with biographies, photos of attorneys, office locations, descriptions of firm practice areas, summaries of recent "wins," and topical articles written by attorneys in the firm. Thus, because these websites provide more information than is available in *Martindale-Hubbell* and can be readily updated as attorneys leave or join a firm, many law firms no longer maintain their *Martindale-Hubbell* profiles. In fact, according to Law.com, approximately ten percent of the nation's highest-grossing law firms no longer list their firms in *Martindale-Hubbell*, saving their firms approximately $200 per attorney per year.

Practice Tip

Martindale-Hubbell

Don't ever go on a job interview without doing some homework about your potential employer by using *Martindale-Hubbell*. Find out something about the firm and mention it during your interview to showcase your research skills and professional savvy. Comment about the firm's new European office, its practice areas, or some other item to demonstrate your familiarity with *Martindale-Hubbell* as well as your level of interest in the firm.

---

b. *Martindale-Hubbell*'s Law Digests

In addition to *Martindale-Hubbell's* directory list of lawyers, the set contains numerous other features that make it a useful and practical research tool. Prior to 2007, the print versions of *Martindale-Hubbell* contained Law Digest volumes, which provided a brief overview of the laws of all U.S. jurisdictions and many foreign countries, so you could quickly determine fees for creating a limited partnership in a state, the

rate of interest in Ireland, and so forth. The state and international digest information is now available on CD-ROM, Lexis, and through the website http://www.martindale.com, which allows one to access the Law Digest volumes for U.S. jurisdictions and foreign countries for free. One may also purchase segments of the Law Digests (for example, the Ohio Digest or the Ecuador Digest) from http://www.amazon.com.

3. *Local Directories*

Directories may be available for a particular region or locality. For example, some local bar associations may publish a booklet listing members of the association. Other local directories may be published by private publishers. An example of a local directory is the "District of Columbia Bar's Lawyer Directory." Some local directories provide only the attorney's name, address, and telephone number, while others may provide brief biographical sketches and even photographs of the lawyers listed in the directory.

4. *Specialized Directories*

A number of directories provide lists of attorneys who concentrate in specialized practice areas or contain information relating to a certain specialized topic. Examples include the following:

> *Directory of Corporate Counsel* (a directory of personnel of the law departments of corporations, both for-profit and not-for-profit, in the United States).
> *Federal-State Court Directory* (a directory of general information about federal and state courts and their personnel).
> *American Association of Law Libraries Directory and Handbook* (a directory of information about American law libraries).

5. *Internet Directories*

All of the attorney information found in the conventional hardbound print volumes of *Martindale-Hubbell* can also be located through the Internet at the sites "Martindale-Hubbell Lawyer Locator" at http://www.martindale.com or Lawyers.com at http://www.lawyers.com. The sites provide free access to comprehensive listings of one million lawyers and law firms in 160 countries around the world. Searching is easily accomplished by name, firm, location, or law school attended.

Another excellent free legal directory on the Internet is provided by FindLaw, West's legal website. Access http://lawyers.findlaw.com to search for attorneys by name or practice area. You may also search for corporate and government attorneys. Articles about retaining attorneys and lists of process servers and other legal consultants are also provided.

Yet another Internet directory is Chambers and Partners at http://www.chambersandpartners.com, which identifies law firms and attorneys throughout the world.

D. Form Books

1. Introduction

One of the typical tasks performed by paralegals is drafting legal documents. Some of the documents may be for use in litigation, such as forms for complaints, answers, notices of depositions, or interrogatories. Other forms may relate to transactional aspects of law practice, such as leases, partnership agreements, or corporate bylaws. Seldom, if ever, do attorneys or paralegals draft documents "from scratch." Generally they rely on forms or models, which have proven useful in other instances.

If you are asked to draft a legal document, there are several alternatives you can pursue. The office you work in may have a central form file, which contains forms for commonly used documents. These form banks are typically located in the firm's computer databases. In such a case you would review the form provided and modify it to suit your needs. Alternatively, you can ask another paralegal, a secretary, or an attorney if any individual client files might have a comparable form you can use as a guide. If these strategies are not helpful, you can consult a form book (sometimes called a "practice set").

A form book is a single volume or, more typically, a multivolume set that contains forms for use in the legal profession. Some sets of form books contain forms that can be used in any aspect of legal practice and include litigation forms as well as forms used in practice areas not related to litigation. Other books provide forms related solely to one state or to one area of the law. An example of such a specialized set of form books is *Murphy's Will Clauses: Annotations and Forms with Tax Effects*, a multivolume set containing numerous forms used in connection with drafting wills, trusts, and other estate-related forms.

2. Well-Known Form Books

Some of the better known sets of form books are as follows:

American Jurisprudence Legal Forms 2d. This set consists of more than 60 alphabetically arranged volumes of forms and provides forms for contracts, wills, and leases as well as for hundreds of other topics.

American Jurisprudence Pleading and Practice Forms Annotated. This set consists of more than 70 volumes of forms and provides more than 40,000 forms relating to litigation, such as forms for

complaints, answers, discovery procedures, motions for change of
venue, motions for new trial, and orders.

Bender's Federal Practice Forms. This more-than-15-volume set
contains litigation forms for use in federal practice, both civil and
criminal.

Current Legal Forms with Tax Analysis by Rabkin and Johnson is a
multivolume set of forms for general law practice.

Federal Procedural Forms. This set consists of more than 25
volumes and provides forms for use in federal practice.

Bender's Forms of Discovery by Lexis is a multivolume set of forms
related solely to discovery matters such as interrogatories, depositions, requests for production and inspection, and medical
discovery.

West's Legal Forms. This set of books, consisting of more than 50
volumes, contains a variety of forms for general law practice, such
as bankruptcy forms, forms for purchase and sale of real estate,
and forms relating to business organizations, including partnerships and corporations.

Some publishers have produced sets of form books devoted strictly to
forms for use in that state. For example, a set commonly used in
California for business or transactional matters is Lexis's *California
Legal Forms: Transaction Guide.* If your state does not have a set of books
containing forms specifically tailored for your state, use one of the
"general" sets of form books, such as *West's Legal Forms* or *Am. Jur. Legal
Forms 2d*, which are designed to provide forms for use in any state. You
may also encounter a set of form books for one specific legal topic, such as
trademark forms, bankruptcy forms, and so forth.

There are also form books prepared strictly for paralegals: *Personal
Injury: Paralegal Forms and Procedures* by Joyce Walden, which contains
sample correspondence, forms, checklists, and pleadings related to personal injury practice; *Paralegal Discovery: Procedures and Forms* by Pat
Medina, relating to drafting discovery documents and case management;
and *Paralegal Litigation: Forms and Procedures*, Third Edition, by Marcy
Fawcett-Delesandri, which includes forms, checklists, and procedures for
drafting litigation documents.

Another source of forms is treatises, which often contain sample
documents and forms. For example, one of the best known treatises on
bankruptcy, *Collier on Bankruptcy, 15th Edition Revised*, contains three
volumes of forms to complete its thorough analysis of bankruptcy practice. Finally, some state annotated codes contain forms. See Figure 7-3 for
samples of forms.

The Internet offers thousands of legal forms. As with many offerings
on the Internet, however, it is unknown who authored the forms or
whether they have been subjected to the rigorous checking and editing
that accompany print publications. Thus, they should be used with
extreme caution. Such forms may nevertheless provide a useful starting
place. References to Internet sites offering forms are provided at the end
of this chapter. Internet legal research is discussed in Chapter 12.

Figure 7-3
Sample Page from Virginia Forms—Criminal Procedure

9-1706   VIRGINIA FORMS

No. 9-1706. Motion for Competency Determination — Commonwealth.

VIRGINIA: IN THE CIRCUIT COURT OF THE _____ OF _____

Commonwealth of Virginia,
        Plaintiff

v.   CRIMINAL NO. _____

J.D. Defendant,
        Defendant

MOTION FOR PSYCHIATRIC ORDER

Comes now the Commonwealth of Virginia by her Attorney for the County of _____, and moves this Court for the entry of an Order directing that the defendant be examined by one or more mental health experts who shall meet the qualifications set forth in §19.2-169.5A of the Code of Virginia for the purposes of determining the defendant's mental state as of the date of the alleged offenses in this case; and further that the Sheriff of _____ County or one or more of his Deputies transport the defendant to said mental health experts and return the said defendant to jail upon completion of such examination.

Commonwealth of Virginia
By _____
Attorney for the Commonwealth
of the County of _____, Virginia

[Certificate of Service]

Note: Code of Virginia, 1950, § 19.2-168.1 as to evaluation on motion of the Commonwealth after notice; § 19.2-169.5 as to evaluation of sanity at the time of the offense; disclosure of evaluation results.

10A Michie's Jurisprudence, *Insane and Other Incompetent Persons* § 44 as to test of insanity in criminal proceedings.

Figure 7-3 *(Continued)*
Sample Corporate Resolutions by Written Consent

Action by Written Consent of Directors

The undersigned, constituting all of the Directors of [name] (the "Corporation") hereby take the following actions by written consent pursuant to Section 709 of the Business Corporation Law of New York and Article V of the bylaws of the Corporation as if present at a meeting duly called pursuant to notice.

> RESOLVED, the Directors approve the hiring of ___[name]___ as ___[identify position]___ for the Corporation to perform such duties and at a salary and upon terms and conditions as determined by the President of the Corporation.

> RESOLVED, the Articles of Incorporation for the Corporation shall be amended to change the name of the Corporation to ___[name]___ which action shall be voted on by the shareholders of the Corporation pursuant to a special meeting to be called therefore by the President of the Corporation.

> RESOLVED, that the Corporation shall instruct its counsel to ___[identify action]___ against ___[identify person]___ for ___[identify reason]___.

The officers of the Corporation are hereby authorized to take appropriate action to effect the purposes of these resolutions.

Date: _____

_____
[Director name and signature]

Date: _____

_____
[Director name and signature]

Date: _____

_____
[Director name and signature]

Some states now offer various forms on their official websites. For example, all states now provide comprehensive forms banks for organizing, maintaining, and dissolving business entities (such as corporations, limited partnerships, and limited liability companies). The forms can be downloaded and printed for free and are generally available on the home page for the state's secretary of state.

Similarly, many courts now offer free forms on their websites. For example, the California Judicial Council offers hundreds of downloadable and electronically fillable forms, from notices of appeal to petitions for changes of name (access http://www.courtinfo.ca.gov/forms). Access your state's judicial site (see Table T.1 of *The Bluebook*) and see if forms are offered. Alternatively, access MegaLaw at http://www.megalaw.com and select "Legal Forms" and then "Government Forms" to see if your state offers free judicial forms.

Ethics Alert

Using Form Books and Metadata

Drafting a legal form requires more than finding a good form and then filling in the blanks. You are required to research the area of law and then modify any preprinted form to comply with the law. Use an annotated form book; it will direct you to primary authorities that endorse use of the language given in the form and provide additional critical references. Because the law changes frequently, using an outmoded form from one of your form files may be malpractice.

In addition, documents created at law firms often contain *metadata,* **or information describing the history, management, and tracking of an electronically created document. For example, if you change the name "Smith" in an older contract that you are now drafting for "Jones," metadata enables a reader to discover that the document was originally prepared for Smith. Metadata also reveals who received documents, comments and deletions made during the drafting process, sequences of changes, delays in sending a document, and other critical information. Many law firms now use sophisticated "scrubbing" programs to eliminate metadata and protect confidential client information. Check your law firm's policies on metadata mining and scrubbing, and be scrupulous about maintaining confidential client information**

---

3. *Locating Form Books*

To locate form books, check the card catalog in your law library, browse the shelves, or consult your law librarian. Often form books are located near other related books. For example, the books containing forms related to federal practice may be found near the sets of books containing federal cases. Similarly, sets of books containing forms for use in criminal law

practice are often located in the "criminal law" section of the law library or the stack that also contains treatises on criminal law and case books devoted solely to criminal law cases. Thus, the easiest way to locate form books is often to browse the stacks devoted to a certain legal topic. Similarly, form books for use in a state are usually located with the cases and statutes for that state.

4. *Research Strategies*

When you have located a set of form books that is pertinent to the legal issue you are researching, you can locate the form you need by either the descriptive word approach or the topic approach.

To use the descriptive word approach, locate the index to the set, generally found in the last volume of the set. The index is alphabetically arranged. You should look up words or phrases that describe or relate to the form you are drafting (contract, trust, complaint, bylaws, venue) and you will then be directed to the appropriate volume and page for the form you need.

To use the topic approach, scan the chapter headings and subheadings in the set. You can then examine the particular form that seems most appropriate.

One of the useful features of many form books is that they are annotated. This means that you will be referred to cases that have approved or supported language used in the form. Moreover, many form books provide analysis and commentary on use of the forms and practical aids such as checklists, providing items to consider in drafting a certain type of form.

Most form books are kept current by pocket parts. Therefore, after reviewing a form, check the pocket part to determine if language used in the form has been revised or if new annotations and comment have been provided.

One of the recent developments in form books is for the publisher to put the forms on disc for use with various software programs or to offer them electronically. For example, West offers *Am. Jur. Legal Forms 2d* and *Am. Jur. Pleading and Practice Forms Annotated*, in CD-ROM form and on Westlaw, allowing you to locate forms quickly with a word search, export forms directly to your word processor, and then customize, copy, and print them with a few keystrokes.

5. *Summary*

Form books provide an excellent starting point for drafting legal documents. You should not view drafting documents as merely an exercise in finding a form and then "filling in the blanks." Carefully review the form to ensure it is appropriate for the document you need to prepare. Feel free to revise the form to make it fit your purposes so long as these revisions are consistent with the law in your jurisdiction. Often you may combine

features or elements of several forms to create the best document. Be alert to forms prepared by others in your office as well as other firms, and start collecting your own set of forms of documents and pleadings you believe are well drafted and effective. In sum, exercise discretion in using form books. "Cut and paste" until you have a form that is best suited to your needs.

The Final Wrap-Up

Use and Citation of Directories and Form Books

Use: Use directories to locate information about lawyers and law firms. Use form books to help you draft forms for both litigation and transactional matters and to give you ideas about how to phrase and structure certain agreements.

Citation: Do not cite to directories or form books. These books are in the nature of finding and practice tools rather than research tools.

E. Uniform Laws

1. Introduction

You have seen that the Restatements were produced as a result of concern by legal scholars that case law was overly complex and uncertain. At about the same time that the American Law Institute (the "Institute") was formed to produce the Restatements, legal scholars became concerned over the great disparity in state statutes on areas of the law that could be treated similarly or uniformly among the states.

The result of this concern was the formation of the National Conference of Commissioners on Uniform State Laws in 1892. The Conference is composed of more than 300 practicing attorneys, judges, law professors, and other legal scholars who are usually appointed by the governor of each state and meet on an annual basis to draft proposed legislation on various areas of the law. These proposed laws, which are the result of considerable time and effort, are then presented to the legislatures of the 50 states with the hope and expectation that the state legislature will pass the Conference's version of the law on that particular legal topic. The Conference can only propose uniform laws. No uniform law is effective until a state legislature specifically enacts it.

For example, after studying statutes relating to partnerships from various states, the Conference drafted its proposed set of partnership statutes, titled the Uniform Partnership Act, and began persuading the various state legislatures in the 50 states to adopt the Uniform Partnership Act in place of their divergent partnership statutes. Once a state

adopts a uniform law, it is then a primary authority in that state. Until they are adopted, however, uniform laws have no such legal effect and thus assume the characteristics of secondary authority. Once adopted, a uniform law is published in the state's annotated codes together with other statutes in that state. After printing the text of the uniform law, the state code will usually provide the text of the Conference's comments about the law and an explanation as to how the state version of the uniform law differs from the original version drafted by the Conference. Cases interpreting the uniform law will follow.

Some states, after holding hearings, debates, and other legislative proceedings, just as for any other state law, will adopt the uniform act "as is." Other states may reject the act, while others may revise the act, adding certain provisions and omitting others. Thus, although the goal of the Conference is to produce a statute that will be uniform from state to state, the end result is a statute that nearly always has some variation from state to state. Nevertheless, many of an act's provisions will be retained intact or with only minor revisions so there will be resulting overall uniformity among the states that adopt a uniform act.

The Conference has approved more than 250 uniform laws, ranging from perhaps the best known, the Uniform Commercial Code (relating to commercial practices and sales), which took ten years to complete and has been adopted in whole or in part by every state, to the Uniform Adoption Act, to the Uniform Simultaneous Death Act.

The Conference also drafts proposed legislation known as "Model Acts." Although a uniform law is one whose adoption is urged in every state by the Conference, a model act is one for which uniformity among the states is not as necessary or desirable. An example is the Model Punitive Damages Act, intended to address the need for consistency in awards of punitive damages throughout the nation. Although the Model Punitive Damages Act serves as a source to which states can looks for guidance in formulating their laws relating to punitive damages, it is unlikely that all states will adopt identical statutes in this area because the manner in which wrongdoers are punished and damages are awarded is a matter of greatest concern to the jurisdiction where the wrong is committed. In sum, model acts are intended as guidelines that states can borrow from or modify when drafting their own legislation whereas uniform acts are intended to be adopted exactly as written. The Conference often works with the Institute in developing uniform and model legislation. For example, the two worked together to prepare the UCC, and the Institute drafted the Model Penal Code.

2. *Research Strategies*

Uniform Laws Annotated. To locate the text of the more than 250 uniform laws and the model acts, you can consult West's *Uniform Laws Annotated.* This multivolume set not only provides the text of uniform laws and model acts but also provides official comments of the drafters explaining the intent and purpose of

each uniform law, a list of the states that have adopted each particular uniform law, the date the law was adopted, brief descriptions of how various states have modified the uniform law, references to law review articles regarding the uniform law, annotations or brief summaries of cases interpreting the uniform law, references to topics and Key Numbers to enable the reader to access West's Key Number System, and references to sections of C.J.S., which discuss that area of the law. The set is kept current by pocket parts and supplements. See Figure 7-4 for a sample page from the *Uniform Laws Annotated*.

Although *Uniform Laws Annotated* thus provides an overview of all uniform legislation, it lacks a comprehensive general index or table of contents. The uniform laws and model acts are, however, grouped together by general subject matter. For example, estate, probate, and related laws are found in books 30 through 33 of the set. Additionally, a pamphlet published regularly in conjunction with *Uniform Laws Annotated*, titled *Uniform Laws Annotated Directory of Acts*, lists all uniform laws alphabetically and will direct you to the location of the law in *Uniform Laws Annotated*. In effect, this directory serves as an index to *Uniform Laws Annotated*. The directory also lists each state and the particular uniform laws it has adopted. See Figure 7-5 for a sample page from *Uniform Laws Annotated Directory of Acts*.

Am. Jur. 2d and C.J.S. The one-volume "Table of Laws and Rules" in Am. Jur. 2d and C.J.S. will refer you to sections in each of the encyclopedias that discuss uniform laws.

Westlaw. The text of all uniform and model acts is also available on Westlaw. Some are available on Lexis.

Internet. All Uniform Laws are available on the Internet. The National Conference of Commissioners on Uniform State Laws posts all final acts on its website at http://www.nccusl.org/Update. The text of all are given, together with a summary of each act, and legislative facts about the adoption of an act in the various states. See also CyberSites at the end of this chapter.

3. *Use of Uniform Laws*

If you are researching a state statute that has been adopted as a uniform law and there are no cases interpreting it, you should review the Official Comment to the uniform law and cases from another state that has also adopted the uniform law. As you will recall from Chapter 1, although cases from one state are never binding in another state, cases from another state interpreting uniform laws may be highly persuasive inasmuch as such cases would be interpreting statutory provisions that are similar or identical to those enacted in your state.

Figure 7-4
Sample Page from the *Uniform Laws Annotated*

INTESTATE SUCCESSION—WILLS   § 2-102

wife which listed as a possible heir the illegitimate child of appellant. In re Raso's Estate, Fla.App.1976, 332 So.2d 78.

Trial court abused its discretion in denying appellant's motion to vacate default judgment where appellant properly alleged excusable neglect for her failure to timely respond to petition for determination of heirs and where appellant properly alleged a meritorious defense. Id.

Section 2-102.   [Share of the Spouse.]

The intestate share of the surviving spouse is:

(1) if there is no surviving issue or parent of the decedent, the entire intestate estate;

(2) if there is no surviving issue but the decedent is survived by a parent or parents, the first [$50,000], plus one-half of the balance of the intestate estate;

(3) if there are surviving issue all of whom are issue of the surviving spouse also, the first [$50,000], plus one-half of the balance of the intestate estate;

(4) if there are surviving issue one or more of whom are not issue of the surviving spouse, one-half of the intestate estate.

COMMENT

This section gives the surviving spouse a larger share than most existing statutes on descent and distribution. In doing so, it reflects the desires of most married persons, who almost always leave all of a moderate estate or at least one-half of a larger estate to the surviving spouse when a will is executed. A husband or wife who desires to leave the surviving spouse less than the share provided by this section may do so by executing a will, subject of course to possible election by the surviving spouse to take an elective share of one-third under Part 2 of this Article. Moreover, in the small estate (less than $50,000 after homestead allowance, exempt property, and allowances) the surviving spouse is given the entire estate if there are only children who are issue of both the decedent and the surviving spouse; the result is to avoid protective proceedings as to property otherwise passing to their minor children.

See Section 2-802 for the definition of spouse which controls for purposes of intestate succession.

Law Review Commentaries

How the family fares. Donald L. Robertson. 37 Ohio S.L.J. 264 (1976).

Modern Wills Act. John T. Gaubatz. 31 U.Miami L.Rev. 497 (1977).

Probate change. 20 Boston Bar J. No. 11, p. 6 (1976).

59

Figure 7-5
Sample Page from *Uniform Laws Annotated*
Directory of Acts

DIRECTORY OF UNIFORM ACTS

List of Uniform Acts or Codes, in alphabetical order, showing where each may be found in Uniform Laws Annotated, Master Edition.

The designation "Pocket Part" under the page column indicates that the particular Act or Code is complete in the Pocket Part. The designation "Pamphlet" under the page column indicates that the particular Act is complete in a Supplementary or Special Pamphlet. The user should always, of course, consult the Pocket Part or Pamphlet for changes and subsequent material when an Act or Code appears in the main volume.

Title of Act	Uniform Laws Annotated Volume	Page
Abortion Act, Revised	9, Pt. I	1
Absence as Evidence of Death and Absentees' Property Act	8A	1
Acknowledgment Act	12	1
Notarial Acts, Uniform Law on	14	125
Administrative Procedure Act, State (1981) (Model)	15	1
Administrative Procedure Act, State (1961) (Model)	15	137
Adoption Act	9, Pt. I	11
Aircraft Financial Responsibility Act	12	21
Alcoholism and Intoxication Treatment Act	9	79
Anatomical Gift Act (1987 Act)	8A	Pocket Part
Anatomical Gift Act (1968 Act)	8A	15
Ancillary Administration of Estates Act	8A	69
Antitrust, State Antitrust Act	7B	711
Arbitration Act	7	1
Attendance of Witnesses From Without a State in Criminal Proceedings, Act to Secure	11	1
Audio-Visual Deposition Act [Rule]	12	Pocket Part
Brain Death Act	12	Pocket Part
Canada—U.S. Transboundary Pollution Reciprocal Access Act	9B	625
Certification of Questions of Law Act	12	49
Child Custody Jurisdiction Act	9, Pt. I	115
Children and minors,		
Abortion Act, Revised	9, Pt. I	1
Adoption Act	9, Pt. I	11
Child Custody Jurisdiction Act	9, Pt. I	115
Civil Liability for Support Act	9, Pt. I	333
Gifts to Minors Act (1966 Act)	8A	181
Gifts to Minors Act (1956 Act)	8A	225
Interstate Family Support Act	9, Pt. I	Pocket Part
Juvenile Court Act	9A	1
Parentage Act	9B	287
Paternity Act	9B	347
Putative and Unknown Fathers Act	9B	Pocket Part
Reciprocal Enforcement of Support Act (1968 Act)	9B	381
Reciprocal Enforcement of Support Act (1950 Act)	9B	553
Revised Abortion Act	9, Pt. I	1
Status of Children of Assisted Conception	9B	Pocket Part
Transfers to Minors Act	8A	Pocket Part

1

A uniform law or model act drafted and approved by the Conference is secondary authority. The official comments of the drafters related to the background, purpose, and effect of a uniform law are also secondary authority, and although these comments provide credible insight into the goals of a uniform law and the ills it is designed to remedy, they need not be followed by a court. Once a uniform law or model act is adopted by your state legislature, however, it is primary authority that must be followed in your state.

F. Looseleaf Services

1. Introduction

You have seen that law books are usually published in a hardbound version or in softcover pamphlets, supplements, or advance sheets. Yet another method of publication is "looseleaf," meaning a ringed binder (or a book with removable covers and pages stacked on posts) with individual looseleaf sheets of paper, which are easily removed and replaced. These are the looseleaf services. The major looseleaf publishers are CCH Incorporated, Bureau of National Affairs, Clark Boardman Callaghan (now part of West), and Matthew Bender (now part of Lexis).

The looseleaf services are a variety of treatise and may consist of one volume or several volumes devoted to one topic of the law, such as labor law, securities, environmental law, Social Security compensation, bankruptcy, tax, criminal law, or family law. In general, looseleaf services are used for areas of the law that are subject to frequent change or that are highly regulated, such as securities law. Similarly, revisions are constantly being made to our tax laws. To publish information relating to taxation in hardbound sets of books would not be efficient or cost-effective, as the hardbound volumes would be out of date almost as soon as they were placed on library shelves. Even frequent updating by pocket parts will not keep pace with our changing tax laws. Therefore, the looseleaf service binder sets are purchased by law firms and law libraries. As changes occur in the law or as new cases are decided, the publisher will send packets of replacement pages to the subscriber with an instruction to remove and destroy certain pages in the set and replace them with the new pages provided by the publisher—an updating technique called interfiling. In this manner, the books are kept current to reflect accurately the status of the law without being cost-prohibitive to the subscriber. Some looseleaf services are updated as frequently as once a week.

Many of the looseleaf services are devoted to rules and regulations promulgated by our federal agencies, such as the service titled *Occupational Safety & Health Reporter*. These will be discussed in greater detail in Chapter 10. Several of the looseleaf services, however, report on areas of the law for which no particular agency is responsible but for which there is general interest, such as criminal law or family law. There are hundreds of looseleafs covering nearly every legal topic.

A typical looseleaf service will include primary and secondary authorities. Primary authority will be found in the statutes or regulations governing a certain area of the law (which are set forth in full text) as well as in the court decisions, which may be included. Often summaries or digests of court cases related to this area of the law are given. Secondary authority is found in the commentary and discussion of this topic and of recent developments in this area of the law as well as practice tips and notices of upcoming seminars or meetings of legal professionals or proposed legislation related to this area of law. The looseleafs thus function to provide a complete treatment of an area of the law, bringing together all information on a legal topic in one set. Some experts call the looseleafs "mini-libraries" because they are comprehensive collections of current legal materials devoted to one area of the law and brought together in one source.

Although a treatise may appear in binder or looseleaf form (such as the seven-volume binder set, *McCarthy on Trademarks and Unfair Competition*), a true looseleaf service is distinguishable from such a treatise because the looseleaf service will contain primary authority, such as cases, statutes, and administrative regulations, as well as secondary authority. A treatise usually includes only comment and analysis of an area of the law with no cases (although statutes may be included in an appendix to the set).

You should feel free to cite a looseleaf service in a memorandum or brief that you prepare. Often, however, the looseleaf services function more as "finding" tools, which provide general background information on a certain area of law and direct you to the primary authorities (statutes and cases) in the field, which you would then cite.

2. *Arrangement of Looseleaf Services*

There is no one uniform pattern for arrangement of looseleaf services. Different publishers arrange the discussion of the law in different ways, and each service is different from the others. Often the best way to determine the arrangement of the service to enhance your research efforts is simply to invest 20 to 30 minutes in reading the editor's introduction to the service and then browsing through the set to familiarize yourself with its features and structure.

In general, however, looseleaf services will consist of multiple ringed binders, each of which has several sections, divided by colorful marked tabs. For example, one tab is usually marked "How to Use." This section provides an overview of the service and guidelines for using the set. Other tabs may be marked "Topical Index," "Table of Cases," "State Laws," "Federal Laws," "Cumulative Index," and "New Developments."

3. *Research Strategies*

To determine if a looseleaf service exists for an area of the law you are researching, for instance, labor law, consult the card catalog in your law

library or ask the reference librarian. Alternatively, you could locate the stacks in the law library that contain labor law materials and simply scan the shelves to determine if a looseleaf service exists. You can also check a publication called *Legal Looseleafs in Print*, which provides information on more than 3,500 looseleafs and will also inform you if the looseleaf is available on the Internet.

Each looseleaf service will have a general index, which will alphabetically list the topics and subjects discussed in the service. Use the descriptive word approach to locate words in the index that describe your research issue. The index will then refer you to the appropriate paragraph or section. Some looseleaf sets have more than one index, so be sure you always check the most current index as well as the "standard" topical index. Alternatively, you can use the table of cases to locate cases reported or discussed in the set. Review the cases to which you are directed.

Note that references in the index are seldom to *pages*. It is typical of looseleaf services that paragraph or section references are used rather than references to pages, as this facilitates the addition of new replacement sheets in the set. Many looseleaf services also use subsections and decimals such as a reference to "¶ 10060.101" to accommodate the insertion of new pages. Thus, it may take you a bit of time to become accustomed to the organization of the looseleaf services. Invest the time it takes to understand how to use looseleaf services because these mini-libraries provide a comprehensive discussion of relevant legal topics.

G. Jury Instructions

1. Introduction

At the conclusion of a trial, a judge will "charge" the jury by providing it with instructions for reaching a decision. Preparing instructions for the jury is done by attorneys and paralegals. Until approximately 60 years ago, new jury instructions were developed for each trial. Often the instructions were erroneous statements of the law, and an appellate court would order a new trial due to the improper instruction. For example, if judges were free in criminal trials to develop their own definitions for "reasonable doubt," convictions of criminal defendants would be based upon differing standards.

Recognizing the duplication of effort required in preparing jury instructions for each trial and the waste of time and excessive cost involved in new trials due to erroneous instructions, a movement for pattern or form jury instructions emerged. Just as there are forms for leases, contracts, and motions for change of venue, there are now form books that contain jury instructions.

The jury instructions are typically drafted by committees of legal scholars or bar associations who study cases and then prepare accurate, brief, and easily understood instructions regarding the law. A new

development is the drafting of jury instructions in "plain English" to improve jurors' comprehension. In many states, the standard jury instructions are so highly regarded that rules of court for the state recommend or require that the trial judge read the applicable instruction. In other instances, jury instructions may be modified to state the law accurately. For example, in 2003, after six years of study, California adopted new civil jury instructions (the Judicial Council of California Civil Jury Instructions) after determining that the state's then-existing instructions were "simply impenetrable to the ordinary juror." The newly drafted instructions are in "plain English" so they are readily understandable to the average juror. Their use is not mandatory but they are designated "official" instructions, meaning that they are to be used unless a judge determines that a different instruction would more accurately state the law and be understood by jurors. All of the jury instructions, together with commentary, directions for their use, and references to primary and secondary authorities supporting their use are available on the Internet at http://www.courtinfo.ca.gov/jury/civiljuryinstructions.

Paralegals often play a major role in preparing jury instructions. Although the primary role of a jury instruction is to provide an accurate statement of the law for a judge to communicate to a jury, a secondary role is to provide research sources. Many sets of jury instructions not only provide the actual text of an instruction but also follow it with commentary directing you to cases, statutes, or treatises that support the language used in the instructions or provide additional information relating to that area of the law. This commentary is an excellent secondary authority source. Moreover, the instruction itself is a source of useful information for researchers. For example, if you were writing a memorandum on a contract matter and needed to list the elements of a cause of action for breach of contract, a jury instruction will likely set them forth. That is, when you read the jury instruction relating to contracts, you will see language similar to the following:

> Ladies and Gentlemen, if you find from your consideration of all the evidence that there was an agreement between the parties, that the parties were legally capable of entering into the agreement, that the defendant without justification or excuse breached the agreement, and that this breach was the cause of damage to the plaintiff, then you should find the defendant liable for breach of contract.

By analyzing the statement, you can easily see that a cause of action for breach of contract arises when three elements exist: an agreement; a breach of the agreement by one party; and damage caused by the breach. Thus, jury instructions serve to provide a quick summary of the key elements of many areas of the law, including contracts, fraud, negligence, infliction of emotional distress, assault, and battery.

2. *Research Strategies*

To locate the jury instructions in your law library, check the card catalog
or ask a reference librarian for assistance. Some law libraries keep the
materials on trial practice in one section, and in such instances you may
be able to locate the jury instructions in that section. Nearly every state
has its own sets of jury instructions for both civil and criminal cases. All
federal circuits have model or pattern criminal jury instructions and most
have approved instructions for civil cases as well.

If there is no set of jury instructions specific to your state, consult
the set *Am. Jur. Pleading and Practice Forms, Annotated.* As you will
recall from Chapter 6, this multivolume set contains thousands of forms
and documents for use in all phases of litigation and also contains
standard jury instructions. For federal cases you may consult a set titled
Modern Federal Jury Instructions, which provides jury instructions for
both civil and criminal cases. Some sets are available in both conventional bound volumes, in CD-ROM form, and on Lexis and Westlaw.

When you have located the books containing jury instructions,
consult the general index to the set. As is typical of indexes, it is usually
found at the end of the last volume of the set and lists alphabetically the
topics covered by the set.

Use the descriptive word approach and locate words describing the
issue you are researching, such as burglary, misrepresentation, or perjury. You will then be directed to the instructions used in such cases. Most
sets of jury instructions are updated by pocket parts. See Figure 7-6 for
sample jury instructions for determining damages in a copyright infringement case.

As discussed earlier, many states and courts now offer their jury
instructions on the Internet. Search your state's judicial website (see
Table T.1 of *The Bluebook* or Appendix 2 of *ALWD*) or review the article
"Reference from Coast to Coast—What Is the Law – Finding Jury
Instructions" at http://www.llrx.com/columns/reference19.htm, which includes links to jury instructions for several states. Use http://
www.uscourts.gov to link to all federal courts for their jury instructions.

———— Practice Tip ————

Jury Instructions

**Don't forget to use jury instructions to obtain a quick answer to a
straightforward research question. If you need to know the
elements of a fraud cause of action or what a plaintiff must prove
to prevail in a sexual harassment case, check your state's jury
instructions for a quick and concise statement of the law and then
a reference to a leading case on the topic.**

Figure 7-6
<u>Sample Jury Instruction</u>

12.8.3 DAMAGES — DEFENDANT'S PROFITS

[In addition to recovering for his actual losses,] Plaintiff is entitled to recover the profits that Defendant made because of the infringement. [Defendant's profits are recoverable, however, only to the extent that you have not taken them into account in determining Plaintiff's actual losses.]

Defendant's profits are revenues that Defendant made because of the infringement, minus Defendant's expenses in [producing; distributing; marketing; selling] the [*insert description of infringing material, e.g. product, advertisement, book, song, etc.*]. Plaintiff need only prove Defendant's revenues. Defendant must prove his own expenses [and any portion of his profits that resulted from factors other than infringement of Plaintiff's copyright].

Jury Instruction

Committee Comments

1. **General authority.** *See* 17 U.S.C. §504(b). The rationale for allowing the copyright owner to recover the infringer's profits in addition to the owner's actual losses is that it prevents the infringer from keeping "windfall" profits that he made from his decision to infringe the copyright rather than to negotiate with the copyright owner for a license. *See Taylor v. Meirick*, 712 F.2d 1112, 1120 (7th Cir. 1983); *Bucklew v. Hawkins, Ash, Baptie & Co.*, 329 F.3d 923, 931 (7th Cir. 2003).

2. **Standard.** *See, e.g., Hamil America Inc. v. GFI*, 193 F.3d 92, 108 n. 7 (2d Cir. 1999); *Robert R. Jones Assocs., Inc. v. Nino Homes*, 858 F.2d 274, 281 (6th Cir. 1988).

References to legal authorities supporting use of instruction

3. **Actual Losses and Profits.** The bracketed language in the instruction's first paragraph should be used only in cases where the plaintiff seeks to recover both actual losses and the defendant's profits.

(2008 ver.)

The Final Wrap-Up

Using and Citing Uniform Laws, Looseleaf Services, and Jury Instructions

Use: Use uniform laws adopted in your state as you would any state statute. If your state has no cases interpreting its particular uniform law, review cases from other jurisdictions as these may be highly persuasive. Use looseleaf services to locate current primary and secondary sources for highly regulated areas such as tax and securities. Use jury instructions when preparing for trial or to find a quick answer to a research question.

Citation: Cite freely to uniform laws. Remember that if adopted by your state, they have the force and effect of any statute. Looseleaf services are highly regarded and enjoy credible reputations, so they may also be freely cited. Cite jury instructions only when submitting them to a court before it charges a jury in a civil or criminal case.

H. Summary

All of the sources discussed in this and the preceding chapter are secondary authorities, meaning that although you may refer to these sources and cite them in memoranda or briefs, courts are not required to follow them. Although secondary authorities are often highly reputable, they remain persuasive at best and lack the force of the primary authorities of cases, constitutions, statutes, and administrative regulations. Keep in mind that some of the secondary authorities such as Restatements and law review articles are highly regarded and often cited, while others, such as encyclopedias, are viewed as elementary in approach and are seldom cited. One of the best indications of the strength of a secondary source is found in Rule 1.4(i) of *The Bluebook*, which provides the following hierarchical order when string-citing numerous secondary authorities: uniform and model acts; Restatements; treatises and books; works in journals, such as law review articles; annotations; magazine and newspaper articles; working papers; unpublished materials; and electronic sources. Encyclopedias are not listed. *ALWD* Rule 45 is substantially similar. All of the secondary authorities do an excellent job of providing commentary on the law and typically direct you to the primary authorities that you should rely upon and cite in your memoranda and briefs. A summary of the secondary sources is provided in Figure 7-7.

I. Citation Form

You should never cite to a directory. Other secondary sources are cited as follows:

1. Attorneys General Opinions:

The Bluebook: 46 Op. Att'y Gen. 496 (1997)
Validity of Statutory Rollbacks, 33 Op. O.L.C. 123 (2009)

ALWD: 46 Op. Atty. Gen. 496 (1997)
Validity of Statutory Rollbacks, 33 Op. Off. Leg. Counsel 123 (2009)

2. Dictionaries:

The Bluebook: *Black's Law Dictionary* 909 (9th ed. 2009)

ALWD: *Black's Law Dictionary* 909 (Bryan A. Garner ed., 9th ed., West 2009)

3. Uniform Laws:

The Bluebook: Unif. P'ship Act § 103, 7A U.L.A. 119 (2002)

ALWD: Unif. Partn. Act § 103, 7A U.L.A. 119 (2002)

4. Looseleaf Services:

The Bluebook: *In re Stevens Textiles Co.*, 4 Bankr. L. Rep. (CCH) ¶ 16,041 (Bankr. D.N.J. Mar. 10, 2003)

ALWD: *In re Stevens Textiles Co.*, 4 Bankr. L. Rep. (CCH) ¶ 16,041 (Bankr. D.N.J. Mar. 10, 2003)

5. Jury Instructions:

The Bluebook: 2 Leonard Sand et al., *Modern Federal Jury Instructions* § 12.04 (1984)

ALWD: Leonard Sand et al., *Modern Federal Jury Instructions* vol. 2, § 12.04 (Lexis 1984)

Figure 7-7
Chart of Secondary Sources

Secondary Source	Overview	Description of Set	Supplementation	Research Techniques	Research and Use Notes
A.L.R. Annotations	Thorough articles or "annotations" on various legal topics.	Multivolume sets	Annual cumulative pocket parts	Descriptive word approach	A.L.R. annotations are very well respected.
Encyclopedias	Alphabetically arranged narrative statements of hundreds of areas of the law supported by cases and other authorities found in footnotes	Multivolume general sets: C.J.S. and Am. Jur. 2d Multivolume state sets Special subject sets	Annual cumulative pocket parts	Descriptive word approach Topic approach	Excellent introductory information. Be cautious about citing to encyclopedias, as they are considered elementary in approach.

	Description	Types	Supplementation	Research/Indexing	Notes
Legal Periodicals	Publications produced on a periodic basis discussing a wide variety of legal topics	Law school publications Bar association and paralegal association publications Specialized publications Legal newspapers and newsletters	No supplementation. Each periodical issue is complete.	*Index to Legal Periodicals & Books* *Current Law Index* Other separately published indexes Online indices	Periodicals range from the very scholarly and well-respected law reviews to the more practical and seldom cited bar association publications and newsletters.
Texts and Treatises	Texts written by legal scholars on one legal topic that discuss cases and statutes in the narrative statements	Multivolume sets that contain thorough and often critical analysis of an area of the law	Annual cumulative pocket parts; softcover supplements; or replacement pages	Descriptive word approach Topic approach Table of cases or statutes approach	Many treatises are highly regarded, and you should feel free to refer and cite to them.

Figure 7-7 (Continued)

Secondary Source	Overview	Description of Set	Supplementation	Research Techniques	Research and Use Notes
Restatements	Statements of the law in clear and unambiguous language	Multivolume sets on selected areas of the law such as torts, agency, or property	Appendix volumes with pocket parts	Descriptive word approach Topic approach	Restatements are probably the most highly regarded of all of the secondary authorities.
Attorneys General Opinions	Written opinions by United States attorneys general and state attorneys general on a variety of legal topics	Multivolume sets for United States attorneys general opinions and opinions of state attorneys general	No supplementation. Each volume is complete.	Descriptive word approach References from other sources	Attorneys general opinions are strongly persuasive and highly respected.
Legal Dictionaries	Books providing definitions of legal words and phrases and references to authorities so defining a word	One-volume alphabetical arrangement of words, phrases, Latin and other foreign terms	No supplementation. Each volume is complete.	Alphabetical approach	While many dictionaries are well known and authoritative, you should cite to and rely on the cases you are directed to rather than the dictionary's definition of a word or phrase.

| *Law Directories* | Lists of lawyers | General directories such as *Martindale-Hubbell* contain lists of all attorneys and other useful features such as uniform laws. Specialty directories list attorneys specializing in certain practice areas or certain geographical regions. | Generally, no supplementation. Replacement sets issued annually or as needed. | Alphabetical approach by state, city, attorney's and firm's name | Used primarily to obtain information about attorneys and law firms. |

Figure 7-7 (Continued)

Secondary Source	Overview	Description of Set	Supplementation	Research Techniques	Research and Use Notes
Form Books	Sets of books containing standard or pattern forms for general use or for use in certain practice areas. Often annotated and containing useful commentary and practice guides.	Multivolume sets of books containing forms for general legal practice or specialty areas such as criminal law, corporate law, etc.	Pocket parts and supplements	Descriptive word approach Topic approach	Used primarily to assist in drafting documents. Seldom, if ever, cited, though used with great frequency.
Uniform Laws	Drafts of statutes proposed by legal scholars for certain areas of the law.	Multivolume set, *Uniform Laws Annotated,* containing text of uniform laws, commentary, references to other sources, etc.	Pocket parts and supplements	Use *Uniform Laws Annotated Directory of Acts* to locate a uniform law.	Cases interpreting a uniform law, even those from another state, may be highly persuasive in your state if your state has also adopted the uniform law.

Looseleaf Services	A variety of treatise devoted to one area of the law (usually a frequently changing area) containing both primary and secondary authority	Multivolume sets of books, arranged in ringed binders containing statutes, cases, case digests, and commentary on one topic of the law	Replacement pages	Descriptive word approach Consult "how to use" section	Looseleaf services provide a thorough overview of an area of the law, though their arrangement and use can be awkward.
Jury Instructions	Sets of books containing instructions for charging the jury in civil and criminal trials, as well as commentary and annotations	One-volume or multivolume sets specific to federal courts, one state, or general in nature	Pocket parts	Descriptive word approach	Used for trials and helpful in obtaining a "snapshot" of an area of the law, though seldom cited in research projects

CyberSites ▬▬▬▬▬▬▬▬▬▬▬▬▬▬▬▬

Attorney General Opinions

http://www.justice.gov/ag	The website for the United States Attorney General provides a great deal of information about the attorney general's duties as well as the text of speeches but does not provide opinions of the attorney general.
http://www.justice.gov/olc/opinions.htm	The website for the Department of Justice's Office of Legal Counsel has posted many opinions of the U.S. attorney general. Search by year.
http://www.naag.org	The National Association of Attorneys General site provides direct links to each state's attorney general, where opinions may be located.
http://www.washlaw.edu	Many states post their state attorney general opinions on their websites. This site provides a direct link to the home page for each state so you can search the site to determine if it offers the attorney general opinions.

Dictionaries

http://www.constitution.org/bouv/bouvier.htm	The complete text of Bouvier's well-known legal dictionary is offered at this site.
http://dictionary.law.com	A legal dictionary is offered at this site.

Directories

http://lawyers.findlaw.com	This website offered by West at FindLaw provides a searchable directory of more than one million lawyers and law firms.
http://www.martindale.com	This website offered by Martindale-Hubbell offers a searchable directory of law firms and lawyers in private and public practice.

Forms

http://www.lectlaw.com/form.html	The website of 'Lectric Law Library offers a variety of forms, including many used for litigation, business, real estate, wills, trusts, and corporations.
http://www.megalaw.com	Mega Law offers a wide variety of legal materials. Select "Legal Forms."
http://www.washlaw.edu	Washburn University School of Law publishes and links to thousands of legal forms, including forms for both state and federal courts. Select "Legal Forms."

(continued)

CyberSites *(Continued)*

http://www.memphis.edu/ govpub/forms.php	The University of Memphis provides a section called "Forms From the Feds" with direct links to numerous useful forms used by government agencies.

Uniform Laws

http://www.nccusl.org	The official website of the National Conference of Commissioners on Uniform State Laws provides the text of all final uniform laws, information and legislative status on uniform laws, and discussion of projects under consideration.
http://www.law.upenn.edu/ bll/archives/ulc/ulc.htm	The website of the University of Pennsylvania provides the text of most uniform laws and model acts and discusses projects currently under consideration.

Looseleaf Services

Although there is no one site providing the text of looseleaf services, the University of Illinois College of Law provides a comprehensive list of looseleafs (together with their publishers) at http://www.law.uiuc.edu/ library/looseleafs_subject.asp.

Jury Instructions

There is no one site to locate jury instructions. Some states, however, post their state-specific jury instructions on their home pages. To locate home pages, access http://www.megalaw.com, then select "State Law" and then select the particular state in which you are interested. The following sites may be helpful as well.

http://www.llrx.com/ columns/reference53.htm	Links to jury instructions from several states are provided at this site.
http://www.ll.georgetown .edu/guides/jury.cfm	Links to federal and state jury instructions can be found at this site.

Writing Strategies

There is a great temptation in using secondary sources such as *Black's Law Dictionary* or form books to use the very language you are provided. Although the use of a definition from a legal dictionary or the use of certain language given in a form book may be technically correct, it may result in "legalese." Legalese produces a document that is difficult for the reader to understand because its meaning is buried in a sea of redundant phrases and archaic word forms.

When discussing the secondary sources explained in this chapter, be on the alert for the following signs of legalese:

archaic words	hereinabove, erstwhile, albeit, opine
Latin or foreign phrases	*inter alia, res gestae*
redundancies	final result, basic fundamentals
nominalizations	"inspection" rather than "inspect," "harassment" rather than "harass," "decision" rather than "decide"
overuse of negatives	"notwithstanding anything to the contrary discussed herein, you are not prohibited from assigning this agreement."

Assignment for Chapter 7

1. Use *Black's Law Dictionary* (9th ed. 2009).
   a. What is the definition of "check kiting"?
   b. To which topic and key number are you directed for this definition?
   c. What does the legal maxim *in generalibus latet error* mean?
2. Use the most current volumes of *Martindale-Hubbell Law Directory*.
   a. Mary K. Barnard is an attorney with the Nashville, Tennessee, law frm Cheadle & Cheadle. Where and when did she receive her J.D. degree?
   b. An attorney named Elisa Santucci is with the Rio de Janeiro law firm Bhering Advogados. Where did she receive her law degree? What languages does she speak?
3. Use *Uniform Laws Annotated* (West's Master Edition).
   a. Has Arizona adopted the Uniform Marriage and Divorce Act?
   b. If your answer in part a. is affirmative, give the citation to the Arizona statute.
   c. Review the Uniform Marriage and Divorce Act. What is the general topic of section 305?
   d. Review section 305. What factors or incidents tend to show reconciliation of a couple?
   e. In what way did Kentucky change the official text of section 305?
4. Use *Federal Criminal Jury Instructions*.
   a. What instruction is used to instruct a jury on the elements of the offense of flight to avoid prosecution?
   b. Review the instruction. Would the instruction be used if a defendant intended to avoid having to testify in a criminal prosecution involving a felony?
5. Use *Am. Jur. Legal Forms (2d)*.
   a. Which general form relates to articles of organization for a limited liability company?
   b. Review the form. To what does article 8 relate?
   c. To which topic and key number are you directed?
6. Use *Am. Jur. Pleading and Practice Forms Annotated*.
   a. Which form provides a complaint against a landlord of residential premises for failure to furnish heat?
   b. Review the complaint. What does paragraph 8 allege?
   c. To which Am. Jur. reference are you directed?
7. Use *Am. Jur Pleading and Practice Forms Annotated*.
   a. Which form provides a complaint against a drug manufacturer for products liability for loss of consortium?
   b. Review the complaint. What does paragraph 19 allege?
   c. To which topic and key number are you directed?

8. Use *West's Legal Forms (3d)*.
   a. Which form relates to an e-mail communication policy in an employment handbook?
   b. Review the policy to which you are directed. Are jokes based on marital status prohibited under the policy?
   c. Under the policy may an employee ask another employee to contribute to a political action committee?

Internet Assignment for Chapter 7

1. Access the website for the National Association of Attorneys General.
   a. In how many states is the attorney general popularly elected?
   b. Identify three typical powers of a state attorney general.
   c. Identify the attorney general for your state and identify when he or she was appointed or elected.
2. Access the website for the Office of Legal Counsel within the Department of Justice. Locate the U.S. Attorney General opinion issued November 24, 2009.
   a. What was the issue handled by the opinion and how was it answered?
   b. Who signed the opinion?
3. Access Law.com's legal dictionary. Briefly, give the definition for "amicus curiae."
4. Access the website for California's Judicial Council Form. Review the form "Adoption Order." What information is required in Space 3 of the form?
5. Access the website http://www.lawyers.com. An attorney named Thomas M. Smith practices in Dallas, Texas. Where did Mr. Smith attend law school?
6. Access the website of the National Conference of Commissioners of Uniform State Laws. Review the Uniform Parentage Act. May a gestational agreement provide for payment to the gestational mother? Answer the question, and state which section governs your answer.
7. Access the website for the U.S. Court of Appeals for the Seventh Circuit. Review the Pattern Civil Jury Instructions. Do notes taken by a juror during a trial constitute evidence? Answer the question, and state which section governs your answer.
8. Access the website http://www.martindale.com. At the top of the toolbar, select "Groups and Topics." In the search box, search for "law digest volumes." How long do trademark rights last in Poland?

Legal Citation Form

Competence in legal citation is expected . . . and an ability to generate accurate citations is viewed as a proxy for . . . attention to detail.

Ian Gallacher, *Cite Unseen: How Neutral Citation and America's Law Schools Can Cure Our Strange Devotion to Bibliographical Orthodoxy and the Constriction of Open and Equal Access to the Law,*
70 Alb. L. Rev. 491, 492 (2006)

Chapter Overview

Paralegals are routinely assigned the task of "cite checking." Cite checking consists of two components: verifying that citations given in a project are accurate and in compliance with rules for citation form (sometimes called "Bluebooking") and then verifying that the authorities cited in a project are still "good law." The guidelines and rules relating to the form of citations will be discussed in this chapter, and the method of

ensuring that authorities relied upon are still correct statements of the law, usually called "Sheperdizing" or "KeyCiting," will be discussed in the following chapter.

This chapter will review the history of *The Bluebook* and *ALWD*, the best-known guides to citation form, and will provide examples of citations for the primary authorities of cases, constitutions, and statutes as well as the secondary authorities of encyclopedias, legal periodicals, treatises, Restatements, and other authorities. Moreover, this chapter will provide information on more intricate citation tasks, such as punctuation, quotations, and the use of signals such as *id.*, *supra*, and *infra*. Note that although numerous examples of citations are provided in this chapter, most are fictitious and are provided solely for the purpose of illustrating citation rules. Note also that the use of italic type is interchangeable with underscoring. References to *Bluebook* and *ALWD* rules are given in parentheses. Note that many examples of citation form are found in other chapters. For example, illustrations of citation form for administrative and international materials and court rules are found in Chapter 10, which discusses those subjects. Finally, for simplicity, pinpoint references to the exact pages on which material appears are often not included in examples until quotations are discussed in Section G.4 of this chapter.

A. Introduction to Citation Form

You may have already observed that legal writings are filled with references to cases, statutes, annotations, and numerous other authorities. The reason for this is that statements about the law must be attributed to their sources. You cannot simply make an assertion such as stating that a trial by jury is waived unless it is requested by a party. Such statements must be supported by legal authority; namely, by primary authorities or secondary authorities. These supporting authorities appear as "citations" or "cites" within the body of your work. Moreover, these citations must appear in a standard and consistent format so that any judge, attorney, paralegal, or other reader, upon viewing your citation, will be able to retrieve the legal authority you cited and verify that you have accurately represented the status of the law.

Because citations communicate information to a reader, it is essential that legal professionals communicate using the same "language" or citation form. You should be able to prepare a legal argument and present it to any court in the United States with confidence that a reader will be able to locate the authorities you cite. If legal professionals cited cases, statutes, and other authorities in varying ways, this would not only impede communication but also would dilute the strength of their arguments. When you present a persuasive argument, you do not want to distract the reader from the argument by using disfavored or incorrect citation form.

Newcomers to the legal field often inquire what will happen if citation form is incorrect in a brief or other document. Improper citation form has an effect similar to spelling errors in a writing: Such errors will

not transform an otherwise winning argument into a losing one. Rather, they result in a loss of respect for the author and cause readers to question the integrity and analysis of an argument. Many readers will conclude that if an author cannot be depended upon to cite or spell correctly, the author likely cannot be depended upon to conduct thorough legal analysis.

Recently, courts have been complaining that too many briefs are riddled with citation errors. *See, e.g., Edison Mission Energy, Inc. v. FERC*, 394 F.3d 964, 969 n.1 (D.C. Cir. 2005) (noting that failure to indicate relevant pages in citations in briefs is sanctionable under the Federal Rules of Appellate Procedure); *Hurlbert v. Gordon*, 824 P.2d 1238, 1245-46 (Wash. Ct. App. 1992) (stating that counsel's errors in briefing and poor citation form made it impossible for the court to find information in the record, hampering the work of the court and justifying the imposition of monetary sanctions against counsel).

B. Citation Manuals

1. *Introduction*

Citation manuals provide the rules for citing legal authorities. Just as writers routinely consult dictionaries and style guides to ensure their writings are correct, legal writers consult citation manuals to ensure that references to legal authorities are in proper form.

There are two primary citation manuals in the United States (and some lesser-known ones, which will be discussed later in this chapter): *The Bluebook: A Uniform System of Citation* (Columbia Law Review Ass'n et al. eds., 19th ed. 2010) (*"The Bluebook"*) and ALWD & Darby Dickerson, *ALWD Citation Manual* (4th ed., Aspen Publishers 2010) ("*ALWD*," pronounced "all wood"). *The Bluebook* is the oldest and best-known citation manual, but the ease of use and readability of *ALWD* have made it highly popular since its inception in 2000. The two manuals are more alike than they are different. This chapter provides separate sections on *The Bluebook* and *ALWD* and gives examples showing citations in both *Bluebook* and *ALWD* form.

2. *Overview of* The Bluebook

The best-known rules for citation form are found in a small wire-bound publication known as *The Bluebook*, which is now in its 19th edition. Its front and back covers are bright blue, and it is the most commonly used guide to citation form. *The Bluebook* was originally produced in the 1920s by the editorial boards of the *Columbia Law Review*, the *Harvard Law Review*, the *University of Pennsylvania Law Review*, and the *Yale Law Journal*. As time has passed, the editors of these law reviews have updated *The Bluebook*, and the 19th edition was published in mid-2010 by the same consortium. Questions and comments about *The Bluebook*

can be addressed to The Harvard Law Review, Gannett House, 1511 Massachusetts Avenue, Cambridge, Massachusetts 02138. Its website is http://www.legalbluebook.com.

Unless you are specifically directed to use some other system of citation rules or unless your jurisdiction has its own system of citation, follow *The Bluebook* because it is the best-known and accepted citation system. If local citation rules exist for your jurisdiction, they must be followed.

Law students, paralegals, and practitioners have long bemoaned the organization of *The Bluebook*, its confusing index, its dearth of sufficient examples, and its lack of articulate explanation of certain citation rules. Although each edition of *The Bluebook* attempted to respond to such criticisms, each new edition seemed to create as much confusion as it resolved. The 15th edition, released in 1991, however, reorganized *The Bluebook*, making it easier to use and of more benefit to practitioners, who often believed *The Bluebook* devoted far too much attention to citation form for various obscure publications and far too little attention to citation problems commonly encountered by practitioners. Similarly, the new 19th edition of *The Bluebook* is more user-friendly than previous editions and has expanded its section called the Bluepages, which includes numerous examples and is designed to assist practitioners with citation form.

In sum, there are few jurisdictions that require use of *Bluebook* form. For example, the rules of the United States Supreme Court impose requirements for nearly every aspect of documents submitted to the Court, from size of paper used to font size for footnotes, yet are silent on citation form. Use of *The Bluebook* is simply expected and traditional.

In early 2008, *The Bluebook* made its content available online. Users pay a modest subscription fee for access to the online *Bluebook*, which affords several advantages, including the following:

- Online searching makes it easy to locate needed information. Users can search by keywords or phrases to locate pertinent citation rules and examples.
- Just as one can mark up and annotate a print copy of *The Bluebook*, users can add their own notes to their online *Bluebooks*, and these notes are fully searchable.
- Group collaboration tools allow several users from the same law firm or practice group to add notes to their online *Bluebooks* so they can communicate needed information to each other about citation formats.

Additional information, including updates to *The Bluebook*, "Blue Tips" for using *The Bluebook*, and video tours are available at *The Bluebook's* website at http://www.legalbluebook.com.

One helpful guide in using *The Bluebook* is *Prince's Bieber Dictionary of Legal Citations* by Mary Miles Prince (7th ed. 2006), which alphabetically lists hundreds of examples of legal authorities following *Bluebook* rules. It is published by William S. Hein & Co., Inc. of Buffalo, New York ((800) 828-7571).

3. *Overview of* ALWD

In 2000, and as a response to continued criticism that *The Bluebook* was not user-friendly, the Association of Legal Writing Directors, an organization of directors of legal writing programs throughout the nation, released the *ALWD* citation manual, now in its fourth edition. *ALWD* is about the same size as *The Bluebook* and is also produced in a wire-bound booklet. *ALWD* is likely easier to use than *The Bluebook*, has numerous examples, and extensively uses color (namely, green) to show spacing, denote examples, and provide headings.

Although *ALWD* actually is longer than *The Bluebook*, most commentators find it far easier to use, and it has been widely accepted since its release. In fact, many law schools and more than 100 paralegal programs throughout the country teach citation form using *ALWD*. Nevertheless, the legal profession is slow to change, and many judges and attorneys in private practice have never heard of *ALWD* and continue to use *The Bluebook*. Thus, although both *The Bluebook* and *ALWD* attempt to provide a standardized and uniform system of citation, the existence of two well-known citation manuals may well cause confusion for some students who will be taught using one manual and yet expected to know the other "on the job." The good news is that although there are clear differences between *The Bluebook* and *ALWD* (see Figure 8-3 for a chart illustrating the differences), those differences are not so significant that legal writers will have trouble using either or both manuals. This chapter will discuss *Bluebook* citation rules and then *ALWD* citation rules, giving examples of both, but with greater emphasis on *The Bluebook* because — as of the writing of this text — it remains the best-known citation system.

PracticeTip

Since its inception in 2000, *ALWD* presented the word "Association" as "Assn." and "Department" as "Dept." (whereas *The Bluebook* always presented these words as "Ass'n" and "Dep't"). *ALWD's* new fourth edition now allows writers to use certain contractions as abbreviations and thus permits writers to present "Association" as either "Assn." or "Ass'n" and "Department" as either "Dept." or "Dep't." Numerous other words listed in *ALWD's* Appendix 3 have multiple acceptable abbreviations. Select one method and be consistent.

---

4. *Other Citation Manuals*

In addition to *The Bluebook* and *ALWD*, there are other guides to citation form, the most notable of which is the *University of Chicago Manual of Legal Citation* (3d ed. 2010), usually called the *Maroonbook*, and used primarily in the Chicago metropolitan area. The *Maroonbook*, first published in 1986, is far easier to use than *The Bluebook*. In fact, it is so

concise (fewer than 90 pages) and it leaves so many decisions about citation form to the discretion of the writer that it has failed to attract widespread interest beyond the Chicago area.

Additionally, in 1999, the American Association of Law Libraries ("AALL") published its *Universal Citation Guide* to create a set of universal citation rules for American legal authorities, whether those authorities appear in print or electronic form. The *Universal Citation Guide* (now in its second version) developed from the work of many groups, including federal and state courts and the American Bar Association. Its full text is available through the ABA's resource center on legal technology (http://www.abanet.org/tech/ltrc/research/citation/home.html) or the AALL site (http://www.aallnet.org/committee/citation).

Finally, in addition to these citation manuals, there is state variation. For example, legal professionals in Texas and California use their own formats and there is significant variation from one local jurisdiction to another. Texas's manual, the *Texas Rules of Form* (12th ed. 2010), is usually called the "Greenbook." California encourages the use of a specific manual published by West, the *California Style Manual* (4th ed. 2000), in citing cases. Cal. R. Ct. 8.204 advisory cmt., although use of *The Bluebook* is acceptable as well. Cal. R. Ct. 1.200. In sum, *The Bluebook* is probably still the best-known citation system with *ALWD* continuing to attract admirers. State-specific rules may require yet different citation formats. Always follow your firm or office practice.

PracticeTip

Citation Form

In citing legal authorities, do not rely on the way books and cases refer to themselves. For example, many volumes of U.S.C.A. include an instruction similar to the following: "Cite This Book Thus: 42 U.S.C.A. §1220." Yet this form is incorrect according to both *The Bluebook* and *ALWD*, which provide the following correct form: 42 U.S.C.A. § 1220 (West 2004), with a space after the section symbol and a reference to the publisher and year. Similarly, many courts in California use the incorrect abbreviation "C.A." rather than the correct abbreviation "Cal. Ct. App." to refer to cases from the California appellate courts.

Thus, always rely on the appropriate *Bluebook* or *ALWD* rules rather than the citation forms you may observe in books or case reports or on Lexis or Westlaw.

C. *The Bluebook*

1. *Organization of* The Bluebook

Although it would be unnecessarily time-consuming to read *The Blue-book*, you should become familiar with its overall arrangement and read at least the Bluepages section in the front of the book. *The Bluebook* is composed of six major sections:

> *Preface.*   The Preface provides a summary of the changes initiated in the 19th edition of *The Bluebook*.
>
> *Introduction.*   The Introduction discusses the structure of *The Bluebook* and general principles of citation.
>
> *Bluepages.*   The Bluepages was added in 2005 and is a how-to guide for basic legal citation form. It is designed for use by legal professionals and includes numerous useful examples. It also includes two tables, one showing abbreviations for use in court documents and one providing references to local citation rules. References in this chapter to Bluepages will be shown as "B."
>
> *General Rules of Citation and Style.*   This section, printed on white paper, provides general standards of citation and style used for legal writings and then sets forth 21 specific rules of citation for primary authorities (cases, constitutions, and statutes) and secondary authorities (books, periodicals, foreign materials, and so on). References in this chapter to Rules will be shown as "R."
>
> *Tables.*   *The Bluebook* contains 18 tables, most of which are printed on white paper with blue trim for easy access describing how cases and statutes from federal courts and each state court are cited and providing abbreviations for court documents, geographical terms, months, and various periodicals.
>
> *Index.*   An alphabetically arranged Index is found at the end of *The Bluebook*. When you have a question or concern regarding citation form, use the descriptive word approach to access the Index, which will refer you to the pertinent page for the citation rule you need.

2. *Typeface Conventions*

Perhaps the single most important fact you should know about *The Bluebook* is that almost all of the examples given in the white pages of *The Bluebook* show how to cite authorities as if you were writing a law review article. Because your cite checking work as a paralegal will in all likelihood relate to authorities cited in court documents and legal memoranda, you must convert the examples you are given by *The Bluebook* that relate to law review format to the format suitable for practitioners.

The Bluebook includes a special section on light blue paper near the front of the book called the Bluepages, which shows you how to adapt the examples you find in the body of *The Bluebook* to the format needed for court documents and memoranda. For example, if you were citing a text in a law review article, it would appear as follows:

1 J. THOMAS MCCARTHY, MCCARTHY ON TRADEMARKS AND UNFAIR COMPETITION § 3:1 (4th ed. 1997).

On the other hand, if you were to cite this same text in a court document or a legal memorandum, it would appear as follows:

1 J. Thomas McCarthy, *McCarthy on Trademarks and Unfair Competition* § 3:1 (4th ed. 1997).

The obvious difference between these two citation forms is that the first, used for law reviews, uses a style of large and small capitals for the author's name and treatise title, whereas the second format, used by practitioners, uses capital and lowercase letters only. It is customary for law reviews to use large and small capitals for state statutes, book titles, author names, periodical titles, and some other materials. This format, however, is not used by practitioners or in non-academic legal documents. In fact, the 19th edition of *The Bluebook* (B1) clearly instructs practitioners, "[l]arge and small caps are never used." Thus, when you see an example given in *The Bluebook* such as the reference to the Florida Law Review as "FLA. L. REV.," you will need to adapt the format to that used by practitioners, namely, "Fla. L. Rev."

Many experts believe that the use of large and small capitals in academic writings is a holdover from the time law review articles were manually typeset. Because documents prepared by practitioners were typed rather than typeset and typewriters could not change fonts to make one capital letter larger than another, practitioners never used large and small capitals (even though the advent of word processing has made this possible). Thus, every time you encounter an example in *The Bluebook*, ask yourself, "Could this format be reproduced on an old-fashioned typewriter?" If not, it is a signal to you that the form is for law reviews, not for practitioners' documents. This dual system of citation (the use of large and small capitals for academic writings and the use of ordinary roman type capital and lowercase letters by practitioners) has continued to exist long past any need for it. Because word processors can readily use a large and small capital format, practitioners could adopt that method of citation, and the dual citation system could be scrapped. Why do two separate systems continue to exist, each with its own rules and requirements? No one knows. One of the nice advantages of *ALWD* is that it eliminates this odd distinction between large and small capitals and ordinary type and requires only the use of "ordinary" type.

Other useful guides to showing you the differences in citation form between law review format and the style used for court documents and

legal memoranda are on the inside front and back covers of *The Bluebook*. The inside front cover is titled "Quick Reference: Law Review Footnotes" and gives you several examples for citation form for use for law review footnotes. The inside back cover is titled "Quick Reference: Court Documents and Legal Memoranda" and gives you the same examples for use in legal writings for practitioners.

Be sure to refer often to the inside back cover. Do not become confused and assume that because an example appears in the body of *The Bluebook* it is correct. It may well be correct — but only for law review footnotes. After viewing an example in the body of *The Bluebook*, check the Bluepages and the inside back cover of *The Bluebook* and adapt the typeface for use in a court document or legal memorandum. Remember that practitioners never use large and small capitals.

Another difference you will note between citations shown on the inside front cover (for law review footnotes) and those shown on the inside back cover (for use by practitioners) is that full case names are neither underscored nor italicized in law review footnotes and yet they are always underscored or italicized by practitioners. In fact, hundreds of examples throughout the white pages in *The Bluebook* show full case names in ordinary roman type (without underscoring or italicization). Do not become confused by the examples shown in the white pages throughout *The Bluebook*. Unless you are preparing footnotes for a law review article, case names will always be underscored or italicized.

3. *Revisions to the 19th Edition of* The Bluebook

The 19th edition of *The Bluebook* retains the same basic approach to citation form as earlier editions. Nevertheless, it does contain some changes, primarily in the rules relating to the situations requiring use of parallel citations and guidance for citing materials in electronic form and on the Internet. Although these changes are discussed in detail in the preface to *The Bluebook* and throughout *The Bluebook*, and in this chapter, some of the more significant changes are as follows:

(i)   The Bluepages (which was new to the previous 18th edition) has been expanded to now include information on citing to Electronic Case Filings.

(ii) Bluepages Table T.2 (providing references to local rules that govern citation form) has been expanded.

(iii) *The Bluebook* now provides an order or ranking for parentheticals when a writer uses several of them. See Rule 1.5 on page 60.

(iv) Much of the information that was previously included in Rule 14 (covering Administrative and Executive Materials) is now in Table T.1.2. Moreover, Table T.1.2 now gives an expanded list of

federal agencies, including information on citing to materials from the Department of Commerce, Department of Homeland Security, and more.

(v) Rule 18, relating to citation to electronic sources (namely, the Internet, Lexis, and Westlaw) has been revised, and citation to these electronic sources is simplified, although *The Bluebook* continues to require the use and citation of traditional printed sources when they are available *unless* there is a digital copy of the source available that is authenticated, official, or an exact copy of the printed source (in which case the authenticated, official, or exact copy may be cited as if to the original source).

(vi) Table T.1 has now been divided into four sections: federal judicial and legislative materials; federal administrative and executive materials; states; and other U.S. jurisdictions.

(vii) Reflecting the increasing cross-border emphasis in legal practice, the rules relating to citation to international materials and Table T.2 (relating to citation to authorities from foreign jurisdictions) have been rewritten and greatly expanded.

D. *Bluebook* Citation Rules and Examples for Primary Authorities

1. Cases

a. Introduction

A typical case citation includes the following components:

- Case name
- References to the set(s) of case reports that published the case and the page on which the case begins (and, as discussed later, a pinpoint citation to the specific page on which material appears)
- A parenthetical that includes the court and jurisdiction and the year of decision
- The subsequent history of the case and other parenthetical information, if any (B4).

Thus, a typical citation to a case cited in a court document in Oregon is as follows:

Smith v. Jones, 329 P.2d 411, 414 (Or. 1979).

b. Case Names

The Bluebook contains numerous rules regarding case names in citations. Carefully review Bluepages B4.1.1 and Rules 10.2, 10.2.1, and 10.2.2 in *The Bluebook* for a full discussion of these rules. Some of the more common guidelines you should be aware of are as follows:

(i) Cite only the last names of the parties to an action.

> **Correct:**   *Talbert v. Carver*
>
> **Incorrect:**   *Luisa N. Talbert v. Jay Carver*

Note, however, that many corporations use an individual's name as part of the business name. In such a case, include the full name of the business entity.

> **Correct:**   *Ruiz v. Edward N. Pauley, Inc.*
>
> **Incorrect:**   *Ruiz v. Pauley, Inc.*

(ii) If more than one party is listed, omit all but the first party on each side.

> **Correct:**   *Hart v. Ward*
>
> **Incorrect:**   *Hart v. Ward, Schiff, and Newley*

(iii) If several actions have been consolidated into one decision, cite only the first listed action.

> **Correct:**   *Marrien v. Jacobson*
>
> **Incorrect:**   *Marrien v. Jacobson, Taylor v. Reynolds*

(iv) Omit any indication of multiple parties when citing published cases.

> **Correct:**   *Galinda v. Dubek*
>
> **Incorrect:**   *Galinda v. Dubek, et al.*

(v) Omit indications of legal status or other descriptive terms.

> **Correct:**   *Brumer v. Crawford*
>
> **Incorrect:**   *Brumer v. Crawford, Executor*
>
> **Incorrect:**   *Brumer v. Crawford, d/b/a The Green Grocer*
>
> **Incorrect:**   *Brumer v. Crawford, Defendant*

(vi)   Do not abbreviate "United States" (or the name of any state) in a case name if it is the entire name of a party and omit the phrase "of America."

Correct:	*United States v. Souther*
	Dixon v. University of Virginia
	Dixon v. Univ. of Va. (in "stand-alone" citation)
Incorrect:	*U.S. v. Souther*
	Dixon v. Va.
Incorrect:	*United States of America v. Souther*
Incorrect:	*USA v. Souther*

(vii) For criminal cases decided by your state, cite as follows:

Correct:	*State v. Eagan*
Incorrect:	*State of Kansas v. Eagan*
Correct:	*Commonwealth v. Nelson*
Incorrect:	*Commonwealth of Pennsylvania v. Nelson*

If the case was not decided by a court in your state (if, for example, the case was later appealed from the Kansas Supreme Court to the United States Supreme Court), cite as follows:

Correct:	*Kansas v. Eagan*
Incorrect:	*State v. Eagan*
Correct:	*Pennsylvania v. Nelson*
Incorrect:	*Commonwealth of Pennsylvania v. Nelson*

(viii) Omit the second "business signal" such as "Inc.," "Co.," or "Corp." if the case name already contains one business signal.

Correct:	*Smith v. Auto Service Corp.*
Incorrect:	*Smith v. Auto Service Corp. Inc.*

(ix)   Omit prepositional phrases of location unless they follow the word "City" or a similar word.

Correct:	*Brown v. Board of Education*
Incorrect:	*Brown v. Board of Education of Topeka, Kansas*

(x) When a case name appears in a textual sentence, for example,
when it appears as a grammatical component of a sentence,
abbreviate only the following words in a case name and widely
known acronyms (such as FBI, CIA, and NLRB) (B4.1.1; Rule
10.2.1(c)):

And	&
Association	Ass'n
Brothers	Bros.
Company	Co.
Corporation	Corp.
Incorporated	Inc.
Limited	Ltd.
Number	No.

When a citation appears or stands alone by itself, rather than
functioning as a grammatical component of a sentence, always abbreviate
any word in the case name that is listed in Table 6 of *The Bluebook*
(B4.1.1, Rules 10.2.1.(c) and 10.2.2). The word is abbreviated even if it is
the first word in a case name.

Note, however, that if one of the eight words listed above (for
example, "Bros.") begins a party's name, it may not be abbreviated.

Examples

Textual Sentence: In *Franklin Hospital Guaranty Co. v.
Southern Division Ltd.*, 780 F. Supp. 91, 97 (W.D. Tex. 1990), the
court held that fraud requires a material misrepresentation.

Stand-alone Citation: Fraud requires a material misrepresentation. *Franklin Hosp. Guar. Co. v. S. Div. Ltd.*, 780 F. Supp. 91,
97 (W.D. Tex. 1990).

This rule is one of the least understood rules in *The Bluebook* and
requires you to focus on the location and use of a citation before you
determine which words can be abbreviated in a case name. For simplicity,
use this rule: If a case name in a citation appears as a textual part of a
sentence (meaning the cite is needed to make sense of the sentence), you
may abbreviate only widely known acronyms and the eight well-known
and commonly used abbreviations provided in Rule 10.2.1., such as "Co."
and "Inc." On the other hand, if a citation stands alone in a clause or after
the end of a sentence and is not needed to make sense of a sentence, you
must abbreviate any of the more than 170 words listed in Table T.6, even
if they are the first word in a party's name. Why? Many experts believe
that because readers are unused to seeing abbreviations in the middle of
sentences, to abbreviate any words other than very commonly used words
would be distracting. On the other hand, if a citation stands by itself,
readers will not be disconcerted by seeing abbreviations such as "Indem."
or "Sur."

The rule requiring abbreviation of the first word in a party's name that appears as a "stand-alone" citation was introduced in 2000 and has caused some confusion. For nearly 100 years, practitioners were firmly instructed, "never abbreviate the first word in a party's name." Thus, the change in 2000 has required some effort for existing practitioners to become familiar with, particularly when the citation might read *Allen v. W. Co.*, 520 U.S. 13, 16 (1998).

(xi)   Generally, omit the word "The" as the first word of a party's name.

Correct: *Washington Post v. Lorenzi*

Incorrect: *The Washington Post v. Lorenzi*

(xii) Entities that are widely known (for example, NAACP, SEC, FCC, FDA) may be referred to as such in case names, without periods.

Preferred: *SEC v. Garcia*

Disfavored: *S.E.C. v. Garcia*
Disfavored: *Securities and Exchange Commission v. Garcia*

The Bluebook (R. 6.1 (b)) gives only a few examples of such entities. Generally, however, if an entity is referred to in spoken language by its initials rather than its full name (for example, one usually says, "He was investigated by the FBI" rather than "He was investigated by the Federal Bureau of Investigation"), it may be used in its abbreviated form without periods.

(xiii) The "v." in a case citation stands for "versus" and always appears in lowercase form. Although you may see some other form for "versus" in a pleading such as a complaint or answer, when referring to decided cases always use a lowercase "v" followed by a period.

Correct: *Marksen v. Sigler*

Incorrect: *Marksen V. Sigler*
Incorrect: *Marksen vs. Sigler*

(xiv) Always underscore or italicize the name of a case in a citation, including the "v.," and any procedural phrases such as "In re." Use a solid unbroken line. Either underscoring (also called "underlining") or italicizing is appropriate (B1). Years ago, underscoring was most popular, as few typewriters were capable of producing italics. With the advent of word processors, which are capable of italicizing, this technique became very

popular. Many legal writers, however, continue to prefer underscoring because it is very noticeable and dramatic on a white sheet of paper. Moreover, the examples given in the Blue-pages section of *The Bluebook* show underscoring. Note these rules for underscoring:

- The line should be unbroken.
- The line should be placed underneath the entire case name, including any periods.

Correct: Peters v. Swanson & Johnson Co.

Incorrect: Peters v. Swanson & Johnson Co.

Whichever method (namely, underscoring or italicizing) you select, be consistent. Check your firm or office practice for preferences.

   (xv) The case name should always be followed by a comma. The comma is not underlined, underscored, or italicized.

Correct: Jeffries v. Purvis,

Incorrect: Jeffries v. Purvis,

Practice Tip

Case Citations

- Note that the correct legal abbreviation for "second" is 2d and the correct legal abbreviation for "third" is 3d, rather than 2nd or 3rd, which are commonly encountered in nonlegal writings.
- Note that the first page given in a case citation is the page on which a case begins and is not introduced with an abbreviation such as "p." which is often used in nonlegal writings.

---

c. Parallel Citations

(1) *Old* Bluebook *Rule*

Until relatively recently, *Bluebook* citation rules required that all citations to all state court cases include all parallel cites; that is, references to the official report and the unofficial reporter(s) that published the case. The parallel citations were provided as a courtesy to the reader because the writer would not know if the reader had access to the official reports or the unofficial reporter(s). The writer would thus provide *all* citations so the reader could easily locate the cited case no matter which set of books or case reports the reader used.

Example
  Liston v. Alpha Co., 129 Va. 109, 381 S.E.2d 12 (1980)

This requirement of providing all parallel cites made citation form awkward and difficult for the writer because the writer would have to obtain all parallel cites and then, if quoting from a certain page in the text, would have to indicate the exact page the quote appeared on in each case report. For California, Illinois, and New York cases, which may have three parallel cites, this rule made the difficult task of citation form even more complicated.

(2) *Current* Bluebook *Rule*

Bluebook Rule 10.3.1 and Bluepages 4.1.3 govern parallel citations for state court cases. *The Bluebook* now makes it clear that you need only include a parallel citation if court rules require such. Note that when court rules do require parallel citations, the official citation is given first, followed by the unofficial parallel citation(s). Remember, however, that many states no longer publish their cases officially, and cases from those jurisdictions will have only one citation.

In all other instances, cite to the relevant regional reporter (for example, *Atlantic Reporter* or *Pacific Reporter*) if the case is in that set, and then indicate the name of the court and its geographical jurisdiction (using the abbreviations found in Table T.1) parenthetically with the year of decision. There is, however, one exception to this rule: Do not include the name of the court if the court that decided the case is the highest court of the state. For example, the highest court in nearly all states is called the supreme court, and Table T.1 in *The Bluebook* indicates that for all states' highest courts, the appropriate abbreviation indicates the name of the state and no other information is given. Thus, Table T.1 states that "Cal." indicates a case from the California Supreme Court and "Ohio" indicates a case from the Ohio Supreme Court. Cases from those states' appellate courts are indicated by the following abbreviations (again, respectively, as shown in Table T.1): "Cal. Ct. App." and "Ohio Ct. App."

Thus, consider the following examples:

- *Green v. Hall*, 68 Mich. 2d 802, 310 N.W.2d 604 (1979) [This is how the *Green* case would be cited if a court rule required parallel citations.]
- *Green v. Hall*, 301 N.W.2d 604 (Mich. 1979)
  [This is how the *Green* case would be cited in any other instance, including in a court document for a court that does not have local rules requiring parallel citations, in a letter to a client, or in an internal office memorandum. Because Table T.1 of *The Bluebook* tells us that the abbreviation for the Michigan Supreme Court is "Mich.," upon encountering this citation, a reader knows the case is from the Michigan Supreme Court.]
- *Taylor v. Fletcher*, 401 Mich. App. 190, 304 N.W.2d 18 (1981)
  [This is how the *Taylor* case, a case decided by the Michigan Court of Appeals, would be cited if a court rule required parallel citations.]

- *Taylor v. Fletcher*, 304 N.W.2d 18 (Mich. Ct. App. 1981)
  [This is how the preceding case from the Michigan Court of Appeals would be cited in any instance other than for a court whose rules require parallel citations.]

Although *The Bluebook* rule does not require parallel cites in an internal law office memorandum, many practicing legal professionals will include the parallel cite knowing that if the memorandum later becomes the basis for a brief submitted to a court that requires parallel citations, such as a motion for change of venue, the parallel cite would be required for that document. Thus, including it in an earlier memo will save time later by eliminating the need to return to the law library to track down the parallel cite. Follow your firm or office practice.

As you will recall from Chapter 4, 22 states and the District of Columbia no longer publish their cases officially, and cases from those jurisdictions appear only in the relevant regional reporter. If you are citing a case from one of these states decided after the date official publication ceased, the correct citation form will refer the reader only to the regional reporter and will include information about the court that decided the case parenthetically as follows:

Gray v. Donoghue, 704 P.2d 118 (Colo. 1999).

To determine which states no longer publish officially and when those states discontinued their official publications, consult the chart in Chapter 4 herein or Table T.1 of *The Bluebook*, which alphabetically lists all 50 states and provides information about correct citation form for each state.

Eleven jurisdictions (Delaware, the District of Columbia, Maine, Montana, Nevada, New Hampshire, Rhode Island, South Dakota, Vermont, West Virginia, and Wyoming) have no intermediate appellate courts. In those jurisdictions, all citations are to the state's highest court, usually called the supreme court, and the parenthetical would always display only the abbreviation of the state (such as "Wyo.") and never any abbreviation that would indicate an appellate court (such as "Wyo. Ct. App.").

Finally, in a few states (including Arizona, Hawaii, Idaho, New Mexico, South Carolina, and Wisconsin), cases from the state supreme court are published in the same volumes as those from the lower intermediate court of appeals. For example, the set *New Mexico Reports* includes cases from the New Mexico Supreme Court and the New Mexico Court of Appeals. Citations to cases from these states may need parentheticals identifying the deciding court. For example, when citing a case from the New Mexico Court of Appeals (assuming local rules require parallel citations), show this as follows: *Cruz v. Harley*, 94 N.M. 861, 729 P.2d 14 (Ct. App. 1993). Without the parenthetical, the reader would assume the case is from the New Mexico Supreme Court. If the case is, in fact, from the New Mexico Supreme Court, the parenthetical need only include the date; it need not include any reference to "S. Ct." Allow the reader to assume it is from the highest court in New Mexico. In sum, if the

name of the reporter unambiguously indicates the jurisdiction and the court, omit that information in the parenthetical.

Do not indicate the department, division, county, or district in citing a case from an intermediate state court unless that information is of particular importance (R. 10.4(b)).

> **Preferred:**   *Crandall v. Brown,* 291 So. 2d 481
> (La. Ct. App. 1981)
>
> **Disfavored:**   *Crandall v. Brown,* 291 So. 2d 481
> (La. Ct. App. 1st Cir. 1981)

Practice Tip

State Cases: **The Bluebook** *and* **ALWD**

Rule 1:   **If the name of the reporter set is the same as the name of the jurisdiction, you need not give the name of the court in the parenthetical with the date.**

Example: 113 Cal. 3d 118 (1999)

Explanation: **You need not include "California Supreme Court" in the parenthetical with the date because Table T.1 of *The Bluebook* tells you that the name of the reporter is identical to the court abbreviation and by looking at the citation, the reader can tell what court decided the case (namely, the California Supreme Court).**

Rule 2:   **You must include the name of the court in the parenthetical with the date if a reader cannot tell what court decided the case from reading the citation.**

Example: 790 P.2d 989 (Or. 1997)

Explanation: **In reviewing the citation, "P.2d" doesn't tell the reader what court decided the case, so the parenthetical must indicate such. The "Or." in the parenthetical tells the reader implicitly that the case is from the Oregon Supreme Court. Otherwise, the parenthetical would have indicated "Or. Ct. App."**

---

(3) *Public Domain Format*

As difficult as *The Bluebook*'s rules are, legal professionals have had, until recently, only this one source to learn. The proliferation of legal materials on electronic databases and the Internet, however, is likely to add further to the confusion already associated with citation form. A controversy has arisen with regard to citation form: how to adapt the traditional citation systems advanced for more than 80 years by *The Bluebook* to an increasingly technological age.

Current citation rules in most states require citations to conventional print forms, the majority of which are published by West, requiring legal professionals to purchase West sets even though cases and other materials are easy and inexpensive (or free) to access on the Internet. Moreover, all states maintain a judicial website, and most post decisions to these websites the day decisions are released. Thus, many legal professionals and consumers advocate the implementation of what is usually referred to as a public domain, neutral, "format-neutral," or "vendor-neutral" citation system, meaning that the citation looks the same whether the reader has accessed the case by conventional print format or by electronic methods, such as CD-ROM, Lexis, Westlaw, or the Internet. These groups argue that *The Bluebook* rules requiring citation to West sets, such as the *Pacific Reporter*, *Federal Reporter*, or the *Federal Supplement*, give West a near monopoly and discourage other legal publishers from entering the market, which would ultimately lead to increased competition with resulting lower costs for consumers.

Although the text of cases and statutes are public domain materials and are thus not subject to copyright protection, when a publisher such as West compiles these materials, adds headnotes, indexes, and other features, it can copyright the resulting product. To end what is perceived as West's unfair market advantage obtained through citation rules requiring or preferring citation to West books, both the American Bar Association and the American Association of Law Libraries as well as numerous professionals support the development of a neutral citation scheme, namely, the *Universal Citation Guide* (version 2.1 2002), discussed earlier.

In February 2003, the ABA passed a resolution committing that it would facilitate discussion with organizations working on legal citation formats to develop a universal American citation system that is equally effective for printed case reports and for case reports published electronically. The ABA is hoping that cooperation among courts, law schools, and others to create a vendor- and media-neutral citation system will benefit the public and make increasing amounts of information available electronically.

Note that *ALWD*'s approach to neutral citations is similar to that of *The Bluebook* and provides that you should use neutral citations when required by local rule.

At the time of the writing of this text, according to *The Bluebook*, the following states have adopted a public domain citation format: Arkansas, Louisiana, Maine, Mississippi, Montana, New Mexico, North Dakota, Ohio, Oklahoma, Pennsylvania (for superior court cases), South Dakota, Utah, Vermont, Wisconsin, and Wyoming. Other states may be considering doing so. No federal court has adopted a public domain format for citations. When states adopt a public domain citation format, it is prospective only and effective only after a certain date (clearly indicated in Table T.1 in *The Bluebook*). Citations to cases decided before the date a state adopts a neutral or public domain format would follow the standard citation format previously described in Section C of this chapter.

The Bluebook (R. 10.3.3) requires that for public domain citations, one give the case name, year of decision, that state's two-character postal code, the Table T.7 court abbreviation (unless the court is the state's highest court), the sequential number of the decision, and, if a parallel citation is available, it must be provided. A pinpoint paragraph rather than a pinpoint page is given. If the case is unpublished, a capital "U" should be placed after the sequential number of the decision.

Bluebook Example

Albert v. Tinley, 1998 ME 116, ¶ 3, 710 A.2d 14, 17.

In the above example, the case name is *Albert v. Tinley*, the case was the 116th case decided in 1998 by the Maine Supreme Court, and the relevant information is located in paragraph 3 of the case. The remaining information is the usual unofficial citation. Thus, the public domain citation replaces only the official citation in state court cases. If available, the unofficial or regional citation must be given as well to ensure easy access to the case by readers.

The ABA recommends the following standard form of citation for a decision from a federal court of appeals:

ABA Example

Baker v. Smith, 2004 7Cir 14, ¶ 17, 231 F. 3d 123.

In the above example, the year of decision is 2004, "7Cir" refers to the U.S. Court of Appeals for the Seventh Circuit, "14" indicates the citation is to the 14th decision released by the court in 2004, "17" is the pinpoint paragraph in the case, and the remainder of the information is the parallel citation to the *Federal Reporter, Third Series*.

Table T.1 of *The Bluebook* clearly indicates which states have adopted the neutral or public domain citation format, and Rule 10.3.3 provides citation rules. As in all citations, if a jurisdiction has adopted its own rules as to citation form, they supersede *The Bluebook* rules, and the same is true for neutral citation format. The website of the American Association of Law Libraries (http://www.aallnet.org/committee/citation/#reports) and the website of the American Bar Association (http://www.abanet.org/tech/ltrc/ research/citation/home.html) provide additional information on jurisdictions that have adopted a public domain citation format. A state's own judicial website (see Table T.1 in *The Bluebook* and Appendix 2 of *ALWD*) may provide court rules giving instruction as to citation presentation. There is a great deal of discrepancy among the adopting states as to spacing in the citations so carefully follow the examples you are given.

Finally, note that most of the states that have adopted a public domain citation format are those that no longer publish officially. Moreover, although neutral citation form engendered a great deal of discussion when states first started adopting it (in about 1994), the issue seems to have decreased in interest, with only Arkansas adopting a neutral or public domain citation format since 2003.

d. Recent Cases

(1) Official Cite Unavailable

West typically publishes its cases a bit quicker than the official publishers. If you wish to cite to a very recent case and the official report is not yet available, you may cite as follows:

Hunter v. Hoffman, _____ Conn. _____, 417 A.2d 704 (2010)

The "blank" lines serve as a signal to a reader that an official citation will exist but it is not yet available. This form is not permitted or recognized by *The Bluebook* but is commonly used by practitioners. *ALWD* Rule 12.13 generally recognizes this citation format.

(2) Slip Form

When a case is not yet reported and is available only in slip or looseleaf form, give the case name, the docket number, the court, and the exact date (Rule 10.8.1(b)).

Correct: *Miller v. Pritchett,* No. 09-CIV-201
                 (N.D. Cal. June 9, 2010)

(3) Cases Available on Electronic Media (B4.1.4, Rules 10.8.1, 18.3.1)

A case may be cited to a widely used electronic database such as Lexis or Westlaw only if it is not reported (meaning that it is not published in print reporters or in slip form). Provide the name of the case, docket number (exactly as it appears), identification of the database (with sufficient information to allow a reader to locate the case), name of court, and the full date of the most recent disposition of the case. If screen or page numbers have been assigned, they should be preceded by an asterisk.

Examples

Gruber v. Edwards, No. 06-829, 2007 U.S. Dist. LEXIS 20104, at *3 (D. Utah Oct. 1, 2007)

McKnight v. Walter, No. 06-10426, 2007 U.S. App. LEXIS 4221, at *4 (4th Cir. Apr. 14, 2007)

Thomas v. Bowman, No. 05-CV-6040, 2007 WL 65102, at *4 (S.D. Cal. July 17, 2007)

Neely v. Younger, No. 06-4091, 2008 WL 46723, at *3 (Cal. Ct. App. Jan. 7, 2008)

(4) Cases Available on the Internet (Rules 18.2.2 and 18.2.3)

Although there are now hundreds of thousands of cases available on the Internet, *The Bluebook* requires the use and citation of traditional printed sources when they are available, unless there is a digital copy of the source available that is authenticated, official, or an exact copy of the printed source. Typically, an authenticated document will have a certificate or logo showing that the document is unaltered. An official document is one that has been designated as official by some legislative mechanism. An authenticated, official, or exact copy of a case may be cited as if to the print source (meaning that no URL information need be given). Because nearly all cases appear in traditional print form within a matter of days after they are decided, *The Bluebook* seems to suggest that citing to the Internet would be exceptional, for example, only for newly released decisions (or for authenticated or official versions found online).

If a printed source can be found, a parallel citation to an electronic source or to the Internet as related authority may be provided if it will substantially improve access to the relevant information or case and the Internet content is identical to that of the print source. Thus, the first citation must be to the printed source and then an electronic or Internet source may be given, introduced with the explanatory phrase *"available at"* (and assuming that the content of the Internet source is identical to the print version), as follows: *Int'l Prot. Servs., Inc.*, 355 N.L.R.B. 47 (2010), *available at* http://www.nlrb.gov/shared_files/Board%20Decisions/355/v35547.pdf.

The Bluebook provides information on citing statutes, books, and journals to Internet locations. Examples of each of these will be found in Section G.9 of this chapter.

e. Abbreviations in Case Citations

Do not assume that you know the correct abbreviations for Colorado, Idaho, or Oklahoma. Although you may know the correct abbreviation for a state for purposes of addressing a letter, *The Bluebook* contains some surprising abbreviations for commonly known geographical terms. Review Table T.10.1 in *The Bluebook* to determine the required abbreviations for the 50 states and for other geographical locations. Similarly, rely upon Table T.7 for abbreviations for court names and on Table T.12 for the correct abbreviations for months of the year.

f. Spacing (*Bluebook* Rule 6.1(a))

The print in *The Bluebook* is very small, and it can be difficult to simply look at the examples given and determine the appropriate spacing in a citation. Therefore, you must memorize three spacing rules given as Rule 6.1 of *The Bluebook*:

• Do not put a space between adjacent single capital letters. For purposes of this rule, the abbreviations for "2d," "3d," "4th," and so forth are viewed as single capitals.

Examples

N.W.2d
S.W.
P.2d
F.3d
U.S.
A.L.R.5th

Each of the examples given here shows adjacent single capital letters. Therefore, do not put spaces between them.

- Multiple letter abbreviations are preceded and followed by a space:

Practice Tip

Superscripts

Ordinals are numbers that show a series, such as "first" and "fourth." In legal citations, the ordinals are replaced by their appropriate abbreviations, for example, "1st" and "4th." Many word processing programs automatically force abbreviations such as "st" and "th" above other text in superscript, as in "1st" and "4th." Both *The Bluebook* and *ALWD* show ordinal abbreviations "set on line" as follows: "1st" and "4th" so their presentation will be consistent with "2d" and "3d," which are always set on line with other text.

In some Microsoft Word versions, you may disable the automatic superscript setting by consulting your "tools" menu bar (select "Tools," then "AutoCorrect," then "Auto Format As You Type," and then uncheck the superscript feature). Alternatively, immediately after a superscript is inserted on your page, click on the "undo" arrow (the backward facing arrow on your menu bar), which will correct the superscript and set the abbreviations on line. *Bluebook* Rule 6.2(b) forbids the use of superscripts. *ALWD* does not prohibit superscripted ordinals (*ALWD* at 10).

Correct:	**1st, 4th, 8th**
Incorrect:	**1st, 4th, 8th**

Examples

So. 2d
F. Supp. 2d
L. Ed. 2d
Cal. 4th
Ill. App. Ct.
S. Ct.

Each of the examples given here includes a multiple letter abbreviation. Therefore, put a space before it and after it.

• In abbreviations of the names of legal periodicals, close up adjacent single uppercase letters except when one or more of the uppercase letters refers to an institutional entity. In this case separate the uppercase letter referring to the entity from other adjacent single letters with a space (*Bluebook* Rule 6.1 (a)).

This rule is confusing. Perhaps the best guide when citing legal periodicals is simply to mimic carefully Table T.13 of *The Bluebook*, which provides more than 700 abbreviations for periodicals.

Examples

B.U. L. Rev.

Because the "B.U." in this abbreviation refers to an institutional entity, namely, Boston University, the capital letters for this entity are separated from the other adjacent single letter.

Note that Table T.13 shows the abbreviation as "B.U. L. REV.," using large and small capitals, as would be used for law review typeface style. Practitioners should always follow the rules on typeface conventions and convert the large and small capitals to ordinary type, specifically "B.U. L. Rev."

With regard to presentation of citations within your project, *The Bluebook* does not offer any guidelines whatsoever. Most experts suggest that you "break" your citation from one line to the next at a "natural" break point, that is, one that is pleasing to the eye and doesn't strike the reader as awkward in appearance.

g. Federal Cases (*Bluebook* B4.1.3; Table T.1)

(1) United States Supreme Court Cases

Despite the fact that cases from the United States Supreme Court are published in permanent hardbound volumes in three different sets of books (U.S., S. Ct., and L. Ed.), *The Bluebook* rule is to cite only to the official set, United States Reports (U.S.).

This rule of requiring a single citation to U.S. and ignoring the sets S. Ct. and L. Ed. is the reason "star paging" was developed, namely, to allow a reader to read a case in S. Ct. or L. Ed. and yet cite to the official *United States Reports*. (See Chapter 4 for discussion of star paging.)

Correct: *Leroy v. Holden*, 368 U.S. 46 (1975).

Incorrect: *Leroy v. Holden*, 368 U.S. 46, 96 S. Ct. 101, 109 L. Ed. 2d 14 (1975).

You may recall that the *United States Reports* have only had that title since 1875 and that before that date, the volumes were named after the individual primarily involved in editing the set (for example, Dallas,

Cranch, Wheaton, Peters). Thus, if you see an awkward-looking case citation such as *Carter v. Lee*, 4 U.S. (2 Dall.) 16 (1798), you should simply recognize that this is a very old case.

If you cannot cite to U.S. because the official report is not yet available, cite to S. Ct., L. Ed., or U.S.L.W., in that order.

Examples

> *Hogue v. Davidson*, 241 S. Ct. 902 (2010).
> *Hogue v. Davidson*, 289 L. Ed. 2d 101 (2010).
> *Hogue v. Davidson*, 63 U.S.L.W. 1226 (U.S. May 19, 2010).

Remember that you should never give a parallel cite for cases from the United States Supreme Court.

(2) *United States Courts of Appeals Cases*

There are no official citations for cases from the United States Court of Appeals; therefore, cases will be cited only to West's *Federal Reporter* (F., F.2d, or F.3d). The reader will need to know the circuit that decided the case. Not only will circuit information confirm the case on point (for example, arguments submitted to the Eighth Circuit Court of Appeals should rely on precedents from the Eighth Circuit), some circuits may have established reputations in deciding certain kinds of cases. Thus, this information must be provided to the reader in the parenthetical with the date. *Bluebook* Rule 10.4 clearly requires that every case citation must indicate which court decided the case unless this information is unambiguously conveyed by the name of a reporter (such as is the case with *United States Reports* or *California Reports*). The information must appear in the parenthetical before the date. Thus, because a reference to "F.2d" tells a reader only that a case is from one of the United States Courts of Appeal, the parenthetical must identify the particular circuit, as follows:

> **Correct:** *Rose v. Capwell Co.*, 721 F.2d 806 (3d Cir. 1988).

(3) *United States District Court Cases*

There are no official citations for cases from the United States District Courts; therefore, cases will be cited only to West's *Federal Supplement* (F. Supp. and F. Supp. 2d). For the same reasons that readers need to know which circuit court decided a case, readers need to know which district court decided a case. Thus, identify the district court (but not the division of the district court).

> **Correct:** *Simon v. Parker*, 760 F. Supp. 918 (E.D. Ark. 1988).

> **Correct:** *Arnold v. Kenney*, 107 F. Supp. 2d 746 (D. Ariz. 1999).

See Figure 8-1 for *Bluebook* abbreviations for our more than 90 district courts.

Practice Tip

Abbreviations for District Courts

Creating the abbreviations for the nation's more than 90 district courts is relatively easy.

- The abbreviation for "district" is "D."
- The abbreviations for the geographical divisions of the courts are as follows:
  - "N." for "Northern" (thus, N.D. stands for "Northern District")
  - "S." for "Southern"
  - "E." for "Eastern"
  - "W." for "Western"
  - "M." for "Middle"
  - "C." for "Central"
- Indicate the geographical division of the court, following the spacing rules given above.
- Indicate the state abbreviation using Table T.10 of *The Bluebook* or Appendix 3 of *ALWD*.

Examples: D. Alaska
               S.D. Cal.
               D.D.C.
               M.D. Pa.

Figure 8-1
Abbreviations for U.S. District Courts

ALABAMA	11th Cir.	**CALIFORNIA**	9th Cir.
M.D. Ala.		C.D. Cal.	
N.D. Ala.		E.D. Cal.	
S.D. Ala.		N.D. Cal.	
ALASKA	9th Cir.	S.D. Cal.	
D. Alaska		**COLORADO**	10th Cir.
ARIZONA	9th Cir.	D. Colo.	
D. Ariz.		**CONNECTICUT**	2d Cir.
ARKANSAS	8th Cir.	D. Conn.	
E.D. Ark.		**DELAWARE**	3d Cir.
W.D. Ark.		D. Del.	

Figure 8-1 *(Continued)*

DISTRICT OF COLUMBIA D.D.C.	D.C. Cir.	**MASSACHUSETTS** D. Mass.	1st Cir.
FLORIDA M.D. Fla. N.D. Fla. S.D. Fla.	11th Cir.	**MICHIGAN** E.D. Mich. W.D. Mich.	6th Cir.
GEORGIA M.D. Ga. N.D. Ga. S.D. Ga.	11th Cir.	**MINNESOTA** D. Minn.	8th Cir.
		MISSISSIPPI N.D. Miss. S.D. Miss.	5th Cir.
HAWAII D. Haw.	9th Cir.	**MISSOURI** E.D. Mo. W.D. Mo.	8th Cir.
IDAHO D. Idaho	9th Cir.	**MONTANA** D. Mont.	9th Cir.
ILLINOIS C.D. Ill. N.D. Ill. S.D. Ill.	7th Cir.	**NEBRASKA** D. Neb.	8th Cir.
INDIANA N.D. Ind. S.D. Ind.	7th Cir.	**NEVADA** D. Nev.	9th Cir.
		NEW HAMPSHIRE D.N.H.	1st Cir.
IOWA N.D. Iowa S.D. Iowa	8th Cir.	**NEW JERSEY** D.N.J.	3d Cir.
KANSAS D. Kan.	10th Cir.	**NEW MEXICO** D.N.M.	10th Cir.
KENTUCKY E.D. Ky. W.D. Ky.	6th Cir.	**NEW YORK** E.D.N.Y. N.D.N.Y. S.D.N.Y. W.D.N.Y.	2d Cir.
LOUISIANA E.D. La. M.D. La. W.D. La.	5th Cir.	**NORTH CAROLINA** E.D.N.C. M.D.N.C. W.D.N.C.	4th Cir.
MAINE D. Me.	1st Cir.		
MARYLAND D. Md.	4th Cir.	**NORTH DAKOTA** D.N.D.	8th Cir.

Figure 8-1 *(Continued)*

OHIO	6th Cir.	**WASHINGTON**	9th Cir.
N.D. Ohio		E.D. Wash.	
S.D. Ohio		W.D. Wash.	
OKLAHOMA	10th Cir.	**WEST VIRGINIA**	4th Cir.
E.D. Okla.		N.D. W. Va.	
N.D. Okla.		S.D. W. Va.	
W.D. Okla.		**WISCONSIN**	7th Cir.
OREGON	9th Cir.	E.D. Wis.	
D. Or.		W.D. Wis.	
PENNSYLVANIA	3d Cir.	**WYOMING**	10th Cir.
E.D. Pa.		D. Wyo.	
M.D. Pa.		**MISCELLANEOUS**	
W.D. Pa.			
RHODE ISLAND	1st Cir.	**CANAL ZONE**	5th Cir.
D.R.I.		D.C.Z. (ceased operations in	
SOUTH CARO-	4th Cir.	1982)	
LINA			
D.S.C.		**GUAM**	9th Cir.
		D. Guam	
SOUTH DAKOTA	8th Cir.		
D.S.D.		**N. MARIANA**	9th Cir.
		ISLANDS	
TENNESSEE	6th Cir.	D.N. Mar. I.	
E.D. Tenn.			
M.D. Tenn.		**PUERTO RICO**	1st Cir.
W.D. Tenn.		D.P.R.	
TEXAS	5th Cir.	**VIRGIN ISLANDS**	3d Cir.
E.D. Tex.		D.V.I.	
N.D. Tex.			
S.D. Tex.		**U.S. COURT OF**	Fed. Cir.
W.D. Tex.		**APPEALS FOR**	
		THE FEDERAL	
UTAH	10th Cir.	**CIRCUIT**	
D. Utah			
		U.S. COURT OF	D.C. Cir.
VERMONT	2d Cir.	**APPEALS FOR**	
D. Vt.		**THE DISTRICT OF**	
		COLUMBIA CIR-	
VIRGINIA	4th Cir.	**CUIT**	
E.D. Va.			
W.D. Va.		**U.S. COURT Of**	Fed. Cl.
		FEDERAL	
		CLAIMS	

h. Subsequent History (*Bluebook* B4.1.6; Rule 10.7)

Whenever you cite a case you are required to provide its subsequent history. Do not, however, give history relating to:

- denials of certiorari or denials of similar discretionary appeals unless the case (not the denial of certiorari) is less than two years old or the denial of certiorari is particularly relevant; or
- history on remand or any denial of a rehearing unless it is particularly relevant.

The rule instructing writers to omit history relating to denials of certiorari (unless the case is less than two years old or the denial of certiorari is particularly relevant) is new since 1996 and has caused some disagreement. Some practitioners take the position that the refusal of the United States Supreme Court to grant "cert" and take a case is always relevant because it confirms that the decision is thus final and not subject to further review. Therefore, some practitioners simply ignore the rule and always note that "cert" has been denied. Consult your firm or office to determine its policy on this much-criticized change.

Correct: *Bernard v. Scott*, 761 F.2d 902 (8th Cir. 1986), *aff'd*, 106 U.S. 921 (1988).

Correct: *Dowell v. Wong*, 629 F.2d 809 (2d Cir. 2009), *cert. denied*, 510 U.S. 466 (2010).

Note that if any subsequent history occurred in the same year as the lower court case was decided, give the year only once, in the last parenthetical (R. 10.5(d)).

Correct: *Walker v. Whiteley*, 701 F.2d 416 (9th Cir.), *rev'd*, 430 U.S. 906 (1985)

A list showing the appropriate abbreviations for subsequent history such as "reversed," "affirmed," "modified," "rehearing granted," all of which must be underlined or italicized, is provided in Table T.8 of *The Bluebook*. You will be informed of the subsequent history of a case when you Shepardize or KeyCite it. Shepardizing and KeyCiting are discussed in Chapter 9.

i. Prior History (*Bluebook* Rule 10.7)

There is no ethical obligation to give the prior history of a case. *The Bluebook* states only that you should give prior history of a case if it is significant to the issue you are discussing or if the case you are citing does not fully describe the issues (such as a memorandum opinion) and therefore you are relying on the lower court case for a full analysis of the issues involved in the case.

This citation rule is logical and eliminates needless citations. For example, virtually all United States Supreme Court cases arrive at the

Supreme Court from some other court and thus have a prior history. Some, in fact, have three or even four prior histories. To include these citations would be confusing and unnecessary because the decision by the United States Supreme Court is the one that is determinative under our system of stare decisis, as discussed in Chapter 1.

j. Parenthetical Information (*Bluebook* B4.1.5; B11; Rules 1.5, 5.2, 10.6, and 10.7)

If you are relying upon or quoting from any part of an opinion other than the majority opinion, you must so indicate in your citation. A reader will always assume that you are relying upon the majority opinion unless you indicate otherwise. Although it is acceptable to cite a dissent or a concurring opinion, remember that only the majority opinion is binding. Dissents and concurring opinions are persuasive only.

> **Correct:**   *Wu v. Bradley*, 490 U.S. 102 (1985) (White, J., dissenting).

Similarly, if you wish to give more information about the weight of the case (for example, 7-2 decision, author of opinion) do so parenthetically as follows:

> *Parker, Inc. v. Simpson*, 504 U.S. 66 (1989) (7-2 decision).

If the citation you rely on quotes from another case, present that information as follows:

> *Costello v. McCarty*, 490 U.S. 102, 106 (1985) (quoting *Lyons v. Wagner*, 488 U.S. 66, 75 (1983)).

Parentheticals must be given in a certain order. Parenthetical information relating to the weight of a decision (whether it is a 6-3 decision or per curiam decision) must precede parenthetical information explaining something about the decision, for example, a brief phrase such as "following the exclusionary rule." Note that explanatory phrases should begin with a present participle (a verb plus an "ing" ending, as in "arguing" or "holding") and a lowercase letter, although they may consist of a quoted sentence or a short statement. Parentheticals should precede any references to prior or subsequent history (Rule 1.5(b)).

k. Different Case Name on Appeal (*Bluebook* Rule 10.7.2)

You may recall that if a case is instituted by a plaintiff, Jones, against a defendant, Smith, and Smith loses the case and appeals, some courts reverse the order of the parties and refer to the case on appeal as *Smith v. Jones*. If the parties' names are merely reversed on appeal, retain the original order, here, *Jones v. Smith*.

1. Order of Preference for Citations

Bluebook Rule 10.3.1 provides an order of preference for citing cases: Generally, if a case is not available in an official or preferred unofficial reporter or as a neutral or public domain citation, cite to another unofficial reporter, to a widely used computer database (such as Lexis or Westlaw), to a looseleaf service, to a slip opinion, to an Internet source, or to a newspaper, in that order of preference.

2. *Statutes*

a. State Statutes (*Bluebook* B5.1.2; Rule 12 and Table T.1)

Citations to state statutes must include the abbreviated name of the code; the section, paragraph, or article number(s) of the statute; and parenthetically the year of the code, as follows: Miss. Code Ann. § 9-9-16 (1986). The "year of the code" is not necessarily the year the statute was enacted but the year that appears on the spine of the volume, the year identified on the title page, or the latest copyright year, in this order of preference (*Bluebook* Rule 12.3.2).

You may recall from Chapter 3 that some states have codes that classify statutes by title, such as an Agriculture Code, a Civil Code, a Corporations Code, an Evidence Code, or a Probate Code. Usually the more populous states have arranged their codes in such titles. The states that have such subject matter codes are California, Louisiana, Maryland, New York, and Texas. If your state organizes its statutes in such a manner, you must indicate the name of the title. Otherwise, if you refer to "Cal. § 301," the reader does not know whether to review Cal. Civ. Code § 301, Cal. Evid. Code § 301, or Cal. Prob. Code § 301. Most states and the District of Columbia do not organize their statutes by subject matter, and therefore you follow the standard statute citation rule and identify the name of the code; the section/paragraph/article number; and the date.

Cite to the official code, if possible. If no official code exists, cite to the unofficial or privately published code, but then indicate the publisher parenthetically with the date. If you cite a statute to an electronic database (because the official or unofficial code or privately published session laws are not available), give parenthetically the name of the database (Lexis or Westlaw) and information relating to the currency of the database as provided by the database itself (Rule 12.50).

Example

Cal. Evid. Code § 52 (West, Westlaw through 2010 Sess.).

Table T.1 of *The Bluebook* lists all 50 states alphabetically and gives instruction on how to cite statutes from every state. For those states such as California, New York, Texas, and the others that classify their statutes by subject matter, be sure to properly abbreviate the subject matter

according to Table T.1. For example, in Texas, the abbreviation for the Family Code is "Fam.," the abbreviation for the Labor Code is "Lab.," and the abbreviation for the Property Code is "Prop."

Examples for states that do not have subject matter codes:

Official Codes:	Mont. Code Ann. § 20-4-201 (1996).
	N.C. Gen. Stat. § 29-10 (1998).
	Tenn. Code Ann. § 7-5-3 (1996).
Unofficial Codes:	Colo. Rev. Stat. Ann. § 11-51-102 (West 2001).
	Fla. Stat. Ann. § 322.01 (West 1997).
	Ohio Rev. Code Ann. § 1701.01 (West 1999).

Examples for states that organize their statutes by subject matter:

Cal. Fin. Code § 1951 (West 1996).
La. Code Crim. Proc. Ann. art. 905.4 (1998).
N.Y. Educ. Law § 293 (McKinney 1994).

Remember that the examples given in *The Bluebook* show large and small capitals, for example, "TEX. LAB. CODE ANN. § 81.001 (West 2006)," the format used for law reviews. As a practitioner, you will need to adapt the style as follows: "Tex. Lab. Code Ann. § 81.001 (West 2006)."

b. Federal Statutes (*Bluebook* B5.1.1; Rule 12)

You will recall from Chapter 3 that all federal statutes are published officially in the *United States Code* (U.S.C.) and unofficially in *United States Code Annotated* (U.S.C.A.), published by West, and *United States Code Service* (U.S.C.S.), now published by Lexis. The elements of a citation for a federal statute are the number of the title, name of set, section number, and year of the code. Once again, the "year of the code" is the year that appears on the spine of the volume, the year shown on the title page, or the most recent copyright year of the volume, in that order. In most cases, this date will *not* be the date the statute was enacted.

Cite federal statutes to the current official code (U.S.C.) if possible. If you cannot cite the federal statute to the official code because it is not available at your law firm or local law library, cite to the unofficial codes (U.S.C.A. or U.S.C.S.). Cite to the actual set in which you located the statute. That is, do not merely drop the "A" of U.S.C.A. to produce an official cite. When you cite to the unofficial codes, you must identify the publisher in the parenthetical before the year of the code.

Examples

U.S.C.	42 U.S.C. § 12406 (2006).
U.S.C.A.	42 U.S.C.A. § 12406 (West 1996).
U.S.C.S.	42 U.S.C.S. § 12406 (LexisNexis 2000).

If a statute is commonly known by a popular name or such information would assist the reader, you may include the popular name as follows (do not include "The" as the first word of a statute name):

Norris-LaGuardia Act § 161, 29 U.S.C. § 221 (2006).

c. Miscellaneous Rules Regarding Citation of Statutes

(1) Spacing

A space should appear between the signal for the section (§) and the number of the statute because the section sign is an abbreviation or replacement for the word "section." A space should also be placed before the parenthetical.

41 U.S.C. § 352 (2006).

(2) Internal Revenue Code (Bluebook *Rule B5.1.5; 12.9.1*)

There are special rules for citing to Title 26 of the *United States Code*, entitled "Internal Revenue." For Internal Revenue statutes, you may drop "26 U.S.C." and replace it with "I.R.C."

Preferred: I.R.C. § 501 (2006).

Disfavored: 26 U.S.C. § 501 (2006).

(3) Pocket Parts and Supplements (Bluebook *Rules 3.1 and 12.3.1(e)*)

If the statute appears only in a pocket part or supplement, indicate as follows:

Alaska Stat. § 8.08.085 (Supp. V 2008).
17 U.S.C. § 101 (Supp. I 2007).

If the original statute appears in the hardbound volume and an amendment to it appears in a pocket part or supplement, cite as follows:

17 U.S.C. § 102 (2006 & Supp. I 2008).

(4) Multiple Sections (Bluebook *Rule 3.3(b)*)

Because of the often awkward numbering system used for statutes, you must be precise when referring a reader to a group of statutes. For example, if you referred a reader to Tenn. Code Ann. § 1764-66 (1996), the

citation is ambiguous. The reader is unsure whether to read sections 1764, 1765, and 1766 or whether there is one particular statute identified as section 1764-66.

Although it is common (and, in fact, required) in references to page numbers to drop repetitious digits, do not do so for statutes. If you wish the reader to review sections 1764 through 1766 indicate as follows:

> **Correct:**   Tenn. Code Ann. §§ 1764-1766
>   (1996).
>
> **Incorrect:**   Tenn. Code Ann. §§ 1764-66 (1996).

For clarity, follow these rules:

- When referring a reader to one section, use one section symbol (§).
- When referring a reader to more than one section, use two section symbols (§§), and do not drop any digits.
- When referring a reader to more than one section, do not use the term "et seq.," a Latin term for "and the following." Such a reference is too imprecise, as it does not tell the reader when to stop reading. For example, the citation 28 U.S.C. §§ 4201 et seq. (2006), strictly interpreted, tells the reader to read the thousands of statutes in the United States Code following section 4201 of title 28.

(5) Section Reference (Bluebook Rule 3.4)

In a "stand-alone" citation, use the sign "§" for the word "section." Most word processors include this symbol, so if it is available, use it. Otherwise, use the word "section." However, spell out the word "section" in a narrative discussion of a statute (except when referring to a provision of the U.S. Code) as follows: The court's interpretation of section 1110 of the Iowa Code was confined to an analysis of the meaning of the term "compensation." (R.6.2(c); R.12.10(c)).

(6) Publisher (Bluebook Rule 12.3.1(d))

Although you may be tempted to omit the parenthetical identification of publisher and/or year in citing statutes, and although practitioners commonly omit such information, *The Bluebook* is unambiguous in requiring such information.

> **Correct:**   16 U.S.C. § 141 (2006).
>   16 U.S.C.A. § 141 (West 1996).
>   16 U.S.C.S. § 141 (LexisNexis 2003).
> **Incorrect:**   16 U.S.C. § 141.
>   16 U.S.C.A. § 141.
>   16 U.S.C.S. § 141.

Practice Tip

Citing Statutes

Although *The Bluebook* and *ALWD* clearly require a parenthetical after any citation to a statute (which parenthetical must include the year of the code and the publisher, unless the set is an official one), practitioners around the country routinely strike the entire parenthetical in citing both federal and state statutes.

Bluebook and *ALWD* style:	11 U.S.C. § 509 (2006).
Practitioner style:	11 U.S.C. § 509.

Note also that individual volumes in U.S.C.A. and U.S.C.S. are replaced only when necessary. Thus, different volumes in a set will have different years in the parenthetical.

---

3. *Rules* (Bluebook *B5.1.3; Rule 12.9.3)*

Cite rules of evidence and procedure and court rules without any section sign or date, as follows:

> Fed. R. Civ. P. 56(a).
> Fed. R. Crim. P. 12.
> Fed. R. Evid. 210.
> Sup. Ct. R. 33(a).

4. *Constitutions* (Bluebook *B6; Rule 11)*

a. State Constitutions

The correct form for citing a state constitution is shown on the inside back cover of *The Bluebook* and in the Bluepages. Note that you do not include a date unless the provision you are citing has been repealed, amended, or superseded.

> **Correct:**   Cal. Const. art. XXII.

b. United States Constitution

Cite current provisions of the United States Constitution without dates.

> **Correct:**   U.S. Const. art. III, § 8.
> U.S. Const. amend. I.

The Bluebook (R.8) requires capitalization of parts of the United States Constitution when they are discussed in textual sentences.

Correct: First Amendment
                 Equal Protection Clause
                 Fifth Amendment

E. *Bluebook* Citation Rules and Examples for Secondary Authorities

Examples for citing secondary authorities will be discussed in the order in which those authorities were discussed in Chapters 6 and 7.

1. *Annotations* (Bluebook *Rule 16.7.6*)

For A.L.R. annotations give the author's full name, identify the item as an "Annotation," give the title of the annotation (underlined or italicized), the reference to the volume and page of A.L.R. in which it can be found, and the year it was written. A.L.R. annotations are cited as follows:

Jack W. Shaw, Jr., Annotation, *Exhibition of Obscene Motion Pictures as Nuisance*, 50 A.L.R.3d 969 (1978).

2. *Encyclopedias* (Bluebook *B8; Rule 15.8(a)*)

Because the encyclopedias are weak secondary sources and are used primarily to give you introductory explanations of the law and to help you locate cases, you should not cite encyclopedias in support of a contention unless you have no primary authorities or stronger secondary authorities. The correct citation form is as follows:

1 C.J.S. *Abandonment* § 14 (1984).
1 Am. Jur. 2d *Abandonment* § 14 (1986).
6 Cal. Jur. 3d *Contracts* § 221 (1988).

Be sure to include and underscore or italicize the topic name in your citation (*Abandonment, Contracts, Deeds*). Otherwise a citation to 1 C.J.S. § 14 (1984) leaves the reader wondering whether to read Abandonment section 14 or Administrative Law section 14, both of which are found in Volume 1 of C.J.S.

3. *Periodical Materials* (Bluebook *B9;* Rule 16)

For periodical articles, give the author's full name (as he or she does), the title of the article (underscored or italicized), the reference to the periodical in which it appeared (abbreviated according to Table T.13 in *The Bluebook*), the page on which the article begins, and the date of publication. Be sure to convert the law review format form of large and small capital letters you see in Table T.13 to ordinary typeface. *The Bluebook* (R.15) provides special rules on articles written by multiple authors.

> **Law Review Articles (*Bluebook* Rule 16).** Steven A. Peterson & Brian T. Carr, *Plea Bargaining in Federal Courts*, 68 Loy. L. Rev. 1421 (1975).
>
> **Student-written Works.** Elizabeth A. Brandon, Comment, *Philosophy of Law*, 48 Ariz. L. Rev. 123 (1998).
>
> **Bar Association Publications.** Lori B. Andrews, *Surrogacy Wars*, Cal. Law., Oct. 1998, at 42.
>
> **Special Subject Publications.** Andrew P. Neil, *Thrift Regulations*, 16 Inst. on Sec. Reg. 411 (1998).
>
> **Legal Newspapers.** Joan M. Cheever & Joanne Naiman, *The Deadly Practice of Divorce*, Nat'l L.J., Oct. 12, 1999, at A1.

Note that a comma is placed after the title of the article.

4. *Books, Texts, and Treatises* (Bluebook *B8; Rule 15)*

For texts and treatises, give the volume the material appeared in (if there is more than one volume to the set), the author's full name as the author gives it, the title of the text, the page/paragraph/section that the reader should review, and in parentheses the edition (for any edition after the first edition) and date of publication, as follows:

> 2 J. Thomas McCarthy, *McCarthy on Trademarks and Unfair Competition* § 18:18 (4th ed. 2004).

If the book has two authors, give the full names of both in the order they are listed on the publication, separated by an ampersand (&). If there are more than two authors, you may give the first author's name, followed by "et al.," or you may list all authors. Always give the full name of any editor or translator, followed by "ed." or "trans." in the parenthetical.

Refer to later editions and pocket parts as follows:

> 6 Daniel R. Donoghue, *Maritime and Admiralty Law* § 7.09 (3d ed. 2006).

Note that there is no comma after the title of a book, text, or treatise, although a comma is given after the title of a periodical article.

5. *Restatements* (Bluebook *B5.1.3; Rule 12.9.5)*

Restatements should be cited to the title of the Restatement, the edition being referred to, the section the reader should review, and the date of publication.

> Restatement (Second) of Torts § 312 (1976).
> Restatement (Second) of Agency § 24 cmt. a (1979).

6. *Uniform Laws* (Bluebook *B5.1.3; Rule 12.9.4)*

If you are referring to a uniform law as adopted by a state, use the standard statutory citation form for that state, as follows:

> Cal. Com. Code § 2-216 (West 1996).

If you are referring to the actual uniform law adopted by the Commissioners, cite as follows:

> U.C.C. § 2-216 (1977).

If you are referring to the set *Uniform Laws Annotated*, cite as follows:

> Unif. Commercial Code § 2-216 (amended 1988), 10 U.L.A. 109 (1992).

7. *Dictionaries* (Bluebook *B8; Rule 15.8)*

Dictionaries should be cited to the name of the dictionary, the page on which the definition appears and, parenthetically, the edition and year of publication, as follows:

> *Black's Law Dictionary* 679 (9th ed. 2009).
> *Ballentine's Law Dictionary* 415 (3d ed. 1969).

8. *Attorneys General Opinions* (Bluebook *Table T.1.2)*

Cite opinions of attorneys general by title of opinion (if desired), the volume, title of set, first page of opinion, and year, as follows:
State attorneys general opinions:
> Pharmaceutical Standards, 64 Op. Md. Att'y Gen. 104 (1995).

United States Attorneys General Opinions:

> 47 Op. Att'y Gen. 16 (1983)
> or
> Applicability of the Emoluments Clause to Non-Government Members of ACUS, 17 Op. O.L.C. 114 (1993).

9. *Looseleaf Services* (Bluebook *Rule 19)*

Cite looseleaf services by volume, title of the service (using appropriate abbreviations (see Table T.15)), publisher, section/subdivision/paragraph, and date, as follows:

> 1 Bus. Franchise Guide (CCH) ¶ 3202 (Aug. 8, 1988).

To cite cases in looseleaf services, cite as follows, unless the case is also published in an official reporter in which case you should cite to it.

> *Anderson v. CFFC Franchise Corp.*, 2 Bus. Franchise Guide (CCH) ¶ 8904 (S.D.N.Y. Jan. 10, 2009).

F.   *ALWD* Citation Manual

1.   *Introduction*

As discussed earlier, the *ALWD* citation manual was created in 2000 and has drawn a great deal of interest because of its user-friendly format, generous spacing and use of color, and numerous examples. Moreover, *ALWD* does not use the confusing "large and small caps" format used by *The Bluebook* and shows all citations in ordinary roman type (or italics).

In many instances, the *ALWD* format for citations is identical to *Bluebook* format. For example, the format for lower federal court cases, most statutes, constitutions, journals and periodicals, and encyclopedias is identical. Rules for spacing and short forms are identical. There are, however, several differences (often in abbreviations for the names of cases

and periodicals). See Figure 8-3 for a chart showing the more significant differences between *ALWD* and *The Bluebook*. Because at the time of writing this text *The Bluebook* is still the best-known citation guide, this section will provide examples of many *ALWD* citation forms but will not provide as much detailed explanation for those forms as the previous section did in discussing *The Bluebook*. The *ALWD* citation manual may be obtained at most school bookstores or from Aspen Publishers at http://www.aspenpublishers.com. Moreover, a great deal of useful information about *ALWD*, other examples, citation exercises, and a list of schools that have adopted *ALWD* is available at the *ALWD* website at http://www.alwd.org.

In the examples to follow, an asterisk (*) indicates that the *ALWD* citation format is identical to that of *The Bluebook*.

2. *Revisions to the 4th Edition of* ALWD

The primary goals for the 4th edition of *ALWD* (released in 2010) were to refine and clarify rules and respond to users' inquiries. Although these changes are discussed in detail in the preface to *ALWD* and throughout *ALWD*, and in this chapter, some of the more significant changes are as follows:

(i)   Rule 11.4 clarifies that legal writers should not use the signal *supra* as a short form unless the document includes footnotes.
(ii) Photos of commonly used sources are included. For example, *ALWD* reproduces a page from the *Southern Reporter* and the cover of the *United States Code*.
(iii) *ALWD* now allows one to use either "U.S." or "United States" when referring to the United States as a party in a document. Previously, only "U.S." was allowed. Similarly, *ALWD* now allows one to abbreviate words such as "Department" either as "Dept." (which was the approach of earlier *ALWD* editions) or as "Dep't" (which is *The Bluebook* approach). This change makes *ALWD* more consistent with *The Bluebook*.

3. ALWD *Citation Rules and Examples for Primary Authorities*

a. Citation of Cases (*ALWD* Rule 12)

ALWD's rules for citing cases are very similar to those of *The Bluebook*. In fact, there are only three major differences for conventionally published cases:

- **Information About Divisions for State Court Cases.** *ALWD* Rule 12.6(b) generally requires that when you cite state cases,

you must include available information about counties, departments, districts, or divisions that decided the case. *The Bluebook* generally does not permit this information.

> *ALWD:*   *Coffey v. Huntley*, 909 S.W.2d 13
> (Ark. App. Div. II 1990)

> *Bluebook:*   *Coffee v. Huntley*, 909 S.W.2d 13
> (Ark. Ct. App. 1990)

- **Parallel Citations for Supreme Court Cases.** For United States Supreme Court cases, *ALWD* permits (but does not prefer) parallel citations whereas *The Bluebook* prohibits parallel citations when citing United States Supreme Court cases.

> *ALWD:*   *Riley v. Harris*, 490 U.S. 909 (2000) or
> *Riley v. Harris*, 490 U.S. 909, 218 S.
> Ct. 78, 211 L. Ed. 2d 445 (2000)

> *Bluebook:* *Riley v. Harris*, 490 U.S. 909 (2000)

- **Abbreviations in Case Names.** *ALWD* Rule 12.2(e) adopts a slightly more permissive approach to using abbreviations in case names than *The Bluebook* and states that you "may" abbreviate any word in a case name when the case name appears as a stand-alone citation, and that it is "traditional" to spell out "virtually all words" in a case name when it appears in text as part of a textual sentence. *The Bluebook* approach is more rigid and requires that you spell out all major words in a case name when it appears in text and requires that you abbreviate words in a case name when it appears as a stand-alone citation. Like *The Bluebook*, *ALWD* allows the following abbreviations: &, Assn. (or Ass'n), Bros., Co., Corp., Inc., Ltd., and No.

In addition to these significant differences, there are some other minor differences as well. For example, the abbreviations used in *ALWD* and *The Bluebook* may vary. *ALWD* abbreviates the word "County" in a case name as "Co." whereas *The Bluebook* uses "Cnty." Similarly, *The Bluebook* requires that when the United States is a party to a case, the case name must read "United States," whereas *ALWD* (Rule 12.2(g)) provides that the case name may read "United States" or "U.S.," as in *U.S. v. Rafferty*. Finally, abbreviations for names of courts may vary. For example, *Bluebook* Table T.1 shows "Conn. App. Ct." for the Connecticut Appellate Court whereas *ALWD* Appendix 1 shows this as "Conn. App."

(1) Spacing (ALWD Rule 2.2)

ALWD's rules for spacing are identical to those found in *The Bluebook*:

- Close up spaces between adjacent single capitals (as in U.S. or N.W.) and treat the ordinal abbreviations as a single capital (as in A.L.R.4th);
- Place a space before and after any multiple letter abbreviation (as in F. Supp. 2d);
- In legal periodicals, set the abbreviations for an institution or geographical entity apart from other capital letters (as in N.M. L. Rev.).

(2) Federal Cases (ALWD Rule 12)

With the exception of the presentation of United States Supreme Court cases (for which *ALWD* permits parallel citations), the presentation of federal cases for *ALWD* is identical to that for *The Bluebook*:

Example of case from United States Supreme Court:

Carroll Bros. v. Allen Co., 490 U.S. 116 (1995)* or
Carroll Bros. v. Allen Co., 490 U.S. 116, 230 S. Ct. 90,
216 L. Ed. 2d 88 (1995)

Example of case from intermediate court of appeal:

Weber v. Franklin, 38 F.3d 119 (9th Cir. 1999)*

Example of case from district court:

Richardson v. McAfee, 98 F. Supp. 2d 778 (S.D.N.Y. 2000)*

(3) Subsequent History (ALWD Rule 12.8)

ALWD's rules relating to subsequent history are nearly identical to those of *The Bluebook*, namely, you must include the subsequent history for the cases you cite, although you may omit denials of certiorari unless the cited case is less than two years old or if the denial is particularly important.

ALWD Example: *Lee v. Nelson*, 109 F.3d 45 (2d Cir. 1998), *aff'd*, 490 U.S. 16 (1998)

Note that *ALWD* provides that when citing a decision with subsequent history in the same year, include the year each time.

b. Citation of Statutes (*ALWD* Rule 14)

(1) *Federal Statutes*

The presentation of federal statutes is the same in *ALWD* as it is in *The Bluebook*. The rules requiring you to include a date parenthetical for federal statutes and the name of the publisher for the unofficial sets (U.S.C.A. and U.S.C.S.) are also identical, although *The Bluebook* uses "LexisNexis" and *ALWD* uses "Lexis."

Examples:	42 U.S.C. § 2220 (2006)*
	42 U.S.C.A. § 2220 (West 1999)*
	42 U.S.C.S. § 2220 (Lexis 2003)

(2) *State Statutes*

Appendix 1 of *ALWD* provides the format for citation for each state's statutes. They are highly similar or identical in form to those shown in *The Bluebook*.

Examples:	Alaska Stat. § 10.45.90 (Lexis 2001)
	Colo. Rev. Stat. Ann. § 6-7-103 (West 2001)*
	N.C. Gen. Stat. § 48-1-103 (Lexis 2000)

4. ALWD *Citation Rules and Examples for Secondary Authorities*

Most of the *ALWD* rules relating to citing secondary authorities are identical to those for *The Bluebook*. Following are examples for the most often cited secondary authorities. Again, an asterisk following an example indicates that the format is identical for both *ALWD* and *The Bluebook*.

a. Annotations (*ALWD* Rule 24)

Cite A.L.R. annotations as follows: Kyle A. Smith, *Private Nuisances*, 124 A.L.R.5th 667 (1999).

b. Encyclopedias (*ALWD* Rule 26)

Cite encyclopedias as follows:	45 C.J.S. *Hospitals* § 201 (1996)*
	24 Am. Jur. 2d *Easements* § 21 (1994)*

c. Periodical Materials (*ALWD* Rule 23)

Generally, cite periodical articles as follows: Jacob N. Scheib, *The Hearsay Rule*, 35 Tenn. L. Rev. 105 (2001).*

d. Books, Texts, and Treatises (*ALWD* Rule 22)

A key difference in the way citations for treatises are presented under *ALWD* rules is that *ALWD* requires that the publisher of the treatise be identified in the parenthetical with the date. *The Bluebook* does not require this information. Another difference is that *ALWD* requires that the volume number of the treatise be given after the name of the set.

> *ALWD* **Example:**   Penny D. Davis, *Corporate Handbook* vol. 3, § 12:8 (3d ed., West 2002).

e. Restatements (*ALWD* Rule 27)

Cite Restatements as follows: *Restatement (Second) of Torts* § 24 (1995).

G.   Special Citation Issues (*Bluebook* and *ALWD*)

1. *Introduction*

Learning the various citation rules can be difficult, and the task is made even more complicated by the work of integrating citations into your legal writing. While citations for law review and other academic articles appear in footnotes, citations in other legal writings such as legal memoranda or court documents usually appear in the body of your narrative text. Because you will typically be preparing or checking cites appearing in text, the information presented in this chapter relates to citing in text. Citations do not exist alone. They appear as part of sentences that must be correctly punctuated, as support for quotations, and together with certain signals that give readers information about the level of support the citation provides for the assertion of law you have made. This section of the chapter will address these special citation issues such as punctuation, quotations, signals, and short form citations you can use when you have once cited an authority in full and now wish to refer to it again. *Bluebook* examples provided will be shown in the form used by legal practitioners.

2. *Punctuation* (Bluebook *Bluepages 2;* ALWD *Rule 43)*

There are three punctuation marks that may follow a citation: a period; a comma; or a semicolon.

a. Citation "Sentences"

Citations appear in legal writings in two ways: as complete "sentences" or as clauses set off by commas within a sentence. If you have made an assertion about the law, it must be supported by legal authority. You cannot make a statement about the law without attributing it to the appropriate authority. If the statement that you have made about the law is a sentence, the citation that follows the sentence will appear as though it were a "sentence" itself.

Example

Landlords are required to provide written notice to tenants before commencing actions for eviction. *Williams Co. v. Sanders Elec. Enter.*, 428 P.2d 102, 106 (Alaska 1996).

In this example, a statement about the law was made in a complete sentence. The citation that supports this legal assertion also appears as a "sentence" in that it starts with a capital letter and ends with a period. The citation informs the reader that the entire preceding sentence is supported by the case *Williams Co. v. Sanders Elec. Enter.* Note that the words "Electrical" and "Enterprise" have been abbreviated because the citation stands alone.

b. Citation "Clauses"

Authorities that support (or contradict) only a portion of a sentence appear in a citation format set off by commas, which immediately follow the statement they support (or contradict). End a citation clause with a period if it is the last clause in the sentence.

Example

It has been held that landlords must provide notice to tenants before commencing eviction actions, *Williams Co. v. Sanders Elec. Enter.*, 428 P.2d 102, 106 (Alaska 1996), although the amount of time provided by the notice may vary from three to ten days, *Hill v. Irwin*, 432 P.2d 918, 921 (Alaska 1997).

This example informs the reader that *Williams Co. v. Sanders Electrical Enterprise* requires landlords to give notice to tenants and that *Hill v. Irwin* provides that the length of time set forth in the notice may vary. Note that because the *Williams* case cite is not needed to make sense of a sentence or clause, it is viewed as a stand-alone cite rather than as part of a textual sentence. Thus, words such as "Electrical" and "Enterprise" are abbreviated.

Do not place a citation in parentheses or brackets. Try to vary your placement of citations. If your writing consists of a series of sentences each of which is followed by a citation, your project will be choppy. Besides varying citations so that some appear as sentences and some appear as

clauses, another technique used by many legal writers to achieve variety and interest in their writing is occasionally to use citations in introductory clauses.

Example

> According to *Williams Co. v. Sanders Electrical Enterprise*, 428 P.2d 102, 106 (Alaska 1996), landlords must provide written notice to tenants before commencing actions to evict those tenants.
>
> or
>
> One of the first cases to address the issue of default notices was *Williams Co. v. Sanders Electrical Enterprise*, 428 P.2d 102, 106 (Alaska 1996), which held that landlords must provide written notice to tenants before commencing actions to evict those tenants.

These phrases provide a different technique for introducing citations and add interest to a project. Again, however, do not fall into the lazy habit of always introducing your legal authorities in the same manner. Occasionally students start each and every paragraph in a project with the phrase "In *Williams v. Sanders . . .*" or "In *Hill v. Irwin . . .*" The reader, on looking at the page, is presented with a series of paragraphs each of which commences with the word "in" followed by a case citation, giving the project a rigid look and a style lacking in interest and variety.

ALWD refers to the technique of incorporating a citation into a textual sentence (as shown in the foregoing examples and as in, "In *Jones v. Smith*, 520 U.S. 106, 109 (1998), the Court held . . . ") as an "embedded citation" and states that some readers dislike embedded citations because they make sentences more difficult to read.

3. *String Citing (*Bluebook *B3.5 and Rule 1.4;* ALWD *Rule 45)*

a. Introduction

Another manner in which citations appear in legal writing is in "strings" or groups of several citations. If you cite more than one authority in support of a proposition, separate each citation from the next by a semicolon and a space and follow the last citation with the appropriate punctuation mark, usually a period.

Example

> Courts from all over the country are in agreement in requiring landlords to provide notice to tenants before commencing actions to evict those tenants. *Samson v. Oak Tree, Inc.*, 761 P.2d 118, 122 (Cal. 1980); *Allen v. Carwood*, 421 A.2d 181, 184 (N.J. 1976); *Fulton v. Garden Apts., Ltd.*, 388 S.W.2d 200, 207 (Tex. 1977).

In general, "string citing" is disfavored. Courts prefer that you select the best authority that supports a proposition and cite it rather than cluttering your writing with citations that do not add anything. In certain situations, however, string citing is acceptable. Thus, as shown in the preceding example, if you need to demonstrate to a reader the breadth and variety of authorities that are in agreement, or if your state has no authorities for a certain issue and you wish to persuade the court to adopt a view espoused by several jurisdictions, you may wish to string cite.

b. Order of Citations in String Cites

When you string cite, however, you must place the citations in a certain order. *The Bluebook* (Rule 1.4) provides that if one authority is considerably more helpful or authoritative than the others, it should be placed first. Except in this situation, you should list the citations in the following order (see *Bluebook* Rule 1.4 for complete list):

(a) Constitutions (list United States Constitution first, then state constitutions, alphabetically by state).
(b) Statutes (list federal statutes first by ascending order of U.S.C. title, then state statutes alphabetically by state).
(c) Cases (list federal cases first, ordering by United States Supreme Court, United States Courts of Appeal, United States District Courts, then state cases, alphabetically by state and from highest court to lowest court).
(d) Secondary authorities (in this order: uniform and model codes, Restatements, books, law review articles, annotations, and electronic sources).

If you have several cases from the same state — for example, Missouri — cite from highest court to lowest court and within each group from newer cases to older cases.

If you have several cases from the United States Courts of Appeal (or the United States District Courts), cite by date, giving the newer cases first.

Bluebook Example

Landlords must provide notice to tenants before commencing actions for eviction. *Alan v. Anderson*, 421 F.2d 101, 106 (4th Cir. 1985); *Darwin v. Balboa Gardens*, 415 F.2d 222, 226 (8th Cir. 1984); *Swanson v. Trudeau*, 399 S.W.2d 14, 17 (Ark. 1988); *McNenly v. Trainor*, 346 S.W.2d 606, 609 (Ark. 1981); *Harrison v. J.T. Alton, Inc.*, 394 S.W.2d 102, 104 (Ark. Ct. App. 1986).

ALWD Rule 45 covers string citing and is nearly identical to *The Bluebook* approach. The order in which authorities are given in the string is also nearly identical to the order directed by *The Bluebook*. Thus, for example,

federal cases are given before state cases (which are arranged alphabetically) and cases from higher courts are given before those from lower
courts. One difference, however, is that *The Bluebook* states that the most
helpful or authoritative source should be given first in the string whereas
ALWD has no such approach. One other difference between *The Bluebook*
and *ALWD* is that *The Bluebook* treats all United States Courts of Appeal
as one court and all United States District Courts as one court. For
example, if you are citing four different cases from four different circuit
courts of appeal, list the newest case first and proceed to the oldest case.
ALWD's approach is different. It requires you to order the federal appeals
courts by circuit number (with "1st Cir." cases coming before "2d Cir."
Cases, and so forth) and to order the federal district court cases in
alphabetical order by state.

4.   *Quotations* (Bluebook *B12 and Rules 3.2 and 5; ALWD Rules 5 and 47)*

a. Introduction

You may find in the course of legal writing that you wish to quote directly
from a case, treatise, law review article, or other legal authority. Your
decision to quote a legal authority rather than merely summarize or
paraphrase it may stem from your desire to emphasize a certain point or
perhaps your determination that the judge's or author's manner of
expressing a legal principle is so articulate that you wish to present the
material in its original form rather than weaken its force by summarizing
it. Quoting from legal authorities is certainly acceptable so long as it is
not overdone and so long as the citation is in correct form.

   You must *always* indicate the exact page a quote appears on to allow
a reader to review the original source and ensure that you have correctly
reproduced the material and have not altered the meaning of the
quotation by omitting or adding material. This reference to the exact page
on which the quoted material appears is often called a "spot cite,"
"pinpoint cite," or "pincite," as you are pinpointing the reader's attention
to a specific page, or a "jump cite," as you are asking the reader to "jump"
from the first page of a legal authority to a specific page within that
authority.

   The reference to quoted material is placed immediately after the
page on which the case or article begins, separated by a comma.

Examples

   Case: *Goodman v. Gray*, 429 F.2d 109, 114 (7th Cir. 1979). This
informs the reader that the case begins at page 109, and the quoted
material is found at page 114.

   Article: Susan L. Hoffman, *The Juvenile's Right to Counsel*, 47
N.C. L. Rev. 411, 446 (1985). This informs the reader that the article
begins at page 411, and the quotation is found at page 446.

If local court rules require you to give parallel citations, you must inform the reader on which page a quote occurs in each parallel cite. In some instances, you will have to locate the quote in several sources.

Example

"A landlord must provide a notice to a tenant before commencing an action to evict the tenant." *Tapper v. Savage*, 201 Wis. 2d 191, 196, 299 N.W.2d 47, 52 (1986).

If the quote spans more than one page, provide the inclusive page numbers but separate them by a hyphen. Retain the last two digits but omit any other repetitious digits. *Bluebook* (R. 3.2(a)). *ALWD* Rule 5.3, however, allows such page spans to be presented in two ways: by retaining all digits or by retaining the last two digits but dropping other repetitious digits.

Correct Bluebook *example*	*Correct* ALWD *examples*
320 F.3d 1071, 1074-76	320 F.3d 1071, 1074-76 or
	320 F.3d 1071, 1074-1076

If you are citing from individual scattered pages from a source, indicate the separate pages as follows: (*Bluebook* R. 3.2(a); *ALWD* R. 5.4).

Example

Bailey v. Pridewell, 412 F.2d 109, 114, 121 (9th Cir. 1978).

The Bluebook states that pincites are "critical." Thus, always include a pincite whether you are quoting directly from material or you are paraphrasing. This practice is a courtesy to readers to enable them to locate easily that portion of the authority you are discussing. If your research is accurate and the legal authority does in fact say what you claim it does, there is no reason not to provide a reference to a specific page. This is the position suggested by *The Bluebook* (R. 3.2(a)), which states that when referring to "specific material" within a source, one should include both the page on which the source begins and the pinpoint. *ALWD* Rule 5.2 is similar.

If a point is continually made throughout a source, use *passim*, a Latin word meaning "everywhere" and interpreted as "scattered here and there," as follows: (*Bluebook* R. 3.2(a); *ALWD* R. 5.6).

Examples

Bluebook: *Taft v. Alpert*, 429 S.E.2d 616 *passim* (W. Va. 1998).

ALWD: *Taft v. Alpert*, 429 S.E.2d 616, passim (W. Va. 1998).

If your specific material appears on the first page of a source, repeat the page number (*Bluebook* B4.1.2 and R.3.2(a); *ALWD* R. 5.2(b)), as follows:

Example

> Allison P. Page, *Statutory Construction*, 46 BYU L. Rev. 109, 109 (1998).

b. Indicating Quotations in Text

The Bluebook and *ALWD* rules regarding quotations conform to the rules regarding quotations that you have been familiar with since high school, that is, that quotations of 49 or fewer words appear in the text of your writing whereas longer quotations of 50 or more words are indented.

(1) Non-Indented Quotations (Bluebook Rule 5.1(b); ALWD Rule 47.4)

Quotations of 49 or fewer words should appear in the body of your text without indentation. Indicate the beginning and ending of the quotation by quotation marks ("/"). If your quote then relies on or incorporates other quoted material, indicate such by a single quotation mark ('). Commas and periods must be placed inside the ending quotation mark. Other punctuation marks such as question marks or exclamation points appear inside the ending quotation mark only if they are part of the matter quoted.

Example

> In one recent case, the court ruled that the defendant could properly be found to have been carrying a knife for use as a dangerous weapon and held as follows: "Although appellant was attempting to check the knife when arrested, his statements permitted the inference that he was prepared to use it, should the occasion arise, but prior to entering and, after retrieving the briefcase, immediately upon leaving the Longworth Building." *Monroe v. United States*, 598 A.2d 439, 441 (D.C. 1991).

Remember that *ALWD* would allow the defendant's name to be shown as "*U.S.*"

(2) Indented Quotations (Bluebook B12.2 and Rule 5.1(a); ALWD Rule 47.5)

Quotations of 50 words or more should be indented (typically ten spaces), left and right, and appear without quotation marks. This "block" quote should be single-spaced. A reader is alerted to the fact that material is being quoted by the indentation itself. Separate the block quote from

the text below and above it with a blank line. If your quotation quotes from some other source or authority, indicate such with quotation marks ("/"). That is, retain all punctuation marks and quotation marks as they appear in the original quote. This is quite different from a non-indented quote, which requires you to use a single quotation mark (') when it is quoting from another source. *The Bluebook* and *ALWD* require that block quotations be fully justified.

Note that *ALWD* also allows any quotation to be presented as a block if it exceeds four lines of typed text. Thus, in the example given above, under *ALWD*, the quotation could have been shown as a block quote because it exceeds more than four lines.

To determine whether you should indent a quote and place it in block form, you must count the words in the quote. Although this is somewhat time-consuming, it must be done. There are, however, a few word processing programs, such as SpellCheck, that will count the words in a quote for you. Again, remember that *ALWD* allows any quotation that exceeds four lines to be presented as a block quote.

Some legal writers indent quotes of fewer than 50 words to empha-size the indented material and make it stand out from the remainder of the narrative. Avoid this practice, as it not only violates *Bluebook* rules but has been overdone, with the result that some readers "skip over" short indented material. Your writing should be sufficiently forceful in itself without resorting to "tricks" to draw emphasis.

One of the mistakes most commonly made by legal writers relates to placement of the citation that supports the quote. The citation does *not* appear within the block indentation. Placement of the citation within the indention indicates that it is part of the quote. The citation should be placed at the left margin on the line of text that follows the quote.

Correct:
XXXXXXXXXXXXXXXXXXXXXX
XXXXXXXXXXXXXXXXXXXXXX
XXXXXXXXXXXXXXXXXXXXXX
XXXXXXXXXXXXXXXXXXXXXX

Monroe v. United States, 598 A.2d 439, 441 (D.C. 1991).

Incorrect:
XXXXXXXXXXXXXXXXXXXXXX
XXXXXXXXXXXXXXXXXXXXXX
XXXXXXX *Monroe v. United States*, 598 A.2d
439, 441 (D.C. 1991).

After you have placed your citation at the left margin, continue your narrative. If you begin a new paragraph, skip to the next line (or skip two lines if you are double spacing) and indent as usual to show a new paragraph is beginning.

c. Alterations of Quotes (*Bluebook* Rule 5.2; *ALWD* Rule 48)

Anytime you alter a quote in any way, whether by pluralizing a word, inserting a word, capitalizing a word that was not capitalized in the original quote, or some other alteration, you must always alert the reader that you have changed the quote. When you change a letter from lowercase to uppercase, or vice versa, enclose it in brackets. Similarly, substituted words or letters or other inserted material should be bracketed. If a letter has been omitted, indicate such with empty brackets — for example, "boy[ ]" for "boys."

   If the original quote was, for example, "The factfinder must consider circumstances surrounding the use of the dangerous weapon," you must indicate an addition to the quoted material as follows: "The factfinder must consider circumstances surrounding [the possession and] use of the dangerous weapon."

   If a mistake or misspelling has occurred in the original material, indicate such by following the mistake by the word *sic*, a Latin word meaning "thus; so; in such manner." For example, if the original quoted material provides, "Defendants was convicted in the Superior Court," indicate the error in the original as follows: "Defendants was [sic] convicted in the Superior Court." Note that *ALWD* Rule 48.6 states that you may retain the mistake, correct it, or use [sic] to show that it appeared in the original quoted material.

d. Adding Emphasis (*Bluebook* Rule 5.2; *ALWD* Rule 48.5)

If the material you are quoting is emphasized in the original by italics, underscoring, or otherwise, retain the original emphasis but do not otherwise indicate such. Thus, do not state "emphasis in original." By including the italicized or underscored word or phrase in the quotation, the reader will assume this emphasis occurred in the original. If, on the other hand, you wish to emphasize something that was *not* so emphasized in the original, you must indicate your alteration of the quote by a parenthetical explanation.

   For example, assume the original quote read as follows:

   "The court refused to hold that merely possessing a dangerous weapon was a violation of the statute." *Franklin v. James*, 681 F.2d 102, 106 (8th Cir. 1988).

   If you wish to emphasize any of the words or phrases in the original material, do so as follows:

   "The court refused to hold that *merely possessing* a dangerous weapon was a violation of the statute." *Franklin v. James*, 681 F.2d 102, 106 (8th Cir. 1988) (emphasis added).

e. Omitting Citations (*Bluebook* Rule 5.2; *ALWD* Rule 49.3(d))

It is possible that the quotation you wish to include is peppered with other citations, resulting in a quote that is disrupted by these intervening cites, weakening the force and effect of the quotation. To eliminate these intrusive citations (or footnotes) and yet remain faithful to the original quoted material, simply indicate to the reader that you have omitted citations.

Example

> The court relied on numerous precedents in refusing to hold that "merely possessing a dangerous weapon was a violation of the statute." *Franklin v. James*, 681 F.2d 102, 106 (8th Cir. 1988) (citations omitted).

If readers wish to review the other cases whose citations have been omitted, they may easily do so by locating page 106 of the case *Franklin v. James*, located at volume 681 of the *Federal Reporter, Second Series*.

f. Use of Ellipses (*Bluebook* Rule 5.3; *ALWD* Rule 49)

If you omit a word, phrase, or sentence from quoted material, you must indicate this omission by the use of an ellipsis, three periods separated by spaces from each other and set off by a space before the first period and after the last period. An ellipsis signals that words have been omitted from the middle of a quotation or the end of a quotation. Do not use an ellipsis to begin a quotation. If you have altered a word or omitted words at the beginning of a quotation, indicate such by changing the first letter of the word now beginning your quote from a lowercase letter to an uppercase letter and enclosing it in brackets. This will signal the reader that you have altered the beginning of a quote.

For example, assume your quote is as follows:

> "In order to prove a violation of the statute, the prosecution must prove defendant's intent."

If you wish to omit the first part of the quote, do so as follows:

> "[T]o prove a violation of the statute, the prosecution must prove defendant's intent."

g. Omissions from the Middle of a Quote

To indicate that you have omitted language from the middle of a quote, use the ellipsis, three periods separated by spaces and set off by a space before the first and after the last period:

Example: "In order to prove a violation . . . the prosecution must prove . . . intent."

h.   Omissions from the End of a Quote

To indicate that you have omitted language from the end of a quote, use three periods separated by spaces followed by the final punctuation of your quote, typically a period.

Example: "Although Appellant was attempting to check the knife when arrested, his statements permitted the inference that he was prepared to use it . . . ."

i.   Using Quoted Language as a Phrase

When using quoted language as a phrase or clause incorporated into your sentence rather than as a full sentence, you need not use an ellipsis.

Example

Justice O'Connor stated that malice and recklessness "will give rise to punitive damages."

j.   Paragraph Structure

If you have indented a quote of 50 or more words and this quote commenced a paragraph, indent further to let the reader know that your quote is from the beginning of a paragraph.

Example

XXXXXXXXXXXXXXXXXXXXX
XXXXXXXXXXXXXXXXXXXXXXXXXX
XXXXXXXXXXXXXXXXXXXXXXXXXX
XXXXXXXXXXXXXXXXXXXXXXXXXX
XXXXXXX.

If you continue to quote another paragraph, skip a line and once again indent the second quote to indicate it commenced a paragraph.

Only indent your block quote(s) if the original quote began a paragraph. Quotations from the middle of paragraphs appear in block style with no additional indentations.

If you are quoting one paragraph of 50 words or more and then wish to omit or skip an entire paragraph and then continue quoting another paragraph of 50 words or more, use four indented periods on a new line to signal that you have omitted an entire paragraph.

Example

XXXXXXXXXXXXXXXXXXXXX
XXXXXXXXXXXXXXXXXXXXXXXXXXX
XXXXXXXXXXXXXXXXXXXXXXXXXXX
XXXXXXX.

. . . .

XXXXXXXXXXXXXXXXXXXX
XXXXXXXXXXXXXXXXXXXXXXXXX
XXXXXXXXXXXXXXXXXXXXXXXXXX
XXXXXXXXXXXXXXXXXXXXXXXXXXX
XXXXXXX.

The Bluebook (R.5.1) shows a standard ellipsis to show an omitted paragraph, but *ALWD* (R. 49.4(d)) requires centering of the ellipsis and five to seven spaces between each ellipsis point. To signal an omission at the beginning of a second or subsequent paragraph, use an ellipsis (even though you may never use an ellipsis to begin a quotation).

5. *Citation Signals (*Bluebook *B3 and Rule 1.2;* ALWD *Rule 44)*

Legal writers often use certain citation signals as a shorthand method of indicating to the reader the manner in which an authority supports or contradicts an assertion. If a citation does anything other than directly state a proposition, identify the source of a quotation, or identify an authority referred to in text, a signal indicating such should be used before the citation. Both *The Bluebook* and *ALWD* recognize four categories of signals: those that show support; one that suggests comparison; those that show contradiction; and one that indicates background material. These signals can be very confusing, and often there are only very subtle shadings of difference between one signal and another. Moreover, the use of signals is complicated by the fact that their use and meaning have shifted from one edition of *The Bluebook* to the next. See Figure 8-2.

    (i) *No signal.* If, after having made an assertion, the author immediately cites a legal authority, this indicates that the legal authority directly states the proposition (or "directly supports" the proposition, according to *ALWD*), identifies the source of a quotation, or identifies an authority referred to in the preceding text.

   (ii) *E.g.* The signal *e.g.* is used to show an example, meaning that the authority you cite is merely an example of several authorities that directly state the proposition but are not cited. The signal *e.g.* may be used with other signals. Note that *The Bluebook* follows the signal *e.g.* with a comma, but *ALWD* does not.

(iii) *Accord.* The word *accord* is used after one authority has been given and indicates that two or more authorities agree with the first.

Example

"Landlords are required to provide notice to tenants before commencing actions to evict tenants." *Li v. Carr*, 420 U.S. 20, 29 (1994); *accord Smith v. Jones*, 681 P.2d 104, 107 (Cal. 1990); *Ivey v. McMullen*, 670 P.2d 13, 18 (Cal. 1985).

(iv) *See. The Bluebook* states that the signal *see* is used when the citation clearly supports the proposition. *See* is used when the proposition is not directly stated by the authority you rely upon but obviously follows from it. The use of *see* has shifted over time. See Figure 8-2. *ALWD* states that the signal *see* is used when the cited authority either supports the stated proposition implicitly or contains dicta that support the proposition.

Figure 8-2
The Evolution of Citation Signals in *The Bluebook*

	[No signal]	See	Contra
Fifteenth Edition (1991-1996)	Citation clearly states the proposition or identifies the source of a quotation or authority referred to in text.	Citation clearly supports the proposition.	Citation directly states the contrary of the proposition.
Sixteenth Edition (1996-2000)	Citation identifies the source of a quotation or authority used in text.	Citation clearly states or clearly supports the proposition.	*Contra* did not exist in the Sixteenth Edition of *The Bluebook*.
Seventeenth Edition (2000-2005)	Citation directly states the proposition or identifies the source of a quotation or authority referred to in text.	Citation clearly supports the proposition.	Citation directly states the contrary of the proposition.
Eighteenth and Nineteenth Editions (2005-date)	Same as Seventeenth Edition.	Same as Seventeenth Edition.	Same as Seventeenth Edition.

(v) *See also.* This signal is used to show additional legal authorities that support a proposition. *The Bluebook* encourages you to use a parenthetical explaining the relevance of the authorities.

(vi) *Cf.* The signal *cf.*, meaning "compare," is used to indicate legal authority supporting a proposition that is different from the main proposition but that is analogous to the main proposition. *The Bluebook* strongly recommends that when using this signal, the writer explain parenthetically how the cited authority supports the proposition.

(vii) *Contra.* The signal *contra* indicates contradiction and is used when the cited authority directly states the contrary of the proposition you have made. Like "no signal" and *see*, the use of *contra* has shifted over time, and, in fact, was omitted entirely from the 16th edition of *The Bluebook*. It was revived in the 17th edition.

(viii) *But see.* *The Bluebook* provides that this signal is used when the legal authority you cite clearly supports a proposition contrary to the main proposition. *ALWD* states that *but see* is used when the cited authority either contradicts the stated proposition implicitly or contains dicta that contradict the stated proposition.

(ix) *But cf.* The signal *but cf.* is used when the legal authority you cite supports a proposition analogous to the contrary of the main proposition. *The Bluebook* strongly recommends a parenthetical explanation as to the relevance of the authority you cite.

(x) *See generally.* The signal *see generally* indicates that the legal authority you cite provides helpful background material related to the proposition. *The Bluebook* recommends an explanatory parenthetical.

These signals are given before your citation. They may or may not be capitalized, depending on the context in which they are used. Capitalize a signal beginning a citation sentence, and do not capitalize a signal that is part of a sentence. The signals are underscored or italicized unless they are used as verbs in ordinary sentences, and an unbroken line is used for signals composed of two words, such as *see generally*.

Most individuals find these signals confusing and very difficult to distinguish. Typically, they are used more often in academic legal writing, such as law review articles, which provide a complete analysis of an issue, including cases in support of a proposition and cases in contradiction to a proposition, rather than in court documents and legal memoranda, which often use citations with no or few introductory signals. Moreover, there are subtle differences in the presentation and meaning of the signals depending on whether you are following *The Bluebook* or *ALWD*. For example, as noted above, *The Bluebook* follows the signal *e.g.* with a comma whereas *ALWD* does not.

Because the meaning of the various signals can be so nuanced, both *The Bluebook* and *ALWD* recommend that when you use most signals, you include a parenthetical explanation after the cited source to describe the meaning and force of the authority. Generally, both *The Bluebook* and *ALWD* require that explanatory phrases begin with a present participle (a verb plus an "ing" ending, as in "arguing" or "holding") and a lowercase letter unless the parenthetical is a full quoted sentence. Note that both *The Bluebook* (R.1.3) and *ALWD* (R.44.8) have fairly complicated instructions on how to order and punctuate these signals when more than one is used in a string citation.

6. *Short Form Citations*

Once you have cited an authority in full, to save time you may use a short form on subsequent occasions when you refer to it in your writing. *The Bluebook* (B4.2) provides that a short form may be used if it will be clear to the reader which citation has been shortened, the earlier full citation appeared in the same general discussion, and the reader will be able to locate readily the earlier full citation. *ALWD* Rule 11.2 is similar.

a.   Cases (*Bluebook* B4.2 and R. 10.9; *ALWD* Rule 12.21)

Assume your full citation is *Singer v. Bryant*, 219 N.E.2d 409, 411 (Ind. 1987). Once you have given this full citation, you may use any of the following short forms:

> *Singer*, 219 N.E.2d at 412.
> 219 N.E.2d at 412. (Note that this form is not acceptable under *ALWD* rules.)
> *Id.* at 412.

For cases in which a parallel citation is required, such as *Lowell v. Allen*, 204 Ga. 102, 104, 68 S.E.2d 19, 21 (1976), you may use any of the following short forms:

> *Lowell*, 204 Ga. at 107, 68 S.E.2d at 23.
> 204 Ga. at 107, 104 68 S.E.2d at 23. (Note that this form is not acceptable under *ALWD* rules.)
> *Id.* at 107, 68 S.E.2d at 23.

The Bluebook and *ALWD* also provide that if you have given a full case citation and later refer to the case in the same general discussion, you may use one of the parties' names without including any further citation (*Bluebook* Rule 10.9(c); *ALWD* Rule 12.20(c)(2)).

Example

> In *Lowell*, the court also discussed punitive damages.

(Note that in most instances, you will probably place a citation to the *Lowell* case at the end of the sentence, including the pincite to the page that supports the assertion.)

Generally, use the plaintiff's name in a short form unless the plaintiff is a common litigant such as the United States, "People," or some government agency, in which case use the more distinctive defendant's name.

b. Statutes (*Bluebook* B5.2(b); *ALWD* Rule 14.6)

Once you have given a full citation to a statute, you may later use any short form (including *id.*) that clearly identifies the statute.

> **First reference:** Ohio Rev. Code Ann. § 1761.01 (West 1988).
> **Later reference:** Ohio Rev. Code Ann. § 1761.01.

c. Constitutions (*Bluebook* B6; *ALWD* Rule 13.4)

Do not use any short form other than *id.* for constitutions.

d. Books and Periodical Materials (*Bluebook* B8.2 and B9.2; *ALWD* Rule 22.2)

The Bluebook requires you to use *id.* or *supra* to refer to these materials after you have given a full citation to them. *ALWD*'s rule is substantially similar (although *ALWD*'s presentation varies depending on whether your document includes or does not include footnotes).

7. *Use of* Id., Supra, Infra, *and Hereinafter*

a. *Id.* (*Bluebook* B4.2 and Rule 4.1; *ALWD* Rule 11.3)

(1) Introduction

Id. is an abbreviation for *ibidem*, a Latin word meaning "in the same place." You may recall using *ibid.* or *id.* in high school or college term papers to avoid having to repeat information in a footnote and to signal the reader that your material originated from the same source as that indicated immediately before.

Id. functions the same way in legal writing. A short court document or legal memorandum may rely almost exclusively on one case, which you discuss over the course of several pages. To avoid having to repeat and retype the citation each time you make an assertion, you may use the signal *id.* to refer the reader to the immediately preceding authority. Note

that although the signal *ibid.* is acceptable in some writings, it is not acceptable in legal writing. Only *id.* may be used.

Id. may be used for nearly any legal authority. That is, *id.* may be used to direct a reader to a preceding case, statute, treatise, law review article, or other legal authority. *Id.* will be capitalized if it "stands alone" or begins a sentence, or it will be introduced with a lowercase letter if it is part of a citation clause or sentence. If underscoring, underscore the period in *id.* If italicizing, italicize the period in *id.*

If you have cited a case or some other authority and you then wish to direct the reader to that immediately preceding citation, use *id.*

Example

In order to prove a violation of the statute, the government must demonstrate only that the defendant carried a dangerous weapon, and intended to carry a weapon. *Monroe v. United States*, 598 A.2d 430, 439 (D.C. 1991). There is no requirement that a defendant evidence a specific intent to use the weapon for a wrongful purpose. *Id.*

The use of the signal *id.* in the example indicates to the reader that *Monroe v. United States* is the source of the assertion that there is no requirement that the government prove that a defendant had a specific intent to use a weapon for an unlawful purpose. The reader is directed to page 439 of *Monroe*.

(2) "Id. *Plus*"

Use *id.* alone if you wish to direct the reader to the exact source and page/section/paragraph as the preceding citation. If, however, you wish to direct the reader to the preceding source, but to a different page/section/paragraph within that source, use "*id.* plus" the change:

Example

"A landlord is required to provide written notice to a tenant before instituting an action to evict the tenant." *Jasper v. Schick*, 692 P.2d 106, 109 (Wash. 1984). This notice must be hand-delivered to a tenant at least three days before the action is commenced. *Id.* at 114.

The reader has been directed to *Jasper v. Schick* but to a different page within that source.

Examples

First reference to a case: *Daly v. Chu*, 661 F.2d 918, 920 (10th Cir. 1986).
Next reference: *Id.* or *Id.* at 921.
First reference to a statute: 42 U.S.C. § 1604 (2006).
Next reference: *Id.* or *Id.* § 1606.

First reference to a treatise: 1 J. Thomas McCarthy, *McCarthy on Trademarks and Unfair Competition* § 18:18 (4th ed. 1997).
Next reference: *Id.* or *Id.* § 18:22.
First reference to a law review article: Carolyn L. Gray, *Tariff Restrictions*, 40 Mo. L. Rev. 161, 166 (1982).
Next reference: *Id.* or *Id.* at 169.

Note that under *Bluebook* rules when you are directing a reader to a different page you use "*Id.* at ____." When, however, you direct a reader to a different section or paragraph, you simply use "*Id.* § ____" or "*Id.* ¶ ____." *The Bluebook* expressly states that the word "at" is not used before a section or paragraph symbol (Rule 3.3).

Correct:	*Id.* § 314.
	Id. ¶ 14.120.
Incorrect:	*Id.* at § 314.
	Id. at ¶ 14.120.

The *ALWD* approach is different and includes the word "at" before a section symbol, as in *Id.* at § 314 (*ALWD* R. 11.3(e)).

(3) Parallel Citations

Remember that local rules may require parallel citations. This requirement makes the use of *id.* somewhat more complicated because you must use the following form:

First cite	*Garde v. Whetsell*, 209 Idaho 106, 108, 309 P.2d 309, 311 (1986).
_Id._ reference	*Id.* at 110, 309 P.2d at 313.

Note that only the official citation is replaced with *id.* The regional reporter citation is repeated. The *ALWD* approach is identical (*ALWD* R. 12.20(f)).

(4) The Use of Id. *in Footnotes*

The signal *id.* may be used to refer to an immediately preceding authority within the same footnote or to an immediately preceding footnote when that preceding footnote contains only one authority. If the preceding footnote or reference contains more than one source, later use of *id.* does not tell the reader which of the preceding sources is being referenced, and thus it may not be used (*Bluebook* B4.2 and R. 4.1; *ALWD* R. 11.3(b)).

b. Supra (*Bluebook* B8.2, 9.2, and Rule 4.2; *ALWD* Rule 11.4)

(1) Introduction

Supra means "above" and informs a reader to look at preceding authorities (although not *immediately* preceding sources, for which you should use *id.*) for the information desired. For example, if you are searching an index for entries related to tenants, you may find the following:

Tenant, see Landlord, *supra.*

This is an instruction that the information you need is arranged and presented under the heading "Landlord," which appears "above" or earlier in the volume, rather than being arranged under the heading "Tenant."

Often in legal writing you may refer to one authority, for example, a treatise, then refer to various other authorities and then wish to refer to the treatise again without repeating the entire citation. In this situation you cannot use *id.* because there are citations that intervene between your first reference to the treatise and your current reference to it. In this instance, use *supra*, which informs the reader that you have given the citation previously in your project, although it was not given immediately preceding.

The Bluebook and *ALWD* are both quite clear that you may not use *supra* when referring to most primary authorities (cases, constitutions, statutes, most legislative materials, or regulations) "except in extraordinary circumstances," such as when the name of the authority is very long (*Bluebook* Rule 4.2). If you have referred to a case, constitution, or statute and then discussed other authorities and then wish to refer again to the case, constitution, or statute, you may not use *supra*. You must use an appropriate "short form" citation, discussed previously in Section G.6, *supra*.

This prohibition against using *supra* to refer to previously cited cases is violated by some practicing attorneys and paralegals. Before embarking on such a violation, determine what the common practice is in your firm or agency. Some firms, usually the larger ones, will rigidly adhere to the citation manuals and would view your use of *supra* to refer to a preceding case as an unforgivable gaffe, whereas other firms would view such a use of *supra* as a practical and effective citation form.

Supra does not "stand alone" like *id.* It must appear with other identification, usually the last name of an author, or, if there is no author, the title of a work.

Examples

First cite:	Carolyn L. Gray, *Tariff Restrictions*, 40 Mo. L. Rev. 161, 164 (1982).
Intervening cite:	*Powell v. Silvers*, 661 F.2d 918 (10th Cir. 1986).
***Supra* cite:**	Gray, *supra.*

To indicate a variation, use "*supra* plus" the variation, such as Gray, *supra*, at 166. If you are underscoring, underscore the word *supra* but not any punctuation following it.

The examples given in *The Bluebook* for practitioners show a comma after *supra* when the "*supra* plus" form is used to refer a reader to a book or article such as Gray, *supra*, at 166 (B8.2). Note that *ALWD* allows the use of *supra* only in documents with footnotes; *supra* cannot be used in documents without footnotes (*ALWD* R. 11.4(b)).

Bluebook **Examples of Short Forms in a Brief or Court Document**

Page 1.	*Taylor v. Ellis*, 501 U.S. 621, 626 (1994).
Page 2.	*Id.*
Page 3.	*Id.* at 629.
Page 4.	6 Judith N. Hunter, *Intellectual Property* § 104 (3d ed. 1991).
Page 5.	*Id.*
Page 6.	*Id.* § 107.
Page 7.	a. *Taylor*, 501 U.S. at 630 or
	b. 501 U.S. at 630 or
	c. In *Taylor*, the Court also . . . .
Page 8.	Hunter, *supra* or Hunter, *supra*, § 108.

(2) *Internal Cross-References* (Bluebook *Rule 3.5;* ALWD *Rule 10)*

Bluebook. It is possible that you may have cited a book or treatise very early in your project and then wish to refer to it many pages later. If your only direction to the reader is "Gray, *supra*," the reader may have to thumb through several pages of your document to find the original citation. As a courtesy to the reader you may wish to include a reference to the specific page in your project on which the original citation appeared. Use "p." or "pp." to direct your reader to the earlier page in your project on which the full citation originally appeared.

Examples

Gray, *supra* p. 3

Gray, *supra* p. 3, at 168. (This signal directs the reader to page 168 of the article written by Carolyn L. Gray and informs the reader

that the full citation appears on page 3 of your project.) Follow *supra* with a comma when you direct a reader to the page or section of the previously cited legal authority. No comma is used after *supra* when you refer a reader to a previous page or section within your own project.

ALWD. *ALWD* prohibits the use of *supra* to refer to sources such as cases or statutes. *Supra* may be used only to send a reader to material that appears earlier in your document, as in *supra* n. 7.

c. *Infra*

Infra is a Latin word meaning "below" or "beneath." It is used to direct a reader to material that will appear later in a project. For example, if you were directed to review some chapter appearing after this one, the signal would be "Chapter 10, *infra*." *Infra* is the direct opposite signal of *supra* and you should follow the guidelines discussed previously for *supra* in using *infra*. Note that neither *supra* nor *infra* may be used to refer to the primary authorities of cases, constitutions, statutes, most legislative materials, or regulations.

As you can imagine, *infra* is not used very often in documents or memoranda prepared by practitioners. It makes little sense to state a legal principle and then give the reader the following citation: Gray, *infra* (meaning that you will be giving the full cite to the article by Carolyn L. Gray later in the project). It is more likely that your use of *infra* will relate to directing a reader to a later section in your document. In this case, use the following form: *See infra* Section V.

d. Use of "Hereinafter" (*Bluebook* Rule 4.2(b); *ALWD* Rule 11.4(d))

If an authority would be difficult to identify repeatedly due to an extremely long name or title, you may identify it in full the first time you cite it and then inform the reader that thereafter you will be referring to it by a shorter name or form.

Earlier editions of *The Bluebook* required that writers identify a session number for a Congress when citing to bills, hearings, committee reports, and other documents. Because astute readers know that the first session of a Congress (1st Sess.) always occurs in odd-numbered years and the second session (2d Sess.) always occurs in even-numbered years, *The Bluebook* no longer requires a reference to a congressional session for any materials published after the 60th Congress in 1907.

Bluebook Example

> ***First citation:*** *Proposed Amendments to the Federal Fair Franchising Practices Act of 1992: Hearing on H.R. 5961 Before the H. Comm. on Energy & Commerce*, 102d Cong. 41 (1992) [hereinafter *Franchising Hearing*]

> ***Later citations:*** *Franchising Hearing, supra.*

The *ALWD* approach is substantially similar.

8. *Capitalization in Court Documents and Other Legal Memoranda*

Bluebook Rule 8 and Bluepages 7.3 require that in headings and titles of documents submitted to courts you should capitalize the initial word, the word following a colon, if any, and all other words except articles (a, an, the), conjunctions of four or fewer letters (or, but, and), and prepositions of four or fewer letters (of, up, to). *ALWD* Rule 3.0 is similar, except that *ALWD* does not require capitalization of any preposition, regardless of its length (unless it is the first word of a title). Additionally, capitalize the following:

- Act — when you are referring to a specific act of a legislature, as in "the Lanham Act."
- Circuit — when you use the word with a circuit name or number, as in "the Eighth Circuit."
- Court — when you name any court in full, as in "the California Supreme Court." (*ALWD* also capitalizes the highest court in a state once it has been identified by full name; *The Bluebook* does not.)

      — whenever you refer to the United States Supreme Court.
      — in a court document when referring to the court that is receiving the document, as in "this Court is respectfully urged to grant Plaintiff's motion."

- Party designations — when referring to the parties in a matter that is the subject of the court document, as in "Defendant's argument to this Court misstates the law."
- Judge, Justice — when referring to a specific judge or justice, as in "Justice Smith" or any reference to any of the Justices of the United States Supreme Court, as in, "The Justices were unanimous in their decision."
- State — when it is part of the full title of the state, such as "State of Florida"; when the wording it modifies is capitalized, as in "the State Attorney General"; or when referring to a state as a litigant, such as "the State argues for conviction."

9. *Electronic Sources, Databases, and the Internet* (Bluebook *Rule 18;* ALWD *Rules 12.12, 12.15, and 38-42*)

The Bluebook (R. 18) announces three general principles for citing to electronic media and other nonprint resources, such as Lexis, Westlaw, and the Internet.

First, *The Bluebook* requires the use and citation of traditional printed sources unless there is a digital copy of the source available that is authenticated (by the use of a logo showing it has been verified by a government entity as complete), official (meaning it has been designated as official by some entity), or an exact copy of the printed source. When such an authenticated, official, or exact copy of a source is available, it may be cited to as if to the original source (without any URL information).

Second, if a printed source can be located, a parallel citation to the Internet may be provided if it will significantly improve access to the relevant information and if the content of the Internet source is identical to that of the printed source. In this case, cite first to the printed source and then give the Internet source, introduced with the phrase "*available at.*"

Third, many articles and materials exist only on the Internet; there is no print counterpart for them. *The Bluebook* refers to these materials as "direct" Internet citations. In such instances, follow *Bluebook* Rule 18.2.2, which provides specific direction on including author names, titles, dates, and the URL. Citations to dynamic sites that are updated frequently should include a time as well as a date.

The *ALWD* approach is similar to that of *The Bluebook*: If a source is available in both print and electronic formats, cite only to the print source if it is readily available to most readers. *ALWD* provides that if it is necessary to cite to the Internet, give the case name and then insert the URL and a parenthetical with the court abbreviation and exact date, as follows: *Kunkle v. Texas*, http://www.supremecourt.gov/opinions/bound volumes/543bv.pdf (U.S. Nov. 18, 2004).

At the time of the writing of this text, the federal government is migrating to a new electronic system, the Federal Digital System (usually called "FDsys" and located at http://www.fdsys.gov), which is intended to provide "one-stop shopping" for nearly all legislative documents, including statutes, regulations, and presidential materials. The documents deposited into FDsys are "authentic," meaning their content is verified as authentic or official and thus one may readily cite to them as if citing to an original print source. Thus, a citation to a federal statute appearing on FDsys would be identical to its print counterpart, as follows: 18 U.S.C. § 2244 (2006).

PracticeTip

What Does "Available" Mean?

Neither *The Bluebook* nor *ALWD* allows you to cite to electronic
sources (such as Lexis, Westlaw, and the Internet) unless material
is not "available" in traditional print sources. What does
"available" mean? Does it mean available to the legal community
in general? Does it mean available in your office? No one knows.
ALWD Rule 38.1 provides some guidance in stating that you should
cite to the print source if it is "readily available to most readers."
Bluebook Rule 18.2.2 suggests that "unavailable" means the
material is so obscure that it is practically unavailable.

Most cases are available in print form within days or weeks. Thus,
it would seem that the window of opportunity for citing solely to
electronic sources is quite narrow: Cite to an electronic source
only during the period of time it takes for the print source to "hit
the shelves," which is typically quite short (or when the material
will not appear in print form, such as when a case is unreported).

---

a. Statutes and Constitutions (*Bluebook* Rule 12.5; *ALWD* Rule 14.5)

Statutes and constitutions must be cited to a traditional print source
when available. If the information is not available in a traditional print
source, one may cite to an electronic database such as Lexis or Westlaw.

Bluebook Example

Cal. Prob. Code § 503 (Deering, LEXIS through 2009 Sess.)

ALWD Example

11 U.S.C. § 105 (WL current through Nov. 14, 2009)

b. Books, Journals, and Magazines (*Bluebook* Rules 15.9, 16.8, and 18.2.2; *ALWD* Rule 23.1(i))

As always, cite books, journals, and magazines first to a traditional source
and only to the Internet when the information is not available in a traditional format or electronic database. Very few books are available in their
entirety on the Internet, but there are now a variety of journals and articles
that are published exclusively online and are not available in print form.

Bluebook Example

Article available only on the Internet: Juliana Gruenwald, *EU
Taking on Net Neutrality*, Nat'l J. (June 30, 2010, 1:29 PM),
http://techdailydose.nationaljournal.com/2010/06/eu-taking-on-net-
neutrality.php.

ALWD **Example (Rule 40)**

> **Article appearing solely on the Internet:** Juliana Gruenwald, *EU Taking on Net Neutrality*, http://techdailydose.nationaljournal .com/2010/06/eu-taking-on-net-neutrality.php (June 30, 2010).

At this time, no one is entirely certain what direction legal citation form will take. In general, practitioners are in favor of the speed and lower costs associated with locating and citing cases to electronic sources such as the Internet, whereas many judges prefer the traditional method of citation. The ABA Standing Committee on Technology and Information Services, the American Association of Law Libraries, and the Judicial Conference's Committee on Automation and Technology continue to meet and discuss citation form in the digital age. As of now, however, cases are relatively easy to locate on the Internet but hard to cite to in legal documents (unless they are authenticated, official, or an exact copy of the printed sources).

See Figure 8-3 for a chart showing the more significant differences between *ALWD* and *The Bluebook*.

10. *Citing to Court Documents (Bluebook B7 and ALWD Rule 29)*

Legal writers frequently cite to various court records, transcripts, appellate records, and other materials in briefs submitted to courts. Both *The Bluebook* and *ALWD* provide guidance on citing to these materials, although their approaches to citing court and record materials and abbreviations used vary to some degree. Following are some general guidelines:

- Abbreviate titles of court documents unless such would be confusing to the reader. Use *Bluebook* BT.1 and *ALWD* Appendix 3 for lists of acceptable abbreviations. Generally, you may omit prepositions and articles unless they are needed for clarity. For example, display "Plaintiff's Motion to Dismiss" as "Pl.'s Mot. Dismiss" and "Defendant's Motion for Summary Judgment" as "Def.'s Mot. Summ. J."
- *The Bluebook* permits (but does not require) citations to court documents to be enclosed in parentheses. *ALWD* allows you to put the entire citation in bold, enclose it in parentheses, or to use both boldface type and parentheses.
- Give dates (in most instances), and use a pinpoint when citing court documents, being as precise as possible. For example, for depositions, give the page and line numbers as shown in the following example:

Example

> Defendant has denied he was driving at an excessive rate of speed. Def.'s Br. 18:1-9. Such is also supported by various witnesses, Peterson Aff. ¶ 4; Hunter Dep. 44:14-18, Oct. 18, 2007, and by the record below, R. at 43:1-6.

Ethics Alert

Finding Local Rules

Both *Bluebook* and *ALWD* provide that any local rules relating to citation form will "trump" or supersede their rules. Thus, you have an ethical obligation to find and follow these local rules. To find specialized, local citation rules:

- Access the website http://www.uscourts.gov for links to all federal court websites, which post their local rules.
- Review each state's judicial website, identified in Table T.1 of *The Bluebook* and Appendix 2 of *ALWD*, for state and local rules.
- Review *The Bluebook*'s Bluepages Table BT.2, which identifies court rules relating to citation form.
- Review Appendix 2 of *ALWD* for a discussion of local rules relating to citation form.
- Call the clerk of the court to which you are submitting a document, and inquire whether any local rules dictate the form for citations.
- Consult a law librarian.

H. Tips for Effective Cite Checking

Whenever you are presented with a cite checking assignment, there are several practical tips you should consider to ensure you perform your task accurately and efficiently.

(i) Ask the individual who assigned the project to you when the deadline is so that you can be sure you do the cite checking in a timely fashion. Often cite checking is one of the last tasks performed in legal writing projects, and you may need to start working immediately on the project so that it can be filed timely.

(ii) Highlight all citations in the document as soon as it is given to you and while you are fresh, so that you will readily be able to find citations and check them even after several hours have passed and your energy level is low. It is easier to locate

citations when they are underscored than when they are italicized. Thus, highlighting italicized citations will help you find these citations when your energy levels are flagging.

(iii) If the document is being filed with a court, you must obtain a copy of the court rules so that you can determine whether the court requires a specific citation form. Some courts insist that documents follow non-standard citation form. For example, some courts in California require that papers submitted show citations in the following format, even though it is unsupported by *The Bluebook* or any other guideline: *Atwell v. Jay* (1985) 142 Cal. 2d 109. If court rules dictate a specific format, you must adhere to that format. To obtain a copy of the rules of the court, call the court clerk and inquire. Alternatively, most states and courts publish their court rules on the Internet. For rules for the United States Supreme Court, access http://www.supremecourt.gov. For lower federal courts, access http://www.megalaw.com. For state court websites, Table T.1 of *The Bluebook* provides a reference to each state's judicial website. *Bluebook* Table BT.2 references some helpful local rules and several jurisdiction-specific manuals that provide guidance on local citation practices. Appendix 2 of *ALWD* contains local citation rules. If no court rules exist with regard to citation form, use *Bluebook* form unless directed otherwise.

(iv) You will quickly learn that some writers are more exacting than others. It is possible that the document you are cite-checking contains complete citations and you need only compare each cite against *The Bluebook* to ensure compliance with *Bluebook* rules. It is equally possible that the document you are given has several omissions and you need to go to the law library or log on to Lexis or Westlaw to obtain dates of decisions, pages of quotes, and so forth. Therefore, as you review the document, use different colored pens, sticky flags, or different symbols to indicate which cites have been checked and are accurate, which need further information supplied, and those for which you have questions. Determine if the author of the document has any preferences as to format, such as preferring underscoring of case names and signals rather than italicizing. Similarly, determine if the author has any special conventions as to format you should follow in lieu of *Bluebook* format. In the absence of instruction, assume *Bluebook* rules govern.

Figure 8-3
Differences in *ALWD* and *Bluebook* Citation Formats

Topic	*ALWD Format*	*Bluebook Format*
Typeface	Ordinary roman type is always used. *ALWD* eliminates use of large and small capital letters.	Practitioners use ordinary roman type. Materials in law review footnotes and academic citations (including names of authors and titles of books and periodicals) appear in large and small capitals.
Capitalization in Headings	Do not capitalize prepositions or conjunctions (unless they are the first word of a title).	Capitalize prepositions and conjunctions of more than four letters.
Parallel Citations for United States Supreme Court Cases	*ALWD* permits (but does not favor) parallel citations for United States Supreme Court cases.	*The Bluebook* does not permit parallel citations for United States Supreme Court cases.
Case Names	• Words in case names are "traditionally" abbreviated if the citation appears as a stand alone and not as part of a textual sentence. • If the United States is a party, cite as "U.S." or as "United States."	• Words in case names must be abbreviated if the citation appears as a stand alone and not as part of a textual sentence. • If the United States is a party, cite as "United States."

Figure 8-3 (Continued)

Topic	ALWD Format	Bluebook Format
Treatises and Dictionaries	• Publisher is included in parenthetical with date. • Volume number is placed after treatise title. • Short form in documents without footnotes is as follows: Smith, *Due Process* at 42.	• Publisher is not included in parenthetical with date. • Volume number is placed as the first element. • Short form is as follows: Smith, *supra*, at 92.
A.L.R. Annotations	The word "Annotation" is omitted from the citation.	The word "Annotation" is given after the author's name.
String Citing	Order cases from the federal courts of appeal by ordinal and then in reverse chronological order; order cases from the district courts alphabetically by state name and then in reverse chronological order.	Treat all federal courts of appeal as one court and all district courts as one court, and list all cases from each in chronological order (placing courts of appeals cases first).
Quotations	Block indent quotations of 50 or more words or any quotation that exceeds four lines of text.	Block indent any quotation of 50 or more words.
Signals	• There are no commas after *e.g.* or *see e.g.* when used before citations. • Separate different types of signals with a semicolon.	• There are commas after *e.g.*, and *see, e.g.*, when used before citations. • Separate different types of signals with a period.

Figure 8-3 (Continued)

Topic	ALWD *Format*	Bluebook *Format*
	• The signal et seq. is not italicized. • The use of *et seq.* for a span of statutes is permitted but not encouraged. • There is a comma before the signal *passim.*	• The signal *et seq.* is italicized. • The use of *et seq.* for a span of statutes is prohibited. • There is no comma before the signal *passim.*
Miscellaneous	• When giving pinpoints, one may retain all digits (example: 1014-1019). • One must use the word "at" before any pinpoint, even a section sign or paragraph symbol (example: *Id.* at § 14). • There are many differences in abbreviations used in *ALWD* and *The Bluebook* (for example, *ALWD* abbreviates "Central" as "C." while *The Bluebook* abbreviates it as "Cent.") • *ALWD* includes local citation rules and forms. • *ALWD* uses "Lexis" in the parenthetical with the date for federal statute citations in U.S.C.S. • *ALWD* does not prohibit superscripts (and would thus allow 11th Cir.). *See ALWD* at 10.	• When giving pinpoints, drop repetitive digits (example: 1014-19). • The word "at" cannot be used before a section sign or paragraph symbol (example: *Id.* § 14). • There are many differences in abbreviations used in *ALWD* and *The Bluebook* (for example, *ALWD* abbreviates "Central" as "C." while *The Bluebook* abbreviates it as "Cent.") • *The Bluebook* does not include local citation rules and forms, although Bluepages Table BT.2 references local rules. • *The Bluebook* uses "LexisNexis" in the parenthetical with the date for federal statute citations in U.S.C.S. • *The Bluebook* prohibits superscripts such as 11th Cir.

   (v) When you find an error, make the correction by interlineating
        or crossing out the error and inserting the correct information.
        You may wish to note in the margin which *Bluebook* rule
        governs your correction as authors can be notoriously defen-
        sive about recognizing errors, and you should be ready to
        support and defend your correction. Because you may not be
        preparing the final version of the document, write legibly so
        that support staff can correctly insert your edits.
  (vi) Because the document may be evolving as you work on it, and
        other attorneys and paralegals may be continuing to edit the
        document, make sure each version is clearly marked with the
        date and the time it is printed. This will help you ensure you
        are working on a current version, not one superseded by a later
        version.
 (vii) If the document contains quotations, check each one for accu-
        racy. Quotations must be faithfully reproduced. If alterations
        and omissions are made, make sure those are indicated by
        brackets and ellipses. You must also verify that the citation
        includes the pinpoint page of a quote.
(viii) Pay attention to short form citations, and verify that the
        author's use of short forms, *id.*, and *supra* are correct. Because
        the document may be subject to revising and editing at the
        eleventh hour, you must always check the accuracy of signals
        in the final version of the document.
  (ix) Make sure that you look beyond the body of the document and
        also check the cites in any appendices, footnotes, table of
        contents, or index of authorities.
   (x) Be consistent. If you underscore case names, underscore book
        titles and signals such as *id.* and *supra*. If you italicize case
        names, italicize book titles and signals.
  (xi) Allow Lexis and Westlaw to help you locate pinpoints, verify
        the spellings of case names, and check the accuracy of quota-
        tions. Remember, however, that only you can determine when
        to use a short form, when you may abbreviate words in a case
        name, and when to use a citation signal.
 (xii) After the document is resubmitted for revision and correction,
        review to ensure that your corrections were incorporated.
(xiii) Validate all primary authorities listed in the document, either
        manually or online, using *Shepard's* on Lexis or KeyCite on
        Westlaw (see Chapter 9).

──────────────── **Practice Tip** ────────────────

What To Do if Your Corrections Are Overruled

In many instances, attorneys are thrilled that you are detailed
enough to catch errors in their citation form. In other instances,
they may become defensive. In still other instances, they
may simply say, "I don't care what *The Bluebook* (or *ALWD*)
requires, I want to cite the case this way."

What should you do if you know your cite checking is correct but
the attorney overrules you? Give in. The author of a document
always has the right to control authorship. You have done what
you were asked to do, namely, correct citation errors, and you
were overruled. If you find that certain attorneys are routinely
submitting briefs with numerous citation errors, and you are
concerned that the firm's reputation for accuracy may be
impaired, raise the issue with your paralegal coordinator or
mentor and ask for help.

It is possible that the author might wish you to do more than simply
correct errors in citation format and might ask that you confirm the
accuracy of the author's conclusions. Thus, if the author has cited *Jones
v. Smith*, 421 A.2d 91 (Pa. 1986), for the proposition that a landlord is
required to provide notice to a tenant before commencing an action to
evict the tenant, you will have to review this case to verify that it does in
fact support the author's conclusion. Similarly, checking citation signals
such as *see, cf.,* and *accord* requires that you read the cited source to
confirm the author has used the correct signal. This extensive type of cite
checking is less common than the usual cite checking assignment, which
typically requires you only to correct errors in citation form and then to
Shepardize or KeyCite.

I. Quick Reference for Citations (*Bluebook* and *ALWD* Form)

1. Cases

Following are examples of the most commonly cited authorities showing
both *Bluebook* form (for practitioners) and *ALWD* form. If only one
example is given, the example complies with both *Bluebook* and *ALWD*
rules.

(i) State Cases (*Bluebook* and *ALWD*)

Sidley v. Steinman, 201 N.C. 118, 429 S.E.2d 16 (1984) [if local rules require parallel citations].

Sidley v. Steinman, 429 S.E.2d 16 (N.C. 1984) [in all other instances].

(ii) Federal Cases

United States Supreme Court:

LaPointe v. Sullivan, 98 U.S. 396 (1984). [Note that *ALWD* permits parallel citations.]

United States Courts of Appeals:

Lawrence v. Mather, 691 F.2d 114 (8th Cir. 1984).

United States District Court:

Blakely v. Yost, 742 F. Supp. 908 (D.R.I. 1986).

2. *Statutes*

(i) State

Ga. Code Ann. § 10-1-440 (West 1998).

N.Y. Gen. Bus. Law § 308 (McKinney 1988).

(ii) Federal:

17 U.S.C. § 101 (2006).

17 U.S.C.A. § 101 (West 1996).

17 U.S.C.S. § 101 (Lexis 2005). [*ALWD* form]

17 U.S.C.S. § 101 (LexisNexis 2004). [*Bluebook* form]

3. *Constitutions*

State: N.M. Const. art. III.
United States: U.S. Const. amend. X.

4. *Encyclopedias*

68 C.J.S. *Trusts* § 302 (1988).
54 Am. Jur. 2d *Trusts* § 114 (1989).

5. *Law Review Articles*

Allan A. Sanders, *The Juvenile's Right to Counsel*, 46 Colum. L. Rev. 891 (1988).

6. *Texts and Treatises*

Bluebook: Joy N. Hildebrand, *Securities Review* § 421 (2d ed. 1991).

ALWD: Joy N. Hildebrand, *Securities Review* § 421 (2d ed., West 1991).

7. *Restatements*

Bluebook: Restatement (Second) of Contracts § 112 (1992).

ALWD: *Restatement (Second) of Contracts* § 112 (1992).

8. *Dictionaries*

Bluebook: *Black's Law Dictionary* 1172 (9th ed. 2009).

ALWD: *Black's Law Dictionary* 1172 (Bryan A. Garner ed., 9th ed., West 2009).

9. *Cases Located on Westlaw and Lexis*

Bluebook: *Daley v. Fisher*, No. 99-CIV-1024, 2001 U.S. Dist. LEXIS 32665, at *4 (E.D. Tex. Oct. 4, 2001).

Harris v. Carter, No. 01-2444C, 2003 WL 43225, at *7 (4th Cir. Jan. 9, 2003).

ALWD: *Daley v. Fisher*, 2001 U.S. Dist. LEXIS 32665 at *4 (E.D. Tex. Oct. 4, 2001).

Harris v. Carter, 2003 WL 43225 at *7 (4th Cir. Jan. 9, 2003).

10. *Summary of Special Citation Issues*

(i) **Quotations:** Always give the page of a quotation. As a courtesy to readers, always include a pinpoint cite even for material paraphrased. Quotations of fewer than 49 words should appear in text with quotation marks. Place periods and commas inside quotation marks. Quotations of 50 words or more should appear indented or in "block" form without quotation marks

and fully justified. Retain the original paragraph structure of a block quotation. Remember that *ALWD* also allows indenting of a block quote if the quotation exceeds four lines of typed text.

(ii) **Short forms:** Once you have cited a case in full you may use a short form.

> **First cite:**   *Parsons v. Geneva*, 92 U.S. 104, 109 (1982).
> **Short forms:** *Parsons*, 92 U.S. at 111.
> 92 U.S. at 111. [*Bluebook* only]
> *Id.* or *Id.* at 114.

(iii) ***Id.*:** Use *id.* or "*id.* plus" to refer a reader to the immediately preceding cite.

(iv) ***Supra*:** Use *supra* to refer the reader to a previous cite that is not the immediately preceding cite. *Supra* may not be used to refer to cases, constitutions, statutes, most legislative materials, or regulations. *Supra* must appear with the name of an author or title of a work. *ALWD* states that *supra* can only be used in documents with footnotes.

11. *Internet Citation Form*

Bluebook:

Article available solely on the Internet: David Lat, *The Supreme Court's Last Day: A Round-Up*, Above the Law (June 28, 2010, 11:04 AM), http://abovethelaw.com/2010/06/the-supreme-courts-last-day-a-round-up.

ALWD:

Article available solely on the Internet: David Lat, *The Supreme Court's Last Day: A Round-Up*, http://abovethelaw.com/2010/06/the-supreme-courts-last-day-a-round-up (June 28, 2010).

CyberSites

http://www.legalbluebook.com This website of *The Bluebook* provides an overview of changes to the 19th edition of *The Bluebook*, asks for comments and corrections, allows ordering of *The Bluebook*, provides introductory material about *The Bluebook*, and offers video tours of the new online *Bluebook*.

(continued)

CyberSites *(Continued)* ████████████████████

http://www.alwd.org	The website of the Association of Legal Writing Directors offers information about *ALWD*, charts and appendices, updates to *ALWD*, and a list of schools that have adopted *ALWD* as their citation manual.
http://lawreview.uchicago .edu/resources/style_sheet .html	The University of Chicago Law School's Style Sheet incorporates the Maroonbook.
http://lexisnexis.com/icw	Lexis offers an "interactive citation workstation" allowing users to quiz themselves on both *ALWD* and *Bluebook* citation formats.
http://www.abanet.org/tech/ ltrc/research/citation/home .html	The American Bar Association website has information devoted to neutral, public domain, or universal citation form and provides the ABA resolution regarding this issue as well as lists of states that have adopted public domain citation formats.
http://www.law.cornell.edu/ citation	Professor Peter W. Martin of Cornell University Law School offers a complete citation primer based on the 19th edition of *The Bluebook* and on the 4th edition of *ALWD*. *Bluebook* and *ALWD* rules are explained and numerous examples are provided.
http://www.ualr.edu/cmbar ger/citations.html	This website provides links to helpful citation resources.
http://www.cit-r-us.com/	The website of Citrus provides a free tutorial showing how its citation formatting system works.

Citation Software Programs

At this time, there is no absolutely reliable way to put your citations in proper *Bluebook* or *ALWD* form other than for you to do the task the old-fashioned way: manually. Nevertheless, Lexis offers a service called StyleCheck (formerly known as CiteRite), which advertises that it will put your citations in proper *Bluebook* or California citation format. Although it is unclear whether StyleCheck can understand all of the idiosyncrasies of citation form (such as when you can abbreviate the word "Surety" in a case name and when you cannot), it is clear that StyleCheck will notify you of improper underlining in a cite, missing parallel cites, or improper punctuation (such as the failure to put a period after the word "Supp.").

── *(continued)*

CyberSites *(Continued)* ██████████████████████████

Additionally, computer-assisted legal research offers some quick approaches to ensure that at least the name and numbers in a case cite have been reproduced accurately.

Another Lexis product, BriefCheck, collects the case and law review citations in your brief, verifies them through *Shepard's* to ensure they are still good law, and checks your quotations, case names, page numbers, and dates for errors. Similarly, Westlaw's KeyCite service (see Chapter 9) also provides citation verification information, such as correct case names and parallel citations. West also offers CiteAdvisor, which can build a table of authorities and suggest correct citation format in either *Bluebook* or *ALWD* format.

A company in Massachusetts, Sidebar Software, has created a software program called CiteIt!, which purportedly formats all citations to *Bluebook* rules or *ALWD* rules. When you wish to enter a citation into your document, you choose a citation source and then select the appropriate citation from ones displayed. Similarly, a company called Dakota Legal Software has recently introduced Citrus, its fee-based software program that automatically generates citations in correct *Bluebook* form (see http://www.cit-r-us.com). Even such systems, however, presuppose some familiarity with *The Bluebook* or *ALWD*; otherwise, how would one be able to select the "correct" citation when several are given? Although all of these programs are helpful, none of them can determine when you should use a signal, when you should include a parenthetical, and other similar decisions that require the use of discretion and an understanding of *Bluebook* and *ALWD* principles.

██

Writing Strategies

When citing authorities in a brief, avoid "string citing" (citing more than one authority to support a contention). Too many citations clutter your project and disrupt the flow of your narrative. Moreover, string cites must be in a specific order according to *The Bluebook* and *ALWD*, making string citing even more difficult.

Similarly, avoid overusing footnotes in writing projects. Upon encountering footnotes, most readers either will stop reading the narrative while they jump to the footnote or will skip over the footnote entirely. Neither result is desired; the first causes a disruption of your argument, while the second renders your research ineffective. Some experts contend that if something is not significant enough to be included in the main body of a text, it should be omitted, and thus there is never a need for footnotes.

To some extent, the overuse of quotations may also result in the reader skipping over them. Use quotations sparingly, in those situations in which what the court has said is so authoritative and persuasive that paraphrasing the statement would dilute its impact. Judicious use of quotations adds drama and variety to your project. Overuse of quotations may cause the reader to wonder if you have taken the easy way out by simply reproducing another's words rather than analyzing those words.

Assignments for Chapter 8

CITATION FORM

There is at least one thing wrong with each fictitious citation below. Correct the citations using the current edition of *The Bluebook* or *ALWD*. You may need to supply missing information such as dates and volume numbers. Punctuation is not needed after the citations. Assume you are preparing a memorandum in your office, and unless otherwise indicated, assume that the citations appear in textual sentences rather than as stand-alone citations. There is no need to include "pinpoints," unless otherwise directed.

1. Samuel Michaels versus Nina Albertson, a U.S. Supreme Court case from 2007, at volume 540, page 344.
2. Fabbiani Brothers versus Lowell Company, reported at page 101 in volume 301 of the Federal Reporter, Third Series, from the Federal Circuit and decided in 2008.
3. Show that the U.S. Supreme Court denied certiorari for the above case in 2009.
4. United States of America vs. Mitchell Murray, reported at volume 201 of the Federal Supplement, Second Series, at page 403, with a quotation from pages 414-417, decided by the Eastern District of Michigan in 2006.
5. Erie Association v. New Morgan Landfill Limited, a Minnesota Supreme Court case from 2001, at volume 722, page 890.
6. LaFleur v. Whitman, a Minnesota Court of Appeals case from 2000, at volume 710, page 788.
7. Ogden Inc. v. Bayview Incorporated, a Nevada Supreme Court case from 2004, at volume 102, page 301. Assume a court requires parallel citations.
8. Anderson v. Berry, a 1999 case from the Ohio Court of Appeals, at volume 340, page 17. Assume a court requires parallel citations.
9. Section 78 of Title 15 of the United States Code.
10. Sections 104 through 107 of Title 11 of the United States Code Annotated.
11. Rhode Island General Laws Section 14-2-109.
12. New York Public Buildings Law Section 14202.
13. Federal Rule of Civil Procedure 54.
14. Restatement of Agency, Second, Section 104.
15. Volume 7 of John T. Haley's treatise "Motor Vehicle Safety," Section 404, (fourth edition 2008).
16. Assume that after your document cites section 403 of the above treatise, you immediately cite section 415 of the treatise (and that there are no intervening citations). How would you present the second citation?

17. A law review article entitled "Securities Regulation, written by Donna A. Burch and David D. Hancock, at volume 48 of the Northern Kentucky Law Review, page 109 (2004).
18. Show how to cite the definition of "mistrial" appearing on page 909 of the current edition of Black's Law Dictionary.
19. Show that the following 2006 U.S. Supreme Court case was decided by a 5-4 decision: Securities and Exchange Commission versus Kaplan, volume 540 of the U.S. Reports, page 118, with a quotation on page 125.
20. Show that Justice Ginsburg dissented in the above-referenced case.
21. Fix any errors in the following:
    Sovereign immunity bars suits against the United States absent an explicit and unequivocal waiver. Department of the Army v. Blue Fox, Incorporated, 525 U.S. 255, 261-263 (1999); Operation Rescue National v. USA, 975 F.Supp. 92, 108-109 (Dist. Mass. 1997); Lyon v. Carey Management Investments Company, 533 F2nd 649, 652 (Cir. 11, 1976).
22. Show how to cite page 430 of the case USA v. Murray (Question 4 above) as a short form (assuming you cannot use *id.*).

MEMORANDUM ASSIGNMENT

There are numerous errors in the fictitious citations in the following brief memorandum. Correct citation errors using the current edition of *The Bluebook* or *ALWD*. You may need to supply missing information.

The business judgment rule generally protects corporate directors and officers. Smithson v. National Management Services Inc, 309 F.3rd 118, 124 (Circuit 9 2005). Corporate managers are thus given wide latitude in their handling of corporate affairs and courts will typically not "second guess" decisions made by those managers so long as those managers act in good faith. Id. at pages 130-132. Thus, if directors act in good faith and in a manner such as ordinarily prudent and diligent persons would act, they are generally protected against liability. Peterson v. Fletcher Professional Marketing Association, 909 Fed. Supp. 2d 440, 445 (Southern District New York 2008). In fact, most state statutes provide that directors are charged with acting with due case and in good faith. See, for example, California Corporations Code Section 11066.

This principle, known as the "business judgment rule," presumes that in making business decision, directors and officers act in good faith and in a manner that is in the best interests of the corporation. James J. Johnson, "Treatise on Corporate Liability," volume 4, Section 109 (fifth edition 2007). "On the other hand, if directors act with clear and gross . . . recklessness, they will not be protected from liability." Smithson, supra at page 139. Thus, if directors clearly and completely abdicate their responsibilities to the corporation, they cannot be protected under the business judgment rule. James J. Johnson, Section 115.

Moreover, in assessing liability under the business judgment rule, courts consider whether corporate managers acted responsibility at the time they made their decision and do not consider what may have occurred since the time of the decision. Peterson. Thus, if directors conduct reasonable investigation and exercise due care when they make their decision, they will generally have no later liability if circumstances change subsequent to the time of their decision. Markson v. Security Life Insurance Co., 909 Fsupp2d 104, 109 (Northern District Calif. 1999), affirmed at 203 F.3rd 118 (Ninth Circuit 2001).

Finally, in making their decisions, directors and officers are entitled to reasonably rely on others. Id. That reliance, however, must be reasonable. Sarah F. Murphy, "Corporate Liability" 48 New York University Law Review 104, 110 (2008). Directors who fail to act with reasonable care, including reasonable inquiry and diligence, are not protected under the business judgment rule. Markson at 109.

Internet Assignment for Chapter 8

1. Access the home page of the Universal Citation Committee of the American Association of Law Librarians at http://www.aallnet .org/committee/citation. Review the Report of the AALL Task Force on Citation Format. Briefly, what is the definition of "public domain citation format"?
2. Access the website for *The Bluebook* and then select "Introduction."
   a. When was the first edition of *The Bluebook* released?
   b. When was *The Bluebook* first released with a blue cover?
   c. What is the central function of a legal citation?
3. Access the website of the Association of Legal Writing Directors at http://www.alwd.org. Select "Publications" and then "ALWD Citation Manual Resources." Access the FAQs. How would you cite a case in which the plaintiff's name is given only as "Nancy P."?
4. Locate Florida Rules of Appellate Procedure 9.800(o). What citation form is required when submitting briefs to Florida courts?
5. Access Professor Peter W. Martin's "Introduction to Basic Legal Citation." Review the information on underlining and italics. Which materials should not be italicized?
6. Access the article *Neutral Citation, Court Web Sites and Access to Authoritative Case Law* by Peter W. Martin (located at 99 Law Libr. J. 329 (2007)). Review paragraphs 55 and 56. Why might it

be easier for states such as North Dakota to adopt a vendor neutral form of citation than for states such as California and New York?

Updating and Validating Your Research

The process of "Shepardizing" a case is fundamental to legal research and can be completed in a manner of minutes, especially when done with the aid of a computer.

Meadowbrook, LLC v. Flower, 959 P.2d 115, 120 n.11 (Utah 1998)

A. **Using *Shepard's* in Print Form to Shepardize Cases**
B. **Using *Shepard's* in Print Form to Shepardize Other Authorities**
C. **Electronic Updating of Legal Authorities**

Chapter Overview

Before you may cite any primary authority in any document you prepare, you must ensure it is still "good law." This is an inflexible rule of legal research. Updating and validating your authorities can be conducted manually (using a set of books called *Shepard's Citations*) or electronically on Lexis (using *Shepard's Citations*) or Westlaw (using its system called KeyCite). Previously, when everyone used the conventional print sources, the process was always called *Shepardizing*; this term is sometimes used today to describe the process of ensuring your authorities are still valid, whether one uses *Shepard's* sources or West's KeyCite.

A. Using *Shepard's* in Print Form to Shepardize Cases

1. Introduction

Few people validate their authorities manually—using print rather than electronic sources—because validating electronically is quicker and provides more current information. In fact, many law firms no longer subscribe to *Shepard's* in print, relying exclusively on electronic

updating. Nevertheless, a thorough grounding in the way the conventional print versions of *Shepard's* work will enhance your understanding of the techniques and value of online updating.

There is a set of *Shepard's Citations* for each set of case reports. Thus, there are sets called *Shepard's Arizona Citations*, *Shepard's Atlantic Reporter Citations*, *Shepard's United States Citations* (covering United States Supreme Court cases), and *Shepard's Federal Citations* (covering lower federal court cases). Most libraries place the volumes of *Shepard's* immediately after the last volume in a set of case reports; some libraries, however, maintain all of the volumes of *Shepard's* in one central location.

A set of *Shepard's* usually consists of two or three hardbound volumes (always a deep maroon color) and one or two softcover advance sheets. White advance sheets are issued approximately every six months, bright red advance sheets are issued quarterly, and gold advance sheets are issued annually or semi-annually. To be sure that you have all of the volumes of *Shepard's* you need, look at the most recent softcover supplement. The front of each supplement displays a notice labeled "What Your Library Should Contain," which lists the volumes of *Shepard's* you will need to complete your task.

2. *Locating* Shepard's *References to Your Case*

Assume the case you are Shepardizing is *Zwicker v. Boll*, 391 U.S. 353 (1968). Because this is a United States Supreme Court case, you will need to locate the volumes of *Shepard's United States Citations*. Open the first volume in the set and scan the upper corners of each page looking for a reference to **Vol. 391**, the volume in which *Zwicker* is reported. This process is similar to looking at the guide words in the upper corners of each page in a dictionary or telephone directory to determine which page will contain the word or name you need.

When you have located the page or pages for **Vol. 391**, scan this page looking for the black boldfaced typed reference –**353**–, because this is the page on which *Zwicker* begins (see Figure 9-1). There are three possibilities.

- **No Reference.** It is possible that there is no reference at all to –**352**–. There may be a reference to –**352**– followed by a reference to –**359**–. Lack of a reference to your page is an indication that during the period of time covered by that volume of *Shepard's*, no case or other authority mentioned *Zwicker* in any manner. If this occurs, proceed to examine the next *Shepard's* volume (again, looking for a reference to **Vol. 391** in the upper corners of each page and then scanning the page for a reference to –**353**–).

Figure 9-1
Sample Page from *Shepard's* United States Citations

UNITED STATES REPORTS — Vol. 391

427NYS2d682
Ohio
30OS2d119
~) 30OS2d128
48OS2d387
283NE155
~) 283NE160
358NE621
P R
122DPR302
1988JTS119
100PRR809
R I
104RI312
111RI253
~) 111RI266
244A2d252
302A2d70
~) 302A2d77
S D
429NW35
Tex
j) 4SW732
Utah
858P2d1016
910P2d1188
Vt
141Vt439
450A2d341
Wash
99Wsh2d859
664P2d1238
W Va
164WV637
264SE855
Wis
d) 269Wis2d [274
d) 674NW601
80CaL745
1975LF305
65VaL909
22LE876n
22LE889n
46LE913n
18A4673n
28A51134n
96A5332n

Citing cases arranged by circuit and then state

—352—
Wilson v Port Lavaca
1968
(20LE636)
(88SC1502)
s) 409F2d1362
s) 285FS85
393US84
395US827
404US2
414US806
419US100
419US812
Cir. 1
309FS1336
Cir. 2
435F2d1250
436F2d1293

Cir. 3
431F2d472
d) 441F2d565
Cir. 5
404F2d913
413F2d323
426F2d144
505F2d915
518F2d892
534F2d610
296FS1343
Cir. 6
454F2d346
j) 515F2d493
Cir. 9
432F2d496
467F2d960
316FS347
Cir. 10
431F2d382
f) 434F2d1233
552F2d915
Cir. DC
513F2d447
522F2d1338
398FS965
15LE904s
17LE1026s

—353—
Zwicker v Boll
1968
(20LE642)
(88SC1666)
s) 270FS131
Cir. 1
309FS726
331FS716
Cir. 2
288FS356
295FS185
Cir. 3
324FS796
329FS1204
441FS1155
Cir. 4
324FS263
Cir. 5
285FS774
296FS180
329FS1328
Cir. 6
432F2d339
Cir. 7
286FS852
288FS206
307FS402
309FS1343
310FS297
311FS770
314FS812
318FS631
322FS1276
327FS1387
Cir. 8
302FS1402
Wis
41Wis2d508

48Wis2d615
99Wis2d583
148Wis2d547
155Wis2d397
164NW518
180NW708
299NW638
436NW291
455NW650
49NYL863
65VaL1319
5A4969n

—359—
Seferi v Ives
1968
(20LE640)
(88SC1665)
s) 155Ct580
s) 236A2d83
Conn
164Ct258
180Ct39
180Ct585
255A2d841
320A2d827
428A2d801
430A2d1287

—359—
North American Van Lines, Inc. v United States
1968
(20LE646)
(88SC1665)
s) 277FS741
105MCC185

—360—
Goldblatt v Dallas
1968
(20LE646)
(88SC1666)
s) 279FS106
Cir. 5
386FS213
Cir. 6
179F3d438

—360—
Howard v Ohio
1968
(20LE647)
(88SC1671)

—361—
Brooks v Briley
1968
(20LE647)
(88SC1671)
s) 274FS538
Cir. 1
343FS903
Cir. 2
321FS679

Cir. 3
441FS1155
Cir. 4
429F2d611
313FS49
324FS262
Cir. 5
434F2d939
j) 434F2d954
285FS774
293FS952
296FS179
311FS107
311FS659
316FS372
320FS671
321FS891
326FS1263
329FS1328
Cir. 6
432F2d339
j) 432F2d346
432F2d535
312FS1122
448FS338
Cir. 8
302FS1400
312FS28
314FS37
Tenn
491SW83
49NYL863
15LE904s
8ARF479n

—361—
Jackson v Nelson
1968
(20LE648)
(88SC1671)
US reh den
392US947

—362—
Walker v California
1968
(20LE648)
(88SC1672)
US reh den
392US947

—362—
Rubeck v New York
1968
(20LE649)
(88SC1672)
s) 28NYAD [1208
s) 286NYS2d [217
Cir. 6
179F3d439

—363—
Federal Power Com. v Pan American Petroleum Corp.
1968
(20LE638)
(88SC1664)
s) 389US1002
s) 376F2d161
5LE1000s

—364—
Branigin v Duddleston
1968
(20LE641)
(88SC1666)
s) 385US455
s) 390US932
s) 255FS155
s) 284FS176
Cir. 5
189FS2d553
Cir. 6
38FS2d529
Cir. 7
435F2d363
12LE1282s

—365—
California v Phillips Petroleum Co.
1968
(20LE639)
(88SC1664)
s) 377F2d278
s) 405F2d6

—366—
Brooklyn Union Gas Co. v Standard Oil Co.
1968
(20LE640)
(88SC1665)
s) 391US9
s) 376F2d578

—367—
United States v O'Brien
1968
(20LE672)
(88SC1673)
US reh den
393US900
s) 376F2d538
j) 393US57
393US113
j) 393US250
394US594
j) 394US616
j) 394US652
395US455

396US372
j) 397US131
398US61
e) 399US263
j) 400US247
403US18
403US224
d) 405US458
j) 405US467
408US101
408US184
409US114
j) 409US128
j) 411US100
413US26
j) 413US103
j) 413US234
415US586
j) 415US599
416US410
j) 417US858
d) 418US409
420US495
422US211
422US934
d) 424US16
j) 425US148
425US771
427US78
d) 427US363
429US265
430US713
430US716
431US93
431US94
433US467
433US476
435US786
436US428
j) 442US283
446US90
j) 446US132
447US462
d) 447US540
450US469
452US69
453US65
j) 453US559
456US226
458US912
j) 459US950
460US580
460US586
461US216
f) 466US804
j) 466US824
468US293
j) 468US308
j) 468US689
j) 468US703
468US847
469US76
f) 470US611
471US228
f) 472US688
j) 473US822
j) 474US1072

Continued

703

- **References in Parentheses.** Citations or references appearing in parentheses immediately below –**353**– are parallel citations for *Zwicker*. The first time a volume of *Shepard's* mentions your case, you will be given parallel citations (assuming they exist). This is an easy and efficient way of locating parallel citations. If you see a reference to an A.L.R. annotation in parentheses, this is a signal that your case has been selected by the publishers of A.L.R. as a leading case about which an annotation has been written. This annotation may provide a thorough review of your topic, so be sure to read it.
- **References Not in Parentheses.** Citations listed below –**353**– that do not appear in parentheses are references to the history and treatment of *Zwicker* as it has traveled through the courts and to sources that have mentioned, discussed, or commented on *Zwicker* in any manner whatsoever.

3. *Analysis of* Shepard's *References*

a. Abbreviations

You may have already observed that the presentation of citations in *Shepard's* is not in *Bluebook* or *ALWD* format. In fact, the citations given you by *Shepard's* have a uniquely peculiar appearance, such as follows:

- 331FS716 (interpreted as 331 F. Supp. 716)
- 455NW^{2}650 (interpreted as 455 N.W.2d 650)

Because *Shepard's* is tasked with presenting so much information as efficiently as possible, it has developed its own "shorthand" references for cases and other legal authorities. You will quickly learn how to correctly interpret the *Shepard's* references. If you have any difficulty, each volume of *Shepard's* contains a Table of Abbreviations placed in the front of each volume decoding its abbreviations.

b. History References

Shepard's will provide you with the subsequent history of your case, meaning you will be informed how your case has been dealt with as it has progressed through the courts. Thus, you will be informed whether your case has been affirmed or reversed, whether certiorari was denied, and so forth. *Shepard's* provides you with this information, called *history references*, relating to the later history of your case by means of an identifying letter placed immediately before the citation. Most of the letters are easy to understand. For example, "a" means "affirmed"; "r" means "reversed"; and "m" means "modified." If you have difficulty understanding the meaning of a history letter, locate the Table of Abbreviations in each *Shepard's* volume. See Figure 9-2 for some abbreviations relating to the history of a case.

Figure 9-2
Common Abbreviations for History of a Case

a	affirmed	Your case has been affirmed on appeal by a higher court.
m	modified	The lower court's decision is modified in some way.
r	reversed	Your case has been reversed on appeal to a higher court.
s	same case	The case is your case, although at a different stage of proceedings.
v	vacated	Your case has been rendered void and has no precedential force or effect.
US cert den		The United States Supreme Court has denied certiorari for your case.

c. Treatment References

Shepard's will not only tell you how your case has been dealt with by higher courts, but will also refer you to every other case as well as selected law reviews, annotations, and other authorities that discuss or even mention your case in passing. *Shepard's* does more than merely refer you to these authorities, called *treatment references*. These sources have been thoroughly analyzed, and *Shepard's* will inform you specifically how your case has been treated by these other sources, namely, whether it was followed by a later case, mentioned in a dissenting opinion, or criticized or questioned by a later authority.

    Shepard's provides you with this information by means of an identifying letter placed immediately before the reference. Once again, most of the letters are easy to interpret ("f" means "followed" and "e" means "explained"), but if you have difficulty interpreting the letters, check the Table of Abbreviations in each *Shepard's* volume. See Figure 9-3 for some common treatment abbreviations used by *Shepard's*.

    Pay careful attention in examining the treatment of your case. If the case you are relying upon is continually being questioned or criticized, you may wish to reevaluate your research strategies, and attempt to locate a case that is more authoritative.

Figure 9-3
Common Abbreviations for Treatment of a Case

c	criticized	The court is disagreeing with the soundness of the opinion in your case.
d	distinguished	The case cited is significantly different from your case, either in the facts or issues involved.
e	explained	Your case is being explained or interpreted in a significant manner.

Figure 9-3 *(Continued)*

f	followed	Your case is being relied on as controlling or persuasive authority.
j	dissent	Your case is mentioned in a dissenting opinion.
L	limited	A later court restricts the application of the opinion in your case. Generally, the court finds that the reasoning in your case applies only in specific instances.
o	overruled	The court has determined that the reasoning in your case is no longer valid, either in part or in its entirety.
q	questioned	The soundness of your case is being questioned.

The absence of an identifying letter before a citation reference means that the later case has mentioned your case in some fashion, but the editors at *Shepard's* have not made any judgment as to the effect of this later case on your case. In many instances, the later case merely mentions your case in passing or in a string cite, and there was no significant analysis of your case.

4. *Arrangement of Later Case References*

When *Shepard's* lists the cases that mention your case, it arranges the references in chronological order so that you are first sent to earlier cases mentioning your case and then to more recent cases. Thus, although *Shepard's* does not provide dates for the cases it lists, you can easily select more recent cases. Also, *Shepard's* references are precise; they direct you to the very page within a case on which your case is being discussed, rather than directing you to the first page of a case. Finally, *Shepard's* will arrange the cases by jurisdiction, when relevant, grouping together entries by circuit or state (see Figure 9-1) so that you can readily locate cases from a specific jurisdiction that discuss your case.

Practice Tip

History and Treatment

The difference between the *history* of a case and the *treatment* of it is readily illustrated by comparing *reversed* (relating to the history of a case) with *overruled* (relating to the treatment of a case). A reversal refers to the later treatment of your case by a higher court discussing that very case. An overruling refers to how a case is treated by some entirely different case, perhaps years later. For example, *Brown v. Board of Education*, 347 U.S. 483 (1954) overruled the much earlier case of *Plessy v. Ferguson*, 163 U.S. 539 (1896).

---

5. *References to Headnotes*

Recall that when a case is reviewed by editors at a publishing company, they will assign headnote numbers for each legal issue in a case. It is possible that you are relying on only a portion of a case in a brief or other document you have written. Assume, for example, that you are relying on headnote 1 of *People v. Briceno*, 99 P.3d 1007 (Cal. 2004). *Shepard's* will not only provide you with information relating to the treatment by later cases of *Briceno*, but will also focus on the cases that have discussed specific headnotes of this case.

These references are accomplished by small elevated or superscript numbers placed immediately after the case citation given to you by *Shepard's*. For example, when Shepardizing *Briceno*, you observe that one of the *Shepard's* entries is 33CaR3d^{2}635 (see Figure 9-4). This indicates that page 635 of volume 33 of the *California Reporter, Third Series*, discusses the point of law discussed in headnote 2 of *Briceno*. This feature of *Shepard's* allows you readily to locate later cases discussing the specific points of law discussed in your case.

Thus, if you relied solely on the issue discussed in the first headnote of *Briceno*, you could quickly run your finger down the column of *Shepard's* entries looking for elevated "1"s. Similarly, if when you Shepardize, you discover that only headnote 4 of *Briceno* has been criticized or questioned, and you are relying solely on the point of law discussed in headnote 1 of *Briceno*, you may be able to bypass those references with elevated numbers other than "1."

Many entries in *Shepard's* have no elevated numbers. This is an indication that a later case discusses *Briceno* only in some general fashion rather than focusing on a specific legal issue analyzed in a particular headnote.

6. *References to Sources Other than Cases*

In addition to validating the case you rely on, *Shepard's* will direct you to a wide variety of other sources that mention or discuss your case. Thus, *Shepard's* functions as a finding tool to expand your research efforts by sending you to a variety of sources, including the following:

- Attorneys General Opinions
- Law Review Articles
- A.L.R. Annotations

Review Figure 9-1 and examine the last three entries for *Zwicker*. You can see that you are directed to a *New York University Law Review* article, a *University of Virginia Law Review* article, and an annotation in A.L.R.4th. See Figure 9-5 for steps in Shepardizing cases using the print volumes of *Shepard's*.

Figure 9-4
Sample Page from *Shepard's Pacific Citations*

PACIFIC REPORTER, 3d SERIES (California Cases) **Vol. 101**

39CaR3d158
41CaR3d389
j 114P3d815
Cir. 2
d 402FS2d440
Cir. 5
f 2006USApp [LX1066
f 163Fed Appx [308
39SFR1045
104McL1407

Vol. 96

—30—
People v Coffman and Marlow
2004
cc 17CaR3d825
cc 96P3d126
2006Cal LX [5392
2006Cal LX [5867
20CaR3d365
22CaR3d24
24CaR3d[74]657
25CaR3d349
25CaR3d713
26CaR3d43
26CaR3d884
29CaR3d599
30CaR3d531
31CaR3d[149] [147
32CaR3d[25]48
32CaR3d[142]51
32CaR3d[26]914
33CaR3d527
37CaR3d[51]127
37CaR3d[52]127
37CaR3d[49]131
38CaR3d126
f 38CaR3d130
38CaR3d171
e 39CaR3d451
40CaR3d147
41CaR3d615
f 42CaR3d45
42CaR3d305
101P3d976
106P3d1001
107P3d823
108P3d217
114P3d773
115P3d[149]460
116P3d[25]515
116P3d[142]517
117P3d[26]608
118P3d560
126P3d962
f 126P3d965
126P3d999
129P3d345
131P3d1014

f 132P3d247
Cir. 9
2006USDist [LX10612
2006USDist [LX13546
92VaL327

—126—
People v Marlow
2004
US cert den
544US953
US cert den
161LE532
US cert den
125SC1706
cc 17CaR3d710
cc 96P3d30

—141—
In re Marriage of Harris
2004
2006CalApp [LX471
29CaR3d247
34CaR3d[3]484
37CaR3d[5]318
37CaR3d[6]318
37CaR3d[3]458
38CaR3d[3]21
f 38CaR3d618
e 38CaR3d618
d 38CaR3d902
39CaR3d793
112P3d634
f 121P3d298
f 127P3d34
e 127P3d34
129P3d5
36GGU121
38LoyL1871
78SCL1529

—170—
People v Haley
2004
~ 23CaR3d401
26CaR3d15
41CaR3d614
f 41CaR3d651
108P3d194
131P3d1013
f 131P3d1044

—194—
Sav-On Drug Stores, Inc. v Superior Court
2004
26CaR3d339
#f 26CaR3d339
29CaR3d416
32CaR3d487
~ 32CaR3d496
34CaR3d[5]576
34CaR3d[2]584

34CaR3d[5]587
35CaR3d[2]100
f 35CaR3d[2]270
35CaR3d[2]270
35CaR3d[7]270
35CaR3d[1]679
113P3d95
116P3d1166
~ 116P3d1173
Cir. 9
2006USDist [LX9010
2006USDist [LX26778

—496—
Claxton v Waters
2004
j 36CaR3d340
37CaR3d[4]212
j 123P3d614

—507—
People v Barker
2004
20CaR3d364
#f 20CaR3d365
20CaR3d500
24CaR3d265
f 24CaR3d268
25CaR3d105
26CaR3d372
26CaR3d883
28CaR3d659
34CaR3d656
38CaR3d633
39CaR3d827
111P3d932
120P3d1050
127P3d48
129P3d34

Vol. 98

—876—
People v Williams
2004
d 28CaR3d10
j 28CaR3d20
d 110P3d1223
j 110P3d1232

Vol. 99

—500—
Stockett v Association of Cal. Water Agencies Joint Powers Ins. Authority
2004
2006CalApp [LX717
25CaR3d57
Cir. 9
2005USDist [LX26941
2005USDist [LX27375
2006USDist [LX6838
f 2006USDist [LX26651
2006USDist [LX28446

—505—
People v Turner
2004
30CaR3d551
32CaR3d42
32CaR3d[11]889
33CaR3d[11]32
33CaR3d433
39CaR3d892
41CaR3d336
114P3d790
116P3d510
117P3d[11]587
117P3d[11]649
118P3d481
131P3d414

—1007—
People v Briceno
2004
22CaR3d277
22CaR3d421
22CaR3d852
f 22CaR3d853
j 30CaR3d579
33CaR3d[2]635
34CaR3d16
f 34CaR3d[10]17
f 34CaR3d18
36CaR3d[3]454
j 39CaR3d188
j 114P3d813

—1015—
McClung v Employment Development Dept.
2004
j 22CaR3d530

25CaR3d[21]456
25CaR3d[6]508
25CaR3d[18]508
26CaR3d535
26CaR3d[3]633
30CaR3d11
36CaR3d548
d 36CaR3d549
f 37CaR3d[1]28
37CaR3d[2]28
37CaR3d[8]29
37CaR3d[11]29
37CaR3d[14]29
38CaR3d502
f 40CaR3d645
j 102P3d914
32WSR155

Vol. 100

—870—
People v Seel
2004
2006Cal LX [6173

Vol. 101

—140—
Graham v DaimlerChrysler Corp.
2004
2006CalApp [LX728
2006CalApp [LX789
2006CalApp [LX801
19CaR3d322
f 21CaR3d375
j 21CaR3d377
23CaR3d470
24CaR3d820
24CaR3d879
25CaR3d523
30CaR3d206
33CaR3d273
33CaR3d[1]281
33CaR3d[2]281
33CaR3d[13]281
f 33CaR3d283
33CaR3d[11]284
33CaR3d779
33CaR3d[1]822
37CaR3d[9]553
37CaR3d[11]645
38CaR3d[11]29
38CaR3d[19]65
38CaR3d[21]65
39CaR3d560
39CaR3d793
40CaR3d220
41CaR3d561
d 41CaR3d566
104P3d827

106P3d316
129P3d5
129P3d407
Cir. 9
f 2005USDist [LX36806
2005USDist [LX40142
f 373FS2d1032
d 407FS2d1122
q 407FS2d1123
42SDL1295

—174—
Tipton-Whittingham v City of Los Angeles
2004
2006CalApp [LX789
j 21CaR3d362
33CaR3d273
33CaR3d[3]282
f 33CaR3d283
33CaR3d[7]283
33CaR3d[2]285
39CaR3d793
41CaR3d566
129P3d5
Cir. 9
d 2005USDist [LX40142
373FS2d1033

—478—
People v Ramos
2004
US cert den
163LE108
US cert den
126SC91
31CaR3d[14]506
31CaR3d[15]506
32CaR3d[26]866
33CaR3d544
35CaR3d787
36CaR3d776
f 36CaR3d777
115P3d[14]1162
115P3d[15]1162
117P3d[26]568
118P3d575
122P3d991
f 124P3d377

—509—
People v San Nicolas
2004
US cert den
163LE79
US cert den
126SC46
29CaR3d849
30CaR3d706
32CaR3d522

Continued

461

Figure 9-5
Steps in Shepardizing a Case Using Print Sources

- Locate the volumes of *Shepard's* you need (state *Shepard's*, regional *Shepard's*, or federal case *Shepard's*).
- Examine the front cover of the most recent issue of *Shepard's* and read the box labeled "What Your Library Should Contain." Make sure you have all of the volumes needed.
- Select the volumes of *Shepard's* that contain citations to cases decided after your case was decided.
- Examine the upper right and left corners of the pages in *Shepard's* to locate the volume number of the case you are Shepardizing.
- Scan down the page looking for the bold page number identical to the page on which your case begins.
- Carefully examine the entries listed, paying particular attention to the parallel citation, the history of the case as it progressed through the court system, its treatment by later cases, and any other sources, such as annotations and law review articles that cite your case.
- If desired, verify that you are Shepardizing correctly by checking one or two cites listed by *Shepard's* to ensure your case is, in fact, mentioned by these cites.
- Repeat, as needed, in other volumes of *Shepard's*.
- Examine and analyze troublesome entries, including later cases that criticize or question your case.

7. *FAQs: Using* Shepard's *and Analyzing Negative Letters*

Following are some of the most frequently asked questions relating to the Shepardizing process:

Question: Must I read every case or source mentioned by *Shepard's*?

Answer: You must certainly read any reference with a "negative" letter, such as "o" for "overruled"; however, if you are pleased with your research project, you believe the cases you have cited clearly and articulately support the arguments you have made, and Shepardizing reveals no negative treatment, your task is complete. On the other hand, if the issue you are researching is an uncertain area of the law or a newly emerging legal topic, read some of the later cases identified in *Shepard's* to obtain better insight.

Question: How can I use *Shepard's* to find better or newer cases?

Answer: If you are not entirely pleased with the cases you have located, or the cases are a bit older than you would prefer, use *Shepard's* as a research tool to locate newer cases, cases from higher courts, or cases that more persuasively explain a legal issue. Look for "f" for "followed" or "e" for "explained" and read these cases.

Question: What should I do if my Shepardizing reveals a negative letter?

Answer: In all instances, retrieve and read the cases that have been assigned any negative letters; however, understand that it is possible that only a portion of your case has been limited or overruled and that the remainder is still authoritative. Carefully examine the elevated numbers to be sure that the part of the case you rely on (and not some other part or headnote) is, in fact, negatively treated.

Question: My case has two parallel citations—which do I Shepardize?

Answer: For state cases with parallel citations, most legal professionals Shepardize in the companion *Shepard's* for their cases. Thus, if you read a case in the *Kansas Reports*, Shepardize it in *Shepard's Kansas Citations* (rather than *Shepard's Pacific Reporter Citations*). This procedure will enable you to most effectively use the elevated (superscript) numbers given by *Shepard's* to pinpoint later discussion of the headnotes from your case. It is not necessary to Shepardize both parallel citations; if your case has received negative treatment, *Shepard's* will inform you of such, no matter what set you use.

Question: When should I Shepardize?

Answer: When to Shepardize is left to your discretion. Consider Shepardizing fairly early in your research process for two reasons:

- To eliminate the possibility of discovering that a key case has been overruled or reversed, causing a last-minute crisis; and
- To locate other valuable research leads to develop your argument.

Some researchers Shepardize almost concurrently with performing legal research. In any event, you must Shepardize before any document with citations is filed

Question: | with a court or given to your supervising attorney, a client, or the adverse party.

Question: How many volumes do I use when I Shepardize?

Answer: When you first learn to Shepardize, use all volumes. As you gain familiarity with the process, you will notice that the spines of the *Shepard's* volumes are marked with volume numbers or dates, and you need not Shepardize for any date before your case was decided. Remember, however, that the volumes of *Shepard's* are not always cumulative; each volume of *Shepard's* relates to a distinct period of time. As a rule of thumb, the older your case is, the more volumes of *Shepard's* you will need to examine.

Question: What if I never find any references in *Shepard's* for my case?

Answer: If your case is new, it is possible that no other cases have yet discussed your case; however, it is possible that you have transposed numbers in your citation. Thus, carefully check your citation for accuracy.

B. Using *Shepard's* in Print Form to Shepardize Other Authorities

1. Shepardizing Statutes, Constitutions, and Administrative Regulations

Just as you must Shepardize a case to determine whether it is still "good law," you must Shepardize the other primary authorities you rely on: statutes, constitutions, and administrative regulations (such as the regulations of the Federal Communications Commission). The process of Shepardizing these authorities is the same as that for cases.

- Locate the volume(s) of *Shepard's* you need, titled *Shepard's [State] Citations for Statutes, Shepard's Federal Statute Citations,* or *Shepard's Code of Federal Regulations Citations.*
- Examine the upper right and left corners of the pages in *Shepard's* to locate the title or article of the provision you are Shepardizing.
- Scan down the page, looking for a boldfaced entry for the particular section in which you are interested.
- Carefully examine the entries listed, paying particular attention to the history of your statute, constitutional provision, or regulation (for example, whether the statute has been amended or

repealed by the legislature) and then to its treatment by later cases (for example, whether a case merely discussed your statute or decided your statute was unconstitutional). Each volume of *Shepard's* will contain a Table of Abbreviations for any abbreviations used. Examine other sources, such as law review articles and annotations, if desired.

- Carefully analyze all troublesome entries. For example, "A2009C37" means that your statute has been amended and that the amending language can be found in Chapter 37 of your state's session laws for 2009.

2. *Shepardizing Other Authorities*

There are several other authorities that you can Shepardize, including the following:

- **Restatement Provisions.** Use *Shepard's Restatement of the Law Citations* to Shepardize Restatement sections you rely on. You will be directed to cases, law review articles, and A.L.R. annotations that have mentioned your Restatement provision.
- **Court Rules.** The volumes of *Shepard's* used to Shepardize statutes are also used to Shepardize court rules so you can locate authorities that discuss any court rules, such as the Federal Rules of Civil Procedure.
- **Specialized Citators.** *Shepard's* publishes specialized citators, such as *Bankruptcy Citations*, *Criminal Justice Citations*, and *Uniform Commercial Code Citations*, whose titles describe their coverage.
- **Treaties.** Use *Shepard's Federal Statute Citations* to Shepardize and validate treaties.

Practice Tip

Shepard's *Daily Update Service*

The print volumes of *Shepard's* are updated approximately every six weeks. To make sure that nothing has happened in the past six weeks that negatively affects your case or statute, use *Shepard's* Daily Update Service. Call (800) 899–6000 to determine what has happened to your case since your last print supplement arrived. Information may be as current as 24 to 48 hours from the time of decision by the courts. The service is also available on the Internet. Send an e-mail to helpcite@lexisnexis.com.

C. Electronic Updating of Legal Authorities

1. *Introduction to Electronic Updating*

For nearly 100 years, legal researchers updated their legal authorities through the conventional print versions of *Shepard's*. Electronic updating, however, provides more up-to-date validation of legal authorities and is easily accomplished. There is no need to learn quirky abbreviations. Negative history, such as reversal of a case, appears in plain English. Electronic updating eliminates the worry that you do not have all of the print volumes in a set of *Shepard's*. Updating and checking your adversary's citations are easily accomplished. Finally, references are available online far more quickly than the print versions of *Shepard's* are published, thus giving you the most recent treatment of your authorities. Consequently, updating electronically is the preferred method for nearly all legal professionals. In fact, most law firms and law libraries no longer subscribe to the print volumes of *Shepard's*, and all updating is accomplished electronically, through the use of *Shepard's* online (offered by Lexis) or through West's online product, KeyCite.

2. *Shepardizing Online*

a. How to Shepardize Cases Online Using Lexis

Assume the case you are updating is *United States v. Falstaff Brewing Corp.*, 332 F. Supp. 970 (D.R.I. 1971).

- If you are viewing this case on the Lexis screen, a *Shepard's* signal indicator will be displayed on the screen. If you click it, *Falstaff* will be immediately Shepardized.
- If you are not currently viewing *Falstaff* on your screen but are instead perhaps validating a written brief that mentions *Falstaff*, follow these steps:
  - Sign on to Lexis.
  - Click the *Shepard's* tab at the top of your screen.
  - Type in your citation (332 fs 970) in the open field.
  - By clicking the word "Check" on your screen, select one of the following options: "*Shepard's* for Research" (also called "FULL"), which will list every authority that mentions *Falstaff*, or "*Shepard's* for Validation" (also called "KWIC"), which will provide you with negative history only, rather than all authorities that mention *Falstaff*. (See Figure 9-6.)

You are now ready to interpret your results. You will be informed, in plain English, whether *Falstaff* has been distinguished, criticized, followed,

and so forth. If you are interested in one of these references, click on it and you will be immediately transported to that reference, thereby eliminating the need for you to run around the library collecting references that distinguish, criticize, or follow *Falstaff*.

Shepard's uses *Signal Indicators* to inform you at a glance of the status of your case. These signal indicators appear at the top of the authority you are viewing on the screen. The following signal indicator graphics are used:

- **Red Stop Sign:** This signal warns that your case has strong negative history or treatment (such as being reversed).
- **Letter "Q" in an Orange Square:** The validity of your case has been questioned by other cases.
- **Yellow Triangle Sign:** This signal indicates that your case may have some negative history or treatment (such as being criticized).
- **Green Plus Sign:** Your case has positive history (such as being affirmed).
- **Letter "A" in a Blue Circle:** Your case has been analyzed in a neutral manner (such as being explained by a later case).
- **Letter "I" in a Blue Circle:** Other citation information is available for your case (such as a law review article that mentions your case).
- **Red Exclamation Point in a Red Circle:** A statute has been treated negatively by a later case.

Figure 9-6
Reviewing Shepard's Results Online

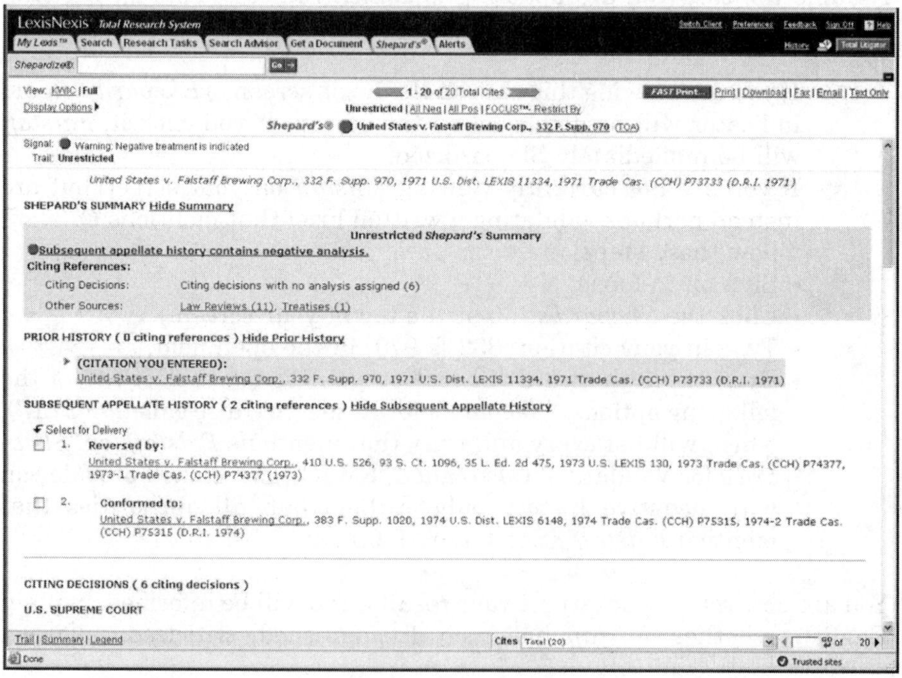

These signals make Shepardizing online extremely easy because they tell you at a glance whether your citation is in trouble or whether it is cleared for your use. Note, however, that a red stop sign does not necessarily mean that your case is no longer good law; it simply means that your case has received some negative treatment that you need to analyze.

Lexis is now available on handheld PDAs, such as BlackBerry devices, allowing legal professionals to Shepardize on-the-go.

b. Features of *Shepard's* Online

Shepard's provides a number of tools to maximize your research efforts:

- **FULL.** If you select "FULL" you will be given all prior and subsequent history of your case and every reference from any case, law review, periodical, treatise, and A.L.R. annotation that mentions your case.
- **KWIC.** Selecting the KWIC option provides a quick answer to the question, "Is my case still good law?" You will not be sent to law review articles and other authorities that merely mention your case. Use KWIC when you are satisfied with your research efforts and only want to confirm that your case is still valid.
- **Summary.** Begin your analysis with *Shepard's* "Summary," which presents a readable summary showing why your case received a signal indicator. For example, you might be informed that your case was distinguished two times, followed once, and mentioned in six law reviews.
- **Custom Restrictions.** *Shepard's* allows you to narrow the results you desire by selecting groups of citations to review by date, jurisdiction, and so forth. For example, you can elect to see only those cases that explain *Falstaff* or only those cases that follow *Falstaff* after a certain date.
- **Table of Authorities.** Assume that *Falstaff* relied on and cited four cases. *Shepard's* validation tool called *Table of Authorities* analyzes those four cases cited in *Falstaff*, allowing you to reevaluate the cases on which *Falstaff* relied (because if their authority is weakened, *Falstaff* may also be suspect).
- **Alerts.** *Shepard's* "Alert" feature allows you to run regularly scheduled updates for the authorities you rely on. You will be automatically notified by e-mail every day, week, or month if there have been any further changes to or mentions of your authorities. This automatic updating feature ensures you receive the most up-to-date information about the cases, statutes, and regulations you rely on or cite to.

c. Shepardizing Statutes and Regulations Online

Shepardizing statutes or regulations online is nearly identical to Shepardizing cases online. To Shepardize 18 U.S.C. § 212 (2006), follow these steps:

- Sign on to http://www.lexisnexis.com.
- Click the *Shepard's* tab at the top of your screen.
- Type in your citation (18 usc 212) in the open field.
- Select "FULL" (and you will be given every authority that mentions your statute) or "KWIC" (and you will be given negative history only, rather than all authorities that mention your statute).

d. Other *Shepard's* Products

Lexis has developed a series of tools that complement its Shepard's validation service. Known collectively as *Brief Suite*, these tools include the following:

(1) *Automatic Validation Through BriefCheck*

One of the most significant advances in validating citations is the availability of software programs that automatically check whether your legal authorities are still good law. Assume your research project cites 20 cases. Keying in 20 separate entries and then reading the results for these 20 cases can be time-consuming.

Shepard's offers a software program called *BriefCheck* (formerly known as CheckCite), which automatically collects all citations in your brief, without the necessity of your keying in a single citation. The program "reads" your brief, locates and extracts your citations, checks them, and then provides the results either on your screen or in a separate printed report. You can elect "FULL" Shepardizing or the "KWIC" option. BriefCheck also checks your quotations for accuracy and locates discrepancies in case names, dates, and page numbers. BriefCheck is also useful for checking your adversary's documents to determine whether authorities cited are still good law.

(2) *StyleCheck*

StyleCheck (formerly known as CiteRite) is Lexis's citation-checking software program that checks your citations for proper form using *Bluebook* rules (or the *California Style Manual*). You will be given parallel cites and informed of errors in punctuation (such as neglecting the period after "Cal"), incorrect abbreviations, and other errors. It is unclear, however, whether StyleCheck can thoroughly master the intricacies of citation form, such as when you may abbreviate "Western." Nevertheless, it is a valuable tool for preliminary checking of citation form errors in both primary and secondary authorities.

(3) *FullAuthority*

Many courts require that briefs submitted to them include a table listing each authority cited in the brief with a reference to the pages in the brief on which the authority is cited. *FullAuthority* reads your brief or document and automatically creates a table of authorities for you, separating federal cases from state cases, and so forth, eliminating the

need for you to create this table manually. Always double-check the table generated by FullAuthority to ensure it is correct and to make sure case names are presented consistently.

(4) Shepard's Link

A new software application called *Shepard's Link* (formerly known as LEXLink) identifies citations in a word processing document (for example, a brief you are drafting), adds *Shepard's* flag indicators so you can immediately spot weakened cases, and creates hyperlinks to Lexis so that readers of your document can instantly link to the cases you cite.

3. *KeyCite*

a. How to KeyCite Cases Using Westlaw

KeyCite is West's service that electronically updates and validates your legal authorities. KeyCite can be accessed on the Internet through http://www.westlaw.com. Although there are some differences between online Shepardizing and KeyCiting, the services are probably more alike than different.

Assume you want to KeyCite the *Falstaff* case.

- If you are viewing this case on the Westlaw screen, a KeyCite status flag will be displayed at the top of your case (red, yellow, or a blue "H") or the word "update" will be displayed. Click the flag or "update" to access KeyCite.
- If you are not currently viewing *Falstaff* on your screen but are instead perhaps validating a written brief that mentions *Falstaff*, follow these steps:
  - Sign onto Westlaw at http://www.westlaw.com.
  - Click the KeyCite tab on the toolbar at the top of your screen.
  - Type in your citation (332 fs 970) in the open field and click "Go."
  - Alternatively, you may type a citation in the "KeyCite this citation" text box that is displayed in the left frame of many screens.

You are now ready to interpret your results. The first thing that appears is any history of the case. Like *Shepard's* online, KeyCite uses signal indicators or graphics to instantly convey information to you about the status of your case:

- **Red Flag.** A red flag warns that your case is no longer good law for at least one of the issues it discusses (such as being reversed or overruled).
- **Yellow Flag.** A yellow flag warns that the case has some negative history, such as being criticized or limited.
- **Blue "H."** The case has some history, such as being explained or having certiorari granted.

- **Green "C."** This signal indicates that the case has been cited by some references but there is no direct history or negative citing references. (See Figure 9-8 for some KeyCite graphics.)

You can easily link to cases that discuss *Falstaff* by clicking on them.

b. Features of KeyCite

KeyCite offers several features (see Figures 9-7 and 9-8) to assist you with your citation updating and validating:

- **Citation History Options.** You can customize your KeyCite results to display different types of case history for your case. By clicking on "Full History," you will be given the complete history of your case; by clicking on "Citing References," you will be directed to other cases and sources that mention or discuss your case, including secondary sources and briefs that cite your case.
- **Graphical Display of Direct History.** A new Westlaw feature shows you the direct history of your case in an easy-to-understand flowchart format. For example, you would be shown in graphical format, using arrows, how your case progressed from trial, through its initial appeal, when certiorari was granted, and then what the United States Supreme Court held. You may easily link

Figure 9-7
KeyCite Screen Showing History of Case

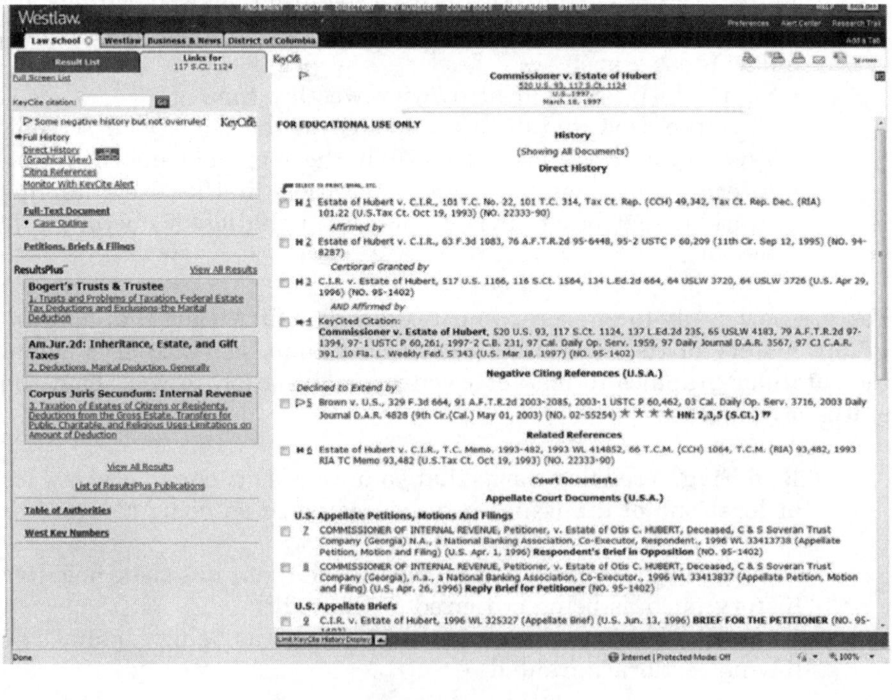

to the court briefs and motions filed at each level of the case's history.

- **Limit KeyCite History Display.** If the list of sources that mention your case is lengthy, you can restrict or narrow your list. Select the "Limit KeyCite History Display" button at the bottom of the screen to narrow results by date, jurisdiction, headnote, and so forth. For example, you elect to view only cases that discuss headnote 2 of *Falstaff*.

- **Depth of Treatment Stars.** As KeyCite lists the cases that mention *Falstaff*, a number of green stars may be displayed next to each citation. These stars tell you the extent to which a citing case discusses *Falstaff*. Four green stars means that the case examines *Falstaff* in depth; three green stars indicates a substantial discussion of *Falstaff*; two stars means there is some brief discussion of *Falstaff*; and one star indicates that *Falstaff* was mentioned in passing, usually in a string citation. (See Figure 9-8.)

- **Quotation Marks.** If KeyCite displays quotation marks (") after an authority, it means that the case or other authority quotes from *Falstaff*. (See Figure 9-8.)

- **Headnote References.** *Falstaff*'s headnote references are clearly displayed. Thus, a reference to **"HN:3"** means that the case discusses the point of law discussed in headnote 3 of *Falstaff*. (See Figure 9-8.)

- **KeyCite Alert.** KeyCite Alert is a clipping service that automatically notifies you of any changes in the treatment of *Falstaff*. You can restrict its coverage so that, for example, you are only notified of later negative treatment of *Falstaff*. You can elect to be notified daily, weekly, and so forth, by e-mail message, ensuring that you always have the most current information about the cases you rely on.

- **Table of Authorities.** Once again, assume that *Falstaff* relied on and cited four cases. West's validation tool called *Table of Authorities* analyzes those four cases cited in *Falstaff*, allowing you to reevaluate the cases on which *Falstaff* relied (because if their authority is weakened, *Falstaff* may also be suspect). This product is identical to Lexis's product (which shares the same name) and is useful for finding weaknesses in cases relied on by your adversary.

- **Petitions, Briefs & Filings.** By selecting this button, you will be linked to various court documents and briefs filed by the attorneys for the parties in the *Falstaff* case.

c.　KeyCiting Statutes and Regulations

KeyCiting statutes or regulations online is nearly identical to KeyCiting cases online. To KeyCite 18 U.S.C. § 212 (2006), follow these steps:

Figure 9-8
KeyCite Symbols

KeyCite.
The Key to Good Law

▶ **Red Flag** - Your case is no longer good law for at least one of the points it contains.

▷ **Yellow Flag** - Your case has some negative history, but hasn't been reversed or overruled.

H   **Blue H** - Your case has some history.

C   **Green C** - Your case has citing references but no direct or negative indirect history.

Depth of treatment stars help you determine how extensively your case has been discussed in a citing case:

★★★★ Examined
★★★   Discussed
★★   Cited
★   Mentioned

" Quotation Marks - Indicate that some language from your case is quoted word for word in the citing case.

HN (Headnote) - "HN#" indicates the legal issue(s) for which your case was cited.

Westlaw.

- Sign on to http://www.westlaw.com.
- Click the KeyCite tab at the top of your screen.
- Type in your citation (18 usc 212 or 6 cfr 9.1) in the open field and click "Go." Alternatively, you may type a citation in the "KeyCite this Citation" text box that is displayed on the screen and click "Go." If you are viewing a statute on your screen, simply click on its flags or signals displayed at the top of your screen.
- After you enter your statute citation in KeyCite, you may either select "History" (to view the history of the statute, including links to recent session laws that amend or affect your statute and historical and statutory notes describing the legislative changes affecting your statute), "Citing References" (to view cases and other authorities that mention your statute), or "Graphical Statutes" (to view a timeline showing you the enactment history of the statute and allowing you to link to prior versions of the statute, conference reports, proposed legislation that may affect your statute, and other pertinent legislative materials).

You may also limit your results by selecting specific jurisdictions that have issued cases citing your statute, selecting documents mentioning your statute during specific time periods, and so forth. KeyCite provides status flags for statutes as well as cases, using a red flag to warn you that a statute has been amended, repealed, or held unconstitutional; a yellow flag to indicate that the statute has been limited or is subject to pending legislation; and a green "C" to show that various authorities cite your statute. The process for updating regulations is nearly identical. You may also monitor changes to your statute or regulation by selecting KeyCite Alert.

d. Other West Products

Similar to BriefSuite, Lexis's package of tools that complements its online Shepardizing service, Westlaw has also developed several tools that enhance its KeyCiting service. They include the following:

(1) Automatic Citation Validation Through WestCheck

Similar to Lexis's BriefCheck, West offers a software program called *WestCheck*, which automatically extracts citations from your document, checks their validity, and produces a printed report with the results of the check. The advantage of using WestCheck rather than KeyCite is that WestCheck automatically "reads" your document and validates your citations, thus saving you the time of keying in each citation you wish to check. WestCheck also reviews your quotations for accuracy.

The process is easily accomplished. Once the software is "loaded" onto your computer, you merely open your brief or other document that contains the citations you wish to check and then click the WestCheck button on your toolbar.

WestCheck is also now available to anyone with Internet access. This product (WestCheck.com) eliminates the need to load software onto your computer. You simply attach your Word or WordPerfect document and run it through WestCheck.com, which will automatically extract and check your citations to ensure they are still good law. Alternatively, you can "cut and paste" your brief into a text box. An easy-to-read online report (using KeyCite flags and symbols) is provided. Access http:// westcheck.com to use the service or take a training tutorial. This Internet-based service allows legal professionals to use their PDAs and perform a last-minute validation check on the way to the courthouse.

(2) BriefTools

West's new product *BriefTools* is a cutting-edge tool that offers the following features (primarily for litigators):

- It inserts KeyCite status flags and creates hyperlinks from the citations in a document you create to the full-text document in Westlaw.
- It monitors the status of authorities you have cited in your brief or document.
- It retrieves all of your firm's internal documents that contain a particular citation.

(3) CiteAdvisor

CiteAdvisor automatically checks the format of the citations in your document (against *Bluebook*, *ALWD*, or state and local rules) and suggests corrections in citation form. CiteAdvisor will also construct a Table of Authorities in your document to show readers where in your document you have discussed the cases and other authorities you have cited.

4. Comparing Shepardizing Online with KeyCiting

Most schools and large law firms afford access to both Lexis and Westlaw, understanding that their legal professionals develop distinct preferences. Although it is impossible to make absolute statements as to pricing and costs (because most firms have negotiated pricing schedules), nevertheless, fees for Shepardizing online or KeyCiting are usually assessed on a per-case basis. Generally, it costs about $7 to check any one citation. Additional fees will be charged by your law firm to the client for your time in performing the updating and reviewing results. Because fees are roughly equivalent, a decision whether to Shepardize online or KeyCite is not usually based on cost.

Beginning researchers often wonder, "Which service is better?" Both offer many of the same features: rapid and easy citation validating; the use of easy-to-understand, colorful graphics (signs and flags) to tell you at

a glance that your citation is in trouble; the ability to limit or narrow your results; and the ability to immediately link to an authority that mentions your case or statute. Both services offer automatic citation updating so that you need not key in individual citations.

In sum, the use of *Shepard's* online or KeyCite is usually a matter of habit, convenience, or preference. Additionally, because deciphering the reports generated by *Shepard's* online or KeyCite can be somewhat difficult (primarily because so much information is given on each screen), legal researchers tend to stick with one service after they have become familiar with its formatting and layout. Note, however, that at least one expert who has compared *Shepard's* online and KeyCite recommends that citations be checked in both databases because in his samples, between 10 and 37 percent of the references were missed if the citation was checked in only one system. William A. Taylor, *Comparing KeyCite and Shepard's for Completeness, Currency, and Accuracy*, 92:2 Law Libr. J. 127, 134 (2000), *available at* http://www.aallnet.org (use the search box to locate the article).

5. *Other Electronic Citator Services*

Although Lexis and Westlaw are the giants in computer-assisted legal research systems, three other systems provide citation updating: Loislaw, JuriSearch, and VersusLaw. These companies generally aim their services at smaller firms or sole practitioners and charge reasonable fees, but they offer much smaller databases than Lexis or Westlaw. Loislaw's citator is called GlobalCite, and JuriSearch's citator is called CheckMate. Their use is similar to that of Sheapardizing online or KeyCiting, but, in general, they offer fewer enhancements and features for customization. VersusLaw offers only rudimentary updating through its V.Cite feature. Loislaw, JuriSearch, and VersusLaw are discussed further in Chapter 11.

───────────── **Ethics Alert** ─────────────

Duty to Update and Validate Cases

A number of cases have reminded legal professionals of their ethical duty to update and validate the cases they cite. In *Gosnell v. Rentokil, Inc.*, 175 F.R.D. 508, 510 n.1 (N.D. Ill. 1997), the court sternly admonished the attorneys involved as follows:

"It is really inexcusable for any lawyer to fail, as a matter of routine, to Shepardize all cited cases (a process that has been made much simpler today than it was in the past, given the facility for doing so under Westlaw or LEXIS). Shepardization would of course have revealed that the 'precedent' no longer qualified as such."

6. *Summary*

Updating and validating your primary authorities is the second component of cite-checking (the first being to place citations in proper *Bluebook*, *ALWD*, or local format). Although the foremost function of updating is to check the status of your primary authorities, a related important function is to allow you to tap into additional legal research, because both *Shepard's* (in print form or online) and KeyCite will direct you to cases, periodicals, attorneys general opinions, annotations, and other sources that mention the authority you are updating.

The determination of when to perform your updating task is a matter of individual discretion, although updating early in the research process will not only alert you to an invalid or weakened case, statute, or regulation but also enhance your efforts by directing you to additional research sources.

Nearly all legal professionals update electronically rather than by using *Shepard's Citations* in print form. The print forms of *Shepard's Citations* will soon be relics. *Shepard's* online and KeyCite provide easy and very recent validation of legal authorities. Moreover, their new software programs (BriefCheck and WestCheck, respectively) offer automatic updating, eliminating the necessity of keying in any citations. Because both Lexis and Westlaw are available on handheld devices such as Blackberrys and iPhones, legal professionals can access and then Shepardize or KeyCite cases on the go.

Once you have Shepardized or KeyCited a few times, you will quickly get the hang of it and will find that it is an easily accomplished task. Do not assume that because Shepardizing and KeyCiting are easy and routine, they are unimportant. On the contrary, updating is one of the most critical aspects of legal research, and no project is complete until every reference to a case, statute, constitutional provision, or regulation has been updated and validated.

CyberSites

http://www.lexisnexis.com/ infopro/training/reference/ Shepards/Shepardscompgd.pdf	This "How to Shepardize" pamphlet offered by Lexis provides instructions on Shepardizing in print form and electronically.
http://web.lexis.com/help/ multimedia/shepards.htm	Take a tour of various *Shepard's* citation services.
http://west.thomson.com/support/ user-guide/keycite.aspx	West offers several User Guides explaining its KeyCiting Services.
http://west.thomson.com/products/ services/brief-tools/default.aspx	Information about West's BriefTools and a demo are available at this site.

(continued)

CyberSites *(Continued)*

http://www.ll.georgetown.edu/tutorials/cases/two/7a_concept.html	Georgetown Law Center offers a tutorial on Shepardizing and KeyCiting.
https://www.lectlaw.com/files/lwr17.htm	The 'Lectric Law Library offers an excellent description on "How to Shepardize."

Be sure to update any citations in an adversary's written project. It is possible that while the cases cited may still be "good law," they may have lost some of their strength by being criticized or questioned. You will then be able to point this out in your project or response as follows: "Although Plaintiff relies upon *Caldwell Co. v. Baldwin Emporium Inc.*, 688 F. Supp. 101, 106 (S.D.N.Y. 1990), that case has been subject to increasing criticism . . . ."

Similarly, if a case cited by an adversary is limited to its own particular facts, point this out to the reader: "The case relied upon by Plaintiff, *Ellers v. McGrath*, 692 F. Supp. 946, 951 (D. Mass. 1991), has been specifically limited to written lease agreements. *Warren v. Chesterton*, 719 F.2d 101, 104 (1st Cir. 1992). Because the present case involves an option to purchase real property and not a written lease, Plaintiff's reliance on *Ellers* is misplaced."

Use updating as a way of enhancing your own writing. If a case you rely on is followed by a later case, bring this to the reader's attention: "In *Satterly v. Jespersen*, 718 F.2d 906, 909 (9th Cir. 1992), the court [noted with approval] or [endorsed] or [followed] the test for defamation set forth in *Handler v. Jacobson*, 689 F. Supp. 614, 617 (C.D. Cal. 1990)."

Assignments for Chapter 9

In the following assignments, you will Shepardize cases, statutes, and other sources using *Shepard's* (available in print and online through Lexis) and KeyCite (available online through Westlaw). Provide the answers as these sources give them to you. You need not use *Bluebook* or *ALWD* form.

RESEARCH ASSIGNMENT USING PRINT VOLUMES OF *SHEPARD'S*

1. Locate the first time *Shepard's* mentions 674 P.2d 145.
   a. Give the parallel citation for this case.
   b. What negative subsequent history is given for headnote 16 of 674 P.2d 145 in this volume?
2. Use *Shepard's Federal Citations* for the first time *Shepard's* mentions 33 F.3d 754.
   a. What Seventh Circuit case followed 33 F.3d 754?
   b. What Fifth Circuit case mentions this case in a dissent?
3. Use *Shepard's United States Citations* for the first time 468 U.S. 491 is mentioned. Which is the first case to explain this case?
4. Use the appropriate volume(s) for *Shepard's Federal Statute Citations* and Shepardize 36 U.S.C. § 5703. Give the negative history for this statute.

RESEARCH ASSIGNMENT USING *SHEPARD'S* ON LEXIS

(Unless otherwise directed, Shepardize using the "Full" rather than "KWIC" option.)

1. Locate the case published at 604 F.2d 530. Select the Shepard's icon. What negative subsequent appellate history are you given?
2. Shepardize 548 U.S. 230. Review the citing references. What is the oldest Second Circuit Court of Appeals case that cites your case?
3. Shepardize 104 F. Supp. 2d 18.
   a. Select "TOA." How many decisions were cited by 104 F. Supp. 2d 18?
   b. Does your case have any negative subsequent appellate history?
4. Shepardize 204 F.3d 652. Give the citation to the denial of certiorari for this case.
5. Shepardize California Corporation Code section 17101. Which California Attorney General Opinion cites this statute?

6. Shepardize California Corporation Code section 15502. What is the history of this statute?
7. Shepardize 92 Cornell L. Rev. 733 (2007).
   a. Cite the oldest law review article that mentions the Cornell Law Review article.
   b. Access this oldest law review article. Where in the article is your original Cornell Law Review article cited?
8. Shepardize 21 C.F.R. § 700.3. Which U.S. District Court for the District of Delaware case cites this provision?
9. Shepardize 35 U.S.C.S. § 112. How many law reviews cite this statute?
10. Shepardize 42 U.S.C.S. § 5791. What is the difference when you Shepardize this statute in "Full" format and when you Shepardize it in "KWIC" format?
11. Shepardize 481 N.W.2d 735.
    a. What is the official citation for this case?
    b. Would you cite this case in a brief you intend to file with a court?

RESEARCH ASSIGNMENT USING KEYCITE ON WESTLAW

1. KeyCite 345 F.3d 467.
   a. Select "Full History." What case distinguished your case? What headnotes were distinguished?
   b. Select "Citing References." What Southern District of Illinois case discussed your case positively and quoted from it?
   c. Select "Limit KeyCite Display" and select the jurisdiction of Indiana. Select "date" and elect to see cases decided after January 1, 2008. What is the earliest case that mentions your case?
2. KeyCite 909 F. Supp. 1023.
   a. Select "C." What is the most recent case that quotes from headnote 14 of this case?
   b. Select the case that quotes from headnote 14 of your case. What page of your original case was quoted?
   c. Select "Limit KeyCite Display." Select to review only A.L.R. annotations. How many A.L.R. annotations cited your case?
3. KeyCite 548 U.S. 557.
   a. What serious negative history is given?
   b. Select "Direct History (Graphical View)."
      (i) When was certiorari granted for your case?
      (ii) What is the citation for your case at the trial court level?
4. KeyCite 446 U.S. 222.
   a. What is the negative history for this case?
   b. Select "Petitions, Briefs, and Filings." Review the Brief for the Petitioner. Briefly, what was the question presented?
5. KeyCite 681 N.W.2d 398.

     a.   How was this case later treated by the Minnesota Supreme Court?

     b.   What later case quoted from headnote 9 of your case?

6. KeyCite 135 Wash. 2d 34. Give the official citation for this case at the appellate court below.

7. KeyCite 18 U.S.C.A. § 1202 and select "Graphical Statutes."

     a.   What was the Public Law Number for the current version of this statute?

     b.   Who testified on June 30, 1994?

8. KeyCite 54 Am. U. L. Rev. 703. What 2010 Michigan Law Review cites this law review?

9. KeyCite 7 C.F.R. § 201.2. Is this provision still valid?

10. KeyCite Okla. Stat. tit. 58, § 215. Select "Citing References." What is the oldest case that cites your statute?

Comparison of Shepardizing Online and KeyCiting

1. Shepardize and then KeyCite Restatement (Second) of Torts § 201.

     a.   What is the most recent case that cites this Restatement provision?

     b.   How many citing references do Lexis and KeyCite disclose for this Restatement provision?

2. Shepardize and then KeyCite 115 P.3d 908 (Or. 2005).

     a.   What *Shepard's* and KeyCite icons are displayed? Why?

     b.   To how many law reviews does each service direct you?

3. Shepardize and then KeyCite Cal. Corp. Code § 15503. Give the negative history for this statute. In which service is it easier to tell the negative history? Why?

4. Locate the case published at 367 F.3d 594 on Lexis and then on Westlaw. What *Shepard's* and KeyCite icons are displayed? Why?

Internet Assignment for Chapter 9

1. Access http://www.lexisnexis.com/Shepards. How soon are *Shepard's* treatment and history analyses updated?

2. Access http://www.lexisnexis.com/literature/pdfs/LO16887-1.pdf ("Shepard's Brief Suite: Four Steps to a Better Brief").

     a.   What is the function of *Shepard's* "Link"?

     b.   What software would you use to verify the accuracy of quotations in your brief?

3. Access http://west.thomson.com/support/user-guide/keycite.aspx (Westlaw's User Guides for KeyCite).

    a.   Review "KeyCite at a Glance." What signal icon would KeyCite display if proposed legislation might affect a statute you are KeyCiting?

    b.   Review "KeyCite Direct History in Graphical View." What is the significance of the size of the boxes that are displayed in KeyCite's graphical view?

    c.   Review "Using KeyCite on Westlaw." Review the section on KeyCite Alert. What materials can be monitored using KeyCite Alert? How often can you elect to be notified of changes in your authority?

Special Research Issues

The only thing that was authoritatively adopted for sure was the text of the enactment; the rest is necessarily speculation.

United States v. R.L.C., 503 U.S. 291, 308 (1992)
(Scalia, J., concurring)

A. **Legislative History**

B. **Executive Materials**

C. **Administrative Law**

D. **International Law**

E. **Municipal Research**

F. **Rules of Procedure and Court Rules**

G. **Citation Form**

Chapter Overview

Most legal research problems can be solved by examining and analyzing the conventional sources of primary authorities and secondary authorities. There are, however, a few types of legal research tasks that lie outside those usual approaches to legal research and that involve sources arranged and published differently from the typical primary and secondary authorities.

This chapter will examine these special research issues and will provide information on legislative histories, presidential documents, administrative law, international law, local and municipal law, and court rules. Although research in many of these unique areas will not be required often, should you need to do any especially thorough research project or should you be employed by a firm concentrating on international or administrative law, you will use the research techniques described herein. A brief introduction to these specialized tasks is needed so you will be able to conduct research efficiently and effectively in these areas if you are asked to do so. Note that administrative regulations,

executive orders, treaties, municipal ordinances, and court rules are all primary law, as are the cases that interpret them.

A.   Legislative History

1.   *Introduction to Federal Legislative History Research*

It is possible that in the course of your research of an issue you realize that the statute relating to the issue is unclear. Usually you would then read and analyze the cases interpreting the statute to determine its meaning. Not all statutes have been subject to court interpretation, however, and you may still be faced with an ambiguous statute and no guidance in determining its meaning. It is equally possible that the cases interpreting the statute are contrary to the position you need to assert on behalf of a client.

In these instances, you should examine the various documents that reflect the activity of the legislature that enacted the statute to assist you in determining the intent of the legislature. This process is referred to as preparing or compiling a *legislative history*. By examining the various versions of the bills, the testimony given before the committee, the committee report, and the debates, you may be able to resolve ambiguities in a statute or argue that a court's prior interpretation of a statute is contrary to the intended purpose of the statute.

Although a well-constructed argument relating to a legislative history and the legislature's intent and purpose may be useful and instructive to a court, a court is not required to adopt an interpretation of a statute based upon the legislature's intent in enacting the law. In fact, many courts view legislative history arguments with skepticism or even hostility. Typically, courts will not examine the legislative history of a statute if the meaning of the statute is clear or "plain" from a reading of it. Only when a court cannot determine the plain meaning of a statute will it resort to reviewing the legislative history of the statute. Supreme Court Justice Antonin Scalia is vehemently opposed to relying on legislative history, noting in 2008 that it is the Supreme Court's job to read statutes, not to write them.

Alternatively, you may be monitoring a piece of legislation as it progresses in order to better assist clients or your employer. This section will first discuss legislative histories for federal statutes and then legislative histories for state statutes. You may wish to review Chapter 3, which discusses the process by which legislation is enacted. In brief, a bill is introduced, referred to a committee, which hears testimony and issues a report, and then the bill is voted on after debate. This procedure is then duplicated in the second chamber of a legislature.

There are three excellent guides explaining and describing the background of legislative histories, the documents to be examined when compiling a legislative history, and the actual process of assembling a

legislative history. Review the following for excellent information and links to relevant materials and websites:

- Carol D. Davis, *Tracking Current Federal Legislation and Regulations: A Guide to Basic Sources*, Congressional Research Service, http://www.fas.org/sgp/crs/98-461.pdf (last updated Jan. 13, 2005).
- Richard J. McKinney & Ellen A. Sweet, *Federal Legislative History Research: A Practitioner's Guide to Compiling the Documents and Sifting for Legislative Intent*, Law Librarians' Society of Washington, D.C., Inc., http://www.llsdc.org/fed-leg-hist (last revised Jan. 2008).
- Law Librarians' Society of Washington, D.C., Inc., *Legislative Source Book*, http://www.llsdc.org/sourcebook (last revised July 1, 2010).

2. Documents Composing Federal Legislative History

There are several documents you might analyze in the process of compiling a legislative history. Each one of these documents may help you achieve your goals of determining the purpose and intent of a statute.

a. Versions of a Bill

One of the steps in compiling a legislative history is examining the various versions of a bill. By studying the evolution of a statute, you may be able to make certain inferences about the intent of the legislature in enacting a law. For example, assume a bill as introduced allows certain benefits for veterans, their spouses, and dependents. Its first amendment limits the benefits to veterans and their spouses, and its second amendment limits the benefits solely to veterans. You may be able to argue that the legislature considered extending the benefits to various groups of people but then narrowed the groups, and therefore the benefits should be limited solely to the veterans themselves and not to the spouses, dependents, or ex-spouses of the veterans. That is, comparison of the language of the various versions of the bill as it proceeds through the enactment process may enable you to draw certain conclusions regarding the intent and purpose of the law. Additionally, the bill may include a preamble or introductory section that explains its purpose and intent.

b. Transcripts of Committee Hearings

You will recall that after a bill is introduced it is assigned to a committee, which holds hearings and receives testimony regarding the proposed legislation. Usually a transcript of the testimony is prepared and published. Keep in mind that although some of the individuals who testify may be neutral and independent consumers, scientists, or experts, others may be celebrities or may be lobbyists paid to advance a particular

viewpoint persuasively. Thus, although the testimony received by the committee may influence the legislators, courts often view the testimony given at committee hearings with a certain amount of skepticism. You may wish to conduct additional research to determine the credibility and reputation of a party who testified before a committee before you advance an argument based on that person's testimony.

c. Committee Reports and Prints

After the committee has concluded the hearings, it will issue a report with its recommendations and its reasons therefor. The published committee report reflects the views of the majority of committee members after a thorough analysis of the bill and after the often lengthy hearing process. A committee may also rely on reports and studies prepared by consultants or staff members. These publications, called committee prints, may include statistical material or legislative analysis. The committee report usually includes the text of the legislation, an abstract of it, and the committee's findings and recommendations. A committee report is viewed by courts as considerably more credible than transcripts of committee hearings. Those members of the committee who disagree with the majority may issue a minority report, which will provide a different point of view on the subject of the legislation. If the bill was sent to a conference committee, it will also issue report, including the text of the compromise legislation and an analysis of how the compromise was reached.

d. Debates

If debate is held on a bill, the remarks of the speakers will be published in the *Congressional Record*, a publication prepared for each day Congress is in session. It is possible that the sponsor of the legislation may discuss the intent or purpose of the bill or that interested parties may explain certain provisions of the legislation. These remarks, published in the *Congressional Record*, form part of a legislative history and may be used to persuade a court as to the intent of the legislature when it enacted a statute. Remarks and statements made by sponsors of legislation may carry more weight than remarks made by other legislators, who may enter material into the *Congressional Record* for purely political reasons. In addition, remarks made by sponsors of the legislation when it is first introduced appear in the *Congressional Record*.

Moreover, the use of debates as a guide to legislative intent is subject to criticism because members of Congress have the right to "revise and extend" their remarks by altering the *Congressional Record*. Although the intent of this right is to allow members to "dot their i's" and "cross their t's," to eliminate minor errors, in some instances members have made more substantive changes, resulting in a *Congressional Record* that is not a verbatim transcript but a revised version of proceedings on the floor of the House and Senate. For example, in April 2004, Representative Jim McDermott (D. Wash.) omitted the words "under God" when he handled the morning duty in the House of reciting

the Pledge of Allegiance. After an inquiry, the presiding officer of the House stated that the words "under God" would appear in the day's *Congressional Record* whether they were spoken or not.

3. *The Process of Compiling a Legislative History*

Many researchers have difficulty compiling a legislative history because the documents are diverse and are seldom located together. Often you will be required to search many sources. This is especially true because a statute may have been enacted one year and then amended on several occasions thereafter. You may have to compile a legislative history for each version of the statute. Moreover, the material is voluminous. Congress's committees produce more than 500,000 pages of material each year. During the 110th Congress, 7,340 bills were introduced in the House, and 3,741 were introduced in the Senate. Do not be shy about asking a reference librarian for help. Reference librarians are aware that conducting legislative history research can be difficult and that few researchers are familiar with the various sources to be used. There are, however, several steps you can take to gather the documents you need.

a. Step One: Getting a Public Law Number

After you read a statute in U.S.C., U.S.C.A. or U.S.C.S., you will be provided with historical notes giving information about the enactment of the statute. For example, immediately following a statute in U.S.C.A., you will be provided with information such as the following:

> Pub. L. 106-78, Title I, Oct. 22, 1999, 113 Stat. 1139.
> In the section immediately beneath the statute, called "Historical and Statutory Notes," you are directed to "see 1999 Cong. and Adm. News, p. 198."

In addition to telling you the public law number of your statute, its date of enactment, and its citation in *United States Statutes at Large*, West also refers you to its publication *United States Code Congressional and Administrative News* (USCCAN), a monthly pamphlet that is later compiled into hardbound volumes, which includes the public laws recently enacted, the legislative history of selected bills, a summary of pending legislation, some committee reports, presidential signing statements, presidential proclamations and executive orders, various federal regulations, and court rules.

Perhaps the most important information you are given is that the statute in question is Public Law 106-78, that is, it was the 78th bill enacted by the 106th Congress. This public law number will assist you in tracking the legislative history of your statute.

If U.S.C.A. directs you to USCCAN, immediately review the materials you are directed to because they are generally excellent sources of

legislative intent and nearly always include committee reports and presidential signing statements. Although only U.S.C.A. sends you directly to the pertinent legislative material in USCCAN, both U.S.C. and U.S.C.S. will provide you with the public law number for the statute you are researching.

Practice Tip

Using USCCAN to Obtain a Public Law Number

If for some reason you do not have or know the public law number for a particular statute but you know the general subject matter of a statute, you should use the subject matter index for USCCAN for the congressional session during which the statute was enacted. Look up the subject matter of the statute (environment, crimes, social security) and you will be given the public law number and other important legislative information pertaining to this statute, which you can then use to locate legislative history materials in USCCAN.

---

b. Step Two: Using a Public Law Number to Obtain Legislative Documents

Once you have obtained the critical public law number, you can locate the documents that make up a legislative history by using any one of three key sources: USCCAN, Congressional Information Service, or CCH *Congressional Index*.

(1) USCCAN

At the end of a congressional session, the monthly USCCAN pamphlets are cumulated into bound volumes. USCCAN is subscribed to by many law firms and is readily available at almost all law libraries.

Use USCCAN's Table of Legislative History (known as Table 4) and look up the public law number of the statute you are researching. Remember to obtain your public law number from the end of the statute you are researching. The easy-to-read Table 4 will inform you what bill number was originally assigned to the statute when it was introduced, such as H.R. 289, meaning the 289th bill introduced in the House of Representatives. You will then be given a reference to which committee report to examine as well as the dates the House of Representatives and Senate considered and passed the bill. You can use these references to locate the pertinent committee reports as well as the debates published in the *Congressional Record*. Official committee reports, conference reports, and statements by legislative leaders on major bills are provided, explaining the background, history, and purpose of the legislation. Presidential signing statements are also included, which often explain the intent of the legislation. Read the materials provided to determine

legislative intent. Some material that is duplicative or unnecessary is omitted from USCCAN. Nevertheless, USCCAN usually provides excellent legislative history materials, including discussion of the background and purpose of the legislation in question.

(2) Congressional Information Service

Congressional Information Service (CIS), part of the Lexis family, is published in monthly pamphlets, which are ultimately cumulated in three bound volumes for each year. Many experts consider CIS the most thorough source for compiling a legislative history because it will refer you to all the documents needed for a complete legislative history. One of the volumes is titled *CIS Annual Abstracts of Congressional Publications*; one is called *CIS Annual Legislative Histories*; and the third is an annual Index to the yearly set.

Each CIS yearly set includes a comprehensive index, which allows you to access documents through a variety of methods. You can look up materials by subject matter (environment, crimes, social security), by name of any witness who testified at committee hearings, by bill number, by popular name of a statute, and by the name of a committee chairperson. The indexing by witness name allows you to check the credibility of a witness by determining other hearings at which the witness has testified.

The CIS index will then refer you to the appropriate pages in the CIS Annual Abstracts volume, which contains summaries or "abstracts" of the bill as introduced, the testimony given at committee hearings, the committee reports, and references to the particular days debates were held so you can readily locate these in the *Congressional Record*. Not only will you be provided with these abstracts, you will also be given references or citations to the exact documents you will need (for example, "House Report 106-451") so you may obtain and analyze the document in full, if desired.

CIS's annual volume titled *CIS Annual Legislative Histories* is arranged by public law number. By "plugging in" your public law number (found immediately after your statute in U.S.C., U.S.C.A., and U.S.C.S.), you will be directed to a brief summary of the law and references to the documents you need to compile your legislative history. For example you will be directed to House and Senate Reports, committee hearings, and the debates that appear in the *Congressional Record*.

CIS then publishes these documents in microfiche in its CIS/ Microfiche Library so you can easily locate the documents you need. CIS also makes its database available on CD-ROM and through Lexis's service called LexisNexis Congressional. This web-based tool offers more than 40 years of congressional information. Searching is easily done by bill number, subject matter, committee name, or public law number. Seamless linking is made to the full range of legislative resources, including bills, hearing transcripts, committee reports, and the *Congressional Record*. Most materials created since the mid-1980s are available. Additional information about LexisNexis Congressional can be found at http://www.lexisnexis.com/academic/1univ/cong/default.asp.

In the event that your law library does not maintain the CIS/ Microfiche Library, CIS will provide you with the stock number of the Government Printing Office documents so you can contact the GPO ((202) 512-1800) and order the documents you need. Alternatively, orders can be placed through the GPO online bookstore at http://bookstore.gpo.gov. In this way, CIS is a complete reference tool for compiling a legislative history.

(3)   CCH Congressional Index

CCH Incorporated (CCH) is the publisher of *Congressional Index*, a looseleaf service, which issues a two-volume set of binders for each congressional session. Each set contains an index to all public laws introduced in that session. This set will direct you to the specific documents you need to examine but does not itself reproduce them in the set. You can access the index by public law number, name of the law, subject matter, or the name of the legislator who sponsored the bill. If you need to obtain a bill number, use the Subject Index to the set.

When you have a bill number, you can look it up in the section called "Status of House Bills" or "Status of Senate Bills." You will then be given a chronological record of actions taken on the bill, including the date it was introduced, when it was referred to a committee, when hearings were held, when amendments were adopted, when it was passed, and when it was sent to and signed by the president. You will also be informed of the bill's public law number and its citation in *United States Statutes at Large*. You can also look up your bill number in a section called "House Bills" or "Senate Bills," which gives a brief description of the legislation and identifies its chief sponsor and the committee to which it was sent. The *Congressional Index* also includes a variety of other information, such as membership rosters for House and Senate committees and subcommittees, information relating to presidential vetoes, and the voting records relating to bills. Moreover, *Congressional Index* is useful in tracking pending legislation.

Congressional Index does not provide references to the *Congressional Record*, meaning that you will be unable to locate debates through the use of Congressional Index.

4.   *Using Electronic Sources and the Internet to Compile a Legislative History*

The ability to conduct research electronically has had a significant effect on the way in which legislative history research is conducted. It is no longer necessary to run around a law library collecting documents, mail requests for documents to the Government Printing Office, and call congressional representatives for assistance. Using Lexis, Westlaw, THOMAS, or FDsys (the new system to which GPO Access is migrating), researchers can easily find the documents they need by searching by bill

number or keywords and then link to related documents, enabling them to assemble a legislative history far more easily than in the past.

a. Lexis

The computerized legal research system Lexis offers easy access to legislative information. After you sign on, select the Lexis database or "Library" called "Legislation & Politics" and then select "U.S. Congress." You can search by Congress number (such as the 109th Congress), by a bill number, public law number, topic of the legislation, committee report number, and so forth. You will then be able to link to the full text of the bill, selected hearing transcripts, committee reports, the *Congressional Record* since approximately 1985, and compiled legislative histories for selected legislation of widespread public interest. You may also select "Legislative Histories" to be given full legislative histories for selected statutes.

Alternatively, after you sign on, you can click on "Get a Document" and then enter the citation to your bill number, the public law number, or to the reference to the *Congressional Record*. You will then be immediately linked to the relevant document.

Lexis's "Alert" feature will notify you by e-mail any time there is a change to any bill you are tracking.

b. Westlaw

Westlaw, West's computerized legal research system, operates nearly identically to Lexis. After you sign on, select the pertinent database. For example, Legislative History (enter "LH") allows searching for legislative history documents for any federal law. The *Congressional Record* (enter "CR") is available since 1985, and legislative history for selected statutes (for example, legislative histories compiled for certain statutes such as the Family and Medical Leave Act of 1993 or the USA PATRIOT Act of 2001) is available by accessing the database called Arnold & Porter Collection-Legislative Histories. Alternatively, you may select "Directory" from the top of your toolbar, then "U.S. Federal Materials," and then "Legislative History," which will allow you to "point and click" to explore various legislative history resources.

Westlaw's WestClip feature (similar to Lexis's Alert feature) allows you to monitor pending legislation and will notify you by e-mail of any change in the legislative status of any bill you wish to track.

c. THOMAS

Although Lexis and Westlaw are easy to use and provide extensive legislative materials, they are fee-based subscription services. Since 1995, it has been possible to obtain many items of legislative history for free, 24/7, through a source called THOMAS. In 1995, the Library of Congress initiated THOMAS, its online database of congressional information and materials named for Thomas Jefferson and located at http://thomas.loc.gov. THOMAS provides a wealth of information, including the following:

- Descriptions of how our laws are enacted.
- Historical documents (including the Federalist Papers, Declaration of Independence, and the U.S. Constitution).
- House and Senate Directories (alphabetical lists of House and Senate members, including their addresses, phone numbers, links to their web pages, and lists of their committee assignments).
- Committee home pages (providing information about the composition and work of House and Senate committees).
- Committee schedules and calendars of upcoming hearings.
- Direct links to other legislative agencies, including the Government Printing Office, Library of Congress, and others.

More important, THOMAS offers easy access to many documents of legislative history. When you access THOMAS, you may select "Legislation in Current Congress," "More Legislation Information" (for previous Congresses), or "Congressional Record." If you elect to search "Legislation," you may search by keyword, bill number, or public law number. You will then be given access to the exact text of the bill or public law, a summary of it, and any action taken on it (such as the date when it was introduced, when it was referred to a committee, when it was voted upon, and when it was sent to and signed by the president). All bills since 1989 are available.

If you do not know or have a bill number or public law number, you can search by word or phrase (such as "patent infringement") or by popular name (such as "Family and Medical Leave Act"). You can search across multiple Congresses in a single search, making it easier for you to locate legislative materials when you do not know in which congressional session legislation was introduced. Once you locate the bill you are interested in, you will be directed by hyperlinks to committee reports (since 1989), the *Congressional Record* (since 1989), and other documents.

THOMAS offers an easy, free, and highly reliable way to compile a legislative history, particularly for legislation enacted in the past ten to fifteen years. Once you locate the bill you are interested in, you can track its progress, locate committee reports, and find references to it in the *Congressional Record* through easy-to-use hyperlinks. Simply click on the topics and documents in which you are interested, and you will be immediately transported to that information. THOMAS is updated several times each day, making the information extremely current. Generally, information about a bill's summary and status is available 24 to 48 hours after any action is taken on the bill. THOMAS has proven to be wildly popular with the public, as witnessed by the fact that nearly 118 million files were transmitted by THOMAS in 2003. (See Figure 10-1 for a sample page from THOMAS.)

d. GPO Access and Federal Digital System

The Government Printing Office offers numerous official publications through its comprehensive and easy-to-use Internet site, called "GPO Access," at http://www.gpoaccess.gov. Congressional bills, transcripts of

hearings, committee publications, the *Congressional Record*, and public laws are available, together with a great deal of other congressional and legislative history information. Most materials since the early 1990s are available. Searching is easily done by bill number, public law number, keywords, subject titles, or *United States Code* citation. Questions or comments can be directed to a toll-free number at (866) 512-1800.

At the time of the writing of this text, GPO Access is migrating to a newer system, the Federal Digital System (usually called "FDsys" and located at http://www.fdsys.gov), which is intended to provide "one-stop shopping" for nearly all legislative history documents, including bills, hearing reports, committee reports and prints, and debates. The documents deposited into FDsys are "authentic," meaning their content has been verified as authentic or official. FDsys will offer easier, more powerful, and improved searching than GPO Access. Locating the pertinent documents needed is easily accomplished by pointing and clicking on the easy-to-understand menus and lists.

See Figure 10-2 for a blueprint for obtaining the documents needed for a legislative history.

Figure 10-1
<u>Sample Page from THOMAS</u>

─────────────────── **Practice Tip** ───────────────────

Online Legislative History Research

Although THOMAS and GPO Access/FDsys offer the ability to
locate thousands of legislative history documents, their databases
are relatively current, meaning that you cannot obtain older
documents from these services. Nevertheless, the fact that you
cannot perform legislative history research for older statutes
using these free services is not a significant drawback, because
legislative history is usually performed for newer statutes. Once a
statute has been in existence for a few years, there will likely be
judicial analysis of the statute and cases discussing it, rendering
the use of a legislative history far less important.

Figure 10-2
A Blueprint for Obtaining Documents
Needed for Legislative Histories

Document	Where to Locate
Bills	• Locate bills and their amendments through USCCAN, Lexis, Westlaw, THOMAS, and GPO Access/FDsys. • Abstracts of bills can be found in CIS.
Transcripts of Committee Hearings	• Committees may post the transcripts of their hearings on their websites. Use THOMAS to link to the pertinent committee. • Some transcripts or prepared statements are available through THOMAS or GPO Access/FDsys. • Abstracts of committee hearing testimony are available in CIS.
Committee Reports and Prints	• Committee reports are published in a bound set called the *Serial Set*. The *Serial Set* (since 1995) is also available through GPO Access/FDsys. • USCCAN reprints selected committee reports.

Figure 10-2 *(Continued)*

Document	Where to Locate
	• Committee reports are available in CIS. • Committee reports are available on Lexis, Westlaw, and THOMAS. • Committee prints are available in CIS, on Lexis and Westlaw, and through GPO Access/FDsys (since 1997).
Debates	• Debates are published in the *Congressional Record*, which is available in bound form. Once you know the date that debate occurred, match the date with the date appearing on the spine of a volume. • Debates can be located electronically through GPO Access/FDsys (since 1994) and THOMAS (since 1989). Search by word, phrase, member of Congress name, or date. • CIS publishes the Congressional Record in microfiche.

5. *Alternative Methods of Obtaining Legislative History for Federal Statutes*

Because compiling a legislative history can be difficult and usually requires you to locate and use numerous sets of books or websites, there are some alternative methods you might use for legislative history research.

a.   Compiled Legislative Histories

A compiled legislative history is a "pre-packaged" legislative history. That is, it is possible that a legislative history may already have been compiled on the statute in which you are interested, thereby eliminating the need for you to perform the task of legislative research yourself. USCCAN provides legislative histories for selected federal laws in its monthly pamphlets.

To determine whether a compiled legislative history exists for the statute you are researching, consult Nancy P. Johnson, *Sources of Compiled Legislative History: A Bibliography of Government Documents, Periodical Articles, and Books,* a book that lists by public law number any published legislative histories and includes citations to articles that discuss and interpret the legislative history of particular statutes. Consult the card catalog at your law library to determine whether these sources are available. Generally, compiled legislative histories exist for legislation that is well known or is of public importance. As discussed earlier, USCCAN, Lexis, and Westlaw offer several compiled legislative histories, especially for significant legislative enactments.

b. Legislative History Worksheets

Recognizing that legislative history can be difficult and time-consuming, some law libraries have worksheets for you to use that provide a step-by-step approach and clear instructions for compiling a legislative history. Ask the reference librarian at your law library if the library provides such a worksheet.

c. Commercial Services

There are several commercial services that will assist you in obtaining documents or in monitoring legislation. Check your local phone book or local legal directory to obtain information about private companies that will obtain government documents for you for a fee. Following is a partial list of some of these companies or services:

    (i) BNA Plus, a division of the Bureau of National Affairs, Inc., in Washington, D.C., will obtain bills and congressional testimony as well as court opinions, agency decisions, or foreign treaties. The toll-free telephone number is (800) 372-1033, or visit http://www.bna.com/products/docs.htm.

    (ii) StateNet, a leader in the field of providing legislative information, will provide legislative materials for Congress and all 50 states. Contact its office at 444 N. Capitol Street, N.W., Suite 725, Washington, D.C., 20001. The telephone number is (800) 726-4566, and the website is http://www.statenet.com.

    (iii) Legislative Intent Service, a well-known company established in 1974, will obtain federal legislative history as well as legislative history for any state. This service also provides expert analysis of materials obtained. Call (800) 666-1917, or visit the website at http://www.legintent.com.

d. Reference Assistance

Legislative history research is a unique and specialized method of attempting to determine the intent of the legislature when it enacted a statute by reviewing the documents that are part of the legislative process. A bill may be introduced in one congressional session and not

enacted and then may be re-introduced in the next congressional session with a different bill number. A bill may be reported out of a committee, voted upon, and then referred to conference if the House of Representatives and Senate pass differing versions. Amendments may be made to the statute in several different years.

These complexities make legislative history research a difficult task, especially to the uninitiated. If you encounter difficulty, ask a law librarian for assistance. Large law libraries and law firms often designate an individual to field inquiries and offer assistance in the area of legislative history research. Law librarians are well aware of the complex nature of gathering the documents needed to compile a legislative history and will not be surprised if you ask for help.

e. Congressional Assistance

Members of the House of Representatives and Senate have office staff assistants whose job it is to perform a variety of tasks, including responding to requests for information by constituents. Call the office of your congressional representative and ask for copies of the bill, the committee report, or other pertinent materials. If you cannot recall the name of your representative, check your telephone directory, as this information is often provided in the first few pages of telephone books. Alternatively, check the House and Senate rosters in THOMAS. Often you will be mailed copies of the materials needed within a few days. If you do not receive the materials you need, call and ask again.

House of Representatives: If you have a bill number, call (202) 226-5200 to check on availability. You may mail a request for a copy of a bill to:

> U.S. House of Representatives
> Office of the Clerk
> Legislative Resource Center
> B-106 Cannon House Office Building
> Washington, D.C. 20515

United States Senate: If you have a bill number, call (202) 224-7701 to check on availability. You may request a bill online by e-mailing orders@sec.senate.gov or mail a request for a copy of a bill to:

> Senate Document Room
> B-04 Hart Senate Office Building
> Washington, D.C. 20510

If you are looking for a bill but do not have a bill number, call the Congressional Research Center at (202) 225-1772, and provide as much information about the statute as possible, such as subject matter, sponsor's name, and date introduced. Alternatively, review the article "How to find bill numbers" provided by the U.S. Senate at http://www.senate.gov/reference/common/faq/how_to_numbers.htm.

f. Law Reviews and Annotations

It is possible that a law review or A.L.R. annotation has already performed the task of legislative history research for you. That is, a law review or other periodical publication may contain a thorough analysis of the statute you are researching and already may have examined the bill, the transcripts of the committee hearings, the committee reports, and the debates and may summarize this legislative history for you.

The best way to determine if an article or annotation discusses your statute is to Shepardize or KeyCite your statute. If *Shepard's* or KeyCite identifies a law review article or annotation as discussing the pertinent statute, examine these sources to determine if they have deduced the intent of the legislature in enacting the statute by examining all of the documents that make up a legislative history.

Alternatively, you could examine the "Table of Laws, Rules, and Regulations" in A.L.R.'s Index to Annotations. This table will direct you to annotations in A.L.R. that cite or analyze statutes.

Practice Tip

Legislative History Research: Three Easy (and Free) Steps

There are many places for you to locate the documents that make up a legislative history. Consider simplifying the process by following these three steps:

1. Obtain a public law number by looking at the end of your statute in U.S.C.A. or U.S.C.S.
2. Look up the public law number (or a keyword or phrase related to the statute) in THOMAS (http://thomas.loc.gov).
3. Read and analyze the pertinent documents, linking to other related documents as needed.

---

g. Web-based Tutorials

A number of websites offer information, guidance, and tutorials on conducting legislative history research for federal statutes. Following are three of the best sites:

- Boston College Law Library's Federal Legislative Histories (www.bc.edu/schools/law/library/meta-elements/pdf/researchguides/legislativehistory.pdf) provides an excellent overview of the legislative history research process with tips on how to compile a legislative history and charts on how to find public law numbers, bill numbers, and so forth.
- Chicago-Kent College of Law's Federal Legislative History (http://library.kentlaw.edu/Courses/tutorials/Leghist%20Tutorial/Intro.htm) is a multimedia tutorial on the legislative history

research process and includes exercises as well as excellent information on legislative history research.

- The Law Librarians' Society of Washington, D.C.'s Federal Legislative History *Legislative Source Book* (http://www.llsdc.org/fed-leg-hist) is subtitled "A Practitioner's Guide to Compiling the Documents and Sifting for Legislative Intent." It provides a thorough overview of the research process and numerous links to excellent sources.

h. Westlaw's Graphical Statutes

One of the easiest ways to locate and compile a legislative history is to use Westlaw's new product "Graphical Statutes." When you view a statute on the Westlaw screen, select "Graphical Statutes," which will show you the evolution of your statute in an easy-to-read flowchart and allow you to link to previous versions of the statute, conference reports, the *Congressional Record*, and other pertinent legislative materials. Graphical Statutes is available for all federal statutes (since 1996) and for select states, including California, New York, Texas, and other larger jurisdictions. This feature allows nearly instantaneous location of legislative history documents.

6. *Introduction to State Legislative History*

You will recall that the process of enacting state statutes is substantially similar to that of enacting federal statutes. Just as there may be ambiguity in a federal statute that would result in a need to research the intent of the United States Congress in enacting a federal law, there may be ambiguity in a statute enacted in your state. If there are no cases interpreting the state statute, you may wish to perform state legislative history research to determine the intent of your state legislature when it enacted the statute.

The process of compiling a legislative history for a state statute is substantially similar to that for federal statutes. Unfortunately, collecting the actual documents involved can be frustrating because many of them are not published, and some are available only at the state capitol.

7. *Documents Composing State Legislative History*

The documents involved in compiling a legislative history for a state statute are identical to those needed for compiling a legislative history for a federal statute: the original bill, together with any of its later versions, transcripts of committee hearings, committee reports, and floor debates.

8. *The Process of Compiling a State Legislative History*

After you have read a state statute, carefully examine the historical notes following it to determine the derivation of the statute. For instance, you may be presented with information such as the following:

Derivation   Stats. 2008, c. 141, p. 621

This would indicate the statute was enacted in 2008 and was initially published at Chapter 141 of the state's session laws and can be found at page 621 of the session laws for 2008.

Consult your law librarian to determine if a legislative service exists for your state. Such a legislative service will operate similarly to USCCAN, CIS, or CCH *Congressional Index* in that it will provide you with a bill number for your state statute and information regarding the committee that considered the bill.

Once you have a bill number or the name of the committee that considered the bill, you can contact the chairperson of the committee or a legislative staffer at your state capitol, and ask for copies of the pertinent documents. Unfortunately, many states do not maintain many of the documents needed for state legislative histories. Although the bill and its versions will be available, the proceedings of committee hearings are rarely transcribed, committee reports are rarely published, and debates are rarely reported. Thus, in many states, the only documents available to you in preparing a legislative history are the various versions of the bill as it proceeds through the state legislature.

To determine what documents are available in your state, consult the following: William H. Manz, *Guide to State Legislation, Legislative History, and Administrative Materials* (7th ed. 2008). This source provides a state-by-state outline of the legislative and administrative documents available in print and electronically for each of the 50 states and the District of Columbia.

9. *Alternative Methods of Obtaining Legislative History for State Statutes*

Due to the difficulties in compiling a legislative history for state statutes, you may find that the following alternative methods of legislative history are the most effective.

- *Compiled Legislative Histories*. Some well-known state statutes may already have been the subject of a legislative history. Your law librarian may assist you in locating these.
- *Legislative History Worksheets*. Check with your law librarian to determine if a worksheet or checklist has been prepared to assist individuals compiling legislative histories of state statutes.

- *Commercial Services.* There may be private companies that will perform state legislative history for you. Because many of the documents are available only at the state capitol, these private companies are often located in the capital city of a state.

  Due to the difficulty of compiling a legislative history for a state statute, making arrangements with a private company to obtain the needed documents may well be the most effective way of obtaining a complete legislative history. Often the fees charged by these companies are moderate, and you may be provided with the documents you need within a matter of days.

  To determine if such a company exists in your state, check with a reference librarian, consult a directory of legal services, call directory information at the capital city, or contact an attorneys' service.

  Following are some fee-based commercial services that provide state legislative history information and documents:

- NetScan, a state legislative history service provided by Thomson/West, provides all proposed state legislation, enacted legislation, and related documents for all 50 legislatures; Committee reports are also available for some states. The toll-free telephone number is (800) 982-2177, and the website is http://www.netscan.com.
- StateNet, headquartered at 21010 K Street, Sacramento, California, 95816, (916) 444-0840, provides legislative materials for all 50 states. Its website is http://www.statenet.com.
- Lexis and Westlaw both provide bill text and bill tracking for all 50 states.

Web-based Tutorials. There are a number of websites that will greatly assist you in compiling legislative history for state statutes.
Following are some of the best:

- The Law Librarians' Legislative Source Book (http://www.llsdc .org/state-leg) links to state laws and regulations and includes valuable website links and phone numbers.
- A research guide and bibliography to finding state legislation is offered through Cornell University Library at http://www.library .cornell.edu/olinuris/ref/statedocs.html.
- The website of the National Conference of State Legislatures (http://www.ncsl.org) is a gateway to state legislative sites, allowing direct linking to the legislative site in each state. Although the site is designed as a source for lawmakers and their staffs, it also provides public users with many reports, meetings schedules, links to the home pages for each state's legislative body, and a method of ordering publications.

Reference Assistance. Be sure to ask your law librarian for assistance if you encounter difficulty in locating the documents you need. You should also check the card catalog at your law library to

determine if there are any books or publications that will provide guidance in compiling a state legislative history.

Legislative Assistance. Contact your state legislators or representatives and ask for assistance or for copies of documents.

Law Reviews and Annotations. Shepardize or KeyCite the particular statute you are researching to determine if it has been the subject of any law review article, A.L.R. annotation, or attorney general opinion. If *Shepard's* or KeyCite directs you to any of these sources, review them because they may provide a convenient summary of the information you need.

Internet Tutorials on Legislative History Research

There are two excellent tutorials that provide guidance on compiling federal and state legislative histories. They are located at the following sites: http://library.kentlaw.edu/Courses/tutorials/Leghist%20Tutorial/Intro.htm and http://law.indiana.edu/library/services/sta_leg.shtml.

---

10. Tracking Pending Legislation

You may need to track and monitor pending legislation for clients who must keep abreast of emerging laws that could affect their business. Clients must prepare for changes before a measure becomes a law. The process of bill tracking to monitor the progress of proposed legislation is different from reviewing the legislative history for statutes already enacted. Following are some sources that will help you monitor pending legislation:

- CCH *Congressional Index* (discussed earlier in this chapter) describes action on a bill and provides weekly updates, allowing you to track when action is taken on pending legislation. Once you have a bill number (easily obtained from the Subject Index to the set), you can "plug it in" the sections called "Status of House Bills" or "Status of Senate Bills" to determine the most recent action taken on the legislation.
- LexisNexis's Congressional provides bill tracking.
- Lexis's service, called "Alert," will provide you with daily, weekly, or monthly updates on pending legislation. You can be notified by e-mail or view the results online. A database entitled BILLS will also provide bill tracking and a report for you.
- Westlaw provides bill tracking through its database "Netscan Legislative History." Its clipping service, WestClip, delivers periodic updates to your e-mail account about legislation you are tracking.
- THOMAS does not automatically alert you to changes in legislation in which you are interested, but by routinely checking the

status and summary of a bill, you can determine the progress it is
making through Congress. Search by bill number or by word/
phrase and then select "Bill Summary & Status."
- StateNet, the commercial service described earlier, will provide
  bill-tracking services for a fee and alert you by e-mail whenever
  legislative action is taken on a bill you are monitoring.

To track the progress of state legislation, use Lexis, Westlaw, or
StateNet. Alternatively, some states automatically provide you with
e-mail updates on the status of pending legislation. For example, in
California the legislature provides a bill status updating service to keep
you informed as bills you are interested in move through the legislature.
The free tracking service (located at www.leginfo.ca.gov) automatically
e-mails you when there are changes in the bill or changes in its status.

Ethics Alert

Tracking Legislation

**If a client retains your firm to monitor pending legislation that
affects the client, you have an ethical duty to monitor the
legislation on a periodic basis and notify the client of the progress
of the legislation. Because legislation tracking is so easily
accomplished, and you can readily arrange to have status updates
delivered to your e-mail account, it will be legal malpractice to
"drop the ball" when you are tracking pending legislation.**

---

11. Summary of Legislative History Research

The primary purpose of compiling a legislative history is to aid a court in
interpreting an ambiguous statute that has not yet been the subject of
judicial interpretation. If there are no cases interpreting a statute, you
may wish to compile a legislative history to present to a court as evidence
of what the legislature intended the statute to accomplish.

The use of legislative history to interpret statutes is often criticized.
Perhaps one of the most vocal critics is United States Supreme Court
Justice Antonin Scalia. Justice Scalia has stated that using legislative
history is "not merely a waste of research time and ink [but] a false and
disruptive lesson in the law." *Conroy v. Aniskoff*, 507 U.S. 511, 519 (1993)
(Scalia, J., concurring). Moreover, former Justice Stevens once remarked
that the use of "frankly partisan statements" by lawmakers can and
should in no way be viewed as reflective of some consensus in Congress.
Demanding that legislatures draft statutes more clearly, many judges
believe that when courts go beyond the plain meaning of a statute by

relying on legislative history they exceed their function as interpreters of the law and are in danger of making law, which is the exclusive province of legislatures.

Keep in mind that, at best, a legislative history is a secondary source. It is not a case, constitution, regulation, or statute, which are binding on a court and which therefore must be followed. A court may elect to follow the findings of a committee report or the comments of the sponsor of the legislation in determining the purpose or effect of the statute. Some courts, however, are reluctant to rely on legislative history and view many of the documents as the product of a political process rather than a careful and reasoned analysis of the statute. That is, remarks made at committee hearings or at debates may be the result of political bias or may be made by legislators who are not totally familiar with the legislation. In such cases, over-reliance on legislative history may be misplaced. Nevertheless, if you have no other argument to advance, you should definitely perform the research needed for a legislative history, present it to the court as clearly and persuasively as possible, and hope for the best. With no other guidance to interpret an ambiguous statute, a court may be persuaded to rely upon legislative history as evidence of the purpose or intent of a statute.

Practice Tip

Hierarchy of Legislative History Documents

Although there is some disagreement, most experts conclude that the documents making up legislative history can be ranked in the following order, from strongest to weakest:

- **Conference and committee reports are usually viewed as the strongest evidence of legislative intent because they reflect the view of experienced members of Congress after careful study of the bill and analysis of testimony at hearings.**
- **Versions of the bill (and its amendments) as it progresses through the legislature are considered highly persuasive.**
- **Statements by a bill's sponsors may show evidence of legislative intent (whether made at a hearing or during debate).**
- **Floor debates by those other than a bill's sponsors are somewhat weak because legislators may use the opportunity to debate for any number of political or personal reasons.**
- **Statements made by various individuals (other than bill sponsors) at committee hearings are weak evidence of legislative intent because many are made by paid lobbyists or persons with political agendas.**

B.   Executive Materials

1. Introduction

The conventional view of the three branches of our government is that the legislative branch makes our laws, the judicial branch interprets our laws, and the executive branch enforces our laws. The executive branch, however, does issue certain directives and documents that affect all of us, although they are of varying legal effect.

2. Proclamations

A proclamation is a statement issued by the president that often has no legal effect. Proclamations are often issued for ceremonial, public relations, or public awareness reasons. For example, Presidential Proclamation No. 6459 declared a certain week to be Lyme Disease Awareness Week. Other proclamations are Presidential Proclamation No. 6461, announcing Buffalo Soldiers Day, and Presidential Proclamation No. 7347, announcing National Disability Employment Awareness Month. Although usually used for ceremonial purposes, proclamations can be used for more substantive statements (such as President Lincoln's Emancipation Proclamation of 1862). See Figure 10-3 for a sample Presidential Proclamation.

Presidential proclamations generally have no legal effect because they do not command or prohibit any action, and no punishment or liability accrues as a result of any "violation" of a presidential proclamation. Proclamations are published in a number of sources:

- USCCAN.
- *Federal Register*, the daily weekday newspaper published by the Office of the Federal Register.
- Title 3 of C.F.R. (the annual codification of the *Federal Register*).
- *Daily Compilation of Presidential Documents* (formerly named the *Weekly Compilation of Presidential Documents*), contains all messages and statements released by the White House.
- U.S.C.S. advance pamphlets.
- *United States Statutes at Large*, the bound volumes containing all public and private laws passed by the United States Congress.
- Lexis and Westlaw.

Title 3 of C.F.R. (since 1994) and *Daily Compilation of Presidential Documents* (since 1993) are both available for free, on the Internet, from the Government Printing Office at the following websites: GPO Access at http://www.gpoaccess.gov and FDsys at http://www.fdsys.gov. Searching can be done by inserting keywords in search boxes or by browsing through tables of contents.

Figure 10-3
Sample Presidential Proclamation

AUTHENTICATED
U.S. GOVERNMENT
INFORMATION
GPO

Administration of Barack H. Obama, 2010

Proclamation 8496—National Former Prisoner of War Recognition Day, 2010
April 9, 2010

By the President of the United States of America

A Proclamation

Our Nation's former prisoners of war faced tremendous challenges and dangers to protect us all. Many gave their last full measure of devotion to defend our freedom, and we are forever in their debt. Each year, on National Former Prisoner of War Recognition Day, the American people pay tribute to these heroes.

Through multiple wars, thousands of American service members have faced unimaginable cruelty and unspeakable treatment at the hands of foreign captors. Many sacrificed their own well-being to protect their fellow prisoners, the war effort, and our country. The families suffered as well, unsure of their loved ones' fates, just as the captured warriors were unsure of what the next day would bring. Not all of these courageous men and women, who persevered bravely and sometimes alone, are prominently noted in our history books. Yet, their stories are etched in our national conscience, and their courage is enshrined in the tradition of honor and bravery that is the mark of our Armed Forces.

America's former prisoners of war gave their freedom so that we can enjoy our own. We may never know the full extent of injuries received nor burdens borne by these heroes and their families, but neither shall we forget their selfless sacrifice and unshakeable resolve.

Now, Therefore, I, Barack Obama, President of the United States of America, by virtue of the authority vested in me by the Constitution and the laws of the United States, do hereby proclaim April 9, 2010, as National Former Prisoner of War Recognition Day. I call upon all Americans to observe this day of remembrance by honoring our service members, veterans, and all American prisoners of war. I also call upon Federal, State, and local government officials and organizations to observe this day with appropriate ceremonies and activities.

In Witness Whereof, I have hereunto set my hand this ninth day of April, in the year of our Lord two thousand ten, and of the Independence of the United States of America the two hundred and thirty-fourth.

BARACK OBAMA

[Filed with the Office of the Federal Register, 8:45 a.m., April 13, 2010]

NOTE: This proclamation was published in the *Federal Register* on April 14.

Categories: Proclamations : National Former Prisoner of War Recognition Day.

Subjects: Former Prisoner of War Recognition Day, National.

DCPD Number: DCPD201000245.

3. *Executive Orders*

An executive order has more legal effect than a proclamation. Executive orders are regulations issued by a president to direct government officials and agencies. These executive orders have the force of law (unless, of course, a court rules to the contrary) and require no action by Congress. An example of an executive order is Executive Order No. 13354 for the establishment of a National Counterterrorism Center. Executive orders can be located in the same sources as proclamations, including through GPO Access at http://www.gpoaccess.gov, except they are not located in *United States Statutes at Large.*

The National Archives and Records Administration provides executive orders and information about executive orders for all presidents since Franklin D. Roosevelt at the following website: http://www.archives.gov. As discussed above, GPO Access/FDsys also provide Title 3 of C.F.R. and *Daily Compilation of Presidential Documents* on their websites, and both of these include executive orders.

State governors also issue proclamations and executive orders. They can often be found on the state's or governor's home page. Access http://www.megalaw.com, and select "State Law," and then your state.

4. Daily Compilation of Presidential Documents

One of the best sources for materials relating to the executive branch is a set of books entitled *Daily Compilation of Presidential Documents* (formerly known as the *Weekly Compilation*). This publication of the Office of the Federal Register contains the following presidential items:

   (i)   addresses and remarks such as remarks made at luncheons or ceremonies, press releases, speeches, and press conferences
   (ii) announcements such as those recognizing certain programs
   (iii) appointments and nominations such as one announcing the assistant secretary for science and education for the Agriculture Department
   (iv) bill signings, bill vetoes, and communications to the United States Congress
   (v)   communications to federal agencies
   (vi) executive orders and proclamations
   (vii) interviews with news media

Access to the *Daily Compilation* is gained through a regularly published index. See Figure 10-4 for a sample page from the *Daily Compilation of Presidential Documents. Daily Compilation of Presidential Documents* is also available for free online from FDsys/GPO Access. Documents since 1993 are available. Searching is usually done by date, keywords, or search terms entered in search boxes. Access the following sites: http://www.gpoaccess.gov/wcomp/index.html or http://www.fdsys.gov.

Figure 10-4
Sample Page from *Daily Compilation of Presidential Documents*

AUTHENTICATED
U.S. GOVERNMENT
INFORMATION
GPO

Administration of Barack H. Obama, 2010

Remarks on the Earthquake in Chile
February 27, 2010

Good morning, everybody. Earlier today a devastating earthquake struck the nation of Chile, affecting millions of people. This catastrophic event was followed by multiple aftershocks and has prompted tsunami warnings across the Pacific Ocean. Earlier today I was briefed by my national security team on the steps that we're taking to protect our own people and to stand with our Chilean friends.

Early indications are that hundreds of lives have been lost in Chile, and the damage is severe. On behalf of the American people, Michelle and I send our deepest condolences to the Chilean people. The United States stands ready to assist in the rescue and recovery efforts, and we have resources that are positioned to deploy should the Chilean Government ask for our help. Chile is a close friend and partner of the United States, and I've reached out to President Bachelet to let her know that we will be there for her should the Chilean people need assistance and our hearts go out to the families who may have lost loved ones.

We're also preparing for a tsunami that could reach American shores later today, particularly in Hawaii, American Samoa, and Guam. A tsunami warning is in place, and people have been alerted to evacuate coastal areas. I urge citizens to listen closely to the instructions of local officials, who will have the full support of the Federal Government as they prepare for a potential tsunami and recover from any damage that may be caused.

I also urge our citizens along the west coast to be prepared as well, as there may be dangerous waves and currents throughout the day. Again, the most important thing that you can do is to carefully heed the instructions of your State and local officials.

Once again, we've been reminded of the awful devastation that can come at a moment's notice. We can't control nature, but we can and must be prepared for disaster when it strikes. In the hours ahead, we'll continue to take every step possible to prepare our shores and protect our citizens. And we will stand with the people of Chile as they recover from this terrible tragedy.

Thank you very much, everybody.

NOTE: The President spoke at 1:48 p.m. in the Rose Garden at the White House. In his remarks, he referred to President Michelle Bachelet Jeria of Chile. The Office of the Press Secretary also released a Spanish language transcript of these remarks.

Categories: Addresses and Remarks : Chile, earthquake.

Locations: Washington, DC.

Names: Bachelet Jeria, Michelle; Obama, Michelle.

Subjects: Chile : Earthquake, damage and recovery efforts; Chile : President; Chile : Relations with U.S.; Natural disasters : Chile, earthquake; Natural disasters : Chile, earthquake-related tsunami warnings :: Hawaii; Natural disasters : Chile, earthquake-related tsunami warnings :: America Samoa; Natural disasters : Chile, earthquake-related tsunami warnings :: Guam.

DCPD Number: DCPD201000134.

1

Numerous other sources provide executive materials. Browse the shelves in the reference section of your law library. Alternatively, consult *Public Papers of the Presidents of the United States*, available online at FDsys/GPO Access, which provides access to presidential papers, speeches, nominations, proclamations, executive orders, and other presidential documents since 1991. Searching is done by dates, keywords, and phrases.

C. Administrative Law

1. Introduction to Federal Administrative Law

In the first half of the twentieth century, it became evident that Congress's lawmaking ability could not keep pace with the demands of modern society. As a result, Congress delegated certain tasks to agencies, each created to administer a body of law. For example, the use of airwaves to communicate information by radio led to the creation of the Federal Communications Commission in 1934.

You will recall that the typical view of our system of government is that each of the three branches of government (legislative, judicial, and executive) exercises one function (making law, interpreting law, and enforcing law, respectively). The administrative agencies are an apparent contradiction to this principle of separation of powers in that the agencies act quasi-legislatively (like a legislature) in enacting their own rules and regulations and also act quasi-judicially (like a court) in settling disputes.

Despite these seeming sweeping powers, there are some constraints on the agencies' powers: Congress, in creating an agency, typically enacts legislation directing how the agency should operate and also exercises some oversight and supervision of the agency to ensure it properly fulfills its function and does not exceed its authority as set forth in the enabling statute that created the agency. The Administrative Procedure Act (5 U.S.C. §§ 500-584 (2006)) is the federal law under which the agencies create and enforce rules.

Each agency administers or regulates a body of law. For example, the Federal Aviation Administration (FAA) regulates aviation, the Federal Communications Commission (FCC) regulates communication, and the National Labor Relations Board (NLRB) regulates labor practices. Note that agencies have different titles, with some being referred to as "Administrations," some referred to as "Boards," and others "Agency," "Commission," "Service," or "Corporation."

Although you may be under the impression that these agencies are far removed from you and exercise only a minor role in your daily life, in actuality these agencies affect you every day in numerous ways. For instance, every time you listen to a radio or watch television, the FCC is playing a role. For every item of food you eat or aspirin you take, the FDA (Food and Drug Administration) is playing a role. Perhaps the most

pervasive agency and the one that affects you in a dramatic way each and every day is the IRS (Internal Revenue Service), a branch of the Department of Treasury.

The individuals who head the agency as well as members of their staffs are usually experts in the area of law that the agency regulates, such as aviation, communication, or securities. The agency heads are selected by the president, are approved by the United States Senate, and serve for a specified term of office.

Because legal practitioners tend to specialize and because administrative law research is highly technical, it is possible that you will never need to conduct administrative law research. On the other hand, you may work for one of the administrative agencies or for a company that engages in a highly regulated field, such as the environment, franchising, or securities. You may be employed by a law firm that specializes in communications law or labor law. In such instances, you will likely become highly familiar with the agencies, their rules and regulations, and the books that publish administrative law. In any event, all legal professionals should be able to conduct competent legal research in the field of administrative law to respond to client or employer needs.

You will need to become familiar with the terminology of administrative law in order to conduct research efficiently in this field of law. The term "administrative law" refers to the body of law created by administrative agencies in the form of rules, regulations, decisions, and other related actions. While the product of a legislature is a "law" or "statute," the product of an administrative agency is a "rule" or "regulation." These terms are synonymous. 1 C.F.R. § 1.1 (2010). Rules or regulations are issued by an agency to implement and carry out the policies and tasks assigned to the agency by the enabling statute. Proposed rules are subject to review by Congress. Violation of a rule or regulation can subject one to punishment just as can violation of a statute. Administrative agencies are often referred to as "regulatory" bodies due to the fact that the function of each agency is to administer or regulate a body of law. Agency rules and regulations are primary law. Some government agencies, including the Internal Revenue Service, issue advisory opinions in response to questions by requesters. The advisory opinion will generally state whether it is legally binding.

2. Publication of Federal Administrative Law

Until 1936, there was no official publication of the rules and regulations of administrative agencies. For example, although radio stations were subject to the regulations of the Federal Communications Commission (FCC), the regulations were published sporadically, making it nearly impossible for those companies regulated by the agencies to determine if they were in compliance with the agency's regulations. Moreover, agencies would each publish their own regulations in separate publications.

This confusing situation reached a climax with the famous case *Panama Refining Co. v. Ryan*, 293 U.S. 388 (1935), in which the defendant company was prosecuted for violation of an administrative regulation. It was not until the case reached the United States Supreme Court that it was discovered that the regulation Panama Refining Company was accused of violating had been revoked before the original prosecution was commenced.

To rectify this situation, the United States Congress enacted the Federal Register Act, which provided for the publication of the *Federal Register*. The *Federal Register* is a pamphlet published weekdays and distributed by the United States Government Printing Office. No agency rule will have legal effect unless it is first published in the *Federal Register*. Thus, the Federal Register provides an organized system for making agency regulations available to the public. It contains proposed, interim, and final rules. The *Federal Register* does more than merely recite the language of the agency regulations. It provides a summary of the regulation, its effective date, a person to contact for further information, and background material relating to the regulation. Additionally, as discussed earlier, the *Federal Register* includes various presidential documents. See Figure 10-5 for a sample page from the *Federal Register*.

Because each daily issue of the *Federal Register* is roughly the same size as an issue of *Time Magazine*, and it is published daily, resulting in publication of approximately 80,000 pages each year, researching the *Federal Register* is a daunting task. Therefore, just as our federal statutes published in the *United States Statutes at Large* were better organized or codified into the 50 titles of the United States Code (U.S.C.), so also has the *Federal Register* been codified to better enable researchers to access administrative regulations. In fact, the *Federal Register* has been codified in 50 titles in a set entitled *Code of Federal Regulations* (C.F.R.). These 50 titles represent the areas subject to federal regulation and many correspond to the 50 titles of U.S.C. For example, Title 29 of both U.S.C. and C.F.R. is "Labor," while Title 27 of the U.S.C. is "Intoxicating Liquors" and Title 27 of C.F.R. is "Alcohol, Tobacco Products and Firearms." Each of the 50 titles in C.F.R. is divided into chapters. Chapters are further subdivided into "parts" covering specific regulatory areas. Within each part are sections.

C.F.R. is a softcover set revised annually with one-fourth of the volumes in the set issued on a quarterly basis. Thus, revision of the set is staggered with one-fourth of the set updated or revised each calendar quarter. Titles 1 through 16 are issued each January 1; Titles 17 through 27 are issued each April 1; Titles 28 through 41 are issued each July 1; and Titles 42 through 50 are issued each October 1. The volumes of C.F.R. are always issued in softcover pamphlet form. Each year the pamphlets are published in a color different from the previous year's pamphlets (except Title 3, containing various presidential materials, which is always white or black) so you can readily locate the issues for the year you need. For example, the 2009 edition of C.F.R. was olive green, while the 2010 edition was aqua blue. See Figure 10-6 for a sample page from C.F.R.

Figure 10-5
Sample Page from *Federal Register*

Federal Register / Vol. 75, No. 82 / Thursday, April 29, 2010 / Notices   22551

comment. The time for individual oral comments may be limited.

Gerald Lawrence, Jr.,
Designated Federal Officer, Davy Crockett National Forest RAC.
[FR Doc. 2010-9809 Filed 4–28–10; 8:45 am]
BILLING CODE 3410-11-M

DEPARTMENT OF AGRICULTURE

Agricultural Marketing Service

[Doc. No. AMS–FV–09–0052; FV–09–326]

United States Standards for Grades of Frozen Blueberries

AGENCY: Agricultural Marketing Service, USDA.

ACTION: Notice; withdrawal.

SUMMARY: The Agricultural Marketing Service (AMS), of the United States Department of Agriculture (USDA) is withdrawing a notice soliciting comments on its proposed revision to the United States Standards for Grades of Frozen Blueberries. After considering the comments received regarding the proposed revision and the withdrawal of the petition requesting revisions, the agency has decided not to proceed with this action.

DATES: *Effective Date:* April 29, 2010.
FOR FURTHER INFORMATION CONTACT: Myron Betts, Inspection and Standardization Section, Processed Products Branch (PPB), Fruit and Vegetable Programs (FV), AMS, USDA, 1400 Independence Avenue, SW., Room 0709, South Building; STOP 0247, Washington, DC 20250; Telephone: (202) 720–5021 or fax (202) 720–9906; or e-mail: *Myron.Betts@ams.usda.gov.* The United States Standards for Grades of Frozen Blueberries are available by accessing the AMS Web site on the Internet at *http://www.ams.usda.gov/ processedinspection.*

Background

On August 22, 2008, AMS received a petition from the North American Blueberry Council (NABC), requesting revisions to the United States Standards for Grades of Frozen Blueberries. These standards are issued under the Agricultural Marketing Act of 1946 (7 U.S.C. 1621–1627).

The petitioner requested the USDA to revise the terminology used for the product description of frozen blueberries. On December 22, 2008, prior to undertaking research and other work associated with revising an official grade standard, AMS published a notice in the **Federal Register** (73 FR 78285) soliciting comments on the petition to revise the U.S. Standards for Grades of Frozen Blueberries. AMS received two comments: one from the USDA, Agricultural Research Service and the other from the American Frozen Food Institute. Both commenters stated that the proposal should include all hybrids and cultivars of the appropriate species.

Given the absence of product samples and additional information on the berries that were the subject of its petition, NABC withdrew its request. Accordingly, after considering the comments received regarding the proposed revision and the withdrawal of the petition requesting revisions; AMS has decided not to proceed further with the proposed revision to the U.S. Standards for Grades of Frozen Blueberries. The notice published in the **Federal Register** on December 22, 2008 (73 FR 87285) is hereby withdrawn.

Authority: 7 U.S.C. 1621–1627.

Dated: April 22, 2010.
David R. Shipman,
Acting Administrator, Agricultural Marketing Service.
[FR Doc. 2010-9869 Filed 4–28–10; 8:45 am]
BILLING CODE 3410-02-M

COMMISSION ON CIVIL RIGHTS

Continuation of Hearing on the Department of Justice's Actions Related to the New Black Panther Party Litigation and its Enforcement of Section 11(b) of the Voting Rights Act

AGENCY: United States Commission on Civil Rights.

ACTION: Notice of hearing.

DATE AND TIME: Friday, May 14, 2010; 9:30 a.m. EDT.
PLACE: U.S. Commission on Civil Rights, 624 Ninth Street, NW., Room 540, Washington, DC 20425.
SUMMARY: The Commission's Hearing on the Department of Justice's Actions Related to the New Black Panther Party Litigation and its Enforcement of Section 11(b) of the Voting Rights Act, conducted on April 23, 2010 and noticed in the March 18, 2010 **Federal Register** at 75 FR 13076, was continued until May 14, 2010 at 9:30 a.m. EDT in Washington, DC at the Commission's offices located at 624 Ninth Street, NW., Room 540, Washington, DC 20425, and will continue thereafter until completed. An executive session not open to the public may be convened at any appropriate time before or during the hearing.

Notice of these hearings was previously published at 75 FR 13076 pursuant to the Civil Rights Commission Amendments Act of 1994, 42 U.S.C. 1975a and 45 CFR 702.3. The purpose of this hearing is to collect information within the jurisdiction of the Commission, under 42 U.S.C. 1975a, related particularly to the Department of Justice's actions in the New Black Panther Party Litigation and Enforcement of Section 11(b) of the Voting Rights Act.

The Commission is authorized to hold hearings and to issue subpoenas for the production of documents and the attendance of witnesses pursuant to 45 CFR 701.2. The Commission is an independent bipartisan, fact finding agency authorized to study, collect, and disseminate information, and to appraise the laws and policies of the Federal Government, and to study and collect information with respect to discrimination or denials of equal protection of the laws under the Constitution because of race, color, religion, sex, age, disability, or national origin, or in the administration of justice. The Commission has broad authority to investigate allegations of voting irregularities even when alleged abuses do not involve discrimination.

CONTACT PERSON FOR FURTHER INFORMATION: Lenore Ostrowsky, Acting Chief, Public Affairs Unit (202) 376–8591. TDD: (202) 376–8116.

Persons with a disability requiring special services, such as an interpreter for the hearing impaired, should contact Pamela Dunston at least seven days prior to the scheduled date of the hearing at 202–376–8105. TDD: (202) 376–8116.

Dated: April 26, 2010.
David Blackwood,
General Counsel.
[FR Doc. 2010-9983 Filed 4–28–10; 8:45 am]
BILLING CODE 6335-01-P

COMMISSION ON CIVIL RIGHTS

Agenda and Notice of Public Meeting of the District of Columbia Advisory Committee

Notice is hereby given, pursuant to the provisions of the rules and regulations of the U.S. Commission on Civil Rights and the Federal Advisory Committee Act, that an orientation and planning meeting of the District of Columbia Advisory Committee will convene at 11 a.m. on Thursday, May 13, 2010, at the U.S. Commission on Civil Rights, 624 Ninth Street, NW., Conference Room 540, Washington, DC 20425. The purpose of the orientation meeting is to review the rules of operation for the Advisory Committee.

Figure 10-6
Sample Page from C.F.R.

Food and Drug Administration, HHS   **§ 164.110**

of nonfat milk solids shall be calculated using only those dairy ingredients referred to in § 163.130(b)(4), exclusive of any added sweetener or other dairy-derived ingredient that is added beyond that amount that is normally present in the specified dairy ingredient.

(b) *Optional ingredients.* (1) Safe and suitable vegetable derived oils, fats, and stearins other than cacao fat. The oils, fats, and stearins may be hydrogenated;

(2) Safe and suitable dairy-derived ingredients; and

(3) Safe and suitable bulking agents, formulation aids, humectants, and texturizers.

(c) *Nomenclature.* The name of the food is "milk chocolate and vegetable fat coating" or "skim milk chocolate and vegetable fat coating", as appropriate. Alternatively, the common or usual name of the vegetable derived fat ingredient may be used in the name of the food, e.g., "milk chocolate and _____ oil coating", the blank being filled in with the common or usual name of the specific vegetable fat used.

PART 164—TREE NUT AND PEANUT PRODUCTS

Subpart A [Reserved]

Subpart B—Requirements for Specific Standardized Tree Nut and Peanut Products

Sec.
164.110 Mixed nuts.
164.120 Shelled nuts in rigid or semirigid containers.
164.150 Peanut butter.

AUTHORITY: 21 U.S.C. 321, 341, 343, 348, 371, 379e.

SOURCE: 42 FR 14475, Mar. 15, 1977, unless otherwise noted.

Subpart A [Reserved]

Subpart B—Requirements for Specific Standardized Tree Nut and Peanut Products

§ 164.110 Mixed nuts.

(a) Mixed nuts is the food consisting of a mixture of four or more of the optional shelled tree nut ingredients, with or without one or more of the optional shelled peanut ingredients, of the kinds prescribed by paragraph (b) of this section; except that when 2 ounces or less of the food is packed in transparent containers, three or more of the optional tree nut ingredients shall be present. Each such kind of nut ingredient when used shall be present in a quantity not less than 2 percent and not more than 80 percent by weight of the finished food. For purposes of this section, each kind of tree nut and peanut is an optional ingredient that may be prepared by any suitable method in accordance with good manufacturing practice. The finished food may contain one or more of the optional nonnut ingredients provided for in paragraph (c) of this section.

(b) The optional shelled nut ingredients referred to in paragraph (a) of this section are:

(1) Almonds, black walnuts, Brazil nuts, cashews, English walnuts (alternatively "walnuts"), filberts, pecans, and other suitable kinds of tree nuts.

(2) Peanuts of the Spanish, Valencia, Virginia, or similar varieties, or any combination of two or more such varieties.

(c) The optional nonnut ingredients referred to in paragraph (a) of this section consist of suitable substances that are not food additives as defined in section 201(s) of the Federal Food, Drug, and Cosmetic Act; or if they are food additives as so defined, they are used in conformity with regulations established pursuant to section 409 of the act. Nonnut ingredients that perform a useful function are regarded as suitable, except that color additives are not suitable ingredients of the food.

(d) The name of the food is "mixed nuts". If the percentage of a single tree nut ingredient or the total peanut content by weight of the finished food exceeds 50 percent but not 60 percent, the statement "contains up to 60% _____" or "contains 60% _____" or "60% _____" shall immediately follow the name "mixed nuts" and shall appear on the same background, be of the same color or, in the case of multicolors, in the color showing distinct contrast with the background, and be in letters not less than one-half the height of the largest letter in the words "mixed

3. Research Techniques for Administrative Law

a. C.F.R.

Because C.F.R. is revised annually, with new volumes issued quarterly, any rule or regulation promulgated a year or more ago can best be located in C.F.R.

There are several methods or indexes you can use to locate information in C.F.R. In many instances you will be directed to the pertinent reference in C.F.R. after you read a federal statute in U.S.C.A. or U.S.C.S. Carefully examine the notes that follow the wording of federal statutes in U.S.C.A. or U.S.C.S. to see if you are directed to sections of C.F.R.

C.F.R. contains an index volume entitled "C.F.R. Index and Finding Aids." This one-volume index is revised annually and can be accessed by subject matter (pesticides, wildlife management) or by the name of an agency (Agricultural Marketing Service, Central Intelligence Agency). The index will direct you to one of the 50 titles of C.F.R. and then to the part within that particular title. There is also a separate index for each of the 50 titles of C.F.R. located immediately after the last part of each of the 50 titles.

The C.F.R. Index and Finding Aids volume also contains a table entitled "Parallel Table of Authorities and Rules" (Table I). If you know the citation to the enabling statute that created the agency or by which authority the agency issues its regulations, you can look up this citation in Table I. Because of the similarity in the organization between C.F.R. and our federal statutes, this research approach is easy and effective. You will then be directed to the appropriate title and part of C.F.R. A list of all 50 C.F.R. titles, chapters, and parts is also found in this index, together with an alphabetical list of agencies. See Figure 10-7 for a sample page from the C.F.R. Index.

West also publishes a separate Index to C.F.R. called *West's Code of Federal Regulations, General Index*, which is designed to provide access to C.F.R. by subject matter (for example, port safety) or by geographic location (for example, Appalachia or Boston). You will be directed to a title and part of C.F.R.

The National Archives and Records Administration also provides indexes to the *Federal Register* and C.F.R. online at http://www.archives.gov.

b. The *Federal Register*

Because C.F.R. is issued annually it will not contain newly promulgated rules and regulations, which are published in the *Federal Register*. To access the *Federal Register*, use the *Federal Register Index*, which is issued monthly in cumulative form. Thus, the *Federal Register Index* for June contains all of the information for the previous five months. Entries in this Index are arranged alphabetically by agency (Agriculture Department, Air Force Department, and National Science Foundation).

Figure 10-7
Sample Page from C.F.R. Index

Tobacco products, cigarette papers and tubes, exportation without payment of tax or with drawback of tax, 27 CFR 290

Turbine engine powered airplanes, fuel venting and exhaust emission requirements, 14 CFR 34

Ultralight vehicles, 14 CFR 103

Water resource development projects administered by Chief of Army Engineers, seaplane operations, 36 CFR 328

Aircraft pilots

See Airmen

Airlines

See Air carriers

Airmen

Air safety proceedings, practice rules, 49 CFR 821

Air taxi operators and commercial operators of small aircraft, 14 CFR 135

Airplane operator security, 14 CFR 108

Alien airmen

Arrival manifests, lists, and supporting documents for immigration, 8 CFR 251

Landing, 8 CFR 252

Parole, 8 CFR 253

Aviation maintenance technician schools, 14 CFR 147

Certification

Airmen other than flight crewmembers, 14 CFR 65

Flight crew members other than pilots, 14 CFR 63

Pilots and flight instructors, 14 CFR 61

Certification and operations

Airplanes having a seating capacity of 20 or more passengers or a maximum payload capacity of 6,000 pounds or more, 14 CFR 125

Domestic, flag, and supplemental air carriers and commercial operators of large aircraft, 14 CFR 121

Scheduled air carriers with helicopters, 14 CFR 127

Customs declarations and exemptions, 19 CFR 148

Federal Aviation Administration, representatives of Administrator, 14 CFR 183

Foreign air carrier or other foreign person, lease of aircraft with crew, 14 CFR 218

General aircraft operating and flight rules, 14 CFR 91

Ground instructors, 14 CFR 143

Medical standards and certification for airmen, 14 CFR 67

Pilot schools, 14 CFR 141

Airplanes

See Aircraft

Airports

Air Force Department, aircraft arresting systems, 32 CFR 856

Air traffic control services and navigational facilities, establishment and discontinuance criteria, 14 CFR 170

Airplane operator security, 14 CFR 108

Airport aid program, 14 CFR 152

Airport noise and access restrictions, notice and approval, 14 CFR 161

Airport security, 14 CFR 107

Certification of airmen other than flight crewmembers, 14 CFR 65

Construction, alteration, activation, and deactivation of airports, notice, 14 CFR 157

Customs Service, air commerce regulations, 19 CFR 122

Defense Department, air installations compatible use zones, 32 CFR 256

Environmental criteria and standards, HUD assisted projects in runway clear zones at civil airports and clear and accident potential zones at military airports, 24 CFR 51

Expenditures of Federal funds for nonmilitary airports or air navigation facilities, 14 CFR 169

Federal aid, 14 CFR 151

Foreign quarantine, 42 CFR 71

General aircraft operating and flight rules, 14 CFR 91

Highway engineering, 23 CFR 620

Land airports serving certain air carriers, certification and operations, 14 CFR 139

Reference to C.F.R. title and part

At the back of each issue of each daily *Federal Register* is a section called "Reader Aids." This section lists any C.F.R. parts affected during the month that issue was published, provides reminders of the rules going into effect that day and within the next few days, identifies the next week's due dates for comments for pending rules, and provides general information for customers needing service and assistance.

Additionally, the United States government periodically offers three-hour free lectures in various locations throughout the United States describing the regulatory process, the relationship between the *Federal Register* and C.F.R., and how to use the *Federal Register*. For dates, locations, and times, check either the inside front or back covers of a few issues of the *Federal Register*.

4. *Updating C.F.R. Regulations*

Because agency rules and regulations are revised or revoked so frequently, you must always check the current status of any regulation you have found. Updating C.F.R. regulations is a two-step process.

a. *List of C.F.R. Sections Affected*

To bring any regulation up to date, consult a publication titled *List of C.F.R. Sections Affected* ("LSA"). LSA is a monthly softcover cumulative publication designed to inform researchers of amendments or changes in any regulation found in C.F.R. By looking up the C.F.R. title and section you are researching, you will be provided a short explanation such as "amended" or "revised" and you will then be directed to the appropriate page of the *Federal Register* on which the amendatory language or other change is found. See Figure 10-8 for a sample page from LSA.

b. C.F.R. Parts Affected

After you have used LSA (which will update the regulation only through the end of last month), you must further check a regulation by determining its status as of today's date. This is accomplished by reviewing the section titled "Reader Aids" at the back of the most recent issue of the *Federal Register*. Each issue of the *Federal Register* includes a section within "Reader Aids" titled "C.F.R. Parts Affected," which will inform you of any changes to any C.F.R. regulations for the period after the most recent issue of LSA. Just as with LSA, you will be directed to the particular page of the *Federal Register* that contains the revisions to a regulation. If you do not locate any entries for your C.F.R. title and part in either LSA or C.F.R. Parts Affected, this means there are no revisions to your regulation during the period covered.

Figure 10-8
Sample Page from LSA

46   LSA—LIST OF CFR SECTIONS AFFECTED

CHANGES APRIL 1, 2010 THROUGH SEPTEMBER 30, 2010

TITLE 20 Chapter V—Con.

606.21 (c) and (d) amended...............57156
606.22 (b)(4), (c)(1), (2), (3) and
   (d)(3) amended.........................57156
606.32 (b) revised 57156
618 Added......................................17000
   Clarification..............................44720
641 Revised 53812

Proposed Rules:

1...49596
10...49596
25...49596
350...20299
404..............................20299, 42639, 51336
416..............................20299, 42639, 51336
672...52671
701...50718
1001..33203

TITLE 21—FOOD AND DRUGS

Chapter I—Food and Drug Administration, Department of Health and Human Services (Parts 1—1299)

1.101 (d)(2)(iii) revised....................20914
2 Technical correction 56858
2.125 (e)(1)(iii), (v), (2)(iii), (iv),
   (4)(iv), (vii) and (viii) removed; eff. in part 6–30–11
   and 12–31–13 19241
5 Revised 16354
10.90 (a) and (c) revised 16346
73.2110 Regulation at 75 FR 14493
   confirmed 34361
106.120 (b) revised...........................32658
107.50 (e)(2) revised 32659
107.240 (b) revised..........................32659
118.11 (a), (b)(2)(i) and (3)(vi) revised.......................................18751
312.32 Revised 59961
312.64 (b) revised 59963
312.140 (a)(1) amended 37295
312.310 (d)(1) revised......................32659
314.440 (a)(2) amended 37295
320.31 (d)(1) and (2) amended;
   (d)(3) added 59963
510.600 (c)(1) table and (2) table
   amended.......20523, 52622, 54016, 55676
   (c)(1) table amended 54017
520.390b (b) revised.........................55676
520.580 (b)(1) amended 52622
520.1616 Heading revised 26646
520.1618 Added 26646

Reference
to revision
of C.F.R.
section

520.1871 (a)(1), (d)(1)(i) and (iii)
   revised; (b)(1) amended.............54018
520.2043 (b)(2) amended...................52622
520.2455 (a) and (b) revised 54492
522.246 (b)(2) amended....................22524
522.533 Heading and (b) revised;
   (c) added; (d) removed 52622
522.558 (c)(2)(ii) revised 60308
522.930 Added 59611
522.956 (d)(2) revised.......................54019
522.1192 (b)(1), (2) and (e)(2)(ii) revised.......................................26647
522.1696a (b)(1), (2), (d)(2)(ii)(A)
   and (iii) revised 54017
522.1696b (b)(1), (2), (d)(2)(i)(A)
   and (iii)(B) revised 54017
522.2005 Revised 20269
   (b) and (c) revised......................38700
524.1044i Added...............................54492
524.1193 (b) and (e)(2) revised 26648
524.1610 Added 16346
529.536 Added 21163
556.90 Removed 24394
558.4 (d) table amended 24394, 34361
558.185 (b)(2) removed; (b)(3) re-
   designated as new (b)(2) 24394
558.325 (a) and (c)(3)(ii) revised;
   (d)(2)(i) table and (iii) table
   amended 55676
558.342 (e)(1)(v), (vi) and (vii)
   amended 60309
558.485 (b)(3) amended 55677
558.500 (e)(2)(viii) amended;
   (e)(2)(xii) removed 20917
   (e)(2)(xii) and (xiii) added............54019
558.630 (b)(5) amended 55677
573.170 Added 41725
801.430 (f)(2) footnote 1 revised
  20914
803.11 (c) revised 20914
803.12 (c) revised 32659
803.21 (a) revised 20914
807.22 (a) revised 20914
807.37 (a) and (b)(2) revised 20914
807.90 (a)(1) revised 20915
812.19 (a)(1) revised 20915
814.1 (a) revised...............................16350
   Regulation at 75 FR 16350
   withdrawn 41986
814.2 Revised...................................16350
   Regulation at 75 FR 16350
   withdrawn 41986
814.20 (b)(3)(i) revised.....................16351
   (h)(1) revised..............................20915
   Regulation at 75 FR 16351
   withdrawn 41986

5. *Electronic and Online Methods of Administrative Law Research*

Lexis and Westlaw both include the full text of the *Federal Register* and C.F.R. in their easy-to-use and search databases. Both of these services, however, charge a fee for their use. The Government Printing Office now offers for free both the *Federal Register* (since 1994) and C.F.R. (since 1996) on the Internet. Access http://www.gpoaccess.gov and select either *Federal Register* or *Code of Federal Regulations*. Searching the *Federal Register* can be done by subject or keyword, agency name, citation, or by browsing tables of contents. Searching C.F.R. can be done by keyword, citation, or by browsing your choice of C.F.R. titles or volumes. C.F.R. and the *Federal Register* are also available on FDsys at http://www.fdsys.gov.

In summer 2010, the federal government launched a new website, *Federal Register*, at http://www.federalregister.gov. The site divides the thousands of federal rules and regulations into six categories: money, environment, world, science and technology, business and industry, and health and public welfare. The site has a clean and crisp appearance and makes locating federal rules and regulations easy; users may browse by agency (Department of Commerce) or topic name (crop insurance).

Proposed and final rules are also available on another new government website, "Regulations.gov," available at http://www.regulations.gov. This site allows searching by key word, name of agency, and more, allowing quick access to U.S. government regulations from nearly 300 federal agencies. You may post comments and sign up for regular e-mail alerts about a specific regulation.

Just as a C.F.R. citation located in print must be updated by using LSA and C.F.R. Parts Affected, a C.F.R. section located online must also be updated. In fact, some information is available electronically prior to publication in the monthly print issue of LSA. First, select "List of C.F.R. Sections Affected" located at http://www.gpoaccess.gov/lsa/index.html (or http://www.fdsys.gov). You can then enter your C.F.R. section in the search box. Second, access "Current List of CFR Parts Affected," which lists C.F.R. Parts affected by changes since the last monthly issue of LSA. It is updated daily. Simply scan down the list of parts affected to see if your specific C.F.R. citation has been changed, amended, revised, and so forth. If so, access the pertinent page within C.F.R. to review the amendments, changes, or proposed rules that affect your C.F.R. provision. In addition, the FDsys/GPO Access websites offer e-cfr, an electronic service that updates the *Code of Federal Regulations* on a daily basis.

Internet Tutorials on Administrative Law Research

Review the following websites for excellent tutorials on performing administrative law research: http://www.ll.georgetown.edu/ tutorials/admin/index.cfm and http://www.archives.gov/ federal-register/tutorial/index.html.

6. Decisions

As discussed earlier, in addition to issuing rules and regulations (acting in a quasi-legislative manner), administrative agencies interpret and enforce their rules and regulations through the process of issuing decisions (acting in a quasi-judicial manner). For example, the Federal Communications Commission issues rules and regulations relating to radio broadcasts. If a radio personality allegedly violates those regulations, the FCC will hold a hearing and issue a decision relating to this matter. The hearing held by the agency is somewhat less formal than a trial conducted in a courtroom, but its basic function — to determine facts and render a decision — is the same. There is no jury, and the individual who renders the decision in the proceeding (called an "adjudication") is an administrative law judge ("A.L.J.") who is an expert in this field. Alternatively, the agency can prosecute violators in court, often by referring the matter to the Department of Justice for prosecution. Thus, the Environmental Protection Agency can ensure compliance with its regulations by instituting a civil or criminal action. There are approximately 1,300 A.L.J.s assigned to more than 30 federal agencies.

These decisions rendered by the administrative agencies will be published so you may gain access to them and review them. There is no one set of books containing the decisions of all of the agencies; however, the United States Government Printing Office does publish sets containing decisions for each agency. Table T.1.2 of *The Bluebook* identifies more than 40 official administrative publications, from *Decisions and Orders of the National Labor Relations Board* to the *Federal Trade Commission Decisions*. Although these publications are official, the sets lack a uniform approach. Indexes are often difficult to use, and the updating can be sporadic. As a result, private publishers such as CCH, BNA, and Matthew Bender have published sets that report agency decisions. Typically, these sets are in looseleaf format (see Chapter 7), and decisions are located through alphabetically arranged Tables of Cases or through the subject matter index for the set, which will direct you to a narrative discussion followed by annotations to cases. To locate the actual case, use the citation given in the annotation. These cases are often published in separate bound volumes that contain both agency decisions and court decisions. Table T.15 of *The Bluebook* identifies more than 100 of these services, from *Aviation Cases* to the *Environmental Law Reporter*. Many services are also identified in *ALWD*'s Appendix 8.

West publishes sets entitled *Code of Federal Regulations Annotated* (for select titles), which is arranged identically to C.F.R. and includes all C.F.R. regulations. In addition, however, the set includes references to law reviews and other authorities and annotations to cases interpreting C.F.R. provisions so that you may easily find authorities interpreting and construing C.F.R. provisions that you are researching.

Additionally, many agencies post their decisions on their own websites. The following site will link you to administrative decisions and actions for many agencies: http://www.lib.virginia.edu/govdocs/fed_decisions_agency.html.

If a decision has been rendered by an agency, you can check its current status, namely, Shepardize it, by using *Shepard's United States Administrative Citations*, which provides update information for decisions reported in more than 30 reports published by federal administrative departments, boards, courts, and commissions. Thus, you can Shepardize an administrative decision or order (using *Shepard's* in print or electronically on Lexis) and ensure it is good law and find other decisions that discuss your case. Alternatively, you can KeyCite the case through Westlaw to make sure it is still good law.

Practice Tip

Administrative Law

Use *Shepard's Code of Federal Regulations Citations* to locate state and federal cases, law review articles, and annotations that interpret or mention C.F.R. regulations, presidential proclamations, and executive orders.

---

7. Review of Agency Decisions

If a party is dissatisfied with the decision rendered by the A.L.J., in most instances the matter may be reviewed at a higher level within the agency and then appealed to a federal court. The enabling statutes dictate the type of review afforded to agency decisions. Because a "trial" has already occurred at the agency itself, the aggrieved party often appeals the agency decision to the appropriate United States Court of Appeals, the intermediate level of court in our federal system, bypassing the United States District Courts, which function as trial courts in our federal system. Further appeal may be made to the United States Supreme Court, assuming certiorari is granted. See Figure 10-9 for a chart showing the appeal process for most federal agency decisions. In some cases, however (such as those heard by the Social Security Administration), after the agency itself has reviewed the decision of an A.L.J., a dissatisfied party may file a civil suit in a federal district court. Statutes governing the agency will specify a forum for review.

8. Locating Federal Cases Reviewing Agency Decisions

There are several techniques you can use to locate federal cases that have reviewed federal agency decisions. You can Shepardize the agency

Figure 10-9
Appeal of Agency Decisions

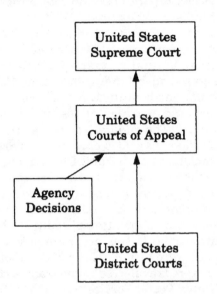

decision in *Shepard's United States Administrative Law Citations*. This will give you the subsequent history of the agency decision by providing you with the appropriate citations to U.S. Supreme Court cases and lower federal court cases that affect or mention your agency decision. You may also Shepardize on Lexis or use Westlaw's KeyCite to find cases and other authorities that mention your case.

Because you are now interested in locating cases from lower federal courts of appeal and from the United States Supreme Court that have reviewed agency decisions, you can also rely on the standard sources you would use to locate federal cases on any topic: digests and annotations.

For all federal court cases, use *West's Federal Practice Digest, 4th Series* (or, if needed, any of the earlier series). To locate United States Supreme Court cases, use West's *United States Supreme Court Digest*. To locate annotations on agency matters, use A.L.R. Fed.

You can check the websites of the agencies themselves to see if they provide their decisions. For example, when you access the site of the National Labor Relations Board (http://www.nlrb.gov), you can immediately link to decisions and search by keyword or date. Similarly, Lexis and Westlaw offer decisions of numerous agencies (although fees are charged to access their databases).

9.   *The United States Government Manual*

One book of particular relevance to administrative law is *The United States Government Manual*, referred to as the "Official Handbook of the Federal Government." This softcover book is prepared annually by the Office of the Federal Register and provides thorough and detailed

information on the agencies (such as the Federal Communications Commission), quasi-official agencies (such as the Smithsonian Institution and the Legal Services Corporation), and international organizations in which the United States participates.

For each agency, the *Manual* provides a list of the principal officials, a summary of the agency's purpose, a brief history of the agency, including a reference to the statute that established it, and a description of the activities engaged in by the agency. The *Manual* also provides miscellaneous information about the three branches of government, such as a list of senators and representatives and information about the federal judicial system. The *Manual* displays a variety of diagrams showing the organization of various executive departments, such as the Department of Homeland Security and Department of Justice, making the division of authority and organization of the various offices and divisions within each department readily understandable.

Finally, the *Manual* provides information regarding terminated agencies. For example, when you attempt to find information relating to the Civil Aeronautics Board, you are promptly informed that most functions of the Board were terminated in 1981, 1983, and 1985, and its remaining functions were transferred to the transportation secretary, the FAA, and United States Postal Service.

Since 1995 the *Manual* has been offered for free online by the Government Printing Office at its site, GPO Access. Access http://www.gpoaccess.gov/gmanual/index.html. Searching can be done by entering keywords or search terms in the search box provided. Using the *Manual* online is an easy and free way to gain information about various government agencies, their addresses, appointees, staff members, and functions. At the time of the writing of this text, the *Manual* can also be located on FDsys at http://www.fdsys.gov, although searching is by date only.

10. State Administrative Law

There are agencies in most states, the actions and activities of which often parallel federal agencies. For example, one of the better-known federal agencies, the Occupational Safety and Health Administration ("OSHA"), is patterned after the California Division of Occupational Safety and Health ("Cal-OSHA"). Whereas the federal OSHA agency regulates health and safety measures on a national basis, the state safety and health agency may impose additional standards for ensuring that work environments and public buildings are safe. Similarly, many state agencies issue regulations for the practice of certain occupations in the state, such as standards for beauticians, barbers, and real estate agents.

One of the best examples of a state agency is your state department of motor vehicles. Although your state statute will set forth the age at which one may drive, testing and licensing procedures as well as other regulations related to the activity of driving typically are determined by the department of motor vehicles.

Some states, usually the more populous ones, publish their agencies' rules and regulations in a fashion similar to the publication of administrative law at the federal level; that is, in separate sets of books devoted solely to agency regulations and titled "Administrative Codes." These usually have indexes, which are arranged similarly to other indexes and are easy to use. Simply look up the word or phrase that describes the issue you are researching, and you will be directed to the pertinent administrative code section.

You may also find that after you read a statute in the state code, you are referred to an administrative regulation in the cross-references or library references that follow the statute. In other instances, in the course of reading a case or a local encyclopedia, you may come across a reference to an administrative regulation. In any of these events, carefully review the administrative regulations, as they typically provide detailed rules, which are subject to strict compliance.

Some state agencies issue decisions. With the exception of tax and unemployment compensation decisions, these are rarely published. Some agencies, however, publish newsletters or other publications that briefly review and summarize their decisions and other activities. These newsletters may be available for subscription or may be available at your law library or through the agency itself.

Both Lexis and Westlaw offer state agency rules and some state agency decisions. Agency rules and decisions may also be available for free on the Internet. Start with your state's home page and look for links to administrative agencies, rules, and decisions. Your state's home page can be accessed by starting with Megalaw at http://www.megalaw.com and then selecting "State law." For example, all of California's administrative regulations can be accessed this way, or by accessing http://www.wash law.edu and then selecting your state's name from the list provided.

For further information contact the pertinent agency. Usually, the main division or office for an agency is located in the state capital. You should begin your search for information and materials there.

D. International Law

1. Introduction

"International law" is broadly defined as the law relating to relations among sovereign nations. Although most individuals regard international law as the exclusive province of international lawyers and as an area of law that has no relevance to their daily lives, international law does impact your everyday existence. For example, the fish you order in a restaurant or the tuna fish you may purchase in a supermarket may have been caught in another country's "economic fishing zone" and is available here pursuant to a treaty. Similarly, individuals in the legal profession who practice near Canada or Mexico often need to become familiar with various aspects of international law. The General Agreement on Tariffs

and Trade ("GATT") and the North American Free Trade Agreement ("NAFTA") have implications for those doing business in foreign countries. Moreover, with more and more companies "going global" and the Internet allowing worldwide communication and commerce, it is important for legal professionals to have a basic understanding of international law research.

One often hears that there are two branches of international law: public and private. "Public" international law is what we typically view as international law: the conduct and regulation of nations, usually called the "law of nations." "Private" international law is an older and more archaic term, used primarily in Europe to describe an area of law more properly classified as "conflict of laws." For example, assume a store in your city ordered a shipment of vases from France that arrived broken. The issue as to which jurisdiction's law would apply, that of France or that of your jurisdiction, is a matter of "private international law." Many contracts include a choice of law clause that governs what law applies and where venue will lie.

Although it is true that international law is a specialized field of law and that most paralegals will not be involved in this practice area, you should become sufficiently familiar with international law sources and research procedures so that, if needed, you can adequately perform a basic research task in this field.

2.   Sources of International Law

International law is derived from four sources:

(i)   International conventions (for example, treaties), which set forth rules for conduct expressly recognized and voluntarily agreed to by signatory nations
(ii)   International custom; that is, some general practice accepted as law or believed to be obligatory
(iii)   General principles of law accepted by civilized nations
(iv)   Judicial decisions and the teachings of international law experts

3.   Overview of International Law Research Procedure

If you are presented with an international law research task, you should use the following procedure unless you know the exact source for the answer to your issue or problem: You should first "get your feet wet" by reading some basic or introductory information relating to your issue. This familiarization process will save you time by ensuring that you do not head off in the wrong direction due to a lack of understanding of the issues involved. After you have familiarized yourself with the issue by reviewing some basic materials and sources, you should determine

whether a treaty covers this issue and provides a definitive answer to your question. If so, you will need to review the treaty and then determine if it is still "good law," that is, if it is still "in force." Finally, you will need to read analyses and cases interpreting the treaty.

To follow this research process, you need to know which sources to consult. This section of the chapter will provide you with the names of the sets of books you should consult in order to perform international law legal research.

4. *Basic Texts and Sources*

There are several sources to consult to obtain introductory information and background on international law. Law libraries usually collect all international law materials together. You should browse the shelves in this section for other useful materials. Some of the better-known general texts and guides relating to international law are as follows:

> Claire M. Germain, *Germain's Transnational Law Research: A Guide for Attorneys* (1991)
> Green H. Hackworth, *Digest of International Law* (1940-1944)
> John B. Moore, *A Digest of International Law* (1906)
> Marjorie M. Whiteman, *Digest of International Law* (1963)

These digests all provide excellent information relating to international law. In many ways, they resemble an encyclopedia in that they are multivolume sets that contain articulate narrative statements of the law and citations to cases that are located in footnotes.

Thus, you are not only provided with a description or summary of an issue, but you are directed to cases as well. Access is gained through the alphabetically arranged index found in the last volume of each set.

You should also consult Restatement (Third) Foreign Relations Law of the United States. This Restatement focuses on international law as it applies to the United States and is an excellent starting place for international law research. The Restatement provides general information on international law, international agreements, and international jurisdiction, judgments, and remedies. The Restatement will also provide you with citations to cases that have interpreted treaties. Additionally, a set of books titled *Foreign Relations of the United States* provides a historical overview of significant foreign policy decisions and diplomatic activities of the United States. Volumes since about 1945 are available online at the State Department website (http://history.state.gov).

Finally, you should consult an excellent periodical, the *American Journal of International Law*. This quarterly publication contains thoughtful and analytical articles relating to various international law topics. Use the index for the set or use the *Index to Legal Periodicals & Books* (see Chapter 6) to determine if an article has been written relating to the issue you are researching.

5. *Treaties*

Once you have gained some background information relating to your research problem, you need to determine if a treaty governs this issue. A treaty is a formal agreement, usually written, between two or more countries. Treaties may be bilateral (between two parties) or multilateral (among several parties). The history of treaty-making goes back thousands of years. Some treaties have ended wars, others have resolved boundary disputes, and still others deal with trade or economic issues. One type of treaty is referred to as a "convention" and usually relates to a formal multilateral agreement with numerous parties, such as "The Geneva Convention Relative to the Treatment of Prisoners of War." While treaties may have been signed and agreed to by representatives of the countries involved, they are not effective until they are ratified or officially approved by each government.

In the United States, treaties are initiated by the executive branch and then negotiated by individuals selected by the president, often foreign service officers employed by the Department of State. They are entered into by the president with the "advice and consent" of the Senate. Two-thirds of the United States Senate must approve a treaty. There are, however, types of agreements called "executive agreements" that can be entered into by the president without Senate approval. There is often a great length of time between the date a treaty is signed by the representatives of the signatory countries and the date it is formally ratified. In some cases, years pass between signing and ratification, and it is quite difficult to obtain the text of a treaty during this interim stage.

According to the Constitution, "all Treaties made, or which shall be made under the Authority of the United States shall be the supreme Law of the Land; and the Judges in every state shall be bound thereby, any Thing in the Constitution or Laws of any State to the Contrary notwithstanding." U.S. Const. art. VI. Thus, treaties are "primary" law in that they must be followed.

6. *Sources for Treaties*

a. Pre-Ratification

During the time between signing of a treaty and approval by the United States Senate, treaties can be located in a series entitled *Senate Executive Documents*. Because the United States Senate, namely, the Committee on Foreign Relations, will hold hearings on a treaty and issue a report much the same way hearings are held and reports are issued for legislation, you can review the report by consulting *Congressional Information Service* (CIS) Index (see Sections A.3 and A.5 of this chapter). Additionally, CCH's *Congressional Index* contains a table reflecting the status of treaties pending before the United States Senate. Finally, access the Senate's Treaty Page (http://www.senate.gov/pagelayout/legislative/d_three_sections_with_teasers/treaties.htm) to locate information on pending treaties and links to legislation relating to foreign relations.

b. Post-Ratification

Since 1945, all treaties and executive agreements to which the United States is a party are published as pamphlets in a set titled *Treaties and Other International Acts Series* (T.I.A.S.). Since 1950, all of the pamphlets published in T.I.A.S. are then published in hardbound volumes called *United States Treaties and Other International Agreements* (U.S.T.). To locate treaties in either of these sets, use the index *United States Treaties and Other International Agreements Cumulative Index*. This Index is easily used. You may locate a treaty by country name (Brazil, Canada, Senegal, United States of America) or by topic (health care, extradition, trademarks, navigation). T.I.A.S. documents since 1996 are available online through the U.S. Department of State's website at http://www.state.gov/s/l/treaty/tias/index.htm.

Another collection of treaties is the *United Nations Treaty Series* ("U.N.T.S."), which publishes treaties filed, registered, or recorded with the Secretariat of the United Nations. Thus, this collection contains numerous treaties to which the United States is not a party. A cumulative index to U.N.T.S. provides access by country and by topic. U.N.T.S. expands at the rate of more than 100 volumes per year.

Treaties are available on both LexisNexis and Westlaw. Searching is easily accomplished by treaty citation, country name, or key words and phrases. Once a treaty is located, it is easily updated to ensure it is still in force.

Many treaties are now available on the Internet. Consult the following sources:

- The United Nations Treaty Collection offers access to more than 100,000 treaties and international agreements and complete access to U.N.T.S. Access http://treaties.un.org. Unfortunately, this is no longer a free service. To obtain access to the entire database, law firms and companies pay a moderate fee, but some treaties and information on the status of certain treaties are available for free viewing and downloading. The United Nations site also offers a glossary of terms relating to treaty actions.
- Perhaps the best free source for recent treaties to which the United States is a party is THOMAS (http://thomas.loc.gov/home/treaties/treaties.htm). THOMAS does not include the full text of treaties but does provide a wealth of treaty information (since about 1968). Searching may be done by treaty number, word or phrase, or type of treaty.
- Treaty documents after 1987 can be located for free through GPO Access. Access the site at http://www.gpoaccess.gov/serialset/index.html, select a Congress (such as the 106th), select "Senate Treaty Documents," and then enter either search terms (such as "hazardous waste") or country name (such as "Canada"). You will then be provided with a summary of the treaty as well as its full text.

- More than 20 treaties related to intellectual property are available for free through the website of the World Intellectual Property Organization at http://www.wipo.int.
- Finally, one of the best new free sites for international law research is the Global Legal Information Network provided by the Library of Congress at http://www.glin.gov, which is a public database of the official texts of laws, regulations, cases, and other sources from more than 50 countries.

7. Determining the Current Status of Treaties

After you have read and reviewed a treaty, you should determine whether it is still in force. Sometimes the treaty itself will specify the date until which it will be in force. For example, the treaty might provide as follows: "The treaty enters into force 30 days after ratification and remains in force for a period of 10 years and continues in force thereafter unless terminated by either party by giving one year's written notice to the other." You should also check an annual publication of the State Department entitled *A Guide to the United States Treaties in Force*, which identifies all of the treaties and executive agreements still in force. *Treaties in Force* is easy to use as it is organized both by country and by topic.

Perhaps the easiest way to determine whether a treaty involving the United States is still in force is to access the Office of the Legal Adviser of the State Department at www.state.gov/s/l/treaty, which provides a link to *Treaties in Force* (with a complete table of contents, allowing easy online searching by country name or treaty topic) as well as to treaty actions and other valuable information. In fact, the print version of *Treaties in Force* is published in limited quantities, so this online version is the best source to use to determine the status of treaties.

8. Interpreting Treaties

To assist you in interpreting treaties, use both secondary sources and primary sources. For secondary sources that have construed treaties, review the digests and the *American Journal of International Law*, described in Section D.4 of this chapter.

To locate primary sources, for example, cases that have interpreted treaties, check the following sources:

> *Shepard's Federal Statute Citations*. Be sure you have obtained *Shepard's* for statutes rather than the volumes for cases. Locate the section called "United States Treaties and Other International Agreements." By looking up the volume and page of the U.S.T. citation and using the same technique for Shepardizing cases and statutes, you can locate judicial decisions and A.L.R. annotations that have mentioned, discussed, or interpreted your treaty.

> *Lexis and Westlaw.* Once you have located a treaty of interest, use *Shepard's* on Lexis or KeyCite on Westlaw to locate cases and other authorities that have cited or discussed your treaty.
>
> *U.S.C.S.* U.S.C.S. contains a separate volume titled "Notes to Uncodified Laws and Treaties," which will provide you with annotations to judicial decisions interpreting treaties.

Once you have located cases construing your treaty, be sure to Shepardize or KeyCite these cases to ensure they are still good law and to help you locate additional pertinent cases.

A hotly debated issue is the use of foreign law by American courts, specifically the U.S. Supreme Court. Some Justices are strong supporters of the use of foreign law, and three recent U.S. Supreme Court cases have cited foreign law or international conventions. Other Justices are vigorously opposed to the use of foreign law, and at the time of the writing of this text a resolution had been introduced in the House of Representatives condemning the use of foreign law and precedents in interpreting the U.S. Constitution. H.R. Res. 473, 111th Cong. (2009).

Internet Tutorials on International Law Research

The following sites provide excellent tutorials for performing international law research: http://www.asil.org/resource/treaty1. htm and http://www.bc.edu/schools/law/library/meta-elements/pdf/ researchguides/treaties.pdf.

9. Citation Form

The Bluebook (Rule 21.4) provides that a citation to a treaty or other international agreement should include the name of the treaty, the parties to the agreement (although if there are more than three parties, their names are not given), the particular subdivision of the treaty relied upon (if applicable), the date it was signed, and the source(s) in which the treaty is located.

For bilateral agreements to which the United States is a party, cite U.S.T., T.I.A.S., or U.N.T.S., in that order.

Example

Treaty on Health Care, U.S. — Can., June 29, 1991, 41 U.S.T. 621.

If there are three or more parties to the treaty (including the United States), cite to one of the following sources: U.S.T, *United States Statutes at Large*, T.I.A.S., or U.N.T.S., in that order. Rule 21.4.5 also provides some other treaty sources that may be cited.

Example
    Treaty on Navigational Waterways, Apr. 14, 1986, 38 U.S.T. 1421.

ALWD citation form for treaties differs slightly from *Bluebook* form, as
follows: Treaty on Navigational Waterways (Apr. 14, 1986), 38 U.S.T.
1421. See *ALWD* Rule 21.

10. *International Tribunals*

There are a variety of methods available to nations to resolve disputes.
Often one country will agree to act as an informal mediator in a dispute
between two countries. For example, in the dispute over the Falkland
Islands between Great Britain and Argentina, the United States attempted to avoid the outbreak of hostilities by acting as a mediator or
liaison between the two nations.
    The Permanent Court of Arbitration was established in 1899 at The
Hague, Holland's royal city. Members of this court serve not as judges but
as arbitrators, and the court offers a broad range of services, including
mediation, arbitration, and fact-finding, for resolving international disputes. It is the oldest institution dedicated to international dispute
resolution.
    In 1920, the League of Nations established the Permanent Court of
International Justice, also at The Hague. This court was renamed the
International Court of Justice in 1946 when the United Nations accepted
responsibility for its operations. It is often called the "World Court." This
court has 15 judges elected for nine-year terms by the United Nations
Security Council and the General Assembly voting independently. The
World Court also provides advisory opinions upon request of the six
principal organs or 15 specialized agencies of the United Nations. In
addition, any United Nations member may bring a dispute before the
Court. The Court renders its decision by majority vote. Its decisions are
final, and there is no appeal. Although the World Court has rendered a
number of decisions, including those dealing with war reparations and a
ruling that Iranian militants had violated international law by taking 52
American diplomats as hostages, its decisions have often been ignored by
the offending nation.
    There is no uniform method of enforcing these decisions of the World
Court. The United Nations General Assembly may, if the Security Council
fails to act on a threat to peace or act of aggression, recommend collective
measures, including use of armed force, to maintain or restore peace. The
United Nations itself has no permanent police force to resolve international conflicts and will send peacekeeping forces when nine members of
the Security Council decide and the disputing countries agree. If any one
of the five permanent members of the United Nations (including the
United States) votes against the proposal, it fails. Since 1948, there have
been 63 peacekeeping operations. At the time of the writing of this text,

16 were currently underway. Many peacekeeping missions focus on monitoring human rights, operating hospitals, and clearing mines.

One of the better-known examples of United Nations action occurred subsequent to the invasion of the Republic of Korea by Communist forces from North Korea. The United Nations Security Council agreed to a "police action," and 16 member nations of the United Nations countries sent armed forces to South Korea, with South Korea and the United States providing most of the supplies and troops.

11. *International Organizations*

There are thousands of international organizations. The best known is the United Nations, established in 1945 and located in New York City. The United Nations now has 192 member nations, including its original 51 member nations.

Other well-known international organizations include the Organization of American States, the oldest regional international organization in the world, composed of 35 North, Central, and South American nations, Caribbean nations, and the United States; the African Union (formerly the Organization of African Unity), an association of 53 African nations; the Council of Europe, composed of 47 members; NATO (North Atlantic Treaty Organization), an alliance of 28 countries from Europe and North America; the European Union, composed of 27 democratic European countries; and the G20 (formerly the G8), a group comprising the eight major industrial democracies (Canada, France, Germany, Italy, Japan, Russia, the United Kingdom, and the United States) and 11 emerging market economies (including China and India) as well as the European Union that meets annually to discuss major economic issues.

Links to hundreds of international and regional organizations can be found at the following two websites:

- Stanford University Library (http://www.stanford.edu/group/Jonsson/igourl.html)
- HG.org, an online legal research source (http://www.hg.org/unitednations.html#other)

E. **Municipal Research**

1. *Introduction*

Often a legal question may arise that is entirely of local concern. For example, if a client wishes to install a swimming pool in a backyard, he or she will need to know what requirements are imposed by the local jurisdiction with regard to fencing around the pool. A client who has a two-acre parcel of land may wish to maintain horses on his or her property and will need to know if this is permissible. Similarly, a client

may desire to put an addition onto a house, bringing the structure within a few inches of a neighbor's boundary line. These and other similar issues are determined by referring to the requirements imposed by the local jurisdiction or municipality rather than the code of the state. To determine the answer to such questions of local concern, you need to know how to conduct municipal or local legal research.

The following is an example of a city code section. "It shall be unlawful to sell or offer for sale any food, beverage or merchandise on any sidewalk within the central business district without obtaining a permit pursuant to section 18-547." Richmond, Va., Code § 18-546 (2006).

2. Terminology

Most municipalities operate under a document called a "charter," which sets forth the powers and activities in which the municipality may engage. A charter for a city is similar to a constitution for a state or the articles of incorporation for a corporation.

Just as your state passes statutes that are the laws for your state, municipalities also engage in lawmaking. These local laws are usually called "ordinances" and are passed by the local governing body. This may be a city council, a city council acting with a mayor, a county board of supervisors, a county executive who supervises a board, or some other local legislative body.

In smaller communities, proposed ordinances are published in the local newspaper, setting forth the text of the proposed ordinance and the time and date of the meeting scheduled to consider and vote on passage of the ordinance. If the measure is passed, its text will also be published in the local newspaper. In larger municipalities, information relating to proposed ordinances and the text of approved ordinances is usually published in a separate journal.

At both the federal and state level, after statutes are passed, they are organized into codes, that is, they are codified. This same process occurs for municipal legislation. The ordinances passed by the local legislature are organized or "codified" so that all of the zoning ordinances are together, all of the health and safety measures are brought together, all of the animal control ordinances are organized together, and so forth.

3. Municipal Research Materials

One of the most difficult tasks in performing municipal research is finding an up-to-date version of the city or county code. Often the law library in your area will maintain the codes for the surrounding municipalities. You can also check your public library, which will usually have the codes. Unfortunately, public librarians are not as familiar with updating and supplementing materials as are law librarians, and the code at the public library may be outdated.

The best place to review a code may be at the appropriate government office: city hall, city clerk's office, county counsel's office, or city attorney's office. These codes should be current and complete.

Practice Tip

Locating Municipal Codes on the Internet

Hundreds of city and county municipal codes are published for free on the Internet by various publishers and local governments. Following are some of the best sites to locate municipal codes on the Internet:

- Municipal Code Corporation (http://www.municode.com) provides codes for more than 1,600 local governments. Searching is easily accomplished: Select a state, select a locality, and search by keyword or by reviewing an index or chapter.
- The Seattle Public Library's website (http://www.spl.org/default.asp ?pageID =collection_municodes) provides links to city and county codes throughout the nation.
- eCode, offered by General Code (http://www.generalcode.com/webcode2.html), provides numerous city and county codes that are easily searched by keyword or chapter.

---

4. *Municipal Research Procedure*

Once you have found the code for your municipality, the research techniques used to locate ordinances are similar to the research techniques used to locate federal or state statutes. The most common method of locating ordinances is the descriptive word approach.

Codes are usually maintained in looseleaf binders that contain all of the municipality's ordinances organized according to topic, such as elections, business regulations, and fire protection. An index is provided at the end of the binder. You use this index to locate ordinances just as you would any other kind of index. Think of words and phrases that describe the problem you are researching, look these up in the alphabetically arranged index, and you will be directed to the appropriate ordinance. Most codes also contain the city or county charter.

5. *Interpretations of Municipal Ordinances*

Municipal codes are rarely annotated. That is, after you read the ordinance relating to the issue you are researching, you are seldom directed to cases interpreting this ordinance. Each ordinance is usually

followed only by a brief historical note indicating when the ordinance was enacted. Thus, conducting research on municipal law is very difficult. In many cases, researchers contact their local planning board or city attorney to inquire if there are any cases interpreting municipal ordinances.

Perhaps the best way to locate cases interpreting ordinances is though Lexis or Westlaw. You can Shepardize local ordinances through Lexis or update them using West's KeyCite. Alternatively, you can insert the name or number of your local ordinance into the search boxes offered by Lexis and Westlaw and you will be directed to cases that have mentioned or cited the particular provision in which you are interested. These cases may provide guidance on how the ordinance has been interpreted or construed.

Moreover, West publishes volumes titled *Ordinance Law Annotations*, which direct you to cases that interpret or apply ordinances. This set is arranged by topic (taxation, traffic, vagrancy) and will provide digests or brief summaries of all cases that have interpreted ordinances relating to these topics. Thus, if you were to look for ordinances relating to pawnbrokers, you would be directed to cases from a variety of jurisdictions that have interpreted ordinances dealing with this topic.

Practice Tip

Conducting Municipal Research on the Internet

Researching local law on the Internet may well be just as complete and current as performing this research using conventional print volumes. Because the print volumes containing local ordinances are rarely annotated (meaning they seldom direct you to cases), reviewing the local ordinances on the Internet may offer the same information as that which can be found in a law library.

F. Rules of Procedure and Court Rules

1. Introduction

As you know, there is an explosion of litigation in this country. If litigants could file their pleadings with courts whenever they liked and in any format they liked, on any type of paper they liked, the backlog in cases would be even more severe than it presently is. To promote efficient operation, courts are usually empowered to enact certain rules relating to various procedures and administrative matters, such as the correct size of paper to be used, when papers must be filed, and the format of papers presented to the court. In addition to rules relating to such procedural matters, there are rules of evidence, rules of appellate procedure, and rules of criminal procedure.

There are several sets of rules of procedure that might be binding in a jurisdiction. For example, all federal district courts follow the Federal Rules of Civil Procedure (FRCP), which contain rules on pleadings, motions, discovery, and civil trials. In addition, the district courts may make their own rules governing practice in their courts. Thus, the United States District Court for New Hampshire follows the FRCP and also has its own "local rules" relating to the maximum length of memoranda submitted to the court.

Similarly, nearly all states have modeled their own civil procedural rules after the FRCP, and in addition have local or court rules governing practice before the courts. For simplicity, this discussion will refer to the more significant rules (such as the FRCP) as *rules of procedure* and the more local rules, which generally govern less significant matters (for example, the format of documents), as *court rules*.

Courts usually insist on strict compliance with all of their rules and will refuse to accept pleadings submitted that are not in conformance with these rules promulgated for the orderly administration of justice.

2. *Federal Rules of Procedure*

The Federal Rules of Civil Procedure (FRCP) became effective in 1938 and govern the conduct of all litigation in the United States District Courts. Many states have patterned their own state rules on the FRCP. Thus, there is often a great deal of uniformity between the FRCP and rules adopted by the various states. The FRCP govern all trial-related matters from the commencement of an action, through the pleadings allowed, to motions and discovery practice, to the trial itself. Appellate practice in the federal courts of appeal is governed by the Federal Rules of Appellate Procedure. Finally, the United States Supreme Court has its own set of rules, composed of more than 50 pages of materials relating to matters such as the time allowed for oral argument, the necessity of a table of contents for briefs in excess of five pages, and the required color for the covers of briefs submitted to the Court (for example, white for petitions for writs of certiorari and yellow for reply briefs).

The rules of civil procedure for federal courts are set forth both in U.S.C.A. and U.S.C.S. In U.S.C.A., the Federal Rules of Civil Procedure are located in volumes following the statutes in Title 28, and the Federal Rules of Criminal Procedure are located in volumes following the statutes in Title 18. In U.S.C.S., there are separate unnumbered volumes, following Title 50, for the Federal Rules of Civil Procedure, the Federal Rules of Evidence, the Federal Rules of Appellate Procedure, and the Federal Rules of Criminal Procedure. After you read the pertinent rule, you will be directed to relevant cases through the use of annotations.

You can locate a pertinent rule by any of the standard research techniques used for locating statutes: the descriptive word approach, the topic approach, or the popular name approach. Once you have located the rule in which you are interested, you can examine the historical notes,

library references, and then the annotations after the rule. The annotations will direct you to cases interpreting or construing the rule. Moreover, West's set titled *Federal Rules Decisions*, discussed in Chapter 4, focuses on United States District Court cases that have interpreted the Federal Rules of Civil Procedure or Federal Rules of Criminal Procedure. Articles commenting on the federal rules are also included.

All of the major federal rules (the Federal Rules of Civil Procedure, Federal Rules of Criminal Procedure, Federal Rules of Appellate Procedure, and Federal Rules of Evidence) are available on the Internet at http://www.uscourts.gov/rules/newrules4.html. Additionally, commentary and background information on proposed rules are provided together with the text of proposed amendments.

Don't forget to Shepardize the federal rules. Use *Shepard's Federal Statutes Citations* to locate cases, articles, and annotations that have mentioned or interpreted the federal rules.

For ready and convenient access to applicable rules, many attorneys and paralegals rely on deskbooks, one-volume paperbacks that contain a complete set of the federal rules (although they do not include annotations to direct you to cases). The deskbooks are replaced every year to ensure their currency.

Several sets of books are useful in interpreting the federal rules, such as *Federal Rules Service, 3d*, which includes the text of the federal rules and will direct you to cases interpreting the rules. Perhaps the two best-known secondary sources for interpreting and analyzing federal rules are the following treatises:

- *Moore's Federal Practice*, a 33-volume set including the full text of the federal rules together with extensive commentary and analysis; and
- *Federal Practice and Procedure* by Charles Alan Wright and Arthur R. Miller (often referred to as "Wright and Miller"), a 67-volume set of books with full coverage and analysis of all aspects of federal civil, criminal, and appellate procedure, as well as relevant forms.

Forms for use in connection with litigation in the federal courts can be found in *Federal Procedural Forms*, a multivolume set that provides step-by-step assistance in drafting forms (such as complaints, answers, motions for new trials, and so forth) for proceedings before federal courts and agencies. Checklists, "how to" guides, and other information make this an invaluable resource. An alternative source for forms is *Bender's Federal Practice Forms*, a multivolume set including a comprehensive range of litigation forms needed by those who practice in federal court.

3. *Federal Rules of Court*

In addition to the significant and substantive federal procedural rules that govern practice in our nation's federal courts, the lower federal courts themselves are free to enact their own more local rules of court.

That is, each of the 94 federal district courts and the 13 circuit courts has rules specific just to that court. Often these rules are administrative and relate to matters such as the maximum length of a brief or citation form. Other rules are more substantive and might impose a duty upon counsel to meet and confer regarding disputed issues or to attend a status conference or settlement conference. No matter what the nature of the rule and no matter how insignificant it may seem to you, the court will expect and demand strict compliance with its rules.

With 94 district courts and 13 circuits, determining the specific rules for each court can be a daunting task. One excellent source you should consult is *Federal Rules Service, 3d* (mentioned above), which arranges all the rules alphabetically by state.

All of the "local" court rules of the lower federal courts are now available on the Internet at http://www.uscourts.gov/rules/newrules8 .html. Simply point and click on the particular lower federal court in which you are interested and you will be immediately linked to its local rules. Finally, *Bluebook* Bluepages Table BT.2 and *ALWD* Appendix 2 now reference some local rules and manuals that provide guidance on local citation practices.

Practice Tip

Interpreting Federal Rules

Use the Shepard's set *Federal Rules Citations* to direct you to federal and state cases, law review articles, and A.L.R. annotations that interpret or mention federal rules (whether they are the Federal Rules of Civil Procedure, Federal Rules of Criminal Procedure, Federal Rules of Appellate Procedure, or Federal Rules of Evidence). You will also be directed to cases and sources interpreting the rules of the Supreme Court and the local rules of the lower federal courts.

---

4. State Rules of Procedure and Court Rules

To promote efficiency in litigation, states have also adopted rules of procedure and rules of court.

Many states have modeled their rules of civil procedure after the Federal Rules of Civil Procedure. These rules are often published together with the state's statutes. For example, in California, the Civil Procedure statutes follow the Civil Code and precede the Commercial Code. You will be provided with historical notes, library references, and annotations, just as for other state statutes. Additionally, many states now publish their rules on their websites. See Table T.1 of *The Bluebook* for each state's judicial website.

In addition to these rules governing statewide practice, courts within the state may also issue specific or local rules governing practice before those courts. These local rules tend to be more administrative than substantive and often address such matters as the size and weight of papers accepted by the court, what time the clerk's office closes, whether pleadings are accepted by facsimile transmission or electronically, and the format of citations. Failure to follow the local rules regarding even such minor matters as the type of paper to be used may result in rejection of documents and pleadings. If your pleading is rejected for nonconformance with local rules and the time limit for filing the pleading expires before you can submit an acceptable pleading, the client's rights may be jeopardized, and your firm may be subjected to a claim of professional negligence.

To obtain a copy of the local rules, contact the clerk of the court and arrange to purchase a set of the rules. The fee for obtaining local rules is usually nominal. Changes in local rules are often announced and published in your local legal newsletter or other publication. To ensure you are using a current set of rules, call the court clerk on a periodic basis to inquire if there have been any amendments or revisions to the rules since the time you obtained your set. Alternatively, access MegaLaw at http:// www.megalaw.com/rules.php, which will link you to many local court rules for each state. Review *Bluebook* Bluepages Table BT.2 and *ALWD* Appendix 2 for references to local rules on citation form.

G. Citation Form

1. Legislative Materials (*Bluebook*):
    Bill: H.R. 1026, 106th Cong. (1999).
    Committee Hearing: *Child Care Costs: Hearings on H.R. 1249 Before the H. Comm. on Educ. & Labor*, 105th Cong. 94-96 (1998) (statement of Rep. Lamar Smith).
    Committee Report: H.R. Rep. No. 94-506, at 6 (1987), *reprinted in* 1987 U.S.C.C.A.N. 109, 114.

    Legislative Materials (*ALWD*):
    Bill: H.R. 1026, 106th Cong. (Jan. 14, 1999).
    Committee Hearing: H.R. Comm. on Educ. & Lab., *Child Care Costs: Hearings on H.R. 1249*, 105th Cong. 94-96 (July 15, 1998).
    Committee Report: H.R. Rpt. 94-506 at 6 (Feb. 12, 1987).

2. Presidential Materials (*Bluebook*):
    Proclamation No. 6361, 3 C.F.R. 906 (1999), *reprinted in* 3 U.S.C. § 469 (2000).
    Exec. Order No. 7125, 3 C.F.R. 477 (1981-1985), *reprinted in* 3 U.S.C. § 297 (2000).

President's Message to Congress Transmitting Nominations, 16
  Weekly Comp. Pres. Doc. 768 (Feb. 26, 1989).
Presidential Materials (*ALWD*):
Exec. Procl. 6361, 3 C.F.R. 906 (1999).
Exec. Or. 7125, 3 C.F.R. 477 (1981).
George Bush, *Message to Congress Transmitting Nominations*,
  16 Wkly. Comp. Pres. Docs. 768 (Feb. 26, 1989).

3. Administrative Materials (*Bluebook*):
Water Pollution Standards, 47 Fed. Reg. 8076 (proposed Mar. 13,
  2004) (to be codified at 38 C.F.R. pt. 47).
25 C.F.R. § 1592 (2009)

Administrative materials (*ALWD*):
Water Pollution Stands., 47 Fed. Reg. 8076 (proposed Mar. 13,
  2004) (to be codified at 38 C.F.R. pt. 47).
25 C.F.R. § 1592 (2009).

4. International Materials (*Bluebook*):
Convention on Nuclear Proliferation, U.S. — Can., art. 14, Oct.
  18, 1989, 46 U.S.T. 107, 119.
International Materials (*ALWD*):
Convention on Nuclear Proliferation art. 14 (Oct. 18, 1989), 46
  U.S.T. 107, 119.

5. Local and Municipal Materials (*Bluebook*):
Seattle, Wash., Mun. Code § 9.12.010 (2005).
San Jose, Cal., Code ch. 7.11 (2006).

Local and Municipal Materials (*ALWD*):
Seattle Mun. Code (Wash.) § 9.12.010 (2005).
San Jose City Code (Cal.) ch. 7.11 (2006).

6. Court Rules (*Bluebook* and *ALWD*):
Fed. R. Civ. P. 12(b).
Cal. Sup. Ct. R. 56.
Sup. Ct. R. 21.

CyberSites

http://www.gpoaccess .gov/index.html	GPO Access, offering access to C.F.R., the *Federal Register*, public laws, the *United States Government Manual*, the *Daily Compilation of Presidential Documents*, United States Congress information, and treaty information

(continued)

CyberSites *(Continued)*

http://www.fdsys.gov	GPO Access is migrating to the federal government's new advanced digital system, FDsys, which provides access to authenticated documents from all branches of the U.S. government.
http://www.federalregister.gov	Newly launched website making federal rules and regulations easy to locate
http://www.senate.gov	Website of the United States Senate
http://www.house.gov	Website of United States House of Representatives
http://www.whitehouse.gov	Website of White House
http://thomas.loc.gov	THOMAS, offering text of bills, public laws, committee information, the *Congressional Record*, treaty information, and other information about the United States Congress
http://library.kentlaw.edu/ Courses/tutorials/Leghist %20Tutorial/Intro.htm	Excellent information about legislative histories with links to relevant materials
http://www.llsdc.org/ Fed-Leg-Hist	Guide to federal legislative history research
http://www.fas.org/sgp/crs/ 98-461.pdf	Guide to tracking current federal legislation and regulations
http://legintent.com	Website of Legislative Intent Service, which provides federal and state legislative histories for a fee
http://www.statenet.com	Website of State Net, a commercial service that provides monitoring and information about federal and state legislation
http://bnaplus.bna.com	Website of BNA Plus, which retrieves documents for a fee
http://www.washlaw.edu/ doclaw/executive5m.html	Washburn School of Law provides direct links to most executive and independent agencies
http://www.gpoaccess.gov/ecfr	GPO Access offers a method for locating updated C.F.R. provisions. Select a title of the C.F.R. and press "Go."
http://www.regulations.gov	Regulations.gov affords easy access to proposed and final rules and regulations from nearly 300 federal agencies.

(continued)

CyberSites *(Continued)* ▆▆▆▆▆▆▆▆▆▆▆▆▆▆▆▆▆▆

http://www.un.org	Website of United Nations, offering text of some treaties, glossary of treaty terms, and links to other information and sites related to international law
http://www.lib.uchicago.edu/ ~llou/forintlaw.html	Primer on conducting international law research on the Internet with links to treaties and websites of major international organizations
http://www.gpoaccess.gov/ serialset//index.html	Select "Congressional Documents" to obtain text of treaties
http://www.state.gov/s/l/	The Office of the Legal Adviser of the State Department provides links to treaty actions and the current edition of *Treaties in Force.*
http://thomas.loc.gov/home/ treaties/treaties.htm	THOMAS provides treaty status information beginning with the 90th Congress. Search by treaty number, type of treaty, or keyword.
http://www.glin.gov	The Global Legal Information Network (provided by the Library of Congress) is a public database of the official texts of laws, regulations, and cases from more than 50 countries.
http://www.municode.com	Site of Municipal Code Corporation, providing text of many municipal codes
http://www.uscourts.gov	Site offering direct links to federal circuit and district courts

Table T.1 of *The Bluebook* provides each state's judicial website, and Bluepages Table BT.2 and *ALWD* Appendix 2 provide references to local citation rules.

Writing Strategies

When writing about the "special" research projects discussed in this chapter, use the following techniques:

Legislative History: To lend credibility to your legislative history results, always use full titles. Refer to *Senator* Richard Lugar, not Dick Lugar. Refer to "the United States Senate Committee on Labor" rather than "the Committee."

Administrative Law: In discussing agency decisions, omit personal pronouns. Do not discuss an agency decision by saying, "he decided . . . ." Instead, state that "the National Labor Relations Board decided . . . ."

International Law: Because treaties are usually cited by their names and those names are often lengthy, unclutter your writing by giving the full name of the treaty only once and then giving it a short descriptive title by saying "hereinafter 'Nuclear Waste Treaty.'"

Municipal Law: Do not use personal pronouns in discussing the entity that enacted municipal legislation. Do not say "*our* ordinance provides . . . ." but rather say "County of Fairfax ordinance 12,345 provides . . . ." or "the relevant City ordinance states . . . ."

Assignment for Chapter 10

LEGISLATIVE HISTORY

1. Use the CIS Index for 2008.
    a. What public law relates to pediatric cancer research programs?
    b. Locate the CIS "Legislative History" volume for this public law.
        (i)   When was it approved?
        (ii)   What was its designation in the House?
        (iii) On which days did debate occur in the House and in the Senate?
2. Use the CIS Index for 2008.
    a. For which piece of legislation did Theresa V. Kough testify?
    b. Review the CIS Abstracts volume for 2008. On what day did Ms. Kough testify?
    c. Who is Ms. Kough?
3. Use *United States Code Congressional and Administrative News*.
    a. To which topic or act does Public Law 111-97 relate?
    b. Use Table 4 for the 111th Congress. Locate the following information relating to this Act.
        (i)   When was this Act approved?
        (ii)   What was its number in the Senate?
        (iii) Give the date on which the Act was passed by the Senate.
        (iv)   Give the date on which the Act was passed by the House.
4. Review the legislative history in *United States Code Congressional and Administrative News* for the Public Law identified in Question 3.
    a. According to Senate Report 111-46, page 3, what is the purpose of Section 2 of the Act?
    b. Review page 6 of the Senate Report. Would enactment of the bill have any effect on the federal budget?
    c. Which volume of the *Congressional Record* includes debates and information relating to this legislation?

ADMINISTRATIVE LAW AND PRESIDENTIAL DOCUMENTS

5. Use the most recent C.F.R. Index.
    a. Which C.F.R. title and part deal with labeling and advertising of wine?

b. Which C.F.T. title and part deal with nuts, specifically, tree nut and peanut products?
   (i) Review this provision and its subparts. If the percentage of Spanish peanuts in mixed nuts is 55%, what must the statement say?
   (ii) Briefly, what is peanut butter?

6. Use the Topic Index (Wages — Hours) for *CCH Labor Law Reporter*.
   a. Which paragraph provides definitions under the Family and Medical Leave Act?
   b. Review this paragraph. What does the term "parent" mean?
   c. Use the Table of Cases in *CCH Labor Law Reporter* (Wages — Hours). Give the citation for the case *Baker v. Dataphase Inc.*

7. Review the case located at 2204-2005 CCH NLRB ¶ 16,694.
   a. What is the name of the case?
   b. Were graduate teaching assistants admitted into the university but not hired by the university who were teaching as part of their academic development held to be "statutory employees" within the meaning of the National Labor Relations Act?

8. Use *Weekly Compilation of Presidential Documents* for the week ending Friday, February 4, 2005.
   a. Who was sworn in as Secretary of Education?
   b. What was the topic of the president's address to the nation on January 30, 2005?
   c. When was the State of the Union address given?
   d. What basketball team was welcomed to the White House?

INTERNATIONAL LAW

9. Use the Cumulative Index, Volume 42, for volumes 2251-2300 for the *United Nations Treaty Series*. Find the agreement between the United States and Madagascar relating to the establishment of a Peace Corps Program in Madagascar. When and where was the agreement signed?

10. Use the Cumulative Index, Volume 41, for volumes 2201-2250 for the *United Nations Treaty Series* and find the agreement between Australia and the United States for the enforcement of maintenance (support) obligations.
   a. Give the citation to this agreement.
   b. When and where was the agreement signed?
   c. Who signed the agreement for each party?
   d. How may the agreement be terminated?
   e. When was it registered with the United Nations?

11. Use Whiteman's *Digest of International Law*.
   a. What volume and page discuss the definition of deportation?
   b. Review this page. Give the definition of deportation.

12. Use Moore's *A Digest of International Law*.
    a. If an incident occurs within two nautical miles from shore, has it occurred on the "high seas"? Give your answer and cite the section of the *Digest* that governs your answer.
    b. Use the "List of Cases Cited" in the Index to the *Digest*. To which topic does the case *La Ninfa* relate?
13. Use Hackworth's *Digest of International Law*. Is the government or War Department liable for injury to a prisoner of war? Give your answer and cite the section of the *Digest* that governs your answer.
14. Use *U.S. Treaties and Other International Agreements*.
    a. What is the general subject matter of 35 U.S.T. 5616 (T.I.A.S. 11016)?
    b. How was this agreement effected?
    c. When did this agreement enter into force?

Internet Assignment for Chapter 10

1. Access the website for THOMAS. Locate House bill 1495 introduced in the 110th Congress. Review "Bill Summary and Status." Give the Public Law number for this legislation.
2. Access the website for either GPO Access or FDsys. What is the subject matter of February 1, 2010, Presidential Proclamation No. 8477?
3. Access the website for either GPO Access or FDsys. Locate the *Federal Register* for Wednesday, May 26, 2010 (volume 75, issue 101).
   a. What Federal Aviation Administration rule was published?
   b. Review this rule. Where will this rule be published in C.F.R.?
4. Access the most recent issue of the *U.S. Government Manual* on either GPO Access or FDsys. Select "executive materials" and review information about the U.S. Department of Agriculture.
   a. When was the Department created?
   b. Review its organizational chart. To whom does the Director of Communications report?
5. Access the website for either GPO Access or FDsys. Review 29 C.F.R. § 570.35. Generally, may a 16-year old work 20 hours during the week when school is in session? Answer the question and cite the provision that governs your answer.
6. Access the State Department's Treaty Affairs Office at http://www.state.gov/s/l/treaty. Select "Treaties in Force" and review the treaties in force in 2010. Locate the information relating to the "Agreement on the Conservation of Polar Bears."

     a.   Identify the parties to this agreement.

     b.   What is the agreement's citation in *U.S. Treaties*?

7. Access the website for the United Nations. Select "Member Countries." When did Chile, Latvia, and the United States each become a member of the United Nations?

8. Access the website MuniCode at http://www.municode.com and select "Municode Library." Locate the Seattle, Washington, municipal code and review the health and safety provisions. If a client operates a facility that is open to the public between the hours of 10:00 p.m. and 6:00 a.m. and which serves liquor and has a maximum capacity of 150 people, is such a "nightclub" within the meaning of the code? Answer the question and cite the provision that governs your answer.

9. Locate the rules for the U.S. Supreme Court. How many copies of a petition for writ of certiorari are required to be filed by a petitioner? What fee must be paid? Answer the questions and cite the rules that govern your answer.

The Digital Library: Lexis, Westlaw, and Nonprint Research Sources

Technology is so much fun but we can drown in our technology. The fog of information can drive out knowledge.

Daniel J. Boorstin, Librarian of Congress, 1983

A. **Introduction to Computer-Assisted Legal Research**
B. **Lexis**
C. **Westlaw**
D. **Final Pointers on Computer-Assisted Legal Research**
E. **Other Competitors in Commercial Electronic Research**
F. **Nonprint Research Tools**
G. **Citation Form**

Chapter Overview

Legal research can be accomplished by means other than using the conventional sources of bound books and journals. There are several newer technologies that allow you to conduct research efficiently and accurately. This chapter introduces you to the digital library, primarily computer-assisted legal research. Legal research using the Internet is discussed in Chapter 12. Being a competent researcher requires use and familiarity with all media, including traditional print courses, computer systems, and the Internet to find the best answer to a legal question in the most efficient manner and at the lowest cost to the client.

A. Introduction to Computer-Assisted Legal Research

1. *Lexis and Westlaw*

There are two major competing computer-assisted research services: LexisNexis (for simplicity, referred to as "Lexis" in this chapter and also commonly known as such in practice) and Westlaw. These research systems provide access to a tremendous variety of cases, statutes, administrative regulations, and numerous other authorities that a law firm or other employer may not otherwise be able to afford. The more familiar you become with Lexis or Westlaw, the more efficient you will be at locating the information you need. Lexis and Westlaw operate in essentially the same manner; most users, however, eventually develop a preference for one or the other. Because both services contain substantially the same materials, it is impossible to declare that one service is superior to the other. The one that is "best" is the one that is best for you.

Each service consists of thousands of databases. The databases include cases, statutes, administrative regulations, hundreds of secondary sources, and other materials for you to access. In general, research using Lexis and Westlaw is highly similar. Both allow easy retrieval of cases, statutes, and other materials when you already have a citation. You merely type the citation into an open field and click on "Go" or a similar button. When you do not have a citation, you will usually access the appropriate database (such as selecting federal cases or Ohio cases) and then formulate a search question by using *Boolean searching* (a search method using symbols, word fragments, and numbers, rather than plain English) or by using plain English, usually called "natural language."

It is important to have a basic understanding of the two computerized legal research systems; however, the best way to learn how to perform computerized legal research is to do it. There is no substitute for "hands-on" experience. Lexis and Westlaw both offer training courses and written materials describing their systems. Often a complete tutorial package is available, consisting of written descriptions of the systems as well as CD-ROMs to demonstrate use of the system. Contact:

LexisNexis	**West, A Thomson Reuters Business**
9443 Springboro Pike	610 Opperman Drive
Dayton, OH 43442	Eagan, MN 55123
24-hour toll-free customer service:	24-hour toll-free customer service:
1 (800) 543-6862	1 (800) WESTLAW
http://www.lexisnexis.com/support/training	http://www.west.thomson.com

---

Ethics Alert

Computer Literacy

Legal professionals are ethically bound to provide competent representation to clients. This duty is broad enough to require that you be sufficiently familiar with conventional *and* electronic research techniques such that you can make an accurate determination as to which sources will yield the best results at the lowest cost for the client. Neither conventional research nor computer-assisted legal research should be used exclusively. Effective researchers use a combination of the two methods and employ selectivity to determine which method is best for a given task.

---

2. Getting Started Using Lexis or Westlaw

Getting started usually requires you to sign on to Lexis or Westlaw with your identification number and password assigned to you by your school or employer. When performing research on the job, you will usually enter a client name or number so that the client can be billed for the time spent conducting the research. In most firms, legal professionals have desktop computer access to Lexis, Westlaw, or both.

The first screen presented to you after sign-on usually allows you to retrieve a document or case (if you know the citation), check a citation (through either *Shepard's Citations* or KeyCite), or construct a search if you do not have a citation.

3. Boolean Searching

You probably know that computers are extremely literal. They will not search for cases containing the word "collision" if you search for "collide." Thus, a method called Boolean searching allows you to use words, symbols, numbers, and connectors (collectively, often called Terms and Connectors) to overcome the literalness of the computer. For example, Lexis and Westlaw both use an exclamation point (!) to substitute for any number of additional letters at the end of a word. Thus "colli!" will locate "collide," "collision," "colliding," and so forth. Of course, words such as "collie" will also be located, so use the symbols carefully. Both Lexis and Westlaw also offer publications that explain the use of their search symbols, numbers, and connectors. See Figure 11-9 at the end of this chapter for a chart of Lexis and Westlaw Terms and Connectors.

These symbols and connectors help you narrow your search and make it more manageable. If you merely entered "first amendment," Lexis and Westlaw would retrieve thousands of documents containing

this phrase. A more effective search would be "first amendment /50 free! and press": This instructs Lexis and Westlaw to locate only those documents that contain the phrase "first amendment" within 50 words of the words "freedom" or "free" and "press." (Of course, documents including words such as "frees," "freely," and so forth will also be located if those terms are found within 50 words of "first amendment.")

4. *Plain English Searching*

Recognizing that many individuals find working with Boolean connectors awkward, both Lexis and Westlaw offer "Natural Language" searching to allow you to enter your issue in plain English or natural language and eliminate the need for symbols, numbers, and connectors. Thus, you could enter in a search question such as "May unmarried or single individuals adopt children?"

Construct your searches before you sign on so that you work efficiently and do not incur excessive costs. Draft some sample queries and search terms. Although using natural language is easier when constructing queries, Boolean searching usually produces more precise results.

———— Practice Tip ————

Boolean or Plain English Searching? Westlaw's Suggestions

Use Boolean searching when:

- **You are searching for particular terms;**
- **You are searching for a particular document; or**
- **You are searching for all documents containing specific information, such as all cases classified under a particular topic name and key number.**

Use plain English or natural language searching when:

- **You are researching broad concepts; or**
- **You are a new or infrequent computer user, or you are unfamiliar with Boolean Terms and Connectors.**

B. Lexis

1. *Getting Started*

Lexis's database consists of a series of *sources* (sometimes called *libraries*) — materials relating to particular areas of law, such as the source titled "GENFED," which contains cases, statutes, and materials

relating to federal legal topics. Within each source are *files*. For example, the GENFED source contains separate "files" for cases from the United States Supreme Court, cases from the United States Courts of Appeal, and other federal materials. In fact, Lexis provides more than 40,000 sources, including cases, statutes, forms, treatises, the Restatements, encyclopedias, dictionaries, jury instructions, and much more. For a searchable directory of Lexis's sources, access the following site: http://w3.nexis.com/sources.

After you log on at http://www.lexis.com, the first screen provides various research options at the top of your screen, including the following:

- **Search.** The "Search" tab at the top of your screen is divided into four subtabs:
  - Search "by Source" is a frequently used starting point and allows you to select a source you want to search (for example, federal cases or state cases) before you enter your search terms. In most instances, when you first access Lexis, this "by Source" screen is pre-selected for you as your starting point. (See Figure 11-1.)
  - Search "by Topic or Headnote" allows you to select the topic you wish to research (for example, "Education") and then customize the sources and jurisdictions in which to conduct your research or elect to view all headnotes relating to a particular topic.
  - Search "by Guided Search Form" lists several broad categories (for example, "States Legal" and "Law Reviews"). When you select a category, you will then be given a search box and a guided form that has several recommended sources already identified for you.
  - Search "by Dot Command" should be used when you know the Lexis library and file name of the source you wish to research (for example, "GENFED").
- **Research Tasks.** Selecting the "Research Tasks" tab identifies more than 20 practice areas (for example, Bankruptcy and Patents). When you select an area of the law, for example, "Patents," you will then be provided a list of patent materials such as treatises, cases, news, and legal developments within which to search further. (See Figure 11-2.)
- **Get a Document.** Use the "Get a Document" tab when you know the citation to a case, statute, law review, or other authority. Type your citation in the open field (for example, 14 p3d 890) and click "Get." You need not use correct citation form.
- *Shepard's.* Use this feature to Shepardize your authorities (primarily, to ensure your primary authorities are still good law). (See Figure 11-1.)

Figure 11-1
Lexis "Search by Source" Screen

2.   *Constructing a Search*

There are three ways to search for materials on Lexis if you do not have a citation: the traditional search using Boolean connectors, the newer plain English search method called "Natural Language" (formerly called "Freestyle"), or Lexis's new Easy Search, a search method similar to popular Internet searching.

a. Boolean Searching

Most experts agree that Boolean searching provides more targeted results than plain English searching. Following are some tips for constructing a search query using Terms and Connectors on Lexis:

- **Lowercase Letters.** Lexis is not sensitive to capital letters (unless you specify such in your search request). Thus, for basic searching, use lowercase letters.
- **Singulars, Possessives, and Plurals.** Forms of singular, possessives, and plurals are automatically found if they are regular forms. Thus, a search for "tenant" will produce results for "tenants" and "tenant's" but a search for "foot" will not find "feet."
- **Universal Symbols.** Lexis offers some *universal symbols* or "wildcards" to help you expand your search:
  - An *asterisk* (*) replaces single letters within words. Thus, "m*n" will find "man" or "men."
  - An *exclamation point* (!) replaces any ending to a word. Thus, "sec!" finds "security," "securities," "secure," and so forth.
- **Connectors.** *Connectors* help you locate needed documents and narrow your search. Following are the most commonly used connectors:
  - **Or.** A search for "teacher or student" will locate documents containing either or both of these words.
  - **And.** A search for "negligence and doctor" will locate documents only if they contain both these terms.
  - **w/n.** The connector "w/n" instructs Lexis to find documents that contain words appearing within a specified number (n) of words of each other. Thus, a search for "tenant w/50 evict" locates documents in which the words "tenant" and "evict" appear within 50 words of each other.
  - **w/s and w/p.** The connector "w/s" finds words in the same sentence and "w/p" finds words in the same paragraph. Thus, a search for "alter w/s ego" (or "alter w/p ego") locates documents in which the words "alter" and "ego" appear in the same sentence or paragraph, respectively.

Lexis offers other connectors as well; they are described in any of Lexis's marketing material and on its website at http://web.lexis.com/help/research/gh_search.asp#TermsConnectors. Multiple connectors may be used in one search request. (See Figure 11-9 at the end of this chapter.)

Constructing a proper search is the most important part of computerized legal research and requires thought and planning. Draft your search query before you sign on and begin incurring charges.

If your search does not produce sufficient results (or perhaps produces too many documents), you may modify your search. Simply select "Edit Search."

Figure 11-2
Lexis "Research Tasks" Screen

b. Plain English Searching

Because many individuals find working with terms and connectors awkward, Lexis allows you to use plain English through its Natural Language feature. First, you must select a Source (such as federal cases). Type your words or phrases into the open field. For example, you could type, "What is the term of a design patent" and select the open circle marked "Natural Language." Click "Search" and modify as needed. Use the "Suggest Terms" tab to see a list of words that can be included in your search.

c. Easy Search

Lexis's new service, *Easy Search*, is a quick search method, which is used similarly to Internet search engines such as Google. Users simply enter their search terms in the open search box without using either Terms and Connectors or Natural Language.

To use this service, click on the "Search" tab, then choose a legal source (for example, federal cases) from the menu, and then select "Easy Search." Type your search terms in the open field and click "Search." Just as you search using Google or another Internet search engine, you may search by phrase ("business judgment rule"), citation (520 us 10) or other relevant terms. As they are by Google, results are ranked by their relevance. (See Figure 11-3.)

Figure 11-3
Lexis Easy Search Screen

d. Display of Search Results

If your search produces numerous documents, you can weed out irrelevant ones by using the following techniques when reviewing your search results:

- **KWIC.** Use the command "KWIC" to highlight your search terms and the 25 words on either side of your search terms so you can review at a glance the portion of the case or document of most interest to you.
- **FULL.** Select "Full" to display the full text of the document containing your search terms.
- **CITE.** When you select "Cite," Lexis displays the citations to documents containing your search terms, together with a list of core terms and often an overview of the case.

Once the search results are on screen, you may move back and forth between documents. (See Figure 11-4.)

Figure 11-4
Viewing Lexis Results

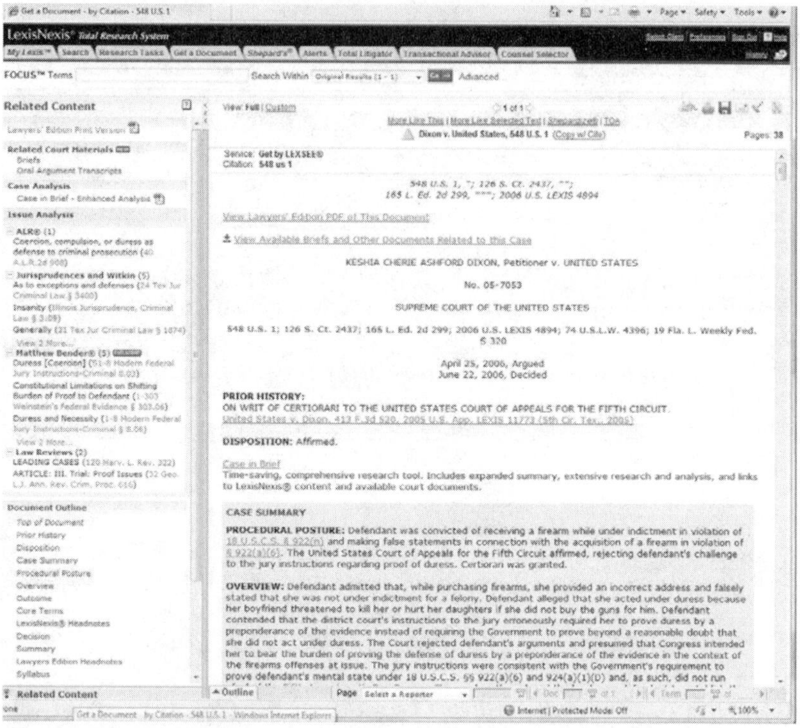

3. *Specialized Searches*

a. Searching for Statutes and Constitutions

- **By Citation.** If you know the precise citation for a federal or state statute or constitution, click the "Get a Document" tab. Type your citation (such as 35 uscs 101) in the open field and click "Get." After reviewing the statute, you can browse through preceding and consecutive sections. You can also review the case annotations following your citation, just as you would in the print version of U.S.C.S.
- **By Topic.** When you do not know a statute or constitutional citation, you must select a library or source (such as "States — Legal" and then "Ohio Statutes"). Construct your search using terms and connectors or Natural Language, as described previously.

b. Searching for Cases

- **By Citation.** If you know a case citation, use the "Get a Document" feature and type your citation (such as 430 us 112 or 222 s ct 1) in the open field. Lexis includes star paging to inform you of

the page number you would be on if you were reading the case in the other parallel sets. A new feature offered by Lexis is a display of some cases on Lexis's screen exactly the way they appear in the official reports. When a case is displayed on the screen, look for the "View Official Reports PDF of this Document" link to view your case in print reporter format.

- **By Party Name.** If you know a plaintiff's or defendant's name, click the "Get a Document" tab and then the "Get by Party Name" tab. Type the party's name in the open field and select "Search."
- **By Segment.** Lexis allows you to search by naturally occurring segments of a case, including the names of the parties, the court deciding the case, the judge, or counsel. After you select a source (such as federal cases), use the drop-down menu to select terms such as "dissent" or "court" to narrow your research. Segment searching is only available when you search by using Terms and Connectors or Natural Language; it is not available if you use Easy Search.
- **By Topic.** When you do not have a citation, use one of the four Search tabs discussed previously.
- **Review by Case Summary.** Lexis's "Case Summary" feature provides a brief snapshot of a case in an easy-to-read format that includes a case summary, headnotes, list of core terms from the case, and other helpful features, given before the full opinion.

c. Searching for Administrative and Legislative Materials

- **By Citation.** If you know the citation to a C.F.R. provision, the *Federal Register*, or a public law number, use the "Get a Document" feature and type your citation (for example, 29 cfr 100.602).
- **By Topic.** If you do not have a citation, select "Search by Source" at the top of your screen and then select the source you desire (for example, "CFR"). Type your Terms or Connectors or use Natural Language in the open field and select "Search." You may also use Easy Search for many administrative materials.
- **Legislative History.** Lexis offers several compiled legislative histories. Select "Legal," then "Federal Legal — U.S.," and then "Legislative History Materials."

d. Searching for Law Reviews and Journals

- **By Citation.** Use the "Get a Document" feature if you know the citation to a law review or journal article.
- **By Topic.** When you do not have a citation, use the "Search by Guided Search Form" tab. Select "Law Reviews" and enter your search terms.

- **By Law Reviews.** Select the "Search by Source" tab at the top of the toolbar and then select "Law Reviews & Journals" and type your key terms in the open field. Click "Search." Alternatively, you may select specific journals in which to conduct your research.

e. Searching for Secondary Authorities

You may search for secondary authorities by selecting the tab "Search by Source" from the toolbar and then clicking on "Secondary Legal," and then selecting the specific secondary source desired, such as "Restatements" or "Area of Law Treatises." Alternatively, you may select the tab "Research Tasks" at the top of the toolbar, and then select a desired area of law (for example, Bankruptcy or Insurance) to be directed to a list of selected sources.

4. *Shepardizing*

As discussed in Chapter 9, Lexis makes it easy to verify that your cases, statutes, and other primary authorities are still valid. To do so, you may click the Shepard's tab, type your citation in the open field, and click "Check." Alternatively, when you are viewing a case or statute on the screen, watch for the "signal indicators" on the screen. For example, a red stop sign is a warning that your case has been subject to some negative treatment (such as being reversed). A yellow triangle indicates caution, meaning that your case has been criticized or limited.

5. *Other Lexis Features*

Lexis offers numerous features to make your research efficient and accurate.

- **Hyperlinking.** As you read a case, statute, or other authority on the screen, references to other cases or authorities are hyperlinked, allowing you to jump to these other documents by merely placing your cursor on the item displayed.
- **Case in Brief.** This new tool provides a comprehensive research report for case law. When you access a new, significant, or high-profile case, select "Case in Brief" and you will be linked to comprehensive materials about the case, including a bulleted list of its holdings, a summary of the parties' arguments, and links to news articles and other commentary about the case.
- **Total Litigator.** Lexis's new Total Litigator feature offers a wealth of tools for litigation, including tips on creating a discovery plan, help for drafting documents, links to court briefs and court rules, the ability to investigate experts and parties, and more.

- **Alert.** By selecting the "Alert" tab, you can save a search and schedule it to run again in the future so you can receive updates by e-mail.
- **Practitioner's Toolbox.** When federal statutes or statutes from selected states are displayed on the screen, a Practitioner's Toolbox will appear on the right side of the screen, directing you to the history of the statute and related helpful research resources.
- **Focus.** Lexis's "Focus" feature looks for additional terms in your search results. Thus, when you are viewing a case or other result, select "Focus" at the top of the page, type additional terms in the open field, and click "Focus."
- **Segment Searching.** Remember that Lexis allows you to restrict your search using segments. For example, you can select "dissent" or "court" to narrow your research. You can also use date restrictions to locate cases before or after a certain date. A menu allows you to select your desired time period.
- **More Like This.** This feature allows you to find other cases or authorities similar to the one you have identified as relevant to your research. You may also highlight the desired text and click "More Like Selected Text" and then "Search."
- **50 State Surveys.** A new feature gives access to all 50 states' statutes on more than 20 state and regulatory topics. For example, if you wish to know the requirements in all 50 states to adopt a child, the 50 State Surveys feature would list, alphabetically, all applicable statutes from all states, thus allowing you to find and compare statutes all over the nation. Select "Search by Source," then "Legislation & Politics," and then "50 State Surveys."
- **Live Help.** Lexis offers student researchers the ability to send e-mail questions asking for help from Lexis's customer support. Real-time chat support provides immediate help and assistance.
- **Affiliated Services.** Lexis offers numerous complementary services. For example, "Company Dossier" provides business information on more than 35 million companies worldwide, including company overviews, financial reports, and more. The "Academic" service offers documents from nearly 6,000 legal, medical, and business publications. "Alerts" is an electronic clipping service that automatically runs searches for you and provides updates to you by e-mail on your desired topics, allowing you to stay abreast of emerging developments.

6. *Quick Review of Lexis*

To use Lexis:

a. Establish your Internet connection and access http://www.lexis.com.
b. Sign on by typing in your Lexis user number, identification number, or password.
c. Type in the client or billing number.

d. If you know a citation to a case, statute, or other authority, select "Get a Document" at the top of your screen, enter the citation, and click "Get."

e. Use one of the four Search tabs when you are unsure where to start your legal research. Click on topics until you reach the most relevant topic, select a jurisdiction, type keywords into the search boxes (using Terms and Connectors, Natural Language, or Easy Search), and click "Search" to access relevant cases, treatises, and other materials.

f. Examine the results. Shepardize all primary authorities.

C. Westlaw

1. Getting Started

The information in Westlaw is contained in *databases* (analogous to Lexis's "sources") and *files*. Westlaw includes more than 16,000 databases, more than 1 billion public records, more than 6,800 news and business publications, and more than 700 law reviews. Within each database there may be several files. For example, within the database called "U.S. Federal Materials" are files for federal cases and federal statutes. You can access Westlaw through the Internet at http://www.westlaw.com. After you enter your password and client identification, the first screen (see Figure 11-5) will provide you with several shortcut choices, including the following:

Figure 11-5
Westlaw Resources Screen

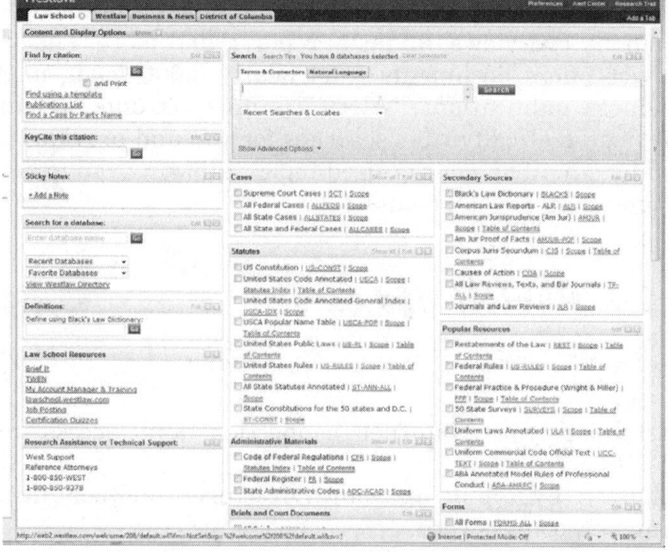

- **Find by Citation.** "Find by Citation" allows you to find a case, statute, or other document by its citation. Type your citation (such as 11p3d 105) and click "Go."
- **KeyCite.** KeyCite allows you to enter a citation and ensure your authority is still valid (analogous to Shepardizing on Lexis).
- **Search for a Database.** This feature allows you to enter a database identifier (such as "ALLFEDS" for all federal cases) and access that database for searching.
- **Resources.** Westlaw's first screen allows you to select a number of resources, including cases, statutes, the Restatements, C.F.R., Am. Jur. 2d, and so on, and then begin your search by entering words into the search box displayed (using Terms and Connectors or Natural Language).
- **Directory.** If you do not know where to begin, select "Directory" at the top of the screen toolbar for access to Westlaw's list of databases. (See Figure 11-6.)

2. *Constructing a Search*

If you do not have a citation, you must construct a search or formulate a *query*. As soon as you access a database, Westlaw will prompt you to enter your query. You may search by Terms and Connectors or Natural Language.

Figure 11-6
Westlaw Directory Search Screen

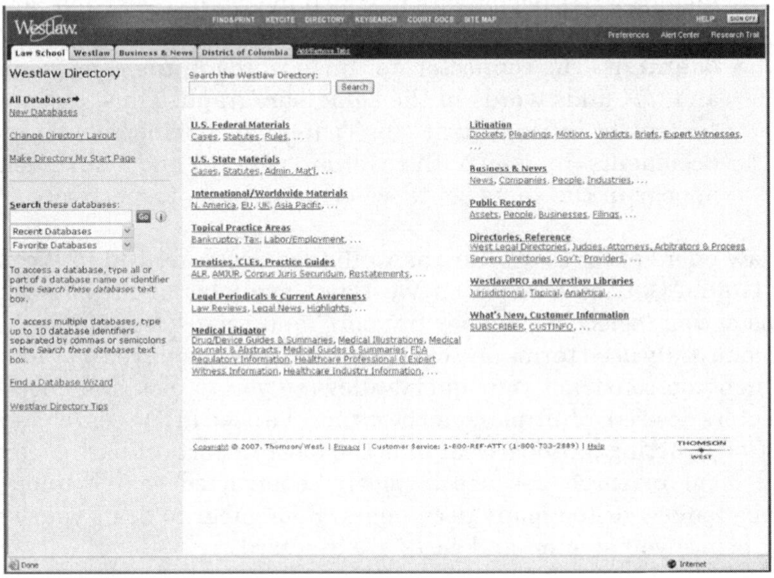

a. Boolean Searching

Following are some tips for constructing a search query using Terms and Connectors on Westlaw. Note that many of these are either similar or identical to the Lexis Terms and Connectors. (See Figure 11-9.)

- **Lowercase Letters.** Like Lexis, Westlaw is not sensitive to capital letters (unless you specify such in your search request). Thus, for basic searching, use lowercase letters.
- **Singulars, Possessives, and Plurals.** Forms of singular, possessives, and plurals are automatically found if they are regular forms. Thus, a search for "patent" will produce results for "patents" and "patent's."
- **Universal Symbols.** Westlaw offers some universal symbols to help you expand your search:
  - An *asterisk* (*) replaces single letters within words. Thus, "franchis*r" will retrieve "franchisor" and "franchiser."
  - An *exclamation point* (!) replaces any ending to a word. Thus, "valu!" will retrieve "value," "valued," "valuation," and so forth.
- **Connectors.** Connectors help you locate needed documents and narrow your search. Following are the most commonly used connectors:
  - **Or.** In Westlaw, the "or" connector is represented by a single space. Thus, a search for "landlord lessor" will locate documents containing either or both of these words.
  - **And (&).** A search for "landlord & covenant" will locate documents only if they contain both these terms.
  - ***/n.*** The connector "/n" instructs Westlaw to find documents that contain words appearing within a specified number (*n*) of words of each other. Thus, a search for "rescission /25 contract agreement" locates documents in which the word "rescission" appears within 25 words of the term "contract" or "agreement."
  - **/s and /p.** The connector "/s" finds words in the same sentence, and "/p" finds words in the same paragraph. Thus, a search for "patent /s infringement" (or "patent /p infringement") locates documents in which the words "patent" and "infringement" appear in the same sentence or paragraph, respectively.

Westlaw offers other connectors as well; they are described in Westlaw's User Guide "Getting Started on Westlaw," available at http://www.west .thomson.com (select "Customer Support" and then "User Guides"). The most commonly used terms and connectors are also displayed on the screen on which you construct your query, allowing you to pick and choose the connectors desired. Multiple connectors may be used in one search request.

Constructing a proper search is the most important part of computerized legal research because a poorly constructed search query will produce too few or too many documents. Remember to draft your search query before you sign on and costs are assessed.

Figure 11-7
Westlaw Sample Query Screen

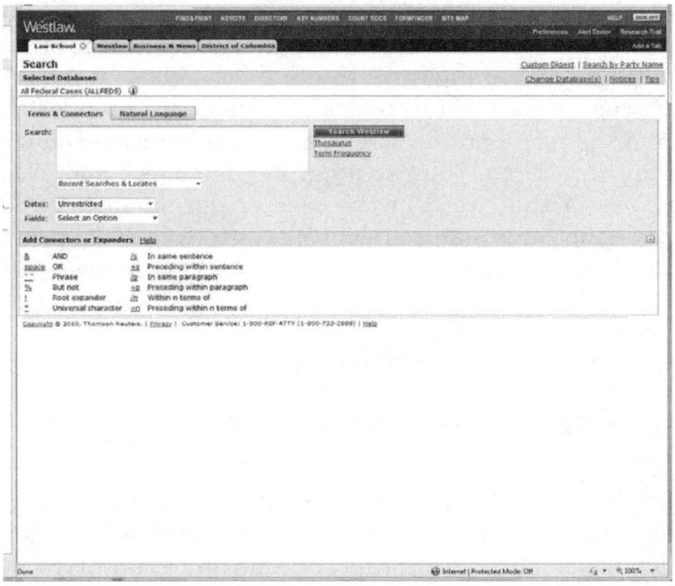

If your search does not produce sufficient results (or else produces too many documents), you may edit your search. Select "Edit Search" at the top of the screen, and modify your search by adding additional terms and connectors.

b. Plain English Searching

Just as Lexis allows searching by plain English, so does Westlaw. When you select a database, and the search box is displayed, simply click on "Natural Language." A new search box is given, into which you type your query in plain English. You may narrow your search by excluding or requiring certain words, and you may be given prompts to add related terms. (See Figure 11-7.)

c. Database Wizard

Just as Lexis's Search tabs help you find the right sources, Westlaw's *Database Wizard* walks you through the process of picking the right database to meet your research needs. After you select "Directory," select "Find a Database Wizard." You will be asked a series of questions about what you are trying to find, and the "Wizard" will help you select the right database by continually narrowing your options.

d. Display of Search Results

Once your search results are shown on your Westlaw screen, there are several methods you can use to browse the materials to determine if they

x

are on point. On the left side of the screen, citations to cases that respond to your query will be listed with your search terms (for example, "patent infringement") banded in yellow. Select as desired. Also on the left side of the screen, the "Results Plus" feature displays additional sources that may be of help, such as references to A.L.R. annotations or articles in *Am. Jur. Proof of Facts*. (See Figure 11-8.)

When you select the full text of a case, you can select "Locate in Result" from the menu on the screen and type in terms you wish to find in the document. Thus, you can type in "damages" and Westlaw will locate any use of that word in the case or document being displayed. Cases include the same features as in West's conventional print volumes, meaning that headnotes and topic names and key numbers are given.

3. *Specialized Searches*

a. **Searching for Statutes and Constitutions**

- **By Citation.** If you know the citation to a statute or a constitution, enter the citation in the "Find by Citation" box displayed on the first screen, or select the tab "Find and Print," type the citation in the search box (for example, 17 usca 109), and click "Go." You will be given the statute, library references, and annotations.

Figure 11-8
Viewing Westlaw Results

- **By Topic.** If you do not have a citation, select a database. For example, for federal statutes, select "Directory" and then select the database "USCA." You will then need to decide whether you will search by Terms and Connectors or Natural Language. Type your search in the search box and click "Search." Westlaw's recently added feature "ResultsPlus" for statutes provides links to other sources (cases, other statutes, administrative code references, and legislative history documents) that discuss your statute. You will also be informed if pending legislation might affect your statute.

b. Searching for Cases

- **By Citation.** If you know a case citation, use the "Find by Citation" box on the first screen, enter your citation in the search box (for example, 520 us 788), and click "Go."
- **By Topic.** If you do not have a citation, select "Directory" and then select an appropriate database, such as all federal cases, cases from the First Circuit, or cases from Texas, and then formulate your query by using Terms and Connectors or Natural Language.
  - Remember to use "ResultsPlus" to expand your research efforts. References to additional sources such as A.L.R. annotations are automatically displayed on the screen with your search results when you conduct case law research on Westlaw.
  - Westlaw includes star paging to inform you of the page number you would be on if you were reading the case in parallel sets for the case.
  - A new feature is the display of cases on Westlaw's screen exactly the way they appear in a printed book. If the note "West Reporter Image PDF" is shown on the screen, you may select this to view your case in the same easy-to-read, dual-column format you're used to seeing in print reporters.

c. Searching for Administrative and Legislative Materials

- **By Citation.** If you know the citation to a provision in either C.F.R. or the *Federal Register*, you may enter it in the "Find by Citation" search box displayed on the first screen after sign-on.
- **By Topic.** You can search through the C.F.R., the *Federal Register*, and other sources by accessing the pertinent database from your first Westlaw screen and then entering your search query in the search box, using either Terms and Connectors or Natural Language. Alternatively, by selecting "Directory" from the top toolbar, you can select "Topical Practice Areas" and then select the field in which you are interested, such as "Energy Law."

- **Legislative History.** Westlaw also includes numerous legislative history documents, including bills, the *Congressional Record*, and compiled legislative histories for certain statutes. Select "Directory" from the toolbar and then "U.S. Federal Materials" and then "Legislative History" (or "Arnold & Porter Collection — Legislative Histories" for numerous compiled legislative histories).

d. Searching for Law Reviews and Journals

When you sign onto Westlaw, the first screen displays the entry "Journals and Law Reviews." Once you select that database, you then enter your search query using Terms and Connectors or Natural Language. Alternatively, you may enter an author's name or title of article, or you may enter a citation to a law review article in the "Find by Citation" box. You may also select "Directory" from the top toolbar and then select "Law Reviews," allowing you to search within specifically named law reviews and journals.

e. Searching for Secondary Authorities

When you sign onto Westlaw, a category titled "Secondary Sources" allows you to search through a number of secondary sources, including the Restatements, A.L.R., and other secondary sources. Alternatively, select "Directory" from the top toolbar, and then review the various sources listed, including "Treatises," "Directories, Reference," and others. Select the database you wish to search and proceed to enter your query.

4. *KeyCiting*

To update and validate your primary authorities when using Westlaw, use its service called "KeyCite." The service and process is highly similar to Shepardizing using Lexis. Westlaw's first screen provides a search box titled "KeyCite this Citation." Enter your citation into the search box, click "Go," and view your results. Alternatively, when you are viewing a case or statute on the screen, watch for the "signal indicators" on the screen. For example, a red flag signals strong negative history, and a yellow flag indicates caution. KeyCiting is discussed in detail in Chapter 9.

5. *Other Westlaw Features*

Like Lexis, Westlaw offers a number of added features to make legal research easy and efficient, including the following:

- **Hyperlinking.** As you read through various authorities, references to other authorities will appear in a bright blue color as hyperlinks, which allow you to click and be immediately transported to them. For example, many cases displayed on the screen

include a hyperlink to "Briefs and Other Related Documents," allowing you to retrieve and review the briefs submitted by the parties to the case.

- **Database Wizard.** To help you select the right database for your search, Westlaw's Database Wizard provides questions and prompts and then suggests the most appropriate database for your use. Select "Directory" from the top of your toolbar and then select "Find a Database Wizard," to access this feature.

- **Key Numbers.** To locate cases on Westlaw using the Key Number System, select "Key Numbers" at the top of the Westlaw toolbar. You can search Westlaw's Key Number Digest Outline, browsing the list of more than 400 topics, until you find the right key number. On Westlaw, key numbers are displayed as follows: "233k166," with the number "233" replacing the topic name "Landlord & Tenant." Alternatively, you can enter descriptive terms into an open search box to locate topic names and Key Numbers.

- **Field Searching.** Like Lexis, Westlaw allows you to retrieve only part of a document or to view documents by name or date. After you select a database, you can restrict your search to search by court, date, judge, attorney, or other fields. For example, if your query is "landlord tenant /20 default da (aft 1990)" Westlaw will search for cases decided after 1990 containing the words "landlord" or "tenant" within 20 words of the term "default." Drop-down menus help you select fields and dates.

- **Graphical Display of Direct History for Cases.** A recently added Westlaw feature shows you the direct history of your case in an easy-to-understand flowchart format. For example, you would be shown in graphical format, using arrows, how your case progressed from trial, through its initial appeal, when certiorari was granted, and then when the United States Supreme Court held. You may easily link to the court briefs and motions filed at each level of the case's history.

- **Graphical Display of Timelines for Statutes.** Westlaw's new feature, called "Graphical Statutes," displays a flowchart of your statute's legislative history (for federal statutes and some state statutes) with links to prior versions of the statute, committee reports, the *Congressional Record*, presidential messages, and any legislative histories compiled for your statute. This display shows the history of your statute in an easy-to-grasp flowchart format. You will also be informed if any pending legislation affects your statute.

- **50 State Surveys.** Like Lexis's feature, this Westlaw service gives access to all 50 states' statutes on more than 250 state and regulatory topics. For example, if you wished to know the requirements in all 50 states to form a corporation, the 50 State Survey feature would list, alphabetically, all applicable statutes from all states, thus allowing you to find and compare statutes all over the nation. Select "50 State Surveys" from the top of your toolbar.

- **Clipping Services.** Similar to Lexis's Alerts service, Westlaw's clipping service, called WestClip, automatically runs your Terms and Connectors searches and periodically delivers updated results to you by e-mail. KeyCite Alert monitors the status of cases, statutes, and regulations and then notifies you by e-mail when those results change.
- **Sticky Notes.** Westlaw's new "sticky notes" feature allows you to jot citations, comments, and other notes to yourself so you can later retrieve notes of interest to you.
- **Live Help.** Like Lexis, Westlaw offers researchers the opportunity to initiate real-time chat to ask for help and assistance. Simply click the "Help" tab, type in your question, and click "Send." Customer support will respond to your question in moments.
- **Affiliated Services.** Westlaw offers several affiliated services, including the following: "Business Information and News," a comprehensive collection of more than 8,000 news and business magazines, newspapers, and other sources; FormFinder, which helps you draft forms; and Westlaw Litigation, a complete service for legal professionals engaged in litigation, affording access to jury instructions, court briefs and records, motions, experts, calendaring systems, and more.

6. *WestlawNext*

In spring 2010, West introduced a new electronic research system called WestlawNext. Generally, WestlawNext mimics the ease of use of Google's search engine. Researchers who use WestlawNext will no longer have to choose a specific database before conducting a search (which often presents problems to researchers who may not know where to begin a search). A single search box presented on a clean, uncluttered screen asks WestlawNext researchers to enter "search terms, citations, databases, anything." The results presented are ranked in their order of relevance, across multiple databases. For example, when searching on Westlaw, one might select a database of federal cases. A search query is entered, and the results presented, of course, are limited to a list of federal cases. A user of WestlawNext, however, enters search terms in plain English in a search box, and the results presented would include cases, statutes, A.L.R. annotations, and numerous other relevant resources.

Users can highlight portions of the results shown on screen and add notes and comments, for example, a note to "include this case in my brief." Research results can be dragged into folders for quick access later. Once you view a case, it is marked with an eyeglasses icon to remind you that you have already looked at the case. If a case has negative history, that history is shown on the screen with the case (currently, when using Westlaw, one is presented with a yellow flag and then must click on the flag to determine the nature of the negative history). As of the time of the writing of this text, WestlawNext coexists with Westlaw and promises to

be a highly user-friendly addition to electronic research. Users who wish access to the new WestlawNext must pay a subscription fee in addition to the fee they pay for Westlaw.

At the time of the writing of this text, Lexis was planning its own revamped system that reportedly will also mimic the ease of using Google.

7. Quick Review of Westlaw

To use Westlaw:

a. Establish your Internet connection and access http://www.west law.com.
b. Sign on by typing in your Westlaw user number, identification number, or password.
c. Type in the client or billing number.
d. If you know a citation to a case, statute, or other authority, select "Find by Citation" at the top of your screen, enter the citation, and click "Go."
e. If you do not know where to start, you must select an appropriate database. Select "Directory" and browse the databases. Select the desired database (or allow the Database Wizard to help you). Enter your query into the search box, using Terms and Connectors or Natural Language. Review the materials presented, and KeyCite all primary authorities.

Practice Tip

Lexis and Westlaw Interactive Tutorials

Lexis and Westlaw both offer free online interactive training and tutorials (as well as useful print products) to help you learn to use their services.

- **Lexis. For interactive training, access http://www.lexisnexis.com/ infopro/training. Take a tour of Lexis at http://web.lexis.com/help/ multimedia/tour.htm. Print materials may be viewed and downloaded at http://www.lexisnexis.com/literature.**
- **Westlaw. For interactive training, access http://west.thomson.com/ support/training/default.aspx. For user guides and reference materials, access http://west.thomson.com/westlaw/guides.**
- **Georgetown University Law Center. Georgetown offers tutorials on performing research using Lexis and Westlaw at http://www.ll.georgetown.edu/tutorials/index.cfm.**
- **Harvard Law School. Harvard offers an excellent tutorial on the use of both Lexis and Westlaw at the following site: http://www .law.harvard.edu/library/research/tutorials/lexisnexis-westlaw.**

D.   Final Pointers on
Computer-Assisted Legal Research

1.   *When to Use Lexis or Westlaw*

Some tasks are best performed by using conventional print research tools, whereas others are best performed by using Lexis or Westlaw. Still other tasks might call for you to blend both methods of research. Knowing which method to use requires an analysis of many factors, including the complexity of your task, the costs involved, and time constraints. Many instructors urge students to first become familiar with the conventional print tools before becoming too wedded to computer-assisted legal research. Strong skills in manual legal research provide a good foundation for using Lexis and Westlaw more effectively.

Use conventional print sources when:

- You need to "get your feet wet" and get some background about an area of the law.
- You need a thorough and comprehensive analysis of an area of the law, such as that provided by a treatise.
- You are having difficulty formulating research queries for Lexis or Westlaw because you are unfamiliar with the issue you are researching.
- It would be more cost-effective and easier to use traditional print sources to get a quick answer to a question than to incur costs by using Lexis or Westlaw.

Use computer-assisted legal research when:

- You already have a citation to a known case or other authority.
- You are looking for cases involving a known party, attorney, or judge.
- The area of law is new or evolving.
- You are looking for the most current information available.
- You are validating your primary authorities (by Shepardizing or KeyCiting).

Computer-assisted legal research is a valuable tool. The services provide rapid access to a wide range of materials that no law firm could afford to purchase or shelve. Nevertheless, computer-assisted legal research may be expensive and will produce useful results only if you understand how to make the systems work effectively for you. This takes practice and experience. Legal research is not as easy as merely inserting some words into a query box. Effective researchers use a combination of computer-assisted legal research and conventional research techniques to obtain the best results for clients.

2. New Developments in Lexis and Westlaw

Lexis and Westlaw continually add new materials and work to make their services affordable, attractive, and easy to use for legal professionals. Lexis has therefore launched "lexisONE" (http://www.lexisone.com), which offers free access to some legal materials, including recent federal and state cases, forms, and other materials. To access older cases or to Shepardize, the user must switch to Lexis and pay a fee. Westlaw now offers a "pay as you go" research plan, Westlaw by Credit Card, allowing you to access its databases on an "as needed" basis without a formal subscription, paying by credit card.

Some Lexis and Westlaw materials are also available in wireless electronic formats, accessible through personal digital assistants, such as BlackBerrys. Both Lexis and Westlaw offer cases, statutes, and validating (through Shepardizing or KeyCiting), thus allowing legal professionals on the run immediate access to many materials. Additionally, some materials (such as *Black's Law Dictionary*) are now appearing as iPhone applications or "apps."

3. Limitations of Computer-Assisted Legal Research

Following are some limitations of computer-assisted legal research:

- **Literalness.** Computers are extremely literal. Thus, a search for "teacher" will not produce results including "instructor." Construct your search query carefully before you sign on and begin incurring costs.
- **Cost.** There are numerous pricing variations for Lexis and Westlaw. Large law firms pay flat rates, allowing unlimited use of Lexis and Westlaw by their legal professionals. Hourly pricing can range from $10 to $800 per hour, depending on the files accessed and the time of day the service is used, with higher fees charged during peak hours.
- **Database Limitations.** There are some limitations to the Lexis and Westlaw databases. For example, both provide the *Federal Register*, but only since about 1980. To determine the date limitations of publications and materials, consult Lexis's and Westlaw's database lists at the following sites, respectively: http://w3.nexis .com/sources and http://directory.westlaw.com/?tf=90&tc=11.

4. The Future of Print Publishing

On occasion, experts wonder whether the new virtual libraries will ultimately replace conventional law libraries with their primarily print collections. In brief, the more reasoned conclusion is that although the

newer technologies (especially Lexis, Westlaw, and the Internet) provide excellent tools, they are unlikely to replace books for some of the following reasons:

- Libraries are permanent archives of materials, whereas the Internet is a temporary host continually being updated, and even replaced, with earlier versions of information sometimes lost forever.
- As the 2004-2005 American Bar Association Legal Technology Survey Report concluded, legal professionals prefer to use print for treatises and other secondary sources. Moreover, the publishers of legal publications report that print is still their dominant format. Catherine Sanders Reach, et al., *Feasibility and Viability of the Digital Library in a Private Law Firm*, 95 Law Libr. J. 370, 375 (2003).
- Certain materials such as articles and texts are copyrighted and are thus unlikely to appear on the Internet because their authors would lose royalties if their works were disseminated globally on the Internet with a keystroke.
- Several years ago, CD-ROMs were touted as the technological marvel that would replace the printed page. Now, most experts recognize their value as complementary sources to conventional printed materials. Similarly, the other newer technologies will likely continue to coexist with their print counterparts.
- Although people can read hundreds of pages at a sitting, research shows that most people only read a few screens of information before printing it out.

In sum, surveys show that legal publishers still have a strong connection to print products, law librarians have concerns about the costs of digital libraries, and legal professionals continue to have a strong attachment to print sources. *Id.* at 381.

Thus, be flexible in your research methods. Be prepared to switch sources when you reach a dead end. No one method is best. Combine the best features of print research approaches with the best approaches of computer-assisted legal research to best serve a client's needs.

E. Other Competitors in Commercial Electronic Research

Although Lexis and Westlaw are the acknowledged giants in the field of computer-assisted legal research, a number of other companies offer access on a fee basis to legal materials through the Internet. Most charge moderate fees and appeal to small firms and sole practitioners. Some cater to government users.

- **Loislaw** (http://www.loislaw.com). Loislaw, a service of Wolters Kluwer, offers case law, statutes, constitutions, administrative law, court rules, and more for all states and the federal courts. Loislaw offers a more comprehensive database than most of the other services described in this section, including all federal and state primary materials as well as treatise libraries for a wide variety of secondary sources, such as estate planning and family law. Moreover, Loislaw offers *GlobalCite*, a service similar to Shepardizing, which refers you to cases that mention or discuss the case you are researching. Searching may be done either through Boolean connectors or through a "find" feature if you know a citation. Low monthly flat fees are charged.
- **Fastcase** (http://www.fastcase.com). Fastcase is a fee-based legal research system that allows its subscribers access to a vast array of federal and state cases and statutes. Secondary authorities are being added. Its libraries are searchable in a variety of ways, from "Google" type searches, to citation lookup, to natural language and Boolean searching. A number of bar associations have purchased Fastcase subscriptions for all of their members. Although Fastcase does not verify or update authorities in the same way that *Shepard's* or KeyCite do, its product Authority Check provides you with a list of other cases that cite your case. Most impressive, Fastcase offers affordable pricing and free iPhone and iPad apps so busy professionals can readily conduct legal research while commuting, in the courtroom, or before an important meeting. After accessing a case on Fastcase, you can easily switch to Lexis or Westlaw to Shepardize or KeyCite the case on a per transaction basis.
- **VersusLaw** (http://www.versuslaw.com). VersusLaw provides access to federal and state cases, statutes, and other legal sources for as low as $14 per month.
- **JuriSearch** (http://www.jurisearch.com). JuriSearch offers primarily California, Florida, and Massachusetts materials for moderate fees.
- **PACER** (http://pacer.psc.uscourts.gov). Public Access to Court Electronic Records (PACER), a service of the United States Judiciary, allows users to obtain case and docket information from all federal courts. The PACER system offers electronic access to a listing of all parties and participants in cases, documents filed for certain cases, case status, and other useful information. For example, if you wish to review Enron's bankruptcy filings, you may access the court files, and review all documents filed in the matter. The fee is presently $0.08 per page, whether pages are viewed, printed, or downloaded.

F. Nonprint Research Tools

In addition to computer-assisted legal research, there are some other nonprint tools that legal researchers should know how to use: microforms, sound recordings, videocassettes, and CD-ROMs.

1. *Microforms*

a. Types of Microforms

Microforms are based on the principle of microphotography: Images are reduced and placed on rolls or sheets of film. A microfilm reader is then used to review the images recorded on the film. The readers resemble a television screen and are usually equipped with printers so you may obtain a photocopy of the material being viewed. There are three main types of microform:

- **Microfilm.** *Microfilm* is a reel of film (usually 16 or 35 millimeters) that is threaded into a reader. Although microfilm saves storage space, it has not been widely used for legal materials. It is, however, often used for government records, bank records, newspapers, and other materials. Many counties preserve their land records on microfilm. The image shown on the screen is often fuzzy, and the prints reproduced are also often difficult to read.
- **Microfiche.** *Microfiche* is a microform displayed on a thin transparent celluloid flat sheet rather than on a roll of film. Each sheet of microfiche may contain images of up to 400 pages. Probably the best-known use of microfiche for legal research is LexisNexis's *Congressional Bills, Resolutions, & Laws on Microfiche,* used to compile legislative histories. Many law libraries maintain their legislative history materials on microfiche.
- **Ultrafiche.** *Ultrafiche* is a type of microfiche with a high reduction ratio. As many as 1,800 pages of text can be held on a single sheet of ultrafiche. West has reproduced many volumes of its *National Reporter System* in ultrafiche, with each sheet replacing one hardbound volume.

b. Summary of Microforms

All microforms save storage space. Although their use for nonlegal purposes has been broad, their role in legal research has never really taken hold. A notable exception is that microfiche is used for the materials making up a legislative history. To determine what materials are published in microform, consult *Guide to Microforms in Print,* an alphabetical list of more than 200,000 books, journals, and other materials currently available in microform. Ask your law librarian what materials are available in microform at your law library.

2. Sound Recordings and Videocassettes

Many continuing legal education programs are offered for those in the legal profession. Professionals may attend the seminars or programs in person or may usually purchase a sound recording, videocassette, or CD-ROM of the program. More recently, legal professionals obtain continuing legal education through webinars, seminars offered on one's own desktop computer, which are often accompanied by materials that may be downloaded or printed.

Law firms often use video for mock trials, helping to sharpen attorneys' skills as well as point out certain characteristics of client witnesses that may bear on credibility. Some firms use videotape presentations to introduce clients to certain routine matters, such as providing clients with basic information about having a deposition taken or the trial process. Videotapes are often used at trials to show the jury an accident scene or in criminal prosecutions to show occurrence of the crime itself (such as bank robbery or shoplifting).

3. CD-ROMs

CD-ROMs are highly efficient storage media; they may contain more than 200,000 pages of text. CD-ROMs have generally replaced the earlier technology of floppy disks. Many legal materials are available in CD-ROM form, including *Martindale-Hubbell Law Directory*. The disks need to be replaced annually. Lexis and Westlaw both make cases, statutes, and practice guides available on CD-ROM. One disc can take the place of several bound volumes. For example, cases reported since 1945 in West's *Atlantic Reporter, 2d Series* are available on seven discs. Searching is easy, making it efficient to locate cases by citation, party name, keywords, or other elements. The CD can be used with a portable laptop computer and small printer, enabling legal professionals to perform valuable research at home or while traveling. Their use at trial can be extremely valuable. If adverse counsel cites an unfamiliar case, you can insert a CD and locate the case. Because discs containing new cases and statutes must be purchased, most publishers issue new discs (for a fee) and take back old ones at periodic intervals. The cost for CD-ROM products is about the same as for their print counterparts. High-speed wireless Internet access to legal materials using laptops and devices such as iPhones may make using CD-ROMs for legal materials a relic of the past.

> **Tips for Efficient Use of Computer-Assisted Legal Research**
>
> - **Construct your search or query before you sign on and start incurring costs.**
> - **You need not memorize all of the commands and root expanders. A quick reference sheet is usually provided at each terminal in a law library.**
>
> *(continued)*

> ### Tips for Efficient Use of Computer-Assisted Legal Research *(Continued)*
>
> - Do not waste time by reading long cases or law review articles on the screen. Such a practice causes strain to the eyes and the wallet. Either print the document or jot down its citation so you can locate it later.
> - To save money, use a smaller file or database rather than a larger one. For example, if you are interested only in California cases, use the database just for California ("CA") rather than one for all 50 states ("ALLSTATES").
> - Because BriefCheck and WestCheck (see Chapter 9) can check cites from a table of authorities, check the cites in an adversary's brief to ensure that the cases relied upon by the adversary are valid and have not been weakened.
> - Use the clipping services to track information about clients and then send the clients articles that mention them. Clients are thrilled when their legal team expresses a personal interest in their business.

G. Citation Form

	Bluebook (for practitioners)	ALWD
Lexis Case	*Smith v. Jones*, No. 05-233, 2006 U.S. App. LEXIS 19334, at *3 (1st Cir. May 15, 2006).	*Smith v. Jones*, 2006 U.S. App. LEXIS 05-233 at *3 (1st Cir. May 15, 2006).
Westlaw Case	*Allen v. Bailey*, No. 05-CV-310, 2006 WL 12656, at *2 (S.D.N.Y. June 10, 2006).	*Allen v. Bailey*, 2005 WL 12656 at *2 (S.D.N.Y. June 10, 2006).
Videotape	Videotape: Shepardizing Made Easy (Shepard's /McGraw-Hill, Inc. 1994) (on file with Georgetown Law Center).	*Shepardizing Made Easy*, Videotape (Shepard's /McGraw-Hill, Inc. 1994).

Figure 11-9
Comparison of Selected Lexis and
Westlaw Terms and Connectors

Lexis Term, Connector, or Symbol	Westlaw Term, Connector, or Symbol	Function	Example	Retrieves documents
!	!	Retrieves words with variant endings	*lend!*	with the words "lender," "lending," etc.
*	*	Replaces one character	*m*n*	with the word "man" or "men"
and	&	Locates two search terms in a document	*Probate and damages* (Lexis); *probate & damages* (Westlaw)	containing both "probate" and "damages"
or	Either "or" or a space between two words	Locates documents with either or both words	*Teacher or professor* (Lexis); *teacher professor* (Westlaw)	containing either "teacher" or "professor" or both
W/*n*	/*n*	Locates documents with one word within a number of words of the other	*patent w/10 infringement* (Lexis); *patent /10 infringement* (Westlaw)	containing the word "patent" within ten words of the word "infringement"
w/p	/p	Locates documents with two terms in the same paragraph	*Wrongful w/p death* (Lexis); *wrongful /p death* (Westlaw)	containing the words "wrongful" and "death" in the same paragraph

Figure 11-9 *(Continued)*

Lexis Term, Connector, or Symbol	Westlaw Term, Connector, or Symbol	Function	Example	Retrieves documents
w/s	/s	Locates documents with two terms in the same sentence	*Wrongful w/s death* (Lexis); *wrongful /s death* (Westlaw)	containing the words "wrongful" and "death" in the same sentence
And not	But not (%)	Excludes documents with certain terms	*Patent and not accounting* (Lexis); *patent % accounting* (Westlaw)	containing the term "patent" but not the word "accounting"
" "	" "	Locates documents in the same order as they appear in quotation marks	*"all elements rule"*	containing the phrase "all elements rule"
Atleast		Term must appear a certain number of times	*atleast4 (RICO)*	containing the term "RICO" at least four times

CyberSites ▮▮▮▮▮▮▮▮▮▮▮▮▮▮▮▮▮▮▮▮▮▮▮▮▮▮▮▮▮▮

http://www.lexis.com	Lexis's home page; select "Products & Services" to learn more about Lexis's features and offerings. Numerous tips and resources are provided.
http://www.westlaw.com	Westlaw's home page allows you to point and click to review its databases, learn about training options, and view its helpful User Guides.

Writing Strategies

While computer-assisted legal research is somewhat mechanical, writing about the results you locate online is not. Because the reader of every project you write will be busy, and some readers may be highly critical, you need to produce a written project that is readable.

To enhance interest in your writing:

- Use the active voice because it is more forceful than the passive voice.
- Use lists and quotations to "break up" long narrative passages and add visual drama to your page.
- Use verbs ("conclude") rather than nominalizations ("drew a conclusion") to create interest.
- Use strong words ("unique" rather than "somewhat unusual").
- Use concrete words ("your lease") rather than vague terms ("your situation").
- Use placement to enhance interest by placing stronger arguments at the beginning and end of your project where they will have more force.
- Use "graphics" such as high-quality paper, headings, and white space to capture the reader's interest.

Assignments for Chapter 11

Lexis Assignment

1. Select "Get a Document" and "Get by Citation." Retrieve the case located at 548 U.S. 331.
   a. What is the Lexis database number or citation for this case?
   b. How does page 576 of the official *United States Reports* begin?
   c. Select the yellow triangle shown for this case.
      (i) Why was the yellow triangle assigned to this case?
      (ii) Which 2009 case from the Southern District of New York followed this case? Give the case name only.
   d. Return to your original case. Review "Related Content." To which A.L.R. annotation are you directed?
2. Select "Search by Source" at the top of your toolbar and then select "Estates, Gifts, and Trusts." Select "Estate Cases, Federal," and then "Easy Search." Locate cases relating to setting aside deeds due to undue influence.
   a. To which 1886 U.S. Supreme Court case are you directed?
   b. Select the case and review its Case Summary. What was the outcome of this case?
3. Select "Research Tasks" at the top of your toolbar and then select "Immigration." Select United States Supreme Court cases. Use Natural Language and locate cases relating to grounds for deportation.
   a. To which 1975 U.S. Supreme Court case are you directed?
   b. Review the case. What *Shepard's* icon is assigned to it? Why?
4. Select "Get a Document" and "Get by Citation." Retrieve the case located at 582 F.2d 654.
   a. What is the name of the case?
   b. Select "More Like This" and then select to review "Federal Court Cases Combined" and then select "Search." To which 1999 case from the Seventh Circuit are you directed?
5. Select "Get a Document" and "Get by Citation." Retrieve 18 U.S.C.S. § 2280.
   a. Generally, to what topic does this statute relate?
   b. To which Am. Jur. reference are you directed?
   c. Select "Shepardize." Identify the name and author of the 2010 *Fordham International Law Journal* article that discusses this statute.
6. Select "Get a Document" and "Get by Docket Number." What is the name of the U.S. Supreme Court case assigned Docket Number 70-74?

7. Select "Search" and then select "Ohio" within "States Legal — U.S." Select to review Ohio statutes. Review Ohio's General Corporation Law.
   a. Generally, what constitutes a quorum for a directors' meeting?
   b. What statute governs this issue?
8. Select "Search" and then "By Topic or Headnote." Select "Family Law" and then "Name Changes." Locate the California statute relating to changing names.
   a. To which statute are you directed?
   b. Select "Suggested Forms." What form are you given?
9. Select "Get a Document" and "By Party Name." Locate the U.S. Supreme Court case in which the defendant's name is Gressette.
   a. Give the name of the case and its citation.
   b. Retrieve the case. Select "TOA." How many decisions were cited by your 1977 case?

Westlaw Assignment

1. At the initial Westlaw screen, use the "Find by Citation" box and retrieve the case located at 14 S.W.3d 9.
   a. What is the name of this case?
   b. Select "Results Plus." To which C.J.S. reference are you directed?
   c. Retrieve the C.J.S. reference. Which Massachusetts case states that an accused may show the general reputation of the deceased as to using firearms or other deadly weapons when engaged in quarrels?
2. At the initial Westlaw screen, select *Black's Law Dictionary* and locate the definition for "collateral estoppel."
   a. What is the definition?
   b. To which topic and key number are you referred?
3. Select "Directory" and continue selecting the appropriate databases to search Indiana cases. Use Natural Language and develop a query to locate cases from Indiana dealing with spite fences as private nuisances.
   a. To which 2008 Indiana case are you directed?
   b. Retrieve this case. Select "Table of Authorities." How many cases are cited in the 2008 Indiana case?
   c. Return to the case. Select "Results Plus." Select the A.L.R. annotation. What section in the annotation discusses that the malicious motive of one erecting a spite fence may justify a remedy?
   d. Return to the case. What KeyCite icon is displayed? Why?
4. At the initial Westlaw screen, use the "Find by Citation" box and retrieve the case located at 550 U.S. 330.
   a. What is the name of the case?
   b. Who delivered the opinion of the Court?

     c.   Access information about the Justice who delivered the opinion of the Court. Where was the Justice born? What are the names of the Justice's children?

     d.   Return to the case. Select "Petitions, Briefs & Filings." Retrieve the Petition for Writ of Certiorari filed on October 24, 2001.

         (i)   What was the question presented for review?

         (ii) Review the Table of Authorities cited in the brief. Select *Pike v. Bruce Church*. Select the KeyCite icon for *Pike*. What case called *Pike* into doubt?

5. At the initial Westlaw screen, select "Find by Party Name" and locate a 2005 Washington case in which the defendant's name is Heidi Fero. What is the citation for the case?

6. Select "Key Numbers" from the top of the toolbar. Browse the Key Number Digest Outline.

     a.   What number is assigned to embezzlement?

     b.   To which topic does Embezzlement Key Number 146k24 relate?

7. Select "Directory" and then "Restatement (Third) of Trusts." What is the definition of a resulting trust?

8. Access the Popular Name Table for U.S.C.A.

     a.   Generally, what is the citation for the short title of the Head Start Act?

     b.   Select the statute. What Senate Report reported on this legislation (for the 1981 Act)?

9. Select the appropriate database for federal statutes.

     a.   What statute deals with cigarette labeling and advertising?

     b.   Retrieve the statute. Give the citation to the 1996 *Catholic University Law Review* comment that discusses this statute.

     c.   Select the law review and retrieve the "citing references" for this law review Comment. How many secondary authorities cite this law review?

     d.   Return to the original statute. Select "Graphical Statutes." Select the House Report prepared for this legislation. Briefly, what was the purpose of this legislation?

10. Retrieve 15 U.S.C.A. § 1672.

     a.   Generally, to which topic does this statute relate?

     b.   Review the annotations following this statute. Are bank checking accounts "disposable earnings" within the meaning of this statute? Give your answer and cite the case that supports your answer. Give the case name only.

11. Select "Directory" and then "FormFinder" and then "Business Law FormFinder." Access the forms for Texas. Using Natural Language, retrieve a form for articles of dissolution of a limited liability company.

     a.   Select the first form to which you are directed. What statute governs dissolution of a Texas limited liability company?

     b.   Who should sign the form?

12. At the initial Westlaw screen, select "Am. Jur. Proof of Facts." Using Natural Language, locate an article written by Angela R. Holder that relates to a plastic surgeon's liability for cosmetic surgery. What does Section 10 provide?

13. At the initial Westlaw screen, select "Am. Jur." Generally, how do courts divide property in a divorce case? What section did you review?

14. Locate a fairly recent *Boston College Law Review* article relating to copyright protection for stage directions.
    a. Who is the author of the article?
    b. Review the conclusion of the article. Why may a director set Shakespeare's play *Henry V* during the American Civil War?

15. Locate the case published at 328 U.S. 395. Use "Direct History — Graphical View." What is the citation for this case at the U.S. District Court?

16. Select "Directory" and then "Litigation." Select "Jury Verdicts, Settlements & Judgments" and then locate Michigan Jury Verdicts Combined. Use the template you are given and locate cases after January 1, 2010, in which a party received more than $2 million for a fractured skull.
    a. To which case are you directed?
    b. Who was the plaintiff's expert psychiatrist?
    c. Which defendants paid most of the damages awarded?

Loislaw Assignment

1. Access the Popular Name Table for the U.S. Code. Give the citation to the Parental Kidnapping Prevention Act of 1980.

2. Browse the Table of Contents for the U.S. Code. Locate 11 U.S.C. § 521. What is the first listed duty for a debtor?

3. Access the Louisiana Code of Evidence. To what topic does Article 510 relate?

4. Locate California Family Code section 4320. Review subsection (a). In ordering spousal support, what is the first factor courts must consider?

5. Use "Find Cases by Citation" and retrieve the case located at 33 P.3d 1.
    a. What is the name of the case?
    b. Select "GlobalCite" for this case. How many cases cite your case?
    c. What is the newest case that cites your case?
    d. Select "Search Within GlobalCite Results" and search for the case in which the defendant's name is Steven DeGraff. Select this case and give its citation.

6. Select "Federal" jurisdiction and then select "U.S. Sentencing Commission Guidelines Manual."
    a. Review Chapter 4, Part B. What is the definition of a "career offender"?

   b. Use the "Search" feature and locate the section in the U.S.
       Sentencing Commission Guidelines Manual that relates to
       "conditions of probation — organizations." To which section
       are you directed?
7. Select the State Library for Florida. Locate Florida Attorney
    General Opinion 2010-31. To what topic does this opinion
    relate?
8. Select the State Library for California. Browse the California
    Code of Regulations. Use the "Search" feature. What is "The
    Quinella"?
9. Select the State Library for California and review the Califor-
    nia Judicial Council Forms. Review the form for a request that
    a court order no travel with children. What does Section 4(b)
    allege?
10. Select "Find Cases by Citation" and locate the case at 978 F.2d
    17.
    a. What is the name of this case?
    b. How does page 24 of this case begin?
    c. Access the statute cited in footnote 1 of the case. Generally,
        to which topic does this statute relate?
11. Use the case law database for the U.S. Supreme Court and
    locate a 2006 case in which the defendant's name is Hallock.
    a. Give the citation to the case.
    b. Who delivered the opinion of the Court?
    c. Who argued the case for the respondents?
    d. Give the citation for this case at the Second Circuit Court of
        Appeals.
12. Select "Find Cases by Citation" and locate the case at 511 U.S.
    863.
    a. What is the name of the case?
    b. Select "GlobalCite" and then "Other Documents." What is
        the first document that cites your case?
13. What is the status of Colo. Rev. Stat. § 18-4-202.1?

Internet Assignment for Chapter 11

1. Access Lexis's Directory of Online Sources at http://
    web.nexis.com/sources. Use the field titled "Publication Types,"
    select "Statutes," select "Regions of Coverage," and then select
    for your state. Give the earliest date for Lexis's coverage for
    your state's statutes.
2. Access Westlaw's Database Directory at http://directory
    .westlaw.com/?tf=90&tx=11.

  a. Give the appropriate database identifier for Georgia state court cases.

  b. Give the database identifier for court rules for all states.

  c. Give the database identifier for U.S.C.A. Popular Name Table.

3. Access lexisONE at http://law.lexisnexis.com/webcenters/lexisone and select "Free Case Law." Locate the case at 29 Cal. 4th 32. Give the case name.

4. Access Westlaw's site for its user guides at http://www.west.thomson.com/westlaw/guides and select "Getting Started with Westlaw" and then "Searching with Terms and Connectors." When should you use the terms and connectors search method?

E-Research: Legal Research Using the Internet

On the Internet, nobody knows you're a dog.

Peter Steiner, cartoon in *The New Yorker*, July 5, 1993

A. **Introduction**
B. **Glossary of Terms**
C. **Conducting Legal Research Online**
D. **Strategies and Tips for Internet Legal Research**
E. **Ethical Concerns Regarding Use of the Internet**
F. **Surf's Up: The Best Internet Legal Research Sites**
G. **Cautionary Notes on Internet Legal Research**
H. **Citation Form**

Chapter Overview

The best legal researchers know how to use a combination of conventional research methods with computerized and electronic research methods to achieve results. Although one need not be a computer guru to satisfy one's duty to perform legal research competently, legal professionals should be sufficiently proficient in using the Internet that they can quickly find a case or statute. The Internet affords researchers the ability to find and review cases, statutes, and a vast array of other materials at no cost, 24 hours each day. Every year more and more materials are available on the Internet. Although the Internet will never replace conventional research methods and while there are some significant drawbacks to Internet legal research, it is an extremely efficient and time-saving method for some research tasks.

Although this chapter provides a glossary of Internet-related terms, one need not be conversant with the jargon of computers to be an effective researcher. In fact, the most useful strategy in conducting Internet legal research is to have one good starting place and then use this to branch out to other sites of interest.

This chapter provides a glossary of Internet terms, tips and strategies on conducting legal research on the Internet, and some cautionary notes about over-relying on the Internet. The chapter also provides the "best of the best" sites for various legal research tasks as well as some sites for non-legal research.

A. Introduction

Today's legal professionals have at their fingertips vast amounts of information that is free and available 24 hours each day. Until fairly recently, a researcher wanting to review a newly issued Supreme Court decision had only two options: drive to a law library or subscribe to a costly computerized legal research service such as Lexis or Westlaw. The advent of the Internet has dramatically changed legal research, allowing professionals immediate access to cases, statutes, federal regulations, forms, legislative materials, treaties, journal articles, and much more. In many instances, cases are posted to the Internet within hours after their release by the clerk of the court. Although the good news is that there is a vast array of legal materials available for your use, the bad news is that the information is so voluminous that making sense of the materials offered can be difficult and confusing.

The Internet was originally developed in the 1970s for military and government use, primarily to provide a secure method of communication in the event of nuclear attack. Use then expanded to the scientific and educational communities and, starting in the late 1980s, people began realizing the Internet's potential for enhancing communication. Use rapidly spread to the commercial sector, which quickly worked to develop the Internet's ability to promote the sale of goods and services. The Internet is now used in nearly every possible field of endeavor, from the military, to the government, to educational institutions, to not-for-profit organizations, to commercial enterprises. Nearly every business, including all large law firms, has a presence on the Internet. In fact, a recent survey by the American Bar Association's Legal Technology Resource Center disclosed that every responding law firm with 50 or more lawyers maintained a website.

Legal professionals typically use the Internet for the following purposes:

- **Communication.** Legal professionals use the Internet to communicate with each other and with clients. Through electronic mail ("e-mail"), clients can be kept informed of the progress of their cases. Legal professionals can become involved in "listservs" to keep apprised of topics of interest to them and to continue their legal education. In many instances listservs or newsgroups will automatically e-mail newsletters or bulletins to subscribers, enabling legal professionals to keep current in their fields of interest.

- **Court Filings.** Many courts and agencies now permit or require pleadings and motions to be filed electronically. Electronic filing allows courts to verify page limit and word count requirements immediately and provides immediate verification that a document has been filed.
- **Marketing.** Most law firms have a website, which is a marketing brochure about the firm that is published electronically rather than in print form. The site will typically describe the firm, its professionals, areas of expertise, and locations, and may provide articles or newsletters on legal topics. State bar ethics codes regulate advertising. Thus, firms need to ensure their websites are in compliance with those regulations.
- **Education.** Legal professionals can take continuing education classes online and subscribe to educational newsletters and other informative materials.
- **Commerce.** Legal professionals can order books, publications, and other materials from publishers and other vendors.
- **Research.** Legal professionals can use the Internet to conduct research, including legal research. One can determine an adversary's address, a client's exact corporate name, when a company's stock "went public" and who its officers and directors are, and a variety of other research tasks. The Internet can also be used for legal research, including finding cases, statutes, regulations, locating forms, reviewing legal journals and periodicals, and locating legislative documents. This chapter will focus on the use of the Internet to conduct legal research.

Although legal research on the Internet can seem awkward and intimidating to the novice, all legal professionals should strive for some degree of familiarity with Internet legal research. The general duty imposed on legal professionals to have a sufficient level of competence to represent their clients is broad enough to require competence in new and emerging technologies, including the Internet. A recent law review article has declared that "[t]he lawyer in the twenty-first century who does not effectively use the Internet for legal research may fall short of the minimal standards of professional competence and be potentially liable for malpractice." Lawrence Duncan MacLachlan, *Gandy Dancers on the Web: How the Internet Has Raised the Bar on Lawyer's Professional Responsibility to Research and Know the Law*, 13 Geo. J. Legal Ethics 607, 607 (2000). In fact, the American Association for Paralegal Education states that to be a successful paralegal, one must possess the "core competency" of being able to use both print and electronic sources of law to locate applicable primary and secondary materials. Moreover, employers and clients are increasingly technologically proficient and will justifiably expect their legal team to be equally proficient, so that clients can be kept apprised of the status of their matters by e-mail, relevant cases can be sent electronically to co-counsel, and others in the firm can be provided immediate access to files and records pertaining to a client's case.

Not only is there a nearly overwhelming amount of information available on the Internet, but also the technology surrounding Internet legal research continues to develop rapidly. For example, legal professionals can now retrieve and Shepardize or KeyCite cases and statutes on their handheld BlackBerry devices, and access primary authorities on their iPhones through Fastcase (see Chapter 11).

There is, of course, some danger in relying too much on the Internet, primarily because not all legal materials are available online. Nevertheless, learning good Internet research techniques will save you a great deal of time. In most instances, Internet legal research should complement your other research techniques — namely, conventional book research and research using Lexis and Westlaw.

Finally, be aware that there is an astounding amount of non-legal information on the Internet. Use the Internet as a tool to track clients' stock prices, determine the weather at the client's headquarters, and obtain basic information about clients' industries. Read the press releases issued by clients. Clients will be pleased and flattered that you took the time and effort to do some homework about their business, location, and financial status.

B. Glossary of Terms

Some otherwise confident professionals are intimidated by the Internet, in many cases because terms commonly used when discussing the Internet, such as "browser," "URL," and "hyperlink," are entirely new to them. Although this section of the chapter provides you with some basic Internet terms, practically speaking, there is little need to know a great deal about how the Internet works or how specific terms are defined. Most of us have no idea how our cell phones and microwave ovens work and yet are entirely comfortable using these devices. The Internet should be viewed the same way: It is nice to know some of the terms commonly used, but it is not totally necessary in order to be able to conduct legal research competently.

Following are some of the terms frequently encountered in the electronic world:

Blog: Abbreviation for "web log," an online journal or diary where a "blogger" posts his or her thoughts, often on a daily basis. The entries, called "postings," are usually arranged in chronological order, with the most recent additions listed first. Blogs devoted to law topics are usually called "blawgs."

Browser: Software that helps access and review information on the Internet and translates HTML-encoded files into text and images that one can read and view. Netscape and Microsoft's Internet Explorer are examples of browsers.

Cable modem: A cable line used to connect to the Internet allowing faster connection than a telephone line.

Chat room: A location in cyberspace fostering real-time communications among several people.

Cyberspace: The electronic or computer world in which vast amounts of information are available; sometimes used as a synonym for the Internet.

Domain name: The name that identifies an Internet site, such as "www.ibm.com." Domain names have two parts: the "generic top level domain," which is the last part of the domain, such as "com," or "gov," and which usually refers to the type of provider of the information, and the "secondary domain," which is more specific and is to the right of "www," such as "ibm" in the above example.

Download: Transferring files or information from the Internet to your personal computer files.

DSL: Abbreviation for "digital subscriber line," a technology providing fast digital data transmission over the wires of a local telephone network.

E-mail: Electronic mail or messages sent through the computer rather than in physical form (which is often called "snail mail").

Extranet: An internal company or law firm Intranet that provides access to selected outsiders on a case-by-case basis.

FAQ: "Frequently asked questions," often included on websites and that respond to the most commonly asked questions about the site or about the information provided by the site.

FIOS: Abbreviation for Fiber Optic Service, a digital technology providing Internet access with maximum connection speed.

FTP: File transfer protocol, a common method of moving files or communicating between two Internet sites or computers.

Home page: The first or main page you are sent to when accessing a person's or business's website.

HTML: Hypertext markup language, a standard language of computer code.

HTTP: Hypertext transfer protocol, a common method of moving files or communicating between two Internet sites.

Hyperlink: A method of instantaneous transport to another destination. Hyperlinks are often underscored or appear in a different color on the computer screen; by clicking the colored line, you will be immediately transferred to that particular site or page.

Internet: A collection of worldwide interconnected computer networks originally developed for defense purposes and linked together to exchange information; the Internet is not owned by any one person or company.

Internet Service Provider (ISP):   A company that provides Internet access, such as AOL or Roadrunner, for a monthly fee.

Intranet: A private network inside a company or law firm that provides access only for internal use to those in the company or firm and not to outsiders; for example, a law firm's intranet could be used only by those in the firm and could not be accessed by any member of the general public.

Link: See "Hyperlink."

Listserv: A system that allows groups of people to e-mail each other and participate in group discussions, usually about a topic of common concern. For example, a listserv comprising law students may automatically send one message to all others in the group.

Log-in: (n.) An account name used to gain entry to a computer system. Unlike a password, it is not secret. Also called a "user name"; log in: (v.) the method of accessing a computer system.

Modem: A device that connects to your computer and to a telephone line or cable line allowing the computer to communicate with other computers much the way telephones allow humans to communicate with each other.

Netiquette: The code of etiquette or conduct for the Internet.

Network: The connecting of two or more computers so that they can communicate with each other and share resources, files, and information.

Newsgroup: An online forum for sharing information and communications. Users view messages, post their own messages, and reply to others.

Online: The process of being connected to the Internet through electronic communication.

Password: The secret code used to gain access to a computer system.

PDF: Portable document format, a format that duplicates on a computer screen what a conventional print source looks like.

Posting: Entering information or messages into a network — for example, cases are "posted" to the website of the United States Supreme Court, and legal professionals "post" messages on a listserv.

RSS: Abbreviation for "rich site summary" or "really simple syndication," a format for automatically delivering updated web content.

Search box: An initially blank box on a computer screen in which you type or key in the word or terms you are interested in researching.

Search engine: A particular service that helps one locate useful information on the Internet, usually through the use of keywords; common search engines are "Yahoo!," "Google," "Bing," and "AltaVista." A search engine is a website that looks for and retrieves other websites. Search engines look for words in the millions of web pages on the Internet and direct you to pages that include the search words or keywords you enter in a search box.

Server: A computer or software package that provides or serves information to other computers.

Spamming: Sending blanket unsolicited messages to others; similar to "junk mail."

Surfing the 'Net: The process of moving or linking from one site to another in the course of reviewing information.

Upload: Transferring files or information from a computer one is using to another.

URL: Uniform resource locator, one's address on the Internet. Most Internet addresses begin with "www" or "http://www." The URL of IBM is "www.ibm.com."

User name: See "Log-in" (n).

WWW: World Wide Web, commonly used to refer to the entire collection of resources that can be accessed in cyberspace through the Internet.

Web: See "WWW."

Web page: A particular file or "page" included in a website.

Website: A collection of web pages; for example, IBM's website (www.ibm.com) will consist of numerous web pages, each of which is devoted to a specific topic. A website always begins with a "home page," which is the first screen viewed when the website is accessed.

WiFi: Abbreviation for "wireless fidelity," a form of wireless data communication.

Glossaries of Internet terms can also be found at http://www. matisse.net/files/glossary.html and http://www.sharpened.net/glossary.

C. Conducting Legal Research Online

1. Getting Started

Following are the steps in accessing the Internet so you can begin conducting legal research. In brief, you will be using your modem and telephone or cable line (or wireless network) to connect to the server of your Internet service provider. When the communication between your computer and the Internet has been established, you will type in a request or click a link, and your browser will send a request for information to the server. The server will send the information to you, and you will view it in your browser. You will "surf the 'Net" by clicking on hyperlinks and jumping to other sites of interest. You may download files or information for later viewing or printing.

- Turn on your computer and proceed to log in, using your log-in identification (sometimes called your "user name") and your password.
- Look for the icon that identifies your Internet service provider, such as AOL.
- Double click on the icon.
- Enter any identifying log-ins or passwords to access your account.
- Type in the word or term you are researching in the search box (if you are in a general search engine such as http://www.yahoo.com).

Alternatively, in the address "box" at the top of the page, type in your favorite starting page, such as http://www.google.com; http://www.washlaw.edu; or http://www.findlaw.com. Use this page as your jumping-off point and begin double clicking on the links that interest you. (See Figure 12-1.)

- Note that although most Internet addresses begin with "http://www" you may not need to type in the initial "http" or "www" information. Most browsers are configured to recognize "www" (or the main site address) by itself. Similarly, in most instances the Internet is not "case-sensitive," meaning that you can usually type in either upper- or lower-case letters and they will be recognized and read.

Figure 12-1
Home Page for FindLaw

2. *Using a Good Start Page*

There is probably no better tip for conducting legal research on the Internet than to always begin your project with one good "start page." Your start page should be reliable and easy to use. It should be formatted in a user-friendly manner so that you can easily read the print on the screen and locate the information you need without confusing graphics, pictures, and distracting scrolling announcements, advertisements, or pop-ups. The advantage of always beginning at the same place or start page is that you will quickly become comfortable and familiar with the page, and it will serve as an excellent jumping-off place for your research tasks.

Although there are many start pages from which you can begin your research, following are some well-known legal favorites:

- http://www.law.cornell.edu. The Legal Information Institute at Cornell University Law School is one of the best-known legal sites. It offers overviews of legal topics such as bankruptcy and corporations and allows direct linking to federal and state cases, statutes, court rules, and administrative regulations. The site is highly respected and credible.
- http://www.law.washlaw.edu. This site of Washburn University School of Law lists legal materials, courts, and states, making it very easy to locate material of interest. Once again, because it is a site offered by an educational institution, it is highly regarded. Its appearance is plain, nearly stark, without any distracting advertising. (See Figure 12-3.)
- http://lp.findlaw.com. This site, FindLaw (now owned by West), is another one of the best-known legal sites. It directs users to a vast array of legal materials, including cases, statutes, forms, reference materials, and legal periodicals. Links to hundreds of sources of interest to legal professionals are provided, including links to each state's bar association, special links for law students, links to help locate attorneys, experts, and consultants, and numerous other links to legal resources. (See Figure 12-1.)
- http://www.megalaw.com. MegaLaw is a commercial site offering links to thousands of useful law-related sites. The site is easy to navigate and offers ready access to federal and state cases, statutes, court rules, legal forms, and more.
- http://www.plol.org. One of the newest competitors in free online legal research is the Public Library of Law (provided by Fastcase), which bills itself as the "world's largest online database of free law." Plol provides access to a wide variety of materials, including all U.S. Supreme Court cases, all lower federal court cases since 1950, state cases, the U.S. Code, state statutes, and more. You may search by key words, citation, or by using terms and connectors. Searching is easy and results are presented in an easy-to-read format. Users must complete a free registration form to use the site.

- http://www.justia.com. Justia provides free case law, codes, regulations, legal articles, and legal blog databases, as well as community resources. Justia also provides information about various legal topics. For example, when you select "Family Law," you are given an overview of this area of law, a glossary of family law terms, and links to articles of interest and other resources. (See Figure 12-2).

Once you choose a "start page" that you are comfortable with, begin your research task with this page and progress from there. After some time, you may encounter other sites that are of more use to you. If you are a beginner in Internet legal research, however, this method of consistently beginning any Internet legal research task with your "one good start page" is the best way to gain expertise on the Internet.

Figure 12-2
Home Page for Justia

Figure 12-3
Home Page for WashLaw

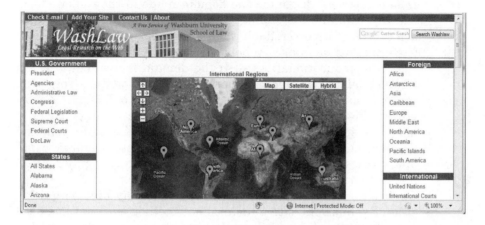

Practice Tip

Using Google Scholar to Conduct Legal Research

One newcomer to free Internet legal research is Google Scholar, located at http://scholar.google.com. Searching of federal and state cases is easily accomplished; you may search by case name, citation, or key words. Results are provided in Google's typical fashion in that they are ranked in order of "importance" (at least, according to Google's determination of the cases' order of importance). You may also easily determine which other cases have cited your case.

---

3.   Assessing the Credibility of Websites

Much of the material that appears on the Internet appears authoritative and reliable; however, many sites are not subject to the rigorous fact checking and editing of their print counterparts. Authors who publish in print form are often the acknowledged experts in their field. On the Internet, it is nearly impossible to judge credibility. Articles often fail to identify an author or date. Contributors to listservs or newsgroups are

anonymous. Consider the following factors in evaluating the credibility of websites:

- *Domain Name.* Examine the domain name in the website (specifically, examine the ending, such as "com" or "org"). Some sites are considered more reliable than others. For example, the "gov" (government) sites are probably most authoritative, followed by the "edu" (educational) sites. If the domain name shows it is a commercial site (through the use of "com" or sometimes "org"), its content may be influenced by its owner or publisher. Review advertising on commercial sites to determine whether there is bias. Consider whether the purpose of the site is to generate revenue. On the other hand, many law firm websites end in "com," and articles posted on a firm's website are usually highly reliable and authoritative.
- *Currency.* Articles posted on the Internet may become quickly stale. Examine the site to determine whether material has been recently updated. Also, if hyperlinks to other sites are outdated, it signals that the site may not be regularly maintained.
- *Author.* A tilde (~) in a web address indicates that the author is an individual rather than an institution. Well-known experts usually like to be paid for their work; thus, "free" articles on the Internet may not be authored by the best-known experts in the field. Check the author's qualifications. Does the author include contact information? Reliable authors often encourage readers to contact them.
- *Appearance.* Review the overall look and feel of the site. If the site is amateurish or accompanied by cartoons and humorous graphics, this may be a sign that its content is not serious.
- *Errors.* If you locate even one error in content (such as incorrect citation form or out-of-date fee schedules), it may well signal that other errors exist. Similarly, errors in grammar, spelling, and punctuation are signs that the material was not subject to thorough editing and review.
- *Attribution and References.* Quotations and statistics should be attributed to their source (and, ideally, there should be hyperlinks to the original source). Most reliable sites include references and hyperlinks to other resources to allow their users to obtain additional information.
- *Richness of Content.* Review a few other websites to compare their content and to serve as a double-check of the accuracy and depth of analysis of your site.

D. Strategies and Tips for Internet Legal Research

It is far easier to get distracted when researching on the Internet than when researching using conventional print volumes. A site piques your interest so you click on it. When you access that site, another site looks promising and you click on it. When you access that site, yet another intriguing link appears. Before you know it, you are no longer researching search and seizure articles but have begun reviewing stock quotes, checking the weather in Seattle, or perusing movie reviews. The vast amount of information on the Internet is a constant source of diversion and distraction. Staying focused is a continuing campaign.

Understand that when you enter a term in a search box — for example, "patent infringement" — and a list of relevant sites is given, the sites are usually listed in order, specifically, in order of how many times your term, "patent infringement," appears on the site, even in coded or hidden form. Thus, the first site identified is not necessarily the best; it is merely the one that uses or displays the term "patent infringement" most often. Because terms can be hidden in websites, you may be directed to a site that offers little or no substantive information about patent infringement. In some instances, you are directed to law firm websites and you must wade through marketing material before you can locate substantive material on patent infringement. Other sites, notably Google (http://www.google.com), list the most relevant and useful sites first, making research easy and productive.

Why use the Internet rather than Lexis or Westlaw? Although search strategies using Lexis and Westlaw are generally more focused and produce more targeted results, Lexis and Westlaw are fee-based services, while the Internet offers free legal research 24/7. Lexis and Westlaw, however, have far more complete databases. For example, state court cases are available on the Internet only for the past few years, while Lexis and Westlaw offer access to nearly all state court cases. Moreover, there is no way to check the validity of a case you locate on the Internet, while Lexis offers Shepardizing and Westlaw offers KeyCiting to determine whether your case is still "good law."

Following are some tips and strategies to help ensure that your Internet research is as efficient and effective as possible:

1. **Take Notes.** Rather than jumping or linking from site to site, jot down the sites that appear promising. You can access other sites after you have come to a dead end in your present research efforts. Moreover, it is possible that you will get disconnected from the Internet. If you have jotted down sites of interest, you will be able to locate them later.

2. **Use the History Lists.** When you research, you will use links to jump from site to site. To return to the immediately previous site, select the "back" arrow at the top of your toolbar. By continually

selecting the "back" and "forward" arrows, you can move through the sites you have visited. Alternatively, you can review the sites you have visited by clicking on the "history" button or on the down arrow at the top of your page that displays the URL of the site you are currently visiting. A drop-down menu will be displayed that identifies the most recent sites you have visited. Select the site in which you are interested and you will be transported there.

3. **Use Bookmarks.** When you determine that there are certain sites you continually visit or that provide you with useful information, "bookmark" them or add them to your "favorites" list, so you can readily return to them. When you are at the website of interest, select "Favorites" from the top of your toolbar. This site will be bookmarked as your personal favorite. Once you add a bookmark, the page name appears whenever you click the "Favorites" or "bookmark" icon.

4. **Avoid Reading the Screen.** Reading material on a computer screen is very tiring and causes eyestrain. If a long article or case appears promising, print it and read it in hard copy form.

5. **Be Aware of Gaps in Information.** Although a law library and Lexis and Westlaw offer all federal court cases, the Internet presently offers only all the United States Supreme Court cases; lower federal cases are often available only for the past several years or decades, and access to state court cases is even more limited. Thus, research on the Internet cannot be a complete substitute for research using conventional print sources or the computerized research systems Lexis or Westlaw.

6. **Never Completely Rely on the Internet.** Although the Internet provides some excellent information and is often the easiest and cheapest way to find a case or statute, it is not a substitute for a law library. Relying solely on the Internet for legal research will result in a research project that lacks in-depth analysis. The best way to find cases interpreting statutes is still the old-fashioned way: reviewing the annotations following statutes in U.S.C.A., U.S.C.S., or the state codes. The Internet, however, is an excellent tool for locating a quick answer to questions such as, "What is the statute of limitations for medical malpractice actions in California?" or "What is the definition of 'copyright' in federal law?" or "What is the citation to the United States Supreme Court case *Brown v. Board of Education*?" To complete a research project, you will need to supplement your Internet legal research efforts with conventional research methods or with computerized services such as Lexis and Westlaw.

7. **Subscribe to a Listserv.** Consider subscribing or signing up to receive news bulletins or updates from a law-related website. You will then be provided with daily or periodic updates related to topics of interest to you. Be cautious: Although many of the update or listserv services (such as those offered through www.findlaw.com) are excellent, subscribing to too many listservs or newsgroups will only result in duplication of materials and a clogged inbox.

8. **Consider Disclaimers.** Review the disclaimer section of a website. It will tell you the limitations of the site and will usually indicate if you are permitted to reproduce the material on the site. Unless otherwise indicated, material on a private, educational, or commercial website is protected by copyright law, and you cannot copy and use it any more than you could photocopy a well-known treatise and then use it. The federal "gov" sites, however, including THOMAS, publish materials in the public domain, and any material on these sites is freely available for printing, using, downloading, or other purposes.
9. **Use RSS to Obtain Updates.** Many websites offer "RSS feeds," which automatically send you updated content from your frequently visited websites or blogs. Thus, rather than having to check continually to see whether a website has changed its content or added new information, you will be automatically notified if new content has been posted. Look for a symbol such as "RSS feed" and click on it to subscribe to updated information. This feature is similar to Lexis's and Westlaw's "alerts" services, which automatically notify you of changes in the status of cases you have Shepardized or KeyCited and of updated information relating to your searches.

E. Ethical Concerns Regarding Use of the Internet

One of the many uses of the Internet is facilitating communication, or e-mail, between legal professionals and their clients. Additionally, in many instances documents are sent electronically to clients for review. Such messages and documents sent to clients travel over a variety of networks in an essentially open environment. One concern regarding such communications is that of privacy. Legal professionals owe ethical duties to clients to maintain their information in confidence. Electronic communications are vulnerable to interception, misuse, and alteration. Thus, law firms using e-mail must ensure that the means used to communicate information to clients are secure so that the attorney-client privilege is not inadvertently waived. Although not every communication between legal professionals and clients needs to be encrypted, some communications may be so sensitive that they should not be sent unless they are protected by encryption software. Before communicating electronically with clients, determine what your firm or office policy is. At a minimum, communications to clients should be accompanied by the type of notice common on facsimile cover sheets, namely, that the communication is intended only for the recipient; it is private and confidential; if it is received in error it should be returned to the sender and may not be copied or disclosed; and so forth. Law firms that market themselves as knowledgeable about the Internet and cyberlaw may be held to a higher standard of care regarding electronic communications.

A number of individuals have considered whether sending unencrypted e-mail over the Internet violates a client's right to confidentiality. In 1999, the ABA resolved the issue in its Formal Opinion 99-413, which concluded that e-mail communications pose no greater risk of interception or disclosure than other methods of communication (such as regular mail) commonly relied upon as having a reasonable expectation of privacy. Thus, sending client material by unencrypted e-mail does not violate the ethical duty to maintain a client's information in confidence. In the past few years, several attorneys have criticized the ABA's opinion, believing that the ABA did not take into account the fact that e-mail is more easily intercepted today than in prior years. Thus, many experts recommend obtaining the client's informed consent before communicating critical information by e-mail.

Another ethical concern that has arisen regarding use of the Internet by legal professionals is whether law firm marketing materials constitute advertising and solicitation. In one instance, a law firm sent an advertisement for its immigration services to thousands of different newsgroups, raising the question whether the advertisement was improper client solicitation. State bar regulations regarding attorney advertising must be carefully reviewed to ensure that all materials posted by a firm on the Internet or sent out to newsgroups are in compliance with state codes regulating advertising and client solicitation. Law firm websites are usually viewed as communications or "advertisements" rather than as unlawful solicitations; thus, so long as their content is neither false nor misleading, they are permissible. Many law firms include disclaimers on their websites that a person's visit to the site does not constitute an attorney-client relationship.

Similarly, legal professionals should be circumspect about providing any information on the Internet that could be viewed as legal advice. The websites of most law firms include broad disclaimers that state that information posted on the site is not legal advice, does not create an attorney-client relationship, and is provided for general information purposes only.

Ethics Alert

Avoiding Copyright Infringement

Be careful not to fall into the trap of thinking that everything on the Internet is in the public domain and can be used without permission. Thus, avoid excessive quoting from Internet sources unless attribution is given or permission is received. In many instances, you can directly e-mail the author of an article or piece and ask for permission to reproduce the material. Look at the site to see whether the author has granted permission to reprint or use. Consider the credibility of the source before relying on it in your writings.

F. Surf's Up: The Best Internet Legal Research Sites

At the end of each chapter in this text, pertinent websites have been given to assist you in your research efforts. As you have noticed, there are hundreds of websites available, so many that research using the Internet can seem overwhelming. For example, federal cases can be located through at least ten different websites. This section of this chapter will give you brief descriptions of some of the best sites for legal and non-legal research.

1. *Best Legal Start Sites*

As mentioned earlier, the best way to conduct efficient legal research on the Internet is to have a reliable and user-friendly starting place. Among the best starting places are the following:

- http://www.law.cornell.edu — Excellent starting place for legal issues, many tools, and links to sites.

- http://www.washlaw.edu — Site offering direct links to cases, statutes, journals, international materials, regulations, and numerous other legal resources by easily arranged links for efficient access.

- http://lp.findlaw.com — Commercial site, devoted to legal topics, offering easy and direct linking to cases, statutes, journals, and a wide variety of other law-related materials, including bar associations, codes of ethics, directories of lawyers, legal reference materials (such as dictionaries), and numerous other law-related sources.

- http://www.lexisone.com — Free cases, forms, articles, headline legal news, links to law-related sites, all offered by Lexis.

- http://www.justia.com — Free cases, statutes, forms, and access to podcasts on numerous legal topics of interest.

- http://www.ilrg.com — Internet Legal Research Group, a meta-index of more than 4,000 Internet legal sites.

- http://www.megalaw.com — Excellent and easy to use site with hundreds of valuable links to legal materials.

2. Best Sites for Locating Cases

- http://www.supremecourt.gov — United States Supreme Court site allowing searching by party name, citation, or docket number and providing schedules of arguments, the Court's calendar, and Court rules.

- http://www.uscourts.gov — United States federal courts home page and gateway to federal courts and their cases, briefs, and rules.

- http://www.plol.org — Site offering access to federal cases and links for each state (availability of state cases varies from state to state).

- http://www.law.cornell.edu — Cornell's site offers access to federal and state cases (availability of state cases varies from state to state).

3. Best Sites for Locating Statutes

- http://www.findlaw.com/casecode — FindLaw's site offers access to all federal and state statutes.

- http://www.law.cornell.edu — Site offering access to *United States Code*. Searching may be done by citation or popular name. Easy browsing of all titles provided. Access is also offered to state statutes.

- http://www.megalaw.com — MegaLaw offers direct access to the *United States Code* as well as all state statutes.

- http://www.law.cornell.edu/ucc/ucc.table.html — Uniform Commercial Code.

- http://www.nccusl.org — Website of National Conference of Commissioners on Uniform State Laws offering text of uniform laws.

4. Best Sites for Government Materials

In many instances, you can "guess" at website addresses for government agencies. For example, the website of the Internal Revenue Service is http://www.irs.gov, and the website of the Federal Trade Commission is http://www.ftc.gov. Following are some useful sites for locating federal and state government materials:

- http://www.usa.gov — The United States government's official web portal (formerly called "FirstGov") is a gateway to all government information, including federal executive, legislative, and judicial materials, information about agencies, and links to state government home pages.

- http://thomas.loc.gov

  THOMAS, offering United States legislative information, bills, voting records, public laws, and other legislative information. (See Figure 10-1.)

- http://www.gpoaccess.gov and http://www.fdsys.gov

  Providing direct links to the Code of Federal Regulations, *Federal Register*, public laws, *United States Government Manual, Compilation of Presidential Documents*, and other government materials. GPO Access is migrating to a newer system, the Federal Digital System (FDsys), which offers enhanced searching and access to authenticated government documents.

- http://www.fedworld.gov

  Guide to federal government resources and reports and links to top government websites.

5. *Best Sites for Locating Forms*

- http://www.lectlaw.com/ form.html

  Forms for litigation, business, real estate, wills, trusts, corporations, and other areas.

- http://www.washlaw.edu

  Select "Legal Forms."

- http://www.megalaw.com

  MegaLaw site; select "Legal Forms" for numerous free forms and links to other sites offering forms.

- http://www.allaboutforms.com

  All About Forms provides more than 2,000 free legal forms.

6. *Paralegal Sites*

- http://www.paralegals.org

  Site of the National Federation of Paralegal Associations, with networking and career opportunities, code of ethics, professional development information, and links to numerous other law-related sites.

- http://www.nala.org

  Site of the National Association of Legal Assistants, with information about the paralegal profession, code of ethics, and links to numerous law-related sites.

- http://www.hg.org/assistants- assoc.html

  Listing of national and state paralegal associations.

- http://www.paralegal management.org

  Site of International Paralegal Management Association (formerly Legal Assistant Management Association), which promotes development of paralegal managers.

7. *Best Specialty Sites*

Note that two sites provide extensive and reliable coverage of numerous law topics: Access Cornell University Law School's site at http://www.law.cornell.edu/topics to select more than 100 topics such as criminal law, employment law, and family law (select "Browse" and then review the list of topics provided); access MegaLaw's site at http://megalaw.com and select "Law Topic Pages" to review more than 230 law topics from aboriginal law to zoning law.

Following are some sites for specialized legal topics:

Americans with Disabilities Act Site

- http://www.ada.gov   Home page for ADA; information and links relating to the Americans with Disabilities Act.

Attorney and Ethics Sites

- http://www.abanet.org/cpr   The American Bar Association's Center for Professional Responsibility offers ethics resources and opinions.

- http://www.martindalehub bell.com   Lawyer locator offered by Martindale-Hubbell.

- http://www.legalethics.com   Comprehensive site providing ethics information and links to other ethics-related sources.

- http://www.law.cornell.edu/ ethics   Links to ethics materials for each state.

Corporate, Business, and Securities Sites

- http://www.sec.gov   Website of the Securities and Exchange Commission, offering full text of filings made by public companies, links to securities laws, and more.

- http://securities.stanford.edu   Securities law and information.

- http://www.hoovers.com   Profiles of more than 12 million public companies. Some information requires a fee.

- http://www.nass.org   Website of National Association of Secretaries of State, with direct links to each state's corporations division for access to state forms, filing fees, and more for corporations, LLPs, and so forth.

- http://www.megalaw.com/top/ corporate.php   Numerous corporate links, including links to text of laws and regulations and recent cases.

Environmental Sites

- http://www.epa.gov   Website of the Environmental Protection
                                      Agency.

- http://www.megalaw.com/top/   Environmental Law Center.
  environmental.php

Intellectual Property Sites

- http://www.uspto.gov   Official site of the United States Patent and
                                      Trademark Office, offering the text of stat-
                                      utes relating to patents and trademarks,
                                      forms, general overviews of trademark and
                                      patent procedure and law, and a fully search-
                                      able database allowing one to search for
                                      trademarks and patents.

- http://www.copyright.gov   Website of the Copyright Office, offering
                                      forms, detailed information on copyright law,
                                      and links to other resources related to copy-
                                      right law.

- http://ipmall.info   Website of Pierce Law Center IP Mall, pro-
                                      viding in-depth coverage of intellectual prop-
                                      erty law and numerous links to other sites
                                      and documents.

International Sites

- http://www.un.org   Website of the United Nations, offering trea-
                                      ties and resolutions.

- http://www.wipo.int   Website of World Intellectual Property Orga-
                                      nization, offering text of various treaties.

Labor and Employment Sites

- http://www.dol.gov   Site of United States Department of Labor.

- http://www.osha.gov   Comprehensive site of Occupational Safety
                                      and Health Administration.

Legal Research and Writing Sites

- http://www.ll.georgetown.edu/   Providing guides describing how to conduct
  research/index.cfm   legal research.

- http://ualr.edu/cmbarger   Site providing research, writing, and advo-
                                      cacy resources and links.

- http://www.gpoaccess.gov/   United States Government Printing Office
  stylemanual   *Style Manual*, the authoritative guide to
                                      writing, spelling, grammar, and so forth.

- http://press-pubs
  .uchicago.edu/garner

  Exercises and information on legal writing from Bryan A. Garner.

- http://www.archives.gov/
  federal-register/write/
  plain-language

  Office of the Federal Register's guides to clear writing.

- http://www.bartleby.com

  Providing links to many sources, including portions of *The Elements of Style*, the classic guide to good writing.

Reference Materials Sites

- http://www.aallnet.org

  Site of American Association of Law Libraries.

- http://www.bartleby.com

  Featuring a thesaurus, *Bartlett's Familiar Quotations*, and a wide variety of reference materials.

- http://www.dictionary.com

  Dictionary and thesaurus.

- http://dictionary.law.com

  Legal dictionary, searchable by word or phrase.

- http://www.usa.gov

  USA.gov (formerly called FirstGov) is the United States federal government's portal to a wide variety of materials, including federal and state resources.

- http://www.refdesk.com

  This excellent all-purpose site offers links for news, encyclopedic information, weather around the world, stock ticker symbols, and much more.

Tax Sites

- http://www.irs.gov

  Site of Internal Revenue Service providing information, forms, and links to other resources.

- http://www.taxprophet.com

  Valuable information and links to other tax sites.

8.   *Best Non-Legal Sites*

Although it is helpful to have a repertory of law-related sites at your fingertips, you also need to be familiar with some basic information sites, so you can determine the weather in the city where tomorrow's deposition will be taken, directions to the client's office, or the last price at which the client's stock was sold. Following are some basic information and reference sites.

- http://www.quotations
  page.com

  Offering quotes (for speeches).

- http://www.internet tollfree.com — For looking up toll-free 800 numbers.

- http://www.usps.com — Providing zip codes in the United States.

- http://maps.google.com — For obtaining a map and directions to a location.

- http://www.2docstock.com/ res-travel.html — Travel resources, including currency converter, maps, weather information, embassy links, and international dialing codes.

- http://www.weather.com — For obtaining weather in a given city.

- http://www.nyse.com — Providing stock quotes for companies listed on the New York Stock Exchange; offering a ticker symbol "look up."

- http://www.nasdaq.com — Providing stock quotes for companies listed on the NASDAQ Exchange; offering a ticker symbol "look up."

9. *Where to Start When All Else Fails*

General search engines can provide excellent information and leads. Whether you start with Google, Yahoo!, or some other site, you merely type keywords into a search box and you will then be given a list of websites that respond to your search terms. In the past few years, Google (http://www.google.com), with its references to more than 8 billion websites and its ranking of results by relevance, has become increasingly popular. Google's search engine is so intuitive that you can enter terms such as "17 usc 101" and be referred directly to 17 U.S.C. § 101.

Two newer features of Google bear mentioning: You may now install Google on your toolbar so that you may do a Google search at any time from any website (access http://toolbar.google.com and follow the directions); Google also provides a variety of special features such as a calculator, stock quotes, and the ability to track UPS packages, check airline flight status, and more at the address http://www.google.com/help/features.html.

Other general-purpose search engines include the following:

- **AltaVista.** http://www.altavista.com
- **Ask.** http://www.ask.com
- **Lycos.** http://www.lycos.com
- **Yahoo!** http://www.yahoo.com

10. *Listservs, Newsgroups, Blawgs, and Apps*

Listservs, newsgroups, and law-related web logs (called "blawgs") help legal professionals keep current on cutting-edge legal issues and share information. Technically, listservs are different from newsgroups in that

listservs operate through e-mail. For example, a listserv system auto-matically sends everyone on the mailing list a message at the same time. In a newsgroup, anyone with an Internet connection may view the messages, post their own, or reply to other messages. A blawg is an online journal or web log related to legal topics.

Following are some excellent websites that allow you to subscribe to newsletters or to access blawgs.

http://www.practical paralegalism.com	Practical Paralegalism is a paralegal blawg with interesting posts, links to other sites, and timely news, tips, and anecdotes.
http://newsletters .findlaw.com	FindLaw allows you to subscribe to daily or weekly newsletters so that you will be noti-fied by e-mail of breaking legal news and re-cently released cases.
http://www.blawg.com	BLAWG will link you to well-known blawgs, including May It Please The Court, a weblog of legal news.
http://blawgsearch.justia.com/ blogs	Justia lists nearly 4,000 blogs, on hundreds of topics, including 12 blawgs devoted to paralegal topics.
http://www.abajournal.com/ blawgs	This ABA site lists hundreds of blawgs, cat-egorized by topic, jurisdiction, and more. Many paralegal blawgs are listed.

One of the newest tech-related developments is the creation of various applications or "apps" that can be used with iPhones, BlackBerrys, and other similar devices. Some of these apps include databases for the Federal Rules of Civil Procedure, U.S. Constitution, tax and other federal laws, federal regulations, *Black's Law Dictionary*, and various state statutes, all accessible anytime and anywhere. Other apps available to legal professionals include those that calculate court deadlines, apps for time and billing entries, and case management tools. As noted in Chapter 11, Fastcase provides a free app for iPhones, allowing access to cases, statutes, and more (access http://www.fastcase.com/iphone to download the app).

G. Cautionary Notes on Internet Legal Research

Many researchers confuse locating information on the Internet with researching. Retrieving a case is not the same as analyzing it. Locating a statute or a case is just the beginning of a research task. Cases that

interpret the statute must be analyzed; treatises and Restatements should be reviewed; and periodicals, looseleaf services, and other materials should be consulted.

Moreover, much of the material that appears on the Internet is anonymous. Thus, you do not know the credibility or reputation of the author. Just as you would not take medical advice from a stranger on the corner, you should not take legal "advice" from strangers on the Internet corner. Most experts prefer to be paid for their work authoring texts and then to receive royalties based on sales of the material. Those who post materials on the Internet may well be reliable experts. Then again, they may not be; there is no way to know for sure.

There are obviously tremendously valuable research materials on the Internet, particularly the *United States Code*, the *Code of Federal Regulations*, state statutes, and federal and state court cases. Note that all of these materials share one thing in common: They are all materials in the public domain. The well-known legal publishers, such as Lexis and West, have not posted their valuable databases on the Internet, and you should not expect that these materials will be made available for free.

Finally, always consider that even the most reputable-seeming sites can be subject to abuse. The CIA's and Department of Justice's sites have both been hacked. Thus, at any given moment, the materials you review on the Internet may be false.

As long as you remember these cautionary notes, the Internet remains a valuable and efficient tool for beginning your research project. It can never be a substitute for a full, in-depth analysis of legal materials, such as those you find in a law library or through the well-known and reliable computer research services, such as Lexis or Westlaw.

Fast Facts: Print Libraries and Digital Libraries

The American Bar Association's recent Legal Technology Resource Center Survey Report disclosed the following:

- Lawyers spend about as much time using conventional print resources as they do using fee-based online tools such as Lexis and Westlaw.
- The respondents spent slightly more time using online fee-based sources for federal and state primary law but preferred to use print materials for law reviews, periodicals, and treatises.
- About one-third of all lawyers use e-mail discussion lists for legal research.
- Of the more than 90 percent of lawyers who reported using the Internet to conduct research of any type, more than half (53 percent) favored Google as their general search engine.
- Legal publishers reported that print materials remain their dominant format and noted a strong attachment to print products by legal professionals.

H. Citation Form

As discussed in Chapter 8, *The Bluebook* requires the use and citation of traditional printed sources when they are available, *unless* there is a digital copy of the source available that is authenticated, official, or an exact copy of the printed source (in which case the authenticated, official, or exact copy may be cited as if to the original source). If access to a print source would be improved by providing an electronic or Internet citation, it may be provided as a parallel citation (introduced by the phrase "*available at*"). Some materials, however, exist only in cyberspace, in which case citation form is governed by Rule 18 of *The Bluebook* and *ALWD* Rules 38-42. Following are some *Bluebook* examples. Additional examples and examples for *ALWD* format are found in Chapter 8.

- Exact copy of print source available on Internet:

    4 U.S.C. § 2 (2006).

- Source available in traditional print format but Internet content is identical, and citation to the Internet will substantially improve access:

    Dolan v. United States, 91 Fed. Cl. 111 (2010), *available at* http://www.uscfc.uscourts.gov/sites/default/files/ CMILLER.DOLAN012610.pdf.

- Sources found exclusively on the Internet:

    Jason Newbold, *Cyberspace Law Issues*, 3 N. Va. Tech. J. 16, ¶ 8 (2004), http://www.findlaw.com/articles/1109-019-45.html.

    Carol Steiker, *Kagan and the Legacy of Marshall*, Nat'l L.J. (July 26, 2010), http://www.law.com/jsp/nlj/PubArticleNLJ.jsp? id=1202463798350&Kagan_and_the_legacy_of_Marshall.

Net Tips

Some advantages of using the Internet:

- Access to Internet sources is available 24 hours a day, from anywhere in the world.
- The Internet provides free access to a wide array of legal materials.
- E-mail, chat rooms, and newsgroup postings allow you to ask colleagues for assistance and information.
- The Internet provides access to many private materials. For example, some paralegals have posted their case briefs on the

Internet and invited others to print and use them. Similarly, law firms often publish articles on selected legal topics.
- The Internet provides direct access to invaluable legal materials including cases, statutes, and regulations.
- Office space for library books and binders is expensive. The web stores incredible amounts of information at no cost.

Some drawbacks to using the Internet:

- Many unpublished cases find their way onto the Internet. On the Internet, with its vast virtual space, no one edits out the "dog" cases. Some courts prohibit citations to unpublished decisions. Thus, exercise care and look carefully for the words "published" or "unpublished" at the beginning of a case.
- Although you can locate many primary materials (including cases and statutes) on the Internet, you cannot determine with certainty whether they are still "good law."
- The Internet is transient. Sites appear, then vanish with no explanation. According to one expert, the average life span of a web page is 100 days.
- The Internet is anonymous. The "experts" providing advice via e-mail or chat rooms are unknown and unproved.
- Accessing the law is far different from understanding and analyzing it.

Be cautious in using terms of art when discussing materials found on the Internet. Provide definitions for terms such as "browser" or "server" and use jargon sparingly so as not to confuse or intimidate readers.

When setting up Internet citations, ensure that the often long string of numbers and letters in the URL break at a natural point at the end of a typed line. Proofread carefully to ensure readers can locate the material you cite. It is easy to transpose numbers and letters in long URL strings.

Both *The Bluebook* (Rule 18.2.2) and *ALWD* (Rule 40.1(d)(3)) allow writers to give instructions on accessing websites (for example, an instruction to "follow hyperlink" or "search History") when a URL is overly long or includes confusing characters such as question marks and percentage symbols.

Assignment for Chapter 12

1. Access the THOMAS website. Locate H.R. 3756 introduced in the 110th Congress.
   a. What is the general subject of this legislation?
   b. Select "Bill Summary and Status" and then "All Congressional Actions." What action occurred on October 10, 2007?
2. Access the THOMAS website. Select "Presidential Nominations." Locate nominations for the 109th Congress and review the confirmed nominations for civilians for the State of Washington. Who was the subject of Presidential Nomination 30-110?
3. Access the website USA.gov. Select "Government Agencies" and locate information on the Government Accountability Office. When was the GAO founded?
4. Access the website http://www.washlaw.edu. Select "Colorado" and then "Code of Colorado Regulations." What is the topic of Colorado Code of Regulations 1503-1?
5. Access Cornell's Legal Information Institute.
   a. Select "Wex legal dictionary/encyclopedia." Generally, what is a Dead Man's Statute?
   b. Access the Federal Rules, specifically, the Federal Rules of Civil Procedure. Generally, how many written interrogatories may one party serve on another?
6. Access Google Scholar. What is the citation for the case *Jimenez v. Quarterman*?
7. Access the Hoovers website and locate information about Office Depot Inc.
   a. Who is the chairman and CEO of the company?
   b. What stock exchange lists the company's stock, and what is the company's stock ticker symbol?
   c. Identify the company's top competitors?
8. Access the website for the Department of Labor. Use the site map to locate information. What is the minimum wage of workers covered by the Fair Labor Standards Act?
9. Access the website MegaLaw.com. Select statutes for California. What is the subject matter of California Business and Professions Code § 6450?
10. Access the website http://www.uscourts.gov.
    a. Review the map of U.S. courts.
       (i) What is the address of the Eastern District of Texas Court?
       (ii) Locate information about Judge Leonard Davis of the Eastern District of Texas. Who is the Judge's courtroom deputy?

      b.   Select "Rules and Policies." Review the Code of Conduct for U.S. Judges. Review Canon 4. May a judge teach a class at your school? Give your answer and indicate the specific Canon that governs your answer.

11. Access the website for GPO Access.
      a.   Select the *Code of Federal Regulations* and browse the table of contents. What is the subject matter of 16 C.F.R. § 310.4?
      b.   Select "Public and Private Laws." Browse the laws for the 106th Congress. Locate and review Private Law 014. What is the title of this Private Law and what was its designation in the Senate?

12. Access the website for FDsys. Select the *Federal Register* for January 29, 2010. Locate the proposed rule for the Department of Labor (OSHA) relating to occupational injury and illness recording and reports requirements.
      a.   What logo and notice are you given in the upper left-hand corner of the document?
      b.   Per *Bluebook* Rule 18, what does this logo mean with regard to citing this proposed rule?

13. Access the website for the Public Library of Law. What is the citation for the case *Barnick v. United States*?

14. Access the website All About Forms. Select "Show All Business Topics" and then "Corporations." Locate a form for bylaws of a corporation. What topic does Article II, Section 8 cover?

15. Access Google. Enter "Arizona statute 13-1202." What is the general subject matter of this statute?

16. Access the website for the Internal Revenue Service. What is the subject matter of IRS Form 6251?

17. Access the website FindLaw. Browse cases and do a citation search for 449 U.S. 1. What is the name of this case?

18. Access the website for the National Association for Secretaries of State. Select "Secretaries of State." What is the fee to organize or form a limited liability company in your state?

19. Access an appropriate website, such as FindLaw. What is the subject matter of Article IV of your state's constitution?

Overview of the Research Process

[R]esearch is never completed . . . around the corner lurks another possibility . . . .

Catherine Drinker Bowen (1959)

A. How to Begin
B. Working with the Authorities
C. When to Stop

Chapter Overview

Among the most difficult tasks in performing legal research are beginning and ending the project. It is easy to become so overwhelmed at the task ahead of you that you become paralyzed at the thought of how and where to commence your legal research. Part of the difficulty lies with the tremendous mass of legal publications: millions of cases, volumes of codes, and so many secondary authorities, including encyclopedias, periodicals, treatises, attorneys general opinions, looseleaf services and other sources, that a researcher does not know where to turn first. Lexis, Westlaw, and the Internet add another layer of complexity to the research process.

Similarly, once you have begun delving into these authorities, you cannot decide when to stop. It seems there is always one more case to read or source to check. This chapter will offer some practical guidelines on beginning your research task and knowing when to end it.

A. How to Begin

1. Introduction

There are few inflexible rules in legal research. It is not nearly so precise as mathematics, which provides step-by-step logical guidelines to enable you to systematically reach a solution to a problem. In legal research you are asked to provide an answer to a legal question. To reach that answer, there are a number of strategies available to you. Although the sheer

number of authorities available to consult offers great flexibility, these numerous authorities can also produce great uncertainty. Where do I begin? How do I begin? These are often the questions that so intimidate legal researchers that they are unable to begin the task itself. Moreover, researching is rarely a straight line but often involves backtracking and revisiting sources, requiring patience and flexibility.

Although this chapter will offer you some guidelines and strategies on getting started, the best approach, as always, is the one that works best for you. If everyone you know prefers to consult an annotated code first but you like to become comfortable with a topic by reviewing an encyclopedia before you start, then that is the best approach.

You should view legal research as a process. Although the answer to a question is the destination you are traveling toward, there are many roads you can follow to reach that destination. Which road you choose to take is not important. In fact, while the number of sources you can examine may be staggering, this in itself is one of the benefits of our system of legal publishing. If you cannot locate a case or statute using one research technique, there are many alternatives available to help you find those authorities.

Ethics Alert

The Two Inflexible Rules of Legal Research

There are really only two inflexible "rules" that you must follow when you perform legal research to ensure you comply with your ethical duties of competent representation:

- If the source you review has a supplement or pocket part, you *must* check it.
- You *must* Shepardize or KeyCite all primary authorities.

As long as you always perform these two tasks, you have tremendous freedom in solving your legal research problem.

---

2.   *Thinking Things Through*

Although it is tempting to run to the library and start grabbing volumes of books as soon as you are given a research task, the time you spend thinking about a project before you begin is time well spent.

It may be helpful to write the issue on a piece of paper. This will help you "frame" the issue and in and of itself may impose some structure on the project and suggest certain approaches to follow. After you write out the issue, develop a list of descriptive words and phrases. Because almost all legal authorities are accessed by alphabetically arranged indexes, and the descriptive word approach is usually the most efficient method of using an index, jot down the words that initially occur to you in

examining the issue. These will be the words you will use in examining the indexes or online sources. Similarly, these will be the words you will use in developing search queries on Lexis, Westlaw, and the Internet.

After you have selected the most obvious words, facts, and phrases, expand your list by thinking of related words, such as synonyms and antonyms. If you cannot think of any such related words right away, consult a dictionary or thesaurus. An online dictionary and thesaurus are available at http://dictionary.reference.com. Consider the following questions, which will help you develop a list of descriptive words or phrases:

Who is involved?
What is the issue being considered?
Where did the activity take place?
When did the activity take place?
Why did the issue develop?
How did the problem arise?

The former Lawyers Co-op recommended that researchers use the "TAPP Rule" in determining which words to look up in an index:

T   Consider the *T*hing involved in the problem
A   Consider the *A*ct committed or the cause of *A*ction (or defense) a party would assert
P   Consider the *P*ersons involved in a problem
P   Consider the *P*lace involved

By focusing on these four areas, you may be able to determine words you can look up in a descriptive word index so you can be directed to relevant authorities.

Once you have given some initial thought to your project and prepared a list of some key descriptive words and phrases, expand your list by adding legal concepts. Consider the following five issues.

• **Criminal or Civil Law.** You must first determine whether the action is a criminal one brought by the federal government or your state government for a wrong done to society or is a civil one, brought by a private party for a wrong done to him or her. The legal authorities, burdens of proof, and punishments and remedies are far different in criminal cases from those in civil cases.
• **Jurisdiction.** You must consider which jurisdiction's authorities you will examine. In other words, is the issue one of Minnesota law, enabling you to limit your research strictly to Minnesota authorities, or is the issue one of federal law? If the issue is one of federal law, narrow the focus again by considering which district or circuit is involved. If your question relates to a lawsuit filed for violation of the United States Trademark Act and the lawsuit was filed in the United States District Court for the Northern District

of Texas, you should initially consult other district court cases
from the Northern District of Texas. Because Texas is in the Fifth
Circuit, you should look for other cases from the Fifth Circuit. All
lower federal district courts that fall within the jurisdiction of a
federal circuit court are bound by its decisions. Each of the
intermediate circuit courts of appeal is free to make its own
decisions independent of what other circuits have held; however,
in practice, the circuit courts are often guided by decisions from
other circuits. Similarly, when performing research related to a
specific state, restrict your search to authorities from that state.
Expand your search to other states only if your state lacks
authorities. Remember that your state need not follow or adopt
the viewpoint of another jurisdiction. Although authority from
outside your state may be persuasive, it is never binding.

- **Action.** Once you have identified the issue as being civil or
  criminal and state or federal and have identified the particular
  jurisdiction (for example, specific state or district and circuit), you
  need to consider the legal issues involved in the case. Ask yourself
  what the plaintiff would allege in a lawsuit based upon this issue.
  Would the plaintiff's action be for breach of contract? Personal
  injuries arising out of a car accident? Trespass to his property?
  Improper search of her house by police officers?

- **Defenses.** Once you have considered the plaintiff's "gripes," put
  yourself in the place of the defendant, and ask how the defendant
  would best defeat the plaintiff. What defenses would a defendant
  assert? Would the defendant allege that there was no agreement
  or, if there was an agreement, he fully performed its terms? That
  the plaintiff's failure to wear a seat belt rather than the defendant's conduct caused the injuries suffered by the plaintiff in the
  automobile accident? That the plaintiff invited the defendant to
  come onto the plaintiff's property? That the police were acting
  pursuant to a proper search warrant?

- **Remedies.** After you look at the issue from the perspectives of
  both parties, consider what remedies the plaintiff is seeking. Is
  the plaintiff asking for money damages for a breach of contract or
  injuries sustained in an accident, or does the plaintiff want to
  compel the defendant to repair damage caused to his property by
  the trespass? If you are unsure as to the theories on which the
  plaintiff would claim relief, what defenses the defendant would
  assert, or what remedies the parties desire, consult West's list of
  more than 400 topics of the law (see Figure 5-2). Use this as a
  "menu," and pick and choose the words and topics that fit your
  problem.

Examining these issues will not only help develop a list of descriptive words and phrases that you can look up in the indexes you will be
using, but it will also help ensure that you have the "big picture" focus,
which is critical in the legal profession. After all, it is deadly to think that
because you have examined an issue from the plaintiff's perspective, you

are finished. The plaintiff may, in fact, have a cause of action enabling her to recover substantial money damages. Nevertheless, the defendant may have a perfect defense, which would completely defeat the plaintiff's action. If you examine questions only from one party's side, you will be sure to miss critical issues.

To develop your list of descriptive words, facts, and phrases, use any approach that works best for you. Perhaps rough notes jotted down on a legal pad are sufficient. You may prefer to use index cards or a word processor. It is not the technique you use that matters at this juncture — far more important is the thinking process and analytical skill you will develop by examining these legal issues in a precise fashion.

Figure 13-1 provides an approach that you may wish to follow to help develop the working outline described herein, that is, the road map you use in reaching your destination. This outline will also help you develop words to use in formulating a search using Lexis or Westlaw. Feel free to copy and use this outline for each project you research.

3. *Tackling the Project*

Once you have formulated the descriptive words, facts, and phrases that you will look up in an index, you need to decide with which sources to start. There are two categories of books you can consider: primary authorities (cases, constitutions, statutes, executive orders, treaties, and administrative regulations) and secondary authorities (everything else). Remember that digests will help you locate cases.

Some research questions will immediately suggest or even dictate the source to consult. For example, if the question is what the statute of limitations is for an action by a patient against a doctor for professional negligence, how many days a defendant has to answer a complaint, or the number of people required to witness a will, the answer will undoubtedly be found in a statute. In such cases, you should proceed directly to an annotated code, look up your descriptive words in the index, read the statute to which you are referred, and examine the library references and annotations following the statute to review how courts have interpreted the statute.

It is altogether likely, however, that you will not know which source to consult initially. In such instances, consider the following strategy.

a. Familiarization

When you are unsure where or how to start a research project, invest an hour or so in becoming familiar with the general area of law involved (contracts, property, wills). The best place to "get your feet wet" is an encyclopedia, which will offer you introductory information on an area of the law. If you live in a more populous state that publishes its own encyclopedia, start with this. If your state does not have a local encyclopedia, familiarize yourself with the topic by reviewing C.J.S. or Am. Jur. 2d.

Figure 13-1
Research Project

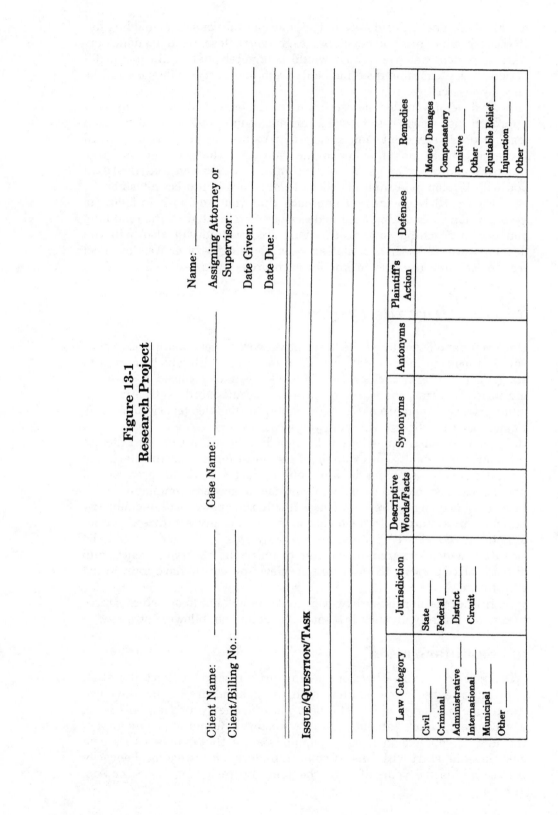

Client Name: _____

Client/Billing No.: _____

Case Name: _____

Name: _____

Assigning Attorney or
Supervisor: _____

Date Given: _____

Date Due: _____

ISSUE/QUESTION/TASK _____

Law Category	Jurisdiction	Descriptive Words/Facts	Synonyms	Antonyms	Plaintiff's Action	Defenses	Remedies
Civil ___ Criminal ___ Administrative ___ International ___ Municipal ___ Other ___	State ___ Federal ___ District ___ Circuit ___						Money Damages ___ Compensatory ___ Punitive ___ Other ___ Equitable Relief ___ Injunction ___ Other ___

If you read either C.J.S. or Am. Jur. 2d, West publications, and you locate a particularly relevant section, make a note of the topic name and key number (**Partnership 14**, **Negligence 121**, **Contracts 42**) as this will unlock the door to other authorities. Similarly, look for relevant annotations in A.L.R., which can provide extremely useful information to you.

Consider also using specialized treatises for your issue. For example, if the question involves corporations or bankruptcy, browse those sections of the law library to see if a treatise exists for that topic. Treatises provide excellent analyses of legal topics as well as references to supporting case law and other authorities.

b. Consult Primary Sources

After you have begun to feel comfortable with the subject matter, consult the primary authorities: constitutions, statutes, and cases (and, if applicable, administrative regulations, executive orders, and treaties).

(1) Constitutions

If your issue is a federal one, it may be governed by the United States Constitution. Both U.S.C.A. and U.S.C.S. contain the text of the United States Constitution as well as annotations referring you to cases interpreting constitutional provisions. If your issue is not federal but may involve your state constitution, consult your state's annotated code, which will contain the state constitution as well as annotations to cases construing provisions of your constitution.

(2) Statutes

Always examine an annotated code because under the American common law theory of stare decisis, it is not merely the language of a statute or law that controls, but the interpretation of that language by a court.

For federal statutes, consult U.S.C.A. (West's publication) or U.S.C.S. (the Lexis publication), look up your descriptive words in the indexes to U.S.C.A. or U.S.C.S., and read the statutes to which you are referred. After you read applicable statutes, review the library references and cases to determine how the statute is interpreted by courts.

For state statutes, examine your state's annotated code, look up the relevant descriptive words in the index to the code, and review the statute to which you are referred, followed by an examination of the library references and cases construing the state statute. Once you have a reference or citation to a specific statute, consider consulting the Table of Statutes construed in a local encyclopedia or a treatise, which will direct you to a discussion of treatment and interpretation of the specific statute in which you are interested.

Always check pocket parts or supplements to a code to determine if a statute has been amended or repealed and to find cases more current than those in the hardbound volume.

(3) Cases

If a review of the annotations for a constitutional or state statutory provision has not yielded any cases on point, use digests, which function as case finders.

Many experts believe that finding "one good case" solves many research problems. If you can find one good case, you can use its topics and key numbers to locate other cases in the American Digest System (if the case is published in a West reporter) and you can Shepardize or KeyCite the case to find other authorities that mention or discuss your case, thereby leading you to a host of other relevant sources. Note that the advice involves finding one *good* case, not one *perfect* case, because there likely is no such thing as the perfect case for a legal issue.

(a) Federal Issues

For a global approach, use the *Decennial Digest System*. For a more focused approach, concentrate on West's federal practice digests (*Modern Federal Practice Digest*, *West's Federal Practice Digest 2d*, *West's Federal Practice Digest 3d*, *West's Federal Practice Digest 4th*). Use the Descriptive Word Index for any of the digests. Look up your descriptive words, facts, or phrases and allow the Index to provide you with a topic name and key number (**Venue 42**, **Larceny 106**, **Zoning and Planning 123**). Look up these topic names and key numbers in the appropriate digest and out will spill the cases you need. Focus on the particular state, district, or circuit you need. All of the West's digests organize the cases according to state or district and circuit, so you may easily locate cases on point.

(b) State Issues

If the issue is governed by state law and you wish to find cases from a particular state, the best case finders are digests. West has published a digest for every state but Delaware, Nevada, and Utah (these states use a regional digest, namely, the *Atlantic Digest* or *Pacific Digest*). Use the Descriptive Word Index available for each set and look up the words, facts, and phrases listed on your research outline. You will be provided with a topic name and a key number such as **Wills 56**. Look up this topic name and key number in your state digest, and you will be provided with other cases from your state dealing with this same issue.

Figure 13-2 provides a chart showing the sets to review when conducting legal research using most primary authorities.

c. Consult Secondary Sources

After you have reviewed the pertinent primary authorities (constitutions, statutes, and cases), consult the secondary authorities to fill in the gaps. Many secondary authorities will refer you to cases, thus ensuring that you find all of the case law relating to your topic. The most commonly consulted secondary authorities are A.L.R. annotations, encyclopedias, periodicals, Restatements, texts and treatises, and law dictionaries.

Figure 13-2
Chart of Primary Authorities

I. *Constitutions*
　　Federal:　　　　Consult U.S.C.A. or U.S.C.S.
　　State:　　　　　Consult your state's annotated code
II. *Statutes*
　　Federal:　　　　Consult U.S.C.A. or U.S.C.S.
　　State:　　　　　Consult your state's annotated code
III. *Cases*
　　Federal:　　　　Consult annotated codes or digests (American
　　　　　　　　　　Digest System or Federal Practice Digests)
　　State:　　　　　Consult annotated codes, your state's digest, or a
　　　　　　　　　　regional digest
IV. *Regulations*
　　Federal:　　　　Consult C.F.R.
　　State:　　　　　Consult your state's administrative code

There are several secondary sources, and you should examine the list of secondary authorities shown in Figure 13-3, and ask yourself if your issue would be addressed by the particular authority in question. If so, review the authority. You need not examine every secondary authority for every issue you research. It is possible that a review of a treatise and an A.L.R. annotation may provide you with such useful information as well as sufficient references to cases that you need not examine other secondary authorities.

d.　Miscellaneous Research Guides

In addition to the primary and secondary authorities discussed above, there are a few other sources that you may wish to consult when performing research. Consider using *Shepard's Citations* or KeyCite not only to let you know whether the authorities you rely upon are still good law, but also to lead you to other sources. *Shepard's* and KeyCite will refer you to law review articles, opinions of the attorneys general, treatises, and annotations that mention your case, statute, or constitutional provision. It is possible that these authorities have so thoroughly examined an issue that for you to conduct additional research would be "reinventing the wheel."

　　Do not forget to use common sense. If the question can be easily answered by an individual or organization, call or write. Thus, if your question relates to zoning in your county, contact your county supervisor or the county zoning officer. If your question relates to the current minimum wage, contact a local employment agency. Many basic questions can be answered by Internet legal research techniques.

Figure 13-3
Chart of Secondary Authorities

Secondary Authority	Coverage	To Use
Encyclopedias		
C.J.S.	All United States law	Consult alphabetically arranged index
Am. Jur. 2d	All United States law	Consult alphabetically arranged index
State-Specific sets	Law of one state	Consult alphabetically arranged index
A.L.R.		
Annotations		
A.L.R. Fed, A.L.R. Fed. 2d	Federal issues	For all A.L.R. sets, consult *A.L.R. Index*
A.L.R., A.L.R.2d, A.L.R.3d, 4th, 5th, & 6th	State and common law topics	
Texts and Treatises	Law related to one topic	Consult alphabetically arranged index or table of contents
Legal Periodicals	Various topics	Consult *Index to Legal Periodicals & Books* or *Current Law Index* (or their online versions)
Restatements	Various topics	Consult alphabetically arranged index to each Restatement
Attorneys General Opinions		
U.S.A.G. Opinions	Federal topics	Consult alphabetically arranged index
State A.G. Opinions	State topics	Consult alphabetically arranged index
Dictionaries	Legal words and phrases	Look up alphabetically arranged words or phrases
Martindale-Hubbell Law Digests	International law	Consult list of countries arranged alphabetically
Form Books	Various topics	Consult alphabetically arranged index
Uniform Laws	Various topics	Consult *Uniform Laws Annotated* and *Directory of Acts* (or http://www.nccusl.org)
Looseleaf Services	Various topics	Consult alphabetically arranged index
Jury Instructions	Federal or state	Consult alphabetically arranged index

Browse the library for useful materials. For example, if your issue deals with bankruptcy, locate the section of the law library containing books related to this topic. Scan the shelves for helpful sources. When you come to a dead end, ask your law librarian for assistance.

Use the Research Game Plan shown in Figure 13-4 to ensure you have consulted all applicable sets of books. Fill out the plan as you perform your research to verify that your research has been thorough and has focused on both primary and secondary authorities. Identify the particular source you consult and then rate its helpfulness or value to you on a scale of 0-10, with 10 being the highest. If you later have only a vague recollection of a source that provided valuable information, the Research Game Plan may jog your memory. It also serves as a reminder to check all pocket parts and to Shepardize or KeyCite all primary sources.

e. Strategies for Effective Research

Following are eight hints to ensure your research is sufficiently thorough:

(i) Use encyclopedias (C.J.S., Am. Jur. 2d, or a local set for your state) to obtain introductory information about the issue you are researching.

(ii) Always examine the statutes. Use an annotated code because it will refer you to cases.

(iii) If you cannot locate cases through an annotated code (because the issue is not dealt with by statutes), use digests: The *Decennial* digests can be used for a global approach; the federal practice digests can be used for federal cases; and state and regional digests can be used to locate cases from a particular state or region.

(iv) If there is a well-known treatise or text on this topic, examine it because it will provide excellent analysis as well as references to cases.

(v) For a complete overview of a topic, consult A.L.R. (or A.L.R. Fed. for federal issues).

(vi) For discussions of new or controversial issues or a thorough examination of an issue, find legal periodicals through the *Index to Legal Periodicals & Books* or *Current Law Index*.

(vii) If a looseleaf service is devoted to the topic you are researching, examine it; it will provide an exhaustive treatment of the topic.

(viii) Use *Shepard's Citations* or KeyCite to validate your primary authorities and to locate other cases, legal periodical articles, attorneys general opinions, and A.L.R. annotations.

Figure 13-4
Research Game Plan

Source	Specific Source & Section Consulted	Date Consulted	Rating
Encyclopedia	_____	_____	_____
Constitutions	_____	_____	_____
Codes/Statutes	_____	_____	_____
Annotations following statutes	_____	_____	_____
Digests (topic _____ , Key Number ____)	_____	_____	_____
A.L.R. Annotations	_____	_____	_____
Texts/Treatises	_____	_____	_____
Legal Periodicals	_____	_____	_____
Restatements	_____	_____	_____
Attorneys General Opinions	_____	_____	_____
Dictionaries	_____	_____	_____
Form Books	_____	_____	_____
Uniform Laws	_____	_____	_____
Looseleaf Services	_____	_____	_____
Jury Instructions	_____	_____	_____
Experts Consulted	_____	_____	_____
Law Librarian Assistance	_____	_____	_____
Computer-Assisted Legal Research	_____	_____	_____
Internet	_____	_____	_____
All Pocket Parts and Supplements Checked	_____	_____	_____
All Primary Sources Shepardized or KeyCited	_____	_____	_____

━━━━━━━━━━━━━━━━ **Practice Tip** ━━━━━━━━━━━━━━━━

Just Ask!

Georgetown University Law Center recommends considering the acronym JUST ASK before you start any research project.

J Consider the *jurisdiction*. Federal? State? Administrative agency?

U Follow *useful* leads by asking experts and colleagues for help.

S What is the *scope* of your project? Is your teacher or supervisor looking for in-depth analysis or a quick review?

T What *terms of art* apply to the project? What terminology do people use when discussing the problem?

A Be sure you know the meaning of any *acronyms* used by others in describing the research issue.

S Ask what *sources* might be of help, such as journals, looseleaf services, and online databases.

K Consider the *key money constraints*. How many hours can be billed to the project?

(from http://www.ll.georgetown.edu/guides/just_ask.cfm)

B. Working with the Authorities

1. *Note-Taking*

As you begin to read the primary and secondary authorities, you need to develop some focused plan for taking notes. Ultimately, the results of your research must be communicated to someone by way of a letter to a client, an internal office memorandum, or a brief submitted to a court, and the notes you take will form the basis for your written project. There is nothing more frustrating than beginning to write your project, having a vague recollection that some source provided a perfect analysis or quote, and then being unable to find a reference to it in your notes. Equally frustrating is having to go back to the law library or go online at additional expense to a client to obtain complete citations because your notes do not reflect the date of a case or the page of a quotation.

These time-consuming tasks can be avoided by effective note-taking during the research process. This way you do not have to waste time later by retracing your steps to locate information you should have obtained earlier. Effective note-taking requires some practice and is often developed through trial and error. Once you neglect to include the page of a

quotation in your notes, thus necessitating another trip to the law library, you will not make the same mistake twice.

Notes that can be used to help you write your project are more than scribbling on a legal pad. If you simply jot down phrases, parts of cases, and isolated sentences on pages in a pad, you will find they are a muddle when you later try to use these notes to construct a written project, with information relating to one issue being hopelessly intertwined with information relating to entirely separate issues.

a. Organizing Your Notes

You should develop a system for taking and organizing notes during your research efforts so you can effectively use these notes to write your project. One of the best approaches is to use a looseleaf notebook that is divided into separate sections through the use of tabs or dividers. You can devote each section to a particular issue. For example, you could use the first section to reflect information relating to the standard of care of physicians, the second section to record information relating to conduct constituting a breach of that standard, the third section to contain notes relating to defenses the doctor could assert, and the fourth section to relate to damages for injuries caused by the physician's breach of the duty of care or malpractice. Consider leaving at least one section untitled for a while because you will invariably discover issues during the course of your research that you had not originally considered.

As you research you may discover that each of these major issues comprises sub-issues. Either insert new tabs or dividers so you can compile information relating to these newly discovered sub-issues, or assign a number or letter to each sub-issue and reflect that in the margin next to any notes relating to it.

If you find that some authorities or cases discuss more than one issue, take notes in one section and in the other(s) simply insert a reminder to review the authority, such as the following: "For discussion of damages in malpractice action, see *Jones v. Smith*, 421 N.E.2d 609, 614 (Ind. 1989), Tab I." Alternatively, you can photocopy the case and "cut and paste" it by placing certain portions of it in your Tab I section and other portions in your notes for Tab III. An advantage of using a looseleaf notebook is that you can shuffle sections of your argument around. If you decide Section II should be discussed after Section IV, it is easy to switch the pages in your notebook.

Some students prefer to use looseleaf sheets (rather than a binder or spiral notebook), label each sheet with a topic name (Duty of Care, Breach of Duty, Damages), and then record information relating to these topics on the appropriate pages. Often students will use different colors of looseleaf paper for different issues so that white sheets relate to the issue of Duty of Care, pink sheets relate to Breach of Duty, and blue sheets reflect notes relating to Damages for such breach.

Other individuals find index cards useful and label each card with a topic name (Duty of Care, Breach of Duty, Damages) and devote a separate card to each case, law review article, A.L.R. annotation, or other

authority, briefly summarizing the case, article, or annotation. Some individuals prefer using different colored index cards for different issues. This system allows immediate recognition and retrieval of the sections you later desire to review.

The advantage to any of these techniques is obvious: When your research is completed, it is already partly organized and prepared for the writing stage. All of your information relating to Duty of Care, Breach of Duty, or Damages is in one place rather than hopelessly scattered among numerous pages.

Another advantage of keeping notes related to separate issues in separate sections is that you can take your separate sheets of paper or index cards and shuffle them around so that you can physically organize the results of your research and determine the order in which you will discuss the cases relating to damages or some other topic. For this reason, try to keep your notes about any one case, law review article, annotation, or other authority to one page or one index card. The purpose of taking notes is to record only the critical portions of a case, not to write out the entire case in longhand.

You can always photocopy or print the case itself so you will have it to refer to when writing your project, but for note-taking purposes, be brief and keep notes to one page or one index card per authority. If you are photocopying cases, invest a bit of time and always maintain them in alphabetical order. Then, when you need to refer to them when writing your project, you will be able to locate the case you need easily. Many individuals prefer to photocopy almost all cases they intend to rely upon (and, in fact, some attorneys insist that finished research projects be accompanied by copies of all cases cited therein).

If you photocopy or print cases, you should mark or highlight the significant portions of the case so when you review it later you can readily locate its relevant sections. Once again, consider imposing some order on this process by using a different color pen or highlighter to reflect different issues so that the portions of the case dealing with a physician's standard of care are highlighted with yellow while the portions of the case relating to damages are highlighted in pink. When you later review the case, you will then be able to quickly locate the portions you need. Do not be afraid to record your own thoughts and reactions on your copies of cases. An interjection such as "perfect" or "oops" may later jog your memory as to the value of a case you read days earlier. You should consider rating the cases on a scale of 1 to 10 so you will have an easier time of weeding out weaker authorities.

New software packages allow students to simulate highlighting, bookmarks, and sticky notes as they take notes on their laptops while in the law library. This form of electronic note-taking is easy and convenient, and hyperlinks to cases and authorities of interest can be inserted in the notes. Any kind of text can be stored in your "infobase," including cases you have downloaded, class notes, or other materials. You can insert notes wherever you like, just as you would attach sticky notes to a text you read. You can highlight portions of text. Finally, you can easily search

the entire text of your infobase, thereby allowing you to locate immediately your notes and information on "jurisdiction" or "venue."

No one method of note-taking is superior to another. The method that works best for you is the best method. For those students who are decidedly "low tech" or "technologically challenged," do not despair: If a great number of judges in the country do not need computers to do their work, it is likely you can succeed as they do and as legal professionals did for hundreds of years — with pen and paper.

b.   Contents of Notes

If your notes are to be of any assistance to you in constructing your written project, they will need to be more than random words or isolated phrases. The best approach for taking notes on cases is to brief the cases. You will recall from Chapter 4 that briefing a case is, in fact, described as taking notes on a case. Thus, any sheet or index card relating to a case should be a mini-brief of the case and should include the following elements:

- complete citation
- brief overview of facts
- procedural history
- issue(s)
- reasoning
- holding

It is not necessary that your sheet of paper or index card be perfect. It should contain only the most important and relevant information. You can "fill in the gaps" when writing your project by referring to your photocopy of the case itself. The sheet of paper or index card is only for reference purposes. Do not expect to be able to put your project together by simply assembling your sheets of paper or organizing your index cards and turning them over to a word processor or secretary. Your notes provide only the framework for your project. They are not the project itself.

For taking notes on other authorities such as law review articles or A.L.R. annotations, simply summarize the most relevant points. Although these authorities may be quite lengthy and often exceed 20 pages, they are secondary authorities, and thus you should not rely too much on them. Such authorities serve as great backups to the cases you rely upon and, because your project will not solely depend upon these authorities, you should be able to record the information you need on one or two pages or index cards. Often, in fact, these authorities are used to introduce you to an area of the law or provide an overview of a topic. Although they may be of invaluable help in educating you on a topic, you may decide not to cite these authorities at all in your project, preferring instead to rely upon the primary authorities to which they referred you.

c. Complete Notes

Your notes will be of little help to you if you are constantly returning to the library or going online to obtain additional information. Your goal upon completion of the research phase of your project is to return to your office to write the results of your research, having everything you need in your notes. If you need to return to the library or log-on again during the writing phase to get a parallel cite or the name of the author of a law review article, your note-taking was ineffective.

It is a great temptation when researching simply to jot down part of a citation and then start taking notes, figuring you will obtain the complete cite later. Resist this temptation, and always include all of the information you will need for citation purposes in your notes. Follow *Bluebook* or *ALWD* form. This will save time later.

For cases, record the complete name of the case, parallel citations, and date. If your notes contain a quote from the case, indicate the page of the case on which the quote appeared so you can later include this pinpoint in your citation.

When taking notes, clearly identify whether your notes reflect a quote or are merely paraphrasing the judge's or author's statements. It is nearly impossible to remember days after you performed your research whether a statement in your notes that "physicians are liable for the harm to their patients proximately caused by their negligent or intentional wrongful acts" is a quotation or your own summary of a case unless your notes remind you. Any system is sufficient so long as it works for you. You may use quotation marks only for direct quotes and then any material not in quotes is a paraphrase; you may label each statement in your notes with a "q" or a "p"; or you may elect to use a different color pen to show a quotation.

It is important to record the page even a paraphrase occurs on because you may wish later to review the original language in the case or you must include in your citation a reference to specific pages and pinpoints, whether or not the statement is a direct quote. Including pinpoints for paraphrasing is expected professional courtesy. Similarly, if your quotation appeared in headnote 6 of a case or you are relying primarily on headnote 6 of a case, indicate this in your notes as **[6]**. When you later Shepardize or KeyCite, you will be able to focus on the treatment of this portion of the case by later authorities and will not waste time reading later cases relating to headnote 12 when you were not relying on that portion of the case.

Your notes should reflect whether you have checked the pocket part or supplement to the authority and whether any information was found therein as this may need to be included in your citation. Similarly, notes relating to primary authorities should record that they have been Shepardized or KeyCited and are still "good law." You can simply include a "box" on each page or index card and complete it as follows:

PP/Supp. ___x___

Info in main vol. ___yes___ or p.p./supp. ___no___

Shep./KeyCite ___x___ on ___2/6.___ Problems/concerns **None.**

2. *Staying Focused*

One of the most difficult tasks in performing legal research is staying focused on a specific issue or question. Students commonly report that as they are in the process of researching an issue such as negligence and reading a pertinent case, they come across a reference to what appears to be a promising law review article. Without completing the reading of the case, they then grab the law review article, which refers to two other cases. These new cases are then pulled from the shelves, and they also refer to other promising authorities. At the end of a full morning of research, the student is surrounded by a pile of books, none of which has been thoroughly analyzed and some of which, when later re-read, are a mystery as to their relevance because they discuss topics completely unrelated to the original issue of negligence.

This hopscotch approach to research will invariably lead you away from your answer rather than toward it. The reason it occurs so frequently is that it is incredibly tempting to interrupt your analysis of an issue with the thought that the "perfect" authority is the next one, or that if you do not grab the authority now you will forget about it later.

Train yourself to stay focused on each specific issue. If you are researching a problem, for example, whether a physician is liable for injuries sustained by a patient during surgery when the patient consented to the risks of surgery and violated the doctor's orders prior to surgery, devote yourself to one topic at a time. Decide that the first morning you will only research the general duty of care required of a doctor. If you come across cases or references that relate to the consent issue or the issue of damages, jot these down in the sections of your notebook corresponding to those topics so you can review them later, but do not interrupt your research on the assigned issue.

After you are thoroughly satisfied that you understand a physician's general duties, assign yourself the issue of whether the patient's consent was valid; that is, whether it is proper for a doctor to obtain, in effect, a release prior to surgery for acts that occur during surgery, and whether the patient had any choice but to sign a written consent without which the doctor would not perform the surgery. If, during the course of research related to these consent issues, you come across other references to the physician's duty of care or damages recoverable in malpractice actions, write them down for future reference, but do not allow yourself to be sidetracked from the consent issue on which you are working. With any luck, when it is time to research your last issue, the question of damages,

you will already have a list of promising cases and other authorities to review, thus eliminating the need for you to start at the beginning with encyclopedias, codes, or digests.

The hopscotch effect also occurs during Shepardizing or KeyCiting. For example, in the middle of Shepardizing one case, you may find a reference to a later case that explains your case. Avoid the temptation to leave your Shepardizing and obtain that case. Once again, jot down the reference and then look it up after you have completed your review of all of the volumes of *Shepard's*. If you interrupt your Shepardizing to read a case, you may forget where you are in the Shepardizing process. Thus, when you return to the task, you may assume you completed Shepardizing the original case when in reality you only examined some rather than all of the requisite volumes of *Shepard's*. The exception to this is in computer-assisted Shepardizing or KeyCiting, which allow you to quickly flip back and forth between *Shepard's* or KeyCite and the authorities that mention or discuss your case.

C. When to Stop

One of the most difficult tasks in legal research is knowing when to stop. No one will come up to you in the law library, tap you on the shoulder, and inform you that time is up and your task is complete. Moreover, it seems as if some issues can be researched endlessly. If you read a landmark case, it may refer to five other cases, which you may also decide to read. When it is time to Shepardize or KeyCite these six cases, you may discover that each of the six cases has been mentioned or discussed in ten other cases (as well as numerous law review articles, opinions of attorneys general, and A.L.R. annotations). You now have 60 other cases that could be examined, each of which refers to other authorities and each, when Shepardized or KeyCited, is in turn discussed by other cases and authorities. This process could continue indefinitely and is a bit like a funnel that gets wider and wider. Eventually, you need to call a halt to your research.

1. *Practical Considerations*

Sometimes there is a practical reason for stopping your research. It is possible that the client's claim is for $40,000. You cannot possibly afford to expend $20,000 in legal research and then present the client with a bill after the trial that charges the client $20,000 for legal research and $10,000 for other costs and attorneys' fees, leaving the client with a mere $10,000 recovery. Thus, in many cases, economics will govern how thorough your research will be. When the client's budget dictates the amount of research that can be performed, you will have to be as efficient and streamlined as possible. Keep track of your hours as you go along, and after a few hours report back to your supervisor on your progress and

estimate how much longer you think will be required. Before you commence the project, discuss the budget with your supervisor, and agree on a strategy and a time to meet and discuss your efforts. When you are given the project, your supervisor may expressly tell you that you should allot five to six hours for research and might even suggest a specific statute or case as a beginning point.

This balance between the duty to research adequately and the economic realities of a case is a delicate one. It is the attorney's task to resolve this issue and give you proper guidance. If you do not receive any instruction, take the initiative and state that for time-management purposes, you would like to inquire as to the date the project is due (this in and of itself may give you a clue as to how thorough the project is to be) and a range of time the attorney estimates for the research. Alternatively, give your supervisor a brief status report after a few hours of research. A quick e-mail will allow your supervisor to redirect you, if necessary.

Research as efficiently as possible. If your research efforts produce a number of potentially relevant cases, all of which look promising but the reading of which would be impractical and time-consuming, adopt a strategy that will produce the best results in the least amount of time. For example, read newer cases before you move on to older cases, read cases from higher courts before those from lower courts, and read cases from your forum jurisdiction before those from a foreign jurisdiction.

If you find that the project is far more complex than you and your supervisor originally anticipated and that the authorities are unclear or conflicting, stop your research and go back to your supervisor, explain your progress thus far and why the issue is more complex than antici-pated, and ask for direction. Your supervisor would much prefer to find out after six hours of your research that you are having difficulty rather than after 30 hours, which cannot be billed to the client.

Do not be embarrassed to ask for direction or acknowledge that you are having difficulties. If the answer to a question was so easy, everyone would already know it, and there would be no need to research it.

Attorneys are always interested in economic efficiency, and if you present your question in a manner that shows you are aware of the economics of a law practice, you will be commended rather than criticized. For example, instead of telling your supervisor, "I can't find any authori-ties on this, so I'm quitting," state, "I haven't yet been able to find any authorities on point. If I can't turn up some leads in the next hour, let's meet and discuss our next step." Alternatively, you can report, "I've spent the six hours you suggested and because the circuit courts are in conflict on this issue, I believe I need two to three more hours. Will the client approve this additional time?"

2. *Complex Projects*

If the project is complex, you may find yourself in the "funnel position," that is, the situation in which there is an ever-expanding list of authori-ties that could be reviewed. Knowing when to stop researching this type

of project is difficult. It is hard to know if you have gotten the "right answer." Seldom, if ever, is there one perfect case or authority that is directly responsive to your research task. It is far more likely that you find numerous cases that are somewhat responsive and that you must patch together to arrive at an answer.

One clue that your research is complete is that you keep bumping into the same authorities. For example, assume that in the course of reading a 1982 case entitled *Jones v. Smith* you make note of a 1970 case referred to therein called *ABC v. XYZ*. When you later read *ABC*, it discusses the same principle discussed in *Jones*. When you Shepardize or KeyCite *ABC*, you are referred to *Jones* and a 1985 case entitled *Henderson v. Powell*. A reading of *Henderson* reveals the same general discussion you read in the earlier cases. When you Shepardize *Henderson*, you are referred to a 1990 case called *O'Connell v. Rowe*. A reading of *O'Connell* discloses a discussion of the previous cases, *Jones* and *Henderson*.

These references to the same authorities are a signal that the principle originally set forth in *ABC* has been continually repeated by later cases. If nothing significant or new is added by the line of cases decided after your "best" case, and Shepardizing or KeyCiting reveals that the cases you rely on are still valid, stop researching. This circular procedure is a hint that your research is complete. You may want to "flesh out" your research by reviewing a law review article or other secondary authority, but if these confirm the results of your earlier research, you will know you have been sufficiently thorough.

Often beginning researchers lack the confidence to stop researching and are convinced there is one perfect case that they will find if they can only devote enough time to the effort. This is a fallacy. Seldom, if ever, is a perfect case sitting on the shelves — for the reason that no two cases are exactly alike. You will find cases that are similar to yours, and you will be able to argue that because the cases are similar the reasoning in the reported cases should apply to your particular problem. It is highly unlikely, if not impossible, however, to find an identical case, so do not waste your time looking for one. Once you have cases "on point" (similar legal issues as your case, similar facts as your case, from the highest courts in your jurisdiction, and that are still valid) this is sufficient.

Another sign of lack of confidence in beginning researchers is their unshaken conviction that they cannot be right, and there must be some case hidden in the library that will render their efforts meaningless. If you have examined the statutes (and, if applicable, constitutional provisions) from your jurisdiction as well as the cases interpreting the statutes and have updated the statutes by checking the pocket parts and Shepardizing or KeyCiting the statutes and cases, and the authorities are in agreement, your research is concluded. It is only when you neglect to review the cases interpreting a statute or fail to update by checking pocket parts and Shepardizing or KeyCiting that your research is an unexploded mine field.

After you gain confidence in your research skills through practice, you will be able to trust your instincts and say, "I'm finished," rather than

thinking, "I can't possibly have found the right answer even though 22 cases all say the same thing so I'll continue to look for something to prove me wrong."

3. Quick Questions

Often your research task is specific and well-defined. You may be asked to check how many days a defendant has to provide answers to interrogatories propounded by a plaintiff or what the statute of limitations is to sue for breach of contract in your state.

Such specific questions are easily answered by examining your state's annotated code. Review the statute and a few cases construing it. Update and Shepardize or KeyCite the authorities to determine they are still valid. Generally, this approach will be sufficient to answer questions that are straightforward.

4. Established Issues and Newly Emerging Issues

If your research task relates to an established area of the law, such as the elements of a cause of action for breach of contract, a landlord's duty to provide habitable premises to a tenant, or the damages recoverable in fraud actions, you may find a multitude of authorities. Some of the authorities may be decades old, and there may be numerous cases, periodical articles, A.L.R. annotations, and discussions in texts and treatises. These authorities, however, may reflect remarkable unanimity. That is, researching an issue related to an established area of law usually results in numerous authorities in agreement.

Determining when to stop researching will be relatively easy because the authorities will begin referring to each other over and over again. Once you update and Shepardize or KeyCite to ensure that the primary authorities are still valid, your task is complete.

Conversely, research in newly emerging areas of law can be frustrating because there will often be substantial conflict among courts as judges grapple with a difficult issue and try to establish rules of law. Thus, research relating to the liability of an Internet service provider for defamatory statements made on a website or research relating to contracts for hiring a surrogate parent will be fraught with conflict. Often periodical articles or A.L.R. annotations will be most helpful because they will offer an overview of new topics and attempt to explain and reconcile conflicts. Update a law review article with *Shepard's Law Review Citations*, and update A.L.R. annotations through the use of pocket parts. Alternatively, you may electronically Shepardize or KeyCite these authorities to locate other, newer authorities. Remember computer-assisted legal research, which has the ability to locate hundreds of documents if you carefully formulate the search query.

Research for these newly developing legal topics is difficult because often you cannot find one single right answer. If this is the case, you simply need to follow the standard research techniques, and realize that your conclusion may well be that the authorities are uncertain and conflicting.

5. *Issues of First Impression*

Often the most difficult research task is the one that yields no results whatsoever. Thus, after hours of research, you may not have found any authorities. There are two conclusions to draw from this occurrence: "There are no authorities relating to this issue" or "I must be doing something wrong because I can't locate any authorities." Beginning researchers will always draw the second conclusion and refuse to stop researching even though they are retracing their steps over and over again.

It is possible that an issue is one of "first impression," that is, one not yet considered in your jurisdiction. Unfortunately, there is no foolproof way to determine this. There is no list produced by the legislature or courts of "topics not yet considered." There are, however, two techniques you can use to assure yourself that it is not your research strategy that has resulted in a total lack of authorities.

First, select a populous and varied jurisdiction such as California or New York, which has a rich body of law. Use the same research techniques, sets of books (annotated codes, digests), and descriptive words that you used in your home jurisdiction. If you obtain results, you will know that your strategies, choice of books, and descriptive words were sound and that the lack of authorities in your jurisdiction is the result of an issue of first impression, not misguided research efforts.

Second, computer-assisted legal research, with its ability to search for thousands of documents that contain specific terms (and sort them by date), will help verify your research techniques. If your search query is "blood and product and infect! and HIV or AIDS /50 bank" and after you have selected the database for all Utah statutes and cases you obtain no references whatsoever, you should feel more confident that Utah has simply not yet considered this issue. To achieve a final comfort level, contact the service representatives for Lexis or Westlaw and ask for assistance in formulating a search.

6. *How Many Authorities Are Enough?*

Beginning researchers usually want to know how many cases or authorities should be cited in a brief or project. There is no answer to this question. As a general rule, however, you will need fewer authorities to support a well-established principle and more authorities to discuss an emerging area of law or one in conflict.

Is one citation enough? It is possible that a single citation may suffice to answer a quick question. Thus, the question of how many days a defendant has to answer interrogatories propounded in a federal court action can be responded to as follows: A party served with interrogatories has 30 days after the date of service to answer or object to the interrogatories. Fed. R. Civ. P. 33(b)(2). A further review of the Federal Rules of Civil Procedure, however, discloses that the answering party has three extra days to respond if served by mail and that if the last day is a Saturday, Sunday, or holiday, the party has until the next business day. Fed. R. Civ. P. 6(a), (d). More complex questions, such as whether a landlord may turn off the heat of a tenant who has not paid rent, may require careful reading of several statutes, cases, and other authorities.

Remember the weight of authorities: Primary authorities (cases, constitutions, and statutes) must be followed by a court. Secondary authorities (encyclopedias, periodical articles, annotations, and so forth) are persuasive only. Thus, you should always aim to have at least one primary authority to support each of your arguments. Do not make the mistake of assuming, however, that if there are 12 cases from your jurisdiction, all of which state that punitive damages are recoverable in fraud actions, you should discuss and cite all 12. Courts are impatient with string citing or repetitive arguments. Exercise discretion, and select the most articulate case or the one most similar to your case. Consider selecting the landmark case in this area and then one recent case from your highest court. See Figure 13-5.

Cite secondary authorities if they provide a concise analysis of a topic or if the author is a well-respected and renowned authority in that legal field. Consider combining primary authorities with a secondary authority to support your argument. Do not, however, believe that legal research is like a recipe and that if you always cite two cases and a law review article your argument will win. Different topics require different levels of analysis, and you will need to exercise your own discretion to determine how many authorities are enough.

Practice Tip

When to Stop Researching

Although there is no perfect rule when to stop conducting legal research, consider that it is time to stop when:

- **You keep bumping into the same authorities and their commentary is much the same;**
- **You have read the same point in a number of different sources, with nothing new added;**
- **The same citations keep showing up; and**
- **Your Shepardizing or KeyCiting reveal no changes to the law.**

Figure 13-5
A Blueprint for Legal Research

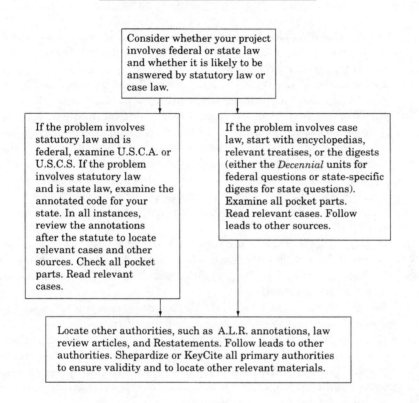

Consider whether your project involves federal or state law and whether it is likely to be answered by statutory law or case law.

If the problem involves statutory law and is federal, examine U.S.C.A. or U.S.C.S. If the problem involves statutory law and is state law, examine the annotated code for your state. In all instances, review the annotations after the statute to locate relevant cases and other sources. Check all pocket parts. Read relevant cases.

If the problem involves case law, start with encyclopedias, relevant treatises, or the digests (either the *Decennial* units for federal questions or state-specific digests for state questions). Examine all pocket parts. Read relevant cases. Follow leads to other sources.

Locate other authorities, such as A.L.R. annotations, law review articles, and Restatements. Follow leads to other authorities. Shepardize or KeyCite all primary authorities to ensure validity and to locate other relevant materials.

CyberSites

http://ualr.edu/cmbarger/Research.htm	This site includes numerous links to sites to enable you to conduct legal research.
http://comp.uark.edu/~ksampson/ legal_research_library.html	This "legal research library" includes good links to state and federal sources as well as a research outline.
http://bc.edu/schools/law/library/ research/researchguides.html	Boston College Law Library offers excellent legal research guides and videos.
http://www.ll.georgetown.edu/ tutorials/index.cfm	Georgetown Law Center provides several valuable tutorials relating to legal research.

Ten Tips for Effective Research

1. **Be prepared.** The time you spend thinking about a project before you begin is time well spent. Give yourself a few minutes to plan your research strategies.
2. **Be flexible.** If the books you need aren't on the shelf or if your efforts are not yielding results, switch to another set of books.
3. **Be thorough.** Check all pocket parts and supplements to be sure you have the most recent materials. Shepardize or KeyCite all primary authorities to make sure the law is still "good." Take complete notes. Be scrupulous in transcribing citations to avoid backtracking. Consider a variety of research methods (print sources, CALR, and the Internet) to achieve the best results.
4. **Be patient.** Research can be a difficult process. Expect some roadblocks.
5. **Be organized.** Tackle one topic or issue at a time. Do not allow yourself to get sidetracked on a minor issue or diverted in another direction. Address each research issue with a laser, not a buckshot, approach.
6. **Be efficient.** Gather together all the materials you need so you don't waste time wandering around the library.
7. **Be creative.** If all of your colleagues are beginning their research in one set of books, begin in another to avoid the crowd as well as the crowd mentality. Try contacting agencies and individuals and asking for assistance rather than depending exclusively on the books in the stacks.
8. **Be wary.** Make sure you approach your problem from all angles. Play devil's advocate. What will the adversary argue?
9. **Be resourceful.** Look for law review articles and annotations on your legal topic. If someone has already written a thorough analysis of an issue, why reinvent the wheel?
10. **Be calm.** If you get stuck, ask a librarian for help. That's what they're there for.

Writing Strategies

As you prepare to write, invest time in "brainstorming." On a piece of paper, jot down anything that comes to mind relating to the project. You can later omit any ideas or topics that are not useful. The mere process of starting to write something will get your creative juices flowing, and some ideas that you originally believe are farfetched may later develop into a creative line of reasoning.

If you initially think of more than one way to express a thought, write down both expressions. Later you can decide which to omit or perhaps you will find a way to combine both ideas.

If an argument or line of reasoning occurs to you during the research process, write it down as clearly and completely as possible. You may later be able to "lift" these notes intact and place them verbatim into the written project. That is, the more complete your note-taking is, the easier it will be for you to write the project. In some instances, your notes will almost be the equivalent of a first draft. If your "note-taking" consists merely of photocopying cases and passages of writings, however, you will need to devote far more time to the initial draft as much work needs to be done to develop what is in those cases and writings into a reasoned and concise project.

Assignment for Chapter 13

Answer the following questions, which are designed to test the research skills you have learned in the preceding chapters, and give the citation to the legal authority that supports your answer.

1. May the U.S. flag be displayed during a violent thunderstorm?
2. Give the definition of "maple sirup" (or "syrup") according to the Code of Federal Regulations.
3. A client in Utah who rents an apartment to a student would like to evict the student for failure to pay rent. Is the landlord required to provide any notice to the tenant prior to bringing an action for eviction? If so, describe the notice required.
4. Our client has been charged with first degree burglary in Colorado by entering a pharmacy to steal a controlled substance. What class of felony is such a crime?
5. A client would like to reserve the name "Party Events by Erin, Inc." in Illinois for a corporation that she plans to form. How long would such a name reservation last?
6. Give the citation to the new federal "Troubled Assets Relief Program" (often called the "TARP program").
7. Our client's daughter, age 15, eloped in Arkansas. Can the parents annul the marriage? Discuss.
8. What is the punishment for bank robbery?
9. An elderly client in Alaska cannot sign her name to her will. Can the will be valid if the client does not personally sign the will?
10. You and your sister have jointly authored a novel. How long will the copyright in this novel last?
11. Our client (a plaintiff in a California lawsuit) recently received a set of interrogatories from the defendant. There are 45 questions or interrogatories that were specially prepared or drafted by the defendant. Must our client answer these interrogatories?
12. Give the citation to the new law known as the Lily Ledbetter Fair Pay Act and then give the citation to the U.S. Supreme Court case that was superseded by this federal statute. Show how you would cite that the case was superseded by statute.

Internet Assignment for Chapter 13

1. Access Georgetown Law Center's site at http://www.ll
    .georgetown.edu/research.
    a. Select "Legal Research" and then "Case Law Research
        Guide." When should one avoid using the Internet for case
        law research?
    b. Select "Secondary Sources" and then "Secondary Sources
        Research Guide." Why should researchers use secondary
        sources?
2. Access the legal research outline located at http://comp
    .uark.edu/~ksampson/flowchart.htm. What are the first and
    last steps identified in legal research?
3. Access the website for Syracuse University Law Library at
    http://www.law.syr.edu/library. Locate the article titled "Suc-
    cessful Legal Research on the Job."
    a. What is the first tip you are given in Section I?
    b. When should you stop researching?

Legal
Writing

Back to Basics

The writer who neglects punctuation, or mispunctuates, is likely to be misunderstood . . . .

Edgar Allan Poe (1848)

A. **The Mechanics of Writing**
B. **Grammar, Spelling, and Punctuation**

Chapter Overview

The goal of legal writing is to communicate. The style of the communication may simply be informative, for example, to inform the reader of certain facts or events, or it may be persuasive, for example, to persuade the reader to adopt a certain point of view. No matter what style or form legal writing takes, its mechanics (grammar, spelling, and punctuation) must be correct. Failure to use good grammar results in cloudy and incomprehensible writing. Incorrect spelling casts doubt on your skill and credibility. Improper punctuation results in an unclear project.

This chapter will review these basics of writing so your final product will effectively communicate to its intended audience, whether it is a client, an adverse party, or a court.

A. The Mechanics of Writing

Even if your research is flawless and you have found primary authorities "on point," these will do you no good unless you can communicate your results to a reader. Flaws in the communication process, such as improper spelling, awkward word usage and sentence construction, and errors in punctuation distract your reader from your message, making the reader doubt your abilities and reflect on your carelessness.

Some legal professionals have strong writing backgrounds and are comfortable with grammar, spelling, and punctuation. Others have more scientific or technology-oriented backgrounds and are unused to writing. Even those individuals who have done a great deal of writing in college or on the job may be unfamiliar with the strictures of legal writing. For example, typical undergraduate writing is marked by more flexible punctuation. Punctuation in legal writing is considerably more rigid

because a misplaced or omitted comma can change the meaning of a statement. There is vigorous debate among grammarians regarding some punctuation marks and usages. Select a well-known text such as *The Chicago Manual of Style* or the United States Government Printing Office *Style Manual* (available online at http://www.gpoaccess.gov/stylemanual), and use it to support your position, if necessary.

After years of communicating primarily by telephone, many people in the business fields are now communicating more in writing. Thanks to e-mail, electronic chat rooms, and blogs, people are writing more now than ever before. Unfortunately, communicating via computer is often so informal that careless errors are perpetuated. Thus, although many of us may be writing more, we're also writing worse, with less attention to spelling, punctuation, and proofing. Do not be seduced into thinking that because e-mail to your supervisor or colleagues is easy and informal, it can be incorrect. The way you communicate communicates a message about you. Invest the time and effort in producing a clear and well-written document or message every time you write, and no matter what the means of communication. A final word of caution about e-mail: Most law firms and businesses have strict policies about the use of e-mail for business purposes only. Moreover, the security of e-mail is open to question. Many employers monitor e-mail use. Therefore, do not use your work e-mail for anything other than business purposes, and do not say anything you wouldn't want your boss to read.

Although there are many guides to writing, perhaps the best known and easiest to understand is *The Elements of Style* by William Strunk, Jr., and E.B. White. First introduced in 1918, *The Elements of Style* (now in its fourth edition) sets forth in clear and concise fashion principles of usage and composition with illustrative examples. Some writing instructors recommend a cover-to-cover re-reading of "the little book" each year to refresh one's understanding of the fundamentals of English style. Portions of *The Elements of Style* are available online at http://www.bartleby.com. Additionally, most dictionaries include sections on grammar, spelling, and punctuation together with useful examples. Finally, any bookstore's reference section will include numerous books on writing and style. Invest in a few reference tools, and keep them near you when you write.

Don't let the rules of grammar and its incomprehensible terms (such as "pluperfect" or "subjunctive") intimidate you. You do not need to know all of the parts of speech to be a good writer, just as you do not need to know all of the parts of a microwave oven to be a good cook.

This chapter will discuss the rules most commonly misunderstood or violated by legal writers.

B. Grammar, Spelling, and Punctuation

1. Grammar Do's and Don'ts

Rules of grammar are used so that we can communicate clearly. Following are some of the most common grammatical errors made by beginning and even experienced writers.

a. Subject-Verb Agreement

A verb must agree in number with the subject of a sentence. That is, if the subject of a sentence is singular, the verb must also be singular. Similarly, if the subject of a sentence is plural, the verb must also be plural. Most problems in subject-verb agreement occur when a subject is used that has more than one word, when the subject is an indefinite pronoun or collective noun, or when several words or a prepositional phrase intervene between the subject and the verb.

(1) Multiple Word Subjects

Examples

Incorrect	*Correct*
Compound subject: The judge and jury was unpersuaded by Smith's testimony.	The judge and jury were unpersuaded by Smith's testimony.

Because the subject of the sentence in the preceding example consists of two words connected by "and," it is plural, and thus a plural verb (were) is needed.

If the subject is composed of singular words connected by "or" or "nor," use a singular verb.

Incorrect	*Correct*
Neither the defendant nor his counsel were prepared.	Neither the defendant nor his counsel was prepared.

If the subject is composed of a singular and a plural word, the verb should agree with the noun or pronoun nearer to the verb, as in "The judge and the jurors have left."

Often confusion regarding subject and verb agreement arises when a word that ends in -one or -body, such as "someone" or "everybody," or a word such as "each," "either," "neither," or "no one" is used. These indefinite pronouns are considered singular, and a singular verb must be

used. Moreover, a singular pronoun (he, she, it) must be used with these words. Other indefinite pronouns, for example, "both," "few," and "many" are clearly plural and therefore take a plural verb, as in "Few were left in the courthouse."

Although it is common to use plural pronouns in speaking or informal writing, legal writing is more formal and one must be scrupulous in using singular pronouns with such words.

Incorrect	*Correct*
Everyone in the courtroom were seated.	*Everyone* in the courtroom *was* seated.
Each of these incidents involve a consumer who mistakenly purchased one product when they intended to purchase another.	*Each* of these incidents *involves* a *consumer* who mistakenly purchased one product when *he* intended to purchase another.
Somebody forgot to file their papers.	*Somebody* forgot to file *his* or *her* papers.

Although the correct examples above show proper usage, you may wish to avoid the words "his" or "he" if they strike you as sexist. As discussed later in this chapter, there are several ways to remedy sexist language.

(2) Collective Nouns

Collective nouns (nouns that stand for a group of people or items) such as committee, crowd, court, and jury are usually singular.

Incorrect	*Correct*
The jury have adjourned to deliberate the defendant's guilt.	The *jury has* adjourned to deliberate the defendant's guilt.
The court are discussing the plaintiff's right to a speedy trial.	The *court is* discussing the plaintiff's right to a speedy trial.
The board of directors have met.	The *board of directors has* met.

If you wish to discuss the individuals composing the unit, for the sake of clarity use the following form:

Correct
The *jurors have* adjourned to deliberate the defendant's guilt.
The *members* of the court *are* discussing the plaintiff's right to a speedy trial.

(3) *Intervening Words*

Subject-verb agreement problems often occur when words or phrases intervene between a subject and a verb.

Incorrect	*Correct*
The remainder of the goods to be distributed are in storage.	The *remainder* of the goods to be distributed *is* in storage.
The deposition, along with many exhibits, show the defendant was speeding.	The *deposition*, along with many exhibits, *shows* the defendant was speeding.

In the preceding examples, the subjects are "remainder" and "deposition." Both of these words are singular and therefore they require the singular verbs "is" and "shows." Focus on the subject of the sentence and ignore intervening words.

(4) *Prepositional Phrases*

Prepositional phrases that intervene between a subject and a verb often confuse writers who may be tempted to match the verb with the noun in the prepositional phrase rather than with the subject of the sentence.

Incorrect	*Correct*
One of the best teachers are available.	*One* of the best teachers *is* available.
A small group of city employees were working.	A small *group* of city employees *was* working.

In summary, always carefully scrutinize your writing to identify the subject. Once you have located the subject, classify it as singular or plural and then select the appropriate verb form, ignoring any intervening words or extraneous words.

Practice Tip

Achieving Subject-Verb Agreement

- **Try mentally replacing multiple word subjects (such as in "the *plaintiff and the defendant* are present") with the word *they* to determine the correct verb, as in *"They are present."***
- **Watch for the word *the* before a noun because it is often a signal that the word should be singular, as in *"The board has declared a dividend."***

b. Sentence Fragments

Sentence fragments, or incomplete sentences, are caused by a failure to include a subject and a verb in each sentence. Often a sentence fragment occurs because the writer has assumed that a dependent clause, that is, one that cannot stand on its own, is a sentence by itself. Sentence fragments can often be avoided by correcting the punctuation or by making the dependent clause into a complete sentence.

Incorrect	*Correct*
I gained two valuable lessons. First, the importance of being bilingual. Second, the need to understand a different culture.	I gained two valuable lessons: first, the importance of being bilingual and, second, the need to understand a different culture.
	or
	I gained two important lessons. The first lesson was the importance of being bilingual, and the second was the need to understand a different culture.

c. Run-on Sentences

In many ways, a run-on sentence is the opposite of a sentence fragment. A run-on sentence combines two sentences into one. Run-on sentences can usually be corrected by inserting the proper punctuation or by dividing the run-on into two separate sentences.

Incorrect	*Correct*
The members of the jury were deadlocked, they could not reach a verdict.	The members of the jury were deadlocked; they could not reach a verdict.
	or
	The members of the jury were deadlocked. They could not reach a verdict.

d. Modifiers

The incorrect placement of a modifier (a word that limits, describes, or qualifies another word or group of words) causes ambiguity. Place modifiers next to or as close as possible to the words they modify. For example, the sentence "Ginny agreed only to lend her sister money" is capable of two interpretations. Does it mean that Ginny agreed to lend her sister money and no other item? Or does it mean Ginny will lend her

sister money and will not lend money to anyone else? It may be necessary to add words to a sentence with a modifier in order to achieve clarity. Either of the following two sentences will reduce ambiguity:

> Ginny agreed to lend her sister only money and nothing else.
> Ginny agreed to lend money only to her sister and not to anyone else.

Similarly, note the following sentence: "A man was put to death in Texas for a murder he committed during a supermarket robbery this morning." The phrase "this morning" must be placed after "Texas" to avoid ambiguity.

Modifiers such as "almost," "ultimately," "frequently," "immediately," "eventually," "finally," and "only" are notorious causes of ambiguity. Exercise caution in using these words.

The typical modifiers are adverbs and adjectives. Once again, try to place these modifiers adjacent to the words they modify.

Confusing	Better
He saw a note on the table that was blue.	He saw a blue note on the table.
	or
	He saw a note on the blue table.

e. Split Infinitives

An infinitive is the word *to* with a verb, as in *to run* or *to plead*. An infinitive is said to be "split" when a word (usually an adverb) is inserted between the word *to* and the verb, as in *to quickly run* or *to convincingly plead*.

Most writing experts now recognize that there is no formal rule against splitting an infinitive, and split infinitives are commonly seen in nonlegal writing, including newspaper articles; however, legal readers tend to be conservative and may be annoyed or distracted by a split infinitive. Because most split infinitives are so easily corrected (by merely moving the adverb that causes the "split" after the infinitive), correct them when you can, and avoid splitting an infinitive unless you want to place emphasis on the adverb.

Awkward	Better
The attorney asked me *to thoroughly review* the pleadings.	The attorney asked me *to review* the pleadings thoroughly.

Do not insert "not" or "never" in an infinitive because the result is awkward and incorrect.

Incorrect	Correct
She agreed to not examine the witness.	She agreed not to examine the witness.

f. Dangling Participles

A present participle is a verb ending in *-ing*, as in *arguing* or *entering*. It is said to "dangle" when it does not modify the subject of a sentence. Also called a dangling modifier, this grammar problem most often occurs when a sentence starts with a word ending in *-ing*, as in *Trying to meet the filing deadline, my computer crashed.* This sentence is incorrect because it lacks an identification of the subject and implies that the computer was trying to meet the deadline. To remedy a dangling modifier, either identify the actor immediately after the introductory modifier, or reword the modifying phrase so that it identifies the actor, as in *As I was trying to meet the filing deadline, my computer crashed.*

Some dangling participles result in unintended humor. For example, the following statement was published in *The Westhampton Beach* (N.Y.) *Hampton Chronicle News*: "Boasting a voracious appetite and stocked with both male and female sex organs capable of producing 1,000 offspring per year, officials at the U.S. Department of Agriculture are warning Long Islanders to report any sightings of the oversized escargot immediately."

Incorrect	*Correct*
Entering the darkened room, his eyes slowly adjusted to the dimness.	As he entered the darkened room, his eyes slowly adjusted to the dimness.

g. Pronouns

(1) Personal Pronouns

Personal pronouns (I/me, he/him, she/her, we/us, they/them) change forms depending on whether they function as the subject of a sentence or the object of the sentence. When the pronoun functions as or replaces the subject of a sentence, use "I," "he," "she," "we," or "they."

Incorrect	*Correct*
It was me who prepared the document.	It was *I* who prepared the document.
James and her drafted the appellate brief.	James and *she* drafted the appellate brief.
Either him or me will do the cite checking.	Either *he* or *I* will do the cite checking.
Us on the jury voted to convict the defendant.	*We* on the jury voted to convict the defendant.
It was them who informed the police.	It was *they* who informed the police.

When the pronoun functions as or replaces the object of a sentence, use "me," "him," "her," "us," or "them."

Incorrect	_Correct_
You must give John and I clear instructions.	You must give John and _me_ clear instructions.
We urge you to release Susan and he from their employment contracts.	We urge you to release Susan and _him_ from their employment contracts.
She has provided the committee and we with the budget analysis.	She has provided the committee and _us_ with the budget analysis.
The prisoner was released into the custody of Janet and they.	The prisoner was released into the custody of Janet and _them_.
Between you and I, the defendant is liable.	Between you and _me_, the defendant is liable.

As an aid to determining which form of pronoun to use, omit or cover up the noun and the word "and" accompanying the pronoun, and this will provide a clue as to which pronoun to use. For example, in the sentence "You must give John and _I/me_ clear instructions," omit "John and" so the sentence reads "You must give _____ clear instructions." This reading makes it clear the correct pronoun is "me." Finally, by custom and usage, the first person pronoun (I/me, he/him, she/her, it) is usually placed second, as in "Joe and I went to Rome" (not "I and Joe went to Rome").

(2) *Reflexive Pronouns*

The reflexive pronouns are the "self" pronouns such as "myself," "yourself," "himself," "herself," "ourselves," "yourselves," and "themselves." Reflexive pronouns usually reflect back on a subject as in "She injured herself." Do not substitute a "self" pronoun for a personal pronoun (I/me, he/him).

Incorrect	_Correct_
Susan and myself attended the trial.	Susan and I attended the trial.
The accident was witnessed by Mrs. Hendrix and himself.	The accident was witnessed by Mrs. Hendrix and him.

(3) *Relative Pronouns*

The relative pronouns include "who," "whom," "that," and "which." To decide whether to use "who" or "whom," you need to determine if the relative pronoun is the subject of the sentence. If so, use "who." If the relative pronoun is the object of a sentence, clause, or prepositional phrase, use "whom."

Incorrect	_Correct_
The man whom is being arraigned is 22 years old.	The man who is being arraigned is 22 years old.
This is the woman who I mentioned earlier.	This is the woman whom I mentioned earlier.

Practice Tip

Who and Whom (Remember "m" for Whom)

When using _who_ or _whom_, rephrase the question or clause and determine whether you would use _he_ or _him_ in its place. If _he_ would be used, use _who_. If him would be used, use _whom_. Remember that the "m" in _him_ matches up with the "m" in _whom_. This tip works in almost all instances.

- **Example: Who is calling?**
- **Test: Rewrite as _He is calling_. Replace _he_ with _who_.**
- **Example: Whom do you trust?**
- **Test: Rewrite as _I trust him_. Replace _him_ with _whom_.**

Use "who" or "that" to refer to humans (as in "the paralegal who was hired," "the project manager who proofread the document," or "the paralegal that was hired"). Note that many writers object to the use of the word "that" to refer to persons, although it is commonly used colloquially. Use "that" or "which" to refer to non-humans, places, or objects (as in "the deposition that was taken," "the exhibits, which were omitted," or "the dog that barked").

"That" is used in a restrictive clause (a clause that is essential to the meaning of a sentence) whereas "which" is used in a non-restrictive clause (a clause that merely adds an idea to a sentence that would be complete without the clause). For example, in the sentence "The pens that were on the desk are missing," the word "that" tells which particular pens are missing (namely, the ones on the desk). Presumably, there are other pens that were not on the desk, and those can still be found. On the other hand, review the sentence, "The pens, which were on the desk, are missing." This sentence tells us that all of the pens were on the desk, and they are all missing. Many writers have difficulty determining whether to start a clause with "that" or "which." Remember these hints:

- If you can drop the clause and still retain the meaning of the sentence, use "which." If you can't, use "that."
- A clause beginning with "which" is usually set off by commas.
- A clause beginning with "that" is not set off by commas.
- "That" introduces essential information; "which" seldom does.

Examples

- My car, which was brand new, was damaged in the collision. (You can drop the "which" clause and the sentence still makes sense. Use "which.")
- The car that was damaged in the collision was my car. (Elimination of the "that" clause causes the sentence to lose meaning. Thus, the phrase is essential. Use "that.")

Writers often substitute pronouns for names in a manner that creates ambiguity. For example, in the sentence "The document Ellen drafted for Teresa was given to her for review," it is unclear whether the "her" refers to Ellen or Teresa. Clarifying such an ambiguous statement usually requires rewriting the sentence. Thus, "The document Ellen drafted for Teresa was given to Ellen for her review" makes it clear which individual received the document for review.

Similarly, the statement "Don likes these cookies more than me" creates confusion (in addition to being grammatically incorrect). Because the word "cookies" is used as the object of the verb, the sentence means that Don likes the cookies more than he likes me. To reduce confusion, rewrite such sentences. Thus, "Don likes these cookies more than I do" makes it clear Don likes the cookies more than I like them.

Use "it" to refer to collective nouns such as jury, court, committee, or association unless you are referring to the members of the group. Also use "it" or "its" to refer to non-human entities or institutions such as corporations.

Incorrect	*Correct*
The corporation held their annual meeting in May.	The *corporation* held *its* annual meeting in May.
The court issued their opinion.	The *court* issued *its* opinion.

(4) Gender-Linked Pronouns

Avoid the use of gender-linked pronouns. For example, the sentence "A nurse should always keep her thermometer handy" is objectionable because it implies that nurses are always female. Similarly, the sentence "A judge must give his instructions to the jury" is objectionable because it presupposes the judge is male.

There are several techniques you can use to avoid offending readers. One technique is to change the singular nouns to plural. This in turn will necessitate a change in the singular pronoun "he" or "she" to a neutral plural pronoun such as "they" or "their." Thus, the first example would read "Nurses should always keep *their* thermometers handy," and the second example would read "Judges must give *their* instructions to the jury."

A second technique is to rewrite the sentence to avoid using any pronouns. The first sentence would then read "A nurse should always keep a thermometer handy," and the second sentence could be rewritten as "A judge must always give instructions to the jury."

Another alternative is to use the noun "one." Using this technique, the first example would be rewritten as "One should always keep one's thermometer handy," and the second example would be "One must always give one's instructions to the jury." As you can see, however, the use of "one" often results in a vague sentence that is stuffy in tone.

Another alternative in some situations is to use the pronoun "you." Thus, rather than writing "The applicant must provide his or her address," write, "You must provide your address."

There are some instances in which none of these techniques will work for you. In those cases you could use "he or she" throughout the document. This, however, can result in a clumsy document if used continually. Avoid the use of "he/she." This construction creates an awkward appearance because slashes are seldom used in legal writing. Their use is noticeable and distracting to a reader. The combination "s/he" is even more noticeable and distracting.

If you are drafting a long document, such as a contract, you may use "he" throughout and at the end include a statement that the use of a masculine gender is deemed to include the feminine. This is a common approach used by legal professionals. Avoid alternating between "he" and "she" in a single document, especially in a single paragraph. This attempt to be fair and gender-neutral is misguided and disruptive to the flow of a project.

When addressing a letter to an individual whose gender is unknown, for example, a letter to the Secretary of State of Utah, check the Internet to see if you can determine whether the individual is a man or woman. If you cannot make that determination, address the letter as "Dear Sir or Madam." While "madam" is an archaic form of address, it is correct in such a situation. Similarly, when you are responding to a letter written by an individual whose name is ambiguous, such as Terry L. Smith, consider calling and asking how the letter should be addressed. Rest assured, you will not be the first person confused by such a name. If contacting the person is not possible or practical, you could address the letter "Dear Terry," "Dear Terry Smith," or "Dear Colleague."

In sum, correct gender-linked pronouns to avoid offending readers if you can do so without causing an awkward and distracting document. For example, the use of specially crafted words such as "personholes" (rather than "manholes") is jarring to a reader. Thus, it is still acceptable to use "he" or "him," if changing the pronouns or rewriting the sentence would result in clumsy and distracting writing.

Practice Tip

Following the Old Grammar Rules

Because legal writing is more formal than other styles of writing, and because legal readers are notorious perfectionists, err on the side of caution so readers will not be jarred by your usage. Thus, whenever possible, comply with the "old" rules of writing in legal documents:

- Don't split an infinitive;
- Don't start a sentence with a conjunction such as *and* or *but*; and
- Don't end a sentence with a preposition.

---

2. Spelling

Poor spellers often announce, "I've never been a good speller," as if this disclaimer were some justification for a writing problem that negatively affects a project and the reader's view of its author. If you know that spelling is your weak spot, you need to work harder on this area rather than shrug it off with excuses. Keep several dictionaries handy — one in your office, one at home, and a pocket one in your briefcase. You may want to go to a professional bookstore that stocks legal books or to the bookstore at a law school to purchase a legal dictionary. A legal dictionary will include words used in legal settings such as "rescission" as well as Latin terms and phrases commonly used. Don't be afraid to write in your dictionary. Circle or highlight words you have reviewed. Chances are you will need to look up the word several times before you memorize the correct spelling. Similarly, you may wish to keep an index card handy with your top-ten list of commonly misspelled words. Refer to it often. Over time, you will learn the words on the list.

Using a dictionary is not a sign of weakness. It is a signal that you are striving for professionalism in your work product. When you look up a word such as "canceled" in the dictionary, you may notice that you are given the spelling "canceled" and then the alternative spelling "cancelled." Usually the entry given first is the preferred spelling, and you should use this form of the word. Similarly, use the commonly accepted spelling of a word rather than some foreign or exotic variety. For example, use "organization" and "behavior" rather than "organisation" and "behaviour," which are British spellings of those words.

One of the wonderful features of many word processor systems is their ability to check the spelling of words. Be sure to use your spell-checking feature to help you catch spelling errors, but do not rely on it exclusively. In fact, many experts believe spelling checkers encourage complacency. Although the spelling checker will let you know if you misspelled "restaurant," it cannot check word usage. Thus, if you used the word "principle" rather than "principal," the spelling checker will not inform you so long as "principle" is spelled correctly.

Be thorough in your review of your finished project, and read through the last draft for spelling errors. You should also keep a list of your own common spelling errors handy and refer to it. If you find it difficult to review your own work, ask a co-worker or friend to read through your project for spelling errors.

One of the most distressing results of misspelling is the effect produced in the mind of a reader. If your aim in writing is to inform or persuade your reader, and the reader is confronted with spelling errors, any value your product may have may well be overshadowed by the misspellings. Readers of legal documents, such as employers, clients, attorneys, and judges, tend to be highly critical and perfectionistic. When confronted with spelling errors, they may react by assuming that if you cannot be trusted to spell properly, you cannot be trusted to have found the correct answer to a legal problem. Thus, spelling errors cast doubt on more than your ability to spell by causing readers to question the correctness of your conclusions. At best, spelling errors make readers believe you are careless. At worst, they may question your intelligence.

Following are some words commonly misspelled in legal or business writing:

Correct	_Correct_	_Correct_
absence	definite	occasionally
accommodate	dependent	occurred
acknowledgment	descendant	offense
admissible	desperately	permissible
affidavit	dilemma	perseverance
allege	dissatisfied	persistent
bankruptcy	environment	possess
basically	exercise	practically
boundary	exonerate	preceding
breach	feasible	predecessor
brief	foresee	privilege
calendar	fulfill	proceed
cancellation	goodwill	publicly
causal	grateful	rarefied
cease	grievous	receive
challenge	harass	recommend
circuit	immediately	relevant
collateral	inasmuch as	renowned
column	indict	rescind
commitment	irrelevant	rescission
complaint	judgment	seize
concede	labeled	separate
condemn	license	sheriff
conscious	lien	sincerely
controversy	lightning	succeed
counselor	marshaled	supersede
deductible	minuscule	statutes
defendant	mortgage	transferred
		warrant

Following are some tips to becoming a better speller:

- Learn some rules. Many spelling rules are easy to remember (although they often have exceptions), such as "place *i* before *e*, except after *c*, or except when it sounds like *ay*, as in neighbor and weigh."
- Use a dictionary. Always consult a dictionary to check spelling and mark and highlight troublesome words. Some dictionaries contain no definitions; they only list spelled words. These dictionaries are useful and portable. The online dictionary found at http://www.dictionary.com is also helpful.
- Don't over-rely on a spell checker. Studies show that papers written with the help of a spell checker are only marginally better than those that are not.
- Use mnemonic devices to help you remember words, such as "the princi*pal* of your school is your *pal*."
- Pronounce your words carefully. It will be difficult to remember the correct spelling of environment if you pronounce it as *enviroment*.
- Write your misspellings several times. If you catch yourself writing "privelege" rather than "privilege," write it ten times to train yourself.
- Proofread carefully. In many instances, a misspelled word will not look "right" to you, and you can then correct the error.
- Use the "find and replace" feature of your word processor to correct common errors automatically. For example, if you routinely type *Untied States* rather than *United States*, the find and replace feature will locate each occurrence of this error and replace it with the correct spelling.

——— Ethics Alert ———

The Duty of Competence

Although errors in spelling, grammar, and punctuation may seem minor or cosmetic, they can and do detract from a polished project. In one case, the court noted with stern disapproval that "the plaintiff's brief is littered with spelling errors, grammatical sloppiness, and incorrect case citations" and condemned this "shoddy professionalism." *Universal Restoration Servs., Inc. v. Paul W. Davis Sys., Inc.*, No. 908-C-2027, 2002 WL 596380, at *7 (N.D. Ill. Apr. 17, 2002). Thus, your duty of competence extends to all aspects of your writing, even the technical aspects such as grammar, spelling, and punctuation.

3. *Punctuation*

a. Introduction

When you speak, you use pauses and changes in voice inflection as well as gestures to signal meaning to the listener. In writing, these signals are given through the use of punctuation. Punctuation makes writing more understandable to a reader. For example, a period instructs the reader that a complete thought or sentence is concluded. Without periods, all of a writing would be one incomprehensible sentence. Similarly, quotation marks signal to a reader that the exact words of another are being used.

This portion of the chapter will discuss commas, apostrophes, colons, semicolons, quotations, parentheses, and the less frequently used marks in legal writing such as dashes and exclamation points.

There is some variation in punctuation. Given the same paragraph, two writers may punctuate slightly differently from each other. Nevertheless, the basic rules of punctuation have remained relatively unchanged since about the mid-1880s. Although the newer, more modern approach to punctuation, referred to as "open" punctuation, uses fewer punctuation marks than the older approach (for example, many modern writers no longer use the serial comma discussed below), legal writing, like business writing, tends to be somewhat formal. Therefore, just as recommended in the section in this chapter on grammar, when in doubt, err on the side of caution and use the more conventional approach to punctuation rather than some unusual approach.

b. Commas

A comma indicates a brief pause and is considered the most troublesome of punctuation marks due to its numerous uses. Use a comma:

(i)   After the salutation of an informal letter and after the closing of any letter:

Dear Aunt Kay,	Sincerely,
Dear James,	Very truly yours,

(ii)   To set off digits in numbers, dates, and addresses:

There are 4,182 pages in the transcript. (Note, however, that *Bluebook* Rule 6.2(a) states to use a comma only where numbers contain five or more digits and would therefore write this number as "4182.")

The plaintiff filed her complaint on June 9, 2010, the day she was fired from her job.

The defendant resides at 2202 Oak Brook Terrace, Evanston, Illinois 07816.

(iii)   To set off an introductory word, phrase, or clause:

According to the plaintiff's testimony, the car was traveling west on Burgener Street at the time of the accident.

Nevertheless, the defendant failed to comply with the
terms of his agreement.

First, the defendant entered Mrs. Smith's dwelling place.

Although she was quite elderly, she made an effective
witness. Use of a comma after a *short* introductory
phrase is optional. Thus, the following is correct: After
the trial I was exhausted.

(iv) To set off interruptive or non-essential words or phrases:

While looking for her pen, however, she found the missing
checkbook.

The defendant, over the strenuous objection of his counsel, insisted on testifying.

(v) To set off appositives (a word or group of words inserted
immediately after another word that explains the previous
word):

William Emery, the noted attorney, consulted on the case.

(vi) Before a coordinating conjunction ("and," "but," "for," "nor,"
"or," "so," or "yet") introducing an independent clause, namely,
one that can function as a complete sentence. You may omit the
comma if the clause is short (five words or fewer). The comma
is not needed after the coordinating conjunction if the clause
that follows cannot stand on its own.

The plaintiff intended to amend the complaint, but the
statute of limitations had expired.

The defendant's answer had been amended several times,
and the judge expressed impatience with the many
amendments.

The defendant's answer had been amended several times
and was poorly written and nearly incomprehensible.

The attorney argued but the jury convicted.

He argued the case and did so clearly.

(vii) To set off items in a series. Although the final comma in a series
is optional in most writing, in legal writing you must place a
comma after each item in the list and before the conjunction.
For example, examine the sentence, "I leave my property
equally to Susan, Bill, Louise, and Tom." A reader would
understand that each individual would receive one-fourth of
the estate. Note that the omission of the last comma could
cause a completely different result, for example, "I leave my
property equally to Susan, Bill, Louise and Tom." The omission

of the comma after "Louise" arguably indicates that the property is to be divided equally into thirds: one-third to Susan, one-third to Bill, and one-third to Louise and Tom together, rather than in equal fourths to each individual. Because the omission of the last comma in a series (the serial comma) can cause ambiguity, always include it. In fact, at least one expert notes that omitting the serial comma is acceptable only in newspapers and commercial magazines. To determine how many commas to use, some writers count the number of items in the list or the series and then use one less comma than the number.

(viii) Before and after quotations:

> "I need the pen," Bob said.
> Lee replied, "I agree."

c. Apostrophes

Apostrophes are used to show possession or ownership or to show omission of one or more letters, as in the contraction *don't*. The use of apostrophes to show possession, especially with regard to proper names, is often confusing.

Use an apostrophe:

(i) to show possession or ownership. Follow three basic rules:

- Add an apostrophe and an *s* ('s) to show possession for all singular nouns, even if the noun ends in s, k, x, or z.

  Correct examples: the girl's coat
                           the shareholder's ballot
                           Arkansas's election
                           Congress's intent
                           Charles's book
                           Xerox's plan

- When a plural word ends in *s*, add only an apostrophe (') to show possession.

  Correct examples: the four girls' coats
                           the six shareholders' ballots
                           the two workers'
                               employment benefits

- When a word is plural and does not already end in *s*, add an apostrophe and an *s* ('s) to show possession.

  Correct examples: the children's toys
                           the women's cars

- To form the plural of most names or to show possession for most names, follow the rules given above.

    Correct examples: Ed Smith's papers were filed today.
                                     The Smiths moved to Chicago.
                                     The Smiths' house is large.

- For names that end in *ch*, *s*, *sh*, *x*, or *z*, however, form the plural by adding *es* and then form the plural possessive by adding an apostrophe after the *es* (*es'*). The singular possessive is formed by following the first rule above (as in *Tim Jones's car is red.*)

    Correct examples: The Joneses moved to New
                                       York.
                                     The Lynches are wealthy.
                                     The Joneses' car is an
                                       Accord.

Practice Tip

Marcus' Pen or Marcus's Pen?

Many grammar books permit the use of an apostrophe alone with a singular word ending in *s* when adding another *s* would make the word difficult to pronounce or look odd. Thus, you may see *Mr. Rogers' sweater* or *Marcus' pen*. Nevertheless, the United States Government Printing Office *Style Manual*, Strunk and White, and most conventional grammar books suggest the *'s*, as in *Mr. Rogers's sweater* and *Marcus's pen*. This form is always correct.

(ii) to indicate omission of letters, as in contractions:

- can't (can*n*ot)
- hadn't (had *n*ot)
- it's (it *is*)
- don't (do *n*ot)

One of the most common errors students and beginning writers make is misusing "it's." "It's" is a contraction for "it is" (or "it has"). The apostrophe is used to indicate that the letter "i" or the pair of letters "ha" has been omitted. To form the possessive of it, use "its." Only use "it's" when you mean to say "it is" or "it has," not when you mean to indicate possession.

    Correct example: *It's* a learned court that has the wisdom to reverse *its* decisions.

Practice Tip

Apostrophes and Plurals of Numbers and Letters

There is some disagreement whether an apostrophe should be
used to show the plural of a number or letter. The better practice
and that of the *Style Manual* is to follow the general rules for
forming plurals and to omit the apostrophe unless the result
would be confusing.

Correct examples: *There are two Exhibit Bs.*
The audit shows all 9s.
The LSATs are difficult.
Be sure to dot your i's.

---

d. Colons

Use a colon:

(i) after the salutation of a formal letter:

Dear Mr. Smith:
Dear Sir or Madam:

(ii) to introduce a list; use a colon especially after expressions such
as "as follows" or "the following":

The defendant asserted the following three defenses:
laches, acquiescence, and unclean hands.

(iii) to indicate that something will follow:

We have instituted a new policy: Goods may not be
returned without a sales receipt.

(Do not use a colon after a verb or preposition. Thus, it
would be incorrect to write, *You will find the answer in:
the case or the statute.*)

(iv) to introduce a formal or long quotation:

The court stated in unequivocal terms: "Liability is
founded on this act of gross negligence."

(Note that this quotation could also be introduced by a
comma.)

Capitalize the first word after a colon if the material following the
colon can stand on its own as a sentence. Conversely, do not capitalize the
first word after a colon if the material cannot stand on its own as a
sentence.

e. Semicolons

Use a semicolon:

(i) to connect two independent but related clauses:

> That was his final summation; it was strong and forceful.

> (Note that these two ideas could also be expressed as complete sentences separated by a period.)

(ii) to connect two independent clauses joined by a transitional word or conjunction such as *therefore, however*, or *nevertheless*:

> The defendant was not credible; therefore, the jury voted to convict her.
> The attorney argued persuasively; however, the judge overruled her.

(iii) to separate items in a list that contains commas:

> Standing trial for embezzlement were Connie Rivers of Portland, Oregon; Samuel Salter of Seattle, Washington; and Susan Stone of Butte, Montana.

(iv) to separate items in a list introduced by a colon:

> The elements to be proved in an action for breach of contract are as follows: the existence of a contract; the unjustified breach of the contract by one party; and damage caused by the breach to the non-breaching party.

> (Note that these items can also be separated by commas.)

f. Quotation Marks

Use quotation marks:

(i) to indicate the exact words of a speaker:

> Patrick Henry said, "Give me liberty or give me death."
> "The motion," said the judge, "is hereby granted."

(ii) to explain or draw emphasis to a word:

> The writer misspelled the word "defendant" in the brief.

Use quotation marks only for quotes of 49 words or fewer. For quotes of 50 words or more, block indent the quote and use single spacing. The indentation of these longer quotes itself indicates a quotation.

Always place commas and periods inside quotation marks. Place colons and semicolons outside quotation marks. When a quotation includes another quotation, single quotation marks (' ') are used:

> "It was the jury foreman," announced Betty, "who said, 'The defendant is guilty.' "

g. Parentheses

Use parentheses:

> (i) to set off interruptions or explanations:
>
>> His primary argument was *res ipsa loquitur* (a Latin phrase meaning "the thing speaks for itself").
>
> (ii) to direct the reader to other information:
>
>> The plaintiff has failed to allege justifiable reliance in the fraud cause of action. (Compl. ¶ 14.)
>
> (iii) to introduce abbreviations:
>
>> The plaintiff, Southwest Avionics Industries ("SAI"), alleged seven causes of action.

If what is included in a terminal parenthetical is a complete sentence, place a period inside the parenthetical. Otherwise, the period is placed outside the ending parenthesis.

h. Dashes

Dashes create drama and draw a reader's attention to a page. In general, however, they are considered too informal for legal writing, and, in most instances, other punctuation marks, such as commas, parentheses, or a colon, would be more appropriate. A dash is made by two hyphens. Use a dash to indicate a break or interruption, as in the following sentence: The defendant — not his brother — testified.

i. Exclamation Marks

Exclamation marks are used to emphasize an idea. They are rarely, if ever, used in legal writing other than when they appear as part of a direct quotation.

j. Hyphens

Use a hyphen:

> (i) to divide words between syllables at the end of a line of text. Avoid hyphenating proper names. Use a dictionary if you are

unsure where to divide the word. The use of word processors with their automatic ability to space words evenly eliminates much of the need for hyphens in dividing words.

(ii) between the parts of a compound adjective when it modifies the next word:

> would-be informant
> employment-related injury
> high-tech espionage

(iii) after certain prefixes:

a. prefixes preceding proper nouns

> anti-American
> pro-Israeli

b. prefixes ending with a vowel when the root word begins with a vowel (other than "re," generally)

> anti-intellectual
> co-op
> de-emphasize
> reexamine

(iv) to form compounds:

> ten-year lease
> ex-president
> on-the-job training

k. Slashes or Virgules

The diagonal slash or virgule causes ambiguity and should be avoided. It means "or," *not* "and," when used between two words. Thus, the sentence "The judge/jury agreed to acquit" means that the judge agreed to acquit or the jury agreed to acquit, *not* that the judge *and* jury agreed to acquit. A slash may be used in dates or fractions.

Dictum

- In choosing "a" or "an," consider the sound rather than the spelling of the following word. Use "a" before all consonant sounds. Use "an" before a silent "h" and before all vowel sounds except long "u."

a uniform	an heiress
a house	an IPO
a unit	an eight-day vacation
a trial	an interrogatory

- Commonly used abbreviations:

B.C.	A.D.
a.m.	p.m.
PST	EDT
Ph.D.	J.D.

- Only one word ends in "sede":   supersede
  Only three words end in "ceed":   exceed, proceed, and succeed
  All other words with the "seed"
  sound end in "cede":   precede, concede, intercede

CyberSites

Numerous website addresses for guidance on writing and grammar are provided at the end of Chapter 15. The following are excellent sources of information relating to grammar, spelling, and punctuation:

http://www.gpoaccess.gov/stylemanual	The Government Printing Office *Style Manual* is one of the most widely accepted manuals on English usage.
http://grammar.ccc.commnet.edu/ grammar	Capital Community College Foundation provides useful information as well as links to other writing resources and quizzes and exercises.
http://owl.english.purdue.edu	Purdue University's Online Writing Lab offers numerous guides and handouts as well as exercises and answer keys.
http://law.case.edu/faculty/friedman/ raw/Writing%20Links,%208-17-00 .html	This site, titled "Rawdata Writing Links," offers excellent links to numerous websites devoted to grammar and style, most of which are law related.

Assignment for Chapter 14

GRAMMAR

SELECT THE CORRECT WORD.

1. Neither the attorney nor the client were/was prepared.
2. The committee of board members were/was responsible for the report.
3. Him/He and I/me prepared the summary of exhibits.
4. Please give the trial transcript to Emma and her/she.
5. The judge is the one who/whom will charge the jury.
6. The jury has rendered its/it's/their verdict.
7. One of the transcripts were/was revised.
8. James and they/them summarized the testimony.
9. Who/Whom do you depend on for cite checking?
10. The exhibit, together with all of the attachments, was/were presented for editing.
11. The orders and the brief was/were lost in the mail.

REWRITE THE FOLLOWING TO MAKE THEM CLEARER.

1. Reading the transcript, the errors seemed obvious.
2. Attorneys often challenge a juror when they appear biased.
3. He was asked to thoroughly edit the brief.
4. Susan and myself prepared the documents.
5. Planning to testify, his notes were helpful.
6. The attorney was late for the trial. Which delayed the day's proceedings.
7. A prosecutor should maintain his files in order.
8. The final argument was powerful, it moved everyone in the courtroom.
9. Tom agreed to not attend the meeting.
10. A court reporter should always be ready to read her notes back to the judge.
11. Everyone had been given their instructions.
12. Its/It's a shame the committee lost its/it's notes.

SPELLING

SELECT THE CORRECT SPELLING.

1.	relevent	relevant
2.	acknowledgement	acknowledgment
3.	accommodate	accomodate
4.	waver of rights	waiver of rights
5.	foregoing document	forgoing document
6.	dependent	dependant
7.	privilege	privelege
8.	forgo one's claim	forego one's claim
9.	rescind	recind
10.	collatteral	collateral

PUNCTUATION

CORRECTLY PUNCTUATE THE FOLLOWING SENTENCES.

1. Neither of the only plaintiffs documents was filed.
2. Jonas sister testified for him.
3. All four of the defendants attorneys were prepared.
4. Jane is a well known paralegal, and is active in the legal community.
5. Following are the claims that should be asserted, fraud, breach of contract and breach of fiduciary duty.
6. The contract dated August 12, 2010 was sent by facsimile.
7. In October, 2010, the sale was completed.
8. Kevin edited the document and he was also responsible for filing it with the court.
9. Judge Bates opinion was brief, it was only three pages.
10. Four shareholders proxy statements were improperly signed.

Internet Assignment for Chapter 14

1. Access the website of the United States Government Printing Office *Style Manual*. For each of the following, either correct it or indicate that it is correct.
   a. Review Rule 3 relating to capitalization.
      • Pennsylvania avenue is the avenue on which the White House is located.
      • Nancy Pelosi is a democrat.
      • One of my favorite types of cooking is Southern cooking.

- The western region of the United States includes many national parks.
  b. Review Rule 5 relating to compounding.
     - Indicate the plural of the words "memento" and "tomato."
     - What is the plural of the word "appendix"?
     - Indicate whether the endings of the following words are "ible" or "able": "access" and "depend"
     - My car was totaled/totalled.
     - I was traveling/travelling on Elm Street.
     - A person from Kansas is called a _____.
  c. Review Rule 6 relating to compounding.
     - Joe is an accomplished horseman.
     - The new transit system is a large scale project.
     - Government employees earn per-diem rates when on government travel.
     - The bill has been rereferred to the committee.
  d. Review Rule 8 relating to punctuation.
     - The ladies' votes have been tallied.
     - We have approved each others ideas.
     - I have considered all the pro's and con's.
     - The boy went home and his sister remained with the crowd.
2. Access http://www.bartleby.com, and review *The Elements of Style*.
  a. Review Section II.1, and use the correct punctuation to make the following expressions possessives: the wallet of Tess; the house of Mr. Graves.
  b. Review Section II.3, and insert the correct punctuation for the following sentence: My attorney, Paul Stevens met with me yesterday.

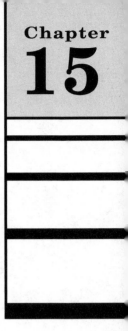

Strategies for Effective Writing

There are two things wrong with almost all legal writing. One is its style. The other is its content.

Fred Rodell, *Goodbye to Law Reviews*, 23 Va. L. Rev. 38, 38 (1936)

Chapter Overview

Once you have mastered the mechanics of writing, you must focus on making your writing effective. This chapter will present techniques to achieve the five hallmarks of effective legal writing: precision, clarity, readability, brevity, and order.

A. Introduction

The cornerstone of the legal profession is communication — communication with a client, colleague, adverse party, or judge. In most cases the communication will be in written form. Even in those instances in which you communicate orally, you will often follow up with a written letter or memo to a file. Because paralegals do not generally appear in court, they often spend even more time than some attorneys in preparing written documents. Thus, effective legal writing is critical to success as a paralegal.

B. The Plain English Movement

One of the recurring criticisms of legal writing is that it is rendered incomprehensible to the average reader by its use of jargon, redundancies, and archaic words and phrases. The use of words and phrases such as "advert to," "aforesaid," and "notwithstanding anything in the foregoing to the contrary" confuses and angers readers.

The increased activism of consumers frustrated with the impossibility of understanding an insurance policy, mortgage, or agreement for the purchase of an appliance led to the requirement in many states that certain documents be written in "plain English." The Federal Trade Commission requires that agreements for the sale of a franchise be written in plain English. Similarly, the Securities and Exchange Commission ("SEC") has issued a "Plain English Handbook" to assist attorneys in creating clear disclosure documents for the SEC (available at http://www.sec.gov/pdf/handbook.pdf). The Commonwealth of Pennsylvania forbids the use of Latin or double negatives in consumer contracts.

Similarly, in 1998, President Clinton issued his Presidential Memo on Plain Language, which requires all federal agencies to write clearly to their customers. The Plain Language initiative rests on three principles:

- Writing should be reader-oriented, clearly showing the author is writing to the customers of the agencies, not to other government employees;
- Writing should use natural expressions, using commonly known and used words; and
- Documents should be visually appealing.

A website provided by government employees at http://www .plainlanguage.gov offers writing tips, writing resources, and numerous samples of documents and letters written in plain language.

The trend toward plain language has also gained acceptance in legal writing. Law students and beginning writers are now encouraged to avoid "legalese" whenever possible and to write in plain English to enhance readability and comprehension of writings.

The plain English movement rightfully shifts the focus away from you as the author to the reader as the recipient. If you have produced what you believe is a beautifully crafted letter and yet the client doesn't understand it, you have failed. A writer is responsible for ambiguity in a document.

Writing in plain English so your reader understands you is not an easy task. Many legal concepts are very complex, and translating them into plain English is difficult. Similarly, some use of "legalese" such as Latin phrases may be unavoidable in certain instances. Falling into the habit of using archaic phrases such as "the instant case at bar" when you really mean "this case" is easy, and you must make a conscious effort to avoid confusing jargon. See Figure 15-1.

Figure 15-1
SEC Guidelines for Plain English

Following is a brief summary of the SEC's guidelines for writing in plain English:

- Use short sentences.
- Use definite, concrete, everyday language.
- Use the active voice rather than the passive voice.
- Use tables and lists to present complex information.
- Avoid legal and financial jargon and highly technical business terms.
- Avoid multiple negatives.
- Avoid weak verbs, abstract terms, and superfluous words.
- Enhance readability through attractive design and layout.

C. Prewriting

Many experts agree that the time you invest in a project before you begin writing can be the most valuable time you spend on the project. Two threshold questions are of particular importance in helping you shape your writing so it is effective and understood on the first reading. Always ask yourself, "What is the purpose of this writing?" and "Who will be reading this writing?"

1. Purpose

There can be several reasons for writing something. It is possible that your purpose is to relay information such as notifying a client that his deposition has been scheduled for next month. Another purpose may be to obtain information such as asking a client to clarify an answer given to an interrogatory question posed by an adverse party. You may be explaining something to a reader, such as in a letter discussing the results of a settlement meeting. Finally, you may be aiming to convince a reader in a trial or appellate brief when your objective is to convince the court to adopt your argument.

If, before you begin any project, you ask yourself, "What is the purpose of this document?" you will set the stage for the tone of the document. After all, there is no point in using persuasive language when your sole mission is to notify a client that a will is ready to be executed. Conversely, you do not want to adopt a neutral and purely informative style if a client's last chance to succeed is your appellate brief. By reminding yourself of the purpose of your writing, you will be able to shape the appropriate tone and style of the project.

2. *Audience*

In addition to considering the purpose of a document, focus on the intended reader. Who will be reading the project — a client, a supervising attorney, adverse counsel, or a judge?

If the writing is prepared for a client, try to obtain a thumbnail sketch of the individual. Some clients may be novices in the legal world and even a term such as "interrogatory," which is commonplace to you, may be puzzling to a newcomer to litigation. Conversely, a client may be a sophisticated real estate broker and a complex discussion of prepayment penalty clauses in promissory notes may be easily understood. In general, use a straightforward style for laypersons. Clients will not be impressed by your command of Latin phrases but will be frustrated by their use. Clients expect to be informed, not mystified, by legal writing. Immediately following the reaction of frustration is one of anger: anger that they had to pay you once to write the letter and then a second time to have you explain the letter. The goal of your writing is to communicate, not impress.

The highly respected and renowned financier Warren E. Buffett explains that when writing Berkshire Hathaway's annual report, he pretends he's talking to his sisters. Though highly intelligent, they are not accounting or financial experts. Mr. Buffett believes that he will be successful if they understand his writing. Similarly, United States Supreme Court Justice Stephen Breyer says that he tries to write his legal opinions so that they are understandable to high school students.

One of the most difficult tasks can be writing for a supervisor. Often the supervisor has not really thought through the way the project should be structured and as a result your approach will not meet the supervisor's expectations. Sometimes the supervisor may have access to certain facts and information you do not have, and your writing may be criticized for being incomplete. You may find that you need to adopt one writing style for one supervisor and an entirely different style for another. As you get to know the people you work with, you will be able to understand their writing techniques and be better able to meet their expectations. Obtain samples of documents written by your supervisors or colleagues so you can get an idea of their styles and approaches. One of the most frustrating tasks is writing for individuals who are so committed to their style of writing that they are never satisfied with anyone else's approach. They will endlessly revise a document, making insignificant small-scale revisions, such as changing all the "glads" to "happys." If you find you can never make such an individual satisfied with your work, try a direct approach and ask outright what the individual likes and dislikes in a writing.

If the letter is to adverse counsel, adopt a neutral and objective style. Avoid language that is confrontational or condescending. Although letters to other legal professionals may include certain terms of art ("The Lanham Act," "The ADA," "ex parte") that need no further explanation, avoid a tone that implies you are giving a lesson on the law. Not only are combative or condescending letters generally unproductive, you never

know when they may be made part of a record in a court proceeding. You do not want a letter written in anger to come back to haunt you.

Writing for judges presupposes a level of expertise, and you need not give definitions or long-winded explanations for commonly known terms or phrases. Nevertheless, keep in mind that most judges rely heavily on law clerks to read briefs and then give an initial opinion to the judge. Thus, you need to make a strong and forceful argument because the judge may only scan the brief and rely on a law clerk's review. Moreover, judges are usually overwhelmed with heavy case loads and will not appreciate an overly long document that resorts to jargon and legalese. They will be much happier if you make the points you need to make as forcefully, persuasively, and briefly as possible, and then move on. As an inducement to legal writers to adopt more concise writing styles, more and more courts, including all of the federal courts of appeal and the United States Supreme Court, are establishing page or word limits for documents submitted. Thus, you must be concise.

By asking yourself, "Who is my reader?" you will automatically tailor the document so it is understood by the reader. The critical question is not whether *you* love your project but whether the reader will immediately be informed or persuaded, that is, whether your writing achieves its purpose.

D. Precision

The most important characteristic of legal writing is precision. Clients will rely on the information and opinions given to them by legal professionals. Judges, administrators, and others will assume the information provided to them is correct. Therefore, being right is fundamental to effective legal writing. No judge will render a decision in a client's favor by saying, "The legal conclusions you have reached are faulty and incorrect, but the brief is so well-written that I will rule in your favor."

Be accurate with regard not only to the "big" issues, such as legal conclusions and arguments, but also as to the "small" elements of a writing, such as names, dates, and dollar amounts. An error in the client's name or address may attract more attention than anything else in the project. Just as spelling errors cast doubt on your ability, so do accuracy errors have a disproportionately negative effect on the reader. The legal profession has become more adversarial in recent years, and even clients (sometimes, especially clients) are quick to point out an error. Similarly, many of your writings are sent to an adverse party who will be more than happy to call attention to a mistake you have made. Thus, because your audience is highly critical, you must be as accurate and precise as possible.

One cause of imprecise writing is an overreliance on forms. Drafting a contract requires more than merely locating another contract in your office and then changing the names and addresses. If this is your approach to drafting, you will no doubt find yourself explaining to a client engaged in accounting services why his or her agreement refers to

restaurants and bars. Using forms as a starting point or guide is perfectly acceptable. Just avoid relying exclusively on forms. When you have used a form originally drafted for another client, proofread carefully to ensure the language is appropriate for this new client's needs. Use the "find and replace" feature in word processing programs to ensure the consistent use of terms.

1. *Word Choice*

The selection of an improper word or the use of vague words causes imprecision in your writing. Similarly, the use of qualifying language or words can cause unintended meanings. For example, no employee would be comforted by reading, "Your department is not in any immediate danger of being downsized." The use of the qualifier "immediate" implies that a danger exists; it simply is not immediate. Select the most descriptive and specific word possible. Descriptive words lend strength and vitality to your writing. Moreover, the selection of an incorrect word can be fatal in legal writing. A document that states, "The Buyer may deposit the purchase price into the escrow account prior to May 15," means something entirely different from one that states, "The Buyer must deposit the purchase price into the escrow account prior to May 15." The second statement clearly imposes an obligation on the buyer whereas the first statement does not.

The use of "will" or "may" for "shall" causes ambiguity and inaccuracy. One writing professor has estimated that more than 1,000 published cases debate the meaning of "shall." Use "may" for optional action, "will" for future action ("I will appear in court on Thursday"), and "shall" or "must" for obligatory action. Some plain English guidelines recommend the use of "must" rather than "shall" on the basis that "shall" is an obsolete word.

Following is a list of words that are commonly misused in legal writing. Just as you use a dictionary to avoid spelling errors, use a dictionary or thesaurus to help you select the precise word you need.

affect/effect

Affect means "to influence" as in "I was greatly affected by the victim's story."

Effect means "to cause or bring about" (as a verb) or "result" (as a noun) as in "He effected a resolution of the case" or "One of the effects of the judgment was impairment of his credit rating."

If you have difficulty remembering the difference between these words, do not use either of them. Use their synonyms (influence, or produce, or result).

among/between

Among is used to refer to *more than two objects or persons*, as in "The agreement was entered into among Smith, Jones, and Andersen."

Between is used to refer to *two objects or persons*, as in "The settlement was negotiated between Peterson and Powell."

and/or

Many experts criticize the use of *and/or*, which can be confusing and ambiguous. Avoid using *and/or*. Use either "and" or "or."

Unclear You must provide a reference and/or a resume.

Preferred You must provide a reference, a resume, or both.

apprise/appraise

Apprise means "to notify or inform," as in "I will continue to apprise you of further developments in this case."

Appraise means to "estimate value," as in "He appraised the value of the property at $100,000."

argue/rule

Courts do not argue cases; lawyers do. Do not write *the court argued* . . . . Similarly, courts do not *contend, believe,* or *feel.* Courts *rule, decide, hold, state, conclude,* and so forth.

beside/besides

Beside means "at the side of," as in "Please sit beside me." *Besides* means "in addition to," as in "Besides leaving Angela his property, Grandfather gave her his jewelry."

compose/comprise

Compose means "to make up," as in "The contract is composed of three sections." *Comprise* means "to include or contain or consist of," as in "Tina's collection comprises rare porcelains." Do not use "of" after *comprise*. Thus, it is as incorrect to write "The brief is comprised of four sections" as it is to write "The brief is included of four sections."

disinterested/uninterested

Disinterested means "neutral" and "impartial," as in "Judges must be disinterested in the proceedings they decide."

Uninterested means "not interested or bored," as in "The jurors appeared uninterested in the masses of statistical evidence presented."

ensure/insure

Ensure means "to make definite," as in "We must ensure the tenant pays all rent due." *Insure* means "to protect against loss," as in "We must insure our valuables for at least $10,000."

fact/contention

A *fact* is something that has occurred or can be verified. Writers often characterize something as a fact when it is merely an allegation or contention. Use the word "fact" only when you are describing an event or something proven. For example, it is a fact that a defendant has blue eyes. It is not a fact that the defendant murdered a victim until the jury or court says so.

fewer/less

Fewer refers to objects or people that can be counted, as in "There are fewer exhibits than I anticipated." *Less* refers to general amounts and things that cannot be counted, as in "I had less time to argue than the defendant did."

guilty/liable

The word *guilty* refers to criminal wrongdoing. *Liable* refers to responsibility for a civil wrong. Thus, it is correct to write that "defendant Smith is guilty of robbery although defendant Jones is liable for damages in the amount of $50,000 for breach of contract."

liable/libel

Liable means responsible for some civil wrong, as in "She is liable for all the harm proximately caused by her negligence."

Libel is a form of defamation, as in "The magazine libeled our client by stating he was a crook."

judgment/judgement

In legal writing and in most American writings, spell as *judgment*. In Great Britain, the word is spelled *judgement*.

memoranda/memorandum

Memoranda refers to several documents (plural) whereas a *memorandum* is a single document.

oral/verbal

Oral means something spoken, as in "The plaintiff's oral testimony at trial confirmed her earlier deposition testimony."

Verbal means a communication in words and could refer to a written or a spoken communication. Thus, the statement *We had a verbal agreement* is confusing because it could refer either to a written or nonwritten agreement. To avoid confusion, use *oral* or *written* and avoid the use of *verbal*.

ordinance/ordnance

An *ordinance* is an act or resolution enacted by a local jurisdiction, as in "Buffalo recently enacted an ordinance prohibiting smoking in public places."

Ordnance is military weaponry, as in "The troops came under heavy ordnance fire."

overrule/reverse

A court *overrules* prior decisions in its jurisdiction. Thus, "The 1954 case *Brown v. Board of Education* overruled the 1896 case *Plessy v. Ferguson*." A court *reverses* the very case before it on appeal as in "The defendant appealed the decision rendered against him; the court agreed with the defendant's reasoning and reversed the lower court's holding."

prescribe/proscribe

Prescribe means to order, as in "The physician prescribed complete bedrest for the patient."

Proscribe means to prohibit or forbid, as in "Massachusetts laws proscribe littering."

principal/principle

Principal is the supervisor at a school or a dominant item, as in "The principal objective to be gained is the prisoner's freedom." Another meaning of "principal" is a sum of money on which interest is paid, as in "The promissory note required repayment of the principal amount of the debt as well as interest."

Principle is a fundamental rule, as in "The principles of physics are complex." Remember to match up the "le" in the word "rule" with the "le" ending of "principle."

respectfully/respectively

Respectfully means "with respect" and is a commonly used closing in a document, as in "Respectfully submitted, Andrew Kenney."

Respectively means in a certain order, as in "The attorneys took their respective positions in the courtroom and the trial commenced."

since/because

Avoid using *since* as a substitute for *because;* otherwise, ambiguity results, as in the sentence *Since the tariffs were lifted, trade has increased*. It is not clear in this sentence whether *since* means after a period of time or whether it means *because*. To avoid confusion, use *since* to refer to the passage of time, as in "It has been four weeks since we filed the appeal," and use *because* to show causation, as in "Because the jury was improperly charged, the judgment was reversed."

2. *Vague Words*

To lend forcefulness to your writing, use concrete and descriptive words. Avoid vague words such as "matter," "development," "circumstances," "system," "situation," "problem," and "process," which provide little, if any, information to the reader. Thus, a sentence beginning "Regarding this matter . . ." offers no guidance to the reader as to what "this matter" might be. A much better approach is to write, "Regarding your lease . . . ."

Similarly, avoid using words such as "above" or "herein." For example, if in an agreement you state on page 18, "As described above . . ." the reader does not know where in the previous 17 pages you discussed the issue. Be specific. State, "as described in paragraph 4(b) . . . ."

The words "it" and "this" are often used in an indefinite and confusing manner. Consider the following: "The court ruled the defendant should be granted probation. This enables the defendant to participate in a work release program." The word "this" could refer either to the court's ruling or the defendant's probation. When using "it" or "this," you should, if necessary, repeat the word that "it" or "this" refers to. Thus, the prior statement would read, "The court ruled the defendant should be granted probation. Probation will enable the defendant to participate in a work release program."

Similarly, avoid "made-up" words. Although you may have heard of, used, and even written "dialogued," "Borked," "liaising," "mentee," or "impactful," these "words" are not generally found in most dictionaries because they are not yet recognized words in English. Our conversation and writing are often influenced by business and technology terms. Thus, a number of terms, such as "cutting edge," "synergy," and "empower," are overused. Do not write, "We need to *interface* to resolve the litigation" when you mean "meet." Do not use "impact" as a verb, as in "His actions will *impact* our ability to obtain a loan." Use "influence" or "affect" instead. Although English is an evolving language, do not use a word before it has evolved into an entry in a dictionary.

3. *Word Connotation*

Many words have more than one meaning. When you select a word, consider its connotation, or suggested meaning. There is a great difference, for example, in referring to an item as "cheap" rather than "affordable." The word "cheap" connotes shoddy or low quality whereas "affordable" conveys either a neutral or desirable meaning. Consider the effect of telling someone he or she is "stubborn" rather than "determined," or "blunt" rather than "candid." Certain words carry hostile undertones and will immediately make the reader defensive or angry.

Use care when selecting words to ensure they have the connotations you intend. If correspondence to an adverse party suggests there is a "discrepancy" in damage figures, rather than simply asking for a

clarification of the figures, you can be sure of an immediate, and probably angry, response.

E. Clarity

The second feature of effective legal writing is clarity — that is, ensuring that your project is easily understood by the reader. Your writing style should be invisible. It is bad writing that is noticeable. Because legal writings are read not for pleasure but for function, readers expect you to make your point clearly and quickly. The three primary legal writing flaws that obscure clarity are elegant variation, the overuse of negatives, and improper word order.

1. *Elegant Variation*

The term "elegant variation" refers to the practice of substituting one term for another in a document to avoid repetition of a term. Writers are often reluctant to repeat a term, in the belief that repetition of a term is boring or unsophisticated. Unfortunately, selecting alternate terms in legal writing creates the impression that something entirely different is intended. Consider the following sentence: "Four of the defendant's witnesses were women, whereas all of the plaintiff's witnesses were ladies." In an attempt not to repeat the word "women," the writer conveys something entirely different about the defendant's group of witnesses.

Elegant variation is deadly in legal writing. For example, if you are drafting a document that continually refers to an individual as a "landlord" and then suddenly you refer to this individual as the "lessor," the reader may believe that the "lessor" is not the same individual as the "landlord." You should therefore be cautious about varying words and terms you have used. Although you may believe that selecting alternative terms shows your extensive vocabulary and lends interest to the document, you unwittingly may be creating the impression that there is a reason that different terms have been selected and that there is a legal distinction to be drawn based upon this variation. Use the "find and replace" feature of your word processing program to ensure terms are used consistently.

2. *Negatives*

The overuse of negatives can be confusing to a reader. Although statutes are often set forth in negative fashion by describing what is prohibited, using more than two negative words in a sentence usually forces the reader to stop and think through what you have said. The phrase "not unlikely" should be converted to "likely" or "probable." Anytime the reader is

interrupted from reading the project, your message is weakened. As a writer, your task is to ensure that a reader proceeds smoothly through the document without needing to puzzle over phrases. For example, the statement "No individual shall be prohibited from refusing to submit to a breathalyzer examination" is confusing. It requires a reader to consider three negative words: "no," "prohibited," and "refusing."

In drafting legal writing projects, keep in mind that there are many more negative words than the obvious ones: "no," "none," or "never." Many words function in a negative fashion, such as "refuse," "preclude," "deny," "except," and the like. Although it is impossible to purge your writing of all negative terms, you should carefully scrutinize your writing to ensure that you have not used too many negative words that obscure your meaning.

The other disadvantage of using negative words is that they are not as forceful as affirmative expressions. For example, it is more effective and shorter to write, "The plaintiff was late for her deposition" than to write, "The plaintiff failed to timely appear for her deposition." To give strength and vitality to your writing, use affirmative and positive terms.

3. *Word Order*

The most common sentence structure in the English language is the placement of the subject first, the verb second, and the object third. Thus, the sentence "The defendant attacked the victim" is phrased in this standard order. Although the thought can certainly be expressed in another way, such as "The victim was attacked by the defendant," readers typically anticipate that sentences will follow the expected pattern of subject, verb, and object. Although you may not want to structure every single sentence in a project in the same fashion, excessive variation from the expected sentence structure will cause confusion and lack of clarity. Just as you should avoid exotic spellings of words because they draw attention to your writing rather than to your message, avoid exotic sentence structure. For example, an article written in a national newspaper began, "The Navy Thursday asked the Pentagon's inspector general to investigate . . . ." Similarly, the famous quote "Backward ran the sentences until reeled the mind" by writer Wolcott Gibbs about the style of *Time* magazine is often cited as a rebuke to *Time*'s often poorly ordered sentences. These oddly structured sentences catch the reader's attention in a distracting way.

Vary from the anticipated sentence structure of subject, verb, object only when you want to draw attention to a thought. Thus, if you have a point you want to emphasize, vary the way it is structured. Keep this technique in mind if you need to "bury" a weak portion of an argument: Phrase it in the manner commonly anticipated because this will draw the least amount of attention to it.

One of the other benefits of using "normal" sentence structure is that you will automatically phrase your thoughts in the active voice.

When you vary from the anticipated order of sentences, the result is often conversion to the passive voice, which creates a weakened point. (See Section F.1.)

Ethics Alert

The Risk of Poor Writing

Courts are becoming more and more impatient with poorly written briefs. In one recent case, the court noted that it could not determine the substance of the defendant's legal argument and therefore denied the defendant's motion for being "incomprehensible." *In re King,* **No. 05-56485-C, 2006 WL 581256 (Bankr. W.D. Tex. Feb. 21, 2006). Thus, poor writing can result in an adverse ruling for a client.**

F. Readability

Because the subject matter discussed in most legal writing is complex, and often rather dry, you need to make your product as readable as possible. Clients will be unfamiliar with legal topics. Judges and other legal professionals will be too busy to struggle through a complex and pompous document. Remember that the more complicated a topic is, the more important is the need for readability. To enhance readability:

1. Prefer the Active Voice

The active voice focuses attention on the subject or actor of the sentence, who performs or causes certain action. The active voice is consistent with standard sentence structure of subject, verb, and object.

The passive voice focuses attention on the object of action by placing it first and relegating the subject (actor) of the sentence to an inferior position.

Active Voice	*Passive Voice*
The corporation held its meeting.	A meeting was held by the corporation.
The defendant's attorney argued for acquittal.	An argument for acquittal was made by the defendant's attorney.
The doctor testified that the patient consented to the operation.	Testimony was given by the doctor that the patient consented to the operation.

The active voice is stronger and more forceful than the passive voice. Readers do not have to search through the sentence looking for the actor or subject. Another advantage of using the active voice is that it usually produces shorter sentences.

There are situations, however, in which the passive voice may be preferable. For example, assume your law office represents a defendant accused of fraud. Instead of stating, "The defendant deposited checks in his bank account," you could write, "Checks were deposited in the defendant's bank account." This use of the passive voice shifts the focus away from the defendant. The reader is informed of what occurred but not who did it. Consider using the passive voice in the discussion of weaker parts of your argument to deflect attention from them. Conversely, be sure to structure the strongest parts of your writing in the active voice because it lends strength and vitality to your writing. A classic example of passive voice is seen in the recent statement of a politician accused of wrongdoing who stated, "Mistakes were made" rather than "I made mistakes." You may also wish to use passive voice when you want to focus on the object of the action or when identifying the actor is not necessary to the meaning of your sentence. In any event, if you decide to use the passive voice, make sure your decision is a conscious one.

Practice Tip

Avoiding the Passive Voice

In many sentences, the person or the thing doing the action is introduced by the words *by the* as in *The policy was announced by the committee*. This is a tip that you have shifted into the passive voice. Use your word processor's find and replace feature to locate your "by the" phrases to determine whether you are overusing passive voice. Similarly, most word processors have a feature that will flag the use of passive voice. This feature is a useful guide but can be distracting.

---

2. Use Lists

Another way to enhance readability is to use lists when discussing complex matters. Lists not only enable readers to comprehend information quickly but also create visual impact and interest because they are usually numbered or bulleted and set apart from the rest of the text. When setting forth items such as the elements of a cause of action or the components of a definition, use a list.

Lists (sometimes called *tabulation*) can be structured in several ways, but to increase interest:

- Set the list off from the rest of your narrative by spaces above and below your list;

- Indent your list;
- Identify the items in your list with numbers, letters, or "bullets" (•); and
- Punctuate correctly by putting a semicolon after each item (except the last item) and include "or" or "and" before the last item.

Not all lists need to be indented. If the list is short, you may separate each item from the other by a comma and include the list as part of your narrative text.

The grammatical structure of all of the items in any list must be identical or parallel. Thus, if the first word in a list is a verb, all of the following items must also be verbs. Similarly, if the first word in the first item ends in "ing," all subsequent items must also begin with words ending in "ing."

Incorrect

The elements of a cause of action for breach of contract are as follows:

- an agreement
- a breach of that agreement by one party
- the act of the breaching party must have caused damage.

Correct

The elements of a cause of action for breach of contract are as follows:

- an agreement;
- a breach of that agreement by one party; and
- damage caused by the act of the breaching party.

Lack of parallel structure is often seen in resumes in which job applicants will describe their experience as follows: "Drafted documents. Prepared pleadings. Assisting in trial preparation." The last item should be "assist*ed*" to retain parallel structure.

Similarly, lack of parallel structure can be seen within a sentence; for example, "It is more important to write the brief than arguing it." Revise as follows: "It is more important to write the brief than to argue it."

3. *Avoid Nominalizations*

A nominalization occurs when you take an adjective, verb, or adverb and turn it into a noun. Although the nominalization itself is technically correct, overuse of nominalizations drains your writing of forcefulness and makes it read as if written by a bureaucrat.

	Nominalizations
The defendant argued.	The defendant made the argument.
The witness concluded.	The witness drew a conclusion.
The contract was enforced.	Enforcement of the contract was accomplished.
We considered our options.	Consideration was given to our options.
We applied for an extension.	An application for an extension was made.

As you can see, nominalizations not only take strong action words such as verbs and convert them into dull nouns, they also tend to make your writing overlong.

Avoid overusing nominalizations by proofreading carefully. Generally, if you use active voice, you will greatly reduce nominalizations. Although not all nominalizations can be avoided, their repeated use will render your writing unimaginative. To avoid nominalizations, watch for words that end in _-ion_, _-ent_, and _-ant_.

4. Avoid Legal Jargon

The use of "legalese" frustrates readers and results in stodgy writing. Legalese or jargon includes not only archaic and stuffy words and phrases such as "accord," "aforesaid," "opine," and "hereinafter referred to," but words and phrases that are unfamiliar to a reader, such as Latin phrases or legal terms (res judicata, mens rea, collateral estoppel). For some years the Texas State Bar held an annual contest called "legaldegook" to draw attention to atrocious legal writing. One "Wooliness Award" was presented for the following:

> For purposes of paragraph (3), an organization described in paragraph (2) shall be deemed to include an organization described in Section 501(c)(4), (5) or (6) which would be described in Paragraph (2) if it were an organization described in Section 501(c)(3).

Try to avoid using legal jargon. Often archaic or jargon-filled phrases can either be omitted entirely or replaced with more familiar terms. For example, an agreement may begin as follows:

> THIS AGREEMENT is made and entered into this fourth day of May 2011, by and between ABC, Inc. (hereinafter referred to as "Landlord") and Susan Andrews (hereinafter referred to as "Tenant") with reference to the premises and covenants hereinafter set forth.

You may easily change the sentence as follows:

> THIS AGREEMENT is entered into May 4, 2011, between ABC, Inc. ("Landlord") and Susan Andrews ("Tenant") regarding the following facts.

The omission or replacement of archaic words and phrases with familiar ones not only enhances readability but also results in a more concise writing.

You may not be able to omit all of the legalese you would like, particularly when drafting wills, deeds, contracts, litigation pleadings, and other legal documents that have more rigid structures. These documents are often drafted in accordance with standard forms and conventions of many years ago, and people are reluctant to change such commonly used forms. In any case, simply try to eliminate as much of the jargon as possible. For example, the phrases "enclosed please find" or "enclosed herewith is" are often used in letters enclosing other documents. Although there is nothing grammatically wrong with these expressions, they are examples of legalese. If something is enclosed, won't the reader find it? Simply use the phrase "enclosed is" followed by a description of the item enclosed.

If you are using legal terms or Latin phrases, be sure to give a brief definition for your reader. The Texas State Bar recognized the following statement by a judge as particularly horrible: "Parens patriae cannot be ad fundandam jurisdictionem. The zoning question is res inter alios acta." Similarly, a client may be completely bewildered by a letter informing him or her that "the doctrine of laches precludes your claim." Rewrite as follows:

> The doctrine of laches (an unreasonable and prejudicial delay in bringing an action) precludes your claim.

Although the insertion of a definition or explanatory phrase produces a longer document, the effect of enhanced readability is well worth the extra words.

Even if a document is prepared for another legal professional who will be familiar with the Latin phrase or legal term, add the definition because it often serves as a smooth transition for any reader. Readers experienced with the terms will not be offended by your inclusion of a definition and will readily be able to skip over it. Other less experienced readers, such as a law clerk or a client receiving a copy of the writing, will be greatly assisted by the "translation" you provide.

5. *Keep Subjects and Verbs in Proximity*

Because the two most critical parts of a sentence are the subject and the verb, readers typically look for these first to make sense of a sentence. Legal writing is known for creating huge gaps between the subject of a sentence and the verb. When too many words intervene between the

subject and the verb, readers no longer remember what the sentence is about by the time they locate the verb. They are then forced to reread the sentence and hunt for the subject.

Although you need not immediately follow every subject in every sentence with a verb, avoid large gaps between these two parts of a sentence. Statutes are especially notorious for separating subjects and verbs by long word strings.

Example

Any *person*, including an organization, institution, or other entity, that presents or causes to be presented to an officer, employee, or agent of this office, or any department thereof, or any state agency, a claim, as defined in subsection 2(g) of this paragraph, that the person knows or has reason to know was not provided as claimed, *is guilty* of a class 1 misdemeanor.

In this sentence, there is a gap of 55 words between the subject (person) and the verb (is guilty). To eliminate these huge gaps, rewrite the sentence, moving the verb closer to the subject.

Better Example

Any *person*, including an organization, institution, or other entity, *is guilty* of a Class 1 misdemeanor by presenting or causing to be presented to an officer, employee, or agent of this office, or any department thereof, or any state agency, a claim, as defined in Section 2(g) of this paragraph, that the person knows or has reason to know was not provided as claimed.

Alternatively, you can make the words intervening between the subject and verb into their own sentence.

Example

The *partnership*, an entity organized and existing under Missouri law and formed after the passage of the Missouri General Partnership Act, *is composed of* Smith, Jones, and Kimball.

Better Example

The *partnership is composed of* Smith, Jones, and Kimball. It is an entity organized and existing under Missouri law and was formed after the passage of the Missouri General Partnership Act.

6. *Use Forceful Words*

Because legal writing is formal, writers often tend to adopt an emotionless, pallid tone in their writing. Although your writing should not read

like a romance novel, the use of vivid and forceful words will not only keep your readers interested but also will aid in converting them to your viewpoint.

Emphasis cannot be obtained by merely underlining or italicizing words or phrases or by adding a modifier such as "very" or "hardly." You need to select a word vivid enough to carry the meaning you desire. Use a thesaurus or dictionary to help you select words that are vivid and forceful.

Weak	*Forceful*
The defendant *stated* he knew where the witness was *located*.	The defendant *boasted* he knew where the witness was *secreted*.
Smith *misrepresented* the condition of the premises.	Smith *lied* about the condition of the premises.
very sad	sorrowful
not allowed	forbidden, prohibited
disagree with	contradict
raining hard	pouring
acknowledge guilt	confess
could not believe	incredulous
withdraw a statement	recant

Conversely, do not take a concrete word, which is strong in and of itself, and dilute it, such as converting "improbable" to "somewhat unlikely" or "rapid" to "pretty fast." In fact, some words stand on their own and are not susceptible to degree such as "unique," which means the only one of its kind. Something cannot be "quite unique" or "very unique."

7. *Repeat Strong Words and Phrases*

Although you want to avoid redundancy in legal writing, there are certain situations in which repetition can add emphasis to your writing. The repetition of a keyword or phrase creates interest and adds drama to writing.

Example
The defendant misled the plaintiff. He misled her by promising the premises were quiet. He misled her by promising the premises were habitable. He misled her by promising the premises were safe.

Each repetition of the words "misled" and "promise" builds on the previous reference. When you use this technique, be sure to structure the sentence so you end with the strongest element.

Example
>   She was a diligent worker. She was a loyal friend. She was a loving
>   mother.

8. *Vary the Length of Sentences*

Short sentences are easier to comprehend than long, complex sentences.
Nevertheless, you do not want a project filled with sentences of approximately the same length. Such a writing would be tedious to read.

Just as you may need to vary the pattern of your sentences from the
standard sentence order (subject-verb-object) to add interest, vary the
length of your sentences to enhance readability. For example, a short
sentence such as "She refused" is concise and powerful. Generally,
sentences that exceed three lines are too long for most readers.

Nevertheless, you do not want a writing filled only with short
sentences. Such a project would have a choppy and abrupt tone and would
read like a telegram. For example, note the clipped tone of the following
sentences.

>   The landlord sent her the rent statement. She refused to pay. He
>   sued to evict her. She countersued. He asked for a jury. The jury
>   ruled in her favor.

The following version has a much smoother and more readable
quality:

>   The landlord sent her the rent statement. She refused to pay and he
>   sued to evict her. She countersued. Although the landlord asked for
>   a jury, the jury ruled in her favor.

Practice Tip

Readability Tests

Several readability formulas can be used to determine the
readability of a project. One of the best-known tests is the Flesch
Reading Ease Formula, which determines readability by using a
calculation based on the average sentence length and average
number of syllables in a word. More information and the Flesch
formula to determine readability can be found at
http://juicystudio.com/services/readability.php. Note that many
readability tests rely on surface or technical characteristics and
cannot test coherence; average sentence length and average
syllables per word cannot completely predict readability of a text.

G. Brevity

The length of a project does not necessarily translate into quality. Some of the most compelling and well-known writings are the briefest. For example, the Lord's Prayer has only 66 words. The Gettysburg Address has 286 words. Yet just one federal statute relating to hospital and medical expenses paid under Medicare has more than 700 words. One of the most dramatic yet brief statements about a person is that written about Machiavelli: "There are not enough words to say his eulogy."

Although almost all writers agree in principle that brevity is an admirable goal in legal writing, brevity is not easily accomplished. One of the reasons brevity is difficult to achieve is that the legal research that is the basis for your project represents time and effort. After going to the library, researching, writing, rewriting, Shepardizing or KeyCiting, revising, proofreading, and editing, writers are loath to abandon the words that evidence their hard work. Like pets and children, we quickly find fault with those belonging to others and defend and love our own. For example, one of the entries in the Texas State Bar "legaldegook" contest was a sentence written by a lawyer that began "Accordingly, in the interest of brevity," and continued for more than 60 words.

Another contributing factor to the length of legal documents is that the topics discussed are often complex, requiring thoughtful analysis. Finally, over-review of a writing causes increased length. Each paralegal or attorney who works on a project will feel a need to improve a writing, generally by adding to it, changing "now" to "at the present time" or "if" to "in the event that." Thus, being concise is difficult.

Although judges complain about lawyers' inability to write succinct briefs, some writing experts suggest that judges themselves contribute to the mass of legal publication by writing longer opinions with more footnotes. One solution proposed by one writing scholar is that judges impose page limits on themselves similar to those imposed on attorneys.

You must be merciless. Your reader's time is at a premium and you cannot afford to frustrate the reader by redundancy and long-winded phrases. Moreover, if the reader continually encounters a rehash of previous material and never encounters new material, he or she may simply abandon the project and never read some of your later, more persuasive arguments. Finally, more and more courts are imposing page limits and word count limits for submissions. Documents that exceed the stated requirements are rejected. Thus, failure to be brief may be legal malpractice.

To achieve brevity:

1. Omit Needless Words

There are numerous phrases in English that we use simply by habit. Many of these can be eliminated or reduced to a more concise word or phrase.

Long-Winded Phrases	_Substitutions_
Due to the fact that	Because
As a result of	Consequently, therefore
In addition to	Additionally
Despite the fact that	Although
At the present time	At present, now, currently
During the time that	While
At such time as	When
With regard to	Regarding, concerning
In the event that	If
As to whether	Whether
In order to	To

Careful writing and revising will help you eliminate extra words. Ask yourself if you absolutely need a phrase and whether there is an effective substitute for it. Many commonly used phrases can be replaced by single words with no loss of meaning. In particular, avoid constructions that include more than one preposition, such as "in regard to." Use "regarding."

2. Avoid "Throat-Clearing" Introductions

"Throat-clearing" refers to introductions that are mere preludes for the main topic that is to follow. Writers often feel compelled to warm up the audience by preparing them for the main idea rather than simply presenting the idea.

Throat-Clearing Phrases	_Substitutions_
In this regard it is important to remember that . . .	Remember
The next issue to be considered is . . .	[none — state the issue]
Attention should also be called to the fact that . . .	[none — state the fact]
It is interesting to note that . . .	Note

Other overused introductory words are "clearly" and "obviously." Writers often add "clearly" before introducing a topic, believing that this word will lend persuasive force. To paraphrase a famous jurist, adding the word "clearly" to a sentence won't make it clear; and if the sentence is clear, you don't need the word "clearly."

The word "obviously" should be avoided for the same reason as "clearly." Moreover, "obviously" carries a hostile meaning. By introducing a sentence or topic with the word "obviously" you signal to readers that you believe they lack the capacity to discern the meaning of the sentence on their own. When you introduce a thought with "obviously" what you really are saying is "even to an idiot such as you it should be obvious . . . ."

3. *Avoid Redundancy*

Those in the legal profession are wedded to redundancy. They cannot resist writing "null and void and of no legal effect." Is all this needed? If something is null, isn't it void? If it is void, can it have legal effect?

The reason legal writing is so prone to redundancy lies in the history of our language. English has its roots in Latin and French as well as in the languages of the Celts and Anglo-Saxons. Often word pairings were used to ensure that readers would understand phrases no matter what their background or station in life. Thus, the French word "peace" joined with the Latin word "quiet." The French "devise" joined the English "bequeath." These redundant doublings have persisted long after their need. Their use today is often the result of pure habit rather than necessity.

If you find yourself using these "stock" redundancies, stop and ask whether one word is sufficient.

> *Common Redundancies*
>> acknowledge and agree
>> alter or change or modify
>> basic fundamentals
>> cease and desist
>> close proximity
>> consented and agreed
>> covenant, warrant, and represent
>> current status
>> due and owing
>> each and every
>> final conclusion
>> force or effect
>> free and clear
>> full and complete
>> give, devise, and bequeath
>> made and entered into
>> null and void and of no legal effect
>> past history
>> previous experience
>> refuse and fail
>> release, remise, and discharge
>> true and correct
>> unless and until
>> vitally necessary

4. *Avoid Repetition*

Once you have stated your contention or communicated the information you need to communicate, stop. Many beginning legal writers believe they should make every point three times by

- telling the reader what the writing or project will say;
- saying it; and
- reminding the reader of what was said.

There is no place in legal writing for such needless repetition. If you write to clients, they will be sufficiently interested in your communication to grasp what you are telling them. Supervisors, adverse counsel, and judges are sophisticated enough or busy enough that they do not need an argument repeated three times. When court rules dictate the maximum number of pages in briefs submitted to that court you will not have the luxury of being able to repeat your argument. The only exception to the rule of avoiding repetition is that in a long document, readers often appreciate a separate conclusion, which briefly and concisely summarizes your analysis.

H. Order

1. *Outlines*

Just as you would never begin a car trip to a far-off destination without a road map, you should never begin a writing without some idea as to how you intend to approach the project. A project that is poorly organized not only fails to inform or persuade the reader but also may so frustrate the reader that it will not be read.

The best system for organizing a writing is to use an outline. Many writers doubt the benefits of outlining and have resisted using an outline since elementary school. Although the most complete outline includes full sentences or topics divided into headings and subheadings, an outline need not be so formal. The looseleaf notebook containing the notes you took while researching, or the index cards containing notes of your research results, are working outlines. By shuffling the index cards or the pages in your notebook, you are outlining, that is, organizing your approach to your writing.

Similarly, your outline can consist of your thoughts on the project scribbled on scratch paper. It is not the format of the outline that is important; rather it is that the mere existence of any type of outline forces you to consider and organize the structure of your writing. The outline should disclose the basic sections of your project and the order in which they will be addressed.

If the notes taken during research are not helpful in preparing an outline, simply jot down on paper all of the words and phrases you can think of that relate to your project. Keep writing and listing the entries; do not worry about organizing these entries. This outlining technique is usually called *brainstorming*. After you have finished listing every topic you can think of, carefully examine the list, and then group related items together. After you have settled on these rough groupings, decide the order in which the groups should be discussed.

Another method of outlining is called "clustering." Place a circle or "nucleus" in the middle of a blank page of paper. Place the keyword or topic of your project in the nucleus. Now write a related topic or issue nearby. Encircle it and draw a line back to your nucleus. Continue by either branching out from the nucleus or the new circle. Trust your instincts to select new words and topics. You may discover a writing approach by considering the connections between words in your cluster. The final product should look like a spider web. Write your project with your web nearby.

When your outline or "cluster" is completed, regardless whether it is a working outline, a formal outline, or your list of topics, you should be able to determine immediately whether you have included all of the items that need to be addressed and whether you are devoting too much time and effort to minor points at the expense of major points.

Another popular outlining technique is storytelling. Talk to a friend or colleague about your project. Start at the beginning by saying, "I have been asked to . . . ." As you tell the story of your project, some organizational patterns may emerge. Allow yourself to ramble a bit. Keep a notepad nearby, and write down ideas as you are speaking. Your notes are then a preliminary outline.

Finally, allow some "down time" before you begin writing so that ideas percolate and bubble up to the surface. Nearly all writers have experienced an "aha" moment while showering or driving that gives them a great idea for a project. Keep your notepad handy so you can capture these ideas.

Some writers prefer to devote substantial effort to outlining. The actual writing stage is then that much easier. In many instances the writer is simply expanding upon the ideas already set forth in the outline, adding citations, and polishing.

2. *Internal Organization*

The way you organize the project can affect the reader's perception of the project. There are four tips to follow in organizing your writing so it achieves your desired objectives.

a. Use Headings

In longer writings, use headings and subheadings to alert the reader to the subject being discussed. It is nearly impossible for a reader to comprehend page after page of narrative containing no breaks or divisions. Similarly, it is very frustrating for readers to suddenly find themselves in the midst of a discussion of contracts when the preceding paragraph related to fraud.

Headings serve as signals to readers to alert them to the topics you are discussing and to show a change in topics. If, for example, your brief states there are four prerequisites to the awarding of an injunction, it will be helpful to the reader for you to label your discussion in four separate parts, each relating to the element to be discussed next.

In persuasive documents such as briefs, try to make your headings as convincing as possible. ("Defendant's Actions Have Caused Plaintiff Irreparable Harm.") In non-persuasive documents, your headings may be neutral and may consist of a mere word or phrase ("Irreparable Harm").

b. Use Effective Paragraphs

Just as you use headings to break up a solid mass of narrative, use paragraphs to break up a discussion into units that are easy to read. Readers will expect that each of your paragraphs relates to a distinct idea and will also expect that the first sentence of your paragraph will "set the stage" for what follows. This first sentence is the topic sentence. Use a thesis statement (described in Chapter 17) to provide structure to your analysis.

Avoid paragraphs that are too long. How long is too long? Most readers have difficulty with paragraphs that cover more than one-half of a page. Not only does the mind crave a break from a long discussion, so does the eye. Remember the visual effect of your writing, and create a project that is pleasing to the eye. Also avoid short paragraphs. The traditional rule is that a paragraph must have more than one sentence. On occasion, however, you may want to use a one- or two-sentence paragraph in legal writing for emphasis and visual effect.

c. Use Effective Transitions

To move smoothly from one sentence, paragraph, or idea to another, use a transition word or phrase. Without transitions, writing would be choppy and telegram-like. Transitions connect what you have said with what will follow. Avoid using the same transition words. Two of the favorite transition words of beginning writers are "however" and "therefore." If you find yourself continually introducing sentences and paragraphs with the same words, examine your project and try to find other transitions to lend variety and interest to your writing.

Commonly used transition words and phrases are as follows:

To introduce a topic
    in general
    initially
    primarily
    to

To show contrast
    although
    but
    conversely
    however
    in contrast
    nevertheless
    on the contrary
    on the other hand
    yet

To show similarity
    in the same way
    just as
    likewise
    similarly

To show examples
    for example
    for instance
    in fact
    namely
    specifically
    that is
    to illustrate

To show conclusions	*To show additions*
accordingly	additionally
as a result	again
because	furthermore
consequently	in addition
for this reason	moreover
inasmuch as	*To summarize*
therefore	finally
thus	in brief
	in conclusion
	in summary
	to conclude
	to summarize

d. Use Position and Voice for Emphasis

In nearly every persuasive writing project, there are stronger points and then points writers wish they did not have to mention. Use the location or placement of information as well as voice to draw your reader's attention to the more compelling parts of your writing and to minimize the impact of "negative" or weak sections of your argument.

The most prominent parts of a writing are its beginning and its ending. Readers tend to start projects with great enthusiasm, lose interest in the middle, and then become attentive again when the end is in sight. Therefore, put your strongest arguments and information at the beginning and ending of your project, your paragraphs, and your sentences.

Bury negative information in the middle of your project, in the middle of your paragraphs, and in the middle of your sentences. These locations will attract the least attention and may even be overlooked. This is another compelling reason for crafting strong topic sentences in each paragraph. These topic sentences, typically placed at the beginning of paragraphs, not only convey the main idea of each paragraph but also may be the only parts of a project read by a busy reader. Thus, if the first sentence of each paragraph may be the only portion of your project that is read, put favorable information in these prominent positions.

Negative information that is buried in the middle of a project, the middle of a paragraph, or in the subordinate clause of a sentence will be less likely to be noticed. Be extremely careful when including these unfavorable portions of your writing because a careless spelling error or typo will immediately draw your reader's attention to them.

There are other techniques you can use to "hide" flaws in your argument. Because active voice is much stronger and more forceful than passive voice, consider using passive voice in discussion of information you believe is negative.

For example, if your client sold a house with defects to the plaintiff, this fact can be disclosed in the following two ways:

Active Voice   The defendant intentionally sold a house
                      with known defects to the plaintiff.
Passive Voice   The house was sold to the plaintiff.

You can easily see that the plaintiff would prefer the first sentence
whereas the defendant would prefer the second. By using the passive
voice you deflect attention away from the actor (the defendant) and onto
the object of the action (the sale of the house). Note how the use of the
passive voice here eliminates any reference whatsoever to the defendant.

Similarly, the techniques discussed above for making writing vivid,
such as selecting descriptive and concrete words and avoiding nominalizations, should not be used in discussions of negative information.
Selecting vague words ("situation," "matter") and including nominalizations ("The plaintiff underwent an operation" rather than "The doctor
operated on the plaintiff") will de-emphasize negative information.

Finally, use detail in describing facts and issues favorable to you and
discuss unfavorable facts and issues in general fashion. For example,
consider the following two descriptions of an accident, one from the
plaintiff's perspective and one from the defendant's.

Plaintiff's version:

As the plaintiff was safely driving within the legal speed limit,
defendant's car ran through a red light and collided with the left
front door of the plaintiff's car. The plaintiff was pinned behind the
steering wheel for three hours. After being forcibly removed from
the totally damaged car by the police and firefighters at the scene,
the plaintiff was rushed to the hospital by ambulance, where she
was treated for her severe and disabling injuries, including a broken
pelvis, a concussion, and internal bleeding.

Defendant's version:

The accident occurred as defendant was traveling westward on
Adams Avenue. After the collision, the plaintiff remained in her car
until she was transported to the hospital, where she received
treatment for her injuries.

Note the detail in the plaintiff's version, which paints a vivid picture
for the reader. In contrast, the defendant's version glosses over the event
by summarizing it in a general fashion. In fact, the defendant's version
doesn't even make clear that the defendant was involved in the collision.

Remember that documents submitted to court are persuasive documents, and their style differs from the objective style used in legal
memoranda. As discussed in Chapter 17, in such objective projects the
writer must disclose possible weaknesses in the case. Consequently, in
these writings, you will not bury negative information but will give it as
much emphasis as positive information.

I. Drafting Techniques

1. Getting Started

For most writers, the most difficult task is getting started. The research is completed, the deadline is looming, and yet the writer cannot begin.

The best cure for this common disease is to write something. Write anything. Just get started. If the idea of beginning an argument paralyzes you, don't begin there. Start writing the section of the document you are most comfortable with, even if this is not the correct order. If you are familiar with the facts, begin with a statement of facts. If you know how you want to conclude a letter, memo, or brief, begin with the conclusion. The mere act of writing any section of a document will relieve some of your anxiety about being able to write.

Use the storytelling technique discussed above to help you organize your thoughts and give you ideas on how to begin writing.

Set a goal for yourself. Challenge yourself to complete a task within an hour. These techniques may help you get started.

2. Finishing on Time

You will often be given deadlines for finishing projects. Similarly, documents prepared for courts may need to be filed by a specified date. If you have a deadline date, you may find it helpful to work backward from this date and establish a schedule for yourself. Set a date by which all of the research will be done, another date for completing the first draft, another for cite checking, and another for revising.

If you are a habitual last-minute worker, always finding yourself operating in crisis mode, it may help to announce a deadline date to someone. Go public. By telling your supervisor, "The first draft will be on your desk by Wednesday morning," you will commit yourself to meet this self-imposed deadline. If there is no deadline for filing the document with the court, ask your supervisor, "When would you like this completed?" Without some deadline date, the project will languish on your desk and continually be relegated to the back burner while you work on other projects.

Once the deadline is established, allow yourself some time for emergencies. The copier may break down, you may get sick, or someone else's project may have a higher priority. If you don't allow room for these last minute crises, you may fail to meet the deadline.

Set small goals for yourself. Tell yourself, "I will have the statement of facts done by 11:00 A.M. today." These self-imposed deadlines will help you tackle the project bit by bit and meet the real deadline.

If you draw a blank while you are writing, just keep going. Move to another section and return to the difficult section later. Mark blank or troublesome sections with sticky notes if writing in longhand and with

"xx" or some other signal if you are word processing. You can use the "find and replace" feature to locate these troublesome passages later.

Avoid self-censoring. Don't worry at this stage that something will sound awkward or unsophisticated. You can clean up problem areas during your revision process.

If you are interrupted while writing, put a sticky note on your notepad or computer screen to remind yourself what you want to write about next. When you return to the project, these notes will help you return to your project efficiently and effortlessly.

3. *Methods of Writing*

There are three primary methods used for the actual writing process: writing by hand, dictating, and writing on a word processor.

a. Writing by Hand

Some people are most comfortable writing in longhand. Although this can be a very effective technique, its primary drawback is that it is extremely time-consuming, especially for a long memo or brief. In fact, some law firms are vehemently opposed to writing in longhand and will insist that a faster method be used. Despite this, projects written in longhand often need less revising than projects dictated or composed on a word processor.

b. Dictating

Dictating is probably the speediest method of drafting. It can take some time, however, to shed self-consciousness when you dictate. Initially, dictating may seem painfully slow. Confidence is rapidly gained, however. Stick with it until you become comfortable.

In the beginning, you may prefer to prepare a mini-outline for your dictating efforts and follow that as you dictate. You may also find that your initial attempts include repetitious sentences and poorly organized paragraphs. With time and practice, however, you will acquire skill at dictating, together with a certain mental discipline enabling you rapidly and effectively to organize your thoughts. This skill at verbalizing complex thoughts may translate into ease and confidence in public speaking as well. This enhanced competence in oral presentation is one of the hidden benefits of dictating.

If you dictate, you will need to insert punctuation and paragraphing so the transcriber knows how to prepare the document. Similarly, you will need to spell certain words.

The popularity of dictating in law practice has declined significantly in recent years as writers have become more comfortable composing with word processors. Nevertheless, it remains an effective and efficient way to draft for some writers.

c. Using a Word Processor

The most popular method of writing is composing using a word processor. Although this method may be very speedy, and allows much flexibility in changing the placement of sections, many individuals tend to spend excessive time revising as they go along. Revising is a task better left until the end of a project. Your project need not be perfect with the first draft. Your initial draft should be focused on including the major issues and arguments needed to be addressed. Try to fight the temptation to engage in micro-editing as you draft on a word processor. Allow your first draft to flow smoothly and then devote effort to revision later.

If you use a word processor, consider the following:

- Save your versions frequently. Use the functions on your computer that allow you to select how frequently the document will be saved.
- To ensure that you don't lose important information, back up your versions on discs, print paper copies of the document frequently in case the disc is corrupted, and e-mail your documents to your personal e-mail account or to a friend for safekeeping.
- Use the features of your word processor to help you. Consider using the "track changes" feature to show changes between drafts. With a single button click, you can then accept (or reject) all changes. This technique, called "redlining," is used when legal professionals negotiate the form and content of a document because it allows each to see the changes made by the other.
- Understand that viewing the project one screen at a time allows you to see only a small slice of the document. Thus, headings and other items may become inconsistent. Carefully review a hard copy to check for consistency in the presentation of such items.

J. Electronic Communications

New forms of communication, namely, electronic communications, have arisen in the past several years, changing the way people communicate at the workplace. Although many of them are great timesavers, others are traps for the unwary. Consider the following when using any of the newer forms of electronic communications.

1. Phones and Voice Mail

Although conference calls and voice mail can both reduce the time you spend on communications, there are some guidelines that will assist you:

- When setting up a conference call, treat it as a meeting and be prompt in dialing in to the conference number.

- Make sure that introductions are made for all participants and that all participants can hear each other. Don't assume that someone is not on a call merely because you did not hear his or her voice or introduction.
- Always ask for permission before placing someone on a speakerphone.
- Always disclose that another is listening with you if you are on a speakerphone.
- Do not leave overly long or rambling voice mail messages.
- Clearly and slowly state your name and phone number in voice mail messages. Repeat at the end of your message for those unfamiliar with you so they do not have to replay the message to obtain your name and number.
- Avoid using voice mail to "dodge" callers and to evade bad news.
- Avoid disclosing confidential information over a cell phone. Messages may be easily intercepted.
- Check your office policy to see if cell phones can be used for business while you are driving. After a large law firm was sued in 2001 for an accident caused by one of its attorneys who was driving while using the cell phone for firm business, many firms now prohibit such use.

2. *Communication by Facsimile*

Communicating by facsimile is so commonplace that many firms use "real" correspondence only for very long projects or for critical matters, such as opinions and status reports. Check your firm or office policy as to documents that may be sent by facsimile. Nearly all facsimile cover sheets include a confidentiality notice indicating that if someone receives the communication in error, he or she should return it to the sender. Such notices are used to maintain attorney-client confidentiality and privilege. Consider sending voluminous materials by mail because even the best facsimile machines produce a copy that is less readable than an original. Always double-check the facsimile number before pressing "send." Once the document is sent, it cannot be recalled.

3. *E-mail*

E-mail has become an increasingly common method of communication, both within the workplace and to clients. E-mail creates an air of informality, and the ease with which a message can be composed and sent causes countless errors. We have all heard stories of people who, much to their chagrin, have mistakenly replied to "all" rather than solely to the sender of a message. Many firms and offices have policies as to the types of communications that can be sent via e-mail and typically include confidentiality notices at the conclusion of each e-mail message. Follow these guidelines:

- Spell-check all e-mail and proof for accuracy. If necessary, print a hard copy of the message, proof it, correct it, and then send it. It is far better to be overly cautious than to be perceived as sloppy.
- Because e-mail is generally "dashed off" without a great deal of thought, it often produces brusque and abrupt communications. The reader will not be able to see your expression, gauge your body language, or hear any intonation. Thus, attempts at sarcasm and humor may be misperceived. Consider receiving a communication writing, "I resent your message." You may be tempted to respond in a curt or hostile fashion before you realize the writer meant to write, "I re-sent your message."
- Never pass along inappropriate e-mail at your workplace. Politely inform the sender that you do not care to receive such information.
- Do not assume e-mail is confidential. Many employers monitor e-mail communications. Moreover, e-mail can be discovered in litigation, so be cautious in corresponding by e-mail.
- Be brief and to the point. Many people receive a great number of e-mail messages each day and won't bother to read a long, rambling message.
- Make the subject line specific. Let the recipient know at a glance what the message discusses. Add "no need to respond" to the subject line to save yourself from receiving excess e-mail messages.
- Be a charitable reader. Resist overreacting to an e-mail communication that may seem abrupt. The writer may have been trying to be brief.
- Avoid using e-mail to resolve disputes or for delicate matters in which tone of voice is important.

4. *Text Messaging*

Text messaging (or texting) is the term used for sending short messages (usually fewer than 160 characters) from cell phones or personal digital assistants such as BlackBerrys and iPhones. Texting has become increasingly popular. The U.S. government has stated that approximately 110 billion text messages are sent each month. The language used when texting is called "text speak," and it is marked by often highly creative abbreviations and acronyms, such as "PLZ" (for "please"), "UR" (for "you are"), and "DQMOT" (for "don't quote me on this"). Many law firms distribute BlackBerrys to their paralegals on the first day of work so that everyone can stay in touch at all times. If you text message anyone about a business-related matter, remember that although you may understand certain abbreviations, the recipient may not. Be sure your message is clear. When in doubt, write it out.

CyberSites

http://www.sec.gov/pdf/handbook.pdf	The website of the Securities and Exchange Commission offers excellent guidance on writing in "plain English," with numerous samples, explanations, and tips.
http://www.plainlanguage.gov	This is the website of the Plain Language Action and Information Network, a government volunteer group working to improve communications for the federal government. Numerous samples and tips are given for writing user-friendly documents, and various links to other useful resources are provided.
http://www.archives.gov	The website of the National Archives and Records Administration offers materials on drafting legal documents. Enter "Drafting Legal Documents" into the search box.
http://law.case.edu/faculty/friedman/ raw/Writing%20Links,%208-17-00 .html	This site, titled "Rawdata Writing Links," offers excellent information on writing and links to other useful writing sites. It is law related and will provide information on legal writing conventions and advice on drafting legal documents.
http://www.ualr.edu/cmbarger/ RESOURCES.htm	This website of a law school professor offers links to references and a variety of resources for legal writers, including tips on grammar, style, and composition.
http://law.lclark.edu/programs/legal_ analysis_and_writing/resources.php	This site offers direct linking to numerous legal writing resources.
http://owl.english.purdue.edu	Purdue University's Online Writing Lab offers handouts on general writing concerns, achieving conciseness, using active voice, developing an outline, overcoming writer's block, parallel structure, and other writing topics. English as a second language (ESL) resources are also provided.
http://www.dictionary.com	This site includes a thorough dictionary and thesaurus to help with accurate word selection.
http://www.law.ucla.edu/volokh/ legalese.htm	This site provides a thorough list of archaic and stuffy legal terms and suggested replacements.

Assignment for Chapter 15

PRECISION

SELECT THE CORRECT WORD IN THE FOLLOWING SENTENCES.

1. The court argued/stated that the statute had been ruled unconstitutional.
2. The deposition schedule will effect/affect our vacation plans.
3. He asked about the effect/affect of the negotiations for settlement.
4. The principle/principal of the doctrine of equivalents governs this patent case.
5. The corporation's principle/principal office is in Ohio.
6. Beside/Besides the exhibits, we also need the statistical tables.
7. The capital/capitol of California is Sacramento.
8. The interrogatories are comprised of/comprise four discrete/discreet parts.
9. The jury found the defendant guilty of/liable for arson.
10. The plaintiff will accept only a written proposal; do not submit an oral/verbal one.
11. From your response, I implied/inferred that you were angry.
12. He billed less/fewer hours than I did.
13. Steven has less/fewer experience than I do.
14. He was reluctant/reticent to question the witness.

CLARITY

REPHRASE EACH OF THE FOLLOWING TO PRODUCE A CLEARER SENTENCE.

1. An invention must be novel, nonobvious, and it must also show usefulness to be patentable.
2. Not only did Susan draft the document, she also was editing it.
3. The employee handbook prohibits unauthorized travel. The manual also requires employees to submit expense forms.
4. Fraud may consist of either an affirmative misrepresentation or the misrepresentation may be omitting to disclose material information.
5. Unauthorized access to the computer files is prohibited.
6. Employees may not use company e-mail for any purpose other than valid business reasons.
7. Persons other than shareholders may not receive distributions.
8. He agreed to draft the brief, edit it, and then to file it with the court.

READABILITY

REWRITE THE FOLLOWING SENTENCES TO MAKE THEM MORE
READABLE BY USING THE ACTIVE VOICE AND OMITTING NOMINALIZATIONS.

1. A determination was made by the ethics committee to close the file.
2. Finalization of the agreement was agreed upon by all parties.
3. A meeting was held by the directors of the corporation for the purpose of consideration of declaring a dividend.
4. A schedule for repayment of the loan was prepared by the finance officer who worked for the bank.
5. The legislature was called into special session by the governor for the purpose of consideration of increasing taxes.
6. A resolution to end the strike was entered into by union officials.
7. A decision to amend the bylaws was given consideration by us.
8. Advancement of the trial date was subject to exclusive determination by the court.
9. Negotiation of the agreement was effected by the corporation's officers.
10. Termination of the lease will be subject to the discretion of the landlord.

REWRITE THE FOLLOWING SENTENCES TO MAKE THEM MORE
READABLE BY ELIMINATING JARGON AND REDUNDANT EXPRESSIONS.

1. The agreement that we have drafted and prepared is enclosed herewith for your review and consideration.
2. The debt in arrears in now due and owing.
3. The methodology and process by which damages were calculated was in accord with the court's directive and order in this regard.
4. The purpose of this letter is to provide you with a full and complete current status report of your claim.
5. Each and every item of correspondence has been reviewed by us.
6. Tenants must and shall provide landlord with advance written notice of tenant's decision to vacate said premises.
7. It is essential and critical for those in the judicial branch to communicate their judicial opinions and writing in a manner that will be comprehensible to members of the public and easily understood by them.
8. I am awaiting your feedback on this memo.
9. Enclosed herewith please find the stipulation to amend the complaint in the instance case, the same having been fully executed by me.
10. Please be assured that I will continue to give this issue my utmost consideration to ensure finalization of this matter in a timely and expeditious manner.

Internet Assignment for Chapter 15

1. Review the SEC's guidance document *Plain English Handbook* at http://www.sec.gov. Review Chapter 6. Review the information on replacing jargon and legalese. Why should you avoid creating acronyms and other words?

2. Locate the case *Walters v. Reno*, 145 F.3d 1032 (9th Cir. 1998), decided in May 1998. What did the Ninth Circuit state regarding the forms used by the Immigration and Naturalization Service?

3. Access Professor Volokh's site relating to legalese at http://www.law.ucla.edu/volokh/legalese.htm. Give the appropriate replacement for the following words and phrases:

   any and all
   cease and desist
   notwithstanding
   substantiate
   utilize

4. Access the site http://www.archives.gov and locate the handout *Drafting Legal Documents*. Review the Principles of Clear Writing. What are the first four principles given?

5. Review *The Law Student's Guide to Good Writing* at http://www.kentlaw.edu/academics/lrw/grinker. Review the information on "throat-clearing phrases." What three examples are given of throat-clearing introductory phrases?

Legal Correspondence

I didn't have time to write a short letter, so I've written a long one instead.

Usually attributed to Blaise Pascal

A. **Letterwriting**
B. **Conclusion**

Chapter Overview

Although television and movies would have you believe that lawyers spend all day arguing interesting and exciting cases in court, the truth is that much of a lawyer's time is spent writing. Lawyers often rely on paralegals to assist in the writing process and often delegate an entire writing task to paralegals.

This chapter will introduce you to one of the most common forms of legal writings: legal correspondence. Letters are written for several purposes, and thus the style and tone you use will vary according to the purpose of the letter.

As you work and have the opportunity to review the writings of others, start collecting samples of the writings you find most effective. Use these samples to build up your arsenal of writing tools.

A. Letterwriting

1. Introduction

In contrast to other legal writings, such as contracts, wills, and appellate briefs, there is no rigid list of elements that must be included in a letter. Although letters should, of course, contain the basics (date, salutation, body, and closing), you will be able to exercise great creativity in

letterwriting based upon the goal you seek to achieve in your letter. The tone you adopt and the order in which you elect to discuss items are at your discretion. To beginning legal writers this flexibility can be intimidating. Without a rigid format to follow, some writers become paralyzed.

Letters can be extremely effective tools. The first letter you send to a client or adversary often establishes the basis for a relationship. If your letter to adverse counsel is hostile and arrogant, you will be responded to in kind, and this will mark the tone of future correspondence. Thus, you need to do some planning and thinking before you write.

The two most important questions to ask yourself before you begin a letter are "Who will be reading this letter?" and "What will this letter say?" The answer to the first question will set the tone for your letter, and the answer to the second question will tell you what type of letter you should write.

a. Who Will Be Reading This Letter?

The tone or style of your letter must be appropriate for the reader. For example, if a letter is directed to an individual who is relatively inexperienced with litigation, you will need to explain the information you present in the most clear and complete fashion possible. If, however, the letter is directed to another legal professional, such as a judge, attorney, or other paralegal, you will know that your discussion of some matters need not be as detailed or elementary as for a layperson.

If you find your letters are becoming stuffy and legalistic in style, there are a few techniques you can use to warm up the tone. One is to use personal pronouns, especially "you." Therefore, rather than writing, "Tenants have a right to withhold rent if the leased premises are not habitable," try writing, "As a tenant you have the right to withhold rent because your premises are no longer habitable." Similarly, contractions such as "can't" and "wouldn't" rather than "cannot" and "would not" tend to make a letter slightly less formal and more personal, although contractions are not commonly used in legal or business writing.

The fact that you will adapt your tone in legal letters to suit different readers is no different from what you already do: A letter or e-mail sent to your friends is written in a style entirely different from a letter responding to a job announcement.

b. What Will This Letter Say?

Before you begin drafting any letter, focus on the central purpose of your letter. Try to distill this to one or two sentences. For example, some purposes may be as follows:

- The client needs to know a deposition has been scheduled for next month.
- The debtor needs to understand that failure to repay the client will result in litigation.
- The client needs to be provided advice regarding cutting down trees on a neighbor's property.

These three examples represent the most basic types of legal correspondence: *general correspondence* or *informative, demand,* and *opinion* letters. Once you decide what type of letter you need to write, a style will come almost naturally.

Before discussing techniques for writing these varieties of letters, we will examine the format and elements of legal letters in general.

2. *The Elements of Letters*

Although there are different types of letters you will write, there are certain "basics" that are common to all legal correspondence. The components of legal correspondence are similar to those used for general business letters.

a. Letterhead

Law firms, government offices and agencies, and corporations all use special stationery, called *letterhead*, that serves to identify the office by name, address, telephone and facsimile numbers, and other relevant information. Letterhead is usually placed at the top of a page. Law firms (unless they have a large number of attorneys) usually list the attorneys associated with the firm on the letterhead. Be careful when drafting and setting up a letter that you recognize how much room the letterhead takes up because you need some space between the letterhead and your writing. Use letterhead for all correspondence connected with your employer because it conveys the message to the recipient that the correspondence is "official." Letterhead is used only for the first page of a letter. The remaining pages match the color and quality of the letterhead page but are not imprinted with the letterhead.

b. Date

Every item of correspondence must include a date, written out in full in the American style by month, day, and year (for example, August 12, 2010). The date is usually centered three lines beneath the letterhead, although occasionally it is placed at the left margin. Because dates in legal matters can be critical, be sure the date given is the date the letter is actually mailed, rather than the date of an earlier draft.

c. Special Mailing Notations

If your correspondence will be sent to the recipient by any means other than first class mail, indicate such as follows: "Hand Delivered," or "Registered Mail," or "By E-mail." This notation should be placed at the left margin two lines below the date and two lines above the address. Similarly, any other special notations such as "Attorney-Client Communication—Privileged and Confidential" should appear before the inside address.

d. Inside Address

The addressee's name and address should appear two lines below the date or any special mailing notations. Always follow the addressee's or organization's preferences for spelling, capitalization, and punctuation. Use titles if appropriate, such as Ellen Cochran, M.D., Stanley L. Williams, Esq., or David P. Kimball, Executive Vice President. If you do not know the marital status of a female addressee, use "Ms." unless you are directed otherwise. The form "Mrs. William Trainor" is acceptable only in social letters. Use "Ms. Madelyn G. Trainor." See Figure 16-1 for sample addresses.

e. Reference or Subject Notation

The reference notation indicates the subject matter of the correspondence. The notation may refer to the title of a case, the topic to be discussed in the letter, or a file or claim number. The reference notation gives the reader an immediate snapshot of what is to be discussed and also helps you later if you need to locate a letter you previously wrote. The reference notation (abbreviated as "Re:") is usually placed two lines below the inside address. As a courtesy to your reader, include his or her file or reference number if you know it, following your own reference notation. If your office uses internal file numbers, indicate those as well, because they often assist in mail-sorting. See Figure 16-2 for sample reference notations.

Figure 16-1
Sample Addresses

Ms. Donna A. Higgins   Mr. Allan N. Navarro
4529 Grandview Avenue   President
San Diego, CA 92110-5401   ABC Distributing Company
                              1429 Burgener Boulevard
                              Chicago, IL 96104

Janet F. Sanderson, Esq.   Director of Human Resources
Mills, Arnold and Smith   Smith Management Company
2900 L Street, NW   2800 Arlington Avenue
Washington, D.C. 20006   Irving, TX 75247-3159

Figure 16-2
Sample Reference Notations

Re: *Calvin v. Temple Motors, Inc.*
    Civil Action No. 09-696-VMA

Re: Estate of Boyer
    Our File: 9204\09-646
    Your File: CN-9220

Re: Punitive Damages in Fraud Actions

f. Salutation

The salutation, or greeting, usually appears two lines beneath the reference notation. Unless you are acquainted with the addressee, err on the side of formality, and address the letter to Mr. Brown or Ms. Taylor, for example. Once again, unless you have been directed otherwise, address letters to females as "Ms." Letters to an unknown recipient such as the attorney general of a state may be directed to "Dear Sir or Madam:" Follow the salutation with a colon in business letters and with a comma in personal letters. See Figure 16-3 for sample salutations.

Practice Tip

Unknown Addressees

If you do not know the name of the recipient of a letter, for example, the Commissioner of the Internal Revenue Service, consider the following:

- **Use a title, such as** ***Dear Commissioner;*** **or**
- **Do some research on the Internet to find out the name of the Commissioner.**
- **If appropriate, use the salutation** ***Dear Colleague.***

---

g. Body

The body of the letter begins two lines below the salutation. The body is the critical part of your correspondence because it conveys your message. The first sentence and paragraph should set the stage for the rest of your letter by indicating the purpose of the letter.

Business letters and legal correspondence are usually single-spaced and then double-spaced between paragraphs. The second and following pages will not be on letterhead but will match the color and quality of the first letterhead page and will usually contain information such as the following (a "header") in the upper left-hand corner of each page:

Mr. Elliot Anthony
December 14, 2010
Page Two

Figure 16-3
Sample Salutations

Dear Mr. Smith:
Dear Ms. Anderson:
Dear Sir or Madam:

h. Closing and Signature

Most letters close with statements such as the following:

> Please do not hesitate to call me if you have any questions.
> Thank you in advance for your cooperation and courtesy.
> If you have any questions or comments you may reach me at the
>   number given above.

The complimentary closing is usually "Very truly yours," "Sincerely," "Best regards," "Yours truly," or something similar, followed by a comma. "Very truly yours" is generally regarded as more formal and is used less frequently than "Sincerely." If the letter is addressed to a judge, senator, or representative, the complimentary closing is typically "Respectfully." Capitalize only the first letter in the complimentary closing, and place it two lines below the body of the letter. The closing is usually centered.

Avoid informal or unusual closings such as "Affectionately," or "Successfully yours." Do not merge your complimentary closing with the last line of your letter. These merged closings were fashionable hundreds of years ago but have a stilted and archaic look. An example of a merged closing is as follows:

> Thanking you for your attention, I remain,
>
> Yours very truly,
>
> Suzanne Forrest

For letters that you will sign, be sure to indicate your title underneath your signature so the reader will know your position in the firm. Allow four lines between the complimentary close and your typed name. Some individuals prefer to use blue ink for their signatures, so readers can easily tell the document is an original rather than a copy.

> Very truly yours,   Sincerely,
>
> Matthew K. Lyons   Paula L. Wagner
> Legal Assistant   Senior Paralegal

> Best regards,
>
> Elizabeth A. Murphy
> Paralegal to Kenneth Tice, Esq.

i. Reference Initials, Enclosures, and Copies

Most letters include a few final notations. Generally, the arrangement of final notations is as follows: reference initials (placed two lines below the writer's typed name and title); indications of enclosures (placed one line below the reference initials), and indications of copies (placed one line below any indications of enclosures). All final notations appear at the left margin, but their presentation styles may differ from author to author.

Reference initials indicate who wrote the letter and who typed it or prepared it. If the author is Maria M. Adkins and the secretary who types it is Gregory L. Huntingdon, the reference "MMA/glh" would appear at the left margin, two lines below the signature block. The use of "mma:glh" is also common. If you prepared the letter yourself, you may omit these initials.

If you are enclosing something in a letter, indicate this by the word "Enclosure" or the abbreviation "Encl." (or "Enclosures" or "Encls." for more than one enclosure). Some writers list or identify the item enclosed, so the reader will quickly know if the correct item has been included. You may also see the notation "Enclosures (2)" for multiple enclosures. Some authors use the word "attachment" rather than "enclosure" when material is physically attached to the letter rather than merely enclosed.

Copies of the letter you write may be sent to others. For example, the client will routinely be provided with copies of letters you write to adverse counsel because this is a way of keeping the client informed of the progress of a case. To indicate the recipients of copies use "cc:" followed by the names of those who will be receiving copies. Although "cc" stands for "carbon copies," which have universally been replaced by photocopies or multiple printouts, the signal "cc:" remains in use.

There may be instances in which you do not want the reader of your letter to know who received a copy of it. In such cases, simply sign your letter, mail it, and then mark the copy that will go to the unidentified individual (assume Theresa Stone) and that will be placed in the file "bcc: Theresa Stone." This is a reference to "blind carbon copy." See Figure 16-4 for sample notations for copies and enclosures.

Figure 16-4
Sample Notations for Reference Initials, Enclosures, and Copies

TLB/amk
Encl.
cc: Susan M. Everett
    Thomas L. Cruz
cc w/encl.: Stephen S. Neal

j. Format Considerations

Letters are written on standard 8½"×11" paper and are usually single-spaced and then double-spaced between component parts (for example, between the date and inside address, between the inside address and reference notation, between the reference notation and salutation) and between paragraphs.

Some letters show no indentations for paragraphs because new paragraphs are clearly indicated by the double-spacing between paragraphs. This style is referred to as "block form" or "left justified." In block form, all elements of the letter, including the date and complimentary closing, begin at the left margin.

Other firms and authors prefer to indent five spaces for new paragraphs even though they are set apart by double-spacing. This style is called "modified block form." Here the date, complimentary closing, writer's identification, and signature are all centered.

When the righthand margin is even and every line ends at the right at the same space (as shown in this text), this is referred to as "right justification" or "full justification." Such letters present a very crisp appearance. One drawback to right-justified margins is that the spacing in some words will be cramped while others may be slightly spread out. Reading studies have documented that word-processed right-justified documents are more difficult to read because the variance in spacing eliminates distinctive word spatial characteristics, which aid comprehension and ease of reading. To a reader, the use of right justification is often distracting. Continuing improvements in word processors are eliminating these spacing problems. Nevertheless, some writers prefer a "ragged edge" at the right margin, believing it has less of a "computer" look and more of a "personally typed" look. Many word processing programs now offer letter templates for business letters in which spacing and common closings are already included, allowing you to "fill in the blanks" of the form. Spacing is preset as well.

Never allow a page to begin or end with one line by itself or one heading by itself. Referred to as "widows and orphans," these single lines or headings present an unprofessional appearance. Use 12-point font for readability. Use a common font such as Times New Roman or Courier.

3. *Types of Letters*

a. General Correspondence

General correspondence or informative letters may include letters requesting information or responding to requests for information, cover letters that accompany some document or other enclosure, confirmation letters that confirm some agreement or arrangement reached with another party, or status or report letters providing a report to a client or insurance

company of the progress of a case. Except for status letters, these letters are often brief and may be only one or two paragraphs in length.

These letters should contain the components of all letters (date, inside address, reference notation). They also should conform to the elements of good legal writing set forth in Chapter 15, namely, precision, clarity, readability, brevity, and order. If you misspell the client's name or send the letter to the wrong address, this will attract far more attention than the content of the letter.

If you are unsure whether a letter should be sent to confirm some matter or clarify some detail, err on the side of caution and write the letter. This will keep the file complete and help establish the progress of the case if you aren't there to explain it. Always send a confirming letter to opposing counsel to confirm dates, amounts, or any other matter. If adverse counsel has offered to settle the case for $20,000, immediately confirm this in writing and then notify the supervising attorney, who will likely conduct negotiations or give you instructions regarding such negotiations. If adverse counsel has granted you an extension to answer interrogatories or produce documents, immediately confirm this in writing by thanking the attorney so no dispute can later arise as to the dates. See Figure 16-5 for several sample general correspondence letters, including confirmation, cover, and status letters.

Ethics Alert

Corresponding with Parties

One of the most basic rules of ethics is that lawyers and those they supervise may not have any contact with parties once those parties are represented by counsel. Thus, never call or write a party without checking whether that party is represented by counsel. If you are unsure, when you make a telephone call, your first question should be, "Are you represented by counsel?" If the person answers "yes," politely end the call, and contact the attorney.

---

b. Demand Letters

Demand letters set forth a client's demands. The most common type of demand letter is a collection letter, which outlines the basis for a debt due to a client and sets forth a demand that it be paid. Other demand letters, however, demand that certain action be taken, such as a demand that a landlord repair a leaking roof or a demand that one company cease using a trademark similar to one owned by another company. Your tone should be firm and businesslike, not strident or nasty. To eliminate any disputes whether the letter was received, send the letter by some verifiable type of delivery, such as registered mail. The only portion of a demand letter that

Figure 16-5
Sample General Correspondence Letters

A. Sample Confirmation Letter

LAW OFFICES
OF
MICHELLE L. MONACO
2300 BIRCH DRIVE
PHOENIX, ARIZONA 60234
(609) 788–4000

November 8, 2010

Stephen L. James, Esq.
6200 Tenth Street
Phoenix, AZ 60244

Re: *Brownell v. Kaplan*

Dear Mr. James:

This letter will confirm that you have granted us an extension to respond to the plaintiff's complaint in the above-referenced action until December 6, 2010. As I explained, the additional time is needed due to my client's hospitalization. Thank you for your courtesy and cooperation.

Please feel free to call me if you have any comments or questions.

Sincerely,

Michelle L. Monaco

MLM/pmr
cc: Sharon J. Kaplan

Figure 16-5 *(Continued)*

B.   Sample Cover Letters

SMITH, CHURCH, AND UPSHAW, L.L.P.
1414 SOUTH ADAMS STREET
SUITE 1000
BOSTON, MASSACHUSETTS
(214) 649–1200

January 14, 2011

Ms. Ann B. Milstead
2001 Elysian Fields Avenue
New Orleans, LA 70015

Re: *Sanderson v. Milstead*

Dear Ann:

I am enclosing a copy of the transcript of the plaintiff's deposition in the above-referenced action. Please review this carefully and call me with any comments you may have. As you know, we are particularly interested in the plaintiff's version of the events in the two hours preceding the accident. Any inconsistencies that you may find in the plaintiff's testimony would be extremely helpful. We look forward to hearing from you.

                                        Very truly yours,

                                        William B. Church

WBC/swa
Encl.

Figure 16-5 *(Continued)*

B. Sample Cover Letters

LAW OFFICES OF THOMAS N. MILLER
1600 ELM STREET
SUITE 202
PORTLAND, OREGON 60102
(402) 657–1990

February 6, 2011

Mr. and Mrs. James E. Bailey
2002 Artesia Boulevard
Portland, OR 60435

Re: Execution of Wills

Dear Mr. and Mrs. Bailey:

    I enjoyed meeting you last week and discussing the preparation of your wills. I have prepared the first drafts of the wills. They are enclosed for your review. After you have examined the wills, please call me with any changes or corrections you have. I will then revise them according to your instructions and schedule a date for you to come to my office to sign them.

    Please feel free to call me if you have any questions or comments.

Sincerely,

Thomas N. Miller

TNM:scg
Encls.

Figure 16-5 *(Continued)*

B. Sample Cover Letters

LAW OFFICES
OF
TAYLOR AND GILBEY
4305 WILLETT STREET
KANSAS CITY, MISSOURI 45609
(421) 678–1299

September 14, 2010

Cynthia A. Chan, Esq.
5000 Missouri Avenue
Kansas City, MO 45609-4265

Re: *Anders v. Patterson*
Your File: CV 1895

Dear Ms. Chan:

In reviewing my correspondence to you of yesterday, I noticed that I neglected to include a copy of Exhibit A to the Complaint, which should have been enclosed with the letter. I am enclosing Exhibit A with this letter and apologize for any inconvenience this may have caused you.

Please feel free to call me if you have any questions or comments.

Sincerely,

Francis K. Taylor

FKT:wlm
Encl.

Figure 16-5 *(Continued)*

C. Sample Status Letter

FENTON, HOGUE AND HOGUE, LLP
1200 B STREET, SUITE 1900
LOS ANGELES, CALIFORNIA 90234
(405) 765–1400

July 16, 2010

Dale L. Curtis, M.D.
3200 Montana Avenue
Los Angeles, CA 90256

Re: *Fontana v. Curtis, et al.*
    Our File: 94081

Dear Dr. Curtis:

This letter will provide you with a brief status report on the progress of the above-referenced action. As you know, we have provided interrogatories, or written questions, to the plaintiff, which he is required to answer under oath and return to us within thirty (30) days. After we have had an opportunity to review the plaintiff's answers, we will be in a better position to evaluate which documents we should request and which individuals and witnesses should be deposed so we may obtain their testimony regarding the acts of professional negligence alleged against you.

The Superior Court has recently notified us that a settlement conference has been scheduled on the matter for Wednesday, August 12, 2010, at 2:00 p.m. in Room 2404 of the Los Angeles County Courthouse, located at 1212 Wilshire Boulevard in Los Angeles. You are required to attend that conference, at which time the judge assigned to the case will explore the possibilities of settlement. The plaintiff will also attend and will be expected to make a reasonable demand for settlement. If we are unable to settle the case at that time, a trial date will be assigned. We expect that the trial will occur after the first of the year.

As soon as we receive the plaintiff's answers to the interrogatories, we will provide you with a copy for your review and comment. Please contact us if you have any questions.

Very truly yours,

Linda J. Fenton

LJF:sfk

will differ from a general correspondence letter is the content of the body. Include these elements:

- *Introduction of your firm.* Identify your firm and specify your role. A simple sentence stating "This firm represents James K. Matthews regarding the automobile accident that occurred on January 8, 2011" is sufficient.
- *Recitation of facts.* You must include the facts upon which the client's claim is based. Because your aim is to motivate the reader to pay your client or take some action, phrase the factual statement as persuasively as possible.
- *Demand.* Set forth as clearly as possible your client's demand. If this is a collection letter, specify the exact amount due. If you are demanding that the reader take some specific action, such as repairing a leaking roof, say so. If there are several components to your demand, you may wish to set them forth in a list.
- *Consequence of noncompliance.* Because your aim in a demand letter is to persuade the reader to pay your client or take some action, you should include a statement telling the reader of the consequence of not complying with the demand letter. These consequences may include the institution of litigation, the cessation of work on a project, or some other adverse action. Although nearly all readers will be offended by heavy-handed threats, there is nothing wrong in clearly and concisely explaining to a reader what will occur if the client's demands are not met.
- *Date of compliance.* You must set forth in explicit terms the deadline for compliance. Do not write "You must pay the sum of $10,000 immediately." When is immediately? Two days? Ten days? Three weeks? Set forth a specific date so the reader will know exactly when compliance is expected.

Follow these guidelines in drafting demand letters:

(i) *Know the facts.* Be sure you have all of the relevant facts. It is not enough to have most of the facts. If the client has informed you that a debtor has breached a contract, determine if the contract is written or oral. If it is written, you need to obtain a copy of it and review it. A mistake in reciting the facts will immediately call forth a response by the recipient pointing out your error, and any momentum you may have had, along with your credibility, will be lost. To be sure your recitation of the facts is correct, send a copy of your demand letter in draft to the client asking that the client review the letter and approve it before it is sent to the other party. If it later turns out that the facts recited in the letter are incorrect, you have protected yourself from your supervisor's or client's wrath by having obtained the client's approval.

(ii) *Know the law.* You cannot send a letter demanding money for breach of contract if enforcement of the contract is barred by the statute of limitations or some other law. You must perform some minimum amount of research to ensure that the client's

claim is valid and enforceable. Similarly, review the code of ethics for your state. It is unethical to correspond with a person who is represented by counsel. Therefore, once you know an individual has retained counsel, all correspondence must be directed to counsel. Most codes of ethics set forth other rules you should be familiar with, such as that it is unethical to threaten criminal prosecution if a demand is not met.

Many states have consumer protection or debt collection statutes, and demands for payment of debts must comply with the requirements of these statutes. Be sure to research any such requirements in your state because failure to follow the statutory requirements may invalidate the demand.

(iii) *Don't argue the case.* A demand letter should set forth the facts underlying the demand, state the demand, and outline the consequences of noncompliance. You need not, and should not, present all the evidence you would need to prevail at a trial of this matter. The debtor will undoubtedly know some of the facts relating to the claim, and you need not provide copies of every item of correspondence and the name of every witness who supports your client's version of the matter. If the problem cannot be resolved by direct negotiation, your firm will have ample opportunity to argue the case at trial. Don't tip your hand at this juncture. Although a few legal authorities may be cited in some instances, routine collection letters rarely include legal analysis.

(iv) *Do what you say.* If you have told the recipient of the letter legal action will be instituted by December 10 unless the amount of $10,000 is paid to the client, you must be prepared to follow through. Nothing jeopardizes credibility more than empty threats. If December 10 comes and goes and you issue another demand letter setting forth another deadline date, the reader will know you do not mean what you say and will understand there is no reason to comply with the renewed demand.

This issue of doing what you say is often a matter of communicating with the client. If the client has no intention of suing or is aware the recipient may have certain counter-claims, the letter can be structured appropriately. For example, rather than stating a deadline date, the letter could leave the issue open and state any of the following:

- We look forward to receiving your prompt response to this demand.
- Please contact us to discuss this matter further.
- Unless we receive a satisfactory response from you by December 10, we will take all appropriate legal action.
- We invite your response to this claim and hope this matter can be resolved amicably.

Note, however, that if you write, "We look forward to a counter proposal from you," you have made a serious concession and have invited the recipient to play "let's make a deal." See Figure 16-6 for a sample demand letter.

Figure 16-6
Sample Demand Letter

DOUGLAS, FRANK, KELLY AND MORGAN
5600 K STREET, SUITE 2500
ALBANY, NEW YORK 12004
(612) 567–8999

August 9, 2010

Mr. Peter M. Todd
Todd Contracting Co.
1255 Stanley Avenue
Albany, NY 12966

Re: Harris Engineering, Inc.

Dear Mr. Todd:

This firm represents Harris Engineering Co. ("Harris") regarding its legal affairs. As you know, on January 4, 2010, Todd Contracting Co. ("Todd") entered into a written contract with Harris. This contract required Harris to provide engineering services for Todd for the construction of Nathan Public Park in Albany, and Todd was to pay the sum of $24,550 to Harris for those services. That contract was signed by you on behalf of Todd.

Our client has informed us that it has provided all engineering services required by the contract. Those services were critical to the improvements performed at Nathan Public Park, and no objections were made by any individual at Todd regarding these services. Our client has further informed us that although it received one payment from Todd in the amount of $15,550 on March 1, 2010, no further payments have been made to it, despite numerous requests therefor.

This letter is a formal demand that the sum of $9,000 be paid to Harris on or before August 19, 2010. Our client has instructed us to inform you that if this sum is not paid as directed, it will institute litigation against Todd for the remaining balance of $9,000 due to it as well as interest and attorneys fees as provided in the written contract that you signed.

Please contact us within the time provided to confirm your compliance with the terms of this letter and to avoid litigation being filed against Todd.

Sincerely,

Anthony P. Kelly

APK:tmb

c. Opinion Letters

Letters offering legal advice or opinions can be signed only by attorneys. Nevertheless, you may find that you are given the task of researching the law and writing drafts of the letter. Thus, although the letter is reviewed, revised, approved, and signed by an attorney, you may be the principal author. Although these opinion letters are usually requested by clients seeking advice on a particular matter, on occasion they may be requested by a third party, such as an accountant who requires a legal opinion as to a client's progress in litigation before the accountant can prepare financial statements.

In addition to the standard components of a letter (reference line, salutation, and so forth), there are eight key elements to an opinion letter. Opinion letters share many elements in common with legal memoranda, although their analysis of legal authorities is more simplified, and they are written to a client rather than to another legal professional.

(1) Date

Although all letters include dates, the date of an opinion letter is especially important because the opinion will relate to the status of the law on that date. Changes in the law after that date may well affect the correctness of the opinion.

(2) Introductory Language

It may be a good idea to remind the client why he or she is receiving an opinion letter. An opinion letter may take several hours to research and prepare and may well be costly. Reminding a client that he or she specifically requested the opinion may protect you from a client's refusal to pay the bill on the ground that this work was never requested. Consider the following introductions:

- We enjoyed meeting you last week. As you requested, we have researched whether a landlord is liable for injuries sustained by a tenant . . . .
- Per our telephone conversation of March 10, 2011, we have reviewed the issue . . . .
- At your request . . . .
- You have asked for our opinion whether . . . .
- According to your instructions of July 18, 2010 . . . .

This introductory language not only protects you from a client's faulty memory but also sets forth the scope of the letter by stating the issue that is addressed by the letter.

(3) Review of Facts

An opinion letter should always set forth the facts upon which it is based. Facts are usually given in a narrative (sentence-by-sentence) form

rather than in an outline or list form. Including the facts gives the client the opportunity to correct you if any of the facts are wrong. Even a minor factual change such as a change in a date or dollar amount can cause an opinion to be incorrect. Thus, include the facts so the reader understands that the accuracy of the opinion depends upon these facts and that changes in the facts may cause changes in the legal conclusions reached. Consider introducing the facts as follows:

- You have informed us that you entered into a written lease on August 18, 2010 . . . .
- As we understand them, the facts are as follows: On June 24, 2010, while traveling west on Ash Street . . . .

(4) Conclusions

The essence of an opinion letter is the advice given to the client. Clients are particularly eager to get to the "bottom line," and many writers immediately give their opinion or conclusion after a recitation of the facts, and then follow the conclusion with an explanation. This is an effective technique if the opinion you give is one the client wants to hear. If, on the other hand, you will be giving the client bad news, such as informing him or her that a lawsuit cannot be initiated because the statute of limitations has expired, you may want to lead the reader to this unfavorable news gradually. By explaining the law first you will be preparing the reader for the unfavorable outcome, so by the time you actually give the bad news, the reader understands exactly why the outcome is unfavorable. Consider introducing the conclusion as follows:

- Based upon the facts you have provided us and the applicable law in this state, it is our opinion that you may initiate an action for wrongful death against Timothy Adams.
- We have concluded that you may bring an action for wrongful death against Timothy Adams. Our conclusion is based upon the facts set forth above and our analysis of the law in this state.

You may have observed that many opinion letters use "we" and "our" rather than "I" and "my." For example, an opinion is often introduced as follows: "It is our opinion" or "Based on the foregoing, our advice is . . . ." This use of "we/I" is a matter of preference by attorneys. Some attorneys believe it is cowardly to hide behind the royal "we" and insist on using the first person "I/me" as in "It is therefore my opinion . . . ." Many attorneys believe the opinion is actually issued by the firm itself rather than by any one particular attorney and thus the "we/our" form is appropriate. You must learn the preference and policy of your supervisor and firm to determine which form to use. If you are working for a sole practitioner, however, "we/our" is never correct.

(5) Explanation of Conclusion

This portion of the letter explains and summarizes the law upon which your conclusions are based. Because most opinion letters are received by laypersons who may not be familiar with the law, avoid detailed discussions of statutes and cases. It is sufficient to summarize the legal authorities in a general fashion.

Should you include citations to cases and statutes? Generally, avoid giving citations unless your reader is sufficiently sophisticated to understand the citations. Similarly, do not merely set out the text of a statute or case; rather, explain what the case or statute means. Refer to the legal authorities as follows:

- Applicable case law provides . . . .
- We have researched the pertinent statute that governs this issue. It provides . . . .
- The legal authorities in this state are in agreement that . . . .

Use headings and subheadings if this portion of the letter is long and you can divide your explanation into easily understood separate sections.

(6) Recommendation

After you have explained the law that governs the conclusion you have reached, provide a recommendation to the client. Be sure that your recommendation is not unduly optimistic. Never inform a client that he or she will recover a substantial amount of money or that he or she "cannot lose," because you will seldom be able to deliver as promised. Phrase your advice as a probability rather than a certainty. Thus, write, "we believe that a court may hold that," rather than "your claim is undoubtedly valid." Do not include any language that could be viewed by a client as a guarantee of success. Similarly, if you need to give the client bad news, try to soften your approach by saying, "Success is extremely unlikely" or "The chances of a favorable outcome are remote at best," rather than a blunt "Taking your case would be a waste of time and money." Be sure, however, that you clearly deliver the bad news. Don't soften your approach so much that you haven't accurately conveyed your meaning. Readers often perceive what they want to, and there is no place for ambiguity in delivering unfavorable news to a client. If you must give bad news, try to find an alternative avenue for the client, as follows:

> Because the statute of limitations has expired, you will not be able to bring an action against your neighbor for trespass. We would suggest, however, that you attempt to negotiate directly with your neighbor. If this approach is unsuccessful, contact the company that issued your homeowners insurance because it may afford coverage for the damage to your property.

Use wording such as "we regret" or "unfortunately" when delivering bad news.

(7) Instructions

The last portion of an opinion letter should be a clear direction to the client to contact the office or take some other action. Consider the following:

> Because the statutes governing this matter require that a claim be submitted to the city within 100 days of the wrongful act, please contact us immediately and provide us with your instructions. Failure to file the claim by May 10, 2011, will bar any action against the city.

(8) Protection Clauses

On occasion, you may not have all of the information you need to provide a complete opinion. For example, the client may have informed you that he is a tenant under a written lease and yet has not provided the lease to your office for your review. In such cases, protect yourself by explaining that you lack certain information, and that the opinion may change depending upon the information you receive. Similarly, if certiorari has been granted for the authorities you rely on, explain this to the reader so if the cases you rely on are reversed or limited, the client will have been forewarned. Finally, think ahead and consider what defenses or arguments the other party may assert. Prepare your client to meet these arguments.

Consider the following examples:

- This opinion is based upon the facts you have provided us. Once we have had an opportunity to review the addendum to the lease entered into between you and your landlord, we will be better able to provide you with our opinion and analysis. Assuming the addendum does not materially alter the original lease, however, it is our opinion . . . .
- The landmark case in this area of the law is *Wolfson v. Dana Point, Ltd.*, 101 P.3d 817 (Cal. 2011). That case is presently being reheard by the California Supreme Court. An adverse opinion by the court could affect the conclusions in this letter. We will continue to monitor this case before the court and notify you once the court has issued its decision.
- Although your employer may argue his business is not subject to the provisions of the Family and Medical Leave Act, we believe such an argument is without merit because . . . .

B. Conclusion

Always write your letter with its intended audience in mind and clearly understand your goals in sending the letter. Do you want to inform? Convince? Settle? This will help you achieve the correct style and tone.

After you have finished the letter, reread it, putting yourself in the recipient's place. This will allow you to focus on whether the letter conveys the information it needs to, whether it will be readily understood by the reader, and whether the tone is appropriate.

Because you will have the opportunity to review correspondence from others, keep copies of those that you feel are well written, and adopt the techniques you believe make the letters effective. Notice the way others order their paragraphs or conclude their letters. Learn from others.

CyberSites

http://owl.english.purdue.edu/ owl/resource/653/01	This site provides information on writing formal business letters and gives sample letters.
http://www.unc.edu/depts/ wcweb/handouts/business .html	The University of North Carolina provides tips on writing business letters.
http://www.jamesmartinpa .com/letters.htm	Attorney James W. Martin offers excellent advice on writing letters for non-lawyers.

Assignment for Chapter 16

You have been given the following fact pattern by Miles Carter, one of the senior partners in your law firm.

Your firm represents Mary Kate Petersen. Mary Kate and her husband, Jon Petersen, have been legally separated. In fact, Mary Kate received a decree of separation last year. Jon died last month, leaving no will (meaning that his estate is "intestate"). Jon's estate is $500,000. Mary Kate would like to know if she is entitled to any share of Jon's estate. The couple has no children, but Jon's mother is still living.

Mr. Carter would like you to prepare an opinion letter (for his signature) to the client, informing the client whether she is entitled to any share of Tom's estate.

By way of background, the Uniform Probate Code includes several provisions relating to intestate estates, shares of spouses, and so forth. Our state (which is not a community property state) has adopted the Act in its entirety. The Act is available through the website of the National Conference of Commissioners on Uniform State Legislation. Assume there are no cases interpreting the applicable provisions of the Act.

Internet Assignment for Chapter 16

1. Access the University of North Carolina's writing website at www.unc.edu/depts/wcweb/handouts/business.html.
   a. Why is writing for a business audience different from writing in other academic disciplines?
   b. When should a writer use "I" and when should a writer use "we"?
2. Access Purdue University's Online Writing Lab at http://owl.english.purdue.edu/owl/resource/653/01, and review the information on writing basic business letters.
   a. Review the information about "Tone in Business Writing." How can you make sure your messages have the appropriate tone?
   b. Review the information on "HATS: Design Procedure for Routine Business Letters." What does the acronym HATS stand for?
   c. Review the information on "Accentuating the Positive in Business Letters." Why will your writing be more successful if you focus on positive wording rather than negative?
3. Access attorney James Martin's information on writing letters at http://www.jamesmartinpa.com/letters.htm. What five things should you do before writing a letter?

Legal Memoranda

[W]riting is the action of thinking, just as drawing is the action of seeing . . . .

Brenda Ueland (1939)

A. **Introduction**
B. **Format of Memoranda**
C. **A Blueprint for Preparing a Memorandum**

Chapter Overview

An office or legal memorandum is a well-known document in legal writing. It calls for you to research an area of law thoroughly and set forth your findings, both positive and negative, in a specific format.

It is only by being completely knowledgeable about the strengths and weaknesses of a case that a law firm can make a fully informed decision whether and how best to

- represent the client
- prepare pleadings and motions
- settle the case
- proceed to trial
- appeal an adverse decision

Thus, office memoranda or "memos" are used to guide those representing the client in every aspect of a case — from the initial decision whether to accept a case to a final appeal. If the law firm knows in advance the weaknesses of a case, it can adopt certain strategies to overcome these weaknesses, and prepare the client for a possible negative outcome. If the memo shows the weaknesses are fatal, the memo saves the client time and money that would be expended in a trial and assists in making a decision to settle the case. A well-written memo can form the

basis for motions to be made later in the case or even a trial or appellate brief. Thus, skillful research and careful analysis at this early stage of a case will contribute to the successful management of a case throughout its progress in your office.

Paralegals frequently prepare legal memoranda, and your employer will expect you to be familiar with the purpose, style, and format of an office memorandum. Preparing and writing a memorandum is often a challenging and satisfying task because it calls for you to integrate both your research and writing skills and to present them in such a way that a reader has a complete and objective "snapshot" of the case, including both its strengths and its weaknesses.

A. Introduction

An office memorandum is a research document designed to provide information about a case or matter. You will be asked to research a question, and your answer will be provided in the form of a written memorandum. It is an internal document, meaning it is prepared for use within a law firm, corporation, or agency. Although a copy of the memo may be provided to a client, it is generally protected by the "work product" privilege and thus is not discoverable by an adverse party.

Because the office memo is not usually discoverable and will only be read by those representing the client (and possibly the client as well), its distinguishing feature is its objectivity. It should set forth not only the strong points of a case but the weak points as well.

Focus on the following three guidelines for effective memoranda writing:

1. Be Objective

The most difficult part of writing a memo is remaining neutral and objective. Once we hear the words "our client," we immediately tend to ally ourselves with the client's position, and ignore the negative aspects of a case while focusing only on the positive. Thus, phrases such as "I believe" or "I feel" have no place in a memorandum. You should be informing the reader of the findings of the authorities you have located, not interjecting your opinions and judgments.

If you are not objective in pointing out weaknesses and flaws in the client's case, you do the client a disservice. It is much better (and far less costly) to determine early in the representation that the other party has a complete defense to your client's action than to find this out at trial.

Force yourself to play devil's advocate. Approach the project as your adversary might and closely examine the cases that appear unfavorable to your position. Your adversary will certainly do so, and you should be as prepared as possible to overcome weaknesses in your case.

2. Be Specific

If you are asked to determine whether a tenant may sublease rented property when the lease fails to address such an issue, focus on this specific question. You need not address the issue as if you were writing a text on the history of landlord-tenant problems from the feudal period to the present. If, during the course of your research, you come across other issues that you believe may be relevant, simply note them and include them in a section at the end of the memo entitled "Additional Research" or "Recommendations."

3. Be Complete

The supervisor who assigned you the task wants a finished project, not a sheaf of notes or series of photocopied cases. Anyone can locate cases and photocopy or print them. Your task is to read and analyze these cases, apply them to the facts of the client's case, and present this as a finished professional research memorandum. Put yourself in your supervisor's place and consider what you would need to know to understand fully the client's case. Assume the supervisor expects a final, polished product that will need no additional work.

B.   Format of Memoranda

Unlike documents filed in court, there is no one rigid format for an internal office memorandum. Some law firms have developed their own formats, and you may wish to ask to review memos previously prepared because these will serve as a guide for you. If you cannot locate a previous memo, use the format suggested below, which is a very common and standard format.

There are usually either six or seven components to an office memorandum, each of which should be set forth as a heading and capitalized and centered or in some other way set off from the narrative portion of the memo. In large part, the elements of a memorandum are similar to those of a case brief, discussed in Chapter 4. See Figure 17-1.

1. Heading

The heading identifies the document, the person for whom the memo is prepared, the person who prepared the memo, his or her position, the subject matter of the memo, and the date it is prepared. The subject matter of the memo (found in the "Re:" line) should include a brief statement of the topic of the memo as well as a file name and number. Thus, a topic description such as "Injunctive Relief" will help facilitate indexing and later retrieval of the memo. Include also your office's file number. See Figure 17-2.

Figure 17-1
Elements of a Typical Memorandum

MEMORANDUM

To:

From:

Re:

Date:

ISSUES

1.
2.

BRIEF ANSWERS

1.
2.

STATEMENT OF FACTS

ANALYSIS

1.
2.

CONCLUSION

Figure 17-2
Sample Heading for Memo

MEMORANDUM

To: Michael T. Gregory, Esq.

From: David H. Hendrix, Paralegal

Re: *Smith v. Jones*
        Our Ref.: 94061
        Sublease of Rented Property

Date: July 15, 2010

2. *Issue(s) or Question(s) Presented*

This section of the memo sets forth the issues that will be addressed by the memo. In some memos, only one issue will be discussed. Other memos may address several issues or questions. If your memo will discuss more than one issue, number each one. Do not number a single issue. Drafting the issues can be very difficult. In fact, you may not be able to formulate the issues until you are almost finished researching the law to be discussed in the memo.

The issues are normally set forth in a question format. They are usually one sentence, although they may include subparts. Be careful that a one-sentence issue is not so long as to be confusing. The issues should be phrased so that they relate to the particular fact the problem presented. For example, questions such as "What is a sublease?" or "What are a landlord's duties?" or "What is burglary?" are far too broad. Incorporate a few facts from your case. Consider the following:

- Under Massachusetts law, may a tenant sublease rented property when a written lease fails to address this issue?
- Under Illinois law, does a landlord have a duty to disclose to tenants information about crimes that have occurred on the premises?
- In New Jersey, has a burglary occurred when an intruder enters a residence through an unlocked and open door?

Some writers prefer the issues or questions to start with the word "whether," as in "whether a tenant may sublease rented property when a written lease fails to address this topic" or "whether a battery occurred when parties involved in a fistfight consented and agreed to fight." Because questions that begin with the word "whether" result in incomplete sentences, many attorneys disfavor this form. Whichever format you choose, be consistent, and use the same format for all questions.

The questions presented should be phrased in a neutral manner so that an answer is not suggested by the question itself. If you have more

than one issue, consider listing the most critical issue first. It is possible that addressing the threshold issue first will cause later issues to be rendered moot. For example, if you first determine there is no breach of contract, any later discussion of damages for breach of contract is unnecessary.

3. *Brief Answer(s)*

This section of the memo sets forth brief answers to the issues you presented together with the reasons therefor. Try to avoid answers that merely repeat the question in a declarative sentence. For example, statements such as "Subleases are common arrangements" or "A landlord has duties to tenants" are hardly helpful to a reader.

Much better answers would be as follows: "A tenant may sublease property rented from another unless there is an unequivocal written lease provision forbidding subleasing" or "Inherent in a landlord's duty to provide habitable premises is a duty to inform tenants of crimes that have occurred at the leased premises." Avoid answers that merely respond "yes," "no," or "maybe." Your answers should incorporate the reason for your conclusions.

Keep your answers brief—no more than one or two sentences. Do not include citations in the brief answers. This section of the memo is only a quick preview of what will be discussed in greater detail later in the body of the memo.

Maintain symmetry in your brief answers. If you have set forth three issues, you must have three answers, each of which corresponds in order and number to the questions previously asked. See Figure 17-3 for sample issues and brief answers.

Figure 17-3
Sample Issues and Brief Answers

Issues

1. Under New Jersey law, may a written contract be rescinded due to one party's fraud?
2. Under New Jersey law, can a failure to comply with the terms of a consent agreement entered in court be the basis for contempt?

Brief Answers

1. Yes. A contract may be rescinded if one party procured the contract through fraud and the other party was misled thereby.
2. Yes. Failure to obey any order of a court, even one based upon the consent of the parties, is contempt of court.

4. Statement of Facts

The statement of facts may precede the issues or follow the brief answers. Either approach is acceptable. Many readers prefer the facts to be given first so they can make sense of the questions the memo will address.

The statement of facts will be based upon what you know about the case, what your supervisor and client have told you, and your review of the file. In brief, you are telling the client's "story." The factual statement must be neutral and objective. Therefore, you will need to include even unfavorable facts. Do not allow your opinions about the case to color your presentation of facts. For example, the statement "He endured four years of employment by Smith" includes an opinion or judgment. State, "He was employed by Smith for four years."

Do not include argument in your memo or conclusions that are not supported by the file. If you are unsure whether a statement or event is true, refer to it as an "alleged" statement or event. If there is a dispute as to the facts, include both versions. It is perfectly acceptable to state, "Although the tenant alleges she provided notice to the landlord of the leaky roof, the landlord disputes this."

Although only relevant facts should be included, the factual statement should be thorough. Do not omit certain facts on the assumption that "surely the attorney who gave me this project knows the facts." It is possible a new paralegal or attorney may be assigned to the case, and your memo may be the first source consulted to become familiar with the case. Therefore, the statement of facts should be self-contained and not require reference to other sources, such as pleadings or correspondence. To eliminate unnecessary facts, reread your statement of facts after you have completed your first draft of the memo. If the statement of facts includes facts that are not later mentioned in the analysis or discussion section, those facts can probably be omitted.

The best presentation of a factual statement is narrative, that is, sentence after sentence, paragraph after paragraph, written in the third person. Presentations of facts in outline form, for example, in separate bullets or numbered sentences, appear choppy and rigid. Use the past tense to narrate your facts unless facts are developing as you prepare the memo. Finally, although other approaches are acceptable, the most typical approach is to present a statement of facts in chronological order. In other words, relate the facts in the order in which they occurred.

At this point, you probably realize that a legal memorandum is unlike any document you have yet prepared. The presentation of questions, followed by answers, followed by facts, is indeed unusual. Remember, however, that your final project will include these critical elements within the first page or two, allowing your reader to review only a portion of the memo and yet comprehend a total view of the case. These three elements provide a snapshot of the essence of the client's situation. The critical questions in the case are enumerated, answers to these questions are provided, and an overview of the facts is given. Simply by reading these first three sections, the reader will know the strengths and weaknesses of the client's position.

5. Applicable Statutes (Optional)

Many memos include a section describing or setting forth any applicable statutory provisions that will be discussed in the memo. This section is optional and need not be included. If you include applicable statutes, you may either paraphrase the statutes or quote from them. If the statute is short, set it out in full. If the statute is long, set forth the pertinent parts and consider attaching a copy to the completed memo. Provide citations to any statutes in *Bluebook* or *ALWD* form.

6. Analysis or Discussion

The heart of the memorandum is the analysis, or discussion, section. This portion of the memo provides an in-depth analysis of the issues presented. Cases, statutes, and other authorities will be presented and discussed. Citations typically appear in the body of the memorandum, not as footnotes. See Chapter 18 for additional information on footnotes. Citations should be prepared according to *Bluebook* or *ALWD* form unless local or other form is used. Keep in mind the critical distinction between primary and secondary sources: Primary sources are mandatory and binding authorities, which must be followed, while secondary authorities are persuasive at best. Thus, do not rely exclusively on secondary authorities unless there are no relevant primary authorities.

There are several things to keep in mind as you write the analysis section of your memo.

Using thesis statements. Many writing experts suggest that authors use a thesis statement when writing projects. A thesis statement distills the central ideas and arguments in your project into one or two assertive sentences. It usually appears at the beginning of a project or issue to give focus and direction to the analysis to follow. Sometimes a thesis statement is called an *umbrella statement* because every part of the discussion to follow must fit beneath it. Thus, later sentences in the paragraph merely elaborate upon the point made by the thesis statement; they do not introduce new material. A thesis statement is not the same as a topic sentence. It is far more assertive than a topic sentence, which generally merely announces the subject matter or theme of a paragraph to follow; a thesis statement, on the other hand, provides a specific conclusion. Consider the following thesis statements:

- To state a cause of action for false advertising, the plaintiff must show that a statement is either literally false or implicitly untrue in that the statement is likely to deceive consumers.
- In order to be enforceable, a noncompetition agreement must be reasonable as to its scope, duration, and geographic area.

You can see that a thesis statement is a strong, conclusory assertion and that it serves to frame the discussion to follow. For example, using

the second illustration given above, after providing the thesis statement, the writer would then proceed to discuss the scope, duration, and geographic area of the noncompetition agreement in his or her case. The thesis statement thus provides the applicable rule and a preview of the analysis to follow.

Using the cases. It is not enough to merely locate authorities and summarize them. Almost anyone can read a case and then restate its holding. You will be expected to do more: to analyze the authorities and discuss how and why they relate to your particular problem. This requires you to interweave and compare the facts of your case with the authorities you rely upon. If the client's particular situation can be distinguished from the situation in the case law, say so. Explain why cases apply and why they do not. Be sure to give some of the facts of the cases you rely on so readers can see how and why they apply to your issue. One warning sign that you are merely providing case summaries rather than analysis is that each paragraph in your memo discusses a single case. If you find this happening, restructure the memo to ensure the cases you rely upon are being analyzed and compared with the client's fact situation rather than merely being summarized. Avoid mentioning a case unless you discuss it at least briefly by explaining how and why it applies to the client's issue.

This section of the memo will require all your effort to remain objective. Thoroughly discuss not only the authorities that support the client's position, but also those that do not. If you find weaknesses in a client's case, continue researching to determine if there are ways to surmount them. If new issues are disclosed by your research, discuss them. Typically, memo writers discuss the cases and authorities that support the client's position before discussing those that are unsupportive. Once all authorities are discussed for an issue, move on to the next issue.

If a direct quotation is particularly apt, use it. Be careful, however, to ensure that your analysis consists of more than a series of quotations. It is easy to read cases and then retype what the judge has stated. Use quotations, but make sure you explain their relevance to your research problem.

Ensuring readability. Retain symmetry in your memo. If you have identified three issues and provided three brief answers, divide your discussion into three parts, each of which corresponds in number and order to the issues you formulated. Each section should be labeled with a descriptive heading. Brief headings, such as "Elements of Contract," "Fraud," and "Damages," are acceptable and clearly alert the reader as to the topic to be addressed. If desired, you may repeat your issues as headings, although this will add to the length of your brief. Use subheadings if these would be helpful to a reader.

Be sure your discussion is readable. If every paragraph starts with a phrase such as "In *Smith v. Jones* . . . the court held . . . ," your finished project will have a choppy, stodgy style and appearance. The most

important part of the memorandum is not a dull recitation of facts and holdings of several cases, but rather your analysis of the effect these cases and other authorities will have on the client's particular situation.

Most effective discussions contain the following three elements:

- A discussion of the relevant authorities;
- An analysis and comparison of these authorities to the client's issues and facts; and
- A conclusion as to the effect of the authorities as they relate to the client's problem.

In many instances, although writing style and techniques should vary to enhance readability, the analysis can be reduced to the following basic format for each separate issue:

> According to . . . [citations], the law is . . . [explain and discuss]. In the present case, . . . [compare with authorities]. Therefore, . . . [conclude] . . . .

Analyzing using the IRAC method. In discussing and analyzing authorities, many writers follow what is referred to as the "IRAC" method. "IRAC" is an acronym for *I*ssue, *R*ule, *A*nalysis or *A*pplication, and *C*onclusion. Many writers, whether writing memos, letters, or briefs for courts, use the IRAC approach in discussing a legal problem.

First, the issue being considered is presented. Introduce the question or topic you will be analyzing. In a memo, the issue is originally set forth in the form of a question, such as "Does the Uniform Partnership Act govern a partnership that has no partnership agreement?" In a discussion section, the issue is often rephrased in the following form: "The key issue is whether the Uniform Partnership Act governs a partnership that has no written agreement." This serves to frame the discussion that will follow.

Next, provide the rule or legal authority that you rely upon to respond to the issue. The authority can be a case, a statute, or some other primary or secondary authority or authorities. If you rely on a case, give sufficient facts from the case that the reader will understand why and how it governs your case. If your rule is a statute, set forth the applicable provisions. Several authorities may be used. In fact, you should have at least one primary authority for every conclusion you reach. Complex matters will require citation of more authorities, including secondary authorities.

The most critical part of an IRAC discussion is the analysis or application of the rule to your case. Explain why the rule you have set forth does or does not apply to your particular case. Do more than merely summarize a case or statute. Summarizing should have taken place when you set forth the rule. Analyzing requires you to compare and contrast the facts of your case to those in the case you rely upon or to review a statute

and show the reader why your client's situation falls within (or without) the activity described by the statute. Apply the reasoning of the case or other legal authorities to your case.

Finally, after a thorough analysis, present the reader with a conclusion based upon your analysis of the rule. If the rule has been set forth clearly and the analysis is complete, the reader will likely be able to draw a conclusion even in advance of your stating it. Nevertheless, presenting a conclusion wraps up your analysis and serves as reinforcement of prior discussion as well as a signal that discussion of a particular topic is complete and that a new topic will likely be presented next, once again using the IRAC method. Readers need closure on one issue before tackling the next.

Many beginning researchers are reluctant to draw a conclusion. They simply summarize applicable cases and then move on to the next topic. You will need to synthesize the authorities you discuss by comparing and contrasting them to each other and then applying them to the client's particular case to reach a conclusion. For example, after discussing the authorities relating to sexual harassment in the workplace, you could conclude by writing, "Because the authorities are in agreement that the conduct an employee complains of must be severe to constitute harassment, it is highly unlikely that a court would find a single passing remark such as the one made to our client to be actionable." See Figure 17-4 for an example of an IRAC discussion.

Figure 17-4
Sample IRAC Discussion

Issue	The central issue in this case is whether a single remark made in a workplace environment (namely, "Hey, babe — looking good") constitutes sexual harassment.
Rule	The cases interpreting the Civil Rights Act of 1964 are in agreement that although a single utterance can constitute harassment, the remark must be so severe and outrageous that it creates an intolerable and hostile work environment.
Application	[Discuss cases and give citations.] In the present case, the remark, although offensive and inappropriate, is not "severe" and "outrageous" as those terms are used in the cases governing this issue.
Conclusion	Thus, the remark is unlikely to rise to the level of actionable sexual harassment.

Following the IRAC approach to discussing problems helps ensure that you conduct a thorough analysis of an issue and is a commonly accepted writing approach both for law students and legal practitioners.

Analyzing using the CRAC method. Some experts suggest a variation of IRAC, often called "CRAC" (for *C*onclusion, *R*ule, *A*pplication, and *C*onclusion). In this analysis, the conclusion is given first, followed by the principal rule of law that supports the conclusion. The rule is applied and illustrated through analysis of cases and other authorities. The rule is then applied to the client's particular case, and the conclusion is restated. Another variant of IRAC is "CREAC" (for *C*onclusion, *R*ule, *E*xplanation, *A*pplication, and *C*onclusion), in which the rule is explained after it is given.

Some writing experts dislike constructs such as IRAC and CRAC because they believe these methods encourage a rigid and formulaic approach to writing. Others believe that IRAC is more useful for writing objective projects such as legal memoranda (because it requires the writer to state the issue in a neutral manner) and that CRAC (with its assertive conclusion given at the beginning) is more useful in persuasive writings, such as court briefs.

Practice Tip

Using Quotations and Paraphrasing

Many beginning writers wonder when to use direct quotations and when to paraphrase. Consider the following guidelines:

- **Use a direct quotation when what has been said is so articulate and apt that to paraphrase it would dilute its meaning.**
- **Use a direct quotation when the author of the quotation is so well known that a quotation from this person would provide instant credibility.**
- **Avoid overlong quotations.**
- **Use quotations sparingly so that they grab the reader's attention and interest.**
- **Paraphrase when the original quotation is difficult to understand or would require so much restructuring (for example, with ellipses and brackets) that it would be distracting to the reader.**
- **Always provide a full citation, with a pinpoint cite, for every quotation and paraphrase in your document.**

---

7. Conclusion

The conclusion should be brief and should be a highlight of the conclusions you reached earlier in the discussion or analysis section of the memo. In many ways, the conclusion will resemble your brief answers,

although it tends to provide more information than the brief answers do. Do not include citations in your conclusion. Simply sum up your analysis. You need not divide the conclusion into numbered sections as you did your questions and brief answers. The conclusion should not present any material that has not previously appeared in the body of the memo.

If you cannot draw a conclusion because the authorities are in conflict, say so. It is not your function to predict the client's chances, but rather to report and analyze the authorities.

It is possible that during the course of your research you determine that certain information is needed or that a certain course of action should be followed, such as locating witnesses or propounding interrogatories to the adverse party. You may include these recommendations as part of your conclusion, or you may prefer to create a new section titled "Recommendations." Similarly, if certain issues have not been discussed, identify those excluded issues. In some instances, tables, photographs, or copies of cases or statutes will be attached to the memorandum in a separate appendix. If your memo is unusually long, you may wish to add a table of contents to help the reader. See Appendix A for a sample memorandum.

Ethics Alert

Being Objective

The duty owed to clients of competent representation requires that clients be fully informed of both the strengths and weaknesses of their cases. Legal memoranda must thus be neutral and objective and must fully analyze cases and other authorities that may be adverse to a client so the client and counsel may jointly make decisions pertinent to the case. Counsel may not bring or file frivolous actions and can be sanctioned for doing so. Fed. R. Civ. P. 11. Thus, you are ethically bound to research all matters relating to a client's case, even unfavorable authorities.

C. A Blueprint for Preparing a Memorandum

Although legal professionals will invariably adopt individual approaches in preparing a legal memorandum, there are several steps you can follow to ensure you provide a thoughtful, complete, and objective analysis of a client's case. The process usually begins with an assignment from your supervising attorney. The assignment may be written but will usually be given to you orally. Take careful notes, ask when the memo is due, and whether it will be sent to the client. Do not be reluctant to go back to the attorney if you later discover you need additional facts or information. Take the following steps:

1. Consider whether the issue is governed by federal law or state law. Next, consider whether it is a matter more likely to be covered by statutory law or case law.
2. Draft a preliminary issue statement based on the information you have. For example, your initial issue might be written, "Under California law, are non-competition agreements entered into by employees valid?"
3. Develop a research plan. If the matter is likely to be covered by statutory law, review the applicable statutes and then examine the case annotations following the text of the statutes. If the matter is likely to be covered by case law, consider starting with an encyclopedia or reviewing digests to find cases. If you are unfamiliar with the topic of law, initially consult a treatise or encyclopedia to "get your feet wet." Prepare a list of key words or search terms to use when examining the indexes to the statutes, encyclopedias, treatises, digests, and other authorities. For example, terms might include "employment," "employer-employee," "noncompetition," and "competition."
4. Conduct research, paying attention to leads to other sources, such as law reviews, A.L.R. annotations, and Restatements. Take careful notes as you read the authorities you locate.
5. Shepardize or KeyCite the primary authorities to ensure they are still valid and to direct you to other authorities on point.
6. Brief the cases you locate if this is helpful to you.
7. Organize your notes, using index cards, notebooks, sheets of paper, or computer files. Use these to construct a working outline.
8. Begin writing. If you have difficulty getting started, begin with the section that is easiest to write. In many instances, this will be the statement of facts. Proceed to other sections, always checking to make sure your writing is balanced and objective. Consider using the IRAC method in the discussion section to ensure you are analyzing cases rather than merely summarizing them.
9. Revise the memo. Check for content. Make sure each conclusion you have drawn is supported by legal authority. Review to ensure that the cases you discuss include sufficient facts that the reader will immediately be able to discern why they do or do not apply to the client's situation.
10. Edit the memo to eliminate unnecessary material and clarify ambiguous portions. Proofread to omit spelling and typographical errors. Do a final check of citation form. Present the finished product to the assigning attorney, along with copies of cases and other authorities. Place a copy in the client's file, keep a "chron copy" (a copy placed in a chronological file you maintain showing your work throughout the year), and place or "save" a copy in the firm's memo bank, if applicable. See Figure 17-5.

Figure 17-5
<u>Examples of Elements in a Legal Memo</u>

	Poor	*Better*
Issue	Does the client have a cause of action?	Under the Civil Rights Act of 1964, does harassment occur when a single remark is made in the workplace — namely, "hey, babe — looking good"?
Brief Answer	No	Because courts consistently require that conduct be severe in order to constitute harassment, the single remark made in this case is highly unlikely to rise to the level of sexual harassment.
Facts	Our client, Grace Parks, was subjected to intolerable conduct in the workplace when her supervisor leered at her and teased, "hey, babe — looking good" when Grace entered a conference room full of employees. Grace was thoroughly humiliated by this remark.	Our client, Grace Parks, is an employee of ABC Inc. Two months ago, when Ms. Parks entered a conference room, her male supervisor stated to her, in front of others, "hey, babe — looking good." Ms. Parks would like to know if this remark constitutes sexual harassment.
Discussion	A poor discussion will: • Merely summarize cases • Fail to include facts from cases • Rely upon non-similar cases, such as those involving physical conduct and touching rather than verbal utterances • Lack objectivity and examine only cases in which harassment is found and ignore cases unfavorable to the client • Finish with mere summaries of cases and fail to draw conclusions as to whether harassment is likely to be found	A better discussion will: • Provide the text of any governing statute • Discuss and analyze cases with similar fact patterns, focusing on cases involving verbal remarks rather than those involving physical conduct and touching • Discuss cases holding that a single remark can constitute harassment and compare and contrast these to client's case in order to reach a conclusion • Use the IRAC method to analyze cases
Conclusion	A poor conclusion will: • Be overlong • Include citations • Include topics not previously discussed in the body of the memorandum	A better conclusion will: • Quickly summarize the major points of the memorandum

Tips for Memo Writing

- Do not use first person pronouns. Avoid statements such as "The next case I found . . . " or "I believe . . . ."
- Use complete *Bluebook* or appropriate citation form so that if the memo becomes the basis for a document submitted to court, you will not have to return to the law library or go online to track down cites.
- Some law firms maintain files or "banks" of previously prepared memos. Before beginning a new project, check the memo bank to see if a memo on your topic has previously been prepared. If no memo bank exists, offer to establish one. Similarly, check with your fellow paralegals to see if anyone else in your office has prepared a memo on a similar topic.
- Some attorneys prefer that all cases cited in the memo be photocopied or printed and attached to the memo for ready reference. Check to see if the individual assigning the memo prefers this practice.
- Gather all documents and materials before you begin to write.
- After you Shepardize or KeyCite, provide your supervisor with copies of cases that negatively affect any cases cited in the memo so they can be reviewed.
- Save memos you have prepared and others you come across in your own mini-memo bank. You may be surprised how often you will need to retrieve previously prepared memos to verify certain legal issues or to use as a starting point for a new project.

CyberSites

http://lscontent.westlaw .com/images/content/ documentation/2009/ OpenMemo09.pdf	West offers a guide on preparing legal memoranda.
http://www.lawnerds.com/ guide/irac.html	This site provides a thorough discussion of analyzing issues using IRAC.
http://www.ualr.edu/ cmbarger/ SAMPLE_MEMO.HTML	A sample memorandum is provided at this site.

Legal Memorandum Assignment for Chapter 17

To: Paralegal
From: Senior Attorney

Our client, Jake Daly, is a famous baseball player. *Celeb Magazine*, a weekly publication similar to *People*, recently featured an advertisement showing an individual who closely resembles Daly. Although the individual's face in the ad is shadowed, the "look-alike" is wearing a baseball uniform and is shown in Daly's highly distinctive pitching stance. The look-alike is holding a can of beer. The text accompanying the ad reads, "The great ones drink the great beer: Mountain Beer." Daly did not authorize the ad, although he does drink Mountain Beer. The magazine also displays a photo of Daly leaving a well-known restaurant with a group of friends. This photo is displayed with those of several other celebrities in a pictorial feature titled "Celebs About Town." Daly did not authorize the magazine to take or print this photograph.

Daly would like to sue Mountain Beer and *Celeb Magazine* for infringing his right of publicity. Please prepare a memorandum for me relating to this matter. The memorandum should be no more than eight pages in length and should be double-spaced. Use *Bluebook* or *ALWD* citation form. Our state has no cases or statutes regarding this issue. Therefore, do not restrict your research to the law of any one jurisdiction.

Internet Assignment for Chapter 17

1. Access West's guide to preparing memoranda at http://lscontent.westlaw.com/images/content/documentation/2009/OpenMemo09.pdf.
    a. What is the first step in writing a satisfactory memo?
    b. What are the ideal secondary sources in which to start one's research?
2. Access Professor Barger's site at http://www.ualr.edu/cmbarger/SAMPLE_MEMO.HTML. Review the note icons.
    a. How should the question presented in a memorandum be phrased?
    b. What should be omitted from a statement of facts?
3. Access the Law Nerds site at http://www.lawnerds.com/guide/irac.html.
    a. What is the most important part of the IRAC equation?
    b. What two parts comprise restating a rule?

Legal Briefs

[W]e must insist that parties not clog the system by presenting us with a slubby mass of words rather than a true brief. Hence we have briefing rules.

N/S Corp. v. Liberty Mut. Ins. Co.,
127 F.3d 1145, 1146 (9th Cir. 1997)

A. Introduction
B. Tips on Writing Briefs
C. Trial Court Briefs
D. Appellate Briefs
E. Ten Pointers for Effective Brief Writing

Chapter Overview

This chapter will introduce you to documents submitted to court. These documents, commonly referred to as "briefs," differ from letters and memoranda in their purpose and audience. While letters and memoranda are intended primarily to inform and explain, briefs are intended to persuade judges. The writing techniques used for briefs are therefore different because each element of a brief must be crafted with its objective in mind: to persuade a court to rule in a client's favor.

A. Introduction

Briefs are formal written legal arguments submitted to a court, and they attempt to persuade a court to rule in favor of a party. On occasion, such a brief is referred to as a "Memorandum of Law" or "Memorandum of Points and Authorities." Be careful not to confuse these court briefs with the internal office memoranda previously discussed. Similarly, be careful

not to confuse the briefs discussed in this chapter with the case briefs or case summaries discussed in Chapter 4.

The fact that the document submitted to a court is referred to as a "brief" does not necessarily mean the document is concise. A common joke is that only those in the legal profession would call a 50-page document a brief!

Briefs are submitted in pending actions and may relate to a variety of issues, including the following:

- a motion requesting a preliminary injunction
- a motion to dismiss a case
- a motion to change venue
- a motion to exclude evidence
- a motion to compel a party to answer interrogatories
- a motion for a new trial
- an appeal of a judgment

There are several types of briefs. Most are submitted to trial courts to persuade the judge to rule a certain way. After a trial is concluded, the losing party may appeal the judgment and will submit a brief, called an "appellate brief," to the reviewing or appeals court. Finally, briefs may be submitted to administrative agencies or other government units.

If an office memorandum has been prepared in a case, it may be a good starting point for a brief because it will contain an analysis and discussion of the authorities pertinent to the case. Although the memo then may serve as a source of cases and other authorities, the manner in which these were discussed in the memo and the manner in which these will be discussed in a brief differ significantly. The style of writing used in a memo is informative and objective because your function as a memo writer is to explain the law. The style of writing used in a brief is persuasive because your function as a brief writer is to persuade the court.

One effective way to learn to write better briefs is to review those of others. A number of websites offer free access to briefs, including http://www.legaline.com/freebriefslinks.html, and Westlaw now offers the world's largest "brief bank" (accessible by keyword or topic searching or through hyperlinks in cases). Lexis also offers briefs, motions, and pleadings through its Total Litigator service. These brief banks enable researchers to locate briefs on the precise point of law for their own cases.

B.   Tips on Writing Briefs

There are three critical rules to follow when writing court briefs:

1. *Be Persuasive*

In some ways, you may find it easier to prepare a brief than a memo. Most writers find it difficult to maintain the neutral and objective tone required

in a memo. It is often easier and more natural to advocate the client's position.

Aim at being persuasive throughout every portion of the brief. Even the Table of Contents and headings provide an opportunity for you to persuade the court. Consider the following two headings:

PUNITIVE DAMAGES

DEFENDANT'S FRAUD ENTITLES
PLAINTIFF TO PUNITIVE DAMAGES

Although both headings inform the reader that the next topic will deal with punitive damages, the second one is considerably more forceful. Many writers include a "reason" in their point headings throughout their briefs. This is an extremely effective technique for drafting point headings. Consider the following point heading:

PUNITIVE DAMAGES SHOULD BE AWARDED BECAUSE
DEFENDANT'S CONDUCT WAS INTENTIONAL,
WILLFUL, AND RECKLESS

Each point heading should have all capital letters, be centered, and be assigned a Roman numeral placed directly above the point heading. Use parallel structure, so if a reader reads only the headings in a brief, the headings provide a clearly written outline of the argument. Maintain consistency in your headings. Headings are usually one sentence. Maintain this approach and do not switch between sentences and phrases. Do not include citations in your headings.

If your headings appear as elements in a Table of Contents, you have another opportunity to reach the reader. The Table of Contents will be the first part of the brief to be viewed. Use this opening as your first attempt to convince the reader to rule in favor of the client.

To achieve a persuasive tone, remember the techniques discussed in Chapter 15:

- Use active voice;
- Use parallel structure;
- Use strong, forceful, and descriptive words;
- Use sentence structure to achieve strength, placing the strongest part of the sentence in the dominant clause;
- Use placement to achieve attention, placing the strongest parts of your argument in the beginning and ending of the brief;
- Use repetition, but sparingly, for drama and emphasis; and
- Use positive statements rather than negative statements.

After you have completed the brief, review it carefully to eliminate words such as "clearly" and "obviously," which are overused, ineffective, and often insulting words inexperienced writers believe will persuade a

reader. Similarly, omit vague and equivocal expressions such as "it would seem that" or "apparently," which have no place in a document aimed at persuading a reader.

Although accuracy, brevity, and clarity are always essential in legal writing, these characteristics are mandated by the United States Supreme Court's rules, which provide as follows: "The failure of a petitioner to present with accuracy, brevity, and clarity whatever is essential to ready and adequate understanding of the points requiring consideration is sufficient reason for the Court to deny a petition." Sup. Ct. R. 14(4). In May 2000, the *National Law Journal* reported that the Kentucky Supreme Court suspended an attorney for 60 days for submitting a "virtually incomprehensible" brief. Similarly, in *In re King*, No. 05-56485-C, 2006 WL 581256 (Bankr. W.D. Tex. Feb. 21, 2006), the court stated that it could not determine the substance of the defendant's legal argument and therefore denied defendant's motion "for being incomprehensible."

2. Be Honest

Although you need not present the adversary's argument, you have an ethical duty to be honest, and bring to the court's attention anything that would assist the court in reaching a decision. If, in the course of your research, you discover cases that do not support your position, mention these in a straightforward fashion, and then show the reader why they do not apply to your situation.

Act on the assumption that your adversary will discover these cases and that if you introduce these problem areas yourself, you will decrease the effect of the adversary's "smoking gun." Moreover, the integrity shown by an honest and direct discussion of these issues will carry over to the rest of your argument. Assertions you make in other sections of the brief will then be likely to be believed and trusted by the reader.

Discussing these authorities does not mean you need to highlight them and make the adversary's case for him or her. Use placement in the brief to assist you and "bury" the most troublesome parts of your argument in the middle of the discussion. Consider using passive voice to minimize the impact of these weak spots.

3. Know the Rules

Most courts issue rules relating to briefs filed before them. Some of these rules relate to the size, color, and quality of the paper used, while others relate to citation form, length of the document, and the elements required in a brief. Many courts establish maximum page or word count limits and require that briefs exceeding certain page limits include tables of contents and authorities. For example, the First Circuit Court of Appeals now requires a copy of all briefs submitted to be on a computer readable disk as well as in hardcopy form, unless the brief is submitted

electronically. Similarly, a newly revised federal rule has reduced the page allowance for principal briefs from 50 pages to 30 pages. Fed. R. App. P. 32. The United States Supreme Court rules require electronic versions of all briefs submitted to the Court. Sup. Ct. R. 25(9). Make sure you have obtained a copy of the court rules and have thoroughly read them before you prepare your brief because failure to follow the rules may be fatal. Nearly all courts have posted their rules on the Internet. You can link to the rules for all federal courts through the website http:// www.uscourts.gov. Each state's judicial website is given in Table T.1 of *The Bluebook*. Additionally, your law firm may have a copy of the rules in its law library. If not, contact the court clerk and order a copy of the rules. Always check the date the rules were issued, and verify that the rules are still current.

C. Trial Court Briefs

1. Introduction

Briefs submitted to trial courts are aimed at persuading the judge to rule in a certain way. These briefs may be accompanied by other documents, such as deposition transcripts, declarations, or exhibits. They may be written in support of a certain position or in response or opposition to another party's argument. On occasion, they are written in response to a judge's request for legal argument on a certain issue.

In some jurisdictions this brief is referred to as a Memorandum of Law or Memorandum of Points and Authorities. Although some jurisdictions have rules relating to the format, citation form, or length of these trial court briefs, these rules tend to be less extensive than the rules for appellate briefs.

As in all legal writing, remember your audience. The judge who will read the brief will be busy and will become frustrated with a lengthy and repetitious document. The other reader, opposing counsel, will have a hostile attitude toward your brief and will scrutinize the brief looking for errors and flaws in everything from citation form to Shepardizing and KeyCiting to the conclusions you draw from your research. Although it is a futile effort to believe you can persuade opposing counsel, aim at presenting a brief that at least cannot be attacked by opposing counsel. A sample trial brief is found at Appendix B.

2. Elements of a Trial Brief

The elements of a brief submitted to a trial court will vary to some degree from jurisdiction to jurisdiction. The following elements are found in most briefs, but you should be sure to review your local court rules to determine if there is a required format.

a. Caption

Because the brief submitted to the court is a pleading, it must display the "Caption" of the case. The Caption identifies the pertinent information about the case: the court, the parties, the docket number, and the title of the document, such as "Defendant's Memorandum of Law in Support of Motion to Change Venue." Rule 8 and Table BT.1 of *The Bluebook* and *ALWD* Rule 3.0 provide instructions for abbreviations and capitalization in headings and titles of court documents.

b. Introductory Statement

The party submitting the brief typically begins with a brief Introductory Statement such as the following: "Defendant Vincent T. Parker respectfully submits the following Memorandum of Law in support of his Motion to Change Venue."

c. Statement of Facts

To save the judge the bother of reviewing all of the pleadings submitted in a case to determine what the case is about, the brief should include a Statement of Facts. Although these facts must be accurate, you should strive to present these facts in a manner most favorable to the client. Use active voice and descriptive words to emphasize facts supporting your position. Use passive voice and placement of unfavorable facts in less noticeable positions to minimize facts that are troublesome. For example, consider the following two ways of describing a defendant's experience with the law:

- Defendant's version: The record discloses prior convictions.
- Prosecution's version: The Defendant has a long history of serious criminal conduct and victimization of innocent parties, including three separate convictions involving violence to women and two additional convictions for assault with a deadly weapon, specifically, a ten-inch jagged-edge hunting knife.

Most facts are presented in chronological order, though you may depart from this order and discuss facts by topic if you wish to emphasize certain facts. Present the facts in the third person and in past tense unless they are still unfolding as you write the brief. Be careful not to jump the gun and argue your case. This section of the brief should be devoted solely to facts, for example, events that have occurred, not legal theories and analysis. Personalize your client by referring to him or her by name (Ms. LaPointe) rather than role (Plaintiff). Although most writers present their Statement of Facts in a narrative, some courts require numbered paragraphs, each of which includes a reference to supporting materials and documents.

Do not overlook the importance of the Statement of Facts. Because most judges have a thorough understanding of the law, they may begin forming impressions and drawing conclusions even as they read the facts.

Moreover, at this stage of the brief, the reader is still enthusiastic and fresh. Do more than merely recite the facts in a dull fashion. Use the Statement of Facts to win over your reader.

d. Argument

The Argument section of a brief is the heart of the brief. This section contains the analysis of the legal authorities that support the client's position and demonstrates why and how those authorities support the position advocated.

Divide your Argument into sections, giving each section a Roman numeral and a heading, and centering the heading on the page. The headings should be as persuasive as possible. You may need subheadings. These can consist of short phrases or even single words. Subheadings are usually preceded by capital letters (A, B, and C). Citations should appear in the body of your brief. Although footnotes are popular with some writers, they are distracting to most readers.

The use of footnotes in legal documents engenders vigorous debate. Footnotes are commonly seen in law review articles and in legal treatises; however, they are seen far less frequently in published cases. There are two schools of thought on the use of footnotes in legal memos and court briefs. Some experts believe that the placement of a footnote number at the end of a sentence jars curious readers who are then compelled to glance at the bottom of the page, leaving the narrative discussion in the body of the text. These experts believe that if the point of a logical argument is to carry the reader through seamlessly from the first sentence to the last, footnotes detract from this objective. Conversely, if some readers are so disciplined that they ignore the footnote notations and continue reading the narrative text, of what use are the footnotes? Despite these criticisms, footnotes continue to be used. Recently, in fact, some writing experts have advocated more extensive use of footnotes on the basis that citations and extraneous comments clutter arguments and are better placed at the bottom of a page. In fact, some judges in California are experimenting with writing citation-free opinions, placing all citations and extraneous comments in footnotes in an effort to create more readable opinions. Other judges have reached the opposite conclusion, believing that if something is important enough to be discussed, it should be discussed in the body of the text; if a point is not important enough to be in the body of the text, it probably doesn't merit any discussion whatsoever. Check your firm or office policy or practice, but in any event avoid "talking" footnotes (those containing argument or discussion) and footnotes that "wrap" from one page to the next, or even beyond. Some readers will leave the narrative discussion, review the footnote that meanders on for several pages, and then simply resume reading where they are, rather than returning to the page on which the footnote began. Endnotes are seen in other disciplines but seldom, if ever, in legal documents.

As you discuss cases and other authorities, emphasize the extent to which favorable cases are similar to the client's case. In the interest of credibility, point out unfavorable authorities and then distinguish them from the client's position by showing why and how they are different and thus inapplicable. Discuss cases in the past tense because references to "this case states" or "the plaintiff argues" will be interpreted as references to your brief itself rather than precedents. Avoid referring to the court by the name of a case. For example, assume you are discussing the case *Horn v. Wagner*, 382 U.S. 116 (1988). In discussing this case, do not write, "The *Horn* Court held . . . ." Although this approach is common, it is nonetheless disfavored by some writing experts. The only way a court is referred to is by its title ("the United States Supreme Court") or by the name of its chief or presiding judge or justice ("the Roberts Court"). In fact, the United States Supreme Court's guidelines for counsel arguing before the Court state, "Do not refer to an opinion of the Court by saying: 'In Justice Ginsburg's opinion.' You should say: 'In the Court's opinion, written by Justice Ginsburg.'" U.S. Supreme Court, U.S. Supreme Court Guide for Counsel 11 (2010), http://www.supremecourt.gov/oral_arguments/guide forcounsel.pdf.

Review your arsenal of writing tips, and organize your Argument so it flows logically. Consider which techniques make for a strong and persuasive document, and give care to techniques that allow you to minimize cases unfavorable to the client's position. Be definite. Avoid expressions such as "it seems" or "it is likely," which immediately convey the message to the reader that the writer is not sure of the position taken.

Avoid any use of the first person. Do not write, "we argue" or "it is my contention." Instead use expressions such as "Defendant will show" or "Plaintiff has contended." This keeps the focus on the parties, not on you as the writer.

Be sure you have done more than merely summarize a series of cases. Analyze and apply the cases and other authorities to the client's case so the reader can readily see why these cases mandate the result you advocate. Consider using the CRAC approach or one of its variants (discussed in Chapter 17) to ensure you thoroughly analyze and discuss each issue. It is perfectly acceptable to rely upon cases in which a different result was reached than the one you desire. Simply write, "Although the Court denied injunctive relief in *Gray v. Smith*, 508 U.S. 110, 112 (1995), that denial was caused by the plaintiff's failure to take prompt action. In the present case, however . . . . Thus, the decision reached in *Gray* is not applicable to this case." Use an assertive thesis statement (discussed in Chapter 17) to give focus to your argument.

Although the aim of your document is to persuade, you need not denigrate the adversary's position. A logical and well-reasoned Argument will command respect. A hostile and sarcastic diatribe will destroy your credibility and render your brief suspect.

```
┌──────────────────── Practice Tip ────────────────────┐
│                                                       │
│  Responding to an Adversary's Brief                   │
│                                                       │
│  When you are responding to briefs filed by           │
│  adversaries, review the authorities cited in his or  │
│  her brief. Dissents in cases relied on by your       │
│  adversary often provide good ammunition for drafting │
│  a reply or response brief.                           │
│                                                       │
└───────────────────────────────────────────────────────┘
```

e. Conclusion

The Conclusion should be a very brief recap of the highlights of the Argument. Because it is a summary, no citations should be included. The last sentence of the Conclusion should remind the reader of the relief requested, such as the following: "For the foregoing reasons, Defendant Vincent T. Parker respectfully requests that the Court grant his Motion for Change of Venue."

Many writers use this request for relief as their entire Conclusion. Although this is easy for the writer because it eliminates the difficult task of condensing a complex argument into a readable summary, do not forgo this last opportunity to persuade, especially because a reader often picks up interest at the end of a project and will thus pay special attention to the Conclusion. The Conclusion should be no more than half a page. Any Conclusion longer than this will likely be ignored.

f. Signature and Date

The brief is typically "closed" much like a letter. The favored closing is as follows:

Respectfully submitted,

Dated: _____   _____

Sandra Taylor Jones
Jones and White
Attorneys for Defendant
Vincent T. Parker

Jones and White
162 C Street, Suite 1725
Chicago, Illinois 97205
Bar No. 764110

g. Certificates of Service and Compliance

For all pleadings filed in court you must verify that all parties have received copies. A Certificate of Service is placed at the conclusion of a pleading and states that a copy of the pleading has been served on all

parties. The method of service, such as hand delivery or first class mail, and the date of service must be specified. Many courts also require that those submitting briefs acknowledge in a separate Certificate of Compliance that they have complied with all court rules relating to the format, length, and other requirements for submissions to the court.

h. Exhibits

You may have attached Exhibits to the brief for review by the court. These may consist of correspondence, transcripts of deposition testimony, answers to interrogatories, affidavits, or other documents. Each Exhibit should be fully described in the brief itself and then should be appended after the end of the brief and clearly labeled. Do not insert Exhibits into the middle of your Argument because they will disrupt the flow of your narrative and detract from the persuasive nature of your brief. Use tabs to make it easier for the judge to locate your Exhibits. If there are several Exhibits, prepare a Table of Contents for your Exhibits.

Remember these three techniques for effective brief writing:

(i)   Be scrupulously accurate in your Statement of the Facts of the case. Include unfavorable facts, and resist the temptation to over-emphasize facts in your favor.

(ii) Focus on your best arguments. If some arguments are "long shots," do not include them. Inclusion of weak or ludicrous arguments causes readers to question the writer's credibility.

(iii) Analyze the cases you rely on rather than merely summarizing them. Describe the cases relied upon, giving sufficient facts so the reader will see how and why these cases are similar (or dissimilar) to your case. Give the holding and reasoning from the cited cases. Then compare and contrast the cases you rely on with the facts of your case. Convince by applying the holding and reasoning from the cited authorities to your case.

See Appendix B for a sample brief for a trial court.

Ethics Alert

Know the Rules

Always check the court's rules to ensure that your brief complies with all requirements as to form, contents, and filing. In a recent case, an appeal brief was filed six minutes late, and the court dismissed the appeal as untimely. *Alva v. Teen Help,* **469 F.3d 946 (10th Cir. 2006). Thus, failure to comply with even seemingly minor court rules and requirements may well be malpractice.**

D. Appellate Briefs

1. Introduction

After a trial court decision or other final ruling, the losing party may appeal the decision. Although the trial court judge who rules on a motion supported by a memorandum of law may be familiar with the case and the facts presented in a trial brief and may, in fact, have been assigned to a case from its filing, appellate judges will have no such familiarity with cases before them. You will thus have to be as articulate and persuasive as possible to convince the appellate court to rule in a client's favor. An appellate brief is a formal document filed with a reviewing court. The appellate brief seeks reversal, affirmance, or some modification of a lower court's action. A sample appellate brief is found in Appendix C.

2. Steps in the Appeal Process

After a judgment is entered in a case, the losing party, usually called the appellant but sometimes called the petitioner, initiates an appeal by filing a notice of appeal. This serves to notify the adverse party, called the appellee or occasionally the respondent, that an appeal has been instituted. This notice of appeal must be timely. In federal court, in a civil case, the notice of appeal must be filed within 30 days (60 days if the United States is a party) after the date the judgment is entered. Most state courts have similarly limited time periods for filing the notice of appeal. Failure to timely file the notice of appeal is fatal, and usually no relief can be granted from the untimely filing of the notice. The notice of appeal is usually filed not in the appellate court but with the trial court.

A filing fee is required when the notice of appeal is filed. The appellant then must order the transcript (or selected portions of it) from the court reporter who transcribed the trial proceeding because it is this record of the proceedings upon which the appeal is based. The trial court record also includes all pleadings filed in the case together with all exhibits entered at the trial.

Rules governing appeal briefs are usually more stringent than rules for any other documents submitted to courts. Moreover, these rules are rigidly adhered to, and a brief that is too long or lacks the proper color cover sheet will be rejected. Briefs submitted to appellate courts may be required to be commercially printed rather than merely typewritten or word-processed. Know the rules.

The appellant sets forth his or her grounds for the appeal in a document called the appellant's brief or opening brief. The appellee will then prepare and file his or her response brief. The appellee's brief must usually be filed within a specified time period (often 30 days) after the appellant's brief. Some courts allow the appellant to submit a brief in reply or rebuttal to certain issues raised by the appellee's brief. In many

cases, however, the appellate court will determine the appeal solely on the basis of the appellant's brief, the appellee's brief, and the record from below. No testimony is received.

The clerk of the appellate court will then schedule oral argument. Each side typically has only a half-hour to present the oral argument. The appellate judges usually sit as a panel of three and may ask questions of the parties. Parties should not make the mistake of believing they will save a persuasive issue for oral argument and omit it from the brief. Briefs should contain *all* of the arguments to be presented to the appellate court because a party may be interrupted by questions from the judges and never have the opportunity to present a certain issue during oral argument.

After oral argument, the appellate court will take the case under advisement or submission and will review the briefs and records, reach a decision, and write the appellate opinion. This may take several months. The parties will then be notified of the decision. If the losing party believes the appellate court has overlooked something, he or she may request a rehearing. Requests for rehearings are usually denied.

The losing party may then proceed to the next higher court, if it exists. In most states, there is an intermediate appellate court, and then the highest state court, usually called the supreme court. Adverse decisions of the highest court in a state may be appealed to the United States Supreme Court only if a federal question is at issue. Even then, the United States Supreme Court may deny certiorari and refuse to take the appeal.

In federal cases, after a party loses a trial in the district court, an appeal is taken to the appropriate circuit court of appeals. For most litigants, this is the end of the process because an appeal from the circuit courts of appeal to the United States Supreme Court is dependent upon issuance of the writ of certiorari by the Court. As you will recall from reading Chapter 2, issuance of the writ is discretionary with the Court, and the vast majority of petitions for writs of certiorari are denied. Because appellate work is complicated, some firms specialize solely in appellate practice and prepare appeals for cases tried by other firms.

3. *Standards of Appellate Review*

The appellant is not entitled to a reversal of the trial court decision simply because he or she is unhappy with the outcome. The appellant must show that an error of law occurred at the trial. For purposes of appeal, the appellate court will assume that the facts found at the trial were true (unless these facts are totally unsupported by the record). Thus, if a jury determines a defendant was driving at a speed of 70 miles per hour and this caused an accident injuring a plaintiff, an appellate court cannot substitute its judgment for that of the jury and determine the defendant's rate of speed was 45 miles per hour. It may, however, decide that a prejudicial error of law was committed at the trial and that this affected the jury's verdict. Examples of such errors of law include admission of evidence, such as hearsay, that should have been excluded,

errors given in the instructions to the jury, and exclusion of evidence that should have been admitted.

Even if an error of law occurred at the trial, the appellate court will not reverse the lower court decision unless this error was clearly erroneous or prejudicial to the appellant. Many errors can occur in a trial. Harmless errors, however, are not reversible. A prejudicial error is one that likely affected the outcome of the case. Additionally, appellate courts review only those errors that were raised at trial. Otherwise, trial judges would not have the opportunity to correct their own mistakes.

Generally, appellate courts give great weight to the trial court's conduct of a trial because the trial court was in the best position to evaluate the credibility of witnesses and to make "on the spot" determinations. Only if the trial court clearly erred or abused its discretion will its decisions be reversed.

Because of the difficulty in meeting these strict requirements and because of the high costs involved, the vast majority of trial court decisions are not appealed.

4. Amicus Curiae Briefs

On occasion, an issue being appealed is of importance not only to the litigants, but also to a wider group of people. The case may involve constitutional issues that will have a substantial impact on a significant number of individuals. In such cases, these individuals, companies, or entities who were not parties to the suit may request that the court allow them to file amicus curiae ("friend of the court") briefs. Appellate courts have discretion to accept or reject such requests, though they will permit amicus curiae briefs if they believe such briefs would be of assistance to the court.

5. Elements of an Appellate Brief

Many of the elements of an appellate brief are the same as the elements of a memorandum of law or trial brief. In some instances, portions of an earlier memorandum or trial brief may be used for the appellate brief. (See Figure 18-1 for a comparison of the elements of trial court briefs and appellate court briefs.)

Following are the elements typically found in an appellate brief, although, as always, you should carefully review the rules of the appellate court to which you are submitting the brief to determine whether there are required rules as to format or elements for the brief.

a. Cover Sheet

The Cover Sheet or title page identifies the following information about the case:

- the specific appellate court hearing the appeal
- the names of the appellant and appellee

- the docket number of the appeal
- the lower court that handled the trial or prior appeal
- the title of the document, such as "Appellant's Brief"
- the attorneys representing the party submitting the brief

Some courts require the party instituting the appeal to be identified first in the caption. This often results in a reversal of the plaintiff's and defendant's names. For example, if the original case was *Davids v. Stephenson* and Stephenson appealed the trial court's decision, some courts require that Stephenson's name be listed first. Due to the confusion caused by this rule, most courts retain the original listing of the parties, no matter who appeals.

Many courts require that the Cover Sheet be a certain color. For example, the United States Supreme Court requires that the appellant's cover color be light blue, the appellee's cover color be light red, and an amicus curiae brief (in support of the petitioner) cover color be light green. This assists the Justices reading the briefs because they can identify at a glance whose brief they are reading.

b. Identification of Parties

Unless all of the parties are identified on the cover sheet, a list of all parties to the lower court proceeding usually must be given, including parent companies and wholly owned subsidiaries. This identification statement (often called a "corporate disclosure statement") allows Justices to review for conflicts and disqualify themselves from cases involving parties they know or with whom they have financial involvement.

Figure 18-1
Elements of Trial Court Briefs and Appellate Court Briefs

Trial Court Briefs	Appellate Court Briefs
Caption	Cover Sheet
Introductory Statement	Identification of Parties
	Table of Contents
	Table of Authorities
	Jurisdictional Statement
	Constitutional and Statutory Provisions
	Questions Presented
Statement of Facts	Statement of the Case
	Summary of the Argument
Argument	Argument
Conclusion	Conclusion
Signature	Signature
Certificates of Service and Compliance	Certificates of Service and Compliance
Exhibits	Appendix

c. Table of Contents

A Table of Contents or Index, with page references, must be included. Although the primary purpose of a Table of Contents is to identify for the reader the location of each element in the brief, a secondary purpose is to serve as an outline of a party's contentions. Many software programs will automatically generate a table of contents.

The Table of Contents should include all of the headings and subheadings contained in the brief. These should be phrased as persuasively as possible. Thus, a heading such as "The best evidence of likelihood of confusion of trademarks is evidence of actual confusion" is considerably stronger than the neutral heading "likelihood of confusion." Headings are usually presented in uppercase letters. Subheadings appear with initial letters capitalized (or with capitalization following *Bluebook* Rule 8) and are usually underlined.

Judges reviewing the Table of Contents will be able to comprehend quickly the scope of your argument. If you organize your brief effectively and phrase your headings persuasively, you are able to make a favorable impression on the judges reviewing the brief even before the argument is begun.

d. Table of Authorities

An appellate brief must include a list of every primary and secondary authority referred to in the brief together with an indication of the page(s) on which it appears. Complete citations in *Bluebook* form must be given (unless court rules provide otherwise). Reference the location of all full citations and all short forms.

Authorities should be grouped together so that all cases are listed together, then all constitutional provisions, followed by statutes, followed by secondary authorities. Within each group, arrangement is alphabetical (or numerical, for constitutions and statutes). For cases, include subsequent history but not pinpoints. If several cases begin with the same name (for example, if the United States is a plaintiff in several actions), alphabetize by the defendant's name, so that *United States v. Baker* appears before *United States v. Coyle*. For secondary authorities with author names, alphabetize by the author's last name, so that a journal article written by Bethany Adams appears before a journal article written by Ann Branson. For additional guidance, review the briefs filed with the United States Supreme Court on the Court's website at http://www.supremecourt.gov.

The Table of Authorities allows readers to identify quickly the location in a brief of a discussion of a certain case or statute. It may be helpful for a reader to compare the appellant's discussion of *Smith v. Jones* with the appellee's discussion of this same case. The Table of Contents and Table of Authorities cannot be prepared until the brief is in final form because it is only then that you will know on which page a certain topic or case is mentioned.

Paralegals often play a major role in preparing the Table of Contents and Table of Authorities. The task requires painstaking care to ensure

you have carefully noted each time a case is discussed and the exact location of each authority. Moreover, because this task cannot be completed until the brief is completed with no insertions or deletions to cause changes in pagination, it is often a pressure-filled task done at the eleventh hour.

Many software programs will automatically generate a table of authorities from your document. The program "reads" your document, locates the cites, sorts them, alphabetizes them, and then notes where the cites appear in your writing. They also correct some common citation errors. Because the programs extract citations from your document, case citations will undoubtedly appear in both "stand-alone" and "textual sentence" format, meaning that, depending on your usage and placement of citations, the word "Technology" may appear as "Tech." in one case name and as "Technology" in another. Thus, you will need to do some revising to ensure consistency in appearance.

Neither *The Bluebook* nor *ALWD* includes any guidance on preparing a Table of Authorities. Many authors prefer to write out case names in full rather than using abbreviations such as "Sur." or "Hosp." in the Table of Authorities, although citations in a table are clearly in stand-alone format. The preference toward using full case names is based upon the fact that the table will be one of the first pages reviewed by a reader, and the presentation of full case names is polished and complete.

If your word processor does not automatically prepare the Table of Authorities, use index cards to list each case and then shuffle them until they are in alphabetical order. Be sure to note if a case is discussed on more than one page. Carefully review the footnotes because they may also include citations you will need to include in the Table of Authorities. Although most word processors automatically compile a table of contents and a Table of Authorities, you should always double-check for accuracy. See Appendix D.

e. Jurisdictional Statement

The appellate brief should include a concise statement of the grounds upon which the court's jurisdiction rests, including a reference to the pertinent authority. This Jurisdictional Statement simply tells the appellate court which statute allows the appeal.

A sample Jurisdictional Statement would read:

> This Court of Appeals for the Eighth Circuit has jurisdiction to hear this appeal pursuant to 15 U.S.C. § 1071(b) (2006).

f. Constitutional and Statutory Provisions

If the case involves constitutional provisions, statutes, ordinances, or regulations, they must be set forth in full together with their citation in *Bluebook* form. If the provisions involved are especially lengthy, you can set forth their pertinent parts. Alternatively, their citation alone will be sufficient so long as they are set forth verbatim in an appendix to the brief.

g. Questions Presented

Many courts require the parties to set forth the issues or questions presented for review. Some writers prefer true question format while others rely on the "whether" format. These questions are somewhat similar to the questions presented in an office memorandum but should be drafted in such a persuasive manner that the desired answer is obvious. An example would be as follows:

> Whether the trial court erred in excluding evidence showing the Plaintiff provoked the disagreement between the parties.

This question includes sufficient facts so the reader understands the issue you intend to address. It suggests an affirmative answer and is written persuasively from a defendant's point of view. The plaintiff's version of such an issue might read thus:

> Whether the trial court properly excluded hearsay evidence relating to Plaintiff's alleged involvement in the incident in which Defendant battered her.

List your stronger issues first, and then proceed to address weaker issues.

Although questions in an office memorandum are immediately followed by brief answers, there is no answer section in an appellate brief because the issues should be phrased such that a "yes" answer is obvious.

h. Statement of the Case

Next to the Argument itself, the Statement of the Case is the most important part of the brief. This Statement of the Case or Statement of Facts includes neither argument nor allegations. The only facts to be included are those that have already been proven at trial. Thus, each fact you state must be followed by a reference to the location in the record or clerk's transcript where such fact was established, as follows:

> Defendant Smith was found to be driving at a speed of 70 miles per hour at the time the accident occurred. R. at 74.

Although you are restricted solely to facts established at trial, you should still strive to present these in a persuasive manner.

In many ways, the Statement of the Case for an appellate brief will parallel the Statement of Facts for a brief submitted to a trial court. You must be honest and straightforward. Establish credibility by being accurate and including all facts, even those unfavorable to the client's position. Remember the techniques of passive voice and placement to de-emphasize unfavorable facts.

The facts are best set forth in a narrative rather than outline form because a narrative is more readable. Present your facts in chronological

order in the past tense. Use descriptive words, verbs, and adjectives to describe favorable fact scenarios. Use parallel structure and careful repetition for drama and impact.

Because the judges reading the brief will be unfamiliar with the case, introduce the Statement of the Case by including background information or procedural history of the case. Some courts require this procedural history to be provided in a separate section, which is called the Statement of the Case and which then differs from a Statement of the Facts. An appropriate statement of procedural history is as follows:

> This is an appeal from a final judgment entered October 12, 2010, by the United States District Court for the District of New Jersey. R. at 79. A jury found Defendant and Appellant ABC, Inc. ("ABC") to have defrauded its customers in the resale of certain automobiles. R. at 70. ABC filed a timely notice of appeal on October 20, 2010. R. at 80.

Do not include argument or legal conclusions in your statement of facts. Thus, do not state that the defendant "battered" the plaintiff (unless such a legal conclusion is supported by the record below). You can, however, recite the facts that the defendant "pushed and shoved" the plaintiff, which will lead the reader to the logical conclusion that a battery occurred.

i. Summary of the Argument

A concise Summary of the Argument is often included. This is a preview or condensation of the argument to follow. This is the first section of the brief that allows advocacy, and you should take advantage of this opportunity to persuade the reader to rule in favor of the client.

Because judges are so busy, they may only have time to skim the entire Argument quickly. This Summary of the Argument, then, may be the best opportunity to win the reader over. Avoid citations in this summary and keep it brief—no more than one page if possible. A mere recitation of the point headings is not sufficient. Present the summary in a narrative fashion.

j. Argument

Like the Argument in a brief submitted to a trial court, the Argument in an appellate brief is the heart of the document. This section analyzes the authorities and convinces the reviewing judges to rule in favor of the client.

Divide the brief into separate sections with each section receiving its own point heading. These point headings should correspond to the questions or issues you set forth earlier. Work at making your point headings persuasive and relevant to your case. If possible, discuss topics in the order in which they were presented in the Statement of the Case. Compare the following point headings drafted for a plaintiff:

A BATTERY IS AN INTENTIONAL AND UNPERMITTED TOUCHING OF ANOTHER.

DEFENDANT SMITH BATTERED EVELYN WOODALL BY REPEATEDLY PUSHING HER AND SHOVING HER TO THE GROUND.

The second point heading is far more likely to grab the reader's attention and persuade the reader that Smith is a horrible fellow. This impression is conveyed as follows:

- By the use of a label, the reader is reminded that Smith is the defendant, that is, "the bad guy";
- The plaintiff is personalized by the use of her name and a reminder of her gender;
- Smith's acts are described in vivid detail.

Written from Smith's perspective, the point heading may read as follows:

BECAUSE PLAINTIFF PROVOKED THE MUTUAL DISAGREEMENT, DAMAGES FOR BATTERY WERE IMPROPERLY AWARDED.

This point heading focuses on the plaintiff's actions rather than the defendant's and provides the critical fact to the reader that the plaintiff provoked the incident. Moreover, the vivid description of the fight is now minimized to a mere "mutual disagreement." Remember to ensure your point headings have parallel structure so that, read in sequence, they provide an outline of the Argument.

Use subheadings within your point headings if needed. Although the point headings should consist of one persuasive sentence, subheadings are typically mere phrases consisting of just a word or short phrase such as "provocation" or "punitive damages."

Through analysis and discussion of legal authorities, the body of the Argument will demonstrate to the reviewing court the errors of law made by the lower court. Do more than merely summarize cases you have located. Compare and contrast the authorities with your particular fact situation so the reader can readily see why the authorities are controlling. Use the CRAC method (or one of its variants, such as CREAC) and set forth your *C*onclusion and the *R*ule that applies; *A*nalyze and *A*pply this rule; and then reiterate the *C*onclusion. Always analogize and compare the facts in the cases you cite to the facts before the court. Use a thesis statement (see Chapter 17) to encapsulate the central argument to follow. In essence, your main point headings serve as thesis statements because they forcefully preview the argument.

Because your Argument will be more credible and respected if you discuss unfavorable precedents and because the adversary will undoubtedly raise them, acknowledge these problem areas. Do so, however, only

after you have set forth the strongest part of your argument and have, perhaps, already gotten the reader "on your side." Discuss why these precedents are not applicable. Explain that the fact pattern in the unfavorable case is so different from the fact pattern in the case being appealed that it cannot serve as precedent; or you may argue that public policy or public interest favors the result for which you argue. If the unfavorable case is older, you can challenge it as antiquated or outmoded. Of course, expect your adversary to characterize it as the landmark or seminal case on the subject. If there are no legal authorities to support your position, argue that public policy and the interests of society compel a change in the law.

k. Conclusion

The Conclusion of an appellate brief often does not summarize the Argument section. This summary has already been given before the Argument. Instead, the Conclusion may merely specify the relief sought, such as requesting that the court affirm or reverse the lower court's decision.

l. Signature

The name of the attorney representing the party is set forth after the conclusion together with an address and telephone number and an identification of the party on whose behalf the brief is submitted.

m. Certificates of Service and Compliance

All documents filed with a court must also be served on all other parties in the action. A Certificate of Service demonstrates to the court that the brief has been provided to all parties and specifies the date and manner of such service, such as hand delivery or first class mail. A Certificate of Compliance verifies that the document submitted complies with word or page count limits or other court rules.

n. Appendix

Appellate briefs often include an Appendix. This may consist of portions of the transcript, pleadings, and the judgment from the lower court action, or exhibits entered as evidence in the trial. When you refer to these materials in your Argument, set forth the relevant portions in the Argument and then refer the reader to the Appendix, where the entire document can be found. Do not interrupt the flow of your narrative with pages of testimony, maps, or graphs. Your aim is to present a logical, persuasive argument. Insertions of extraneous materials disrupt the argument and distract the reader. Make it easy for the reader by using exhibit tabs, including a table of contents for the appended materials, and highlighting relevant material. See Appendix C of this book for a sample appellate brief.

E. Ten Pointers for Effective Brief Writing

Whether you are submitting a brief to a trial court or to an appellate court, remember the following ten tips:

1. Know the rules of the court to which the brief will be submitted.
2. Do more than summarize cases. By following the IRAC or CRAC methods (or a variant), show the reader how and why the cases and other authorities apply to the client's situation. Use a strong thesis statement to give direction to the argument to follow.
3. Write from the client's perspective. Omit any references to yourself as the writer, such as "we believe" or "we argue." The brief is not a forum for your personal opinion but a logical and persuasive argument. Use the third person.
4. Avoid a rote or routine method of writing. If each paragraph discusses one case and ends with a citation to that case, the brief will have a rigid appearance and tone. Variety in the method of analysis of the cases will enhance readability.
5. Avoid string-citing unless there is a definite need to do so. Select the best case supporting a contention and use that case.
6. Avoid sarcasm, humor, or irony. Although these techniques may provide drama in oral argument, they are often misinterpreted in written documents. Maintain a respectful tone toward the court.
7. Avoid the overuse of quotations. It is often the case that a judge has said something so articulately and eloquently that you prefer to use a direct quote. Used sparingly, quotations give force and impact to your writing. Overuse of quotations, however, dilutes their strength. Anyone can retype language found in a case. Do more: Analyze why this language applies to the case at hand.
8. Keep the focus on your argument. If you spend too much time refuting the opponent's position you will shift the focus of the brief from the client's point of view to that of the opponent. Fully argue the client's position before you respond to the opposition.
9. Do not distort or overstate your position. If any portion of the brief is not supported by valid authority, the entire brief is undermined.
10. Use prominent placement to emphasize the strongest arguments. Bury weaker portions of the argument in the middle of the brief, the middles of paragraphs, and the subordinate clauses of sentences.

Appellate Brief Dicta

1. The highest number of amicus curiae briefs filed for one United States Supreme Court case is more than 200 (filed in the 2003 cases *Gratz v. Bollinger* and *Grutter v. Bollinger*, relating to affirmative action in college admissions). Eighty-five percent of all United States Supreme Court cases include at least one amicus brief, often filed by organizations such as the ACLU or AFL-CIO.

2. The United States Supreme Court accepted its first brief in CD-ROM form in 1997. Such CD-ROMs allow direct access to court transcripts, records, and other documents through hyperlinking, making review easier for many Justices. Effective October 2007, the Court requires that all briefs be submitted electronically at the same time they are filed in hard copy.

3. The private company that printed most briefs for the United States Supreme Court ended its hot-metal printing process and went digital in mid-2000. Printing a brief using the hot-metal process generally took three weeks, while digital printing enables reproduction of a brief in three days.

4. New Supreme Court rules recognize brief writers' tendency to try to squeeze additional wording into a brief by using a small typeface and yet still complying with page limits. Thus, effective October 2007, the Court imposed word count limits on briefs, and clarified that words in footnotes count toward these word limits. Sup. Ct. R. 33.

CyberSites

http://ualr.edu/cmbarger	Professor C.M. Barger offers numerous resources and excellent information on legal writing and advocacy, including tips and links relating to appellate briefs.
http://www.legaline.com/freebriefslinks.html	This site provides direct links to numerous free briefs filed with trial and appellate courts.
http:www.uscourts.gov	This site allows direct linking to all federal courts, which post their rules on their own websites. Most courts also post briefs filed, so you can readily review the formatting and presentation of briefs.
http://www.megalaw.com	This site allows access to each state's judicial website, nearly all of which post their rules on their sites.

Court Brief Exercise for Chapter 18

To: Paralegal
From: Meredith Garcia, Partner

On November 15, 2010, our client, Franklin Olsen ("Olsen"), was arrested and charged with burglarizing the home of Lindsay Young ("Young"). Young told police that she found Olsen in her home on October 15, 2010, at dusk, and had the opportunity to see him for about one minute before Olsen left the premises. Young stated that Olsen was dark-haired, wore all black clothing, and was very tall. When Olsen was taken into custody, Young was asked to identify the burglary suspect in a police lineup. Olsen had an attorney represent at the lineup and was one of six white males in the lineup.

The five participants in the lineup other than Olsen ranged in height from 5´8" to 5´10," all had dark hair, and all wore light-colored clothing. All ranged in age from 28 to 35 years.

Olsen is 6´3" tall and is 30 years of age. At the lineup he was instructed to wear all black clothing and was the only individual asked to repeat the phrase, "I've got a gun and I'll use it," which Young had told the police the perpetrator told her at the time of the burglary. At the lineup, Young stated that she thought Olsen "might be" the burglar.

Please prepare a brief (or memorandum of law) in support of a motion to suppress that will persuade our state court (the Anywhere County Court in Anywhere State) that the lineup identification was so suggestive that it should be suppressed and that it lacked such independent reliability that any later in-court identification based on the suggestive lineup must be excluded. Our state has no cases or statutes regarding this issue. Therefore, do not restrict your research to the law of any one jurisdiction.

Court rules impose a ten-page limit on all briefs. In addition, court rules require that the brief be typewritten and double-spaced, and that current *Bluebook* or *ALWD* citation format be followed.

Assignment for Chapter 18

You have been asked to prepare the Table of Authorities for an appellate brief to be filed in the United States District Court for your district. There are no special rules for citation form. You should use the rules set forth in the current edition of *The Bluebook* or *ALWD*. Do not worry about the page numbers. The following citations will appear in the brief.

Or. Revised Statute § 421.650

42 U.S. Code Section 101

Turner v. Armontrout, 845 F. 2nd 165 (Eighth Circuit 1988)

Neil v. Biggers, 409 U.S. Reports 188, 195 (1972)

Estelle v. Williams and Henry General Insurance Company, 425 U.S. 501

Or. Revised Statute § 752.101

Federal Rule of Evidence 801

People v. Watley, 630 N.W.2d 43 (Michigan 2004)

William H. Grey v. State 178 P.3rd 154 (Or. 2008).

Dias v. State 601 P.2d 706, 708 (Oregon Ct. App. 1979)

United States v. John Miller, 146 F.3d 274 (Fifth Circuit 1998)

Russell v. Rolfs, 893 F.2nd 1033 (Ninth Circuit)

Aiken v. Spalding Manufacturing Association, 841 F. 2d 881 (9th Circuit)

Colorado v. Christine Connelly, 479 U.S. 157 (1986)

Eamons v. State of Oregon, 807 P.2nd 718 (Oregon 1991), *affirmed*, 13 P.3rd 420 (Oregon 2000)

U.S. v. Owens, 484 U.S. 554, 560 (1988)

David H. Kaye, *The New Wigmore: A Treatise on Evidence*, Volume 3, Section 20:140 (3rd edition 2004)

28 U.S.C. § 9042

Federal Rule of Evidence 702

Eugene Gressman, et al., *Supreme Court Practice*, 190 (9th ed. 2008)

People v. Coy, 620 N.W. 2d 376 (Mich. App. 2000)

Brandon L. Garrett, "Claiming Innocence," 92 Minnesota Law Review 1629 (2008)

Teague v. Lane, 489 U. S. 288, 301-04 (1989)

Internet Assignment for Chapter 18

1. Read Judge Richard A. Posner's article "Against Footnotes" at http://aja.ncsc.dni.us/courtrv/cr38-2/CR38-2Posner.pdf. What is the "obvious objection" to footnotes?
2. Access the rules of the U.S. Supreme Court.
   a. What color must the cover be for a petition for a writ of certiorari?
   b. What are the word limits for a petition for a writ of certiorari?
   c. Do word limits include footnotes?
   d. What is the typeface required for footnotes?
3. Access the site http://ualr.edu/cmbarger/App_res.htm. Select "Persuasive Strategies for Appellate Brief-Writing." Review the sixth strategy. Identify three characteristics that will strike a reviewing judge as "bogus."
4. Access the site http://www.appellate.net/briefs. Review the amicus curiae brief filed in *American Atheists, Inc. v. Duncan*. What is the argument heading for Argument II.C? Do you think this is a neutral heading or a persuasive one? Why?
5. Access the website for the U.S. Supreme Court and select "Case Handling Guides." Review the "Guide for Counsel in Cases to be Argued Before the Court." Review Section II.E.3, relating to Protocol.
   a. What should counsel's argument focus on?
   b. If an argument relates to a statute or regulation, what should counsel do?

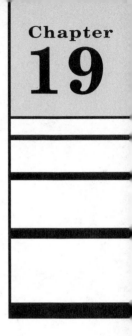

Postwriting Steps

The best writing is rewriting.

E.B. White

Chapter Overview

Paralegals not only engage in the drafting of documents for themselves but also are often asked to review and revise the writing of others or perform proofreading for others. Although these tasks are typically accomplished at the end of a writing project, their importance cannot be overlooked. It is at this stage of the writing process that unclear passages should be revised, redundant phrases should be deleted, and spelling and grammatical errors should be corrected. Even a minor typographical error will impair the professionalism of your project.

This chapter focuses on reviewing and revising your writing, proofreading, and polishing the finished product so its appearance enhances readability.

A.   Reviewing and Revising: Stage One

When you have the first draft of your project in hand, the difficult tasks of reviewing and revising begin. Your initial review should be to ensure that the writing accurately conveys all the information needed. At this stage, focus on content. Try to review the project from the perspective of the intended reader, and ask if the reader will understand the writing. Consider the following strategies:

- Keep the purpose of the project in mind. If the project is a brief, its purpose is to persuade. If the project is a memorandum, its purpose is to inform. Ask yourself if the writing meets these goals. Consider whether the tone is appropriate for the reader and whether the project is either too formal or too informal.
- Review to ensure the writing flows smoothly and that its organization assists the reader's comprehension. Move paragraphs and sections to other locations if you believe they would be better placed elsewhere.
- Be careful not to engage in micro-revision during the writing process itself. Agonizing over the choice of each word and continually striking out or rephrasing sentences may be a waste of time and energy because you may eventually omit a section you spent considerable time revising during the first effort.
- Do not interpret this advice to mean that no revisions should be done during the writing stage. It is both necessary and helpful to revise throughout the process of writing. Do not, however, write your initial draft expecting that the first typed version will be suitable for submission to court. You may even wish to insert reminders to yourself in the initial draft such as "work on this" or "revise" to remind you that further work needs to be done for a certain section. When writing, if you cannot decide between two ways of expressing an idea, initially include them both. When you read through your completed first draft, you can then decide which version to retain.
- Try to allow at least a few hours (and, if possible, overnight or longer) to pass between the completion of your first draft and your initial review. It is extremely difficult to review effectively a project with which you are too familiar. If you can come to the review "cold," you will be better able to detect flaws and gaps in the writing.
- Focus 100 percent on the review. Ask someone to hold your calls, and find a quiet space where you can concentrate on your task. If you attempt to review a project and are interrupted by phone calls and e-mails, you will be unable to devote the effort you need to make a critical evaluation of the project and may unintentionally skip over sections.

- You may find it helpful to close the door to your office or the library and read aloud. This will enable you to hear repetition or awkward phrasing or to realize something is missing from the project. Make sure each draft of a project includes a date. Often, several versions of a project will accumulate in a file. Because some drafts will vary only slightly from each other, sorting out the current version can be nearly impossible unless each draft is identified by date, and perhaps even time, for example, "DRAFT 1/16/11 10:30 a.m."
- If you have collaborated on the project with another writer, be especially alert to ensure your headings, numberings, and presentations of lists are consistent.
- If you are aiming to improve your writing skills in general, focus on one or two problem areas (such as overly long sentences or overuse of nominalizations), work on correcting these, and then move on to other weak spots.

B. Reviewing and Revising: Stage Two

The first review and revision of your project should alert you to major problems in content and organization. Use the second review to focus on four specific areas.

1. Sentence Length

Go through your second draft and place a red slash mark at the end of each sentence. Observe whether a pattern of overly long sentences emerges. If most sentences are several lines in length, you need to trim your writing. Use sentences of varying length to create interest. Various software programs assist by informing you of average sentence length in a project.

2. Needless Words and Phrases

Read through the project looking for unnecessary words. It is easy to become attached to your product. Writers often have difficulty omitting words and phrases because they are reluctant to omit anything after hours of research and hours of writing. Be merciless. Most writers are far better at adding words than at deleting them. Watch carefully for modifiers such as "clearly," "obviously," or "naturally." These should be omitted for two reasons: They add nothing to a sentence, and they often create a patronizing tone.

3. *Legalese*

Keep alert to the use of jargon and legalese, including the overuse of archaic words and phrases and the overuse of nominalizations such as "discussion" or "exploration" instead of strong words like "discuss" or "explore." You can detect nominalizations by looking for words ending in *-ent, -ant,* and *-ion*.

4. *Passive Voice*

The overuse of passive voice will result in a distant and weak project. The active voice, coupled with the selection of forceful words, will lend strength and vigor to your writing. You can detect passive voice by looking at a noun introduced with the phrase *by the* (as in "The report was filed by the company").

C. Proofreading

The third and final review of your writing should focus on technical errors such as grammatical errors, spelling mistakes, and typos. The more familiar you are with a project, the more difficult this task becomes. Your mind will automatically supply the word you intended, and you will not be able to see your errors. Do not rely exclusively on the spelling and grammar checker programs of your word processor. A spelling checker will not inform you to use "from" rather than "form" because both words are properly spelled. Do not proofread on a computer screen. Print a copy of the document and work from that. Reading a hard copy is easier on your eyes. Moreover, it is presented in the way it will be to the ultimate reader, allowing you to see it as it will be seen by its audience. Consider photocopying the document in an increased size, for example, to 120 percent of its original size, to allow you to read the document easily and make notes in the margin.

Although there are a few techniques you can use to assist you in proofreading, the best tip is to allow as much time as possible, preferably two to three days, to elapse before you begin this final step in writing. This break will allow you to come to the project with a fresh approach and will counterbalance the familiarity that hampers a careful scrutiny of your writing. In many instances, and in busy law firms, it is not always possible to allow time to elapse between drafting and proofreading. Energy levels are often higher in the morning, so try to schedule your proofreading as the first thing you do in the day.

Do not underestimate the difficulty of proofreading and editing. All major publishers require that writings be edited by professional editors and proofreaders for the very reason that authors are notoriously unlikely to catch their own errors.

Because a normal reading of your project will naturally focus on content, and you will read groups of words and phrases rather than isolated words, you need to force yourself to slow down and focus on each word. Try the following techniques:

(i)   Place a ruler under each line as you read the document. This will prevent you from jumping ahead to the next sentence or thought and force you to focus on each word.

(ii) Read the project backwards, from the last page to the first page and from right to left. Although this technique is excellent for finding typos and spelling errors, it will not help you pick up a missed word or ensure that you have used a word such as "united" rather than "untied."

(iii) Read the document aloud with a partner. Each of you will concentrate on the individual words, but the listener will focus more on the mechanics of the writing instead of the content. If your partner stumbles over certain sections, you will know these need to be fixed.

(iv) Read sections of the project out of order. Read Section V first, then the Conclusion, then Section III, then the Statement of Facts, and so on. You will not be able to focus on the flow of ideas, and your concentration will then be aimed at the mechanics of spelling, grammar, and typos.

(v)   Devote extra attention to the parts of the project that were prepared last. More errors occur when you are tired.

(vi) To ensure accuracy in complicated passages, such as in patent claims and in descriptions of real property in deeds, read the original description into a tape recorder, and then play it back, listening and proofreading against your text.

If you find yourself getting tired or losing concentration, stop and take a quick break. Get up and walk around the office. Get some juice or a fresh cup of coffee and then return to the task. Because you are not reading for content, but for mechanics, these interruptions will do no harm.

You can also ask someone else to proof the project for you. Having someone else review the project can be extremely helpful because this newcomer will have no familiarity with the writing. He or she will be able to review the writing with a fresh approach and no preconceived ideas or expectations. If you only want the reader to review for mechanical errors, say so, or you may receive a project with substantial corrections and suggestions. It is an intrusion on someone else's time to review your work; therefore, if you have asked for help, you should give the reviewer the courtesy of considering his or her comments or suggestions without becoming defensive. If you have difficulty accepting comments and criticism from others about your writing, do not ask for help. It is a waste of the other person's time if you are not able to keep an open mind about accepting suggestions.

Be alert to the dangers of over-reliance on word processor spell checking programs. Although these programs can be of great assistance and can offer suggestions for word choice, they do not recognize contextual misspellings. Thus, if you mistakenly referred to the complaint as "compliant," the spelling program will not alert you because the word "compliant" is correctly spelled. Although spell checking programs help speed up the editing and proofing process, they also encourage complacency. There is no substitute for human proofreading, as witnessed by the fact that a review of some recently published court decisions disclosed 23 cases referring to "Santa Clause" and 817 cases referring to the "trail court."

Similarly, the use of templates and forms prepared for an earlier transaction increases the risk of importing incorrect terms into later documents. Thus, a document prepared for a tenant needs to be scrupulously checked when it is later used for a subtenant. Make sure that defined terms are used consistently. For example, if an agreement uses the term "Franchisor," check to make sure the term is defined in the agreement, that it is always capitalized, and that it is consistently spelled and used. Use the "find and replace" feature in your word processing program to check for consistent presentation and use.

Ethics Alert

Competency in All Aspects of the Representation

Remember that the duties imposed on those in the legal profession are the highest duties of competency and that they extend to every aspect of the representation. In one 2004 case, a United States Magistrate reduced an attorney's fees from $300 per hour to $150 per hour, in part because of numerous typographical errors in pleadings. *Devore v. City of Phila.*, Civ. A. 00-3598, 2004 WL 414085 (E.D. Pa. Feb. 20, 2004). Thus, your duty to represent the client competently is broad enough to encompass even seemingly minor matters such as proofreading, editing, and cite checking.

D. Proofreading Projects by Others

If you are asked to review someone else's work, obtain clear instructions so you know if you should review for content or review only for mechanics such as typos, spelling mistakes, and grammatical errors. Reviewing for mechanical errors in someone else's writing is fairly easy. If you are not familiar with the content, the errors will fairly leap off the page at you (just as they will for the ultimate reader, such as the client or the judge).

If you are asked to review for content, be judicious. All writers are sensitive about their product, and overcriticizing may result in the writer believing you have a grudge and then discounting everything you suggest.

Recognize that each writer has a unique style. Just because a thought is not expressed in the exact way you would express it does not mean it is inaccurate or vague. Limit your corrections to meaningful items. It is unproductive to change "glad" to "happy" or "concerning" to "regarding." Your credibility as an effective reviewer will be jeopardized if you engage in such meaningless changes.

Comments such as "weak," "poor," or "expand" placed beside a paragraph are nearly useless. Specifically explain to the writer why the section is weak and make a suggestion for improving it. Harsh comments such as "What are you thinking?" or "Ridiculous!" will cause the writer to avoid seeking your help and to become a passive writer. Try phrasing suggestions diplomatically, such as "Have you considered . . . ?" or "Let's discuss some alternatives . . . . " These approaches focus on the two of you as colleagues committed to producing a quality product rather than on the writer's perceived inadequacies.

In some instances, a letter to a client or a memo may bear the notation "dictated but not read," which means that the author dictated the project to someone else but has not reviewed it for errors. Avoid such a notation. The message it conveys to a reader is either "I'm too busy for you" or "Don't blame me if there are errors in this document."

E. Proofreaders' Marks

Although there is some variety in the marks writers use to show errors, most legal writers employ the standard marks, called proofreaders' marks, used by professional editors. Many attorneys learned these marks while writing articles for law reviews. Their use in law firms and among legal professionals is common.

Most dictionaries will provide descriptions and illustrations of proofreaders' marks. These marks are designed to show clerical staff where and how to make corrections in your project. Be sure all of your working drafts are double-spaced with generous margins so you will have sufficient room to note corrections. The most commonly used proofreaders' marks are shown in Figure 19-1.

F. Polishing Your Writing

Even if your project is well written, clear, and readable, it should be presented in such a manner that it creates a favorable impression on the reader. One of the reasons some appellate courts insist that a brief submitted must be commercially printed rather than merely typed or produced on a word processor is that printed briefs are easier to read and present a uniform appearance.

Figure 19-1
<u>Commonly Used Proofreaders' Marks</u>

Mark	*Explanation*	*Example*
≡	Capital letters	president bush
/	Lowercase letters	the eleventh Juror
∼	Boldface	April 16, 2008
⊂	Close up space	in as much
¶	Begin new paragraph	¶The plaintiff
ℓ	Delete	The hearing was was
stet	Let original text stand	Many courts have concluded
∧	Insert item	The plaintiff and his attorney argued
#	Add space	the court.The defendant
∼	Transpose	compliant
⊏	Move left	⊏ any jury
⊐	Move right	⊐ any jury
∧	Insert comma	the Plaintiff John Brownell argued
∨	Insert apostrophe	its a fact that
⊙	Insert period	the court The jury also requested
◯ or (SP)	Spell out	Jan. 10, 2008

Many factors play a part in making a project readable, including quality of paper, typeface, margins, and headings. If your goal in writing is to communicate, you must avoid producing a document so messy in appearance that it frustrates a reader or one that is simply not read because of its physical appearance.

Visually appealing documents are easier to understand. Replace blocks of text with headings, tables, lists, and more white space. Make sure the layout of your project is uncrowded.

1. Paper

Use the highest-quality paper possible. Some courts require that the paper used for documents submitted be of a certain quality. The United States Supreme Court, for example, requires all 8½ × 11-inch documents to be produced on unglazed, opaque, white paper. Sup. Ct. R. 33.2(a).

Select a paper of sufficient weight so that page two of a document doesn't show through to page one. Although some law firms use cream or ivory colored paper, most use white. White is the more traditional color, and many readers find it easiest to read because black type provides a greater contrast on white paper than on cream colored paper.

2. Typeface

Use ordinary Roman type for most of your writing. Italics (or underscoring) must be used for names of cases; titles of books, law review articles, and other publications; citation signals; and foreign words and phrases. Italics (or underscoring) may be used to emphasize certain words or phrases. Use boldface only for headings or special purposes, such as emphasizing a deadline date in a letter to a client.

Word processors can easily create italics. Some writers prefer italics to underscoring because they create an elegant look. Other writers believe underscoring draws more attention to a word or phrase.

As to type of font, many experts prefer a "serif" style, which is one that adds small decorative strokes to the edges of letters. Serif styles are generally viewed as enhancing readability because they draw the eye from one word to the next. Old-fashioned typewriters always used a serif style. Well-known serif styles include Garamond, Times New Roman, and Century Schoolbook. This text is presented in a serif style. "Sans serif" styles (those without extra strokes) such as Arial might be acceptable and dramatic for headings. In any case, do not select a font style that is so different as to be distracting to a reader. Do not use all capital letters, except for short headings, because they are difficult to read.

Practice Tip

Document Design

Consider the following tips to ensure the design of your document enhances its readability:

- Don't mix typefaces in a document. Variations in typeface make a project look too much like an advertisement. Moreover, readers assume that headings in the same size and font style signal information of the same importance.
- Use visuals (graphs, charts, and so forth) sparingly. Keep visuals simple, and make sure they are helpful rather than merely "eye candy."
- Typefaces may be monospaced (meaning that every letter takes up the same amount of room) or proportional (meaning that, for example, a capital M takes up more room than a capital I). Most readers find proportionally spaced typefaces (such as this text) easier to read.

---

3. Type Size

Word processors can provide you with numerous choices for type size. Type size is measured in "points," such as 10-point type or 12-point type, with the larger the number showing larger print. Many courts require documents to be printed in a certain size type. Similarly, some statutes require certain information, such as language disclaiming a warranty, to be of a specified type size. If there are no rules you must follow with regard to type size, select 12-point type, which is easily read. Rules of the United States Supreme Court dictate that the text of documents submitted to the Court be typeset in a "Century family" (such as Century Schoolbook) in 12-point type. Sup. Ct. R. 33.1(b). Most readers prefer 12-point type due to its ease of readability.

On occasion a client may insist that certain information be included in a contract, invoice, or other form. In order to fit all of the information or terms in the document, you may need to use a much smaller type size, such as 6-point or 8-point. Alternatively, many photocopy machines will reduce an image. These reductions, however, impair readability.

4. Length of Document

If court rules require that a document not exceed a specified page limit, you will need to be able to calculate and estimate the length of a project. The average typewritten or printed page, measuring 8½ × 11 inches, double-spaced, contains 250 words. If you are handwriting a document, count the words on any one sheet of your handwritten draft. Multiply this

by the number of pages in your draft and divide this figure by 250. This will provide a rough estimate of how many typed pages your handwritten draft will produce. Some courts exclude certain sections, such as tables of contents and tables of authorities, from page or word limits. Always check your court rules. Word processing programs easily provide statistics on document length and word counts.

If your project exceeds a maximum length requirement, you have several alternatives:

- Revise the project, omitting extraneous material.
- Alter your margins so that more words fit on each page.
- Use a smaller point type size to include more text on each page.

Although these last two techniques will allow you to squeeze extra material into the document, many court rules mandate margin size and type size. The rules of the United States Courts of Appeal flatly require one-inch margins on all sides. Fed. R. App. P. 32.

It is increasingly common for courts to require that documents comply with word count limits rather than page limits (otherwise, writers would "cram" extra text into footnotes, using smaller typeface than in the body of the page). For example, the United States Supreme Court requires that principal briefs not exceed 15,000 words (including footnotes) and that a certificate be attached to all documents verifying that they comply with the word count limitations. Sup. Ct. R. 33.1(g), (h). Additionally, briefs must now be submitted electronically to the Court (which allows the Clerk of the Court to verify compliance with the word count limits easily). *Id.* at 25.9.

The other disadvantage of squeezing material into a document is that it creates a more cramped appearance, and few, if any, readers will be fooled by artificial techniques adopted to meet length requirements. Pages filled with text from the upper left corner to the lower right corner cause eyestrain and frustration. Using adequate white space will cause headings and quotations to be more easily noticed. Although the technique of leaving ample white space on a page, including adequate or generous margins, may seem like an artificial device, reading studies have demonstrated that it results in a more readable project.

Another formatting device that contributes to a pleasing appearance is the use of right justified margins. A right justified (or "fully justified") margin is one in which all of the words end at the exact same location at the right side on the page. This type of margin creates a clean and crisp-looking document. The only disadvantage is that to ensure the margin is even at the right side, spacing between letters and words may be uneven from one line to the next. This uneven spacing can reduce ease of reading. Carefully proofread any document with right justified margins to make sure the spacing is acceptable. If it is not, use a ragged right edge.

5. Headings

Headings not only provide the reader with an idea as to what will follow, but also create visual drama on a page. Main headings should be in all capital letters, centered, and single-spaced. Each should be given a Roman numeral. Some writers use boldface print to make sure the headings stand out. Subheadings that occur with a main heading should use capital letters only for the first letter in each major word, such as nouns, verbs, adjectives, and adverbs. Do not capitalize the first letter in articles and short prepositions, such as "in," "of," or "the," but be sure to capitalize "is," "its," "be," and other short verbs, nouns, and adverbs. Follow *Bluebook* Rule 8 or *ALWD* Rule 3 for instructions on capitalizing words in headings. Label each subheading with a capital letter and underline or use boldface for emphasis. All headings should be separated from the remainder of the narrative by double-spacing above and below. If the heading is a complete sentence, follow it with a period.

The structure and labeling of headings and subheadings may be as follows:

I.

A.
B.
    1.
    2.
    3.
        a.
        b.
        c.
C.

II.

A.
B.
C.
    1.
        a.
        b.
        c.
            (i)
            (ii)
    2.
D.

III.

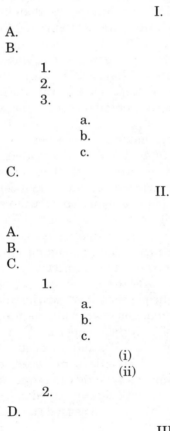

Do not use an "I" or an "A" unless a "II" or a "B" follows. On your final proofreading effort, scan through your project examining only the lettering and numbers of the headings to make sure you haven't skipped over or repeated a letter or number.

6. *Quotations and Lists*

Quotations and lists can serve to provide relief from a long narrative. Select quotations with care and be careful not to overquote. Follow *Bluebook* rules and keep quotes of 49 or fewer words in text. Indent quotes of 50 words or more. *ALWD* rules are similar.

Lists also create interest and are an effective tool for presenting information. Overuse of lists, however, can make your project have an outline-look to its appearance. Be consistent in presentation of lists. Don't use bullets in some lists and dashes to introduce others. Review lists to make sure the presentation of the material is in parallel structure.

G.   The Final Review

Just before your writing is sent to the reader, check these four items:

(i) *"Widows and orphans."* A "widow" or "orphan," respectively, is a heading or isolated line occurring at the top of a page or an isolated line occurring at the bottom of a page. Correct that awkward placement. It is distracting to the reader and results in an unprofessional-looking project. Remember to keep at least two lines of text together.

(ii) *Hyphenated Words.* Do not hyphenate a word between one page and the next. Most software programs automatically correct this error.

(iii) *Numbering.* Quickly scan the project to make sure the page numbering is correct. If the document has a table of contents, review it to make sure all references to pages are correct. If footnotes are used, check their accuracy.

(iv) *Exhibits.* Make sure all exhibits or attachments to the project are included and are properly marked.

See Figure 19-2 for a Project Checklist you can use to ensure all projects are in final form.

Figure 19-2
Sample Project Checklist

Project Checklist

Moving target _____   Type of project _____

Nearing final form _____   Client _____

Final form _____   File/Billing No. _____

Due date _____   Supervisor _____

Proofread   _____

Cite-Checked   _____   *Bluebook* / *ALWD* / Other ____

Shepardized/KeyCited   _____

Quotations Checked   _____

Defined Terms Consistent   _____

Consistency in Headings   _____

Consistency in Exhibits   _____

No Widows or Orphans   _____

All Exhibits Attached   _____

Court Rules Checked   _____

Create Table of Authorities   _____

Create Table of Contents   _____

Number of Copies   _____

Special Filing/Mailing Notes _____

H.   Conclusion

Although the foregoing comments relating to paper quality, type size, and white space may seem inconsequential, remember that if your objective is to inform or persuade your reader, any device that keeps the reader's interest is significant. View these techniques as weapons in your arsenal of writing tools. Your goal is to produce a writing that is accurate and readable. Errors and typos impair the accuracy of a writing, and an unprofessional project impairs the readability of a writing. If you discover

errors, don't be afraid to send the document back for correction. Better that you are viewed as a perfectionist than as someone uninterested in quality.

Strive for excellence. Make every project something you and your fellow legal professionals will be proud to sign.

Common Writing Errors

Watch for the following common errors:

- Repeated words at the end of one line and the beginning of another.
- Errors in figures, dates, monetary amounts, and names.
- Substitutions of letters in small words, such as a change of "now" to "not" or "of" to "or."
- Transpositions of letters such that "complaint" becomes "compliant" and "trial" becomes "trail."
- Misspellings of compound words such as "every one" rather than "everyone" or "can not" for "cannot."

CyberSites

http://www.unc.edu/depts/wcweb/ handouts/proofread.html	The University of North Carolina provides information on proofreading and editing.
http://owl.english.purdue.edu/ owl/resource/561/01	Purdue University's Online Writing Lab provides strategies to improve proofreading and editing.
http://www.ualr.edu/cmbarger	Professor C.M. Barger offers numerous hints and valuable guidance on formatting various legal documents.
http://www.prenhall.com/ author_guide/proofing.html	Prentice Hall provides examples of common proofreaders' marks.
http://www.sec.gov/pdf/ handbook.pdf	The SEC offers information on document design in *A Plain English Handbook*.

Assignment for Chapter 19

CAREFULLY PROOFREAD THE FOLLOWING PASSAGE AND MAKE THE NECESSARY CORRECTIONS.

In the Untied States, under a principal know as the "business judgement rule," corporate officers and directors are generally imune from laibility for corporate actions if they acted in good faith and had a reasonable basis for they're business decision. The concept is based on a pragmatic approach courts have taken: courts are reluctant to to impose liability to freely on corporate mangers for fear that none would agree to manage a corporation if their actions were constantly second-guessed by couts. Thus, if directors and officors can demonstrate some valid busness purpose for their actions, they will generally be protected from liability of there corporation suffers some harm as a result of their actions. In essense, a presumption exits that the bored acted with sound business judgment, and so long as some rational business decision can be found for board action inaction the corporate managers will be protected form liability.

In fact, in may states, a corporation can include in its original chartre or certificate of incorpration that directors and officers will only be liable for conduct that involves ilegality, a breach of the duty of loyalty, personal financial benfit, in tentional misconduct or or payment of an unawful divident. The approach taken by the Model Business Corporation Act ("MBAC") is simlar.

Thus do to this judgment business rule, although many law suits may be filled by furious sharehodlers, few may suceed, absent a showing of direct fraud. Law suits against accoutants, attorneys, and others have often proven more successful.

Internet Assignment for Chapter 19

1. Access the site http://www.umsl.edu/services/css/workshops/proofreading.html.
   a. What is the fourth tip for successful proofreading?
   b. What are the proven proofreading techniques?
2. Access the SEC's document titled *A Plain English Handbook*. Review Chapter 7.
   a. What is the maximum number of headings or levels recommended for a document?
   b. When is it best to use a sans serif typeface?

      c.   What is the recommended maximum number of typefaces in a document?

      d.   What is a comfortable line length for a reader?

3. Review Rule 33 of the Rules of the United States Supreme Court. What is the word limit for a brief for an amicus curiae submitted in support of a plaintiff?

4. Locate the article "Painting with Paint" written by Ruth Anne Robbins, which is available on the website of the U.S. Court of Appeals for the Seventh Circuit. Review the information on proportionally spaced fonts. Why did writers place two spaces after ending punctuation?

Sample Legal Memorandum

MEMORANDUM

To: Joanne DeRoache, District Attorney

From: Lane Gammon, Paralegal

Re: *State v. Davis*
         Terroristic Threatening

Date: January 30, 2011

ISSUES

1. In Delaware, does the offense of terroristic threatening require that the threat be communicated to the person threatened?
2. Is a threat to kill protected under the First Amendment?

BRIEF ANSWERS

1. No. A threat need not be communicated directly to the person threatened for terroristic threatening to have occurred.
2. No. An unequivocal threat to kill another is not speech that is protectable under the First Amendment.

FACTS

Our client, Robert Davis ("Davis"), was recently charged by the State of Delaware with "terroristic threatening," a violation of Del. Code Ann. tit. 11, § 621 (2002). The charge arose out of the following incident. After his girlfriend, Gina Gersten, broke up with him, Davis saw Ms. Gersten with another man. Davis angrily told his friend, Allen Franklin, "I'll kill Gina if I ever see her with another man again. You know I have a gun, and I'll do it." Concerned, Mr. Franklin told Ms. Gersten about Davis's threat. Ms. Gersten reported the threat to the police who charged Davis with "terroristic threatening," a violation of Del. Code Ann. tit. 11,

§ 621 (2002). Davis contends that because the threats were not uttered to the intended victim, Ms. Gersten, that they cannot constitute terroristic threatening. Davis has also contended that his statement is protected free speech under the First Amendment.

DISCUSSION

Terroristic Threatening

Del. Code Ann. tit. 11, § 621 (2002) provides, in pertinent part, that "a person is guilty of terroristic threatening when he or she . . . threatens to commit any crime likely to result in death or in serious injury to person or property." The language of the statute does not specify that the threat must be made directly to the person to whom the threat is addressed. Moreover, there is no case law in Delaware addressing this issue. Case law from other jurisdictions, however, with statutes similar to those of Delaware supports the conclusion that a threat to a third party, rather than to the threatened person directly, can constitute the offense of terroristic threatening.

In *State v. Alston*, 865 P.2d 157, 162 (Haw. 1944), the defendant, Alston, was seated in a restaurant and threatened a waitress who was scheduled to be a witness against him in court. Two police officers were present and asked Alston to go outside with them. While outside, Alston pointed at the waitress through the window and angrily told the officers that he was "tired of that [expletive]" and that if he were arrested, he would "go home and get his pistol and tie up this end once and for all." Alston immediately told another woman present to go to his home and get his gun so he could "take care of that [expletive] once and for all." *Id.*

Alston was charged with terroristic threatening for the threats to the waitress made in front of the two police officers. He argued that the threats made in front of the officers could not constitute terroristic threatening because the threat was never communicated to the person against whom the threats were made. The Hawaii Supreme Court held that the threat did not need to be communicated to the victim. The court noted that for one to be subject to criminal prosecution for terroristic

threatening, "the threat must be conveyed to either the person who is the object of the threat *or to a third party*." *Id.* at 168. Once the threat is communicated to anyone, terroristic threatening has occurred.

Similarly, in *State v. Chung*, 862 P.2d 1063 (Haw. 1993), a teacher (who was holding a clip of bullets) made a threat against the school principal in front of other teachers, but without the principal present. The court held that this threat constituted terroristic threatening. Moreover, the court noted that actual terrorization is not a material element of the offense of terroristic threatening. To be subject to criminal prosecution for terroristic threatening, one need only make a threat either to the person who is the object of the threat or to a third party. *Id.* at 1071.

In *Richards v. State*, 585 S.W.2d 375, 377 (Ark. Ct. App. 1979), the defendant, Richards, while holding a gun, stated that that intended to shoot a former co-worker, Roberts. The threat was made to a third party, and Roberts did not hear it. The third party promptly communicated the threat to Roberts. On appeal, the defendant challenged his conviction on the ground that the threat had not been communicated to the intended victim. The Arkansas statute prohibiting terroristic threatening was nearly identical to the Delaware statute at issue in this case. The court held that because the statute did not include language specifying that the threat must be communicated directly to the person threatened for the offense to occur, terroristic threatening can occur although the intended victim does not hear or know of the threat. Thus, Davis's threat to kill Ms. Gersten constitutes terroristic threatening under the Delaware statute even though the threat was made to a third party and not directly to Ms. Gersten.

First Amendment Defense

Davis has asserted that his statement that he would kill Ms. Gersten if he ever saw her with another man again is protected by the First Amendment right of free speech and expression. *See* U.S. Const. amend. I.

The U.S. Supreme Court has already addressed the issue whether an unequivocal threat is protected under the First Amendment and has firmly stated "a statement that amounts to a threat to kill . . . would not be protected by the First Amendment." *Rankin v. McPherson*, 483 U.S. 378, 386-87 (1987). Although threats made in jest and which when taken in context are not true threats because they are conditional are protected under the First Amendment, *Watts v. United States*, 394 U.S. 705, 708 (1969), if language used in a threat conveys a gravity of purpose and likelihood of execution, it is not protected speech. *United States v. Kelner*, 534 F.2d 1020, 1026-27 (2d Cir. 1976). If a statement on its face and in the circumstances in which it is made is so unequivocal and unconditional as to convey a gravity of purpose and imminent prospect of being carried out, such is not protected speech under the First Amendment. *Id.*

In the present case, Davis's threat was made in anger, not in jest, and stated his clear and unequivocal intention to kill Ms. Gersten. Davis's statement included specific details as to how this killing would occur. Moreover, Franklin understood the threat to be sufficiently serious that he immediately conveyed the threat to Ms. Gersten. Such an unequivocal and unconditional threat is not protected free speech.

CONCLUSION

Because there is nothing in the Delaware statute requiring an applicable threat to be made directly to the threatened person, a threat made in front of a third party who later communicates it to the victim can constitute terroristic threatening. Thus, Davis has committed the crime of terroristic threatening. Moreover, because Davis's threat was un-equivocal and unconditional and not made in jest, it is not protected free speech under the First Amendment.

Appendix

B

Sample Brief
for Court

The following trial court brief was submitted by the United States government in the Microsoft Corporation antitrust case. Note that not all citations comply with *Bluebook* or *ALWD* rules.

IN THE UNITED STATES DISTRICT COURT
FOR THE DISTRICT OF COLUMBIA

UNITED STATES OF AMERICA, 　　　　　　Plaintiff, 　　　　　v. MICROSOFT CORPORATION, 　　　　　　Defendant.	Civil Action No. 98-1232 (TPJ)
STATE OF NEW YORK *ex rel.* Attorney General ELIOT SPITZER, *et al.*, 　　　　　　Plaintiffs, 　　　　　v. MICROSOFT CORPORATION, 　　　　　　Defendant.	Civil Action No. 98-1233 (TPJ)

**PLAINTIFFS' RESPONSE TO MICROSOFT'S OBJECTION TO
PARTICIPATION BY PROFESSOR LAWRENCE LESSIG AS AN
AMICUS CURIAE**

Microsoft has objected to participation by Professor Lawrence Lessig of Harvard Law School as an amicus curiae. Professor Lessig's participation in that role is proper, and Microsoft's objections are ill conceived and unfounded.

I.

Background

By Order dated November 19, 1999, the Court invited Professor Lessig to participate as amicus curiae. The Court also permitted the two plaintiffs and Microsoft each to designate an amicus curiae. In a conference with counsel the day before its Order, the Court explained that it asked Professor Lessig to submit a brief that addresses the legal issue of technological tying. Transcript of Proceedings, November 18, 1999, at

10-11. The Court's Order followed the entry of the Court's detailed findings of fact. There is no suggestion in Microsoft's papers, nor could there be, that the amicus process has anything to do with issues of fact.

II.

Legal Standard

Although there is no federal rule or statute governing participation by amicus curiae at the district court level,[1] *see United States v. Gotti*, 755 F. Supp. 1157, 1158 (E.D.N.Y. 1991), a federal district court has the inherent authority to invite participation by amicus curiae to assist the court in its proceedings. *United States v. Louisiana*, 751 F. Supp. 608, 620 (E.D. La. 1990); *United States v. Michigan*, 116 F.R.D. 655, 660 (W.D. Mich. 1987). The decision to invite or accept participation by an amicus is committed to the sound discretion of the court. *Alexander v. Hall*, 64 F.R.D. 152, 155 (D.S.C. 1974).

The classic role of the amicus curiae is to assist in a case of general public interest, supplement the efforts of counsel, and draw the court's attention to law that may otherwise escape consideration. *Miller-Wohl Co., Inc. v. Commissioner of Labor and Indus.*, 694 F.2d 203, 204 (9th Cir. 1982); see also *New England Patriots Football Club, Inc. v. University of Colorado*, 592 F.2d 1196, 1198 n. 3 (1st Cir. 1979) (historically, the role of an amicus was "to aid the court in resolving doubtful issues of law"). There is no requirement that an amicus be disinterested. *Funbus Systems, Inc. v. California Public Utilities Commission*, 801 F.2d 1120, 1125 (9th Cir. 1986); *Hoptowit v. Ray*, 682 F.2d 1237, 1260 (9th Cir. 1982), although in this case there is no reason to believe that Professor Lessig is other than disinterested.

---

[1] Federal Rule of Appellate Procedure 29 governs participation by *amici* in the Courts of Appeal.

III.

Argument

A. Microsoft's Arguments

First, Microsoft asserts, without any explanation of its foundation or reasoning, that the Court's Order inviting Professor Lessig's participation is sufficiently broad to constitute a request for proposed conclusions of law. Microsoft also contends that Professor Lessig does not meet requirements to participate as an amicus because he does not have a "particularized 'special interest'" in the legal issues presented in the case, but then goes on to argue, seemingly paradoxically, that he should not participate because he is not impartial. These objections are specious.

B. Legal Argument By Amici Will Not Usurp The Judicial Function

The intended import of Microsoft's puzzling suggestion that the invitation to Professor Lessig to submit an amicus brief "is sufficiently broad as to constitute an invitation to submit proposed conclusions of law from a non-party," Microsoft's Objection at 2, is unclear and, in any event, does not provide any basis for revoking the invitation. First, Microsoft's suggestion ignores the Court's clear statement to counsel that Professor Lessig was being specifically requested to address the issue of technological tying. Transcript of Proceedings, November 18, 1999, at 10-11. Indeed, the Court made clear the straightforward purpose of its invitation of the limited brief of Professor Lessig and those of other amici: "I am asking for amici help." *Id.* at 10.

More importantly, that Professor Lessig and the other potential amici may discuss how they believe that the Sherman Act should be applied to the facts as the Court has found them is neither unusual nor improper, and indeed is the traditional role of an amicus. *See, e.g., Funbus Systems, Inc. v. California Public Utilities Commission*, 801 F.2d 1120, 1125 (9th Cir. 1986) ("perfectly permissible role" for amicus to "take a

legal position and present legal arguments in support of it"). Submitting a brief as amici involves *no* delegation of judicial authority or duties, raises none of the same concerns that appointment of a special master would raise, and is unobjectionable.

C. If The Court Believes That Professor Lessig Would Bring A Helpful Perspective To Legal Issues In The Case, It Is Appropriate For Him Participate As Amicus

"There are no strict prerequisites that must be established prior to qualifying for amicus status; an individual seeking to appear as amicus must merely make a showing that his participation is useful to or otherwise desirable by the court." *United States v. Louisiana*, 751 F. Supp. 606, 620 (E.D. La. 1990). Although some courts have required that the amicus possess some "unique information or perspective," this does not require any particular quantum of expertise beyond the expectation that the amicus will add significantly to, not merely parrot, the contributions from the lawyers from the parties. *See Ryan v. CFTC*, 125 F.3d 1062, 1063 (7th Cir. 1997); *see also United States v. Gotti*, 755 F. Supp. 1157, 1158-59 (E.D.N.Y. 1991) (rejecting proffered amicus brief that merely parroted arguments of defendants).

In this case, Professor Lessig has written at length and taught law school and multidisciplinary courses on the Internet and the law. Contrary to Microsoft's current assertion, *see* Microsoft's Objection at 3, Professor Lessig does possess expertise in antitrust law, having taught antitrust law at Harvard and elsewhere. *See* Microsoft's Memorandum In Support Of Its Motion To Revoke Reference to the Special Master, CV-94-1564, at 7. If the Court believes that he brings a special perspective to the issues raised in this litigation and that his contribution would be useful to the Court, it is appropriate and well within the Court's discretionary authority to invite him to submit his views.

**D. Microsoft Has Not Demonstrated That Professor
Lessig Is Biased Against It**

Microsoft again raises the issue of Professor Lessig's purported bias
against it. These allegations are not only wholly meritless; they also are
irrelevant as there is no requirement that an amicus be impartial in order
to participate.

When Microsoft first raised the issue of Professor Lessig's purported
bias in connection with the consent decree enforcement proceeding, this
Court found that Microsoft's bases for its allegations of impartiality were
"both trivial and altogether non-probative." *United States v. Microsoft*,
CV 94-1564, Memorandum and Order, at 2 (January 14, 1998). Having
scoured Professor Lessig's record since that time, Microsoft renews its
allegations of bias based on two items: (1) that Professor Lessig serves on
the advisory board of a non-profit organization devoted to open-source
software which is affiliated with, and has received financial support from,
Linux vendor Red Hat Software, and (2) that he has expressed the view
that the experience of *United States v. AT&T* may be of some interest
when thinking about the instant case. Underlying its specific allegations
of bias seems to be Microsoft's concern about one theme of Professor
Lessig's work, that the open nature of the Internet has engendered
tremendous competition and innovation, that this openness is neither
accidental nor inevitable, and that society will benefit if this openness
continues.

Like Microsoft's previous allegations about Professor Lessig, its
current allegations of bias are unfounded. Professor Lessig's affiliation
with a non-profit organization devoted to open source software is a
non-issue. Microsoft has not shown that this organization has any
purpose beyond its stated one, *i.e.*, "to take the principles of open-source
software and apply them in a variety of scientific and educational projects
'for the greater good of the general public.'" Exhibit A to Microsoft's
Objection, at 1. Indeed, the article Microsoft attached to its motion notes
that the group will have a "board of academics and technology experts."

Id. That the group has connections with Red Hat, a participant in the open-source movement, is also of little moment. Microsoft has not alleged, nor are the plaintiffs aware of, any economic interest of Professor Lessig in the outcome of this litigation. At most, Microsoft has shown that Professor Lessig has views about the public welfare implications of developments in the software industry. None of this indicates that Professor Lessig has any bias against Microsoft that would disqualify him to participate as an amicus.[2]

Microsoft's allegations concerning Professor Lessig's comments about the AT&T break-up are even more puzzling. Read in context, Professor Lessig's comments merely reflect his recognition of the seriousness of the issues presented by this litigation, not any animus toward Microsoft. Exhibit B to Microsoft Opposition, at 3-4.

IV.

Conclusion

For the foregoing reasons, the plaintiffs submit that it is entirely proper and appropriate for the Court to invite Professor Lessig (and others solicited by the parties) to participate as amicus curiae in this important case. Microsoft's motion is nothing more than an attempt to manufacture some appellate point to use to distract attention from defendant's clear and continuing violation of the antitrust laws. Having

---

[2] In any event, there is no requirement that an amicus be impartial or disinterested. *E.g., Funbus Systems, Inc.*, 801 F.2d at 1125; *Hoptowit*, 682 F.2d at 1260; Krislov, *The Amicus Curiae Brief: from Friendship to Advocacy*, 72 Yale L.J. 694 (1963). Indeed, "by the nature of things an amicus is not normally disinterested." *Strasser v. Doorley*, 432 F.2d 567, 569 (1st Cir. 1970); *see* Tigar, *Federal Appeals: Jurisdiction and Practice*, at 133 (1993) ("An amicus brief is rarely disinterested; usually it supports one party or the other.") For example, to the extent that Microsoft and the plaintiffs invite amici who are themselves or who represent participants in the software industry, these persons will have economic interests that may be affected by this litigation or by Microsoft's conduct far more directly than the non-profit board position that Professor Lessig holds. Thus, even if there were any merit to Microsoft's allegations of some degree of partiality, those allegations would provide no grounds for rescinding the invitation to participate as an amicus.

In an excess of caution and in the interests of full disclosure, the plaintiffs suggest that the Court may wish to consider whether there is any merit in Professor Lessig filing a statement of interest, such as that required by Fed. R. App. P. 29, or disclose in some other format any interest he may have in the litigation, including any relevant information about his role in the Red Hat Center for Open Source.

no plausible basis for appealing any of this Court's findings of fact, and having no plausible argument that those findings do not make out a clear violation of the antitrust laws, Microsoft resorts to an attempt to create an appellate question by unfounded attacks on Professor Lessig and this Court's procedures. The Court may wish to consider whether it should accede to Microsoft's tactics simply to avoid adding another issue to this case. However, the law is clear that either decision is well within the Court's discretion.

DATED: December 20, 1999

Respectfully submitted,

_____/s/_____

Christopher S Crook
Chief
Phillip R. Malone
John F. Cove, Jr.
Jeremy Feinstein
Attorneys
David Boies
Special Trial Counsel
U.S. Department of Justice
Antitrust Division
325 7th Street, NW, Rm. 615
Washington, DC 20530
(202) 514-8276

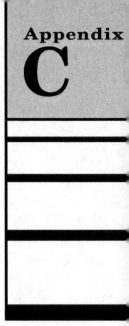

Sample Appellate Brief

The attached appellate brief (a Brief in Opposition to a Petition for a Writ of Certiorari) was submitted to the United States Supreme Court. Note that not all citations comply with *Bluebook* or *ALWD* rules.

No. 03-878

In the Supreme Court of the United States

PHIL CRAWFORD, INTERIM FIELD OFFICE DIRECTOR,
PORTLAND, OREGON, UNITED STATES IMMIGRATION
AND CUSTOMS ENFORCEMENT, ET AL.,
PETITIONERS

v.

SERGIO SUAREZ MARTINEZ

On Petition for a Writ of Certiorari
to the United States Court of Appeals
for the Ninth Circuit

BRIEF IN OPPOSITION

Christine Stebbins Dahl
Assistant Federal Defender
101 SW Main Street, Suite 1700
Portland, Oregon 97204
(503) 326-2123
Counsel for Respondent

QUESTION PRESENTED

In *Zadvydas v. Davis*, 533 U.S. 678 (2001), this Court considered the government's authority under 8 U.S.C. § 1231(a)(6) to continue to detain for the purpose of removal those persons whose removal from the United States could not be accomplished in the reasonably foreseeable future. This Court interpreted the statute to limit such detention to a "reasonable time," and applied it to former permanent residents. In this case, the Ninth Circuit Court of Appeals, citing *Lin Guo Xi v. INS*, 298 F.3d 832 (9th Cir. 2002), summarily affirmed the application of *Zadvydas* to Sergio Suarez Martinez, a Mariel Cuban who had been paroled into the United States in 1980 and was ordered removed in 2001. Although it detained Mr. Martinez under section 1231(a)(6) for nearly two years, the government made no effort to remove him, conceded it was unable to do so within the foreseeable future, and ultimately asked the Ninth Circuit to summarily affirm the district court's conditional release order pursuant *Lin Guo Xi*.

Given that section 1231(a)(6) draws no distinction between individuals who are removable on grounds of inadmissibility and those removable on grounds of deportability, this case presents the question whether the Ninth Circuit correctly applied *Lin Guo Xi*, in which it adhered to this Court's statutory construction of section 1231(a)(6) in *Zadvydas*.

TABLE OF CONTENTS

TABLE OF AUTHORITIES

FEDERAL CASES

FEDERAL STATUTES

BRIEF IN OPPOSITION

Petitioners Phil Crawford, Interim Field Office Director, Portland, Oregon, U.S. Immigration and Customs Enforcement, and John Ashcroft, Attorney General of the United States, seek a writ of certiorari to review the judgment of the United States Court of Appeals for the Ninth Circuit. The government has asked this Court to hold its petition pending final resolution of the petition to review *Benitez v. Wallis*, 337 F.3d 1289 (11th Cir. 2003), *cert. granted*, 2004 WL 67860 (U.S. Jan. 16, 2004) (No.03-7434). The respondent, Mr. Martinez, opposes the issuance of a writ in his case. Although the question presented here cannot seriously be distinguished from that in *Benitez*, the Ninth Circuit resolved it correctly and the Eleventh Circuit did not. Because his conditional release is at stake, Mr. Martinez opposes holding this petition pending final disposition of *Benitez*. Instead, Mr. Martinez requests consolidation with *Benitez* for argument should the Court grant the writ.

OPINIONS BELOW

The order of court of appeals is unreported and appears at 1a of the Appendix to the Petition for Writ of Certiorari. The order of the district court is unreported and appears at 2a of the Appendix to the Petition.

JURISDICTION

This Court has jurisdiction to review the judgment by writ of certiorari under 28 U.S.C. § 1254(1). The government's petition appears to have been timely filed.

STATEMENT

Certain errors in the government's statement require correction. The government has never before suggested that Mr. Martinez attempted to enter the United States illegally. *Petition* at 2 ("Respondent is one of approximately 125,000 Cuban nationals, many of them convicted of crimes in Cuba, who attempted to enter the United States illegally during the 1980 Mariel boatlift."). In fact, he did not. He fled Cuba by boat as part of the "Freedom Flotilla" that enjoyed U.S. government approval.[1] Mr. Martinez arrived in Key West, Florida on June 8, 1980, and was immediately paroled into United States pursuant to 8 U.S.C. § 1182(d)(5). *Gov't Supp. Mtn. to Hold in Abeyance* (CR 12) at 2.

---

[1] Comments by President Carter at a press conference in Miami on May 5, 1980, indicated government approval of the flotilla:

> [L]iterally tens of thousands of others will be received in our country with understanding, as expeditiously as we can, as safely as possible on their journey across the 90 miles of ocean, and processed in accordance with the law. . . . But we'll continue to provide an open heart and open arms to refugees seeking freedom from Communist domination and from economic deprivation, brought about primarily by Fidel Castro and his government.

United States v. Frade, 709 F.2d 1387 (11th Cir. 1983).

2

The government omits to state that it identified section 1182(d)(5) as an independent source of authority to detain Mr. Martinez for the first time before the Ninth Circuit. *Compare Petition* at 3. In its district court pleadings, the government identified only section 1231(a)(6) as the source of its authority and made no attempt to distinguish *Lin Guo Xi. E.g., Gov't Supp. Mtn. to Hold in Abeyance* (CR 12) at 4; *Appellants' Response to Petitioner-Appellee's Motion for Summary Affirmance and Request for Summary Affirmance* (CA 03-35053) (July 9, 2003) at 2. The government did not suggest section 1182(d)(5) provided independent authority to detain Mr. Martinez until it moved for summary affirmance in the Circuit. *Appellants' Response to Petitioner-Appellee's Motion for Summary Affirmance and Request for Summary Affirmance* (CA 03-35053) (July 9, 2003) at 7.

Finally, while noting annual custody reviews pursuant to parole regulations applicable to Mariel Cubans, 8 C.F.R. § 212.12(g), *Petition* at 8, the government omits to state Mr. Martinez alleged these regulations were constitutionally deficient and yielded an unreliable result because they do not provide detainees a meaningful opportunity to challenge continued detention and are so lacking in important safeguards as to create a significant risk of erroneous deprivation of liberty interests. *See Brief in Support of Petition* (CR 9) at 25. The government never addressed this argument, and the district court's order granting the habeas petition

did not disclose whether this argument informed its decision. *Compare Order Granting Petitioner's Motion to Dissolve Stay and for Immediate Release* (CR 24).

REASON FOR DENYING THE PETITION

The petition should be denied because the Ninth Circuit correctly concluded it was bound by this Court's statutory construction of section 1231(a)(6) in *Zadvydas*, and applied the same statute in the same manner. Because Congress chose to treat all of the categories of aliens the same in section 1231(a)(6), this Court has no occasion to rewrite the statute. It has the same meaning for everyone to whom it applies.

Contrary to the Eleventh Circuit's analysis in *Benitez*, the Ninth Circuit began with the statutory construction issue, and having resolved the issue in favor of the petitioner, concluded it had no occasion to address the underlying constitutional issues.

> Just a year ago the Supreme Court held that 8 U.S.C. § 1231(a)(6) "limits an alien's post-removal-period detention" to a reasonable time period and "does not permit indefinite detention" by the Immigration and Naturalization Service ("INS"). *Zadvydas v. Davis*, 533 U.S. 678, 689 (2001). We are now presented with the question of whether this statute bears the same meaning for an individual deemed inadmissible to the United States under 8 U.S.C. § 1182. The answer is yes. Our analysis of § 1231(a)(6) begins and ends with *Zadvydas*. Because the Supreme Court construed the statute, we are bound by that framework and thus are not called upon to address the scope of any constitutional claims of an inadmissible alien.

Lin Guo Xi, 298 F.3d at 833-34.

The Ninth Circuit, employing traditional canons of statutory construction, looked first to the language of the statute and concluded that it expressly applies to both inadmissible (formerly referred to as excludable) and removable (formerly referred to as deportable) aliens. *Id.* The plain language of the detention statute provides:

> An alien ordered removed who is [A] *inadmissible under section 1182* of this title, [B] removable for violations of [nonimmigrant status or entry conditions, violations of criminal laws, or threatening national security,] or [C] who has been determined by the Attorney General to be a risk to the community or unlikely to comply with the order of removal, may be detained beyond the removal period and, if released, shall be subject to the terms of supervision in paragraph (3).

8 U.S.C. § 1231(a)(6) (emphasis added).

The Ninth Circuit found that although *Zadvydas* only concerned the second category (removable aliens), this Court's construction addressed the statute as a whole, and thus, the holding of *Zadvydas* was not limited to the second prong:

> Although *Zadvydas* concerned the second prong of the statute—relating to deportable aliens—the Court's ultimate holding addresses the statute as a whole: "we construe the statute to contain an implicit 'reasonable time' limitation, the application of which is subject to federal court review." 533 U.S. at 682. In assessing the applicability of the statute, the Court spoke broadly, noting that it "applies to certain categories of aliens who have been ordered removed, namely *inadmissible* aliens, criminal aliens, aliens who have violated their nonimmigrant status conditions, and aliens removable for certain national security or foreign relations reasons . . . ." *Id.* at 688 (emphasis added). Concluding that the statute "does not

permit indefinite detention," the Court pointedly used the term "aliens" as opposed to "deportable aliens":

> [W]e read an implicit limitation into the statute before us. In our view, the statute, read in light of the Constitution's demands, limits an alien's post-removal-period detention to a period reasonably necessary to bring about that alien's removal from the United States. It does not permit indefinite detention.

Lin Guo Xi, 298 F.3d at 835 (quoting *Zadvydas*, 533 U.S. at 689).

The Ninth Circuit rejected the INS's argument that the statute should be construed differently depending upon the category into which the alien fell. The Ninth Circuit found the plain language of the statute forbids such a "bifurcated construction," and such an approach would be "untenable." *Lin Guo Xi*, 298 F.3d at 836-37. Because the statute no longer distinguishes between "excludable" and "deportable" aliens, there is no sound or principled basis to interpret and to apply it one way for one category, but a different way for the other. *See Zadvydas*, 533 U.S. at 710 (Kennedy, J., dissenting) ("Section 1231(a)(6) permits continued detention not only of removable aliens but also of inadmissible aliens, for instance those stopped at the border before entry. Congress provides for detention of both categories within the same statutory grant of authority").

The INS argued as much in its briefing to this Court:

> [The Supreme] Court has long recognized that, when Congress uses the same language even in different parts of the same

statute, it generally intends the language to have the same meaning. That rule is "at its most vigorous when a term is repeated within a given sentence." *Brown v. Gardner*, 513 U.S. 115, 118 (1994). *A fortiori* here, where Congress enacted a single grant of authority to the Attorney General over several categories of aliens, *Congress must be understood to have intended the same language to confer the same authority with respect to each category.*

Brief for the Petitioners at 47, *Ashcroft v. Ma* (No. 00-38) (U.S. June 28, 2001) (emphasis added). Any argument by the government that the statute should now be interpreted differently for inadmissible aliens must be rejected. *See also Zadvydas*, 533 U.S. at 710 (Kennedy, J., dissenting) ("[I]t is not a plausible construction of § 1231(a)(6) to imply a time limit as to one class but not to another. The text does not admit of this possibility."); *id.* at 717 ("[T]hat Mariel Cubans and other illegal, inadmissible aliens will be released . . . would seem a necessary consequence of the majority's construction of the statute.").

The Ninth Circuit properly concluded it was bound by this Court's construction of section 1231(a)(6).

We thus abide by the Supreme Court's interpretation of § 1231(a)(6) and hold that Lin may not be subjected to indefinite detention. *See Rivers v. Roadway Express, Inc.*, 511 U.S. 298, 312-13 (1994) ("It is [the Supreme Court's] responsibility to say what a statute means, and once the Court has spoken, it is the duty of other courts to respect that understanding of the governing rule of law. A judicial construction of a statute is an authoritative statement of what the statute mean[s] . . . ."); *Elmendorf v. Taylor*, 23 U.S. (10 Wheat) 152, 160 (1825) ("[T]he construction given by this Court to the constitution and laws of the United States is received by all as the true construction . . . .")

298 F.3d at 836. The Ninth Circuit's having correctly applied in *Lin Guo Xi* this Court's binding precedent and the clear language of section 1231(a)(6), there is no reason for this Court to disturb the order pursuant to which the government released Mr. Martinez on reasonable conditions.

CONCLUSION

The petition for writ of certiorari should be denied. In the alternative, Mr. Martinez requests consolidation for argument with *Benitez*.

Respectfully submitted,

Christine Stebbins Dahl
Assistant Federal Defender
101 S.W. Main Street, Suite 1700
Portland, OR 97204
(503) 326-2123
Counsel for Respondent

January 2004

Sample Table of Authorities

The following Table of Authorities is from an actual brief filed with the United States Supreme Court and offers guidance on compiling a table that refers to numerous sources. Note that not all citations comply with *Bluebook* or *ALWD* rules.

TABLE OF AUTHORITIES

CASES Page

Glossary

A.L.R.: *See American Law Reports.*

***ALWD* citation system:** A system introduced in 2000 by the Association of Legal Writing Directors ("ALWD") to provide an easier, more readily understood citation format.

Act: A series of statutes related to one topic.

Adjudication: An administrative proceeding before an administrative law judge.

Administrative agency: A governmental body that enacts rules and regulations on a specific topic and settles disputes relating thereto, for example, the FCC, FDA, or NLRB.

Administrative law: The law relating to administrative agencies.

Administrative law judge: An individual who presides over an administrative adjudication.

Advance sheets: Temporary softcover books that include cases prior to their publication in hardbound volumes.

Am. Jur. 2d: *See American Jurisprudence 2d.*

American Digest System: West's comprehensive set of digests designed to help researchers find cases.

American Jurisprudence 2d: A general or national encyclopedia published by West covering all United States law.

American Law Reports: Sets of books publishing appellate court decisions together with comprehensive essays or annotations relating to the legal issues raised by those cases.

Amicus curiae: Literally, "friend of the court"; a brief submitted to a court by one who is not a party to the action or proceeding.

Annotated: Literally, "with notes"; generally, a reference to one-sentence descriptions of cases that follow statutes in codes such as U.S.C.A. or a state code.

Annotated code: A set of statutes organized by subject matter that contains material accompanying the statutes, chiefly references to cases.

Annotated law reports: *See American Law Reports.*

Annotation: A one-sentence description of a case; an article or monograph about a legal topic published in A.L.R.

Appeal: Review by one court of a lower court's decision.

Appellant: A party who initiates an appeal; sometimes called a petitioner.

Appellate brief: A document presented to a reviewing court to obtain affirmance, reversal, or some alteration of a lower court's ruling.

Appellee: A party who responds to an appeal; sometimes called a respondent.

Apps: Law-related databases accessible on iPhones, iPads, Black-Berrys, and other similar devices, allowing legal professionals access to federal laws and other materials.

Attorneys general opinions: Opinions by executive officials on various legal topics; opinions by the U.S. Attorney General or individual state attorneys general.

Auto-Cite: A computer service provided by *Shepard's* showing the appellate history of a case, used primarily to confirm that the authority in question is still good law.

Bicameral: A two-chamber legislature.

Bill: A proposed law.

Bill of Rights: The first ten amendments to the United States Constitution.

Binding authority: Legal authority that must be followed by a court.

Blawg: An online journal related to legal topics.

Block form: Style of letter writing in which all the elements, including the date and the closing, begin at the left-hand margin.

Block quotation: A quotation from another source of 50 words or more, indented (typically ten spaces) left and right, that appears without opening and closing quotation marks.

Blog: An online journal or diary (short for "weblog").

Blue and White books: Books published by West for individual states that include conversion tables for locating parallel cites.

Bluebook: The best-known and used guide for citation form; subtitled A *Uniform System of Citation*, now in its 19th edition.

Bluepages: Section of *The Bluebook* printed on light blue paper, providing rules and examples for practitioners (rather than the citation form used for law review articles).

Boolean searching: A method of conducting research online using symbols and characters rather than plain English.

Brainstorming: A pre-writing strategy that results in a type of outline listing all words related to a project.

Brief: A summary of a case; or a written argument presented to a court; *see also* Memorandum of Law.

BriefCheck: Lexis's software program that extracts citations from a document, checks their validity, and produces a printed report with results.

BriefTools: West's software that monitors the status of authorities cited in a document and retrieves internal firm or company documents that contain a certain citation.

Browser: Software that helps access and review information on the Internet and translates HTML-encoded files into text and images that one can read and view; Internet Explorer and Mozilla Firefox are examples of browsers.

CALR: *See* computer-assisted legal research.

CCH *Congressional Index:* Sets of books used to compile legislative histories.

CD-ROM: Literally, "compact disc, read-only memory"; a hard disc containing thousands of pages of information.

C.J.S.: *See Corpus Juris Secundum*

CRAC: An acronym for "Conclusion," "Rule," "Application or Analysis," and "Conclusion"; a method used to analyze legal authorities and issues in a brief or other document.

CREAC: An acronym for "Conclusion," "Rule," "Explanation," "Application or Analysis," and "Conclusion"; a method used to analyze legal authorities in a document.

Cable modem: Equipment used to connect to the Internet over cable TV lines, allowing faster connection than a telephone line.

Case of first impression: An issue not yet decided by a jurisdiction.

"Case on point" approach: System used by a researcher following West's headnotes and Key Numbers to locate other similar cases by inserting a topic name and Key Number into the various units of the Decennial Digest System.

Certificate of Compliance: A verification that a document or pleading complies with court rules as to word count, page count, or other rules.

Certificate of Service: A verification that a document or pleading has been "served on" or presented to a party.

Certification: The process by which a court of appeals refers a question to the United States Supreme Court and asks for instructions and direction.

Certiorari: Writ of certiorari; the most widely used means to gain review of a case by the United States Supreme Court; issuance of the writ (meaning a decision to review a case) is discretionary with the Court.

Cert pool: The group of United States Supreme Court law clerks who takes turns evaluating petitions for certiorari and writing memos.

Cert worthy: A case for which certiorari has been granted.

Chamber opinion: An opinion written by a United States Supreme Court Justice in his or her capacity as the Justice assigned to a particular circuit rather than in the capacity of writing for the majority of the Court; also called "in-chambers opinion."

Charter: The governing document for a municipality.

Chat room: A location in cyberspace fostering real-time communications among several people.

Checks and balances: The system whereby each division of the United States government is to exercise its own powers and function separately from the others.

Chief Justice: The presiding Justice of the United States Supreme Court.

"Chron" copy: A copy of a legal document placed in a chronological file for law office purposes.

Circuit: A geographical area in which courts are located; the United States is divided into 11 numbered circuits and two unnumbered circuits, each with its own court of appeals.

Citators: Sets of books published by Shepard's or Westlaw's KeyCite that direct one to other materials discussing or treating legal authorities.

Cite-checking: The process of verifying that citations in a document are accurate and in compliance with rules for citation form and then verifying that the authorities are still "good law."

Civil law: A body of law depending more on legislative enactments than on case law, often seen in non-English-speaking countries.

Code: A compilation of statutes or regulations arranged by subject or topic.

Code of Federal Regulations: The codification of administrative rules and regulations, by subject, into 50 titles.

Codification: The process of organizing laws or regulations by subject matter rather than chronologically.

Comment: A shorter piece in a law review authored by a student; also called "Note."

Committee print: A report or study prepared for a congressional committee.

Committee report: Document reflecting decisions reached by legislative committees considering proposed legislation.

Committee transcript: Report of proceedings before committees considering proposed legislation.

Common law: The body of law that develops and derives through judicial decisions rather than from legislative enactments, usually seen in English-speaking countries.

Compiled legislative history: "Prepackaged" legislative history, usually compiled for significant legislation.

Complimentary close: The ending of a letter, such as "Sincerely."

Computer-assisted legal research: The process of conducting legal research through computer rather than conventional print sources.

Concurrent jurisdiction: The sharing of jurisdiction over a case by federal and state courts so that a litigant can select which forum in which to bring the action.

Concurring opinion: Opinion written by a member of the majority who agrees with the result reached in a case but disagrees with the reasoning of the majority.

Congress: The lawmaking body of the federal government, composed of the Senate and the House of Representatives.

"Congressional": Source provided by Lexis on the Internet offering more than 25 years of congressional information, including bills, hearing transcripts, committee reports, and the *Congressional Record*.

Congressional Information Service: Sets of books used to compile legislative histories.

Congressional Record: A publication that publishes the remarks of the speakers debating a bill prepared for each day Congress is in session as well as other remarks and speeches made on the floor of the House or Senate.

Constitution: The document that sets forth the fundamental law for a nation or state.

Constitutional courts: Courts such as the United States Supreme Court that exist under the United States Constitution and whose judges are protected as to tenure and salary reductions.

Convention: A type of treaty, usually relating to a single topic.

Corpus Juris Secundum: West's general or national encyclopedia covering all United States law.

Court reports: Sets of books that publish cases.

Courts of Appeal: Intermediate appellate courts; in the federal system, these are sometimes called circuit courts.

Courts of first resort: Trial courts.

"Current Awareness Commentary": A section of the monthly issue of U.S.C.S. Advance that includes summaries of pending legislation.

Current Law Index: Separately published index designed to direct researchers to periodicals, such as articles in law reviews.

Cyberspace: The electronic or computer world in which vast amounts of information are available; sometimes used as a synonym for the Internet.

Database: A collection of information organized for access through a computer system; one of Westlaw's groupings of materials offered in its computer-assisted legal research system.

Database Wizard: A service offered by Westlaw designed to help researchers select the right computer database; Database Wizard assists in selecting a database and narrowing research options.

Decennials: Digest books published by West that arrange cases in ten-year (or more frequent) groups; *see also American Digest System.*

Decision: Technically, the final action taken by a court in a court case; generally, the term "decision" is used synonymously with "opinion," "judgment," or "case."

Demand letter: A letter setting forth a client's demands or requirements.

Depository library: A library designated by the United States government to receive selected government materials and publications.

Descriptive word approach: A method of locating legal materials by looking up words describing a problem or issue in an index that then directs the reader to relevant information.

Dictionary (legal): An alphabetical arrangement of words and phrases providing the meaning or definition of those words and phrases.

Dictum: Technically, "obiter dictum"; a remark in a case said for purposes of illustration or analogy; dictum is persuasive only.

Digests: Books or indexes that arrange one-sentence summaries or "digests" of cases by subject.

Directory: A list of lawyers.

Dissenting opinion: An opinion written by a judge in the minority who disagrees with the result reached by the majority of a court.

District courts: The 94 trial courts in our federal system.

Diversity jurisdiction: A basis upon which federal courts take cases, due to the different or diverse citizenship of the parties in the case.

Docket number: A number assigned to a case by a court to track its progress through the court system.

Domain name: The name that identifies an Internet site, such as "www.ibm.com." Domain names have two parts: the "generic top-level domain," which is the last part of the domain name, such as "com," or "gov," and which usually refers to the type of provider of the information; and the "secondary domain," which is more specific and is to the left of the generic top-level domain, such as "ibm" in the above example.

Download: Transferring files or information from the Internet to your personal computer.

E-mail: Electronic mail or messages sent through the computer rather than in physical form (which is often called "snail mail").

Ellipsis: Three periods separated by spaces and set off by a space before the first and after the last period, used to indicate omission of a word or words.

Embedded citation: A citation appearing in the middle of a sentence, often introduced by a phrase.

Enabling statute: A statute that creates an administrative agency such as the FDA or FCC.

En banc opinion: Literally, "in the bench"; an opinion in which all judges in an appellate court participate.

Encyclopedias: Sets of books that alphabetically arrange topics related to legal issues; treatment of legal issues is somewhat elementary; the best-known general sets are C.J.S. and Am. Jur. 2d; some state-specific sets exist.

Engrossed bill: A final version of a bill passed by one legislative chamber.

Enrollment: A process wherein a bill that has been passed by both the House and the Senate is then printed by the Government Printing Office, following which the bill is certified as correct and signed by the Speaker of the House and by the vice president.

Exclusive jurisdiction: The basis upon which a court's ability to hear a case is exclusive to the federal court, such as a bankruptcy case, and which cannot be heard by another court.

Executive agreement: An agreement entered into with a foreign nation by a president acting without Senate approval.

Executive branch: The branch of the United States government that enforces laws.

Executive order: Regulations issued by a president to direct government agencies.

Extranet: An internal company or law firm intranet that provides access to select outsiders on a case-by-case basis.

FAQ: "Frequently asked questions," often included on websites and that respond to the most commonly asked questions about the site or about the information provided by the site.

FIOS: Fiber Optic Service, a digital technology providing Internet access with maximum connection speed.

FTP: File Transfer Protocol, a common method of moving files or communicating between two Internet sites.

FULL: A feature of "Shepard's for Research," a software program provided by Lexis that lists every authority that mentions a case.

Federal Appendix: West's set of books that prints unpublished federal courts of appeal cases.

Federal Digital System (FDsys): Website maintained by the federal government offering easy access to official, authenticated government documents, including federal statutes, Code of Federal Regulations, and numerous other primary sources; formerly GPO Access.

Federalism: Sharing of powers by the federal and state governments.

Federal question jurisdiction: The power of a federal court to hear a case based upon the fact the case arises under the United States Constitution or a United States law or treaty; sometimes called "subject matter jurisdiction."

Federal Register: A pamphlet published every weekday relating to administrative law and publishing agency rules and regulations.

Federal Reporter: West's unofficial publication containing cases from the federal courts of appeal.

Federal Supplement: West's unofficial publication containing cases from the federal district courts.

FindLaw: Internet site providing free access to many legal authorities.

Flesch Reading Ease Test: A test used to determine the readability of a written document.

Form books: Sets of books including forms for use in the legal profession; may be general or related solely to one area of law.

Freestyle: *See* Natural language.

FullAuthority: A software program that automatically creates a Table of Authorities from a written document.

G20: A group comprising the major industrial democracies.

GPO Access: Online source offering free direct links to information about government agencies, their addresses, appointees, staff members, and functions, as well as direct links to the Federal Register, C.F.R., congressional, and executive materials; the site is now migrating to an updated system, FDsys. *See* Federal Digital System.

General encyclopedia: *See* Encyclopedias.

GlobalCite: Loislaw's citation validation service, used to ensure cases are still good law.

Guide to Microforms in Print: List of books, journals, and other materials available in microform format.

HTML: Hypertext Markup Language, a standard language of computer code.

HTTP: Hypertext Transfer Protocol, a common method of moving files or communicating between two Internet sites.

Header: Information found on the second and any following pages of letters in the upper left-hand corner listing the addressee, page, and date.

Headnotes: Short paragraphs prepared by editors, given before a case begins to serve as an index to the points of law discussed in a case.

History references: References provided by *Shepard's* relating to the subsequent history of a primary authority.

Home page: The first or main page sent when accessing a person's or business's website.

Hornbook: A one-volume treatise devoted to one area of the law, such as contracts, torts, or real property.

Hyperlink: A method of instantaneous transport to another destination in cyberspace; hyperlinks are often underscored or appear in different color on the computer screen; by clicking the colored line, you will be immediately transferred to that particular site or page.

IRAC: An acronym for "*I*ssue," "*R*ule," "*A*pplication" or "*A*nalysis," and "*C*onclusion"; a method used to analyze authorities and legal issues in a memo or brief.

Id.: A signal used in citation form to direct a reader to an immediately preceding citation.

Indefinite pronoun: A pronoun that does not refer to a specific person, such as "anyone."

Index: An alphabetical arrangement of words and terms designed to direct researchers to relevant cases, statutes, or legal information; usually contained in the last volume of a set of books or in separate volumes after the last volume.

Index method: *See* Descriptive word approach.

Index to Legal Periodicals & Books: Separately published index designed to direct researchers to periodicals such as articles in law reviews.

Infra: A signal used in books or citation form meaning "below" directing a reader to a later (though not immediately following) citation.

Interfiling: An updating technique used in looseleaf binders or sets by replacing individual pages.

International Court of Justice: A court under the responsibility of the United Nations, created to hear and decide disputes between and among nations; also called the World Court.

International law: The law relating to relations among nations.

Internet: A collection of worldwide inter-connected computer networks originally developed for defense purposes and which are linked together to exchange information; the Internet is not owned by any one person or company.

Internet Service Provider (ISP): A company that provides Internet access, such as America Online or Roadrunner, for a monthly fee.

Intranet: A private network inside a company or law firm that provides access only for internal use to those in the company or firm and not to outsiders; for example, a law firm's intranet could be used only by those in the firm and could not be accessed by any member of the general public.

Judge: Individual who sits on a lower court.

Judiciary: The branch of the government that interprets laws.

Jump cite: *See* Pinpoint cite.

Jurisdiction: The power of a court to act.

Jurisdictional statement: A statement in a brief explaining the grounds upon which the court's jurisdiction to hear the case rests.

Jury instructions: Sets of books containing proposed instructions to be used to charge a jury in a civil or criminal case.

Justice: Individual who sits on the United States Supreme Court or the highest court in a state.

KWIC: A computer program offered by Lexis that provides subsequent appellate history of a case; used primarily to confirm that the authority in question is still good law by showing negative history only. Also a method of displaying a band or window of words around a requested search term or phrase.

KeyCite: A citation service offered through Westlaw providing valuable and automatic information relating to the validity of primary authorities cited in a document.

KeyCite Alert: A software clipping service that automatically notifies a researcher of changes in the treatment of a case.

Key Number: West's assignment of a number to a particular topic of law, allowing researchers to retrieve numerous cases dealing with the same point of law.

Law: *See* Statute.

Law review: The periodic publication by a law school providing scholarly treatment of a legal topic; sometimes called "law journal."

Legalese: The overuse of legal terms and foreign words and phrases in legal writing.

Legal Looseleafs in Print: A publication that identifies which topics are covered by looseleaf publications.

Legal Periodicals & Books: The online version of *Index to Legal Periodicals & Books*.

Legis: A Lexis database library for legislative information.

Legislative courts: Specialized courts, such as the United States Tax Court, which do not exist under the Constitution and whose judges are appointed for specific terms.

Legislative history: The documents reflecting the intent and activity of a legislature at the time it enacts a law.

Legislature: The branch of the government that makes law.

Letterhead: Information printed on stationery identifying the correspondent.

Lexis: The computerized legal research system offered by Reed Elsevier.

LexisOne: Lexis's free research service accessible through the Internet.

"Library References": A feature of U.S.C.S. comparable to that of U.S.C.A. in that it provides cross-references as well as directing the researcher to books, encyclopedias, annotations, and a wide variety of law review articles.

Link: *See* Hyperlink.

Listserv: A system that allows groups of people to e-mail each other and participate in group discussions, usually about a topic of common concern; for example, there may be a group comprising law students, and when one message is sent by a user, it is automatically sent to all others in the group; sometimes called "newsgroup."

Log in: (v.) To gain access to one's account on a computer system by entering one's user name and password.

Login: (n.) The account name that is used to gain entry to a computer system and that is not secret, as is a password; also called a "user name."

Loislaw: The computerized legal research system offered by Wolters Kluwer.

Looseleaf (or looseleaf service): A set of materials collected in ringed binders due to the need for frequent updating and related to a specific area of law such as labor law or tax; includes both primary and secondary authorities.

Majority opinion: Any judicial opinion written by a member of the majority after a court reaches a decision.

Maroonbook: A citation manual published by the University of Chicago and used in the Chicago area.

Martindale-Hubbell Law Directory: A comprehensive directory of lawyers in the United States and in foreign countries.

MegaLaw: Internet site providing free access to many legal authorities.

Memorandum (legal): A document explaining legal issues involved in a case in a neutral and objective manner.

Memorandum of Law: Document presented to a court to persuade the court to rule in a party's favor; also called a brief; occasionally called Memorandum of Points and Authorities.

Memorandum of Points and Authorities: *See* Memorandum of Law.

Memorandum opinion: An opinion that provides a result but offers little or no reasoning to support that result.

Merged closing: The disfavored combination of a complimentary close with the last sentence of a letter.

Metadata: Information relating to the history, management, and tracking of electronically created documents.

Microfiche: A strip or sheet of celluloid film containing images of archived documents.

Microfilm: 16-mm or 35-mm film containing images displayed on screens and often used for efficient storage of voluminous records.

Microform: A type of technology embracing microfilm, microfiche, and ultrafiche, based on photography and that stores material more efficiently than print sources.

Model act: Proposed law intended to be used as a guideline for actual legislation.

Modem: A device that connects to your computer and to a phone line, allowing the computer to communicate with other computers, much the way telephones allow humans to communicate with each other; *see also* Cable modem.

Moot: Resolved; cases that have been resolved or settled in some manner are said to be moot.

National Reporter System: A set of unofficial court reporters published by West and including federal and state cases.

Natural language: A "plain English" computer method of conducting legal research offered by Lexis; previously called "Freestyle"; in contrast to using Boolean connectors.

Netiquette: The code of etiquette or conduct for the Internet.

Network: The connecting of two or more computers so that they can communicate with each other and share resources and information.

Neutral citation: *See* Public domain citation.

Newsgroup: Electronic communications method allowing its participants to view, post, and reply to messages.

Nexis: An online library affiliated with Lexis offering the full text of almost 700 general news, business, and financial publications.

Nominalization: The conversion of an adjective, verb, or adverb into a noun, for example, the conversion of the verb "decide" into "render a decision."

Noncritical: Treatment of a legal topic in explanatory rather than analytical or critical manner.

Note: *See* Comment.

Obiter dictum: *See* Dictum.

Official: Publication of cases, statutes, or other legal materials as directed by a statute.

On all fours: *See* On point.

Online: The condition of being connected to the Internet through electronic communication.

Online catalog: An electronic database used by libraries in place of a conventional card catalog to catalog materials owned by the library.

Online journal: A journal that is published exclusively online, not in print form.

On point: A case that is factually similar and legally relevant and that controls another case; sometimes called a case "on all fours."

Opinion: A court's explanation of the law in a particular case; also called "case" or "decision."

Opinion letter: A letter setting forth advice to a client.

Ordinance: A local law.

Original jurisdiction: The ability of a court to act as a trial court.

Overrule: The overturning of a case by a higher court considering a different case on appeal.

PACER: Service of the United States Judiciary, allowing access to documents filed in federal courts.

PDF: Portable Document Format, a format that duplicates on a computer screen what a conventional print source looks like.

Parallel cite: Two or more citations to the same case allowing researchers to read a case in two or more sets of reports.

Parallel structure: The requirement that the grammatical structure of all items in a list be identical or parallel.

Password: The secret code used to gain access to a computer system.

Per curiam: An opinion by the whole court.

Periodical: A publication issued on a periodic, such as monthly or quarterly, basis; for example, the *Computer Law Journal*.

Permanent law: A law that remains in effect until it is expressly repealed.

Personal digital assistant (PDA): A handheld computer device such as the BlackBerry or Palm Pilot, which provides wireless access for updating and validating through both *Shepard's* and KeyCite.

Persuasive authority: Legal authorities that a court is not required to follow but might be persuaded to do so; secondary authorities are persuasive.

Pinpoint cite: A reference to the exact page in a source to which a reader is directed; also called a "pincite," "jump cite," or "spot cite."

Plain English movement: A modern approach to legal writing calling for the use of plain English and an end to stuffy, archaic, and jargon-filled writing.

Plurality opinion: The result reached when separate opinions are written by members of a majority.

Pocket part: A booklet or pamphlet inserted into the back of a hardbound volume to provide more current information than that found in the volume.

Popular name: A name used to refer to a statute or case, such as the names of the sponsoring legislators, the parties to the case, or a name coined by the media.

Popular name approach: A method of locating cases or statutes by looking up their "popular names."

Posting: The entering of information or messages into a network, for example, cases are "posted" to the website of the United States Supreme Court and legal professionals "post" messages on a listserv.

Primary authority: Official pronouncements of the law, chiefly cases, constitutions, statutes, administrative regulations, and treaties, all of which are binding authorities.

Private international law: The law relating to which country's law will govern a private contractual transaction or arrangement.

Private law: A law affecting only one person or a small group of persons, giving them some special benefit not afforded to the public at large.

Procedural history: The path a case has taken, for example, from trial to appellate court.

Proclamation: A statement issued by a president having no legal effect.

Proofreading: The process of reviewing a writing to correct errors.

Public domain citation: A citation that does not refer to a particular vendor or to a particular type of source; also called *neutral citation* or *universal citation*.

Public international law: The law relating to the conduct of nations.

Public law: A law affecting the public generally.

Query: A search request used to access a computer-assisted legal research system.

Quick Index: An easy-to-use one-volume index published by West that directs the researcher to annotations in A.L.R.3d, A.L.R.4th, A.L.R.5th, and A.L.R.6th. Note that there is also an A.L.R. Federal Quick Index.

RSS: Abbreviation for "rich site summary" or "really simple syndication," a format for automatically delivering updated web content.

Ratio decidendi: The "reason of the decision"; the holding of a case.

Redlining: A method of showing changes to a document.

Reference notation ("Re"): An indication of the subject matter of a document.

Regulation: A pronouncement by an administrative agency; sometimes called a rule.

Regulatory body: An administrative agency.

Remand: An order by a higher court that returns a case to a lower court, with directions.

Removal: Sending of a case from one court to another.

Report: Set of books publishing cases, generally official sets.

Reporter: Set of books publishing cases, generally unofficial sets.

Resolution: A proposed local ordinance.

Restatements: Publications of the American Law Institute designed to restate in a clear and simple manner legal doctrine in specific areas, such as contracts, torts, or trusts.

Reverse: The overturning of a lower court decision by a higher court considering that same case on appeal.

Root expander: A device provided by Lexis in computerized legal research, such as an asterisk or an exclamation point, that substitutes for a character or any number of additional letters at the end of a word, respectively.

Rule: *See* Regulation.

Rule of Four: The decision by four of the nine United States Supreme Court Justices to grant certiorari and take a case.

Rules of court: Procedural requirements issued by courts and that must be followed by litigants.

Rules of procedure: Rules governing practice before a court, such as the FRCP, which govern significant matters.

Running head: The printed line across the top of published cases that identifies the parties' names and case citation.

Salutation: The greeting in a letter, such as "Dear Ms. Howard."

Sans serif style: Print style without embellishments of extra lines forming letters, such as the Arial font.

Scope note: A brief paragraph outlining the matters treated in a legal discussion and those to be treated elsewhere.

Search box: A blank box on a computer screen, in which you type or key in the word or terms you are interested in researching.

Search engine: A particular service that helps one locate useful information on the Internet, usually through the use of keywords; common search engines are "Yahoo!" "Google," "Lycos," and "AltaVista." A search engine is a website that looks for and retrieves other websites. Search engines look for words in the millions of web pages on the Internet and direct you to pages that include the search words or keywords you enter in a search box.

Secondary authorities: Legal authorities that are not primary law and which explain, discuss, and help locate primary authorities; persuasive authority; includes encyclopedias, A.L.R. annotations, law reviews, texts, and treatises.

Selective enforcement: A defense raised whereby a party asserts that he or she has been singled out for prosecution.

Selective publication: The process whereby not all cases are published but rather only those that advance legal theory are published.

Serial Set: Conventional bound pamphlet set of books publishing congressional committee and subcommittee reports.

Series: Newer or more recent editions of cases or other legal materials.

Serif style: A style of print that adds small decorative strokes to the edges of letters, generally

viewed as enhancing readability, such as Garamond and Times New Roman fonts.

Server: A computer or software package that provides or serves information to other computers.

Session laws: The chronological arrangement of laws prior to their arrangement in a code.

Shepardize: The process of ensuring that authorities are still "good law."

Shepard's: Sets of books that allow researchers to verify that primary authorities are still "good law."

Shepard's Link: Software that identifies citations in a document and creates hyperlinks to them.

Short form citation: An abbreviated form of a citation used after a citation has been given in full.

Signal indicator: A symbol showing on the computer screen that informs the user of the precedential status of a case or other authority by indicating through colors or letters the history and treatment of the case or other authority.

Signals: In citation form, words indicating how a citation supports or contradicts an assertion; references to preceding or later-given citations in a legal writing.

Slip law: A piece (or pieces) of looseleaf paper containing language of a law; the manner in which laws are first published.

Slip opinion: A court decision available on looseleaf sheets of paper; one not yet available in a published reporter.

Sources: Lexis's databases of materials; also called "Libraries."

Spamming: Sending blanket, unsolicited e-mail messages to others, similar to "junk mail."

Spot cite: *See* Pinpoint cite.

Stack: Shelf in a library.

Standing: Personal injury or damage sustained by a plaintiff enabling the plaintiff to bring suit.

Stare decisis: The concept whereby courts follow and adhere to previous cases.

Star paging: A technique to convert page numbers in cases published in unofficial sets to page numbers in cases published in official sets.

Statute: An act of a legislature declaring, commanding, or prohibiting something.

String citing: The somewhat disfavored practice of citing more than one authority in support of a proposition.

StyleCheck: *Shepard's* citation checking software program that checks citations for proper form using *Bluebook* or *California Style Manual* form.

Subject matter jurisdiction: *See* Federal question jurisdiction.

Supplement: A softcover pamphlet that updates material found in a hardbound volume.

Supra: A signal used in books or citation form meaning "above," directing a reader to a preceding (though not immediately preceding) reference or citation.

"Supreme Court Update": A feature of U.S.C.S. *Advance* that includes summaries of recent United States Supreme Court cases.

Surfing the 'Net: The process of moving or linking from one site to another in the course of reviewing information.

Syllabus: A comprehensive but unofficial summary preceding an opinion of a court, prepared by the court's reporter of decisions or the publisher.

Synopsis: A brief summary of a case prepared by editors to provide a quick overview of the case and given before the case begins.

TAPP: An acronym for "*T*hing, *A*ction, *P*erson, and *P*lace" and referring to a technique used to determine words to insert into an index to locate relevant research materials.

THOMAS: Website for legislative information provided by the federal government that offers text of proposed and enacted legislation, committee information, calendars for hearings scheduled, and House and Senate Directories.

Table of Authorities: List of authorities cited in a brief or document and that must be arranged in a certain order.

Temporary law: A law that has specific language limiting its duration.

Terms and Connectors: A method of searching on a computer, using words, symbols, and characters rather than plain English; often called "Boolean searching."

Text messaging: A style of communication using wireless electronic devices and using abbreviated words and symbols.

Thesaurus: A book providing synonyms and antonyms for words and terms.

Thesis statement: An initial sentence or two at the beginning of a project that encapsulates the central argument to follow; also called *umbrella statement*.

Titles: Categories of statutes or regulations.

Topic approach: A method of locating legal materials by bypassing the general index and going directly to the appropriate title or topic in a source.

Total Client-Service Library: Collectively, the sets of books published by the former Lawyers Co-op and including U.S.C.S., Am. Jur. 2d, A.L.R., *Proof of Facts, Am. Jur. Trials*, and various form books.

Transitions: Words or phrases that connect preceding language with that which follows.

Treatise: A scholarly book (or set of books) devoted to the treatment of a particular legal topic, such as *Treatise on the Law of Contracts*.

Treatment references: References provided by *Shepard's* relating to the later treatment and discussion of primary authorities by other cases, attorneys general opinions, law review articles, and so forth.

Treaty: An agreement between two or more nations.

URL: Uniform Resource Locator, one's address on the Internet. Most Internet addresses begin with "www" or "http://www." The URL of IBM is "www.ibm .com."

Ultrafiche: An enhanced microfiche holding a great many images.

Unicameral: A one-house legislature.

Uniform law: Model legislation prepared by the National Conference of Commissioners on Uniform State Laws on various legal topics, such as the Uniform Commercial Code, and designed to be adopted by the 50 states.

Uniform Resource Locator: *See* URL.

United States Code: The official publication of all federal laws, arranged by topic.

United States Code Annotated: West's annotated version of the *United States Code*, including all federal statutes arranged by subject.

United States Code Congressional and Administrative News: A publication including public laws, legislative history of selected bills, summaries of pending legislation, presidential proclamations and executive orders, various federal regulations, and court rules.

United States Code Service: Annotated set of federal statutes arranged by subject and published by Lexis Publishing.

United States Government Manual: A manual or handbook

providing information about the United States government, particularly the administrative agencies.

United States Law Week: A weekly publication that prints the text of significant public laws.

United States Reports: The official publication containing cases from the United States Supreme Court.

United States Statutes at Large: The set of books containing all federal laws, arranged in chronological order.

Universal Citation Guide: The citation system promulgated by the American Association of Law Libraries.

Universal symbols: Symbols and characters used in constructing a search on Lexis or Westlaw; sometimes called root expanders.

Unofficial: Publication of cases or statutes not directed by statute.

Unreported case: A case marked "not for publication" by a court; persuasive authority only, although it may be available from Lexis, from Westlaw, or on the Internet.

Unwritten law: A reference to the common law tradition of dependence upon cases.

User name: See Login (n.).

Versus Law: A commercial legal research system offering cases via the Internet for a moderate fee.

WWW: World Wide Web, commonly used to refer to the entire collection of resources that can be accessed in cyberspace through the Internet.

Web: See WWW.

Web page: A particular file or "page" included in a website.

Website: A collection of web pages; for example, IBM's website (www.ibm.com) will consist of numerous Web pages, each of which is devoted to a specific topic. A website always begins with a "home page," which is the first screen viewed when the website is accessed.

Weekly Compilation of Presidential Documents: Publication including materials relating to the executive branch.

WestCheck: A West software program providing automatic validation of all cases cited in a document.

West CiteAdvisor: A West software program that checks the format of citations in a document and constructs a Table of Authorities.

West Document Retrieval: A fee-based service established by West providing public records and court documents by overnight delivery, e-mail, or fax.

WestFind&Print: A fee-based Internet service established by West allowing one to download cases and other authorities and KeyCite cases.

Westlaw: The computerized legal research system offered by West.

WestlawNext: A new, user-friendly research platform that allows easy "Google"-type searching of Westlaw, with results ranked in order of importance.

Widows and orphans: Headings or isolated words or lines occurring at the top (widows) or bottom (orphans) of a page.

Words and Phrases: A multivolume set of books directing researchers to cases that have construed certain terms.

World Court: The United Nations court, officially named the International Court of Justice, which provides final decisions regarding international disputes.

World Wide Web: See WWW.

Writ of certiorari: See Certiorari.

Written law: A reference to statutes.

Index